RURAL CHANGE

RURAL CHANGE

The Challenge for Agricultural Economists

PROCEEDINGS

SEVENTEENTH
INTERNATIONAL CONFERENCE
OF AGRICULTURAL ECONOMISTS

Held at Banff, Canada
3rd – 12th SEPTEMBER 1979

Edited by
Glenn Johnson, Department of Agricultural
Economics, Michigan State University, USA
and
Allen Maunder, Institute of Agricultural Economics
University of Oxford, England

INTERNATIONAL ASSOCIATION OF AGRICULTURAL
ECONOMISTS
INSTITUTE OF AGRICULTURAL ECONOMICS
OXFORD

1981

ALLANHELD, OSMUN

© The International Association of Agricultural Economists 1981

Published in the United States of America in 1981 by Allanheld, Osmun & Co. Publishers, Inc., 6 South Fullerton Avenue, Montclair, New Jersey, 07042

Library of Congress Cataloging in Publication Data

International Conference of Agricultural Economists,
    17th, Banff, Alta., 1979.
    Rural change.

    Sponsored by the International Association of
    Agricultural Economists.
    1. Agriculture – Economic aspects – Congresses.
    2. Agriculture and state – Congresses. I. Johnson,
    Glenn Leroy, 1918–   II. Maunder, A.H.
    III. International Association of Agricultural Economists.
    IV. Title
    HD1405.I58   1979   338.1   80-27966
    ISBN 0-86598-043-8

Printed in Great Britain

CONTENTS

SECTION III – NATIONAL

SECTION IV – SUPRA-NATIONAL

SECTION V – MULTI-NATIONAL, PARASTATAL AND STATE TRADING AGENCIES

PREFACE

This book reproduces the main papers and reports which were presented at the Seventeenth International Conference of Agricultural Economists held at Banff, Alberta, Canada from 3 to 12 September 1979.

A further selection of contributed papers will be published in the series of Occasional Papers of the International Association of Agricultural Economists.

The Association is grateful to its Editor, Mr. Allen Maunder, of the Agricultural Economics Institute, University of Oxford for his valued work in preparing this volume.

The Banff Conference programme was prepared by Professor Glenn L. Johnson, of Michigan State University. Readers cannot fail to appreciate the immense amount of work which he devoted to the creation of an event which built upon the traditions of the Association's previous conferences but also had its own unique features of design and integration.

Prominent in the Conference proceedings was the Leonard Elmhirst Memorial Lecture on "Development Strategy in a Limping World Economy", delivered by Professor Sir Arthur Lewis. It was with great pleasure that the Association subsequently learned of his award of a Nobel Prize for Economics, together with the same award to Professor T.W. Schultz, the 1976 Elmhirst Lecturer.

The Association gratefully acknowledges the assistance of the Government of Canada and the Government of Alberta in ensuring the success of the Conference, and particularly wishes to put on record its thanks to Murray Hawkins who, as President of the Canadian Council for IAAE, acted as Chairman of the Committee responsible for local arrangements.

DENIS K. BRITTON
President, International Association of
Agricultural Economists

INTRODUCTION

This "proceedings" volume contains the major portion of the formal papers and discussion at the Seventeenth International Conference of Agricultural Economists held at Banff, Canada, from 3 to 12 September 1979. These were the papers delivered at the plenary and at the invited paper sessions of the conference.

At the first plenary session the Elmhirst Memorial Lecture was given by Professor Sir Arthur Lewis. This was followed by the Presidential Address on the conference theme by Professor Denis Britton. The sessions which followed were grouped under the six sub-divisions of the conference theme.

In this volume each paper is followed by the remarks of whoever was invited to open the discussion and these are followed by an account of the general discussion. The editor wishes to express his thanks to the openers* who (with one exception) turned in their written contributions before the end of the conference; and also to the rapporteurs who had the onerous task of summarizing the general discussion and the paper reader's reply. Thanks are also due to Mrs Pearl Maunder, whose immediate typing of these contributions made the task of editing both easier and more accurate.

As was the case with the preceding conference, the contributed papers, together with summaries of their discussion, will appear in an *IAAE Occasional Paper*; while the reports of the meetings of the thirty-two Discussion Groups will appear in an *IAAE Members' Bulletin*.

This being the fiftieth anniversary of the first International Conference of Agricultural Economists, it is appropriate to include in this volume not only a photograph of the site of this seventeenth conference but also one of our predecessors who met fifty years ago at Dartington Hall in Devon.

A.H. Maunder
IAAE Editor

---

* The editor regrets the omission in the Sixteenth Conference Proceedings of the contribution of Dr M.R.I. Molla as an opener to discussion of the paper by Dr H. Walker.

First conference held at Dartington Hall, Devon, England in 1929

Seventeenth conference held at the Banff Centre, Canada in 1979

OPENING SESSION

PRESIDENTIAL ADDRESS

DENIS K. BRITTON

Fifty Years of Agricultural Economics – and What Next?

This is the fiftieth anniversary of the first International Conference of Agricultural Economists, held at Dartington Hall, England from 28 August to 6 September 1929. Today, in this place and at this hour, seems to be the right moment to look back to that small but auspicious beginning of an unbroken chain of events which explains our coming together now in Banff, from all corners of the world – the right moment to look back over the intervening years and to look forward into the future.

Let us first recall some of the personalities of those early days, and their declared aims. By the invitation and generosity of Mr and Mrs L.K. Elmhirst, fifty people attended that first conference, from twelve countries. The programme planners were Orwin (Oxford), Currie (Dartington Hall) and Ladd (Cornell), and it is interesting to note that the triangle Oxford – Dartington – Cornell appears to have formed the operational base of subsequent activities for a number of years, with Elmhirst at the centre of gravity – somewhere in mid-Atlantic, one might say.

The purposes of the first meeting (as recorded in the foreword to the Proceedings volume which was printed as a hardback book of 356 pages, including a photograph of the participants, in that same year) were: to bring together agricultural economists from many countries to discuss research results and research methods that were of common interest; to discuss national and international problems in the field of agricultural economics; and to promote a more effective and more rapid exchange of agricultural economics information. Elmhirst was a strong believer in the value of exchanging experience and information. His travels, principally in Asia, and his residence for several years in a rural area of India, had convinced him that people doing similar work in different countries should know more of what was being done elsewhere. Thus I am sure that he would approve if we choose to spend most of our time here telling each other what we are doing, and that he would wish that our paper-reading and other activities should not impede such discussion. He said that we should measure the success of our conferences by the quality of the relationships we establish with one another.

In preparing that first meeting our founders had emphasized the need

3

for an *informal* gathering, and informality certainly seems to have been the keynote of the pre-war conferences which to some extent we may have lost because of our much greater numbers and the organizational problems to which they give rise. We have moved away from the intimate conversational atmosphere, so conducive to what one member in 1929 described as "amiable disagreement", to that of the vast auditorium; the carefully prepared statement with its lack of the excitement of spontaneity; the mediation of professional interpreters; and the hard-headed advice of consultants on conference techniques.

Those high-minded and dedicated men of 1929 (there were no ladies in those days, or if there were they were kept out of the official photograph) also persuaded each other that it was necessary to meet "away from the distractions of the great cities". Just what distractions they had in mind and whether we shall entirely escape them in Banff I am not sure, but it is a fact that most of our seventeen conferences have taken place, if not away from cities, at least within easy reach of rural areas which our members were able to visit, no doubt in a mood of quiet contemplation. It is recorded that they also played cricket and baseball, though these games were not to everybody's taste. Arthur Ashby for one – the man who, incidentally, did more than anyone else to get me started in agricultural economics – confessed at the second conference held at Cornell in 1930 that when he felt the need to "get away from these eighty papers" he would "find his way down to the creek and listen to the drip and murmur of the falls".

Indeed, while we do honour, as is certainly our duty and pleasure today, to the memory of Leonard Elmhirst, I hope we shall not forget the contribution made by Arthur Ashby who was another of our founders. It was to him that was entrusted the task of drafting our constitution, much of which has survived to this present day. He was also elected chairman in 1930 of a committee to make plans for future conferences. Besides taking on these administrative duties, he delivered a paper in that year on "Agricultural Economics as Applied Economics" which still rings true and indeed could be said to have been prophetic in some respects. He had no hesitation in embracing normative studies, even if he did not call them that. He stressed the underlying assumption of all applied sciences that the results of study will lead to desirable change, to development and progress. He spoke not of elegant solutions to problems confined within very specific and often highly artificial sets of assumptions, but of the need to formulate a course of action leading to "intelligent modification of existing forms and conditions". He saw that weaknesses discovered in those forms and conditions should be given greater attention than evidences of strength or of stability. He would therefore have found himself to be entirely in tune with our chosen theme for 1979 of Rural Change; yet he was far-sighted enough to envisage that the time might come, as the science developed, when "knowledge would lead quite as clearly to preservation or conservation as to change". Meanwhile, being acutely conscious as were many others of that generation, quite as much as our own contemporaries, that rural people generally had been neglected and deprived a due share of the benefits of economic progress, he affirmed that "the outstanding fact ... about agricultural economics is that its knowledge will be used for purposes of manipulative or directive acts in the sphere of economics or politics". He was sceptical of the classical economic philosophy because it afforded no guarantee that all people would receive a proper share of the benefits of civilized life.

In that same 1930 paper Ashby observed that our problem, as agricultural economists, is that of "combining the pursuit of least cost with that of the highest possible degree of order and security"; or, as we might say today, of making efficiency objectives compatible with equity objectives. He perceived and feared that the pursuit of efficiency standards by farmers might lead only to the enrichment of other people. During and after Ashby's time we have tended to persist in giving much more attention to efficiency than to equity, and I would venture to suggest that this is because we believe that the former is more amenable to quantitative analysis and therefore more respectable from a scientific point of view. We tend to forget that efficiency can only be considered relative to a stated goal or goals. There is little point in devoting much of our time to minimising the cost of achieving low-priority objectives. To do so is almost as irrational as to suppose that high-priority objectives must be pursued, and can be attained, without counting the cost and without any regard to the implications for secondary objectives.

If I have dwelt rather long upon certain ideas expressed fifty years ago it is because I am convinced of their relevance today. Our founders laid down certain guide-lines, and they were profoundly conscious of what they were doing. We would do well to consider whether we have heeded their guide-lines, or whether we have modified or discarded them as our subject has grown, and if so, whether we should revert to them. In particular I suggest that we recall today that the first objective of our Association, as set down in the Constitution, is "to foster the application of the science of agricultural economics in the improvement of the economic and social conditions of rural people and their associated communities". The deliberate focusing of attention upon the improvement of human situations in rural areas is basic to the original conception of our purpose in holding these conferences, and if we have at any time moved away from it we should recognize the fact and be ready to justify it. This reference point should prove valuable, for instance, when we are discussing, as we do from time to time, whether our studies should embrace the whole complex of agri-food industries; whether fish-farming comes within the purview of agricultural economics; and whether our university departments should abandon the label "agricultural economics" in favour of "resource economics" or "food energy economics". Disputes about demarcation of intellectual territory can, of course, be a great waste of time and are often quite unnecessarily acrimonious; and I acknowledge that in the long-run most people will contrive to study what interests them, regardless of the label. Nevertheless I think that labels should have a fairly consistent and widely-accepted meaning, and should not be altered too readily to satisfy fashions or aspirations which may prove to be short-lived.

What could we in the agricultural economics profession today show to our founders by way of achievement? We could, I suppose, proudly parade our statistics of increased attendances at conferences and our exponential growth in membership of the Association. We could point to a shelf full of bound volumes of conference proceedings. No doubt our founders would be duly impressed, and rather pleased with themselves at having fathered such a numerous and distinguished looking lineage. But being the men they were, for whom the quality of life meant so much, they would not be taken in by mere numbers or bulk. They would ask for evidence of the real value of our efforts, in terms of the progressive advancement of knowledge and what they called "the economical provision of the material requirements of the good life for rural people".

As regards the first criterion, the progressive advancement of knowledge, I am very glad that this gives me the opportunity to mention that since we last met, at Nairobi in 1976, a very significant landmark has appeared in our ever-widening field of activity. I refer to the monumental *Survey of Agricultural Economics Literature* which has been published in three volumes under the auspices of the American Agricultural Economics Association and edited by Lee R. Martin. I should like to express my admiration and gratitude, personally and I hope on behalf of you all, for the imagination and perception of need which put this enterprise in hand; the sound organizational basis of consultation, selection and appraisal on which it was constructed; and the depth of knowledge, sustained intellectual effort and wise judgement of those who were primarily responsible for drafting the respective parts of this massive work. As I wrote in my review of Volume I of this *Survey of Agricultural Economics Literature* (in the *European Review of Agricultural Economics*, Vol. 4 No. 4, 1977), "it gains a great deal from the fact that the authors have felt free to give their own comments on the adequacy of the research which has so far been accomplished in our field; they frequently draw attention to unresolved conflicts of evidence or opinion; and they make suggestions for future research into relatively neglected areas'.

The cumulative effect and level of achievement which these three volumes describe are impressive indeed, and I am confident that even the most critical of our founders would pay his respects. If they wanted still more evidence of our progress in research and of our comprehensive coverage of an ever-widening field, we could refer them to other scholarly review articles such as those contained in various issues of the Australian *Review of Marketing and Agricultural Economics* and the British *Journal of Agricultural Ecomomics*. We could also confront them with just one year's output of the *World Agricultural Economics and Rural Sociology Abstracts* (WAERSA) and its recent offshoots, *Rural Development Abstracts* and *Rural Extension, Education and Training Abstracts*. To those who wished to trace the evolution of ideas in agricultural economics in the context of Europe, we could transmit a copy of Joosep Nou's encyclopaedic study published in 1967, though this would not give any indication of the rising flood of studies resulting from the establishment of the European Community and its common agricultural policy.

Despite all this testimony to the activity of one and a half generations of agricultural economists who have been working since 1929, the task which the present generation inherits is undiminished. We are probably more conscious of its sheer magnitude than they were, because of our greatly increased liability to exposure to the needs of others through our much higher travel-mileage per member and our self-imposed elaborate information network, which makes it relatively easy to assemble or gain access to visual and statistical evidence of the human condition. All this evidence points to a deterioration for much of the world's population. There is no positive relation between the rate of economic growth and the reduction in rural poverty; and economic growth itself is slowing down. On the second criterion of our founders, that of promoting "the economical provision of the material requirements of the good life for rural people", we would therefore have to admit to a notable lack of success.

As one conference follows another we pass on this undiminished task, throwing new light on some of its aspects, breaking off chunks of it for separate study, reassembling other parts which call for a more multidisciplinary approach, redefining concepts here, discarding untenable theories there, removing layers of ignorance or obscurity only to discover new strata of problems of unsuspected depth and intractability. Even if agricultural economists may have had a powerful positive influence, the negative forces have been too strong for us. It therefore seems inappropriate for me to spend more time today in trying to chronicle our successes when so much remains to be done.

On behalf of our Association I recently attended, along with our President-Elect Professor Dams, the World Conference on Agrarian Reform and Rural Development which was organised by FAO and took place in Rome. Among the national delegations we were pleased to find our former President, Professor Westermarck, our Vice-President, Professor Nazarenko, and the former President of the European Association of Agricultural Economists, Professor Barberi. It would be wrong, however, to give the impression that agricultural economists had a major rôle to play in that conference. Fundamentally it was concerned with the need for changes in the power structure surrounding and permeating the rural economy, and clearly this is an issue which will have to be resolved mainly by politicians, for whom the exercise and distribution of power are vital considerations. Yet because power has economic as well as political muscle, we cannot abdicate all interest in this particular manifestation of the twentieth-century world-wide power struggle. I therefore propose to make a few comments on it.

In its documentation and in the speeches of delegates this FAO Conference repeatedly emphasized the imbalance which is to be found in almost all rural communities. This imbalance, usually but not exclusively expressed in terms of disparity of incomes, is to be found between urban and rural people and between rich and poor within rural communities, as well as internationally between the more developed and the less developed nations. Priorities in national planning have too often neglected the rural sector. Insufficient efforts have been made to build the rural infrastructure which agricultural development requires. In some countries a small, dynamic modern element has established itself in the rural community, but it is greatly outnumbered by the great majority for whom the traditional patterns of poverty persist, so that the progressive élite may be more of an aggravation than a source of benefit. Landlessness is increasing. Fair rent laws are not enforced. Rural people have borne a disproportionate burden in the financing of general economic development, whether the discrimination against them be through pricing, taxation or the unfavourable terms of trade. In several countries agricultural production has slowed down while population increase has accelerated; production per caput was thus lower in the 1970s than in the 1960s. About 500 million people in the world have "less than the critical minimum energy intake", and their number is increasing, in spite of FAO's categorical but somewhat distracting statement that total food supplies could meet the nutritional needs of the world's population if properly distributed.

The underlying concern, rightly or wrongly, is with equity and not with productivity. The point was most forcibly and persuasively made by President Nyerere of Tanzania. Claiming that national and international action over the past fifteen years had provided a lesson in how *not* to succeed in tackling rural poverty, he maintained that the fundamental division is that between those with and without access to resources. Effective land reform must be accompanied by giving the poor access to credit, to improved seeds and tools and to new knowledge. Any rural production surplus above immediate needs must not be "extracted" for use in urban centres, but must be re-invested in rural development, which is people's development of themselves. They cannot do it if they have no power to mount effective pressure nationally and to participate in the determination of priorities.

President Nyerere admitted that such transfers cannot be done painlessly, and that they require a revolution in the present patterns of government expenditure and of taxation. What he calls the "flow of wealth towards wealth" has to be stopped and reversed.

Whether this line of thought will prevail at our present conference here in Banff remains to be seen, but clearly it is one which cannot be ignored. The debate will continue, probably more vigorously than before, between those who put wealth creation as the first priority, even if it means some widening of the gap between the richest and the poorest, for only so can the necessary welfare services be financed; and those who put distributive justice and reform of the social structure first, even if it means some lowering of material standards for considerable numbers of people. Economists will no doubt continue to be found in both groups. As I have already indicated, Ashby and others saw the dilemma fifty years ago, and did not shrink from the need to contemplate and promote change in economic and social systems if these failed to give expression to the aptitudes, abilities and desires of large sections of the population.

The line-up of economists in the current world-wide debate may be partly a matter of temperament, or of attitude to their work. On the one hand there may be those who, by training or by habit, are mainly concerned to find ways of making the best of a given situation, where most of the major factors are considered to be exogenous; on the other hand there may be those who are mainly concerned with creating a different (and better) institutional framework within which optimising behaviour can then begin to operate to better effect. The latter are bound to be more politically involved than the former. They are probably also more numerous, relatively as well as absolutely, than they were in the days of our founders; for one can discern a general mood in the post-war world of questioning outmoded systems, whereas in the 1930s there seems to have been a stronger inclination to accept the *status quo* and work within it.

Glenn Johnson put his finger on this same division of activities within agricultural economics when he wrote a review article on developments in the field of production economics for the *Australian Journal of Agricultural Economics* in 1963. Too much concentration on the theory of equilibrium, with its insistence on equating returns at the margin, had distracted economists from the really relevant farm problem of inadequate resources – of "getting ownership of enough property and command over enough skill to earn a decent living." This critique can be linked directly with the re-ordering of priorities which President Nyerere and others are now demanding in rural development.

What, then, of our professional rôle in the future? Once again I find a rich source of ideas in the *Survey of Agricultural Economics Literature*, in which the contributing authors were invited to indicate research priorities in their respective fields. I cannot do justice today to their very positive and fruitful response to that invitation, but will pick out a few general areas of activity which particularly caught my attention.

Harald Jensen, reviewing the field of farm management and production economics, argued that our science is not yet sufficiently effective in solving current social problems. Increasing the complexity of our models does not result in delivery of solutions which have a strong practical appeal. Farm management, as well as exploring certain narrowly-defined fields in depth, must also continue to draw on various neighbouring disciplines in its problem-solving activity. It must help farmers to define their multiple goals, and cope with situations in which various parties with diverse interests and objectives enter into a decision-making process.

Ben French, reviewing the field of analysis of productive efficiency in agricultural marketing, was also looking for a shift of emphasis away from the efficiency of the individual firm to the attainment of an optimum structure of firms within the industry. He anticipated that "efficiency in marketing" might tend to disappear as a separate study and be merged with questions of production and price policy on a commodity level.

G.E. Brandon, looking over the field of policy studies for commercial agriculture, emphasised that there would be a continuing need for accurate knowledge of how the agricultural economy works, reliable quantification of key relationships within the system and an awareness of the political processes by which policy is made. One specific topic which I am sure is ripe for study in many countries is the analysis of the difficulties which family businesses experience in transferring ownership from generation to generation, and the policy measures needed to reduce these difficulties. Brandon also calls for more studies of the personal distribution of income and wealth, both in a descriptive sense and as a criterion for farm policy. Should we be actively designing policy instruments which would scale down the benefits going to the wealthier producers? How would they affect efficiency and total output?

Looking at agricultural price analysis and outlook studies, William Tomek and Kenneth Robinson ask some pertinent questions about our provision of economic forecasts, and specifically, why do equations with high R^2s and seemingly logical coefficients provide poor forecasts? Policy-makers will continue to look to us for indications of the likely consequences of alternative decisions. Tools of analysis and methods of forecasting must be improved and must be able to cope with new types of questions.

These are only a few examples from selected fields, and I must leave the specialists among you to consider other major fields which I have not even mentioned. I would like to round off this brief sketch of some suggested priorities and research criteria by going back to Harald Jensen's concluding remarks, in which he quoted with approval the following passage from an article by D.R. Fusfeld in the *Saturday Review*.

> A humane economy requires more than prosperity and economic growth, more than efficient allocation of resources. It demands changes in the framework of economic institutions to achieve greater equality and freedom. It requires dispersal of the economic power and governmental authority that support the present disposition of income, wealth and power. It requires a social environment that brings a sense of community and fellowship into human relationships. It demands compatibility among man, his technology, and the natural environment. And all these things must be done on a world-wide scale. These are the goals of the future, to which economists and everyone else will have to devote their energies.

The IAAE is neither a pressure group nor an action group. Our founders did not intend to forge such an instrument. We have not come to Banff to pass resolutions, nor to try to organize some dramatic piece of world-wide collective activity which with one supreme effort will heave our shipwrecked humanity higher up the beach to a place of safety. As economists we should appreciate the value of a less conspicuous contribution which aims at marginal increments of improvement at the points of greatest opportunity and greatest need, increments which individually may have no impact which is perceptible beyond a restricted locality but which cumulatively may generate enough leverage to move the world.

None of us, I trust, has come here with an exaggerated idea of the net benefit of our deliberations to the rest of mankind. But we have a rare opportunity to give to and obtain from one another a better personal orientation, both vertically and horizontally: vertically, in the sense that we can lift our range of vision to see world-scale problems and place our national and local preoccupations in proper relation to them; horizontally, in that we can increase our awareness of work in other countries than our own on the problems which interest us, whether these are specific or general, local or global, methodological or operational in character.

Our Vice-President in charge of the programme of this conference, Glenn Johnson, has prepared for us with great care and forethought and not without considerable trouble, a feast of intellectual food, with many courses to suit all tastes. I am sure that it is not necessary for me to wish you *bon appétit*; I only trust that your digestion will be sufficiently robust to meet the challenge. And I will close by repeating the hope expressed by G.F. Warren at the Cornell Conference in 1930, that "the intellectual stimulus will be a spur to more work and clearer analysis".

ELMHIRST MEMORIAL LECTURE

W. ARTHUR LEWIS

Development Strategy in a Limping World Economy

My purpose is to look at some aspects of economic growth in the developing countries since the second world war, and to speculate on changes in economic strategy which may already be appropriate, or which may become appropriate in the immediate future, to cope with a world economy that settles into relatively slow economic growth.

As is well known, the period since the second world war, down to 1973, has been one of unprecedented growth for the world economy as a whole, as well as for developed and developing countries separately. In the last golden age of capitalism – the four decades before the first world war – world industrial production increased at about 3.5 per cent per annum; whereas the rate from say 1953 to 1973 averaged just under 6 per cent per annum. World agricultural output grew at under 2 per cent in the earlier period, compared with under 3 per cent in the later period. The growth of world trade jumped in the same way, from about 3.3 per cent before the first world war to about 8 per cent in the quarter century ending in 1973.

The developing countries have shared in this unexpected performance. Their growth rate of national income, averaging about 5 per cent, or 2.5 per cent per head, exceeded the growth rates that were achieved in the nineteenth century or the first half of the twentieth century by any of the now developed economies.[1] This upward leap was unexpected, and caught many economists off their guard. Because of the sharp contraction of world trade in the 1930s – the growth rate from 1913 to 1937 averaged less than one per cent per annum – and the rise in tariffs, exchange control and restrictions of every kind, most economists assumed that world trade would grow very slowly after the war, and could not again serve as an engine of growth, as it was supposed to have done in the nineteenth century. Development economists therefore created a set of theories appropriate to a world in which foreign trade is stagnant – including the theory of balanced growth, the two-gap model, structural inflation, regional integration – each of which is valid and important if exports cannot be increased, but none of which belongs in a world where trade is growing at 8 per cent per annum. Acting on the assumption of a stagnant world

12

trade many countries, notably India, and several in Latin America, neglected their trading potential until late into the 1960s, when the facts could no longer be ignored. We may now be in danger of falling into the opposite pit. World trade has expanded more slowly since 1973 and nobody knows whether it will resume the fast pace of earlier years. Yet many of us continue to take it for granted, as in last year's *World Development Report*, that export-oriented policies will also yield the highest payoff over the next two decades. Part of my purpose today is to consider what differences in strategy may be appropriate to differences in the rate of growth of world trade.

II

But before getting there I want to spend a moment with agriculture, which has been the weakest link in the development chain. Industry in LDCs has grown at around 7 per cent per annum, the number of children in school has multiplied by four, the domestic savings ratio has risen by three percentage points – the picture is everywhere bright until one turns to agriculture, where the dominant fact is that in LDCs as a whole food production has failed to keep pace with the demand for food, thereby causing or aggravating a whole series of other problems.

The basic reasons for this failure are well known, so I will list but not dwell on them.

The first has been fast population growth. Population has grown at around 2.5 per cent per annum and demand per caput has pushed the growth of total demand well beyond 3 per cent, while output has grown at significantly less than 3 per cent, turning what used to be an export surplus into an import surplus of food.

Secondly, the technological revolution in tropical food production has only just begun, research in the colonial days having been confined almost but not exclusively to commercial crops exportable to the world market. We have made spectacular progress with maize, wheat for subtropical conditions, and rice for areas of controlled irrigation, but have still far to go with other rice, with sorghums, and millets, and with livestock management.

Third, even where there is new technology to impart, the agricultural extension services and the network for supplying modern inputs to the farmer, especially seeds, fertilisers and pesticides, are gravely deficient and in many areas virtually non-existent.

Fourth, investment in rural infrastructure is inadequate. Road systems have improved immensely, and the penetration of the countryside by buses and trucks is altering the patterns of rural life. But not enough has been invested in irrigation, or in storage facilities.

Fifth, everyone speaks in favour of land reform, but very few governments have done it in any of its various forms, whether distributing land to the landless, or converting from rental to ownership tenures, or fixing rental ceilings. The case for some sort of land reform remains unquestionable from the standpoint of justice; the case from the standpoint of its effects on production is now stated with greater sophistication, recognising the extent to which higher output is tied to improved technology, extension and investment. Indeed several writers now speak not of land reform but of "the land reform package", to distinguish what they see as good land reform from bad land reform.

And finally to complete our list of factors that have inhibited agricultural output we must add poor terms of trade. The prices of agricultural commodities in world trade fell throughout the 1950s and most of the 1960s, while industrial prices rose all the time. This was anomalous, since prosperity usually improves agriculture's terms of trade. The basic factor was the enormous increase in agricultural productivity in the United States, resulting in the build up of stocks of cereals; since agricultural commodities compete with each other either on the demand side or on the supply side, this depressed all other agricultural prices. Add to this that in several LDCs governments wanted to keep farm revenues low, whether by imposing taxes on exportable crops, or by placing price ceilings on food for the domestic market. This is at first sight a curious phenomenon. One would expect that farm populations, being more than half the nation (in most cases) would carry enough political clout to be able to defend themselves against such measures and would on the contrary be manipulating the terms of trade in their favour, but this is not automatic. European farmers were doing this at the end of the nineteenth century, but the contemporaneous efforts of American farmers, though they were still in the majority, were a failure.

III

Let me now turn from the causes of the low level of agricultural output in the LDCs to some of its effects. Agricultural failure is not the sole cause of the problems I shall mention, but makes in each case a significant contribution.

Take first the probability that inequality of the income distribution has increased along with recent growth. This is not a novel phenomenon. Increased inequality is inherent in the classical system of economics because population growth keeps labour income down while profits and rents increase. Given the long and strident debate between economic historians as to what happened to European living standards in the first half of the century, no modern economist should have assumed that economic growth would automatically raise the incomes of those at the lower end of the scale. Rapid population growth has also played its negative role in our day, restraining the wage level and farm income per head. Since the majority of the labour force in LDCs consists of farm people, who also have the lowest incomes, the standard of living of the great bulk of the population can be raised only by raising farm income. Discussions of the effects of growth on income distribution or income distribution on growth lead nowhere unless farm income is at the centre of the alleged relationship.

The worst effects of population growth combined with technological standstill are to be seen in the arid zones of the tropical world, where some 500 million people live, especially along the fringes of the African and Asian deserts. There we have the largest concentration of human poverty; the numbers continue to grow rapidly; and we have not yet had the technological breakthrough in dry farming that might promise higher productivity. To raise the living standards of these hundreds of millions is the greatest challenge to those who work for development.

Consider next the huge flow of migrants from the countryside into the towns. Central to this of course is the growth of population. Relatively under-populated countries can cope with population growth by opening up new land, as has been happening over much of Africa, but in less favoured countries population growth means smaller farms, more land-less labourers and lower output per head. Unless a green revolution is set in motion, the natural reaction of farmers caught in this situation is to put pressure on the young to migrate to the cities, which they will do if the cities show signs of expanding employment. This is not a complete solu-tion. The towns cannot provide employment for the whole of the natural increase in the countryside, not to speak of women now also leaving the family tasks and seeking wage employment; so unemployment mounts. The government is also trapped. The towns exert great pressure for expansion of the public services – of water, bus transport, schools, hospi-tals and so on – eating up more funds than exist, and leaving nothing to spend in the countryside. So that the differential in amenities between town and country widens all the more, and the stream of migrants is increased. Unemployment in the towns cannot be ended by spending more in the towns. The basic solution is rather to make the countryside economically viable, with a larger cultivated area, with rising productivity on the farms, more rural industry, and better social amenities.

Note "the larger cultivated area". Development economists have been mesmerised by European experience into assuming that the development process always involves a decline in the number of persons in agriculture. This is true of relative decline, but it extends to an absolute decline only in the later stages of development. For example, around 1850 in Western Europe the agricultural population was only 50 per cent of the whole, and the rate of natural increase about 1.25 per cent. So the agricultural population would decline absolutely if the non-agricultural population grew at over 2.5 per cent a year. Whereas with 70 per cent in agriculture and a rate of natural increase of 2.5 per cent, an absolute decline of the agricultural labour force requires non-agricultural employment to expand at 8.3 per cent per annum, which it cannot do.

An increase in the absolute numbers engaged in agriculture is therefore an essential item in coping with the current flood of population. The fact that the green revolution in cereals is labour-intensive helps, especially if the natural propensity of the more enterprising farmers to invest in labour saving machinery can be restrained. But there is no escaping the need to bring more land under cultivation, by opening up roads, irrigation, terracing, drainage, and other investment in infrastructure. Some governments are actively engaged in colonisation schemes of this sort, which, if highly planned to meet modern standards, are costly and troublesome. The subject is neglected in our textbooks. It needs more research and experimentation, leading to action.

A third consequence of the weakness of agriculture is that it is one of the reasons why so many LDCs have had balance of payments troubles, have incurred large external debts, or have found themselves defaulting on their obligations. It is not just that a larger output would earn more foreign exchange, or save on food imports. Indirectly it would reduce urbanization, the high cost of which is the prime cause of their needing so much capital and having to borrow so much. Also, in countries suffering from the two-gap disease, it would facilitate the translation of domestic saving into foreign exchange.

A fourth and final consequence of the weakness of agriculture has been to inhibit the growth of manufacturing industry because of the farmers' low purchasing power. The physical output of LDC commercial export crops grew rapidly, aided on the supply side by the expansion of internal transport, and on the demand side by the unusually rapid growth of the developed countries. But the prices at which these commodities sold were poor; exports are a small part of agricultural output, so their prices are linked on the supply side to the price of food, which as we saw earlier, was depressed by American surpluses. The individual LDC can do well out of exporting agricultural raw materials or tropical beverages; but for the group of LDCs as a whole the elasticity of supply of these commodities is so high, at prices yielding roughly the same incomes as domestic food production, that the factoral terms of trade stay much the same despite increases in demand or improvements in technology. The road to riches does not run in these directions.

At the same time farm incomes from domestic production were also low, for reasons which we have already considered. So import substitution of manufactures, which was the starting point of industrialization, was limited by the narrowness of the domestic market. LDCs soon discovered that if industry is to grow at 7 per cent per annum, in the face of a peasantry with only a small marketable surplus, industry must look to foreign markets. By the year 1970 this lesson had been learnt, and nearly every LDC had begun exporting some manufactures to developed countries. Unfortunately this range was very narrow, dominated by textiles and clothing; broadening only as the protests and restrictions of MDCs forced the more advanced LDCs into light metals, electronics and other fields. The LDC effort was clearly successful, since LDC exports of manufactures were growing at 10 per cent a year, despite the barriers erected by the MDCs. Whether world trade will revive, and if so whether

LDC exports of manufactures will again grow at 10 per cent are crucial questions for LDC development strategy, to which we shall come in a moment. But no matter how they may be answered, it will be to the advantage of LDCs to raise their agricultural productivity, since this would simultaneously raise the living standards of their farmers, create a domestic market for their manufactures, and improve their terms of trade.

IV

Let me come back to my starting point, which was the observation that the world economy grew faster after the second world war than it had ever grown in the preceding century.

The speed of growth of LDC economies is linked to that of the MDCs mainly through trade: specifically by the demand of MDCs for the products of LDCs. In primary commodities the relationship is quite tight. World trade in primary commodities grew slightly less than 0.9 times as fast as world industrial production, between 1873 and 1913, and we get exactly the same coefficient for 1950 to 1973. Allowing for faster industrial growth in LDCs than in MDCs since the war, it is not surprising that GNP has grown at about the same rate in both groups. To continue with the links, the terms of trade also fluctuate with the growth rate of MDCs, within the limits permitted by the high elasticity of supply of tropical raw materials, and by the link between agricultural materials and the price of cereals. A new trade linking, emerging since the war, is the export of manufactures from LDCs to MDCs, which depends on the rate of growth of GNP in MDCs, not merely because this affects consumer demand, but also because it influences the willingness of MDC governments to allow such imports to come in rather than to shut them off with quotas. The effect of these links is multiplied by the further link between prosperity in LDC export trades and industrialisation for the domestic market. Other links are via the flow of international investment. As MDC income accelerates, so does MDC demand for minerals; prices rise, and more capital is invested in LDC mines. In fact more capital is invested in LDCs generally, because their prosperity makes it easier for LDC governments to raise funds, whether concessional or on commercial terms. Another postwar link has been migration from LDCs to take jobs in the tight labour markets of MDCs. These migrant workers send home remittances, which stimulate LDC trade and investment.

The closeness of these ties seem incompatible with one of the objectives of development economists, namely that LDC per capita income should rise faster than that of MDCs, and so narrow the gap between rich and poor nations. (Perhaps I should say one of the *former* objectives of *some* development economists since these same scholars are now in the forefront of denouncing economic growth as an objective for LDCs.) If MDCs grow more slowly than LDCs their imports will slow down, the terms of trade will move against LDCs, and the growth rate of LDCs will slow down. *Given the continuation of these links* what LDCs need is that MDCs should grow as fast as possible.

These issues have come to a head since 1974, when the onset of international recession brought all growth rates down, and especially the growth rate of international trade, which has since averaged about 4 per cent, in contrast with the 8 per cent of the two preceding decades. This has brought two questions to a head. First, were the high postwar growth rates to 1973 a mere flash in the pan, not due for repetition, or will the previous pace be restored? And secondly, if the developed countries now settle into slow growth, can the LDCs delink themselves and continue with high growth on their own?

V

I am not able to answer the first question – what is going to be the rate of growth of the world economy? – since my crystal ball is not working properly, but I would like to make a few agnostic remarks.

Many people now assert that the world economy has made one of those major turns that it makes from time to time, as it did in 1873, when world trade settled into a growth rate only about two-thirds of that of the preceding half century. However, part of the evidence they adduce is merely evidence of cyclical and not secular decline – high unemployment rates, low profits, low investment ratios, low savings and a slower growth rate of productivity are the familiar elements of cyclical downswing, and throw no light on long term trends.

Over the past century the United States has experienced a series of great depressions, each of which took ten years to complete itself, except for that of 1929, which took twelve years. The starting points of these depressions were 1873, 1893, 1907, 1929, 1957 and 1974. Chart 1 shows US industrial production on a semi-logarithmic scale, where the straight lines indicate the rate of growth along the peaks, and the potential output at that rate. The difference between actual and potential output is shown in Chart 2 for each of these great depressions separately. The depression at the top of the page is the one we are now experiencing. It seems to conform to pattern. For example, suggestions that the US economy was "overheated" at the end of 1978 (year five) seem implausible. In the absence of the crystal ball we cannot assert that the US economy will be back on trend by year ten, but the odds suggest that this will happen.

If then we reject all evidence that can be explained by five years of depression, we are left with a number of arguments that are being advanced to suggest that the prosperity of 1950–73 was special and not repeatable. I shall merely list them, because to pursue each of them would take us too far off course. Here are the leading six:

1   The fast growth of Europe after the second world war was due to catching up on a backlog of innovations whose feasibility and profitability

Chart 1 US Industrial Production
1865–1913 and 1950–1978

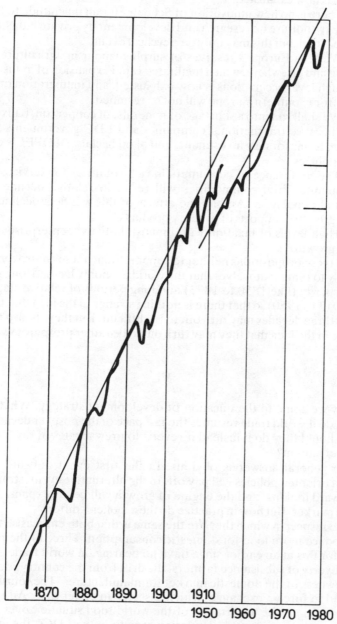

the USA had demonstrated by 1950, but whose utilization had been delayed in Europe by two world wars and the great depression – telephones, automobiles, refrigerators, television, aeroplanes and so on. This backlog is now exhausted.

2 There is no new innovation of Schumpeterian magnitude to take its place. Expenditure on research and development by private industry may have declined, but this may only be a cyclical event.

3 Western Europe's reserves of surplus labour in agriculture, petty retailing and elsewhere, which facilitated rapid expansion of industry and other high level occupations is now exhausted, and immigration of cheap labour from Southern Europe will not be resumed.

4 We shall run into a shortage of minerals: of copper, tin, bauxite and others because transnational companies and LDC governments cannot agree on terms for new investment; and of oil because of OPEC's conservation policies.

5 The preference of consumers in rich countries for services rather than manufactured commodities will result in relative decline of the industrial population. Among the effects of this will be a decline in the rate of growth of imports of primary products.

6 High levels of taxation will diminish initiative, enterprise and the rate of growth.

I list these propositions neither to support them nor to controvert them, but only to remind ourselves that the world economy has had long periods of prosperity (like 1850 to 1873) and long periods of relative stagnation (say 1913 to 1950) so that there is nothing strange in the idea that the next two or three decades may turn out to be difficult. But there is also nothing strange in the idea that they may turn out to be rather prosperous.

VI

Finally we come to the question of development strategy. What should LDCs do if world trade resumes the fast pace of the postwar decades; and what should they do if instead it reverts to prewar rates of say 3 to 4 per cent per annum?

The general answer is obvious. In the first event outward looking export oriented policies will pay off. In the alternative event, strategy will be inward looking, and the engine of growth will be the expansion of the home market. But how in practice do these policies differ?

One respect in which they are the same is that both emphasise the need to produce more food for domestic consumption. Three of the reasons I gave for this at an earlier stage have no bearing on world trade – namely the poverty of subsistence farmers, the drift from the countryside and the narrowness of the domestic market for manufactures. The fourth reason related to foreign exchange, which is scarce in either case. Add to these considerations the uncertainty of the world food situation over the next two decades, given rapid population growth in the LDCs, the exodus of

Chart 2   US Great Depressions
Deviation of Actual
from "Capacity" Industrial Production

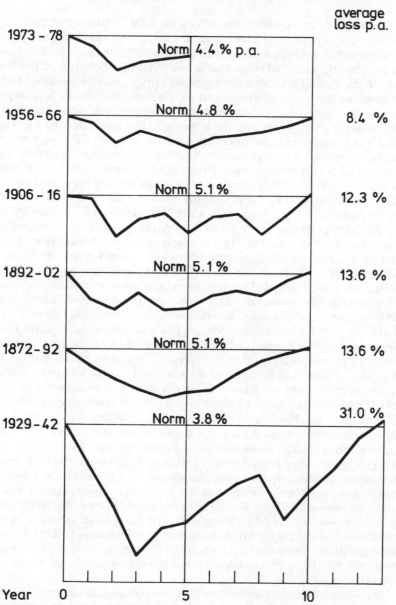

average
loss p.a.

1973 - 78
Norm 4.4 % p.a.

1956 - 66
Norm 4.8 %
8.4 %

1906 - 16
Norm 5.1 %
12.3 %

1892 - 02
Norm 5.1 %
13.6 %

1872 - 92
Norm 5.1 %
13.6 %

1929 - 42
Norm 3.8 %
31.0 %

Year   0   5   10

labour from LDC farms, lagging food production in Russia, and the unpredictability of China. LDCs ought clearly to free themselves from dependence on MDCs for food. This does not mean that each of over one hundred countries must become self-sufficient; it means only that the group should be self-sufficient in food, in a context which I shall elaborate in a moment.

I want now to consider the effect on LDC agricultural prices of increased productivity in LDC food farming. The results vary according to whether the analysis is for a small country or for the group as a whole, and in the latter case whether one is analysing the short run or the long run. In the case of a small country market prices may be assumed to be determined by world demand and supply, and to remain unchanged despite a rise in productivity in food. Production of agricultural raw materials (in which we include the beverages) becomes uneconomic. Less food is imported and more food exported. In the case of a large country, or the group as a whole, food prices fall immediately, carrying raw material prices down with them. Prices fall too low, in order to promote movement out of farming whether in LDCs or MDCs; then rise again as this is accomplished. In the new equilibrium the factoral terms of trade are improved for LDC farmers against MDC industrial workers by the amount of the increase in productivity (assuming that there are no rents); the price of food is as high (same assumption); and the price of raw materials has risen in the same proportion as productivity in food.[2]

This is the framework for approaching the question whether LDCs should allow themselves to become sources of raw materials; a role which allegedly has no future, and in which they are exploited. There is no future in the sense that once the area suited to a crop is fully planted with that crop, further investment ceases. For example, how will the Ivory Coast continue to develop when it has planted in oil palm, coffee and cocoa all the acreage suited to these crops? This is an easy question. By then the country will be covered with infrastructure, will have a large educated cadre, and will have a higher savings potential than countries which have not had areas to plant in commercial crops, such as Mali or Guinea. So it will have superior potential for investment in industry and in other opportunities. As for the exploitation, this derives from the factoral terms of trade between food and raw materials. As we said earlier a bigger demand for raw materials makes little difference to their price; and higher productivity in raw materials over the group as a whole (and new technology soon spreads over the group as a whole) merely lowers the price proportionately. What raises the price of raw materials is a rise in the income that could be earned in producing food, whether due to increased demand for food or to increased productivity in food.[3] Given an appropriate rise in potential income from growing food, it will become as profitable for the tropics to export tea as it is for farmers in the temperate world to export wheat.

Meanwhile one must remember that comparative advantage differs as between one LDC and another. In general, food productivity is higher in

Latin America than in West Africa, while productivity in cocoa or coffee or sugar is about the same. Hence West African farmers will find cocoa or coffee a profitable alternative to food at prices that would drive Brazilians or Colombians out of growing such crops. By keeping prices low over the first seven decades of this century the market has been making space for African output at the expense of Latin America.

The same force, comparative advantage, is at work between LDCs as a whole and MDCs as a whole, in that LDCs could export much more to MDCs if they were permitted to do so – of such commodities as sugar, cotton, meat, rice, maize and fruit. The future height of MDC trade barriers may be related to the state of trade, in the sense that they are more likely to be reduced if the economy is growing rapidly than if it is growing slowly.

To summarise our conclusions so far: first, increases in food productivity should be sought whether world trade is growing fast or slowly. Secondly, fast growth favours investment in export agriculture because it will raise prices (via food prices) and reduce barriers; if slow growth is predicted for the MDCs, such investment should be restricted.

Thirdly we come to manufactures. Fast growth of world trade makes room for LDC exports of manufactures to MDCs, both by expanding demand, and also because MDC governments become more tolerant towards imports. Already manufactures are one-third of the exports of non-OPEC LDCs, and if a return of world prosperity permitted a resumption of the growth rates of the 1960s, manufactures would soon be more than half of LDC exports. Slow growth of world trade postpones this turning point, and mandates a greater effort to increase the domestic demand for manufactures by increasing the farmers' marketable surplus. The two sets of policies are quite different. Production for the domestic market can be high cost and inefficient, protected by high tariff walls or other restrictions. Production for export requires good quality at low prices, and this requires the winds of competition. The export manufacturer has also to quote prices months in advance, frequently in foreign currencies; so he is damaged by inflation and an overvalued rate of exchange. These two are less troublesome to the producer for the home market.

VII

I have been speaking of LDCs turning inward and developing domestic markets as if every LDC had the option of determining how large a percentage foreign trade should be of its Gross Domestic Product. This is not so. Most LDCs are too small to have either a wide range of raw materials or a wide range of opportunities to produce for a domestic market on an economic scale. And now that the stage of import substitution is highly advanced, even the large LDCs have reduced their imports by as much as it is economical to do, if not more so. We may therefore assume that if LDCs set themselves a growth target of 6 per cent per year for output, they will need a 6 per cent per annum increase in imports, and therefore also in exports to pay for imports. The problem is how to achieve this if the rest of the world trade is growing only at 3 per cent per year.

One possibility would be for LDCs to raise their share of MDC markets. The generalised system of preferences is supposed to do this, but we know how reluctant MDCs have been to translate this piece of rhetoric into valuable trade concessions. It seems that MDCs fear exports from LDCs even more than exports from each other, for they keep reducing their barriers to each other in the succession of GATT negotiations, while simultaneously raising barriers to LDC imports. The World Bank has calculated that LDCs could export an extra $20 billion a year of manufactures and agricultural commodities to MDCs but for quotas and other non-tariff barriers. These barriers may be reduced if fast growth is resumed, but our present context is what may happen if growth is slow, and the answer seems to be that the share of LDCs in MDC trade is more likely to fall than to rise if MDC trade is growing slowly.

The other possibility is for LDCs to buy more from each other: to look "inward" in the sense of towards each other rather than to their trade with MDCs.

The big items in LDC dependence on MDCs are food, fertiliser, cement, steel and machinery. Taken as a group LDC could quickly end their dependence for the first four, and gradually throw off their dependence for machinery. It could be that they would do better to retain their trade with MDCs for these commodities, but if MDCs will not play the game, i.e. will not take imports from LDCs, then LDCs have no option but to trade with each other. Perhaps in order to scare MDCs into recognising what they may lose if they do not play it is now customary to point out what a large share of MDC exports goes to LDCs – 24 per cent in the case of the United States; it remains to be seen how persuasive this may be.

The case for LDCs to trade more with each other and less with MDCs was much discussed in the 1950s, in the context of the general expectation that international trade would grow slowly; and of the development theory of the day, with its assumption that exports were inflexible. The discussion centred on advocating regional integration through regional customs unions and other discriminatory trade arrangements. The case was accepted, and was written into the charters of our international institutions. Over a dozen customs unions or free trade regimes have been created, the precise count depending on how one classifies the series of agreements on West Africa.

Experience of these arrangements has been mixed, but disappointing. Customs unions are fragile at two points. First, the union is particularly advantageous for sharing out industries with significant economies of scale. It runs up against the desire of each member country to retain its own light industries and in the absence of economies of scale, is unpersuasive in arguing for internal free trade in such industries. The moral is to exclude light industries from the agreement, and confine oneself from the start to those industries where economies of scale are really significant. The second point of fragility is that in a set of neighbouring countries some are much more advanced than others in industrial achievement and potential. The advanced countries attract more new industries than the less advanced, who feel that they are being exploited. The union then survives only if the more advanced countries will contribute funds to make the less attractive industrial locations more acceptable to potential investors; and this is hard to negotiate.

The future of regional agreements is therefore somewhat doubtful, but it may also not be particularly relevant to the problem in hand. Inter-LDC trade is not necessarily going to develop through each country selling more to its next door neighbours. Indeed when one bears in mind its more important targets – oil, food, fertilizers, cement, steel and machinery – and adds to this the geographical similarities of next door neighbours, distant trade between one region and another seems more to the point. One can conceive of the Middle East offering oil and petrochemicals, West Africa offering maize, Brazil and India offering machinery, and so on.

It is not clear that special measures are needed to foster inter-LDC trade at this level. If they are, the nucleus exists in the Protocol Relating to Trade Negotiations among Developing Countries which came into force in 1973, with the blessing of GATT, and which provides for negotiated preferential arrangements among sixteen of the bigger and more advanced LDCs. One may doubt, however, whether such different countries will travel much distance on the basis of mutual concessions. The fundamental requirement for a large expansion of mutual trade is a set of prices and foreign exchange rates which reflects comparative advantage and makes it cheaper for them to buy from other LDCs than to buy from MDCs, who by the definition of the problem, are unwilling to take payment in LDC exports. There are also two supplementary financial requirements. One is a loosening up of restrictions on foreign lending, so that loans from MDCs can be used to finance the sale of capital goods from LDCs. Secondly, some kind of clearing arrangements may be necessary for LDC currencies; otherwise LDC traders will tend to do business with each other in one or more MDC currencies, and will be constrained by the relative scarcity of such currencies (given our assumption that MDC imports are growing slowly).

In the end the question whether LDCs can continue to grow rapidly while MDCs stagnate turns not on trade but on the dynamism of the LDCs themselves. Trade will sort itself out if prices are allowed to reflect real costs. But growth has in the past been driven by trade; whereas our scenario calls for trade to be driven by growth. What then will drive growth? In Rostow's terms it will then turn out that some of the LDCs have already reached the stage of self-sustaining growth, while others have not. The self-sustainers are going to make it whether the rest of the world grows fast or slowly. The rest still need a background of world prosperity if they are themselves to prosper. So the sooner the world economy can recapture those postwar rates of growth, the better it will be for all of us.

NOTES

[1] There was wide variation in "performance" among developing countries. A systematic variation was that those with higher per caput incomes grew faster than those with lower per caput incomes. An important element of this is that the latter were more agricultural, and agriculture had the lowest sectoral growth rate. Thus, suppose two countries have the same sectoral growth rates (e.g. industry 7, agriculture 2.5, services 6) but the labour force distributions are 2, 3, 5 in one and 1, 6, 3 in the other, the overall growth rates will be 5.2 and 4.0, translating to say 2.7 and 1.5 per caput – a difference of a whole percentage point.

[2] This formulation presupposes (for simplicity of exposition) that there are no rents. If food is produced at increasing cost in MDCs, the price of food is lower in the new equilibrium, and the rise in raw material prices is correspondingly smaller.

[3] The price can also be raised by agreement among producers to curtail supplies, but it is difficult to enforce such agreements.

SECTION I

Micro

EARL O. HEADY

Micro-Level Accomplishments and Challenges for the Developed World

There has been a somewhat uniform trend among micro-oriented agricultural economists over recent decades. This trend has been in deep training and abilities in economic theory and related quantitative methods. The micro agricultural economic fields are supported by a strong body of economic theory and a rather wide range of advanced quantitative methods. It is now common to find a newly finished PhD in agricultural economics as well trained in these tools as is the general economist.

Going back a half century in world agricultural economics, however, this degree of homogeneity did not prevail so generally. Agricultural micro analysts came from a diverse set of backgrounds and training. Many originated as technical agriculturists and added an agricultural economics layer to become teachers and research workers in farm management, farm marketing or farm finance. Each was somewhat a specialist in the source of the data he analysed or the analytical approaches he used. Some built their analyses and communications around farmer-kept records. Others used farm surveys subjected to several forms of cross classifications relative to farm profits. A few were applying farm budgeting as a forerunner of mathematical programming. Rather than tabular cross classification of variables which might explain the magnitude of farm profits, a few statistically oriented persons were using multiple regression with some quite general models for similar purpose. Also a number were beginning to group around the central theory of production economics. Training thus extended over emphases ranging from accounting, descriptive, institutional and foundation economics. How one viewed the field largely depended on the data he used, where he worked and where he had graduate training. This diversity was expected in a field which was completing only two decades of existence. With no previous inventory of trained people, the profession had to draw people from related fields where they were available and where their interests or training encouraged them to pursue economic problems of farms, market firms and financial institutions. With so little previous research to draw on, it perhaps was best that the profession of the time was made up by persons with varied training, backgrounds and approaches in their

29

research and education but who knew agriculture well. A major accomplishment of these diverse micro economic analysts was an ability to bring economics problems of farming, marketing and financing into sufficient focus to attract financial resources and the attention of administrators, so that greater funds were available for developing the profession. Also their results were of sufficient relevance and use that farmers demanded them.

As mentioned previously, a relatively small number of institutions provided advanced graduate training in these early times and it was diverse and of varying content. In recent years, however, there has been a great convergence in the types of graduate training providing the core tools of agricultural economists, and particularly those with emphasis on micro economics. Possibly this training has become too homogeneous with respect to emphasis on neoclassical economic theory, mathematical economics and statistical and quantitative methods. While there still are ample grounds for philosophical debate, it sometimes appears that we are on the verge of producing a class of economist clones. However, this homogeneity of training need not be dangerous. What is important is that the array of theoretical and quantitative tools available be applied in the context of "here is a relevant real world problem, what is the most efficient tool for its solution", rather than ask "here is a shiny tool, where is a problem to which I can apply it". If the tools are used in the context of the former, analysis is likely to stay in touch with real world clientele and research will be conducted on its behalf with tools which are best adapted to it. If the latter approach dominates, analysts will insulate themselves from urgent problems and their solutions. To an extent, the somewhat tight orientation to illustration of tool application over recent decades has been in this direction.

In any case, a large and highly refined set of economic concepts and quantitative tools are available for analysis of the micro problems surrounding agriculture and its related sectors. No other field of agricultural economics has better backup in basic theory and quantitative method. These theories and quantitative methods have allowed analysts of the last three decades to make great progress in a more systematic collection and application of data for decision-making at the firm level. Too, these theories and methods have allowed them to process and apply much more data and larger data sets than did the tools of a half century back. Early micro analysts for agriculture made a quantitative quest for those factors which determine farm profits. Later analysts, using neoclassical firm theory, knew the conditions under which profits were maximized and ordered their search for data accordingly. Concepts of marginal and other cost functions led them to engineering syntheses and budgeting approaches which allowed estimation of cost functions relevant to decision making or knowledge of cost economies relating to firm size. Marginal concepts and their potential application in profit maximizing led agricultural economists to interdisciplinary studies with physical and biological scientists. A large range of crop and livestock production functions have been estimated and used in extension recommendations to farmers, in classroom teaching and to further research designs. These trends have enough momentum that biological and physical scientists now can carry most response research by themselves.

Production economists and farm management specialists were quick to put computers, mathematical programming, simulation and related methods to use in analysing the potential structure of farms and in guiding farm decisions. Of course, much larger models and greater farm coverage were possible than with less formal budgeting techniques. Application of these approaches has progressed so rapidly that extension specialists now offer farm planning and analysis systems by means of programming models, computerized record systems, farm simulation models and prog-rammable hand calculators. There has been a general growth in the demand for advanced systems information and in the ability of clientele to absorb it. This is not only true at the farmer level but also courses in linear programming and simulation models of farm and market firms are taught to undergraduates in most agricultural colleges of developed countries. The high level of education of farmers in developed countries will cause these trends and possibilities to continue.

Perhaps greatest advances in micro analysis and communication have been in a normative setting where certain assumptions prevail with respect to the objective function, the farmer's knowledge of production and price parameters, capital levels and tenure conditions. The optimiz-ing tools such as conventional theory and mathematical programming have facilitated this progress. However, as is detailed later, important progress was made over recent decades in positive analyses and in pre-dicting farmer response behaviour. True, these time series analyses have been aggregations of quantities for a nation, region or state. But the models which underlay them are based on postulates of firm behaviour. These positive analyses have been useful in policies and market outlook work in developed countries, but especially in proving farmer responses in developing countries to favourable commodity and input pricing policies.

Some progress was made on problems of decisions under conditions of risk and uncertainty, the real world environment of farm and market firm decision and management. The need for progress in this area has been emphasized continuously for three decades.[1] Some refinement of con-cepts and development of empirical procedures extended over this entire time span. Generally, problems of decisions under uncertainty were recognized but given limited space in books written on farm and market firm management. Only in the last decade have entire books been devoted to agricultural decisions under uncertainty. Hopefully this mod-ification and extension of decision theory, and some parallel empirical applications by various persons, will gain greater momentum and have more resources devoted to it in the future. Our progress in this realm, especially in availability of useful risk management procedures for appli-cation in firm decision-making, has been too small in the last thirty years.

Farmers have indeed used decision procedures adapted to uncertainty. But they, rather than the professional agricultural economist, have constructed the models. One finds literature which micro analysts have written mainly for each other in illustration of decisions under risk, but one finds very little written or in a form to explain these procedures to farmers. Is this void due to a gap in communication between research and extension workers or to a still existing inability to communicate modern decision theory to farmers? If it is the latter, some reallocation of resources is justified – with a greater proportion going into translation of these procedures for farmers.

Agriculture in developed countries has gone through mammoth structural change since World War II. These structural changes have arisen because of the favourable real prices of capital relative to the price of labour and a flow of technologies giving rise to extended cost economies. Except where institutional conditions restrained them, these are resulting in a vast decline in the number of farms and people employed in agriculture. Some farm families decide to stay and enlarge operations; others seek employment elsewhere. Decisions on these changes are made in micro units. The extent to which they are aided by micro economists is unknown and varies among countries and states depending on the magnitude of public investment in agricultural economics research and extension. The emphases of agricultural micro analysts have probably been biased towards large farms and farm enlargement. Hence, more assistance has been given to those who stay and enlarge, than to those who give up and leave.

THE FUTURE

With large technical, financial and size changes still going on, we are challenged to determine who our relevant clients are, and the consequences of emphasizing different clients. By restricting ourselves to one set of clients, we are likely to work ourselves out of employment. The computerized record systems, on-line programming models to help select crop and livestock systems and similar services of extension education so far have been directed at the larger farm. What incentives can be developed to encourage similar efforts on behalf of small farmers, part-time farmers and beginning farmers?

With the larger-scale power and machinery units of high capital costs now available, a further leap in farm size, specialization and industrialization is in sight. Prospects are that while a ragtag collection of small and part-time farms may prevail in market economies, a small number of large industrial farms eventually will dominate the supply of food commodities in developed countries. These steps are nearly accomplished in Eastern Europe and are progressing rapidly in the West. What should be the micro analyst's role in this process? Should he help to hurry it – through the problems and clients he selects and the techniques he uses?

Agricultural economists in developed countries seem highly concerned about small farms and their progress in developing countries, but more oriented to work with big farms in their own countries. As stated previously, economic research, extension and teaching directed at farmers over recent decades generally have had the large commercial farm as their focus. Even the concepts and the tools encourage this emphasis. If one is to keep in style his research should be of an orientation entailing computerized models with some degree of mathematical sophistication and fair sized computer applications. Large farms provide these potentials better than do small farms. Also, the persons who can best use the results of sophisticated models are well educated farmers operating on a large scale with a continuous quest for knowledge to help optimize, satisfice, finance and expand their operations.

These farmers will have a growing demand for agricultural economists who can aid them in their quest. This opportunity and prospect excites many micro analysts because it calls for more complex models and computer applications. And while it is an intellectually exciting opportunity, it also has its pitfalls. Eventually, as farms grow large enough, there may be so few of them that public support of analysts to service them may decline. Under technology now available, the state of Iowa could be farmed by a tenth of its present or 13,000 large-scale operators. When this time arrives, as it eventually will, how many farm management specialists and production economists should the public supply to aid farmers' decision processes? Or should it supply any, letting these large business firms pay for management services from private consulting companies as is done by medium sized firms in other sectors of market economies?

An interrelated problem of size, client served and capital relates to long-run inflationary tendencies and related levels of land prices. Under the high prices for agricultural land which have arisen, investing in land for purposes of returns from farming *per se* gives an extremely low return. Investment is profitable only in terms of further inflation in land prices and prospective capital gains. Mainly it is the wealthy farm families which can pay these high land prices and buy for these purposes. Hence, with continued land price and general inflation, the financial sieve eventually retains only wealthy farmers to serve as clients of the farm management or production economics specialist.

Other questions arise in this complex: should micro analysts continue to focus their efforts on this sector of large farms and aid them in becoming larger? Or should they turn their efforts to effective means of restraining growth of large farms and stimulating small farms? The answers to these questions will vary by country and the values different societies attach to traditional farming versus industrialized agriculture. Legislation in Saskatchewan province of Canada emphasizes aid to the beginning small farmer.

In the same philosophical framework, we may ask: when the stage of development becomes so high that only a very small percentage of a nation's population and work force remain in agriculture and farms become very large, will society abandon its long-held unique concern for traditional farmers? If so, does or should the public's role in supplying economists to analyse and solve problems of agriculture revolve more nearly around its own interests in reasonable and stable food supplies and prices, or in improving the efficiency of the marketing and processing sectors whose components dominate the price of food at retail? Is the function of the farm management, production economist and credit specialist then to serve the interest of farmers or consumers?

Some economists suggest that agriculture has lost its uniqueness as an industry and as an institution, and that policy for it now has drifted away from the traditional concern over farm prices and income. A large number of issues and factors are now focused on the farming sector and have interest in programmes and policies for it. Consumers are interested in the drugs and chemicals used by farms and their migration through the system as residuals in food. Environmentalists are concerned with the pollution impacts of pesticides, fertilizers, livestock production systems, cropping systems and other farm technologies which produce sediment. The energy intensiveness of developed agriculture will be of increasing concern in most countries, as will competition for water in some. As mentioned elsewhere, the structure of farms has importance to rural communities and the amount of nonfarm employment and income which is generated in them. Other issues relate to nutrition, tax equity and land use. This complex of concerns represents another reason why the focus of many micro analysts may need to shift from being mainly the servant of the farmer in aiding him to increase income and asset values, to analyses directed toward the external interests in farm technology as it relates to food contaminants, the environment, energy and water use, etc. For the latter focus, farm research will need to measure and emphasize alternatives to, and the real costs of, resource uses required or prohibited in meeting these external interests. These outward interests are important, and may become dominant, in societies where no more than 10 per cent of the population is in agriculture, as many developed countries are or will soon be. In the future perhaps micro analyses of farms should have major objectives of helping policy makers who must administer regulations and social goals in the use of agricultural resources. These programmes and decisions on them are implemented at the firm level of action.

Vertical integration of farm production and growing linkages of farm decisions and management to financial services and input suppliers has caused agricultural economists to coin new designations for agriculture and its related sectors. Some suggest that we should no longer look upon farming as a distinct industry but as part of a continuum making up the national food system, or as part of a continuum denoted as the agribusiness complex. If we consider these systems, rather than their components, to be the dominant concern of agricultural economists, then does the micro analysis concentrate on (for example) the integrating or central firm, with the farm component simply being a linkage to it? Instead of building systems models of farms, should we build them of this larger complex with the farm as simply one "box" in the overall system?

EXTERNALITIES

Where farm decision results on technology and size give rise to negative externalities, it can be questioned if micro economic research is sufficiently complete in all cases if it is concluded at the boundaries of the farm or market firm. This negative spillover of farm adjustments and change is unique in some countries. It falls on people in rural areas who are especially disadvantaged in education, spatially separated from labour markets, females with meagre employment opportunities and others. As a minimum compensation, groups bearing the negative incidence of the technologies employed by and the large adjustments of farms are owed as much research and guidance as goes into research and extension education for the farms that erode their economic opportunities, institutions and environment. Hence, to each micro analysis with implied negative externalities there should be attached an analysis directed at restoration of the welfare of its victims.

ONGOING AND UPDATED MODELS

In earlier times each micro research project was a discrete activity. Data were gathered and analysed, and a manuscript was published. A completely new study then was initiated. Under current research technology, there is the tendency to develop models with continuous updating so that new data for a farm, or data of different farms, can be plugged into it to provide a stream of solutions or results over time. Once the setup costs of developing the model have been met, this can be an economical means of continuously supplying extension specialists, farmers and marketing or other firms with information for decisions. For models directed at repeated use to aid farmer decision making, the question can be asked: does the continued application of the model with additional data for other farms, or the same farm in another year, represent research? There now is a much greater need than in previous times for joint appointment of extension personnel to some research time. The research portion might be used for developing models, updating and extension of developed models, with the extension portion allocated to their continued application as aids in farm decisions. This total activity, which has started, has room for much greater development and application.

INTERDISCIPLINARY OPPORTUNITIES

In earlier times agricultural economists worked long and hard to enlist physical scientists in co-operative research which would provide data of more appropriate form for decisions. This situation is changing rapidly and as often as not, the physical scientist now searches out the economist. The interest of highly commercial farms in economic outcomes and analyses had caused animal scientists, agronomists and others to attempt to understand and apply what they term systems analysis. To an extent, what these groups term systems analysis is more or less a synonym for economic analysis. They sometimes embrace orthodox marginal analysis or linear programming as readily as conventional systems simulations. Add these resources to the growing number and capabilities of farm production economists and further impetus is provided to highly capitalized and large farms which wish to accentuate these characteristics. However, it also provides a widening opportunity for co-operative activity between economists and technical scientists. This generation of technical scientists generally has studied economics and mathematics, at least at the undergraduate level. They have abilities to move ahead rapidly in team efforts. The complexity of agricultural systems and decisions in highly developed agricultures will need more of this interdisciplinary activity in the future. Economists can contribute to estimates of the payoff from developing different characteristics in animals and plants for different market and financial environments; physical scientists can identify the restraints and possibilities in these developments. Together, too, they need to design experiments and analyse them in a manner to reflect the risky responses of the real world.

Although there are some outstanding exceptions, economists dealing with micro problems of agriculture have insulated themselves from co-operative endeavours with other social scientists more than with other technical scientists. We need to assess the possibilities of greater aid from and interaction with other social scientists in tackling ongoing and upcoming facets of highly commercialized agricultures. Evidently the values and objective functions of these decision makers is changing rapidly. Today's able young managers have occupational goals greatly different from those of their grandfathers. Many prefer to compare their goals of income and living styles with those of a medium sized corporation president. Then there also are questions of the values of society towards farm structure. If, as some suppose, societies of developed countries are now interested in farms only as links in a food system, in contrast to a decade back when they paid heavy public subsidies to keep farms solvent for the sake of the farm family *per se*, the micro analyst is given a licence to work only with and to rapidly incorporate the most commercial of commercial farms, so that they more rapidly grow fewer in number and larger in size – as long as he cleans up the impacts on other social groups resulting from externalities created by adjustments to larger farms. This licence will not exist under other values relating to farms and their families.

While decisions under risk should draw more attention in the future, refinement and extension of the theory may require little participation of other social scientists. However, quantifying models in the real world (e.g., in measuring utility and risk aversion and in establishing the components of multi-goal objective functions) and making them of actual widespread use stand to benefit greatly from participation by psychologists, sociologists and anthropologists.

FORWARD PROBLEMS

We need to look ahead to major problems which will emerge and have research answers forthcoming when they arrive. Much of the progress made by developed agricultures over the last fifty years has been linked to a growing use of cheap energy. During the next fifty years energy will play an equally important role, but more because of its relative scarcity and high price. Completely new technology sets and farming systems may be required. Biomass harvested for energy production could become important in the product mix of farms. For problems which are going to become so major as those revolving around future energy supplies and prices, research should run ten years ahead of the time these problems actually embrace farms. We need an increasing proportion of our research devoted to these problems of the longer-run future.

A large effort has gone into the quantification of the returns from public investment in agricultural research and education over the last two decades. It has been proven several times that "agricultural research does pay off" and that the "returns are quite high as compared to other investment alternatives". These findings have been replicated for numerous commodities in several developed countries; they have been repeated in several developing countries. From the results, it seems only that research administrators need go blindly forward and invest in research. Still, the "sorting out" has not been completed. Not all research in agriculture gives the same marginal return to investment, as past studies nearly imply. Given present states of technology, what should be the priorities for further investment? For which commodities and which technologies will the marginal return from research investment be high or low? It seems more challenging to answer these questions, and thus supply better guidance in allocation of research resources, than simply replicate more studies that show "in general, agricultural research pays a handsome return". Being close to agriculture, as many farm management and production economists are, they seem excellently experienced to provide this guidance. But can they do so any better than their physical and biological counterparts? It is a challenge for the future, both in avoidance of more duplicating studies and in guiding investment to those points where return is the greatest.

THEORY AND OPTIMIZATION

Some extreme propositions have been made about the theoretical framework within which farmers operate and the implied utility of this theory. Schultz supposes farmers are active optimizers and refined marginal tuners in his statement:[2] "Farmers the world over, in dealing with costs, returns and risks, are calculating economic agents. Within their small, individual allocative domain, they are fine tuning entrepreneurs, tuning so subtly that many experts fail to see how efficient they are. . . ." Johnson supposes that optimization theory has to be highly qualified and may even have impaired the work of farm management workers in North America and Europe.[3] So, what theory should micro-level workers use in the future?

Concentration of graduate study in theory at most major training universities is in conventional static theory of the firm where it is supposed price and production function parameters are known with certainty, and production functions are continuous. While this optimization paraphernalia is considered to provide useful concepts and, where used appropriately, has been employed as useful background for quantitative analysis of agriculture, it also has been long known that real world decisions and adjustment to changing price, technical and other parameters is conditioned by risk aversion, utility maximization, adjustments in distributed lags, capital restraints, equity, multi-goal objective functions, firm-household interactions and related phenomena.

Perhaps conventional optimizing theory was used more widely in recent decades because theory related to time and stochastic phenomena was not yet sufficiently operational. A sizeable number of commodity supply or resource demand studies have been made and suggest with quantitative success how farmers do respond to changing technology and market values and which implicitly assume that farmers are profit motivated and adjust in the direction of increasing returns or lessening losses (even if they don't have in mind the first and second order conditions which define a maximum or minimum).[4] At somewhat early times, a number of studies incorporated distributed lags, lagged variables, interyear restraints on responses (flexibility restraints), and cautious optimizing, in recognition that farms do not make instantaneous, pure and complete shifts for each incremental change in price and technology parameters. In general, these studies provided quantitative verification that farmers both (a) respond to price and technological change in the general theoretical manner expected, but (b) these responses are restrained in the short run, with greater elasticity quantified for the long run. For some time it has been supposed that farmers may maximize things other than profit, such as utility. For more than a decade, quantitative work has been underway to relate utility to decision-making. Recent efforts include attempts to incorporate risk and risk aversion considerations directly into the estimation of supply response.[5]

A major complex of problems for developed countries in the decades ahead will be a better understanding of the process and goals of change in agriculture. Unless the world develops offsets to fluctuating weather, wide shifts in international grain trade and rapid inflation, farm decisions will continue to be made under great uncertainty and high resource prices. While progress has not been as rapid as we might have wished, considerable progress was certainly made over the last two decades in quantifying this change as it is modified by alternative decision strategies for uncertainty, resource fixity, multi-goal objective functions, maximization of utility as related to level and variance of expected income, distributed lag and recursive types of responses and other constructs and phenomena which depart from the static theory of the firm. In some cases, such as *Agricultural Decision Analysis* and *Decisions Under Uncertainty*,[6] some large forward leaps have been made in theory and initial applications. We need more of these focused and concentrated efforts to modify theory, measurement and empirical method where they are too weak to explain farmer behaviour or to provide him guidance in a relevant real world decision framework. The present "assessment of the state of the arts" suggests that we have a considerable distance to go in (a) meaningfully measuring risk preference, utility curves, subjective probability distributions and related phenomena, and (b) using them either better to understand decision-making under uncertainty or applying them in manners useful to farmers in the actual decision-making process.

So while micro analysts are better supplied with theoretical tools and quantitative methods than other fields of agricultural economics, they are challenged to fill voids where they exist. To inventory the voids is a useful activity but at some point it becomes more urgent to develop or adapt the theory needed to fill them. Never has the profession been better manned to do so. It has a large number of extremely well trained young people who not only know the theory and can adapt it but also can apply it quantitatively. It is even possible that the firepower of these "soldiers" is entirely superior to the target which they need to attack. If so, the need is to get an appropriate number of them directed to developing and adapting the theory needed to fill the voids.

NOTES

[1] For example, see: Heady, Earl O. "Elementary Models in Farm Production Economics Research", *Journal of Farm Economics*, Vol. 31, pp. 201–25, 1948; and Johnson, G.L. et al. *Managerial Processes of Midwest Farmers*, Iowa State University Press, Ames 1961.

[2] Schultz, T.W. "Economics and Politics in Agriculture" in *Distortions of Agricultural Incentives*, Indiana University Press, Bloomington 1978, p. 4.

[3] Johnson, G.L. "A Critical Review of Selected Studies of Agrarian Change Done Prior to TACAC," *European Review of Agricultural Economics*, Vol. 3–213, p. 188, 1976.

[4] Examples include: Johnson, G.L. *Burley Tobacco Control Programs*, Kentucky Experiment Station Bulletin 580, 1952; Judge, G.G. *Econometric Relationships of The Demand and Supply Relationship for Eggs*, Connecticut Experiment Station Bulletin 307, 1954; Hildreth, C. and Jarrett, F.G. *A Statistical Study of Livestock Production and Marketing*, John Wiley and Sons, New York 1955; Mundlak, Y. and McCorkle, C.O. Statistical Analyses of Supply Response in Spring Potatoes *California Journal of Farm Economics*, Vol. 38, pp. 553–69, 1956; Grileches, Z. "The Demand for Fertilizer; An Economic Interpretation of Technical Change", *Journal of Farm Economics*, Vol. 41, pp. 591–606, 1958; Nerlove, M. *The Dynamics of Supply – Estimation of Farmers' Response to Price*,

John Hopkins Press, Baltimore 1953; Dean G.W. and Heady, E.O. "Changes in Supply Elasticity and Response for Hogs", *Journal of Farm Economics*, Vol. 40, pp. 845–60, 1953; Heady, E.O. et al. (ed.) *Agricultural Supply Functions*, Iowa State University Press, Ames 1961; and Heady, E.O. and Tweeten, L.G. *Resource Demand and The Structure of The Agricultural Industry*, Iowa State University Press, Ames 1963.

[8] Hazell, P.B.R., Norton, R.D., Malathi, P. and Pomeroda, Carlos *The Importance of Risk in Agricultural Planning Models*, World Bank Staff Working Paper No. 307, Washington, 1978; Boussard, J.M. "The Introduction of Risk into a Programming Model: Different Criteria and The Actual Behavior of Farmers", *European Economic Review*, Vol. 1, pp. 92–121, 1969; Just, R.E. "Investigation of Importance of Risk in Farmer's Decisions", *American Journal of Agricultural Economics*, Vol. 5, pp. 14–25, 1974; Len, W. "Measuring Aggregate Supply Response Under Instability", *American Journal of Agricultural Economics*, Vol. 59, pp. 903–7, 1977.

[6] Anderson, J.R., Dillon J.L. and Hardaker, B. *Agricultural Decision Analysis,* Iowa State University Press, Ames 1977; Halter, A.N. and Dean, G.W. *Decisions Under Uncertainty*, Southwestern Publishing Co., Cincinnati 1971.

DISCUSSION OPENING – ARNE LARSEN

A considerable part of Professor Heady's paper relates to the scope of work undertaken, or the scope of work which should be undertaken by the micro-level agricultural economists. Consequently it relates to the training of the agricultural economist. It underlines that the agricultural economist now generally is well trained in economic theory and in quantitative methods, and that the training gives a large homogeneity. There can hardly be any doubt that the training in economic theory has been very beneficial and has greatly enhanced the credibility of the agricultural economist. When it comes to the training in and application of quantitative methods there is probably reason for more scepticism. While quantitative methods are essential tools for the economist, has there not been a rather one-sided emphasis on these tools at the expense of training concerning the institutional and human framework within which the tools are used? Sometimes one even has the feeling that the emphasis on quantitative methods is a convenient escape from real life realities. Not least at the micro-level sophisticated quantitative methods have often failed because of the predominant importance of individual managerial skills in a family-farm dominated agriculture. While complicated quantitative tools may be important for gaining new knowledge, they still have to be reasonably understandable for the users in order to avoid a credibility gap. The question is whether there is a reasonable balance between emphasis on the tools used and knowledge of the changing society in which they are used.

A number of challenges for the future, as mentioned by Heady, is closely connected with the remarks made on the training of agricultural economists. Within the agricultural production sector further work on inflationary, interdisciplinary and uncertainty aspects is needed. The inflationary aspect does not only influence the farmer's investment decisions, but it also influences his decisions concerning output-mix, when for instance pensionable farmers hang on to the farm in order to reap additional capital gains. Surprisingly little research has been carried out on the effect of capital gains and most farm level economic analyses are still carried out without consideration of the influence of expected capital gains. There also seems to be plenty of scope for interdisciplinary work with the technical disciplines. Particularly in establishing the framework for investment decisions the economist should take the lead in bringing together the involved disciplines. Concerning uncertainty aspects for the farmer, there is clearly a need for a systematic framework usable at the farm level.

In his paper, Heady returns several times to areas of work which have not traditionally involved the agricultural micro-level economist. While this is somewhat related to the shrinking number of farmers, it is also a response to public demand, on the one side, for larger considerations of environmental, food quality and other less tangible technical aspects, and, on the other side, for more consideration of the social problems appearing in the wake of continuous productivity increases and an ever increasing farm specialization and farm capital concentration. While these areas provide plenty of opportunities for agricultural economists, the question is whether we are prepared to take up the challenge. Agricultural economists and agricultural researchers in general are occasionally accused – and undoubtedly with some reason – of being too inbred with the farm – food sector. Such questions of credibility must not be allowed to arise when agricultural economists become heavily involved in research concerning agriculturally related areas.

As the general economic outlook for the coming years is probably not too bright for most of the world, the increasing demand for establishing stricter priorities for research investments is likely to be further underlined. Agricultural economists should help in establishing these priorities by estimating the likely returns in different research areas. The process of priority setting would also provide the researchers with an opportunity to explain the value of research to politicians and interest groups.

While further micro-level work on agricultural production aspects could give plenty of scope for discussion, I suggest that the discussion here might concentrate on whether the training of the agricultural economist is sufficiently wide in scope, particularly to cope with the challenge raised by "new agenda" problems.

GENERAL DISCUSSION – RAPPORTEUR: LARS BRINK

Several points were raised in the discussion. The possibility of using models of medium and large farms as components of a Leontief type model was indicated, but a concurrent concern about the usefulness of such an undertaking was voiced. Dr Heady stressed that he did not argue for the use of any particular model, but wanted to make the point that fewer agricultural economists may be needed if farms are fewer.

The priority to be put on work with small farms, as compared to large farms, was discussed. This priority would depend on the particular country in question. Farm size projections for the US Midwest made thirty years ago have now become true. The question of whether agricultural economists should work with small or large farms could have been asked and discussed already at that time in the same vein as today.

The role of agricultural economists working in developing countries, but trained in developed countries, was discussed. Reference was made to Collinson's paper (page 43). The interface between agricultural economists with a macro perspective and those with a micro perspective, as well as farmers themselves, was seen as a possible problem (such as relating farm level decision making to demand and supply projections). Extension activities in some countries are dealing with this problem.

Participants in the dicussion included Edmund A. Nightingale, John R. Raeburn, Ramesh C. Agrawal and R. Thamarajakshi.

MICHAEL P. COLLINSON

Micro-Level Accomplishments and Challenges for the Less Developed World*

Having taken on the job of writing this paper I found access to sources on Asia and Latin America well nigh impossible. I apologise for the African bias in the paper. It brings a strong emphasis on manpower constraints as an influence on the appropriateness of methodologies and neglect, perhaps, of social structure as an important determinant of economic activity. I trust delegates with relevant experience will help offset this bias as they see fit in the discussion.[1]

I hope we have a consensus that at the micro-level the profession should be seeking the improvement of agricultural productivity, increased employment opportunities and a wide distribution of benefits across the millions of small farmers making up the major part of the populations of LDCs. The sequence of micro-level research in farm economics is the same in developed and less developed agriculture. Investigation is followed by analysis and the sequence completed by planning and advice. However the way this sequence is institutionalised, the balance between these three phases and the methods useful in each phase varies with the circumstances of the agricultural economy and with the characteristics of the farmers under research. These circumstances and characteristics differ from developed to less developed agriculture, where a cost effective micro level sequence must deal with types of farms rather than the individual.

The paper is divided into three parts; first the context of micro-level research is briefly described, secondly some history of our efforts in this context is recalled and discussed, and thirdly some of the challenges ahead are identified.

THE CONTEXT

For those accepting the better welfare of millions of small farmers as a goal the challenge lies in the circumstances of agriculture and the charac-

* Read by Derek Byerlee in the absence of the author.

43

teristics of farmers in LDCs. I outline here this context which influences the choice of an effective approach to Farm Economics Research.

Fifty to ninety per cent of the total population in most LDCs are small farmers; therefore very large numbers of farmers must be covered. Development efforts must be cost effective as the other sectors are not large or strong enough to subsidise agriculture. With relatively small urban populations, market opportunities tend to be limited and homogeneous over wide geographical areas. Social homogeneity dominates eating habits and influences agricultural practices. Social customs, obligations and hierarchy may distort the effects of market forces on farmers' decision-making. Rudimentary market development creates uncertainty in crop sales and retail purchases, and thus inhibits specialisation. Price and policy instability enhances the risks attached to market dependence. Apart from the farmers themselves, government agricultural research services are the main source of new technology. Governments also operate farmer advisory services. Low levels of qualified manpower are available to these government services and the opportunity costs of using it at the farm level are very high.

Small farmers by definition operate small units. The value of annual output generally ranges between US$ 200 and US$ 600. In an environment of weather and market uncertainty they often operate complex farming systems to meet a predominant objective of day to day food supply. Food is often produced on the farm because of the vagaries of markets. The threat to basic needs from uncertainties of the weather and markets leads to risk averse behaviour and security oriented management strategies. The low level of surplus production achieved and the risk-averse nature of small farmers result in low levels of capital use. The same capital scarcity and risk aversity inhibit dramatic changes from their existing situation. Small farmers change in small steps consistent with their resource endowments and risk preferences.

This then is the context – large numbers of small farmers often operating complex farming systems to satisfy a food security objective threatened by uncertainties of markets and weather.

SOME ACCOMPLISHMENTS IN MICRO–LEVEL RESEARCH IN LDC AGRICULTURE

Let us have a look at the major thrusts of micro-level research in LDC agriculture over the last twenty-five years. With its foundation in 1939 the Indian Society of Agricultural Economics is probably the earliest professional association in a LDC. Evidence of the profession in other parts of Asia, Africa and the Caribbean began to filter through in the 1950s but in a very *ad hoc* way (Conklin 1957, Clayton 1957, Jolly 1957). I have divided early professional activities into four types. I discuss each type briefly. The first two use approaches inherited from developed countries; the Comparative Approach, in which standards derived from surveys are used to diagnose weakness in the farm business under investigation, and the individual Farm Planning Approach, in which data from the farm are used to plan partial changes in resource allocation or to determine an optimal allocation.

1 *The use of developed country approaches in large-farm sectors.* Several LDCs have large-farm sectors within dualist agricultural economies where both the Comparative Approach and the Individual Farm Planning Approach have been applied under similar condition to those of the developed countries. Kenya for example has had a Farm Economic Survey Unit from 1957 onwards which carries out farm and enterprise cost studies and draws up standards for farms in the commercial sector. This category is not discussed further since it is irrelevant to the unique problems of small farms in LDC agriculture.

2 *The use of developed country approaches among small farmers.* Several LDCs have effected a direct transfer of approaches used in developed countries to their small farm sector. Kenya extended the Comparative Approach to its small farm sector in 1962 (MacArthur 1968) and still has District guidelines as enterprise standards against which individual farm performance can be compared, and from which farm plans can be designed. India recognised farm planning as a tool for improved productivity and launched a farm planning programme in seven IADP Districts in 1960. Even in India where the skilled manpower situation is less pressing, considerable professional controversy arose over the efficacy of planning at the level of the individual farm. Many South East Asia countries, including the Philippines, Thailand, Korea and Taiwan also have Farm Management Research and Extension services focused on the planning of the individual farm unit. In general these approaches borrowed from developed countries have been inappropriate for the same reason; professional competence is required at the level of the *individual* farm for implementation. Coverage of the small-holder sector is negligible and costs per farm unit are very high because of the large numbers of farms involved and the scarcity of skilled manpower.

3 *Research and development in methodology.* Two streams of research can be identified in the development of methodology appropriate to small farmers circumstances – one is data collection methods, the other in the application of planning techniques to analyse farm level data.

While India has a very strong base of data collection instruments underwritten by highly capable statisticians and although farm classification is inherently easier in smallholder agriculture, the sampling problems due to the multi-variate nature of Farm Management Surveys are compounded by scarce funds and personnel and by the illiterate populations under investigation. Personal interview is the only method of enumeration and is associated with high levels of observational error. It can be supplemented by objective measurement techniques (e.g. crop cutting) necessarily expensive of time and people. Much of the work in the early 1960s was used to assess which parameters in which circumstances could be collected by low cost limited visit collection techniques and which required frequent visits throughout the agricultural season. The results of much of this work emerged in the early 1970s (Hunt 1966, Collinson 1972, Spencer 1972, Norman 1973, Kearle et al. 1976). While there is a better understanding of the circumstances under which low cost limited visit surveys can be used, there is no clear professional consensus on their usefulness for the collection of labour use and output data and indeed on the costs of errors in these variables when using the data.

Recent emphasis has placed priority on survey work drawing on anthropological methods and aimed at understanding rather than quantifying the farming system – what are farmers doing and why are they doing it that way? These methods seek a low cost/rapid approach as an essential starting point for a bread and butter contribution from the profession.

The other stream of development in methodology has emphasized planning techniques for manipulating farm level data. In the early 1950s Jolly established Unit Farm as "test-beds" for examining small farmer problems (Jolly 1952, 1957). These were repeated extensively, certainly in Africa (Collinson 1969), but were largely superseded in the early 1960s by paper models once holistic techniques for farm planning became widespread in developed countries. These experiments in farm analysis were a direct transfer from the profession in developed countries, with linear programming (Clayton 1963) and programme planning (Collinson 1963) predominant. There was perhaps more concern with the effects of uncertainty (Heyer 1972), seen to be of greater importance to small farmers, and more priority on food supplies in resource allocation. In India, Kahlon (1962) drew attention to the Representative Farm as a possible way around the implementation bottleneck for individual farm plans. Most of the experiments in the 1960s recognised this and were made on a typical farm basis at the area level.

In the mid 1960s the professional focus took a new turn – the relevance of agricultural research efforts began to be called into question both in LDCs (Belshaw and Hall 1964) and in developed countries (McMeekan 1964, Davidson and Martin 1965). This was based perhaps on a growing emphasis in agricultural development theory on the importance of new agricultural technologies to break the Schultzian "steady state". This questioning of the efficacy of traditional crop by crop agricultural research was particularly strong in francophone Africa where a systems orientation emerged, for example in Senegal, as early as 1966 (Elliot 1977). This growing disillusionment was given weight by two other thrusts; one emphasising the economic logic of many small farmer practices given their circumstances (Norman 1974), the other emphasising the need to evaluate innovations in a systems context to understand their consequences for small farmers (Collinson 1968, 1972). From these three thrusts a link has been forged in the last few years, between Farming Systems Research (FSR) and adaptive agricultural experimentation. This link which is discussed later in this paper has begun to attract the attention of professionals working at the micro-level in many LDCs (Hildebrand 1976, Norman 1978, CIMMYT Economics Group 1979).

4 *Improving Theories of Agricultural Development*. A burgeoning interest in the theory of agricultural development in LDCs stimulated considerable spin-off in understanding small farmer behaviour. Micro-level research became a tool used by both planners and academics for improving plan orientation and theory. Many of these initiatives were by developed country universities (IFO, Munich Africa Study Series 1962 onwards, e.g. Ruthenburg 1968, African Rural Employment Study Series, MSU 1971). In this category might also be included the extensive adoption studies carried out in small farmer populations and throwing light on the priorities, capacities and attitudes of small farmers (Roy et al. 1968, CIMMYT 1976).

After reviewing these four categories, it seems fair to conclude that the profession has made little *direct* contribution, that is at a bread and butter level, to the improvement of incomes of the millions of small farmers dominating LDC economies. The reasons for this seem clear.

First, our profession, and of course others, had no clear target in view, and therefore no clear criteria for an appropriate approach to micro-level research. Politicians of the newly independent states had a need for visual evidence of progress. In agriculture this was manifested in machines and concrete. Research was viewed as unproductive and improvement through extension as painfully slow, and the aid agencies were dominated by the strategy of sector transformation through settlement and irrigation schemes. It took until the late 1960s to see that the structural changes and management intensity implied by machines, concrete and transformation necessarily focused all available funds and manpower on a tiny proportion of the rural population.

Second, the state of the arts in micro-level research in LDC agriculture has been rudimentary. There seems to me to have been a tremendous confusion in the profession active in LDC agriculture in the 1960s – a confusion between R & D in techniques and efforts to develop an approach for a bread and butter contribution to agricultural improvement. I must lay some of this confusion at the door of the heavy emphasis on technique in American universities over the period. A "have tool will travel" mentality was evident in graduate students converging on the LDCs on the initiative of their professors. Much of the academic interest was in micro-level research to throw light on theory and strategy in agricultural development, certainly one useful emphasis at that time. Undoubtedly however, it contributed to the fact that up until the mid 1970s the profession had little to offer smallholder agriculture in LDCs at the "bread and butter" level.

Thirdly, and still a continuing factor, is the traditional technical establishment in LDC agriculture. In many LDCs the improvement of agriculture remains synonymous with achieving higher yields per unit of land. Moreover research has been insulated from the farmer. This narrow orientation and the farmer isolation from research were inculcated by expatriates trained in the technical tradition of their homelands. Many local professionals have the same metropolitan training and, with it, the same orientation and insularity. This is particularly damaging in the small farm sector. Large farmers have the education to sift research results for themselves and often the authority to orient research efforts to their problems. Small farmers rely entirely on "improvements" channelled to them, through the extension service, as prescriptions from a doctor. But the farmer/research link is rarely developed; the doctor never sees his patient, a lack of concern which reflects a teacher/pupil mentality permeating the predominantly technical establishments.

The profession with little conviction as to its role, uncertain of the validity of its techniques and with numbers very thin on the ground, had little to offer over the sixties and seventies. But all innovations are proved by "fire and water" and perhaps the trials of the sixties and seventies have provided us with a sound basis for the years ahead. I turn now to the opportunities and challenges for the profession to make a direct contribution to the improved well-being of small farmers across LDC agriculture in the future.

OPPORTUNITIES AND CHALLENGES IN MICRO–LEVEL RESEARCH

1 *The Contribution*. Farming Systems Research is the key to our contribution for the future. It brings the small farmers' perspectives to the planning of zone oriented adaptive experiments to provide appropriate content for area based agricultural development programmes. It begins with the assumption that the farmer manages his resources to give a balance of production, with his knowledge and ability, which meets his priorities. Almost inevitably, at some point in the system, the allocation of resources to one commodity implies a compromise in the management of other commodities and other resources.[2]

FSR seeks to understand these compromises. It describes what farmers are doing and why they are doing it that way. Its holistic perspective is also the farmers' perspective as a decision-maker. It describes compromises being made and the resources imposing them. FSR focuses adaptive agricultural experimentation by identifying areas of management where the farmer is flexible and where improved management will contribute to higher productivity in the system as a whole. Wider sources of improved productivity can be tapped. Manipulating the level or timing of land, labour or capital commitments may allow a larger area to be managed, greater cropping intensity, higher value crop combininations or higher yields. As an extreme a new crop variety with lower yields than existing varieties but with a pattern of resource absorption over the agricultural year complementary to other system activities, may improve system productivity more effectively than a new crop variety with higher yields but a conflicting resource absorption pattern. For example FSR in one area demonstrated several benefits of a maize variety maturing in 90 days compared to a higher yielding maize variety used by farmers but maturing in 120 days. First, because of a mid-season rainfall trough there would be less risk to the earlier variety of drought at flowering. This reduced risk would enable farmers to switch from insurance crops such as sorghum to their preferred food crop, maize, and to cash crops. Finally the earlier maize variety would increase the probability of a legume crop planted on residual moisture after maize (CIMMYT, 1977).

So the perspective of the decision-making inherent in FSR gives wider sources of farm improvements. Adaptive experimentation, whether in crops, animals or machines, focused by FSR is immediately problem oriented and solutions or opportunities investigated are within the capacity of target farmers. Positive results from experimentation are likely to be rapidly absorbed. Because it is integrative in character FSR needs to draw on the natural sciences for technical relationships and insights – hence the emphasis on the link with agricultural experiments and experimenters. It is a link which appears to me to offer a major advance in the generation of technology relevant to the needs and capacities of the millions of LDC small farmers.

I will outline the sequence of an approach for FSR to make this bread and butter contribution to improving small farmer productivity in LDCs.[3]

1 Zoning: farmers with the same problems and potentials are grouped to allow cost-effective Research and Development efforts. Major groups reflect homogeneous farming systems with respect to present technology and resource endowments. Identified groups form a framework on to which policy objectives can be brought to bear to decide priorities for research and development.

2 Exploratory survey: within each identified target group the farming systems economists and the relevant technical specialists conduct informal discussions with target group farmers. Discussion aims at understanding the farming system and then identifying areas of management which could be modified to improve farm productivity. The economist and agronomist have complementary roles in establishing hypotheses of feasible and compatible management improvements. The economist analyses farmer priorities and the impact of resource limitation and risk on present management strategies for meeting priorities. The agronomist analyses crop potential and the likely effects of management variations on crop performance under local conditions. The economist specifies critical areas of resource absorption and offers guidelines to improved productivity such as reduced labour use or higher yields. The agronomist offers changes in management practices which he believes would have favourable effects on these critical areas. The economist evaluates the compatibility of these changes with the priorities and constraints manifested in present management strategy. This interaction is the core of the whole sequence in identifying appropriate experimental content.

3 Verification survey. A formal single visit farm survey is carried out among the target population to verify that the understanding gained in the exploratory survey is indeed generally true for the target popula-

tion. Hypotheses on resource allocation compromises and risk avoiding management strategies are tested, and farmers' attitudes towards conclusions on possible management improvements are sought. The incidence across the population of characteristics, opinions on resource use and constraints, the hazards and attitudes towards management improvements, are plotted in frequency distributions. Quantification is limited to key parameters needed to test hypotheses which can be measured usually by recall in the course of a single two-hour farm interview.

4   Planning local specific experiments. The exploratory and verification survey provide the content for adaptive experimentation designed to improve productivity on farms in the target group.

(a) Practices in which target farmers' management is flexible and in which *ex ante* evaluation suggests improvements in productivity could be expected; these make up the experimental variables.

(b) The degree of flexibility, for example the level of capital likely to be made available where purchased inputs are involved, sets the feasible range of treatments for those variables.

(c) The description of present management including location, soil type used and practices employed is the basis for the management of the non-experimental variables in the experiment. The Control treatment is farmer practice.

We urgently need a consensus on how to make a bread and butter contribution in the small farm sector of LDCs. We have had twenty years' R & D – surely we have enough experience to synthesise a relevant approach. Of course professional discussion is vital to crystallize detailed methodologies, but let it focus on this pertinent and pressing issue, and let constructive argument build on a basis which has a consensus. Farming System Economists are extremely thin on the ground. Without a consensus we will not gain the authority necessary to influence the establishments, particularly on the vital question of research orientation.

There is a great deal of confusion about FSR. A recent review of FSR at international research centres reflected the professional chaos over the subject; most centres doing different things and none doing FSR as the Review team defined it (CGIAR (1978)). Donor agencies are increasingly interested in FSR but many donor activities, and the pre-occupation with monitoring and evaluation is a good example, still assume that the technology being offered to farmers is good for them. Effort is wholly focused on the delivery system. Moreover, emphasis is often placed on developing new Farming Systems. Except in the very narrow sense that a shift in one variable gives a changed and therefore a new system, this is misconceived. Farmers operate farming systems, they do not adopt them.

Looking to the future there seem to be three "balances" to be addressed in further experience.

First, there is a grey area in the balance between "understanding" and "quantification". Can quantification only add to our understanding or can it make a more concrete contribution? Perhaps understanding should identify key areas of existing systems and quantification be limited to relationships within these key areas. This would obviate the need for whole farm modelling and limit the data collection needs.

Second, understanding the whole system in detail in burdensome in terms of field investigation, particularly in detailing the management of each crop. One version of the approach outlined pre-identifies the key crop or enterprise, usually that absorbing most of the limiting resources, and focuses effort on this enterprise on the grounds that this offers the best change of manipulating the system. Fieldwork concentrates on explaining how the system compromises the management of that one enterprise. This approach is consistent with the commodity orientation of many technical research programmes. Does this method, which allows cheaper and quicker fieldwork penalise the approach too much?

A third balance, mentioned earlier, is between the top down movement of policy, based on national considerations and the bottom up movement of local, especially farmer, considerations. National and local interests must be reconciled to find local acceptance; devices for reconciliation are' price changes, subsidies, credit and infrastructural change. Guidance is needed on reconciling these two flows and on effectively institutionalising the interface.

Finally, in research organisation and in training major challenges are evident. Location specific circumstances of farmers require a location specific research orientation toward specific groups of farmers. This implies major changes in research organisation in many LDCs. A two tier organisation suggests itself with an economist working with two or three technical specialists at the local level. These local researchers are generalists dealing with whatever enterprise represents a development opportunity for local farmers. They are backed up by regionally located, discipline oriented, centres with specialists who are called in to work on technical problems arising in the course of the location specific work.

The approach outlined for Farming Systems Research implies a systems perspective on the part of both the economist and the local technical scientists. Agriculturalists should be encouraged to generalise. They need to understand how small farmers' priorities and circumstances influence each aspect of their farm management. The production economics involved needs a dilution of anthropology and sociology. Agronomists need an environmental perspective; the ability to evaluate the suitability of a range of crops and to analyse crop performance and management. All disciplines need a strong awareness of the stochastic perspective and its importance in farmers' decision-making. Such a changed orientation offers a serious challenge to agricultural economics teaching at universities and colleges.

The evidence is overwhelming. Small farmers enthusiastically absorb new techniques that improve their lot. I believe we are close to a mechanism for radically increasing the opportunities available to them. A little extra professional effort at the "bread and butter" level could clinch it.

NOTES

[1] Thanks are due to Derek Byerlee and David Norman for their comments which have improved the structure and flow of the paper.

[2] For example, commodity oriented research at one research centre showed the optimal planting time for six crops, grown by local farmers to be the first week after the rains. Working by hand with hoes, local farm families could prepare about one-third of a hectare for planting within the first week. If they had stopped planting then they would have earned perhaps one-fifth of current income levels. In practice they continue to plant over a three-month period.

[3] Other references with a similar sequence and orientation are Hildebrand (1976) Norman (1978) CIMMYT Economics Group (1979).

REFERENCES

Belshaw, D.G.R. and Hall, M. (1964) "The analysis and use of agricultural experimental data", East African Agricultural Economists Meeting.
Consultative Group on International Agricultural Research (1978) "A Review of Farming Systems Research at the International Agricultural Research Centres".
CIMMYT, Economics Programme 1976 Series of Adoption studies: 1977 Eastern African Programme; Report 2; 1979 Towards a methodology for Developing Technology appropriate to farmers (IAAE contributed paper).
Clayton, E. (1957) "A note on Research Methodology in Peasant Agriculture", *Farm Economist*, XVIII, 6.
Clayton, E. (1963) *Economic Planning in Peasant Agriculture*, Department of Economics Monographs, Wye College, University of London.
Collinson, M.P. (1963) Farm Management Survey No. 3, Western Research Centre, Ministry of Agriculture, Tanzania; (1968) *East African Journal of Rural Development* 1.2, "The evaluation of Innovations in Peasant Agriculture"; (1969) *East African Journal of Rural Development* 11.2, "Experience with a Trial Management Farm in Tanzania"; (1972) *Farm Management in Peasant Agriculture*, Praeger, New York.
Conklin, H.C. (1957) "Hanunoo Agriculture, a report on an integrated system of shifting cultivation in the Philippines", FAO, Rome.
Davidson, H.A. and Martin, B.R. (1965) *Australian Journal of Agricultural Economics IX*, "Relationships between Field and Experimental yields".
Elliot, H. (1977) "Farming Systems Research in Francophone Africa, Methods & Results", Paper for Ford Foundation seminar on Farming Systems, Tunis.
Heyer, J. (1972) *Journal of Agricultural Economics* XXIII, 2, "Analysis of Peasant Farm Production under uncertainty conditions".
Hildebrand, P. (1976) "Generating technology for traditional farmers, a multi-disciplinary methodology", A paper for the Rockefeller Bellagio Conference.
Hunt, K.E. (1966) *Agricultural Statistics for Developing Countries*, OUP.
Jolly, A.L. (1952) *Tropical Agriculture* 29, 7, "Unit Farms"; (1957) *Journal of Farm Economics* XXXIX, 3, "The Unit Farm as a tool in Farm Management Research".
Kahlon, A.S. (1962) "An analysis of Farm Planning Structure in Ludhiana I.A.D.P. District" in Farm Production Planning and Programming, ISAE, Seminar series IV.
Kearle, B. (ed.) (1976) "Fieldwork in the Social Sciences; Experiences in Africa and the Middle East", ADC Inc.
MacArthur, J.D. (1968) *Journal of Agricultural Economics* XIX, 2, "The Economic Study of African small farms – Some Kenya experiences".
McMeekan, C.P. (1964) *Proceedings of the IAAE Conference*, "Co-ordinating Economic and Technical Research".

Michigan State University, Department of Agricultural Economics, 1971 "African Rural Employment Study".
Norman, D.W. (1973) "Methodology and Problems of Farm Management Investigations, Experiences from Northern Nigeria", MSU African Rural Employment Paper No. 8; (1974) *Journal of Development Studies II*, "The Rationalisation of a Crop mixture Strategy adopted by farmers under Indigenous conditions; the example of Northern Nigeria"; (1978) *American Journal Economics*, December, "Farming Systems Research to Improve the Livelihood of Small Farmers".
Roy P., Fliegel, F.C., Kelvin J.E., and Sen, L.K. (1968) *Agricultural Innovation among Indian farmers.*
Ruthenburg, H. (ed) (1968) "Smallholder Farming and Smallholder Development in Tanzania", IFO Series No. 24.
Spencer, D.S.C. (1972) "Micro-level Farm Management and Production Economics Research among Traditional African Farmers; Lessons from Sierra Leone", MSU: African Rural Employment Study No. 3.

DISCUSSION OPENING – D.W. NORMAN

The important paper written by Dr Collinson provides an overview of work by agricultural economists in the developing parts of the world during the last two decades. He is – with his very extensive experience particularly in the East Africa area – in an excellent position to undertake such a task. Those of us who have also had somewhat similar experiences can, I am sure, relate to the frustrations that come through in the paper.

The underlying theme of the paper is one of acceptance of the realities of the local situation in the developing parts of the world and attuning the methods and roles of agricultural economists to them. This is being reinforced by: (a) the increasing commitment of many governments in such countries to help the large numbers of small farmers, and (b) the increasing accountability for funds spent on research. The increasing frustration with the gap between experimental station results and those at the farm level has led to an increasing trend to focus attention on interdisciplinary work with technical scientists, this being consummated in the so called Farming System Research (FSR) approach. The rationale for this approach, which is characterized by the inclusion of the farmer in the research process, has been further enhanced by an increasing realization of the value of many practices currently undertaken by farmers and the need to develop technologies that will be compatible with the realities of their situation.

I have no basic disagreement with Dr Collinson's paper. Rather than dwell on the accomplishments of agricultural economists at the micro level which to date would appear to be somewhat limited, I would like to raise a few issues and challenges – some of which Dr Collinson mentions – that I believe are pertinent in legitimatizing and making the role of agricultural economists at the farm level more effective in the next decade.

1 *The issue of Farming Systems Research*
I share with Dr Collinson the belief that the successful application of this

approach could be a critically important ingredient in the development of relevant improved technology that will result in the improvement of the welfare of small farm households, in societies where farmers can voluntarily decide whether or not to change their farming systems. There are however problems of a philosophical, methodological, implementation and credibility nature that are likely, initially at least, to inhibit its potential impact. Very briefly philosophical objections are likely to some extent to be a function of the difficulty of solving the other problems. The methodological problems basically stem from characteristics that are somewhat unique to FSR. These consist of the notion of the technology developed being a variable rather than a parameter, the research process being holistic rather than reductionist in nature necessitates considerable interdisciplinary co-operation, and the inclusion of the farmer himself in the research process. Although I agree with Dr Collinson that it is likely that a consensus could fairly easily be reached in terms of cost effective ways of solving methodological problems, there are to my mind some major problems in its successful implementation. These include needed adjustments in institutional arrangements for undertaking such research which cross both discipline and commodity boundaries, the issue of training, and the relationship between international and national research institutions in terms of responsibilities for undertaking FSR. Agricultural economists have a particularly important role to play relating to the contributions of sociologists/anthropologists and technical scientists. In order to provide such a function it is important that they understand what other disciplines are doing and are able to communicate with them in the context of their disciplines. Unfortunately, apart from institutions located in the developing world itself, there are to my knowledge, no institutions in the high income countries – where most of the advanced degrees are still earned – where training programmes have been implemented to answer this need. Finally there is the problem of credibility in terms of ensuring financial and manpower support in the long run. The evolutionary nature of FSR is not likely to give such spectacular results as has, for example, been achieved with Green Revolution technology. However such results may be more pervasive and more equitably distributed.

2   The issue of income growth and distribution

The Schultzian emphasis on allocative efficiency – efficient but poor farmers – unquestionably helped legitimize expenditure of substantial amounts of funds on the development of improved technology. This obviously is desirable. However, although production increases as a result of adoption of improved technology have substantially increased the incomes of some farmers, it is apparent that in many locations incomes have become more unequally distributed. The FSR approach may partially correct this through stimulating the development of relevant improved technologies for all types of farmers. However, it is now becoming apparent that our preoccupation with allocative efficiency has tended to blind us to differences in technical efficiency among farmers which appear to contribute to differences in incomes within communities. Reasons for such differences cannot be blamed solely on differences in managerial ability or motivation. In addition technical, economic and social characteristics and relationships can contribute to such differences. Thus strategies other than simply the development of relevant improved technology may be able to contribute to improving the incomes of poorer farmers and decreasing the unequal distribution of incomes. I believe agricultural economists in conjunction with other disciplines have a major role to play in analysing the causes for differences in technical efficiency and for devising practical strategies to minimise them, and hence improve the welfare of poorer farmers.

3   *The issue of private versus social interests*
A major problem in many parts of the developing world is the increasing prevalence of short-run private returns or benefits which result in long-run social costs. For example, mining of the land resource in the short run without replacing lost soil nutrients can result in an irreversible decline in its potential contribution in the long run. The challenge is of course to devise improved technologies and strategies that will encourage convergence rather than divergence between the interests of the individual and society. Agricultural economics along with other disciplines have a vital role in resolving such an issue.

4   *The issue of a linkage between micro and macro*
Dr Collinson has already mentioned this issue. FSR involves working from the farmer upwards. Development strategists are also increasingly advocating some decentralisation. Although anthropologists/sociologists and political scientists probably have the most critical roles to play in the interface area between government and the local community, I believe the agricultural economist still has a contribution to make. Such a role goes beyond the farm management area to include work in terms of institutions.

5   *The issue of reward systems for agricultural economists*
Unfortunately, there has been a tendency for agricultural economists trained in and/or originating from high income countries to relate to peer groups within those countries. As a result, as Dr Collinson quite rightly points out, reward systems have tended to be based on R & D and not on bread and butter issues that are relevant to the societies in which they are working. This is even more true in terms of work in fringe areas such as the interdisciplinary type work advocated in the FSR approach. This reward system has to change if agricultural economists are going to be more relevant to the needs of developing countries.

It seems to me that agricultural economists at the micro level in the developing world need to address themselves to these issues and challenges if they are to play a significant role in contributing to improving on a sustainable basis the welfare of small farmers in the developing countries of the world.

GENERAL DISCUSSION – RAPPORTEUR: FELIX I. NWEKE

Most of the participants in the discussion felt that the paper greatly underestimated micro-level accomplishments in the 1960s. It was through the efforts of the profession in the 1960s that the problems of the small farmers came to be appreciated and became priority issues in policy. Some speakers hoped that in advocating FSR the paper was not suggesting that other approaches be neglected. Detailed micro-level studies would complement FSR to enhance the profession's accomplishments. The difficulties likely to be experienced in convincing other agricultural scientists to go along with the approach, as well as the problems of bias likely to arise from non-sampling error possible with the approach, were among other issues that were also raised.

Participants in the discussion included Judith Heyer, Ramesh C. Agrawal, David A.G. Green, A.S. Kahlon and Howard Osborn.

EIVIND ELSTRAND

Sub-Arctic Farming

WHAT IS SUB–ARCTIC FARMING?

I have not found any clear definition of the concept "sub-arctic farming". The word "sub-arctic" naturally reminds one of similar concepts as tropical, sub-tropical, temperate and arctic zones. According to this the sub-arctic zone must be the area between the temperate and arctic zones. This means areas of the earth located fairly far north, close to the polar circle.

I have not given the concept "sub-arctic" such a clear limitation. The reason is, that when I was asked to present a paper on sub-arctic farming, I understood that the programme committee wanted a paper concerning agriculture in the northern parts of Canada, Scandinavia and the Soviet Union. It is especially in these areas that we find agriculture under hard climatic conditions, which differ clearly from agriculture in the temperate zone.

If you look at the southern hemisphere and are moving northwards, you find only oceans in all directions. The south point of South America is located at 56°S. latitude, and the south point of New Zealand at 47°S. latitude. On the northern hemisphere we find that the 60°N. latitude passes close to Oslo, Stockholm and Helsinki, moves further into the middle of Siberia in the Soviet Union, fairly far north in Canada and touches the south part of Alaska. In other words, it is only in the northern hemisphere that we find areas of interest to study in connection with sub-arctic farming.

The extension of arable agricultural land towards the north varies substantially from one country to another. In Scandinavia we find arable land up to 71°N. latitude, while in Canada we only find rather small areas of arable land farther north than 55–60°N. latitude. Also in the Soviet Union we find that the northern extension of arable land is further south than in Scandinavia.

One way of limiting the sub-arctic farming area might be to define it as the areas located north of the boundary at which wheat and barley may be profitable to produce. On the map of Scandinavia in Figure 1 I have drawn these boundaries for barley and wheat. In Canada we find most of the wheat and barley in south Alberta, Manitoba, Saskatchewan, Ontario and Quebec, i.e. south of the closed boreal forests, see Figure 2. In the northern part of the Soviet Union we find mostly forests and rough grazing land, see Figure 3.

In Table 1 is shown some basic data from countries with sub-arctic farming.

It is only for Scandinavia that I have been able to get separate data for northern and southern parts. According to what I have said and shown on the maps I will reckon the whole of Alaska, most of the land areas in

TABLE 1 *Some basic data for countries having sub-arctic farming within their borders*

	Fin-land	Swe-den	Nor-way	Ice-land	Can-ada	Ala-ska	USSR
Population, million	4.6	8.1	4.0	0.2	21.6	0.4	242.0
of which in north%	13	15	12	—	..	—	..
Arable land, 1000 ha	2641	3342	900	2431[1]	69830	10[2]	233307
of which in north%	16	11	9	—	..	—	..
Forests in 1000 ha	18697	23466	8330	27	322281	53568	914900
of which in north%	58	56	19	—	..	..	..
Cattle in 1000	1763	1878	944	62	13704	8	111034
of which in north%	20	12	9	—	..	—	..
Pigs in 1000	1193	2556	701	7	5485	..	57900
of which in north%	3	3	1	—	..	—	..
Sheep in 1000	180	330	1782	740	523	5	141436
Reindeer in 1000	135	170	166	..	..	..	..
Arable land/farm, ha							1000[3]
Whole country	11	26	8	23[1]	171	..	5000
In north	8	15	5	..	..	..	..
In south	14	28	10	..	..	..	..

.. Data not available to the author
[1] Rough grazing land, meadows and permanent grassland included.
[2] 950 000 hectares of rough grazing land, meadows and permanent grassland in addition.
[3] Collective farms.

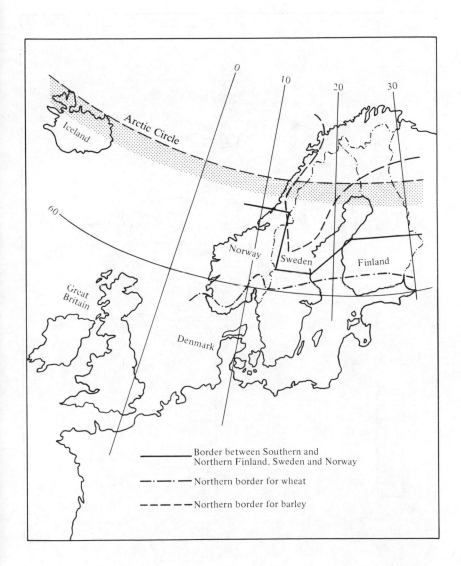

FIGURE 1 Scandinavia and Iceland

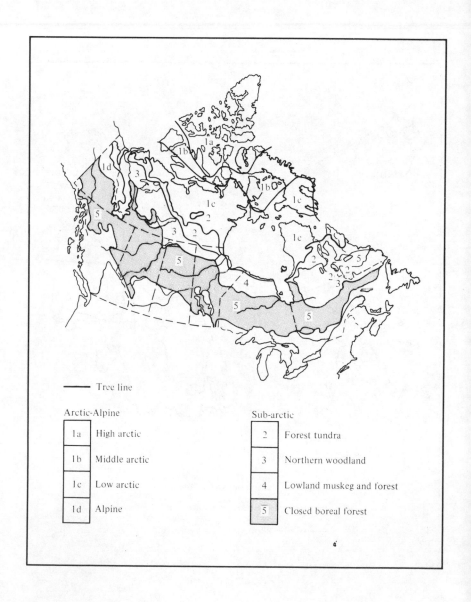

FIG. 2   Vegetation of Arctic and Sub-arctic Canada *Source*: Wonders (22)

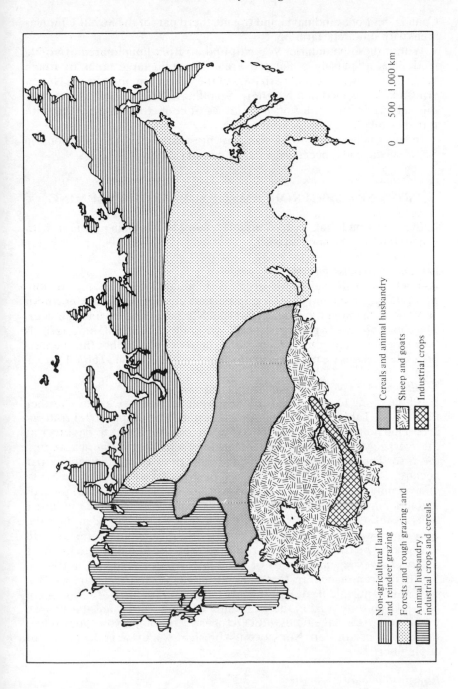

FIG. 3   Types of farming in the Soviet Union *Source*: IAAE (5)

Canada, half of Scandinavia and the northern part of the Soviet Union as areas with sub-arctic farming.

Within these boundaries you will find a rather limited area of arable land. It is a sparsely populated area. You find large areas of rough grazing, mainly in the northern part of the Soviet Union, Alaska, Northern Canada, Iceland and Northern Scandinavia. In the southern part of this sub-arctic area you find huge areas of cool coniferous forests with rather small plots of arable land within.

In my further analyses I will pay most attention to conditions in Scandinavia, and especially my native country, Norway.

SOME SPECIFIC PROBLEMS OF SUB–ARCTIC FARMING

In the following I shall try to summarize some of the main problems with which sub-arctic farming is faced.

Few alternatives for farming

Agriculture in the sub-arctic areas is dominated by grass production. Thus, dairy, sheep and goats are important enterprises. In the northern part and in the mountain areas with rough grazing land we find reindeer. The choices between types of farming are limited. You find some agriculture based on concentrate feed, but experience shows that these enterprises decrease as we move northwards in Scandinavia (see Table 1).

Smaller farms in Northern than Southern Scandinavia

It is interesting to notice that the farms get smaller as we move further north (see Table 1). Why should it not be the opposite? From an economic point of view we should think that farms ought to be larger as the average yield per hectare is getting lower. In North America we find this is so. The largest farms are found on the prairies, with low yields per hectare. One reason for the existence of small farms in Northern Scandinavia may be the natural conditions, i.e. there are many small plots of arable land which it is difficult to amalgamate and to operate in larger units. Another reason may be of an historical nature. In olden days the agriculture was based on self-sufficiency on the individual farm. A third reason may be the short summer seasons, and the fact that one family is able to harvest a smaller area of grass in Northern Scandinavia than in Southern Scandinavia. In Denmark for instance, they can start work in the fields in the middle of April, while the farmers in the Northern part of Norway can only start in the beginning of June. In the fall the Danish farmer can work in the fields until October and perhaps November, while the farmers in Northern Norway must finish in August or in the middle of September.

Low productivity

The short summers in the north force the farmers to have some over-capacity in their labour and machines in order to manage all their work during the season. This phenomenon together with small farms and low yields per hectare will necessarily lead to lower productivity.

With respect to yields it can be mentioned that the averaged yield of barley in South Sweden is about 4000–4500 kilo per hectare compared to 2500–3000 kilo per hectare in North Sweden. In Table 2 is shown the average yield of barley in various countries in Europe.

Besides the lower yields in Scandinavia compared to countries farther south in Europe, we also notice that the increase in yield per hectare per year is lower in Northern Europe.

Analyses clearly indicate that the increase in productivity in agriculture in Northern Norway is much lower than in Southern Norway. It seems also clear that the productivity of the total agriculture of Norway increases at a lower rate than in countries farther south (see Figure 4).

COMMENTS ON VARIOUS ENTERPRISES

Forestry
When I mention forestry first, it is because of its dominant role in the sub-arctic farming areas (see Table 3).

The part of the coniferous forest called "cool coniferous forest" (mainly spruce and pine) has probably more than 90 per cent of its extent in Canada, Scandinavia and the Soviet Union. Obviously, the great forests will influence agricultural production structure in these areas. In Scandinavia we also find that the combination of forestry and agriculture is very common. About 25 per cent of all the holdings in Sweden and Norway are combined with forestry. These farms are supposed to have about 20 per cent of the total forest areas in these two countries. A typical farm in Norway with combined agriculture and forestry would have about 10 hectares of arable land, 10 milk-cows and about 25 hectares of forest land.

TABLE 2   *Yields per hectare of barley in some European countries*

	Yield in kilo per hectare 1972/74	Increase in yield. Kilo per hectare per year 1967/70–1972/74
Finland	2260	26
Norway	3270	52
Sweden	3380	80
Denmark	3960	24
France	3840	128
West Germany	4020	90
Great Britain	4040	100

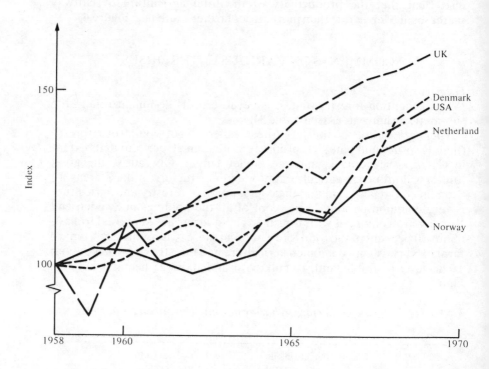

FIG. 4   Changes in net productivity *Source*: Romarheim (13)

TABLE 3　*Coniferous forests: million hectares*

USSR	553
North America	400
Europe	75
of which in Scandinavia　36	
Other countries	112
Total	1140

Dairy

This is the most important farm enterprise in northern Scandinavia. However, there seems to be a limited market for milk products in these areas, because of the sparse population. In Norway for instance, we find that about 9 per cent of the dairy production is located in Northern Norway, while the area has about 12 per cent of the inhabitants. The figures for Sweden are of similar size, while Finland has a somewhat larger proportion of its cattle in the North compared to its proportion of the population (see Table 1).

The dairy production in these northern areas is based on grass from local areas and concentrate feed imported from regions further south. The production is characterized by short grazing seasons and cold winters. Thus, there is a need for expensive insulated buildings in order to carry out the production during a long winter season. A typical dairy family farm may have 10–15 hectares of arable land and 12–15 milk-cows.

Sheep

Sheep farming is quite common in Norway. It is more common in Norway than in Sweden and Finland. In Iceland sheep is the most important type of production. Norway has 1.7 million sheep while Iceland has 0.7 million sheep. This is very few compared to Great Britain which has 26 million sheep and Australia and New Zealand which have 232 million sheep together.

A typical sheep farm in Norway will have about 5–10 hectares of arable land and 80–120 sheep in the winter time. In addition the farms have access to sufficient rough grazing for their herds during the summer season. It is very common to combine sheep and dairy in many parts of Norway. These farms will have about 50 sheep and 8–12 milk-cows.

Reindeer

In Northern Scandinavia we find reindeer. However, we must go to Alaska and the Soviet Union to find the large areas suited for reindeer. A typical Norwegian family farm based on reindeer will have about 230–350 reindeer.

HOW TO MAINTAIN AGRICULTURE IN THE SUB–ARCTIC AREAS

It is well known that the agricultural population has decreased drastically in all the industrialized countries during the last decades. This is also the case in Scandinavia, and forecasts seem to prove that about 3–5 per cent of the total economically active population will have their work in agriculture in the future. This may have drastic consequences for agriculture in many regions of Scandinavia, and especially for regions which are sparsely populated. Obviously, it raises a conflict between the goals of establishing a productive agriculture on one hand and the wish for maintaining viable communities on the other hand. This problem has been focused in the agricultural policy discussions in Scandinavia, and particularly in Norway. In a report from the Norwegian Parliament in 1977, "On Norwegian Agricultural Policy", it is stated that great emphasis should be laid on the possibility of establishing viable communities in the rural districts of Norway. Expansion of agriculture in these areas is looked upon as an important measure for reaching this goal.

However, are there also other reasons for this change in agricultural policy? Let us make a short historical review. During the last decades agriculture in Northern Scandinavia has been reduced. This may be explained by the general competition in producing agricultural commodities. Internationally we had surpluses of several agricultural products until 1974. Consequently, many of the least competitive areas for agriculture were reduced or abandoned. In 1974 there was the international wheat crisis, and several countries changed their policy regarding their productions volumes. They wanted to be self-sufficient for the most important agricultural commodities. This was also the case in Norway which has a very low degree of self-sufficiency (40–50%). The agricultural policy is now based on an increase in the volume of agricultural production. The land resources in the marginal areas should also be considered. Furthermore, it is desirable that a certain degree of self-sufficiency is attained within the various regions. For instance, it is desirable that Northern Norway should be self-suffcent for fluid milk.

Strong measures are needed to maintain agriculture
This is obviously seen in the light of the different natural and climate conditions we find in much of the areas of sub-arctic farming. It is also necessary if you want to give these farmers an equal income compared to the farmers farther south. In Norway several investigations in this field have been carried out. In Table 4 I have shown some figures indicating the differentiation of product prices and direct payments to the farmers in northern and southern Norway.

In order to get more exact data for how strong a differentiation is needed, several model-farms have been worked out for Norway. Altogether there are 17 model-farms which are supposed to cover the country with respect to region, size of farm and type of farming. In Table 5 is shown two

TABLE 4   *Differentiation of agricultural support to farmers in Southern and Northern Norway. Based on a farm with 14 hectares of arable land and 15 milk-cows.*
Year 1976.   US$ per farm.

Type of support	Southern Norway	Northern Norway
Price support[1]	—	7,600
Direct payment of various kinds	4,800	6,400
Sum	4,800	14,000

TABLE 5   *Model-farms in Norway used as a basis for estimating the necessary differentiation of product prices and supports. Also used to measure the income level in agriculture versus other industries.*
Year 1977.   US$

	Southern Norway	Northern Norway
Arable land, hectares per farm	22	12
Milk-cows per farm	18	12
Labour, hours per year	3900	3300
Net factor income per farm	24,100	18,900
Family labour income per farm	19,600	16,100
Labour income per man-hour	5.90	6.60

models of which one is located in Southern Norway and the other in Northern Norway.

It will be noticed that the farm in Southern Norway is larger than the comparable farm in Northern Norway. Further, we notice that the difference in income has been substantially levelled out by means of various kinds of agricultural measures during the last years. The future goal is to reach even more complete parity regarding income. As mentioned in the table, the models are also used to compare income in agriculture and industry. In 1976 the Parliament of Norway decided that farmers gradually should be given the same level of income as industrial workers. This goal shall be reached by 1982. According to the latest estimates (1979) farmers' incomes are now 95 per cent of the incomes of industrial workers.

An important question is the level of productivity which should be used in the farm-models. This question is solved by negotiation, and the productivity level is adjusted from period to period. It is accepted that productivity is lower in North Norway compared to South Norway.

Also in Finland and Sweden it is accepted that extra supports are needed for farmers in the northern areas. We find various kinds of investment supports and direct payments. At present (1967–77) the *differences* in the price of milk between southern and northern parts of Finland, Sweden and Norway are as follows:

	US$ per litre	US$ per gallon (=3.79 1)
Finland	0.079	0.30
Sweden	0.061	0.23
Norway	0.074	0.28

However, in spite of these extra price supports on milk and other extra government grants, the farmers in North Scandinavia attain a relatively lower profitability than their colleagues in South Scandinavia (business year 1975 in Finland and 1976 in Sweden and Norway):

	South	North
Finland	100	83
Sweden	100	88
Norway	100	92

Production structure and type of farming in sub-arctic areas. What is natural?

What is the optimum farm structure: small units as we find them in North Scandinavia or large units as we find them in Canada and the Soviet Union? Norway had chosen an agriculture policy which to a great extent allows the small unit to exist. One argument has been the natural conditions which make it difficult to establish large farm units. Another argument has been the fear of depopulation of many rural districts in North Norway. In North Sweden they want larger units and the natural conditions are also more appropriate for this. In a Swedish report concerning the establishment of viable farms in Northern Sweden it is stated that the farms must at least have 22–30 hectares of arable land, 30–35 milk-cows and forest land in addition.

The farm sizes I have mentioned from Scandinavia are very small compared to what we find in, for instance, Canada (see Table 6).

The figures from Canada are average for the whole country. I will guess that the figures for the sub-arctic areas in Canada are somewhat different.

The choice between alternatives for farming may include several problems. An important question is whether one should choose a labour-consuming type of production, as for instance milk, or a less labour-consuming production, as sheep and reindeer. In Iceland many farmers have chosen sheep, probably because of the quality of the rough grazing which does not allow intensive dairy production. Many places in Iceland also have the problem of land erosion. The rough grazing areas may easily be overcrowded with sheep and often the result is increased wind erosion.

Another important question relates to the enterprises based on concentrate feed, for instance pigs and broilers. By locating these types of production to sub-arctic areas you often get extra transport costs both of concentrate feed and of the final commodity.

As mentioned earlier, the combination of agriculture and forestry seems to be a very important type of activity in Scandinavia. Earlier, the combination of agriculture and fishery was very common along the Norwegian coast and in the northern areas of Norway. However, this combination seems to be decreasing very rapidly.

Individual versus regional plans
The need for co-ordination of the plans for the individual farm and the plans for the total region seems to be more important in many cases in the sub-arctic areas than is found in the typical farm regions further south. The reason is partly the limited resources that should be divided between several farmers and partly that an increase in the production in one area will make it difficult to increase the production in the adjacent region due to the limited market for agricultural products in the local area. In other words, which region should be allowed to increase production? Or to what extent should production be increased in the various regions in order to attain an optimum use of the total resources and a balance between supply and demand for agricultural commodities? Also in Scandinavia several complicated econometric models have been worked out to solve the question of distribution of agricultural production among regions. However, I think there is a long way to go before we may say that these models give the complete answer to how agriculture in the sub-arctic areas should be organized.

How to establish viable regions in sub-arctic areas? The multiplier effect of agriculture and forestry. The need for other industries
An important task in the sub-arctic areas is to create satisfactory production and social surroundings for farming. One problem is the long distances to the processing industries for agricultural and forest products. Another problem is schools, health services, transportation facilities, shops, agricultural extension services and other social services that are

TABLE 6   *Average size of farms in Canada.*

Types of farming	Average size, hectares per farm
Wheat	270
Cattle, pigs and sheep	208
Livestock combination	135
Dairy	78
Mixed farms	135
Forestry	144

needed in a modern society. Much attention is paid to these problems in Norway, and not least in Northern Norway. Complete plans that include agriculture, forestry, industries and service institutions have been carried out for this part of the country. The aim of these plans has been to maintain the population in the area. Several measures have been utilised to encourage new industry to move into the region (regional development fund).

Agricultural economists are responsible for the agricultural part of this problem. In Norway the economists have been interested in measuring the multiplier effect of agriculture with respect to employment and income. The idea behind this is that agriculture creates activities for agricultural and forest processing industries, for the transportation system and for the service industries in the region. As an example it was found that the total employment in agriculture and forestry in a Norwegian region was 2,250 man-years. The indirect employment was estimated to be 830 man-years. Thus, the direct and indirect employment amounts to 3,080 man-years, and the multiplier effect of agriculture and foresty was $3080/2250 = 1.4$. Similar analyses have been carried out with respect to the factor income in the region. It was found that the total factor income in agriculture and forestry in the region was 7.2 million US$, whereas the indirect or multiplier effect was 4.6 million US$. That means a total impact of 11.8 million US$ altogether, or a multiplier corresponding to $11.8/7 = 1.6$.

The investigations indicated that the multiplier effect varied substantially from one industry to another. Analyses of this kind should be very useful in planning the set of industries and services that are needed in a region to create the necessary employment, if this is an important goal.

Also in Northern Sweden and Finland substantial support is given to manufacturing industries which want to establish themselves in the area. It is increasingly realised that it is necessary to make regional agricultural policy more a part of general developing area policy.

However, we also have a competition between agriculture and other occupations, and this competition may be even harder in the sub-arctic areas with low productivity in agriculture. In connection with the new oil activity in the North Sea, many politicians feared that low income industry including agriculture would be left along the Norwegian coast. Several investigations have been carried out in order to shed light on this problem. Agricultural economists have also been involved. Surprisingly, very few farmers took part in the oil industry, in spite of substantially higher wage rates compared to agriculture. Those farmers who took part still kept their farms, but reduced their activity in agriculture. This was the short run implication.

Altogether, several investigations seem to prove that low income industries including agriculture may exist side by side with high income industry. The explanations may be more or less security for future employment, environmental differences from one industry to another and personal preferences. In Norway, another explanation may be the increase in income that is promised by the Government. So far, there seems to be a sufficient number of people, and also young people, who want to go on with farming also in the sub-arctic areas of Norway.

Finally, part-time farming should be mentioned, which is practised on two-thirds of all Norwegian farms. I have mentioned the combination of forestry and agriculture, but just as common is the combination of agriculture and industry. What happens in many areas with growing industry outside agriculture is a change to less labour-consuming enter-prises in agriculture and thus an increase in the number of part-time farmers.

CONCLUDING REMARKS

The item "Sub-arctic farming" is placed under "Micro-level, plenary session", and many readers might certainly have expected more evalua-tions of typical micro economic problems. When I have emphasized the macro economic and agricultural policy aspects, it is to stress the impor-tance of clear goals when advising the individual farmer in these areas. It may be a waste of resources to establish agricultural units which may be left or substantially reduced after a short period of time. Or let me put it in another way. The process of working out individual plans for the sub-arctic farmers includes almost the same problems as you find in regions further south. The enterprises may be somewhat different and the choices between type of farming are more limited compared to the situation in the south. However, the principles for estimating optimum solutions on individual farms are the same. What is really different may be the market situation, far distances, risky conditions and the lack of environmental stimuli. Thus, I have laid stress on the need for complete plans for the sub-arctic regions that include all activities, also those outside agriculture.

I have raised questions like: what is the desirable size of the farm and what types of farming should be preferred? What kind of agricultural policy measures are needed to maintain agriculture in these areas? Other questions might have been raised, such as how should the agricultural extension service be organised in sparsely populated areas, i.e. private or public? The municipalities in the sub-arctic areas are often economically weak, and what kind of aid should be given to these municipalities in order to improve agriculture and other activities? What type of non-agriculture industries should be preferred, and what about the infrastruc-tural investments?

We have been in a period in which the importance of sub-arctic farming has been declining. This has mainly been caused by the surplus tendencies of agricultural production, and due to the fact that sub-arctic farming has lost its market proportion because of less productivity compared to agriculture farther south. My analyses also show that total farm produc-tion in the sub-arctic areas counts for a rather small part of the total agricultural production in the world. Anyway, this is the situation if we keep the wheat-producing areas in Canada, Scandinavia and the Soviet Union outside the sub-arctic area. However, the wheat crisis in 1974 clearly indicated that it may be of interest to maintain – and perhaps increase – agricultural production in the sub-arctic areas. It is also probably true that substantial areas of potential arable land are hidden in the n.ighty coniferous forests we find in the sub-arctic areas today. Thus, reclamation of new agricultural land is possible in these areas. But is it a wise resource allocation? It might have climatic consequences which we are unable to foresee, and timber might be a scarce resource in the future, just like food.

SELECTED REFERENCES

Andersen, F.G. and Eid, O. *Combined Agriculture and Forestry*, Norwegian Institute of Agricultural Economics, Oslo 1979.

Dybdahl, I. and Leiramo, A. *Combined Agriculture and Fishery in North Norway*, Norwegian Institute of Agricultural Economics, Oslo 1978.

Fågeras, E., Hoffmann, J. and Romarheim, H. "The Multiplier Effect of Agriculture, Forestry, and Agricultural-based Industries in a Rural Area", Report from The Agricultural University of Norway and The Norwegian Institute of Agricultural Economics, 1975.

Holstrøm, S. *Swedish Farming, Agriculture and combined agriculture/forestry*, Agricultural Economic Research Institute, Stockholm 1977.

IAAE, *World Atlas of Agriculture*, Instituto Geografico De Agostini-Novara, Italy 1969.

Knapskog, K. *Agriculture and Oil Industry*, Norwegian Institute of Agricultural Economics, Oslo 1977.

Kolesnikov, L. "Agriculture of the Soviet Union", published at the XIV International Conference of Agricultural Economists, Minsk 1970.

Lantbruksekonomiska Samarbetsnämndens Rationaliseringsgrupp: Utvecklingsvegar i lantbruket, Samanfattning av en serie undersøkningar, Stockholm 1975.

Lomacka, L. "Agriculture of Northern Scandinavia", *Nordisk Jordbruksforskning*, hefte 3–4, 1958 og supplement 1960. Published by the Nordic Association of Agricultural Research Workers.

Oxford Regional Economic Atlas: United States and Canada, Clarendon Press, Oxford, London 1967.

Persson, L.O. *Supports to Agriculture in Northern Sweden*. Importance and Regional Consequences. Preliminary report from the Agricultural University of Sweden, Uppsala 1979.

Persson, R. *World Forest Resources*. Review of the World's Forest Resources in the early 1970s. Department of Forest Survey, Royal College of Forestry, Stockholm 1974.

Romarheim, H. *The Productivity Development in Norwegian Agriculture*, Norwegian Institute of Agricultural Economics, Oslo 1975.

Scott Wood, K. *The North Norway Plan*. A Study in Regional Economic Development. The Chr. Michelsen Institute, Bergen, Norway 1964.

Sigtorsson, B. "Agriculture in Iceland", reprint from *Iceland 874—1974*, handbook published by the Central Bank of Iceland, Reykjavik 1975.

Symons, L. *Russian Agriculture*. A Geographic Survey. University College of Swansea, G. Bell & Sons Ltd, London 1972.

Sørland, R. *Reindeer in Norway*, Economic Analyses, Report from the Norwegian Institute of Agricultural Economics, Oslo 1978.

The Norwegian Parliament "On Norwegian nutrition and food policy", Report No. 32, 1975–76, to the Storting, Oslo; "On Norwegian Agricultural Policy", Report No. 14, 1976–77, to the Storting, Oslo; "The Implementation of the Development Plan for North Norway", Report No. 60, 1976–77, to the Storting, Oslo.

Torvela, M. "Main features of Milk Subsidy", paper presented at a Symposium on the Problems of the Agricultural Development of less-favoured areas, held in Geneva, May 1978. Arranged by FAO and ECE.
Wonders, W.C. *The North*. Studies in Canadian Geography, Montreal 1972.

GENERAL DISCUSSION – RAPPORTEUR: WAYNE E. BURTON

The speaker presented the Northern Scandinavian case of sub-arctic farming as being a peripheral extension of temperate zone farming into the harsh environment of the far-north, and being characterized by small farms, animal agriculture based on grass, low crop yields, high costs, and few alternatives. Constraints were identified as rough topography, short seasons, weak or absent service industries and institutions, distances from factor-input sources, and high costs for infrastructure. Forestry was mentioned as a typical enterprise combination with agriculture in sub-arctic farming. A primary goal for farming in the northern region is to maintain viable communities. The primary policy stratagem appears to be income parity with industrial employment, brought about by regional price differentials and investment supports.

The discussion opened with a description of a second type of northern agriculture; that found in conjunction with industrial developments in the remote locations of the northern Soviet Union. In this case, agricultural production has been developed to support settlement in previously undeveloped areas for the purpose of petroleum, mineral, and transportation industry development. Dairy products, potatoes, and vegetables are produced to satisfy settlement needs and total economic development. Recognition is given to the fact that such agricultural development provides amenity values above and beyond nutritional values. Recognition is also given to the fact that new technology must be created for these northern locations, and is being provided through research institutes developed for that purpose. Capital investment costs are high, and this is met through increased direct government investment in agriculture or through increased industry investment as part of the social cost of development.

A third type of sub-arctic farming would be that found in Alaska and some areas of Northern Canada, ranging from large greenhouses at urban centres, producing vegetables and ornamentals, and large dairy farms, to subsistence gardening and feed production for recreational horses; yet all being few in number. While agriculture was introduced by early fur trading companies and gold miners, it was not incorporated into the indigenous cultures. Reindeer production was introduced by the respective governments for socio-economic development among the indigenous population, but was of limited time duration even though a residual does remain. Quite recently, some three years ago, the situation has changed. Commercial agricultural development has been recognized as a goal of Alaskan socio-economic development. Subsistence gardening is being developed in remote indigenous villages. State project lands, some 24,000 ha. each, are being sold to individuals in 1,200 ha. units. Small-farm project lands are also being sold in 8 to 64 ha. units. It is anticipated that some 265,000 ha. will be sold to individuals for agriculture-only in the period 1978–1983. Native-claims-settlement lands, some 1.2 million ha., are beginning to come under scrutiny for possible agricultural development by rural villages. Primary purposes for farming development include substantial self-sufficiency for a rapidly growing population which imports more than 90 per cent of food supplies, amenity support for an urban-emigrant population, and socio-economic development in isolated rural areas. The stimulus for sub-arctic farming development in this area has primarily resulted from ongoing petroleum industry developments and the need for socio-economic development in rural village areas.

Questions were raised regarding the boundaries of sub-arctic farming. Responses regarding both Northern Scandinavia and the Soviet Union indicated that this type of farming was north of the grain growing areas. However, subsequent discussion concerning crops that do biologically well in the sub-arctic indicated that breeding changes have extended barley for animal feed to the arctic circle. Other crops that do well in sub-arctic farming areas are improved and wild grasses, rape for silage, many vegetables and potatoes, and several types of berries. While the yields of some crops may not directly compare with more southerly locations others compare quite well, even though only a single crop may be raised. It should be noted that the insular nature of settlement, particularly in the Soviet Union and Alaska, places an importance on sub-arctic farm production beyond the nutritional values obtained. Questions were then raised regarding the critical size of human settlement for communities and sub-arctic farming to survive. Responses indicated that, depending on the degree of isolation, probably some 200,000 to 300,000 in a 1–3 day drive will provide a full range of services that make for permanency of settlement, but in much lesser degrees of isolation, populations of 15,000 may survive quite well. A final question was directed to the willingness of young people to go into farming in the sub-arctic. The response indicated that such was now the case since incomes have improved and many social services are now available.

PETER H. CALKINS

Small Farm Structure and Output in Selected Regions of Nepal, Taiwan and the United States

Traditionally, economists have been concerned with achieving Pareto-optimal output combinations for the evolving resource structure of growing economies, but they have focused little on the relative contributions – and fates – of small and large farms. Do agricultural economies fall into general types? What output mix characterizes each? What is the role of small farms in each? If certain classes of farm are disadvantaged by technological change, what countervailing short-run policies might help to guarantee their survival as unique actors in the agricultural sector?

There are two types of definitions for "small" farms:

1 Those that focus on size, and set some arbitrary break-point between classes in terms of land controlled or value of farm sales. Such definitions fail to illuminate the causes of small physical size or low sales volume and may include farms that actually achieve high profits.

2 Those that focus on structural disadvantages of certain farms. "Structure" refers not just to the quantities of land, labour, capital and management available, but also to the relative balance among these production factors on a given farm. Small farms are those which suffer from having either too few resources or an inappropriate balance among them to take advantage of new technologies and prevailing government policies.

The second type of definition seems preferable because it distinguishes structure from size. Disadvantage has its clearest roots in structure, and a given structure in turn dictates a most efficient output mix for a given farm. For example, labour is often the least limiting resource of farms small in size. Such farms have a comparative advantage in producing commodities which are labour-intensive. If tastes and preferences in the society favour such commodities, "small" farms will actually improve in relative income. Thus, the terms small and disadvantages are not always synonymous.

75

TYPES OF AGRICULTURAL ECONOMIES

We may group agricultural economies into at least four broad types.

1   Subsistence agriculture. More than 60 per cent of the workforce is directly involved in producing food, primarily grains and grain legumes to meet calorie-protein needs. The production possibility frontier (Figure 1a) would allow the production of more non-grain products, but society's utility curves favour a preponderance of resources to be devoted to grain production. These utility curves reflect an inelastic demand for grain crops in the face of inelastic supply schedules for both grains and non-grains (Figure 1c). The low level of technological development accounts for the inelasticity of supply, a consistent technology across farms of different size, and hence a very short and high long-run average cost curve (Figure 1b).

Although international trade may occur in the subsistence economy, it is either insignificant or takes the form of a plantation sector with little effect on most operators. Therefore, Figure 1a shows society under autarky. Examples of subsistence agricultural economies include Nepal, Indonesia, and Bangladesh.

2   Intensive mixed agriculture. Between 25 and 60 per cent of the workforce is in food production. Technological advances allow society to satisfy calorie–protein needs on limited land. Consequently, there is sufficient land to devote to producing non-grain commodities. The supply curves for both grain and non-grain commodities lie farther to the right and are more elastic than in subsistence economies. The demand for grain is also more elastic, but non-grain demand is comparatively less elastic because the better-off populace considers animal and horticultural products fixed components of their diets. Compared with subsistence economies, the production possibility frontier lies farther out for both grain and non-grain commodities, but the shift is relatively more pronounced for non-grains. The intensive mixed agriculture has a relatively high number of workers per ha cropped and an absolute or comparative advantage in producing labour-intensive horticultural commodities for export. Trade allows society to consume on a higher utility curve than possible under autarky (Figure 1a). Because of technological advances, the long-run average cost curve for agricultural production lies lower than and to the right of that for subsistence economies. These advances impart a structural advantage to large farms in grain production. However, the income distribution does not worsen because smaller farms are rewarded for producing commodities which favour labour. Intensive mixed economies include Taiwan and Korea.

3   Extensive monoculture. Less than 25 per cent of the workforce is in agriculture and land is abundant. Increasing income, investment in production, and improvements in internal markets and transportation allow for specialization and trade within the country. Smaller land areas provide the grain and horticultural portions of the diet, and more land is left for the production of feed crops. The very technical advances which allow

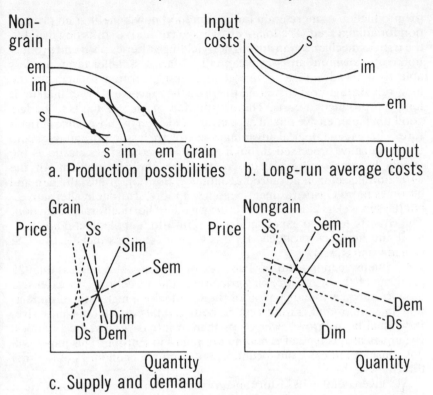

FIG. 1   Structure and output in three types of agricultural economy (s = subsistence, im = intensive mixed, em = extensive monoculture)

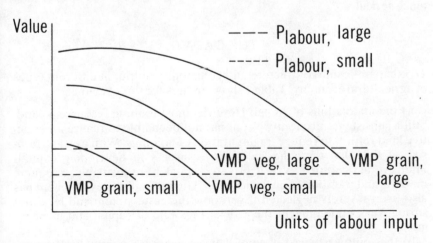

FIG. 2   Labour productivity in small- and large-scale farms for grain and vegetables

the production of more grain for human food now benefit grain production for animal feed. The long-run average cost curve shifts down and to the right as mechanization and higher-yielding varieties push unit production costs down on large-scale capitalized farms. Smaller farms are less able to take advantage of this change and are often so high on the long-run average cost curve that the price they receive is lower than their long-run production costs. The distribution of income tends to be less good than in intensive mixed agriculture and even in subsistence agriculture, where technological advantages of size are less important. Demand for grain (now processed through animals) becomes less elastic as the supply becomes more elastic, creating the chronic problems of the agricultural sector in advanced economies. For non-grains, the demand becomes more elastic (as meat becomes a more affordable alternative), but the supply less elastic as land is drawn out of horticultural production. The country tends to export grains in return for supplemental horticultural and livestock products. Extensive monocultures include the US, Canada, and Russia.

4   Intensive monoculture. This type of economy also has less than 25 per cent of the workforce in agriculture, but in contrast to extensive monocultures, is found in areas of the world with a high ratio of population to arable land. Production is both capital- and labour-intensive. Individual farms grow fewer crops than in intensive mixed economies. Examples of this type of economy are found in Europe. This paper will not consider intensive monoculture, but compare economies of the first three types.

At a given point in its history an agricultural economy may be a mixture of two or more of the above types. For example, Japan currently combines intensive mixed with intensive monoculture, and many South American countries have extensive monoculture co-existing with subsistence agriculture.

THE DATA

To compare resource structure and commodity output in different types of agricultural economy, Table 1 shows indices for three regions:

a) the middle hills of Nepal. Here the most limiting resource is land. Still a subsistence economy, Nepal has not been able to realize an effective land reform to reduce fragmentation of holdings. With average farm size at 0.35 ha, there has been little success in developing capital-intensive agriculture. Even if private capital were available, adequate markets and transportation do not exist. Human capital development has also been severely neglected. Even now the caste system and lack of a strong work ethic prevent the efficient pooling of capital and management.

b) the southwest coast plain of Taiwan, whose economy has successfully passed from subsistence to a well-developed intensive mixed agriculture. The family structure allows for the ready transfer of savings from rural to urban and from agriculture to industry, and for the pooling of capital among friends and neighbours. Partnerships, formal and informal, have allowed the people to take advantage of economies of size. Input-intensive agriculture has freed workers now employed in skilled-labour industries. Land has always been the limiting resource.

c) the cornbelt of the United States, whose agriculture economy has evolved to a heavily-capitalized extensive monoculture. As throughout the United States, the limiting agricultural resource of states like Iowa has been labour. Because the economy has moved through technical change to a lower and longer long-run cost curve, larger operations have been favoured. This has made matters difficult for small-scale or beginning farmers in two ways: additional land is worth more to established farmers, who can bid up its price; and nonreal capital has become a costly *sine qua non* for adopting the new technology.

Appropriate technology in each economy should use labour and capital in inverse proportion to their prices. Table 1 shows that this is indeed the case for general farms in each economy. For example, the US with the highest cost of labour and lowest of capital uses the most capital per unit of labour.

The problem is that small farms in all economies command relatively less capital (and land) than labour. They must either acquire control of more non-labour resources to operate efficiently or produce different commodities from general farmers. Since other factors are limiting on small farms, the marginal physical product and value of the marginal product will be lower for equal inputs of labour on small than larger farms whether they produce grain or vegetables (Figure 2). But production processes for vegetables are generally labour-intensive. Therefore, the VMP curve for vegetables on small farms will lie above that for grains. In intensive mixed economies, where research and consumer demands favour technological improvements and price increases in horticultural over grain crops, small-scale producers will gain. Moreover, because small-scale farms already have relatively large amounts of labour, its opportunity cost may be lower than that for larger farms. If so, small farm benefits from labour intensive commodity emphases will be even greater.

BARRIERS TO IMPROVED EFFICIENCY ON SMALL FARMS

Before operators of small farms in subsistence and extensive monoculture economies can be induced to produce the labour-intensive crops in which their resource structure has an advantage, at least four major barriers must be alleviated:

1 Inappropriate research and extension. Government could devote more resources to the development of higher-yielding, more flavourful vegetable commodities suited to the often inferior microclimates in which small farms operate.

TABLE 1   *Indices of Agricultural Structure and Output*

Index	Nepal 1972–4	Taiwan 1976–8	Iowa, US 1920–5	Iowa, US 1976–8
% national population in agriculture	93*b*	34	30*d*	4
Av. farm size (ha)	0.35	1.20	63	107*a*
Overall cropping intensity*	0.61	1.00	0.35*gh*	0.37*c*
Vegetable cropping intensity**	0.23	0.36	0.002*g*	.002*cf*
% Vegetables marketed	1.6	96	26*gh*	12*acf*
% Vegetable value of gross crop value	18	32	3.2*g*	0.13*c*
Number full-time adult workers/farm	2.9	1.7	1.89*h*	1.26*a*
Man:land ratio (adults/cropped ha)	5.4	0.5	0.03*h*	0.01*a*
Labour use (man-days/ha/year)	1718	486	n.a.	6*a*
Capital use ($US/ha/year)	44	2462	n.a.	510*e*
% farms owning power tillers/tractors	0	17	9*g*	99*a*
M.t. chem. fertilizer applied/farm	0.009	11.8	n.a.	13.2*c*
M.t. organic fert. applied/farm	29.1	1.6	n.a.	n.a.
Years' education per farm	0.9	36.8	38.0*h*	46.7*a*
Risk level	high	low	mod./ high	mod.

* $\frac{\text{Total ha cropped} \times \text{mos. cropped}}{\text{Total ha available} \times 12 \text{ mos.}}$

** $\frac{\text{Total ha cropped to vegetables} \times \text{mos. cropped}}{\text{Total ha available} \times 12 \text{ mos.}}$

Sources:

a Hoiberg, E. and W. Huffman, 1978, Profile of Iowa Farms and Farm Families: 1976, Cooperative Extension Service Bull. P–141, Iowa State University, Amex, Iowa.

b Nepal, His Majesty's Government of, 1972, Agricultural Statistics of Nepal, Kathmandu.

c Iowa Crop and Livestock Reporting Service, 1978, Iowa Agricultural Statistics, Des Moines, Iowa.

d Hyami, Y. and Ruttan, V., 1971, Agricultural Development: *An International Perspective*, Baltimore.

e Herbst, 1976.

f Dr. Henry Taber, Department of Horticulture, Iowa State University, personal communication.

g United States, Government of, 1920, Fourteenth Census of the United States, State Compendium for Iowa, Washington.

h Iowa, State Government of, 1925, Iowa Census, Des Moines, Iowa.

All other data from Calkins, 1978a.

2   Unfavourable financial environment. Raup (1978) shows that the historic lack of ceilings on farm price support payments to individual operators plus the inequities of investment tax credits, deductibility of interest on borrowed funds, accelerated depreciation, preferential taxation on capital gains, non-accrual accounting, and fewer avenues to credit, put small-scale farms at a disadvantage in the United States.

3   Lack of markets. Transport, storage and processing facilities would allow small producers in subsistence and extensive monoculture economies to specialize in labour-intensive commodities. In intensive mixed-culture economies such as Taiwan, such facilities are generally available to all farmers. Contracts with factories, group marketing, pick-your-own operations, and roadside stands are other ways to give the small producer a market outlet.

4   No insurance. Crop insurance is now limited largely to row crops in the cornbelt and does not exist in subsistence Nepal. Such insurance could be extended to labour-intensive commodities in which small growers have a comparative advantage.

THREE CASE FARMS

Figure 3 shows the land and labour resources and output mix of three "small" farms.[1] The subsistence farm (Figure 3a) at 0.20 ha was the smallest of four representative farms in the middle-hill region of Nepal (Calkins, 1976). The farm was only 36 per cent irrigated, and the operator's major objectives were survival and variety in the diet. By contrast, the largest Nepal farm studied (1.31 ha) was 74 per cent irrigated and had much higher quality land overall. The larger scale farmer was mainly concerned with maximizing the value of output and devoted more than half of his non-rice land to vegetable and fruit crops. The operator of the larger farm also had much greater access to debt capital for hiring labour and bullocks.

In 1974, the operator of the small subsistence farms grew paddy, wheat and twenty-five other types of crops, sixteen of which were vegetables. Thus, overall cropping intensity[2] was high (0.85). Although vegetables showed the highest return per ha planted and had great potential for more fully utilizing family labour (Figure 3a), the relative cropping intensity of vegetables[3] was only 0.15 in 1974.

When linear programming was used to determine improved allocation of resources on this subsistence farm, the overall cropping intensity rose to 0.90 and the relative vegetable cropping intensity to 0.74. The shift to raising more vegetables would also increase employment on the farm and slightly reduce variability in month-to-month labour use (from a co-efficient of variation of 46 to 43 per cent). The main barriers to adopting the new pattern were lack of markets and inexperience with growing vegetables on a large scale. Such beliefs as the necessity of removing green leafy vegetables and citrus fruits from the diets of sick children further served to undervalue the importance of vegetables.

The intensive, mixed farm (Figure 3b) was of 0.47 ha, the smallest of six farms studied in southern Taiwan (Calkins, 1978). The operator had few capital assets. He had one pumping set, compared with between two and four for the larger Taiwan farms studied; and he had neither a power tiller nor draft animals (in contrast to the three largest Taiwan farms). Still, since the farm was 100 per cent irrigated, the farmer could use his labour to achieve a very high overall cropping intensity (0.93), with a relative vegetable cropping intensity of 0.40. Because of the small size of the farm, the operator and his spouse engaged in off-farm employment. Although there were technically no "full-time" workers; with seven in the family, the number of total workers per hectare (14.9) was more than adequate to maintain the high intensity of vegetable cropping.

The operator's major objective in choosing crops was to maximize farm income per hour. Operators of larger farms in Taiwan endeavoured to maximize returns per ha and, especially as size increased, to reduce the level and variability in labour use from month to month. Thus, the goals of small-scale farmers differed from those of large-scale farmers.

A linear programming format was used to try to bring about a 20 per cent improvement in the objective function (higher income per hour of labour). The farmer also listed 20 per cent returns to investment and 50 per cent higher income per ha as subsidiary goals. However, no farm reorganization could better the current cropping pattern (compare the small subsistence farm). The operator could increase his income per hour on the farm, but in so doing would have to give up some of his higher-paying off-farm work. Nor was the return to off-farm investment high enough to meet the farmer's criterion for change. Though not an explicit concern, Figure 3b shows that the farmer reduced labour variability in 1976–77 by limiting the area planted to cauliflower in September (the period of rice harvest), and by planting fresh-market tomato and lima bean, which complemented these crops in labour use. Under the best alternative cropping pattern, month to month variability in labour use would jump from 55 to 74 per cent. Thus, in the current economic situation of southern Taiwan, where the operators of small farms have the option of working off the farm, they seem ill-advised to adopt changes in their farm plans to further utilize their abundant labour resource.

The Illinois farm shown in Figure 3c was located in the cash grain area of east-central Illinois, near very good markets for grain, cattle, and hogs. The operator did not have enough land to buy large machinery to take advantage of the capital-intensive mechanization which would allow him to move out farther on the long-run average cost curve. He had no confinement buildings for hogs and owned equity in only half the land he operated. Thus, even though the acres operated were of medium size, the resource structure would become inappropriate if the operator could not acquire the control of more capital through loans, business reorganization, and/or further leasing.

The major objective of the operator of the extensive monoculture farm

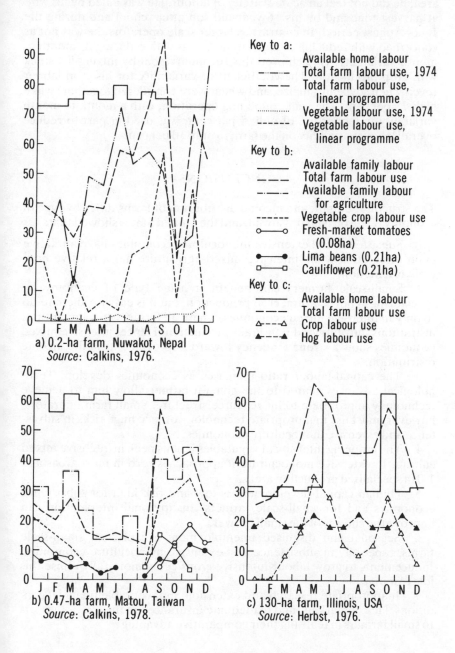

Key to a:

——— Available home labour
—··—··— Total farm labour use, 1974
——— Total farm labour use,
       linear programme
············ Vegetable labour use, 1974
------ Vegetable labour use,
       linear programme

Key to b:

——— Available family labour
——— Total farm labour use
—··—··— Available family labour
       for agriculture
------ Vegetable crop labour use
o———o Fresh-market tomatoes
       (0.08ha)
●———● Lima beans (0.21ha)
□———□ Cauliflower (0.21ha)

Key to c:

——— Available home labour
------ Total farm labour use
△--△ Crop labour use
▲--▲ Hog labour use

a) 0.2-ha farm, Nuwakot, Nepal
Source: Calkins, 1976.

b) 0.47-ha farm, Matou, Taiwan
Source: Calkins, 1978.

c) 130-ha farm, Illinois, USA
Source: Herbst, 1976.

FIG. 3   Month-to-month patterns of labour use on farms

was to maximize net farm income. In contrast to many larger farms in the area, he did not feel an acute scarcity of labour. He was aided by his wife at harvest time and by his 16-year-old son after school and during the June–August period. In contrast to larger scale operators, he was not as concerned with reducing overall labour use as with reducing its month to month variability. He achieved this secondary goal by mixing livestock with crop production. The coefficient of variability for his crop labour (even when soybeans, maize, and wheat were considered together) was a high 78 per cent. The year-round hog operation, with a month to month variability in labour use of only 5 per cent, was used in part to reduce overall labour variability on the farm to only 30 per cent.

CONCLUSIONS

The structure, output, and income distribution of farms differ by type of economy. Data on Nepal, Taiwan, and the United States showed that:

1   Subsistence and extensive monoculture economies have a relative grain orientation while intensive mixed agriculture has a relative non-grain orientation.

2   Small-scale farmers can benefit in each type of economy by specializing in horticultural crop production, but it is easy for them to do so only in intensive mixed economies, where all farmers and agricultural institutions move toward non-grain production. Hence, intensive mixed economies show a strong tendency toward improvements in the income distribution.

3   The capital-labour ratio increases as economies develop. Technological advances geared to the general farmer allow him to achieve technology appropriate to his resource structure. Small farm operators, however, must use inappropriate technology or face huge risks in subsistence and extensive monoculture economies.

4   The cropping intensity of vegetables is at its peak in intensive mixed culture. In extensive monoculture it approaches zero in most areas and 1.0 in specialised production areas.

5   Human capital development is low and risk high for subsistence economies and for small-scale farmers. Institutional intervention can improve the choices of the small grower.

6   Seasonal and disguised unemployment is worst on small-scale farms, especially in subsistence and extensive monoculture economies. Inducements to grow labour-intensive crops could more fully utilise this idle resource.

7   Inappropriate research and extension, unfavourable financial conditions, lack of markets, and inadequate insurance are the major barriers to small farmers in realising their comparative advantage.

NOTES

[1] Because of lack of data, the Illinois farm shown is medium sized. In the short run it is in no danger of extinction; however, it has just the number of acres (320) commonly cited as the borderline for remaining competitive in the long run. The farmer also has equity interest in only half the farm: the other half he rents.

[2] $\dfrac{\text{total crops grown} \times \text{ha-mo planted to each}}{\text{total hectareage of farm} \times 12 \text{ mos.}}$

[3] $\dfrac{\text{vegetable crops} \times \text{ha-mo planted to each}}{\text{total crops grown} \times \text{ha-mo planted to each}}$

BIBLIOGRAPHY

Calkins, P.H. (1976) "Shiva's Trident: The Impact on Income, Employment, and Nutrition of Developing Horticulture in the Trisuli Watershed, Nepal, unpublished doctoral dissertation, Cornell University, Ithaca, NY.
Calkins, P.H. (1978) "Why Farmers Plant What They Do: A Study of Vegetable Production Technology in Taiwan", AVRDC Tech. Bull. 8 (78-74), Shanhua, Taiwan.
Calkins, P.H. (1978a) "Labour and Other Input Availability in Determining Vegetable Production Technology in Asia", *Acta Horticulturae*, Vol. 77, pp. 331–40.
Herbst, J.H. (1976) *Farm Management – Principles, Budgets, Plans*, fourth revised edition, Champaign, Illinois.
Raup, P.M. (1978) "Some Questions of Value and Scale in American Agriculture", *American Journal of Agricultural Economics*, Vol. 62, No. 2.

DISCUSSION OPENING – JOAQUIM J.C. ENGLER

First of all, I would like to thank the Executive Committee of the Association for the invitation to open the discussion of the paper presented by Dr Peter H. Calkins.

I think that it is clear that "small farm" and "poverty" are not the same thing. For this reason, it is fundamental that, in analysing the agricultural economy the structural "balance" or the relative ratio among production factors be considered, and not only size of farm.

Dr Calkins analyses the agricultural economies of three broad types:

1   Subsistence agriculture: with over 60 per cent of the workforce involved in producing food, especially grains, with inelastic supply and demand, insignificant international trade, low technological level and intensive labour. In his paper, this type is represented by Nepal, where the limiting resource is land.

2   Intensive mixed agriculture: with 25 to 60 per cent of the workforce engaged in producing food, where technological advances release resources for the production of other commodities and international trade is significant. Technological advances do not worsen the distribution of income because small farms produce commodities which favour labour, such as horticultural products. This type is represented by Taiwan, where input-intensive agriculture has freed workers for the skilled labour industries.

3   Extensive monoculture: with less than 25 per cent of the workforce

in agriculture, abundant land, investments in production, improved market and transportation conditions, higher market integration, and regional specialisation within the country. Mechanisation and higher yielding varieties favour the large producers and worsen the distribution of income. Under this type, grains are exported and horticultural and livestock products are imported. In Dr Calkins' paper, this type is represented by the US cornbelt, with its heavily capitalised extensive monoculture, and where labour is the limiting resource.

Improvement of the efficiency of small farms faces four main barriers:

1   Inadequate research and extension;
2   Unfavourable financial conditions;
3   Lack of market facilities such as transportation, storage and processing;
4   Lack of crop insurance.

These barriers encountered by small farmers in subsistence and extensive monoculture economies, such as Nepal and the US cornbelt, also occur in Brazil.

By using linear programming, Dr Calkins attempted to determine a better allocation of resources for the small farms of the three types of economies mentioned.

For the small subsistence farms (Nepal) a higher proportion of horticultural products would increase employment and decrease monthly variation. The adoption of this production pattern is made difficult by lack of markets and inadequate qualification of the available labour.

For the small intensive mixed farm (Taiwan), with the option of off-farm work, no reorganisation would be better than the present production pattern, since an improvement in agricultural income would sacrifice the gains from off-farm work.

The small extensive monoculture farms do not own land enough to take advantage of mechanisation and their facilities are also insufficient. In this case, we have a problem of resource structure versus technology.

The main conclusions of the paper which, in my view, merit further discussion are:

1   The small farm is not a problem in itself. The high ratio of labour to land may result in a comparative advantage for certain products, such as horticultural products.

2   The small scale of operation may be a problem depending upon the context in which it is located. Thus, the farm structure presents itself together with research, infrastructure, product, and labour market problems. The best income distribution in Taiwan, for example, results from technology, infrastructure and from the existence of adequate product and factor markets.

3   The typification of the agrarian structure merely in terms of resources and their ratios will not reflect the problem of poverty and efficiency. What is really important is to verify in what situation the small farm is problematic and why. As a rule, the problem is outside the small

farm and its causes are associated with research, extension and infrastructure policies. In such cases, it is essential that changes be made to allow the release of labour and capital from agriculture through increased productivity and that:

(a) the income generated outside the sector create a strong demand for labour-intensive products;

(b) there exists a market capable of absorbing eventual labour surpluses through migrations or off-farm work;

(c) the technology created by research is not biased in favour of large farms.

GENERAL DISCUSSION – RAPPORTEUR: JUAN CARLOS MARTINEZ

The general discussion of Dr Calkins' paper was developed basically around the following issues:

1 The regions in which the typology was based face a different situation in terms of policy setting. Would this have any implication in terms of the validity of the typology?

2 Dominating the analysis is the idea that 0.3 ha farmers can exist. Are we talking about mere subsistence or some meaningful change?

3 Could the consideration of income outside agriculture contribute to explain the concept of smallness?

Dr Calkins' replies could be summarized as follows: policy setting faced by the farmers will have clear implications for the typology. More specifically this was one of the elements used in the analysis to define the different types of farming.

AMIR U. KHAN

Small Scale Machinery Development for Labour Surplus Economies

INTRODUCTION

The countries of the tropical Asian region have predominantly rural economies, with nearly 42 to 95 per cent of the population dependent on agriculture (Table 1). The total population of fourteen tropical Asian countries is about one billion, which represents nearly 30 per cent of the world population. These countries are characterised by high population growth rates and varying degrees of unemployment.

TABLE 1 *Population and numbers in agriculture; rice production area, total production and yield per hectare for selected Asian countries*

Country	Population		Rice		
	Total*c*	Agri-cultural	Area	Pro-duction	Yield
	(Million)		(Mil. ha)	(1000 MT)	(Ton/ha)
Bangladesh*a*	70.2	*d*66.4	9.48	10.99	1.2
Burma	27.7	17.5	4.97	8.4	1.7
Cambodia	7.1	5.5	1.88	2.7	1.4
India	554.6	372.6	38.8	66.5	1.7
Indonesia	121.2	83.2	8.46	18.6	2.2
Laos	3.0	2.3	0.66	0.90	1.4
Malaysia	10.8	6.2	0.52	1.53	3.0
Nepal	11.2	10.1	1.20	2.30	1.9
Pakistan*b*	66.7	26.2	11.25	18.0	1.6
Philippines	38.1	26.7	3.2	5.44	1.7
Sri Lanka	12.6	6.5	0.61	1.62	2.6
Taiwan	14.0	6.2	0.98	3.36	3.4
Thailand	36.2	27.4	6.73	13.27	2.0
S. Vietnam	18.0	13.6	2.5	5.6	2.2

Source: FAO Production Yearbook, Vol. 25, 1971. FAO, Roma.
a Source: CERES FAO Review, Vol. 5 No. 5, 1972.
b Total population for Pakistan, 131.3 less 70.0 for Bangladesh.
c Source: East Pakistan Statistical Digest, No. 2, 1964.
d Source: 1970 World Population Data Sheet.

Broadly speaking, these countries have somewhat similar agro-climatic and socio-economic conditions. With the exception of arid and semi-arid zones in India and Pakistan, the rest of the region has a humid, tropical climate. The rainy season starts about June or July and lasts for approximately four to five months, with rainfall varying from 26.0 to 93 inches per year.[1]

The important agricultural crops in the region are rice, wheat and corn. Wheat is an important crop in the semi-arid regions of India and Pakistan. For the rest of the tropical Asian region, rice is the single most important crop and the economies of these countries are heavily dependent on it. It has been estimated that nearly 90 per cent of the world's rice is grown in this region[2] Table 1 includes figures on the major rice-producing countries in Asia. Rice is grown on 91.24 million hectares with an estimated annual production of 159.21 million metric tons in the tropical Asian region.

Land and labour productivity is quite low in tropical Asia, which results in a poor standard of living for a majority of the rural population. The average farm is small, with over 95 per cent of farm holdings falling below 10 hectares in size.[1] Almost all of the crops produced on small farms in the tropical Asian region are presently cultivated by non-mechanical methods. Small holdings, low farm incomes, and different production practices are often cited as the major problems in transferring agricultural mechanization technologies from the temperate regions. In addition, many fear that mechanization of tropical agriculture may lead to serious unemployment and socio-economic imbalances in the region. Recent developments, however, are beginning to create a more favourable climate for agricultural mechanization in Asia. An important issue facing most Asian countries, is concerned with the strategy that must be followed for mechanizing their agriculture to increase food production without creating any undesirable imbalances.

PRESENT STATE OF MECHANIZATION

Mechanization of tropical agriculture is a rather complex question due to its social and economic impact on the rural population. The author firmly believes that the techniques that produce 20 kg of rice with only 5 to 7 minutes of labour in the United States have little justification for application in the labour-surplus economies of tropical Asia. At the same time, however, low labour productivity in tropical agriculture must be raised through mechanization to provide a decent standard of living for a majority of the Asian farmers.

The power available in agriculture, both per hectare and per man, is a good indicator of the level of agricultural mechanization in a country. Table 2 indicates the horsepower per hectare and per man in eleven tropical Asian countries along with data from Japan which has one of the most mechanized agricultures in the world. Many authorities have under-

TABLE 2 Some agricultural mechanization indicators in eleven rice-producing countries in Asia.

Country	Arable land per holding (ha)	Agri-working population per ha	Horsepower per hectare				Hp per agricultural worker	Labour hours for rice cultivation/ha
			Human	Animal	Mechanical	Total		
India	2.62	0.90	0.090	0.204	0.008	0.249	0.009	1000
Iran	6.17	0.37	0.037	0.048	0.154	0.292	0.418	n.a.
Japan	1.06	2.16	0.216	0.120	2.664	3.000	1.231	1400
Korea	0.90	1.96	0.196	0.236	0.003	0.435	0.0013	830
Nepal	1.22	2.49	0.249	0.480	0.004	0.733	0.0016	n.a.
Pakistan	2.37	1.09	0.109	0.288	0.013	0.410	0.012	n.a.
Philippines	3.66	0.71	0.071	0.104	0.023	0.198	0.030	800
Sri Lanka	1.59	1.20	0.120	0.148	0.110	0.378	0.009	n.a.
Taiwan	1.11	1.95	0.195	0.164	0.146	0.505	0.074	1300
Thailand	3.64	1.10	0.110	0.184	0.054	0.348	0.050	n.a.
Vietnam	1.57	2.10	0.210	0.244	0.023	0.477	0.004	n.a.

Source: APO Expert Group Meeting on Agricultural Mechanization, APO Project SYP/III/67, Tokyo, October 1968, Vol. II.

standably pointed out that insufficient power in agriculture is a major problem in the developing countries. In the tropical Asian countries average power input from all sources, human, animal and mechanical, is 0.19 hp/ha in agriculture.[3] It has been estimated that at least 0.5 hp/ha is required to achieve respectable crop yields.[4] For a variety of reasons, it seems doubtful that additional power could be provided in these countries from human or animal sources.

If agricultural mechanization is to be one of the means for economic and social uplift of a large segment of the rural society, it must cater to the needs and aspirations of the small farmers. Today the majority of small farmers are facing a dilemma. On one hand, they must intensify cultivation, which can be economically done only through mechanization, on the other hand, mechanization technologies to meet their crop production requirement within their economic and social framework is generally not available.

THE CURRENT DEBATE

Two somewhat opposed premises are often put forward for the mechanization of tropical agriculture: (1) That mechanization of agriculture will create unemployment and will lead to many socio-economic problems, hence, mechanization is not only unnecessary but also harmful. (2) Shortage of power is the essence of the agricultural mechanization problem and large, high-powered equipment can provide this power in the most economical manner, hence, mechanization of tropical agriculture with large tractors and equipment would be most economical and desirable. Proponents of these two diametrically opposed viewpoints put forward seemingly convincing arguments to support their hypotheses.

The fear that mechanization of agriculture will lead to large labour surpluses in the developing countries seems a little unjustified. Recent studies in the Philippines indicate that the progressive farmers who adopt new seed-fertilizer technology are more inclined towards intensive cultivation through mechanization. Japan is another interesting example where, in spite of the most mechanized agriculture in the world, labour utilization in rice production is still among the highest in Asia (Table 3).

These cases clearly indicate that mechanization is possible without displacing labour for farming. It is important however that mechanization strategies for the developing countries must not only be based on a thorough understanding of the functional requirements and constraints but must also consider the socio-economic implications and the aspirations and goals of the developing countries.

AGRICULTURAL DEVELOPMENT

Developments in the seed-fertilizer technology have demonstrated that it is possible to raise crop yields in the tropics by several-fold. To obtain maximum benefits from modern seed-fertilizer technology, farmer must keep his land in near continuous production. Many studies have indicated that demand for labour in rural Asia is highly seasonal. In spite of high rural unemployment in many parts of Asia, labour shortages are beginning to occur in peak labour demand periods. Many farmers find that they cannot effectively till, transplant, and harvest their crops with traditional methods due to a shortage of labour. In addition, the cost of labour in most Asian countries has been rising steadily over a number of years. In Pakistan, of which I have more recent personal experience, availability of farm labour is becoming a serious problem in many parts of the country. The shortage is so serious that some farmers have been reported to have left their land fallow due to non-availability of labour.

Matsubayashi, et al.[5] found that in Japan the major labour-consuming operations are: land preparation 15 per cent, transplanting 15.3 per cent; weeding, 15.41 per cent, harvesting and threshing, 33.5 per cent. They also found that labour requirements in the peak-labour demand months is about 60 times that of the minimum monthly labour requirement. A study of farm labour requirements in the Laguna Province and the Central Luzon areas of the Philippines[6] indicates that the labour requirements for land preparation, transplanting, and harvesting–threshing of paddy are 32 per cent, 23 per cent, and 27 per cent, respectively, of the total labour inputs in paddy cultivation. In the double-cropping areas, harvesting–threshing of the first crop and the land preparation and transplanting of the second crop require 82 per cent of the total labour inputs in a short period of four to five weeks. Timeliness of operations is an important factor in the double-cropping areas because the second crop must be transplanted in time to take maximum benefit from the late rains. The mechanization of cultivation is, therefore, an urgent necessity in many parts of tropical Asia.

TABLE 3   *Labour hours for rice cultivation in some selected Asian countries*

Country	Land preparation	Transplanting	Harvesting	Total (including others)
India	170	229	227	1000
Japan	50	240	220	1400
Korea	160	160	160	830
Nepal	240	240	240	n.a.
Philippines	190	120	170	800
Taiwan	60	190	220	1300

Source: APO Expert Group Meeting on Agricultural Mechanization, Vol. II, (APO Project SYP/III/6767), October 1968.

TECHNOLOGY TRANSFER

There are two distinct agricultural mechanization technologies that have evolved to suit different agro-climatic, socio-economic and industrial conditions in the world. The Western approach emphasizes dryland farming with large, high-powered equipment. A remarkable saving in labour input has been achieved here either through the use of large, high-powered equipment or by combining many farming operations in a single pass of the machine. Widespread application of such a labour-saving technology in the tropical region would certainly cause serious dislocations. Crops and cultivation practices of the tropical Asian region, as well as the scale of farming operations, are quite different. In addition, Western farm equipment is designed for manufacture with highly capital intensive, mass production methods that are not available nor recommended for developing countries of Asia.

Agricultural mechanization in Japan has not followed the Western pattern. Small farm holdings, high price support for rice, coupled with rapid industrial growth, has resulted in the mechanization of Japanese agriculture with small, low-powered but highly sophisticated machines. Japanese farm equipment has been primarily developed to meet the complex requirements of farmers who are more prosperous, better educated and more mechanically minded than those in tropical Asia.

Experience indicates that the Japanese agricultural mechanization technology is uneconomical and too sophisticated for tropical Asian conditions. The Japanese transplanters, reaper binders, combine harvesters are interesting examples of popular Japanese farm equipment which have failed to find a market in tropical Asia.

An important factor which cannot be ignored in introducing foreign manufactured equipment is that the balance of payment problems for most countries in tropical Asia is not expected to improve in the near future to permit any large scale imports of agricultural machines.

IMPORT VERSUS LOCAL PRODUCTION

Considerable scope exists in the developing countries for the manufacture of tractors and other agricultural machines. Mechanization of agriculture and local production of farm machines are so closely related that the establishment of a local farm equipment industry is almost a prerequisite for widespread agricultural mechanization. Manufacturing technology in the industrialized countries has advanced to a highly capital intensive level. The socio-economic climate in the developing countries does not lend itself to such an advanced technology.

Quite often a convincing argument is put forth by established farm machinery manufacturers from the industrially advanced countries that sufficient demand does not exist in the developing countries to justify local production. There is no doubt that economies of scale are very important in the high labour-wage economies of the industrialized world. More often, however, low volume production with labour intensive methods can be economically organized in the developing countries if machinery designs and production methods are appropriately tailored to suit local conditions.

During the last few years, many interesting cases of economic low-volume production have been successfully demonstrated in Asia. Local production of small four wheel riding tractors and power tillers in Thailand and in the Philippines are excellent examples. The manufacture of the Jeepney in the Philippines, on an almost cottage industry basis, is another interesting example of product and production process adaptation for low volume production. Similarly, locally developed three wheel auto rickshaws and farm trucks are being economically produced by small metal working firms in Taiwan.

Production of the IRRI power tiller in the Philippines is another interesting example. The tiller design was started in late 1971 at the International Rice Research Institute with the specific objective of developing a simple machine that could be fabricated by small metal working shops with standard equipment. Care was taken to limit the production operations to simple cutting, bending, welding and machining operations. Extensive use of readily available components such as air cooled engines, motor cycles and automotive parts, roller chains and sprockets were utilized in the power tiller design. Within a short period of about eight years this tiller is being widely produced in the rural areas of the Philippines and Thailand.

MECHANIZATION STRATEGIES

In most developing countries of Asia, agricultural land holdings can be broadly categorized in three size groups; small (less than 2 hectares), medium (2–10 hectares) and large (above 10 hectares). The small farm holdings group is characterized by subsistence farmers and comprises the largest number of farm families. The medium size farm holdings cover a substantial cultivated land area and support a fairly large number of farmers. The large farm holdings usually cover a relatively small cultivated land area with few farmers dependent on such holdings.

From a socio-economic point of view, the small and medium size farm holdings are of much greater importance in the developing countries. Medium and large farm holdings, however, play a significant part in producing surplus food that is needed to feed the urban population. Mechanization of these three levels of farm holdings require somewhat different strategies. A brief discussion of the suggested strategies for these three categories of farm holdings is given below:

1   *Small farm holdings (less than 2 hectares)*
This category of farm holdings consists primarily of subsistence farmers

who do not have much surplus cash resources to mechanize agriculture with individually owned machines. Primary focus for increasing food production for this operational level needs to be placed on providing improved divisible inputs such as seeds, fertilizers, insecticides etc. along with improved labour intensive cultural practices. This group of farmers depend primarily on manual or animal drawn implements for their farming operations.

Most farms in this category are too small to be attractive to large tractor pool operators or contract operations. Attempts to mechanize operations on such farms through large Government operated tractor and machinery hiring pools are not expected to produce any significant results in most developing countries. A more promising approach for providing an intermediate level of mechanization would be to encourage renting of tractors and farm equipment from medium and large size neighbouring farms. Such a strategy has proved rather successful in South East Asia where small farm machines such as power tillers, threshers as well as large tractors and other farm machines are being used for contract operations on neighbouring farms.

There is, however, considerable scope for introducing new and improved manual and animal drawn implements on such farms. Past experience in most developing countries however indicates that efforts on the design and development of new or improved manual and animal equipment have not been too productive. It would be more beneficial to transfer promising manual and animal drawn equipment from other countries with similar agro-climatic conditions. Thus a mechanization strategy based on testing and evaluation of new farm equipment from other regions and extension and local manufacture of the promising equipment would be more appropriate for mechanizing such holdings.

Since location specificity is rather high for manual and animal drawn implements, extension of such equipment among farmers as well as rural workshops would require considerable efforts from the public agencies. Most manual and animal drawn implements are fairly low in cost and are not amenable to manufacturing in centralized plants and marketing on a national basis. For this reason, manufacture of such equipment in close proximity to the end users, i.e. in villages and rural towns, would be the appropriate strategy.

2 *Medium size farms (2-10 hectares)*
Most farms in this category can afford an intermediate level of farm mechanization. Because of a lack of appropriate equipment, such farm holdings are forced to use traditional methods. Tractors and other farm machines from the industrialized countries, are often too large and high priced for this group of farmers. Traditional farm equipment are also uneconomic for their operation. Such farmers are in a dilemma for even though they could mechanize their farm operations, appropriate machines to meet their needs are not generally available. Lack of commercially viable designs of power tillers, small tractors, implements and

other farm machines are serious bottlenecks in the mechanization of this major farm group today.

In most industrialized countries farm equipment is developed by machinery manufacturers to meet local farming requirements. This equipment is subsequently marketed in the developing countries to expand sales. It is somewhat unrealistic to expect that industrialized countries manufacturers would develop appropriate farm equipment for the medium size farm holdings in the developing countries. The developing countries, must, therefore, look to themselves for generating appropriate small farm equipment designs to meet their own needs. Since farm equipment manufacturers in Asian countries are not yet capable of developing appropriate equipment, greater efforts are needed from the public research institutions on the design and development of appropriate farm equipment for the medium size farms. This medium category of farms will generally require farm machines that would be powered with small 5–12 hp. medium and high speed diesel engines. Efforts must, therefore, be made to manufacture such engines to accelerate the development of appropriate mechanization technologies for the medium size farms.

While this category of farms could benefit from centralized Government tractor and farm machinery hiring services, efficient management of such services is generally a chronic problem. For this reason, development of private tractor and machinery hiring contractors and hiring by neighbourhood farms offer much greater hope, as discussed earlier. Since equipment for the medium size farm holdings will be of a somewhat higher complexity than for the small farm holdings, production of such intermediate would have to be organized in the larger market towns and medium size cities in the country.

3   *Large farms (over 10 hectares)*
This category of farm holdings can be adequately served by the mechanization technology that is currently being imported from the industrialized countries. Some degree of selective mechanization may be necessary to minimize undesirable socio-economic effects. Some restrictions are necessary to limit imports of tractors and equipment to a few makes in the developing countries. This will permit development of stronger marketing and distribution channels and would ease the problems of spare parts and service availability. Wherever market demand justifies, production under a limited period licence from the original manufacturers is a desirable strategy to maintain product quality and encourage indigenous production in the country.

IRRI MACHINERY DEVELOPMENT NETWORK

Machinery design and development is primarily an industry function in the industrially advanced countries. Because of the struggling state of the farm equipment industry in the developing countries, industry is not in a position to invest funds in R & D. Consequently, little commercial style R & D is done in the developing countries.

Recognizing this bottleneck, the International Rice Research Institute in the Philippines started a programme in 1967 on the development of low cost rice production machines for local manufacture in the Asian countries. The IRRI Machinery Development Programme is primarily focused towards meeting the requirements of the medium size farmers. With modest beginnings in the late sixties, the IRRI programme has developed into a major source for designs of appropriate wetland rice cultivation equipment for the medium size farm holdings. The IRRI machines are now being commercially produced in thirteen developing countries and are gaining popularity in other parts of the world. Table 4 indicates the growth in the production of the IRRI machines and the funds expanded on the IRRI machinery development programme. As of December 1977 a total of 95,000 IRRI designed machines were commercially produced by co-operating IRRI manufacturers in Asia.

In order better to disseminate and adapt the machinery designs to other areas, three regional industrial extension programmes have been established in Thailand, Indonesia and Pakistan. The Institute also has co-operative industrial extension programmes with Universities and research organizations in nine other countries. The IRRI–PAK Agricultural Machinery Programme in Pakistan is focusing its attention on adapting and introducing the IRRI machines to rain-fed and irrigated dryland farm conditions that are prevalent in this region.

Experience gained with the IRRI outreach machinery programmes indicates the importance of local adaptation in introducing new technologies. The IRRI industrial extension programmes have introduced many IRRI machines to manufacturers in their respective regions after testing and adapting these to suit local conditions. The IRRI Programme has amply demonstrated the returns that could accrue through appropriate R & D efforts for small farmers in the developing countries.

REFERENCES

[1] Asian Productivity Organization (1968) – APO Expert Group Meeting on Agricultural Mechanization, Tokyo, Vol. I and II.
[2] Stout, B. (1966) "Equipment for Rice Production", FAO Agricultural Development, Paper No. 84, Food and Agriculture Organization, Rome.
[3] Food and Agriculture Organization (1971) in UNIDO, TS 6022/16, Low cost tractors suited to the needs of the developing countries, 20 September, Vienna, Austria.
[4] Giles, G.W. (1967) Towards More Powerful Agriculture, Report to the Government of West Pakistan on its Agricultural Power and Equipment Needs, The Planning Cell, Agriculture Department, Lahore, West Pakistan.

[5] Matsubayashi, M. et al. (1956) "Theory and Practice of Growing Rice", in Stout B. "Equipment for Rice Production", FAO Agriculture Department, Paper No. 84, FAO, Rome 1966.
[6] Johnson, S. (1969) Terminal Report on the General Engineering and Economic Research Portion of Contract No. AID/CSD-834, The International Rice Research Institute, Los Banos, Philippines.

DISCUSSION OPENING – HAROLD C. LOVE

I 1 Mr. Khan's paper deals with some of the most challenging and important problems of developing world agriculture. He gives a progress report on relevant and innovative research conducted by the International Rice Research Institute.

   2 Twenty-eight Asian countries produce about 90 per cent of the world's rice. Mr. Khan's paper selects 14 Asian countries for study. These countries produce 50 to 55 per cent of Asia's rice.

   3 The paper considers three facets of mechanization in agriculture:
      (1) Population and labour problems;
      (2) The dilemma between mechanization and surplus labour and,
      (3) Research and development of locally produced tractors and tillers for developing countries by IRRI.

   4 All Tables in the paper (except No. 4) use 1968 to 1972 data. It is therefore appropriate to support and emphasize Mr. Khan's major headings with recent trends 1970–77 for the countries selected. We begin by adding Table 1-A.

II Population and labour problems
   1 Note: a) The trends in Table 1-A and
             b) Total population grew at an annual rate of 3.5 per cent.

   2 The working force, or economically active population's annual growth was 2.1 per cent.

   3 During the seven years, the agricultural working force declined 5.3 as a per cent of the economically active population.

   4 Annual growth of agriculture's economically active work force was only 0.92 per cent. This low growth trend is one major stimulant for mechanization in agriculture.

   5 Finally, note lines four and five of Table 1-A. In spite of favourable production conditions during 1977, per caput domestic production was 7.5 kilograms below 1970. (In 1977 Taiwan and Japan were in export positions for rice and were encouraging the production of maize and other crops. Indonesia was still a net importer.)

III *The dilemma between mechanization and surplus labour*
   1 Most of Asia's production of rice and other crops depends on human power. They are about where US agriculture was 150 to 200 years ago.

TABLE 4 *Expenditures and sales patterns for IRRI agricultural machinery development programme, 1962–77*

Year	Programme expenditures			No. of machines produced	Sales value	R & D expenditures as % of sales	Av. selling price
	CA-CORE	USAID 1208	Total				
	US$	US$	US$		US$	%	US$
1962	3,639.85	—	3,639.86				
1963	9,414.61	—	9,414.61				
1964	10,213.91	—	10,213.91				
1965	20,535.44	—	20,535.44				
1966	56,307.49	—	56,307.49				
1967	101,330.58	—	101,330.58				
1968	131,782.85	—	131,782.85				
1969	108,549.05	—	108,549.05				
1970	123,982.05	—	123,982.05	50	19,248.01	644.0	384
1971	194,366.31	—	194,336.31	2,200	831,011.91	23.0	377
1972	236,270.79	—	236,270.79	4,400	1,662,023.82	14.0	377
1973	253,534.50	—	253,534.50	6,600	2,493,872.60	10.0	377
1974	366,343.53	—	365,343.53	8,900	3,362,543.66	11.0	377
1975	273,000.00	36,367.31	309,367.31	17,258	5,765,000.00	5.0	336
1976	340,000.00	262,147.32	602,147.32	30,451	11,187,697.40	5.0	367
1977	437,000.00	393,204.22	830,204.22	34,847	12,302,787.80	6.0	367
Total	2,665,270.97	691,718.85	3,356,989.82	104,706	38,124,185.20	9.0	364

2   A country may judge its relative stage of development by the percentage of its population in agriculture. In Mr. Khan's selection Nepal and Taiwan represent the range with 93 and 48 per cent respectively. Yet Taiwan with its high rice yields and mechanization uses 1300 hours of labour per hectare and Japan with even greater mechanization uses 1400 hours.

3   The number of agricultural tractors in use each year in the fourteen Asian countries is only a rough measure of mechanization. Such data does not indicate horsepower per unit, or hours of use annually. However, in 1967–71 these countries had 185,000 tractors; but in 1976 there were 369,000 in use. This is a compound annual growth rate of 12.2 per cent. It is an impressive trend toward mechanization.

4   Timely operations during tillage, seeding and harvest are critical for double cropping rice production. Yet severe labour shortages occur in many Asian countries especially at harvest time. In the future, a type of mechanical harvesting will be needed to alleviate this shortatge.

5   Providing some mechanization for millions of small holder rice producers remains a critical challenge. Mr Khan's paper suggests: (1) custom work hired from neighbouring larger farms; (2) new and improved manual and animal drawn implements; (3) testing and evaluation of new farm equipment from other regions and extension and local manufacture of the promising equipment; and (4) manufacture of such equipment in close proximity to the end users, e.g. in nearby villages or small towns.

IV   *Research and development by IRRI*
1   The IRRI machinery development programme is a good example of how new machines and techniques can be introduced.
2   Based on the IRRI's progress to date the governments of developing countries may begin to give high priority to investing some of their scarce resources in this type of research and development. As agricultural economists we can support and encourage such action.

GENERAL DISCUSSION – RAPPORTEUR: JUAN CARLOS MARTINEZ

The general discussion of Dr Khan's paper was developed basically around the following issues:

1   Is the mechanization discussed in the paper economic from the perspective of the farmer, assuming he is paying the full cost of the equipment, operating and maintenance cost?
2   Is the small farmer financially able to handle the increased capital requirements associated with mechanization and its implications in terms of increased flows of production?

3   The experience in project evaluation in labour surplus economies involving mechanized technological alternatives has consistently given negative benefit/cost relationships. Can we then advocate these types of technologies for these countries?

4   The concern of the paper deals with labour surplus economies. What will be the implications of adding to this the consideration of the energy situation; in particular, the increase in the price of petroleum?

Dr Khan's replies are summarized as follows:

1   The evidence indicates that it is economic and financially feasible from the point of view of the farmer to meet the capital as well as the operating and maintenance cost of the type of mechanization discussed in the paper. One of the reasons for this is that the costs are not too far off the ones implied in the traditional methods. This is one of the innovative aspects of the type of mechanization advocated in the paper.

2   The negative benefit/cost ratio currently found in project evaluation for mechanized technologies refers to designs coming from the developed world and not to the kind of mechanization advocated in the paper.

3   There is no question that shortage and increase in the cost of energy will complicate the situation. Simultaneously, cost of labour is also increasing in most countries. In any case, it is becoming essential that more intensive cultivation be introduced; which seems difficult, if not impossible to do without mechanization.

TABLE 1–A   *Population and production trends for 14 selected Asian countries for the years 1970 through 1977*[1]

Year	1970	1977
Total population (millions)	925.31	1,176.18
Annual population growth %		3.5b
Annual rice production (1000 metric tons)	153,341a	186,013a
Per capita domestic production (kilograms)	165.7	158.1
Net change (kg.)		7.5
Economically active population (millions)	383.43	442.99
Annual growth rate %		2.1b
Economically active population in agriculture (millions)	265.82	283.56
As % of active population	69.3	64.0
Annual growth rate %		0.92b

Sources: 1971 and 1977 FAO Production Yearbooks; 1978 Yearbook Encyclopedia Britannica; USDA Foreign Agricultural Service, and 1978 Commodity Yearbook, Commodity Research Bureau, New York.
[1] Bangladesh, Burma, Cambodia (Democratic Kampuchea), India, Indonesia, Laos, Malaysia, Nepal, Pakistan, Philippines, Sri Lanka, Taiwan, Thailand and Vietnam.
a   The selected countries produce 52 to 55 per cent of total Asia rice production.
b   Computed as an annual compound rate $(1 + i)n$ from data given.

MICHAIL POLYAKOV, FRIEDRICH KUHLMANN AND BO OHLMER*

Computerization of Farm Management Decision Aids

INTRODUCTION

The aim of this paper is to discuss some main principles of computeriza-tion of farm management decision aids. Since the authors have different backgrounds, represent different economic and social systems and differ-ent scientific schools which result in stressing different aspects of com-puterization, the goal was to develop and outline general principles and approaches for the development and implementation of these kinds of decision aids valid for any country and farming system. The paper is the result of discussions on the problem the authors had during their stay at Michigan State University in 1978–79.

Agricultural researchers are producing new information and know-ledge at an increasing rate, which means new production alternatives and techniques that farmers have to consider. The farm growth is continu-ously resulting in increasing capital investment and bigger operations, so the farmer's management work requires more details and data, and a mistake will have greater consequences. Production links are becoming more complex, farms are getting involved in deepening processes of specialization, co-operation, co-ordination and integration. However, farmers' comprehensive capacity and managerial time is limited. Some managerial tasks may be too complex and difficult for a farmer to solve, and others can be more effectively solved with the aid of new facilities or even outside the farm.

Many universities, research institutions, and private firms have developed and are developing different computerized farm management tools. Some of them represent what we now call Computerized Farm Management Information Systems (CFMIS). Much work is being done with the help of these systems, but much more still needs to be done.[1,2,4,5,7,10]

* The authors wish to express their appreciation to Glenn L. Johnson, Stephen B. Harsh and David L. Watt for their fruitful suggestions and critical comments provided during the drafting of this paper.

METHODS TO HELP FARMERS IN DECISION–MAKING

Computerization of farm management decision aids is based upon the fact that a farm is a controlled continuous and dynamic system having its own specific goals and principles of operation, utilizing certain methods to achieve given goals, and fulfilling a set of functions. The recent two decades of theoretical studies and experiments with different computer-supported farm management tools have given us a rather sound basis for defining farmers' needs, for modelling managerial processes, for designing information systems, as well as for their implementation.[7,6,11]

Since most of the systems now existing to help the farmer with his managerial tasks are developed according to the different methods of extension and advice, let us first take a short look at those approaches. This will facilitate the definition of the contents and the boundaries of a general farm management information system.

Aside from changing the farmer's environment by political means so that his managerial tasks are easier to fulfill, e.g. by fixing product prices, there are commonly four methods of improving the farmer's ability to perform his managerial tasks more efficiently in a given environment.[10]

The first kind of help is to provide the farmer with information about relevant data (e.g. available facilities and services), about problem situations, and about analysis and planning methods. This kind of help utilizes written material and broadcasting. It is directed to many farms.

The second kind of help is to increase the farmer's knowledge and managerial skills so he will be able to perform the management task by himself. This means education about the situation (problem), relevant information, analysis and planning methods, available facilities, and available service. Each activity within this kind of help is directed to a group of farmers.

A third kind of help is face-to-face service, i.e., an extension or commercial agent helps the farmer in doing a part or all of the management tasks.

The fourth kind of help is to provide facilities which the farmer can use by himself and then be able to perform the management task. Each of these facilities is used by a single farmer, although the facilities can be mass-produced.

These different ways of helping farmers with management do not, however, exclude each other. On the contrary, it is even desirable to offer farmers many alternatives within each kind of help.

The computer can be used in each of the four kinds of help. With the aid of a computer, it is possible to use a more detailed description of the reality and to consider more of the relevant factors in the analysis of the situation and in the determination of the best prescription. How advantageous this is eventually depends upon the possibilities available to execute the prescriptions, and upon how much better the production results will be compared to the additional cost of using the computer. In some situations the use of a computer may also result in lower costs for fulfilling a particular managerial task, e.g. in accounting where a lot of data has to be treated.

But in the process of developing computer based means to help the farmer with his managerial tasks, it became more and more obvious that using the computer alone does not solve all the problems. At the same time the tasks of data gathering, data transmission, and of model maintenance had to be taken into account. It is, therefore, now necessary to consider, and first of all to define, the whole system of computer supported farm management in a more comprehensive way. This definition will be the next step of our investigation.

COMPUTERIZED FARM MANAGEMENT INFORMATION SYSTEM ORGANIZATION

The most appropriate way to define a complex system like the one under consideration here is to apply the now well established systems methodology.[8] In particular, to define the system it is necessary to give the definition of the exact boundaries, system structure, and characteristics of internal and external links. The changing of the links and modes of operation gives us a certain spectrum of possible alternatives. The latter allows us to judge about possibilities of the complete or partial solutions of particular managerial problems.

Analysing a defined system, one should include here all the components of the CFMIS as far as one intends to utilize the corresponding technical and personal facilities.

In spite of the fact that the considered system is intended to be used by farmers, the CFMIS is regarded as an external system having its own problems, goals, structures, etc. Those problems do exist, for example, related to the so-called "delivery system", or to the low rate of CFMIS acceptance by farmers, or to the gap between technical levels of existing operational CFMIS and others that are technically feasible now and in the immediate future.

An information system represents "not only (1) a data system, but also (2) the analytical and other capabilities necessary to interpret data, and (3) the decision maker as well. . . . An information system is the total process by which knowledge is generated and brought to bear on social decisions – public and private. It is social information processing with which we are concerned as social scientists and statisticians. The design of the information system establishes the nature of the relationship between the decision maker, the information on which decisions are based, the analytical process which transforms data into information, and the design and collection of data. . . . When the phenomenon that is being represented changes rapidly . . . the conceptual base of the information system must be redesigned frequently to keep up with the changes in reality being represented and the problems being studied. If the rate of change is high enough, the need for conceptual redesign becomes nearly continuous. This is the fundamental problem in the design of information for agriculture".[7]

Having analysed different types of systems, developed in different countries, and processes of research, design, implementation, and usage, we have come to the conclusion that any CFMIS should be considered as consisting of two main blocks:

(1) operational, and
(2) "system development facilities"

The first block can also be subdivided into

(a) on-farm computer "self-service" facilities, and
(b) "delivery system" (see Figure 1)

As an organizational structure, the CFMIS can be either an on-farm, or off-farm or mail-in, or mixed system, or a computer network depending upon the location and number of central processors, and the type of means for data transmitting.

Institutions involved in any kind of activity related to the CFMIS form a high level organizational structure having personnel, hardware, software, data and documentation its low level structural components. The role of institutions is very important as far as no activity in research, design, implementation, supervision and usage of any CFMIS takes place anywhere but within these institutions. They establish goals, provide necessary means for the CFMIS creation, development and maintenance. These institutions are characterized by their content and include farms, research units, extension services, computer companies, communication agencies, private firms, etc. The institutions use their experience and capability to fulfill different functions in a problem-solving process.

There can be named at least four functional areas of activity: research, design, implementation, and supervision and evaluation of the CFMIS. Depending upon the level of consideration, these areas can also be subdivided in groups of functions or stages of management. As far as problems both farm management and computerized information systems have been linked together, some specific groups of farm management functions have the same meanings and importance for the whole CFMIS, and they take place in the development or exploitation of the system. Projecting and forecasting, planning and programming, accounting, analysis and operative control are needed to properly organize and supervise the system creation and usage. At the same time these functions are the farm management functions; therefore in given context they are related to corresponding models.

Other functions are more specific, for example, data gathering, coding, preparation, transmitting, processing, storing, and retrieval. This group of functions is needed to organize the process of converting data into information. Functions of surveying, development, selection, modeling, programming, testing, training and education, and evaluation are main functions of the CFMIS creation, whereas consulting, service, up-dating, interacting, performance, administration and evaluation represent the main functions of the system usage.

Personnel distributed among institutions execute functions mentioned above. Personnel include people of different specialities and skills, users, developers, producers, service people and so on. They are farmers, economists, programmers, extension personnel, etc. In respect of the CFMIS, all of them have certain duties and responsibilities and deal with hardware, software, data and documentation related to the CFMIS.

The hardware is the equipment including communication facilities. General components of the hardware are a processor, memory, I/0 devices and channels, mass storage, data preparation devices, means of communication and, in some cases, measuring and controlling devices.

Different kinds of hardware can be distinguished according to their costs and performance. Micro- and minicomputers can be used either as self-contained computers or as terminals to a maxicomputer. It is also possible to use terminals with a minicomputer.

The system software consists of three main types of programmes – a) system programmes and/or operating system, b) data base management programmes (system), and c) user's programmes. The degree of the software development and, therefore the capability of the CFMIS to solve complex problems, is defined by the system software supplied with hardware, and the power of the system development facilities.

User's programmes developed by personnel should be considered and classified in accordance with corresponding models serving to solve practical problems. This classification is based first of all on the following characteristics a) functions, b) subject area of activity, c) time, d) methodology, e) mode, f) type, and g) level; therefore it has several dimensions.

The performance efficiency of any CFMIS depends on the model structures and the flexibility of the models to a particular situation adjustments. Considering models as the reflection of reality, we should design them in such a manner as to provide the most effective way of application.

Modern farming is characterized by the processes of deepening specialization, therefore farms are now becoming simpler to model, and corresponding models are simpler to generalize and to structure. On the other hand, more and more farms are getting involved in different types of co-operation and integration. Farms are receiving more alternatives in selecting means of production, advanced technologies and services. All these make some models have broader boundaries and include more components and links.

The first group of classification characteristics include forecasting, projecting and planning, analysis, accounting and operative control. The second group is connected with agricultural inputs and outputs – resources, crop and livestock production, and also with marketing, tax management, inventories and cash flows. All these tasks can be either permanent or connected with some specific problem which has to be

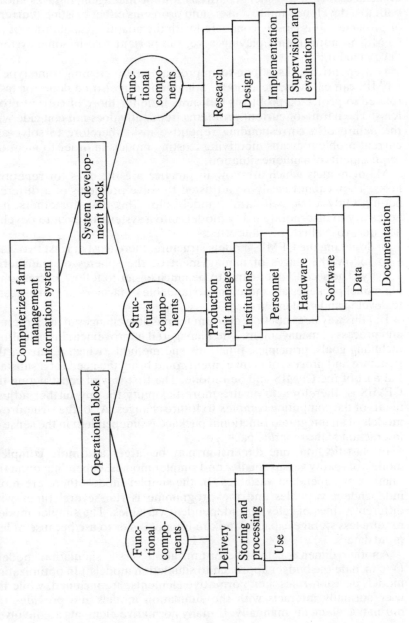

FIG. 1   Example of organization of a computerized farm management information system

solved only once. In other words, there can be distinguished two options in the CFMIS usage requiring different modes of operation and resulting in the necessity to consider separately routine management tasks known both to a developer and to a user, and problems either existing (current) or projected. It is closely connected with the adaptive capabilities of the CFMIS to adjustments playing a very important role in some systems development.[15]

For repetitive tasks, a long-term programme for creating some type of CFMIS can easily be developed. Something can also be done for tasks related to projected problems but quite little for those of current problems. The nature of current problems frequently does not coincide with the nature of a corresponding repetitive task; therefore to solve any current problem means modifying existing models in order to meet the requirements of a unique situation.

Major models which are now in practice are the ones for repetitive tasks. They cannot easily be adjusted to solve problems of a different nature. Only a few "all-farm" models allow this (6a); for others, it is necessary to incorporate many models into a system, or even to develop new ones to evaluate possible effects.

In designing the CFMIS models structure, there exist at least two ways – to follow the stages of management or the spheres of managerial activity. The second one seems to be much easier to follow, corresponding model packages are more understandable to farmers. It is also easier to develop and implement them.

But this way does not fully account for possible changes in the structure and process of management. The managerial improvement in agriculture including goals, principles, functions and methods, which results in the structure and process of management could bring the need for a substantial part of the CFMIS and be redone. The first way of constructing the CFMIS is, therefore, to ensure more flexibility for any further adjustments of the computing complex to future changes. Also, the structure of models of an integrated functional package is independent in the sense of interaction of the separate packages.

In classification, one dimension may be larger and more complete models of reality versus smaller and simpler models, depending upon the number of dependent variables. In the simpler models there are more independent variables and the programme is run several times with different values of relevant independent variables. The simpler models require less storage capacity and are usually easier to use because of less input data.[10]

Another dimension may be optimization versus simulation models. (We include the budget approach to simulation models.) In optimization models decision-rules, i.e., normative elements, are included, while the user normally interacts with the simulation models and provides the normative elements manually. If many normative elements are involved in a decision process, it may be difficult to find a relevant optimization model. This may be the case in long and medium range management, where most of the resources are variable, and the solution will have great influence on the structure of the farm and the situation of the farm family. In these cases a simulation model will be more generally accepted. In short run management on the enterprise level, optimization models will be easier to accept, e.g., feed planning.

A third dimension may be interactive versus batch operation. The interactive execution is advantageous especially in combination with simulation models or simpler models where the programmes are run several times. The user wants to solve the task without interruptions, and when he still is acquainted with the problem. When dealing with an interactive system more realistic and effective results can be obtained in many cases, even more effective than some optimization models can give us. But it depends on both the heuristic ability of a user and the degree of the interactive programme sophistication.

Data in the CFMIS can be represented by records, data sources, codes and data banks. This component of the CFMIS is linked with a) institutions by possession and usage, b) personnel by development, usage and up-dating, c) hardware by special equipment for data gathering, transmitting and usage, d) software by data base management programmes, and e) documentation by the description of data organization and manipulation.

Finally, the CFMIS documentation developed or being developed also relates to other structural components of the system, and its content is defined by the content and function of corresponding components.

A very important feature of the system, is the so called "delivery system".[12] It has several components. Major components are marketing and the provision of introductory information about how to use the equipment and the available software; maintenance, especially of the software; an organization (institution) providing extension or commercial agents; personnel for input and output processing (i.e., coding and transforming data from one media to another), and an organization (institution) for operating the central maxicomputer.

Some computerized methods need simpler delivery systems with less of the above components than others. Skill and interest of the involved agents are important factors.[3] In computerized methods not involving agents, the skill of the user, i.e., the farmer, has, of course, the same importance, while the interest of the farmer had to be present in both cases.

The delivery system has to be considered already in the development of the computerized tools, so the hardware and software will suit the available delivery system.[10]

CFMIS DEFINITION AND STAGES OF CREATION

With this in mind, the CFMIS can now be defined as a man-and-computer organizational structure directed towards accomplishing farm management tasks through data gathering, transmitting, storage and processing and converting data into information to facilitate the farmers' decision making processes and having facilities for its further development, implementation and maintenance.

The main task of the CFMIS is to provide the best ways of rational resource utilization (labour, land, capital investment, water, energy, etc.) in the process of agricultural production, processing and marketing in accordance with farmers' goals by the means of farm management improvement based on modern economic mathematical methods, computer techniques and means of communication.

In our definition we stress the fact that any CFMIS possesses facilities for its future development. It is connected with the unique feature of this system to add a new quality to it by developing more sophisticated programmes and data bases to solve practical tasks and problems, to be an educational tool improving farmers' managerial skills and enriching their abilities. On the other hand, "if agricultural information is to be accurate and reliable, the capacity for redesign must be a normal internal function of the information system".[1]

In fact, and as a rule, such a development never stops, although it is mainly related to the software, data and documentation because of its relative simplicity. It is more costly to change hardware, and it is much more difficult to modify and organize a new organizational structure.

The CFMIS follows three stages in its development. The creation of the CFMIS should be started with preliminary surveys of the existing system of management, farmers' needs for computerized farm management decision aids, and theoretical investigations in the field of agricultural economics, farm management and technical disciplines. The goal is to define problems, and outline possible solutions, to structure tasks, to study sources and flows of information, to develop testing methods and models, and system requirements and recommendations as well.

In the stage of designing, the CFMIS type and mode are determined, the hardware is also selected, software, data system and documentation are developed and tested. Based on research methods, the evaluation of the expected performance efficiency has to be provided.

At the same time, some work on implementation can take place. Here, personnel education and training, hardware purchasing or renting, data transmitting and processing organization has to be done.

To build up a complex system such as CFMIS requires a lot of resources. These resources are as a rule limited; therefore it is impossible to create it in a full volume at once. Rapid computer technology and means of communication improvements strictly influence the structure and process of data services that are to be designed or modified.[4] That is why it is necessary to have system development facilities in a row with the CFMIS supervision as an administrative functional component providing measures on the operational system maintenance and development by interacting institutions.

Different operational CFMIS have different components and elements, modes of operation, types of computers, and forms of organization. Ohlmer and Nott (1979) have studied four main alternative combinations of these components for different computerized methods (systems). The methods have been characterized mainly by the type of hardware utilized, namely (1) on-farm use of programmable hand calculators; (2) on-farm use of micro or minicomputers; (3) on-farm use by an agent with or without remote processing, and (4) mail-in systems with a maxicomputer.

The methods are numbered in reverse order of their development. Mail-in has been used the longest; programmable hand calculators are the newest. For delivering effective management aid to farmers, Method 3 seems to have the most potential. The delivery system provides expert consultants and interpretation of output as needed. The computer processing is immediate if the hardware is operating. Many software packages already developed for Method 4 can be made accessible to Method 3 with minimal effort. Some problems can be observed with rural area telephone lines and access to the computer during certain hours of the day. For smaller problems, and for automated production control, minicomputers and Method 2 would be noticeably more reliable. Land grant universities and farmer organizations may need to review their role in creating a delivery system for Method 2. In the future all four methods are expected to exist, each serving farmers in the situations where they are cost effective.

Linking elements of structural or functional components into a CFMIS, it is possible to evaluate alternatives in the process of analysis or synthesis while dealing with any problem of the CFMIS, on the basis of the systems methodology it is also possible not only to develop structural or functional components, but to design a comprehensive programme for implementing a particular system.

TYPICAL DECISIONS AND SITUATIONS

In recent years, many models have been developed to solve the very same problems. The number of these models is rapidly growing in spite of the fact that their modification is not significant. Major parts of the models do not need to be redone, but this is done because it is sometimes difficult to build in a new module into existing models.

In some countries, this problem is beginning to be solved with the help of so-called "typical decisions" modules standardized enough to be used in making up models of any complexity and configuration. Special requirements have to be developed for these modules libraries and be used by developers and model-builders. Typical decisions cover models (model modules), hardware (typical hardware packages for farms, county offices, etc.), software (applied programme packages), documentation (typical operating instructions), etc. They represent a flexible and economical tool in the design and adoption of a particular CFMIS.

FARM SYSTEMS INTEGRATION

With computer technology developments, more and more alternatives are becoming feasible. Much is expected to be done in combining functions of automatic devices with functions of the CFMIS into an integrated CFMIS (ICFMIS).

Utilizing the idea of "distributed processing" for controlling technological processes on the farm, and simultaneously feeding the central computer with rectified data for further processing, it is possible to create an effective ICFMIS. An effect of any CFMIS is mainly created in production. So, to be effective, the CFMIS should be linked with production processes as closely as possible. Experiments with dairy farm automation on the basis of ICFMIS have confirmed this statement.[9]

On the other hand, farm management information systems should be linked with other information systems also employed for the agricultural sector, e.g. Pest Management Systems. Such a consideration requires much more effort and in some countries they are being made in the design and implementation of agricultural computing networks. There the farm level of management is considered to be the lowest level in a hierarchical structure.[11]

CONCLUSION

The CFMIS performance efficiency depends on the degree of correspondence and fitness of its components. These components should be equally effective and developed, and they should provide the way for future improvements.

Many questions in the CFMIS creation are still open. Some of them are the result of the uncertainty which takes place in any attempt at modelling reality. In this respect, any CFMIS can be considered as a model of farm management organized on a new scientific and technical basis. Impressive figures of user numbers or computer runs witness only to the need for computerization of farm management decision aids; but they do not reflect that what is done is what ought to be done. Absence of reliable methods for CFMIS analysis and synthesis creates problems needed to be solved. At the same time, great variety of models, available software for farm management, and hardware used within differently organized CFMIS can give us what is necessary to develop descriptive models of CFMIS, analyse their problems, and outline possible way of synthesis.

REFERENCES

[1] Bonnen, J.T. "Assessment of the Current Agricultural Data Base: An Information System Approach", *A Survey of Agricultural Economics Literature*, Vol. 2, University of Minnesota Press, Minneapolis 1977, pp.386–407.

[2] Chapman, C.A., Infanger, C.L., Robbins, L.W. and Debertin, D.L. "Computers,

Information and Community Development: A Review of State Extension Programmes",
Taking Computers to the Community: Prospects and Perspectives, (ed.) Carol A. Chapman
et al., Kentucky Coop. Extension Service, 1978.
³ Harsh, S.B., Black, J.R. "The Michigan Computerized Forward Planning System",
Agricultural Economics Misc. 1971–72, Dept of Agricultural Economics, Michigan State
University, 1971.
⁴ Harsh, S.B. "The Developing Technology of Computerized Information Systems",
Amer. J. Agr. Econ. 60 (1978): 908–912.
⁵ Infanger, C.L., Robbins, L.W. and Debertin, D.L. "Interfacing Research and Extension
in Information Delivery Systems", *Amer. J. Ag. Econ.* 60 (1978): 915–920.
⁶ Johnson, G.L., Halter, A.N., Jensen, H.R. and Thomas, D. (eds) "A Study of Managerial Processes of Midwestern Farmers", Ames, Iowa 1961.
⁶ᵃ Kuhlmann, Friederich, "The Farm Firm Simulator SIMPLAN and Its Application to
Research, Extension and Decision Making" Ag. Econ. Staff Paper 79–24, Michigan State
University, East Lansing, Mi. 1979.
⁷ LaDue, E.L. "Impact of Alternative Remote Access Computer Systems on Extension
Programmes". *Amer. J. Agr. Econ.* 60 (1978): 135–138.
⁸ Manetsch, Thomas G. and Gerald L. Park, *System Analysis and Simulation with Applications to Economic and Social Systems*, Part 1 and Part 2, 3rd edition, E. Lansing,
Michigan, August 1977, Chapter 2.
⁹ Minister, P. "Into the Computer-Controlled-Wide Blue Yonder", *Dairy Farmer*, February 1978.
¹⁰ Ohlmer, B. and Nott, S. "The Need and Design of Computerized Farm Management
Tools." Ag. Econ. Report No. 353, Michigan State University, 1979.
¹¹ Polyakov, M.A. "The Automated Control System for the Management of Agriculture
(ACSMA): Creation Problems and Future Developments". A Seminar Paper, Dept. of
Electrical Engr. and Systems Science, Michigan State University, East Lansing, Michigan
1978.
¹² Pugh, C.L. "Farm Management Information Systems – A Practical Approach", Farm
Management, Vol. 3, No. 5, Spring 1977.
¹³ Schmidt, J.R. "Documentation of EDP Programmes for Extension". Paper presented
at the North Central Farm Management Extension Workshop, Michigan State University,
May 1973.
¹⁴ Thompson, S.C., "Central Computing Facilities for Information Systems", Draft for
Agricultural Information Systems, 1978.
¹⁵ Thompson, T.L., Kendrick, J.G. and Stark, A.L. "AGNET – A Management Tool for
Agriculture", ASAE Paper No. 78–5001, St. Joseph, Michigan.

DISCUSSION OPENING – TED NELSON

The authors have given us a comprehenisve taxonomy of Computerized
Farm Management Information Systems and the large number of combi-
nations of equipment, software and delivery methods available to build
CFMIS.

I fully endorse the addition of a delivery component parallel to the
structural and design blocks in Figure 1. It seems to me that we need to
consider three questions about the application of these systems at the
farm level and this seems naturally to follow the presentation.

1   Are the concepts and models used understood by the farmer? If not,
the best hardware and software can be expected to fail, until such time as
the user has been taught (with or without the aid of computers).
2   Who is to accept the responsibility for developing computer-use skills

by field agents and farmers? (Agricultural economists do not teach basic mathematics or reading but may have to teach a few hours of computing skills to farmers for the use of calculators and micro-computers to be successful).

3   How can we provide useful software for hardware currently available, with cheaper and better hardware becoming available so often, which will displace the hardware (and probably software) of each yesteryear?

GENERAL DISCUSSION – RAPPORTEUR: LEONARD KYLE

The general discussion was comprised of the following questions regarding (1) measurement of benefits of computers to farmers; (2) whether programmes are designed to reflect the way professionals or farmers think; (3) the usefulness of various types of computer and in particular micro-computers; and (4) the cost of farm advisers and their training.

In reply, the authors felt that (1) was difficult because more tasks would be done in less time and farmers would also increase their managerial input in other areas. Regarding (2), the system had to be designed with farmers in mind if it were of a kind where they had access. In other cases some compromise was possible. Under (3) the most immediate use was that of financial control. Larger and more complicated computers can be used for planning and decision making. Within their limitations, micro-computers can be similarly used. It was felt that (4) represented the major item of cost, by comparison with which the cost of the computer was of minor significance.

Participants in the discussion included Keith Butterworth, Stephen B. Harsh, Stephen C. Thompson, A. Hartmann and John C. Duncan-Watt.

JOHN C. ABBOTT*

Technical Assistance in Marketing: A View over Time

This review first analyses attitudes towards marketing improvement in the developing countries and towards some component elements, then the assistance forthcoming from bilateral and multilateral sources. It concludes with some remarks on directions for the future.

"MARKETING" AS A CONCEPT

While the word marketing has rung out loud and clear in North America and in many British Commonwealth countries, it was accepted much later in countries with French and Spanish cultural backgrounds.

Within FAO the focal point for work on marketing has remained consistently with the "Marketing Branch". However, this unit has shifted through Commodities, Economic Analysis and Rural Institutions divisions to Agricultural Services.

A new set of overlays has come up in recent years. For FAO and the aid agencies "food security" and the "reduction of post harvest losses" have international appeal. In vogue at the universities now are "Agribusiness" and "Food systems" – again activities that include a lot of marketing. In FAO circles, however, agribusiness has been a bad word. Indeed "Marketing" itself has not been very popular with its governing bodies. Their members tend to be drawn from ministries of agriculture concerned only with production. Other governing body members have a strong social orientation for which the word "marketing" is too commercial.

Awareness of marketing as a concept and as a vital element in their economies needing attention has nevertheless, extended greatly in the developing countries since the 1950s. Large numbers of young people from those countries have taken courses in marketing at American universities, and more recently also in Europe. Gradually they are moving up into influential positions. FAO has also made an important contribution through its series of Marketing Guides which were first transmitted

* The views expressed in the paper are those of the author and do not necessarily represent those of FAO.

directly to governments and then reprinted many times in response to commercial demand. A series of FAO regional training centres financed by the UNDP in the sixties also had a substantial impact.

GOVERNMENT SERVICES FOR MARKETING

Still in many countries there is no government department specifically responsible for agricultural marketing policy or carrying on practical research as a basis for it. In the majority of Latin American, African and Asian countries elements of marketing services and controls are operated by different bodies without much co-ordination. Departments of agriculture, commerce, co-operatives, development banks and municipalities are all involved. Without an adequate government marketing support service there is little hope of implementing any measures that require public initiative and consistent follow up.

Lack of awareness of the importance of marketing also showed up in the content of national development plans in the 1950s and early '60s. None assigned a major role to marketing of agricultural products in their development strategies. In only three out of thirteen examined in a 1966 study did the financial allocation to marketing, exceed 6 per cent of total expected investment in agriculture.[1] In 1970 Spinks'[14] review of government attitudes towards marketing in Asia showed that this was a field about which most government officials knew very little and that major decisions were frequently taken without adequate information on what was actually going on.

FAO has sought fairly consistently to build up information, advisory and policy formulating units in the ministries of agriculture of developing countries or in the ministries of commerce if responsibility for agricultural and food marketing was located there. USAID has followed the same path. In Iran there was a full Ministry of Marketing and Consumer Goods at one time but it cut across too many interests. Slowest to consolidate marketing responsibilities and mobilize the requisite expertise in one department have been governments of countries with French and Spanish cultural backgrounds. This is now being done in Mexico, Colombia and Ecuador in Latin America , but there, and in francophone Africa, there is still much to do.

WHAT TO DO TO IMPROVE MARKETING

In comparison with extended irrigated land and breeding higher yielding crops, what constitutes an improvement in marketing is not so obvious. Large numbers of people are involved, important interests are affected. Even after a decision is taken or legislation passed implementation remains uncertain. For such reasons many administrators of aid programmes have shied away from an area which they saw as complex and difficult. They also saw it as full of politics – international, national and local.

As a United Nations organization, FAO has been protected from many of the pressures on aid-giving governments. There have been queries on its policy *vis-à-vis* private and public enterprise and some pressure for support to co-operatives, but in practice those concerned with marketing assistance have been able to maintain a neutral alignment. FAO is equally able to assist the Government of Tanzania build an efficient state marketing system and to help that of Kenya strengthen a blend of private, co-operative and marketing board structures.

PHYSICAL ELEMENTS IN MARKETING

Packing, transport and storage
This might seem to be the least controversial area of marketing assistance where even casual visitors to developing countries can see that much needs to be done. There are limits, however, to the introduction of new methods and equipment set by the extent of local know-how and related development, by costs in relation to scale of enterprise and consumer incomes, and by social considerations. Access to aid funds can easily lead to the purchase of mechanized sorting, handling and packaging machinery that is never used. Too often advisers backed by foreign equipment manufacturers recommend storage construction along lines adapted to quite different conditions. Economic advisers and government planning departments are increasingly concerned about possible disadvantages of technical improvements in marketing. Proposals to use technology in place of labour must be appraised both for their direct employment effects and their implications for employment at other stages in the production–assembly–distribution chain.

In the area of transport too some expensive lessons have been learnt over the last decades. Air and refrigerated transport can bridge gaps in the movement of perishables to the better-off consumers. However, in the developing countries better feeder roads, bridges over seasonal streams, rubber tyres for bullock carts and spare parts for trucks often pay off much better than the introduction of radically new transport equipment. Access to return loads and out-of-season business to reduce costs, and adequate maintenance, are related issues. Often they point to ownership by a private carrier rather than a specialized agricultural marketing organization and this has raised problems for some aid agencies.

There is a view that the establishment of some physical facilities – a plant to pack or process an agricultural product – will stimulate an expansion of output in the area around. A review of 70 canning, slaughtering, storage and related plants established in Africa and subsequently failing, evidences the risks of disappointment if a more thorough consideration of the marketing element is not undertaken.[10]

Quality control and grading
The heterogeneous nature and appearance of the produce offered on
their markets has been of continuing concern to developing country
governments and the subject of many requests for assistance. It is fairly
easy to have quality standards and grades promulgated but very difficult
to see them applied. This is easiest in export marketing, notably when
some major importing country sets standards which must be met if entry
is to be allowed. In domestic marketing the application of simple standards in the purchasing of grain or other produce by an official price
stabilization agency can be a potent influence, but one difficult to maintain.

Market planning and construction
As urban populations increase more and more, cities need larger and
better situated marketing facilities. An FAO specialist who recommended the establishment of a wholesale market for fruit and vegetables
in Malta and prepared detailed plans for it, was pleasantly surprised to be
invited to the official inauguration of the market he planned – ten years
later. This is quite fast going for city wholesale markets. New central
markets for Baghdad, Beirut and Tehran have each been under discussion and planning for 20 years now: they are still not built. In Latin
America, on the other hand, high rates of inflation have led politicians to
build markets as big and as fast as possible – often not too well adapted to
local needs. FAO's view is that many national sponsors of new markets
and associated international advisers build too expensively and too sol-
idly when only a simple shed is required. In addition to taking up money
that would be better spent on "soft ware" services and staff training these
structures are difficult to modify later as needs evolve.[11]

Marketing organization
This is usually a blend of private, co-operative and marketing board or
state enterprise. *Private enterprises* have a bad public in many countries.
To technical and financial assistance agencies they are well nigh
anathema. If they are near-monopolists they will have the ear of someone
in the government and cannot be touched. If they are foreign owned or of
different ethnic background they cannot be helped. If they are small they
will be difficult to identify and contact; they will also lack the resources
and risk capacity to try out the new ideas of the foreign adviser.
    Faced with an apparent multiplicity of small enterprises the approach
of some administrators has been to restrict their numbers in the hope that
some will then get bigger. The neoclassical economist is against this
because it restricts competition. Many of us pinned our faith on government facilitating measures – improvement of roads, transport means,
public provision of market information and easier access to credit. Even
this relatively safe ground can prove shaky. For years the establishment of
market news services was the stock in trade of the marketing improvement adviser. Now there are disturbing questions as to whether such

information is ever used. Credit is available in plenty for large farmers and beneficiaries of government projects, but how to organize it for small scale traders?

Co-operatives
Arguing from successful farmers' associations in their own countries and reinforced by political support, aid agencies have consistently favoured co-operative solutions to organization problems. They also find co-operative organizations, most amenable to proposals to try new techniques and pilot activities. How far this path of idealism and convenience has led into the wilderness of disappointment is masked by the finite duration of most aid projects, and the arrival on the scene of fresh enthusiasts with more funds.

A recent analysis of experience in East Africa and Asia concluded that an over-reliance on co-operatives can become a major impediment to agricultural development.[5] The Government of Tanzania has now officially abandoned "co-operative marketing" in favour of state directed bodies. The easiest role for a new co-operative is as assembling agent for an established marketing board. It has a sure outlet and no sales risk. From this base it can go on to distribute seed and fertilizer on credit and undertake other related activities.

Marketing boards and other state marketing enterprises
In the developing world these were set up first for export crops in the British Commonwealth countries of West Africa and the Caribbean in the late 1940s and '50s. Some of them set up to handle perishable crops grown for local consumption may be judged a disservice to the countries concerned. They asked too much in management and political responsibility. At this stage FAO (and USAID also) hesitated to be involved. Setting up marketing boards in the developing countries smacked of a political decision directly affecting other existing enterprises. Behind this lay anticipation that the initial phases might not be smooth and the agency associated with them would pick up the blame. Later, when it became common for countries gaining independence to nationalize important segments of their marketing systems that were in foreign or alien hands and to seek help in operating them, FAO saw its responsibility clearly. In 1966 its *Marketing Guide No. 5 Agricultural Marketing Boards: their Establishment and Operation* came out in English, French and Spanish. In 1970 a Michigan State University team on a US Government contract undertook a thorough going review of the marketing board system in Tanzania and recommended consolidation into a single marketing corporation.

FAO and AID have both worked on domestic price stabilization systems, buffer stock agencies and other agencies set up to implement guaranteed prices at the farm level. Considering, however, their strategic role in developing country economies it could be expected that major marketing boards would be subject to continuing reviews of operating methods, management and costs. In practice these are extremely rare. Board managements seem able to ward off outside assistance in such areas and to have allies in the Government committed to their protection.

Integrated marketing systems and entrepreneurs
Integration of production with marketing through linked ownership or firm contracts has been common in the developing countries for tobacco, oilseeds and other crops for processing. It has been more difficult to organize for crops sold fresh and where there are many producers of varying quantities. The follow-up of AID financed Michigan State University marketing surveys in Latin America featured attempts to develop integrated systems serving the big cities. FAO also supported public programmes to develop centrally managed and voluntary retail chains with unified purchasing. It has become clear, however, that there must be a leader for the integration to work – a "channel captain" in contemporary terminology. The entrepreneur can be directing a private, cooperative or publicly owned system, but an entrepreneur there must be.[4]

TRAINING OF STAFF FOR MARKETING

In most of the developing countries lack of trained personnel is a major constraint on marketing development. Especially difficult to organize is in-service training particularly when the enterprises are small and family based. The main credit for the present build up of qualified people in marketing must go to American universities and the Government of the USA which has both provided scholarships for people of the developing countries to attend these universities and arranged for marketing professors to teach in those countries. By preparing training materials specifically for the developing countries and organizing a series of training centres on a regional basis FAO met a crucial need in the late 1950s and '60s. Now most developing countries have their own universities. The main issue at this level seems to be to secure sufficient time for marketing in a general agricultural or economic curriculum. In 1975 the average course allowance in a number of African universities was only ten hours.[3]

How best to organize medium and lower level training in marketing in developing countries remains an open issue. Supported by the Coffee Growers' Federation and leading banks FAO trained several hundred candidates in the more practical aspects of grain and other produce marketing and in marketing management in Colombia. Now they may be found in strategic jobs throughout the Colombian economy.

Marketing in rural development
The contemporary situation is marked by concern for the welfare of rural populations as a whole. Recent meetings of FAO/RED in Bangkok and IICA in San José have been directed towards policy guidance on how to organize marketing to help raise small farmer incomes. Strategies being

tried out include: (a) group action by farmers to reduce transport costs and improve bargaining power (b) introduction of contract systems for crops adapted to small farmer production, (c) fostering positive action by private entrepreneurs and (d) extending assembly market systems further into rural areas.

There is particular interest also in the extention of fertilizer and input distribution systems to reach the smaller and more outlying farmers. Help to the traditional small scale marketing enterprise has also been stressed by FAO and by Uma Lele in a review of rural development projects in Africa financed by the World Bank.[8]

Social marketing

From the early 1960s the FAO Marketing Branch has been concerned with protein food marketing and projects to make available more nutritious products to low income consumers.[17] More recently it has helped in the establishment and operation of agencies to supply basic food at low prices to vulnerable urban consumers.

MARKETING IMPROVEMENT POLICIES BY LEVEL OF DEVELOPMENT

FAO's work on the "Indicative World Plan" also sparked attempts to sort out the investment, training and other improvement measures that might generally be associated with a particular level of development. A subsequent study endeavoured to relate levels of marketing and other strategic services with stages of agricultural development using a statistical correlation approach.[15] A 1972 US Department of Agriculture formulation of tentative marketing development priorities for (a) predominantly subsistent countries (b) countries with transitional production oriented agriculture and (c) countries with market oriented agriculture and mainly urban population was further discussed at the International Conference on Marketing Systems for Developing Countries held in Israel 1974.[16,6]

QUANTIFICATION OF COSTS AND BENEFITS OF MARKETING IMPROVEMENT

This may be another issue to which marketing specialists have not faced up fully because of the difficulty both of measurement and of achieving agreement on what should be measured. The regulation of assembly markets in India was at one time estimated to save farmers $18 million in market charges.[2] These benefits were easy to measure, but what about the effect on competition, on prices and on farmers' and traders' convenience? A beginning in assessing the benefit value of a reduction in food marketing margins in Argentina and of the introduction of innovations at successive stages in the marketing of grain, potatoes and other produce has been made by Dieter Link.[9] What degree of precision on the benefits of a market news service, the cost of bureaucratic procedures, the benefits of maintaining competitive channels should we expect? Lack of convincing figures for estimating internal rates of return exceeding 12 per cent may be one of the factors in both the low allocation of World Bank funds to marketing and the relative lack of interest on the part of development planners.

MARKETING COSTS AND MARGINS

FAO has often felt that it should be reviewing annually the cost of moving food from producer to consumer along representative channels in developing countries. This has been done for many years in the USA. The main area where comparative studies have been carried out in developing countries has probably been in fertilizer marketing case studies. These have focused attention on the wide distribution margins between port of entry and the farmer-user in various developing countries. Recognizing the obstacles raised by differences in conditions, high rates of inflation and arbitrary exchange rates it may still be maintained that much more could usefully be done in this area.

MARKETING ASSISTANCE TO DEVELOPING COUNTRIES BY AGENCIES

FAO was already recruiting specialists in marketing to advise the governments of developing countries in 1955 and had a small technical support unit of two men at its headquarters. A year or two later the FAO programme was made up as follows:

1   *Provision of technical experts* (around 20) to assist governments of developing countries.
2   *Training courses* in meat marketing (Santiago 1955) and grain marketing (Argentina 1956) averaged six weeks' duration per year each accommodating 25–35 trainees.
3   *Fellowships* of 6 to 24 months' duration enabled the personnel of government departments and marketing organizations to receive specialized training and first hand experience in other countries.
4   *Direct information, advice, publications etc.* A series of marketing guides designed specifically to serve developing countries had been initiated, also an international marketing bibliography service.

The establishment of the UN Special Fund for Development in 1958 opened the way to a much larger programme, but some years lapsed before major projects in marketing were supported. A review of the arrangements made for assistance in the preparation of some half-dozen area development plans in Mediterranean countries showed a participation by marketing specialists of only 3 to 5 per cent.[1]

During the course of work on the FAO Indicative World Plan for Agricultural Development, a major FAO project of this period, estimates of investment requirements through 1985 in central and livestock auction markets, refrigerated and other storage, flour, rice, and oilseed mills, sugar processing, slaughterhouses, dairy plants and fruit and vegetable packing and canning in five western Latin American countries were made. They amounted to 2.6 per cent of the annual value of agricultural output.

In 1976 FAO had 63 marketing specialists on advisory assignments in the developing countries with a technical support staff of 9 at headquarters. In addition there were 5 associates in the field and at headquarters. Major projects (budgeted around $1.0 million) supported government marketing services in Iran, Kenya and Tanzania respectively, assisted marketing boards and supply and price stabilization systems for basic grains in Guatemala and Uganda, and livestock marketing organization in Mali. Most FAO area and rural development projects now included provision for work on marketing, also the second generation of projects founded on irrigation programmes.

In FAO, the allocation of funds for marketing work, out of its regular programme budget is about $600,000 a year – around 1 per cent of FAO's technical and ecomomic programme budget for agriculture, forestry and fisheries. A similar allocation is made in field activities funded by UNDP. Some $3.5 million a year or less than 2 per cent of the total UNDP projects carried out by FAO now goes for marketing and related project activities.

The *World Bank* had been the major source of multilateral investment funds for agricultural development, but little has gone into marketing. A $17,000,000 investment in local assembly markets for the State of Bihar is now under way. It is recognised in the Bank that administrative considerations have stood in the way of making funds available for the small scale investments often required for marketing. A project to help small scale traders in the Caribbean is currently in formulation by FAO.

Of the regional banks only the *Inter-American Development Bank* has paid significant attention to marketing improvement to date. Specific marketing investment projects include the financing of grain storage in Ecuador and Paraguay and of rural and central market facilities in Jamaica and Trinidad.[12]

Over the last fifteen years the *International Trade Centre* in Geneva has mobilized a significant programme of assistance to the developing countries in export promotion. A major supporter has been the Swedish development assistance programme. Of its ongoing and proposed projects in 1977, 37 or 44 per cent were for agricultural, fish and forest products. In collaboration with FAO are studies of import markets for livestock by-products and on the feasibility of organizing a market news service for tropical fruits and vegetables on European markets.

USA

For many years bilateral assistance in the marketing of food and agricultural products has come predominantly from the various aid programmes of the United States Government. During the 1950s US technical assistance took the form mainly of individual advisors drawn from federal and state government advisory services, from private industry and agricultural co-operatives who were outposted in ministries of agriculture and commerce, and of professors helping to establish marketing courses in developing country universities. Farmers' co-operative marketing projects were a means of introducing new methods and equipment. Recognition in a number of developing countries of the need for government marketing units to provide information, advice and facilitating services owes much to American technical assistance at this period.

Around 1965, to simplify its task of recruiting qualified specialists and ensuring technical support, AID developed the system of contracting assistance programmes to particular universities. In this way, some were able to develop special expertise in particular areas: Michigan State in Latin America, Stanford in Africa, Cornell in India, together with helpful language abilities.

United Kingdom

Direct assistance in the organization of food and agricultural marketing and in the establishment of marketing facilities has been a continuing UK government responsibility towards developing countries in the British Commonwealth. The export monopoly set up in West African countries became models that many of their francophone neighbours eventually followed. British administrators and advisors have also promoted the establishment of co-operative structures for marketing; notably as assembling agents for monopoly boards. Outstanding examples were coffee and cotton co-operatives in Uganda and Tanzania, and in Cyprus co-operatives of citrus and grape growers. Of integrated marketing and processing programmes initiated by the UK, notable models are the livestock assembly, processing and meat export system established by the Commonwealth Development Corporation at Lobatse in Botswana and the earlier cotton production, ginning and marketing system operated under the Gezira Board in the Sudan.

France

A parallel programme of assistance to developing countries linked with France has been maintained by the French Ministère de Coopération and preceding government agencies. Proportionately, the French aid programme in total has been more generous than those of most other developed countries. The marketing assistance having most impact on the farmers in the developing countries has been French support for the price of their export products. Much more emphasis has been placed on assuring market outlets at favourable prices than in building up national marketing structures to compete on foreign and domestic markets.

Nevertheless, help has been provided in establishing marketing enterprises and facilities, notably as part of integrated production and marketing systems operated by companies with strong French links. Such companies have organized the production and marketing of coffee and cocoa in Cameroon, fruit in Ivory Coast, cotton in Chad, to mention only a few examples. Characteristically French implants in many francophone African countries have been the "caisse de stabilisation" into which exporting firms paid when export prices were high and from which they received balancing allocations when prices were low, and the export quality control and inspection service. A French initiative of the 1950s which became a model of international interest was the establishment of integrated holding grounds, abattoir and meat export by air from Chad to coastal African cities.[7] Relatively less was done to build up indigenous enterprises.

Other European bilateral aid
Danish aid has for many years been directed towards the improvement of meat and milk handling featuring provision of processing equipment and the training of staff to work with it. Many developing country dairy technicians were trained in association with the Bombay milk scheme. However, "marketing" *per se* has not been a line of Danish assistance.

Over the last decade, Swedish aid has been among the highest in terms of percentage of national GNP. It has also aimed high in terms of changing policies and building up progressive institutions, in contrast to the provision of materials and equipment. Assistance to marketing has emphasized co-operatives. Under the Nordic programme more than 50 advisors have been working with co-operative unions in East Africa for a number of years. Aid to co-operatives and credit in Afghanistan was used as a lever to secure the passage of co-operative legislation. An earlier target of 100 multi-purpose co-operatives has been raised to 1,000 by the new government. In Ethiopia co-operative milk and grain marketing were lead elements in a package of services for integrated area development.

The Federal Republic of Germany is now a major force in marketing assistance. Support capacity has been developed through expert meetings on marketing issues, early participation in the FAO associate expert programme and the financing of senior students to carry out marketing research in developing countries for advanced degrees. Since 1974, increasing numbers of projects have been set up exclusively to promote agricultural marketing.[13]

The Netherlands government has been one of the main underwriters of the FAO Food Security Programme. Bilaterally, processing, particularly of fish and meat, and new marketing systems for horticultural products have been assisted. Switzerland has supported storage development in various countries. Canada also is paying special attention to post-harvest problems. Recently, some Latin American countries have received technical assistance from Spain and Israel.

Regional and group programmes
The Colombo Plan whereby the more developed members of the British
Commonwealth – Australia, Canada, New Zealand and the UK – assisted
other members in training, advisory and investment projects is an early
example. Travelling seminars in livestock and fruit and vegetable marketing were organized for Iran, Pakistan and Turkey through the Cento
Agreement. The Inter-American Institute of Agricultural Sciences,
IICA, has 13 staff members engaged on marketing programmes, focusing
on the development of internal food markets and support institutions. In
the late 1960s a marketing training and development centre was established in Brazil.

Outstanding group aid programmes are those of the Common Market
countries to associate countries in Africa and the COMECON group to
some communist-oriented developing countries. With assistance from
these sources major rail and road construction projects have been undertaken and processing, storage and other marketing infrastructure provided.

Private aid
Here the most influential source of marketing assistance has been the
Ford Foundation. Its advisory teams have usually worked in central
planning departments with corresponding scope for influencing government decision-making. Ford Foundation recommendations were behind
the opening of fertilizer distribution to private enterprise in Pakistan
during the 1960s with the consequent rapid expansion of fertilizer distribution. The Agricultural Development Council has promoted some
discussions between specialists engaged in marketing assistance but has
not taken a major role.

Perhaps the most interesting conclusion from this tentative review of
assistance programmes is that constructive impact on national government decisions and follow through is the crucial goal. A well-timed
government decision can mobilise vast domestic human and material
resources. Construction of storage and processing plants that are not
integrated into stable marketing systems or require sophisticated servicing, or initiation of marketing enterprises that are too complex for local
people to maintain may appeal to governing bodies in aid giving and
receiving countries, but are of limited use on the ground.

ISSUES FOR CONSIDERATION

Concern of developing country governments for the organization of food
and agricultural marketing has increased greatly over the last two
decades. For many of them marketing policy is of crucial importance. It is
now time to face up to some of the more intransigent issues in marketing
assistance.

1 *Special marketing programmes for small farmers*
The meetings at Bangkok and San José assembled information but produced little guidance for policy. Is it worth pursuing examination of ways in which the smaller farmers can be helped by special marketing programmes?

2 *Training of staff for small-scale marketing operations*
Management and technical training is being provided for intermediate-level staff of government departments, public enterprises and co-operatives. Only in Kenya is training of small marketing entrepreneurs being attempted. How can this best be carried forward. Or must it be left to the entry of new people with a better general level of education?

3 *Marketing management for state enterprises*
Relatively little is being done here, possibly because of reluctance to face criticism. Can an acceptable approach be devised?

REFERENCES

[1] Abbott, J.C. "Marketing issues in agricultural development planning" in *Markets and marketing in developing economies* (eds) Moyer and Hollander, Irwin 1968, pp. 87–116.

[2] Chatterji, N.P. "Agricultural marketing in India", *Agricultural marketing* 3(1) Nagpur 1961.

[3] FAO, *Training in agricultural and food marketing at university level in Africa*, Report on FAO/AFFA expert consultation held in Nairobi, 10–20 November 1975.

[4] FAO, *The role of the entrepreneur in agricultural marketing development*, Report of an international expert meeting held in Berlin 8–13 Nov 1971.

[5] Hunter, G. "Cooperatives: effects of the social matrix" in *Cooperatives and rural development in East Africa* (ed.) Widstrand, New York, Africana Publishing Co. 1970.

[6] INCOMAS Proceedings *Agricultural marketing for developing countries* (eds) D. Izaeli, D.N. Israeli, F. Meissner, J. Wiley, New York 1974.

[7] Lacrouts, M. and J. Tye carried out a series of livestock resource studies for Benin, Ivory Coast, Madagascar, Mali, Mauritania, Niger and Senegal in the early 1960s.

[8] Lele, U. *The design of rural development: lessons from Africa* John Hopkins University Press, Baltimore 1975.

[9] Link, D. *La modernizacion de la distribucion de alimentos* Informe al Gobierno de Argentina, FAO, Rome 1974.

[10] Mittendorf, H.J. "Marketing aspects in planning agricultural processing enterprises in developing countries", FAO *Monthly Bulletin of Agricultural Economics and Statistics*, (4) April 1968.

[11] Mittendorf, H.J. *Progress in improving wholesale markets in developing countries*, paper presented to the 10th International Congress on Wholesale Markets, Nice September 1977.

[12] OECD/FAO, *Critical issues on food marketing systems in developing countries*, report of an OECD/FAO Joint Seminar, Paris October 1976.

[13] Schubert, B. *Die Agrarmarktkomponente bilateraler deutscher Agrarhilfeprojekte*, Berlin 1977, p. 78.

[14] Spinks, G.R. "Attitudes towards agricultural marketing in Asia and the Far East", *FAO Monthly Bulletin of Agricultural Economics and Statistics* 19(1) January 1970.

[15] Szczepanik, E.F. *Agricultural policies at different levels of development*, FAO 1975.

[16] United States Department of Agriculture, *Improving marketing systems in developing countries: An approach to identifying problems and strengthening technical assistance*, Washington Feb. 1972.

[17] Wickstrom, B. *Marketing of protein rich foods in developing countries*, Rome, FAO/WHO/UNICEF Protein Advisory Group 1971.

DISCUSSION OPENING – A.T. BIROWO

The author of the paper is a long experienced officer in FAO in charge of marketing activities. Hence the paper was prepared with long years of experience as background, particularly in the international arena. Indeed, the paper is rich in its wealth of interesting cases and supplied with a relevant list of appropriate bibliography.

The flow of thinking presented in the paper reflects the fact that the author has all the necessary background to discuss the problems of marketing. However, the author may have been impressed by time constraints. The items described in many sections are too sketchy, and at times the flow of statements are discontinuous. The richest of all, is the section describing the marketing assistance to developing countries by agencies. As the title of the paper suggests, this section should be the main portion of emphasis of the paper.

But if one refers to the theme of the Conference: "Rural Change: the prospective role of the agricultural economists", the paper should have dealt more with fundamental questions relating marketing with rural change, and the perspective discussion with more illustrations on future thinking in marketing assistance to the developing countries.

Marketing as a concept
In many developing countries marketing is crucial in at least three aspects. Firstly, it is an essential activity to accelerate the transition from a subsistence economy to commercialization of the agricultural economy. Secondly, marketing and trade capacity are an indispensable environment for a smoother forward linkage from agriculture to industry, and thus very crucial in the modernization process of the agricultural sector. Thirdly, marketing activity is instrumental in providing new and expanded entrepreneurial capability required for modernizing agriculture.

Many "scholars" and political leaders in the developing countries have long been aware of these important roles of marketing, even during the periods when their countries were still colonial territories of the present developed countries. I have to disagree with the author when he wrote "Awareness of marketing as a concept . . . extended greatly in the developing countries since the 1950s. Large numbers of young people from these countries have taken courses in marketing at American universities, and more recently also in Europe. Gradually they are moving up into influential positions". Awareness was there long before the 1950s and concerns leaders who may never have had the opportunity to study abroad – not to mention the luxury of attending US or European universities. These leaders were aware of the tight entanglement of marketing with politics and power structure in the agricultural economy in general and the rural scenery in particular. They could not afford to express their "awareness" strongly, until major transformational and structural rural change took place. What was needed for them to be able to express their concern strongly, was not US or European marketing education, but an appropriate political climate for structural changes in the rural areas. To illustrate an extreme case at the other end of the arena, there are examples where bright US and European graduates with brilliant education in marketing were confused and frustrated to understand the reality of market monopoly and monopsony in the rural areas of the developing country. Many agricultural economists, graduates from US and European universities, started to question the relevance of the theories they obtained abroad to understand the marketing problems they face in their respective countries.[1] Rigorous empirical research is now carried out in many areas to test the relevance of US and European theories in understanding and solving marketing problems in the developing countries. Probably, they have to learn more from China, Japan and Korea rather than from the US or Europe.

Marketing as development policy
In many developing countries, marketing of agricultural products have been usually induced initially by the trade relationships between US/Europe and their previous colonies. International trade has been very powerful in shaping the progress or stagnation of the developing economy. This kind of historical legacy was one of the main reasons why many marketing practices in the current developing countries are more export-oriented than directed towards the development of domestic markets. Or put in other words, marketing for export commodities are more developed than markets for linkages with domestic industry. This also helps to explain why in many developing countries government services in marketing are not well established relative to the important role of marketing in the agricultural development of the country.

As a policy instrument for development, marketing improvement should be directed more to develop the institution for domestic markets, both for final food consumer and processing establishments in the industrial sector.

Future direction of marketing assistance
Marketing assistance in the future should be directed towards strengthening the role of marketing in the development process of the agricultural sector. Emphasis should be given to strengthen marketing institutions as well as training activities to improve marketing capabilities, especially of small farmers.

Creating viable marketing organizations with well-trained personnel may be more relevant than erecting prestigious buildings at wrong environments. I strongly support the thesis of the author that training for middle managers and low-level marketing personnel should receive more attention in future technical assistance in marketing.

Economic co-operation among the developing countries should be stimulated, as this may prove to be a more efficient transfer of know-how than large scale training in the developed countries.

Conclusion

In general I should like to congratulate the author for preparing such good discussion material for this session. The materials presented in his paper have been rich with illuminating real cases. My contribution in opening the discussion would be to suggest areas of fundamental interest where further dialogue can be stimulated.

NOTE

[1] See Proceedings of the First Conference of the Agricultural Economic Society of South East Asia, Balikpapan, Indonesia, 1977. In this conference a special session was devoted to a discussion of the relevant foundation of agricultural economics to South East Asia.

GENERAL DISCUSSION – RAPPORTEUR: FELIX I. NWEKE

Among issues raised on Dr Abbott's paper was that assurance of market outlet at minimum prices must be an integral component of policies for agricultural development, because if expenditures on research, extension and organization of input supplies are to bear full fruit, reasonable prices for the agricultural products are essential. For the implementation of government policy in this regard institutional arrangements that would avert the emergence of explosive situations, such as non-availability of essential commodities and consequent social unrest, are needed. This is because in developing democratic countries there is demand for a public distribution system for essential commodities to assure that the needs for vulnerable sections of the population are met. Such arrangements may involve higher costs than private trade, however, and economy and efficiency in operation are important and should receive full consideration in developing para-statal market support organizations.

Other issues to which attention was drawn included the need to integrate improvements in post-harvest technology into the on-going marketing system; whether the input supply and output marketing structures set up under some area development projects were too elaborate to be replicated over a country as a whole; and the role of taxes in marketing. These taxes range from village level cesses in East Africa to the rice premium in Thailand and the substantial profit margins of some export marketing organizations in West Africa and Latin America.

Participants in the discussion included H.L. Chawla, George T. Jones, John D. Strasma and Deryke G.R. Belshaw.

H.J. MITTENDORF*

Useful Strategies for Developing Countries Striving to Improve Food Marketing Systems

Three major issues dominate any discussion of strategies for the development of more effective marketing systems which, through the provision of economic incentives and the stimulation of innovation will make a major contribution to economic development. These are:

(a) the need to design marketing systems able to deal satisfactorily with the increased food supplies required to feed rapidly growing urban populations;

(b) the means by which the subsistence and semi-subsistence producers can be integrated into the marketing system; and

(c) the effective use of pricing policies as an important stimulant of agricultural production.

This paper will review the first two of the above mentioned issues, namely urban and rural marketing organizations and will focus on the type of applied marketing research and training considered necessary to bring about the desired improvements. The paper will not deal with pricing policies as these have already received wide attention in other publications,[10] particularly so far as the price level needed to stimulate agricultural production is concerned. Reference will, however, be made to aspects of price policy implementation as related to (a) and (b) above.

The need to direct more attention to the promotion of efficient internal marketing systems is highlighted by the fact that rapid urbanization coupled with agricultural and economic specialization will expose internal marketing systems to continuous stresses as they develop more specialized, diversified and complex systems requiring the application of greater managerial skills. The volume of food that will have to be handled by internal marketing systems in the year 2000 will be about three times greater than in 1975 if account is taken of rapidly growing urban populations and the higher level of food exchange in rural areas.

* The views expressed in the paper are those of the author and do not necessarily represent those of FAO.

131

TABLE 1   *Growth of urban populations in developing regions*

Region	1971	2000	Annual growth rate in % against 1975
	'000 millions		
Africa	98.2	3'7.6	4.3
S. America	137.8	811.0	3.7
Asia	595.6	1,386.4	3.1
Near East	73.6	202.4	3.5
Total	905.2	2,207.4	3.6

Source: UN Population Estimates and Projections, April 1974.

STRENGTHENING FOOD MARKETING IN URBAN AREAS

The pressure to provide food at low prices to urban centres, an important political factor to most governments, is likely to increase in the years to come. The question raised constantly is whether full advantage has been taken of all opportunities available to organize food marketing on a least cost basis. An analysis of the problems of food marketing in large urban areas, say of more than 0.5 million inhabitants, should distinguish between the issues that arise at the retail and wholesale level.[8]

RETAILING

Of the three main traditional food retail outlets in developing countries, namely public retail markets, grocery stores and self service stores, the first named are still the most popular and often account for more than 50 per cent of total food sales, particularly highly perishables. The main problems facing public retail markets are those of organization and management.

Finance. Because of pressure from retailers, the fees charged for use of the market are often so low that they are barely sufficient to cover maintenance costs let alone provide for the recovery of invested capital. Most municipalities with responsibility for markets are, therefore, unable to undertake an expansion of the existing facilities or to increase their number. Consequently, markets become overcrowded and antiquated, and increasingly inefficient.

Maintenance. Many markets are badly maintained, and have low standards of hygiene and waste disposal.

Planning. The few new markets that are built are often planned on the basis of architectural considerations or as prestige projects without due attention to the economic sensitivity of the investment. The markets that have been built are often not used to capacity. In this connection, the steady pressure of unemployed people for more market buildings as a means of providing job opportunities in marketing has to be recognized. This pressure has induced politicians, as for instance in Latin American cities, to authorize the expenditure of scarce financial resources for new market investments far in excess of the capacity that can be economically utilized. To remedy this situation, better planning, management and financial methods are essential. In planning new retail food markets, particular attention has to be paid to the size and capital outlay to ensure that this is realistic. Account has to be taken of alternative retail food outlets such as zonal and central retail markets where customers are in the habit of purchasing at weekends, retail markets, where customers within walking distance of their homes are able to attend daily, and the availability of other independent grocery stores. Financing food retail markets can be strengthened by setting fees at a level that covers not only administrative and cleaning charges but also allows for the amortization of capital costs. Private entrepreneurs can be encouraged to invest in public markets by being allowed to purchase or rent stalls on the same basis as in "shopping centres", a course that has already been adopted in Argentina, Brazil, Mexico and Indonesia.

Apart from the food retail markets, there are the neighbourhood or grocery shops which serve as major sales outlets for staple or dry foods. The main issues bearing on their productivity are related to:

> the establishment of optimum stock assortments to enable all customers to be adequately supplied;
> the minimization of stocks, i.e., higher stock rotation; and
> group purchasing to improve their bargaining position and to obtain lower prices by bulk purchase. This would, at the same time, promote vertical co-ordination and encourage a larger scale of operations.

All three measures can be applied effectively through closer vertical co-ordination with the wholesale trade in the form of retailer co-operatives and voluntary chains. Some experiments have been made in Bogotá, Colombia, which led to a strengthening of some privately owned store groups. As these measures constitute a realistic attempt to improve the efficiency of distribution, efforts should be made to launch pilot schemes to test such operational procedures under different conditions, as proposed by Link for Argentina.[7] Consumer co-operatives, with their popular appeal, have barely made a start in the developing countries in spite of the support they have received, notably from Scandinavian aid. One problem has been the difficulty they experience in competing with small-scale retailers whose opportunity costs of labour are generally well below the salaries and social charges payable for the sales assistants employed by consumer co-operatives; in addition their overhead costs are usually higher.

WHOLESALING

The more obvious problems in food wholesaling in the developing countries arise out of the lack of appropriate and adequate wholesale market
facilities, so essential for highly perishable foods such as fruit and vegetables, meat, fish and dairy products which by their nature call for fast and
timely handling. In most cases where congested and unhygienic wholesale
market facilities constitute a major bottleneck, the establishment of new
wholesale markets on the periphery of the cities they are intended to
serve is the only answer to the present unsatisfactory situation. Again, the
key to the problem is not so much lack of available finance restricting
investment but more the dearth of reliable economic and technical feasibility studies. The information and analysis needed for a feasibility study
has been set out in recent publications.[8] Still there are a number of major
issues that call for more careful consideration:

Size and layout of stalls. Experience has shown that many new market
stalls are too large and therefore difficult to rent on a cost-covering basis.
Types of buildings. In spite of frequent indications that economically
viable projects can afford only low cost simple buildings, architects are
still inclined to suggest sophisticated and prestigious structures which
wholesalers are unable to support financially and which cannot reasonably be amortized.
One or more wholesale market? While it is argued in some advanced
countries that one central wholesale market is the answer, in multi-
million cities served mainly by small traders who do not own a motor
vehicle, one central market able to deal with 50 to 60 per cent of total
supply, supplemented by satellite distribution markets, may be preferable. The satellite markets provide a convenient supply point for the
small-scale retailers in outlying residential areas who must rely on non-
motorized means for moving their purchases.
Co-operation with wholesalers. In principle, wholesale markets are constructed for use by wholesalers, but wholesalers are often not involved, or
are even ignored, in the planning of new markets. This often tends to
reduce the possibility of the market being used by or supported by
wholesalers because it does not provide adequately for their needs.
Policies on rents. Unduly low rents are often a major impediment to new
investments in wholesale markets and an obstacle to increasing productivity and promoting the growth of more efficient organizations.
Dynamic management. A major constraint on the modernization of
wholesale markets has often been the absence of an autonomous agency,
fully supported by both local government and the trade, that is able to
succeed in achieving a concerted approach by the various groups and
vested interests involved as well as being competent to prepare and
implement plans effectively.

To summarize the situation, there is considerable scope for improving
the planning and operation of food marketing for urban areas, but while

the basic principles of planning are understood, research based on case studies could help considerably in promoting concepts suitable for profitable adoption in particular cases. Areas calling for applied marketing research are:

The changing role of different types of retail food outlets, such as retail markets, including street markets, grocery stores and self service stores as the process of economic development unfolds, and the factors that determine the most favourable combinations of retail outlets in different conditions;

The changing role of wholesale markets in different stages of economic development and the factors that determine number, size and layout in various conditions;

The nature and degree of intensity and vertical co-ordination of wholesale and retail food marketing possible and necessary in different conditions and stages of development.

There is also much scope for specialized training for different types of personnel such as those responsible for:

The planning and implementation of wholesale and retail food marketing facilities at city and enterprise level. Such training has to include the installation of practically orientated concepts of marketing planning and operation;

The marketing of food, such as wholesalers and retailers, on food handling methods, sales promotion and business procedures. This training has to be specific and tailored to the individual needs of particular target groups and has to be organized in close co-operation with, and preferably through, trade associations. It has to be preceded by a detailed survey designed to highlight existing shortcomings, be organized in close co-operation with the trade, and be aimed at removing shortcomings. At present, this approach is undertaken in Brazil with some success by a local agency in co-operation with FAO.

As important as the wholesale market, or even more so, is the food wholesaling enterprise. No other business has, in recent years, been subjected to such regular criticism and been held responsible for various evils in marketing, particularly hoarding and conflict with government price policies, than the food wholesaler. Since he must play an increasingly important role as "channel captain", and as main co-ordinators of the marketing channel, government policies will, in future, have to give greater recognition to the key nature of their role. Government marketing and price policies have to take into account the condition at the enterprise level to recover capital invested in stocks and storage facilities and the labour costs of marketing operations.

Only if future policies succeed in providing requisite incentives for investment and offer a consistency of policies, will wholesalers be induced to play to the full their role, particularly in respect of extending the marketing system effectively to the rural areas.

In summing up suggested strategies for improving food marketing systems for urban areas, there has to be a sharper focus on the systematic planning of the marketing system to make better use of scarce resources. There has to be adequate recognition then of the importance of vertical co-ordination in a fragmented system and higher priority for training of personnel. Price policies have to be designed to provide greater incentives to the trade to make investments in facilities and for improving their operational procedures.

PROMOTING SMALL FARMERS INTO THE COMMERCIAL SECTOR

Bringing 700 million small farmers into the commercial sector is an important priority[5] if they are to participate in the growth stimulated by the need to feed expanding urban populations. The minimum "marketing mix" or minimum package of marketing and credit services required at farm level to achieve the proposed development target remains in many conditions an open question in view of the complexity of the problems, which are not only economic but also human and social in nature. It may, therefore, be of value to review some of the more important components of the marketing package in this context:

Physical infrastructure. The provision of an appropriate infrastructure at village level, access roads, and the availability of effective communication services, particularly the telephone and mail service, is generally a high priority. There is a question as to the extent this infrastructure could be provided through some form of self help organization, which would mobilize at least some local resources for construction and maintenance. Considerably more thought and evaluative work is required to analyse the factors which determine the success of self help projects and the manner in which they must be phased in order to achieve maximum success.

Farmers' marketing co-operatives have been the chosen instrument for development of many governments and bilateral aid agencies in the last decade, but they have not often achieved the results expected. After many failures, those concerned have become much more realistic as to what can be achieved through co-operative marketing enterprises.[10] A much more careful approach and a more realistic phasing of the co-operative development, including consideration of alternative forms of marketing organization, is needed for a better use of scarce resources.

Vertically co-ordinated production–processing–marketing schemes. Various attempts have been made to advance the progress of smallholders by integrating them into closely co-ordinated smallholder production–export marketing schemes. This has been done for tea (Kenya, Tanzania, Ruanda), bananas in Central America, flowers in Kenya, palm oil in Malaysia, tobacco in various countries and cotton in the Francophone countries of Africa. It has been demonstrated that smallholders respond favourably to involvement in closely co-ordinated production–export schemes provided the requisite highly qualified management skills can be developed quickly enough and the necessary technical expertise and discipline can be grafted on to a traditional farming community framework to meet export require-ments in a relatively short time. Where this management ability was not available and the task of training the farmers was underestimated, schemes have failed.

Rural markets as service centres. Rural markets are the main market outlet of the small farmer. The price he receives there determines to a large extent his income. A rural market is also an important centre of communication and innovation and a convenient point for the provi-sion of additional services. For these reasons policy makers have in recent years given increasing attention to the need to strengthen rural market centres. The Government of India has expanded the regulated market system designed to ensure fair and competitive prices for small farmers and to offer better physical conditions of marketing. The extent to which rural markets can be developed as *dynamic service* centres for small farmers by providing such additional services as credit, marketing promotion, marketing extension and inputs, requires much more investigation, trial and development work. The mere build-ing of new markets and their regulation is not enough. A rural market has to be co-ordinated vertically with the next wholesale market or with the wholesale supply agent in the case of agricultural input supply. The form and degree of forward and backward linkages of the rural market must be determined with accuracy. A stronger dynamic note for rural markets could be developed if the management of such markets were made fully aware of their potential position and if they were able to mobilize to the full all available resources of the production-marketing system. A manager of a rural market, for instance, should be fully aware of the farmer's potential in the market procurement area and be able to co-ordinate fully the efforts of both farmers and traders. There is, therefore, much scope for developing efficient and dynamic managers for rural markets if such markets are to become centres for small farmer development. The rural market centre should, however, never be considered as an objective in itself but only as a means to achieve small farmer development in a practic-able and efficient manner.

The role of rural assembly markets will of course change as develop-ment proceeds. As vertical co-ordination proceeds, more produce will move directly to wholesale markets as is the case now in South Korea, where rural markets have declined in popularity at the expense of direct marketing. Elsewhere in developing countries, grain is delivered directly to millers and wholesalers, thus bypassing the rural assembly market. The decisive question is for what commodity and in which situations is selling at the nearby rural assembly market more favourable than is selling directly to wholesalers. To facilitate this decision, competing alternative channels must be available.

The role of private traders. One of the major problems experienced in developing government strategies for rural development has often been attitudes more critical than constructive towards the private trade. In many instances, the private trade is considered responsible for all the shortcomings of the marketing system including the instability of government policies. The numerous conflicts which developed between government policies, particularly price policies, and those at enterprise level in the past few decades have discouraged the private trade from making a greater contribution to rural development and have definitely discouraged the flow of investments into the marketing system, including storage and processing. Small rural traders, with links to wholesale buyers, including government grain market stabilization agencies, could become much more effective agents of change if they were fully integrated into a rural development strategy. The rural trader can become more effective in the distribution of agricultural inputs if he is given technical support and expertise so that he can become an adviser on fertilizer application to the small farmer with whom he is in frequent contact. Access to institutional credit can help the trader to finance a more timely purchasing and stock holding of agricultural inputs and purchase of farm output. A change in the basic pattern of behaviour and attitudes in the private trade sector is needed if it is to become a dynamic force for rural development. This requires government understanding and co-operation in mobilizing local entrepreneurial abilities.

A brief review of the various forms of marketing organization at the rural level reveals the variety of approaches that can be followed. What matters more in moulding future development is not so much the form of ownership be it private, co-operative or state, but more important is the development of adequate managerial capacity in the marketing sector. It must be able to recognise shortcomings, to identify the minimum package of marketing improvement services required and to decide who is best able to implement them most effectively.

Vertical co-ordination of production and marketing activities to integrate the trading sector into rural development as strategic potential "change agents" calls for much greater attention than it has received in the past.

DEVELOPING MARKETING RESEARCH AND TRAINING UNITS TO ADVISE ON NATIONAL POLICIES

An analysis of existing shortcomings in marketing organization and methods shows that these are not primarily due to a lack of finance but are more a question of decision-making, management, institution building, motivation and incentives. Two supporting services which in most of the developing countries are at present extremely weak or non-existent require strengthening, namely, field orientated marketing research and advisory services and practical training.

More development orientated marketing research
According to the type of economy applied marketing research and planning services are needed for central and provincial government, the larger municipalities and major marketing institutions and universities. In recent years, some governments have strengthened their marketing advisory services. The Government of Tanzania has established a Marketing Development Bureau, and the Government of Mali an Office Malien de Betail, a marketing advisory and planning institute for the livestock industry. Many others lag behind and need assistance in developing effective marketing advisory services.

A distinction can be made between three major areas of marketing research: market analysis, including market forecasts and market information; marketing organization and methods; and government marketing intervention.

In market analysis and forecasting the main problems are in establishing an adequate data basis to provide for timely and accurate forecasts for government decision making on price and market intervention policies. More accurate and timely data on production, production prospects, supply and storage are, for the time being, more important than the development of more sophisticated methods and models.

There is a growing interest on the part of governments to improve the performance of marketing systems by the introduction of more efficient marketing techniques such as packaging, refrigeration, improved handling of grains in bulk as opposed to bags, the marketing of meat as against livestock. These all have an impact on the scale of operations and the type of marketing organization required. In order to comply with the proposals for changes in the type of marketing organization and methods an effective advisory service is required which is technically competent to advise on these issues and to guide systematically the changes required in the marketing system.

Since marketing development is, in many conditions, basically a learning process, any well conceived applied research work will continue to leave open a number of questions. These could be clarified more systematically if greater use were made of well planned and organized pilot operations. Such pilot operations would, for instance, clarify more clearly the time and training involved in bringing about the required changes in the behaviour of personnel. Such pilot operations have been particularly useful where it is intended to reach new markets, to test new packaging and grading standards or to develop new forms of vertical co-ordination as, for example, required in the introduction of voluntary food supply chains for large urban areas. Much greater use could be made of the pilot marketing project by the market researcher. This would help to identify more clearly the most critical factors likely to determine the success or failure of a project and would accelerate development.

In spite of the progress that has been made in recent years in the formulation of development principles, there is still considerable scope for refining concepts of marketing development, particularly for operational purposes. For example, the determination of an adequate standard of performance for a marketing system under well defined conditions and objectives, and how it has to move over time as the general data on economic development change, is still subject to personal judgement.

The project on the rural market centre development in Asia recently instituted by FAO[8,11] in co-operation with the governments concerned, has already illustrated that aspects of pricing and innovative efficiency in rural markets require considerably more research before they are to be useful for practical operational advisory work. Another issue is the attainment of the optimum scale of marketing operation under different conditions which depends largely on the cost relationship of labour and capital and the structure of the markets to be supplied or served. A further issue is how to determine with precision the right type of package of marketing services required for a specific target farmer group. These issues are closely related to the development of dynamic entrepreneurship in marketing which is so essential in developing countries, particularly in those cultures where levels of entrepreneurship are very low. More conceptually orientated marketing development research work, supplemented by comparative case studies could make a considerable contribution to our knowledge as to what makes a marketing system more dynamic in one situation, as opposed to another. In many conditions this would probably require a multidisciplinary approach in order to cover the non-economic aspects as well.

The various government marketing intervention schemes, as they have developed over the last decade, in the domestic grain, sugar and fertilizer trade, in export marketing and in food retailing in urban areas call for regular evaluation in terms of the objectives established, the means applied, costs and margins involved and the pricing policies followed. Since it is likely that government intervention schemes will show greater expansion in view of the social objectives which many governments hope to achieve by operating special marketing schemes, the demand for regular reviews of these government initiated schemes will tend to increase. In this connection, reference is made to subsidized food distribution programmes to low income groups[2] and subsidized fertilizer distribution schemes to specific target farmers. It is necessary not only to analyse whether the objectives could be achieved more effectively by other means than through the marketing system but also to determine how the schemes could be organized at lower cost, by such means as improving the productivity of the personnel engaged, or sub-contracting operations to independent operators under competitive conditions. The question of providing adequate incentives in administered countries is a critical issue in many conditions.

More development orientated marketing training at various levels
Many problems of marketing development and the lack of understanding about issues are due to inadequate training in marketing concepts and principles. A recent review of training programmes devoted to agricultural and food marketing initiated by FAO at African and Asian Faculties of Agriculture, has revealed that present training programmes are not meeting development requirements.[3,4,12] The number of hours devoted to marketing at undergraduate level must be extended and directed to satisfying local development needs. While these undergraduate courses can only provide an appreciation of marketing development problems, there is a need for more specialized courses, either at a postgraduate level in the form of a master's programme or as a diploma course for people who would like to specialize in agricultural and food marketing. Such programmes should be set up in developing countries and should give adequate attention to aspects of agribusiness and micro economics at present neglected. The training has to be supported by field research programmes which at present are extremely weak and this would tend to bring many teachers into closer contact with reality. Another major constraint is the lack of medium level marketing personnel and marketing technicians. A number of reasonably well formulated policies are simply not implemented or only partially implemented because the necessary number of sufficiently motivated and qualified middle level managers and foremen are not available. Government must give a higher priority to middle level training; so little has been done in this field in the past. The trading sector has itself to play a vital role in the organization of such training programmes in order to ensure that training is directed to the attainment of well defined and realistic goals.

CONCLUSION

In conclusion it is proposed that future strategies for the development of effective marketing systems call for greater emphasis on:

the systematic planning of food marketing systems intended to serve large urban areas; this should include the promotion of vertical co-ordination of marketing functions, and the training of personnel;

alternative forms of marketing organization at farm level, meeting the differing requirements of target farmers and promoting the integration of trading sectors into rural development programmes;

marketing facilitating services particularly applied marketing research, designed to provide more systematic policy guidance and practical advice in the development of more complex marketing systems including the promotion of pilot marketing schemes to test new methods and forms of organization;

strengthening training programmes in marketing and agribusiness management and offering programmes more tailored to development requirements.

promoting the exchange of experience and technical co-operation in marketing development between developing countries.

SELECTED REFERENCES

[1] Abbott, J.C. "Case Studies of Advances in Marketing in Tropical Countries", *International Conference of Agricultural Economists*, 14th Conference 1970, Oxford p. 468–85.

[2] Abbott, J.C. "Adjustment of Food Distribution Systems to Meet National Needs", *Bibleotheca Nutritio et Dieta* No. 28, Basel 1979.

[3] FAO Report on the FAO/AFAA Expert Consultation on Training in Agricultural and Food Marketing at University Level in Africa, held in Nairobi, Kenya, 10–20 November 1975.

[4] FAO/OBM Workshop on the Improvement of Agricultural Marketing Training in Asia, 2–6 April 1979, Bangkok, Thailand.

[5] German Foundation for International Development, in cooperation with BMZ, FAO and IAAP, Marketing "Dynamic Force for Rural Development", "Report on International Expert Consultation on Marketing and Rural Development", "Improvement of Agricultural and Food Marketing Systems with Emphasis on Small Farmer Development", Feldafing, Federal Republic of Germany, 27 November to 3 December 1977.

[6] Haines, M. "Training in Agricultural and Food Marketing at University Level in Asia", report prepared for The Ministry of Overseas Development and The Food and Agriculture Organization of the United Nations, September 1978.

[7] Link, D. "La Modernización de la Distribución de Alimentos en Argentina", FAO N.A.T. 3279, 1974.

[8] Mittendorf, H.J. "The Challenge of Organizing City Food Marketing Systems in Developing Countries", *Zeitschrift für ausländische Landwirtschaft*, 1978, pp. 323–41.

[9] Mittendorf, H.J. "Marketing Aspects in Planning Agricultural Processing Enterprises in Developing Countries", *Monthly Bulletin of Agr. Economics and Statistics*, Vol. 17, No. 4, April 1969.

[10] OECD/FAO "Critical Issues on Food Marketing Systems in Developing Countries", Paris 1977.

[11] Reusse, E. "Economic and Marketing Aspects of Post-Harvest Systems for Staple Food Crops in Semi-Subsistence Transitional Economics with Special Reference to West and Central Africa", *FAO Monthly Bulletin of Agricultural Economics and Statistics*, September 1976.

[12] Yon, B. "Renforcement de la formation dans le domaine de la Commercialization Agricole et Alimentaire en Afrique Francophone", Ministère de Coopération Paris and Organization des Nations Unies pour l'Alimentation et l'Agriculture, December 1968.

DISCUSSION OPENING – JUAN PABLO TORREALBA

Dr Mittendorf has presented a useful summary of the problem areas in the marketing systems of developing countries, together with a set of orientations useful to find concrete solutions in each country, or better, in each situation. The basis of his paper is his large experience as technical advisor of FAO and important studies and conferences, some of which are listed in the paper's references.

The paper refers to "developing countries", which is becoming increasingly a less meaningful category as more knowledge and data is available. This is especially true if we are talking about strategies in marketing, which commonly have to be designed in a "tailor-made" way.

The paper emphasizes the issue of the need to improve the food marketing system's evaluation techniques. Market performance evaluation criteria can and should be reviewed; least cost cannot always be the decision criterion, but, rather, a set of criteria which must be consistent with development goals. Employment and income distribution considerations would then be considered. This revision of performance criteria would allow the presentation of better quantitative strategies as applied to given situations and policy objectives.

Public retail markets and wholesale markets no doubt can help in reducing food marketing costs. However, there is evidence that undesirable employment and income distribution effects might result if project planning does not consider the marketing organization of the wholesale and retail trades.

Dr Mittendorf refers to small farmer marketing, which is of great importance in Latin America since there is a great number of small farmers facing great difficulties to enter effectively into the marketing systems. Large farmers, on the other hand, generally have been able to create and modernize their marketing channels to capture market opportunities.

The paper shows us the successes and limitations observed in the strategies outlined to incorporate small farmers; unfortunately without referring to the kinds of farmers, product markets or organizational characteristics. This is limiting the lessons of the conclusions arrived at, for comparative purposes or for orientations, since there is no such concept as a "small farmer" but, rather, a wide variety of farmers with different characteristics and potentiality.

At the Inter-American Institute of Agricultural Sciences we have developed a marketing strategy for small farmers which is based on the selection of groups of farmers, by micro-region and production potential, which have a reasonable probability of success in group or associated marketing operations. The implementation of the strategy calls for specially designed marketing services directed to these groups. The strategy assumes that not all small farmers can be selected and that marketing improvements cannot always increase substantially the well being of small farmers.

Finally, I must mention some issues that could be discussed by this select audience:

1. In the latter years a great deal of information and analysis of marketing in developing countries has been done, yet little has been done to construct further the theory of marketing development – in quantitative terms. This could considerably help in diagnosing problems, in

medium and long range market planning as well as in setting better project goals. Recognition must be given to the Latin American Market Planning Conference at Michigan State University for advances in this area.

2. There is a need to increase research on the impact of small farmer marketing projects and their methodologies, as well as the need to increase the training of small farmers and technicians.

3. As Dr Mittendorf suggests, more marketing research and training is needed, but it must be orientated to develop "necessary" or "appropriate" marketing systems.

4. Research and methodologies of economic evaluation of post-harvest losses is urgently needed.

GENERAL DISCUSSION – RAPPORTEUR: LEONARD KYLE

A speaker from India commented that rural markets in that country had operational problems. More emphasis was needed on off-farm storage and more linkage between the public sector and growers. In response to a question about guaranteed fixed prices, Dr Mittendorf commented that without a seasonal incentive a guaranteed fixed price produced a glut on the market near villages of small farms. More storage was needed and competitive prices were preferable. A single government fixed price is sometimes inefficient although it can be used effectively in the case of export crops.

Other speakers wondered how small farmers could be motivated to integrate into the marketing system and why the present paper was optimistic while that of Dr Abbott (also from FAO) was on the pessimistic side.

In reply, Dr Mittendorf agreed that efforts to include small farmers must be built into new and existing programmes for market development. The need for such development has to be appreciated by governments. At present the response was rather variable.

Participants in the discussion included R. Thamarajakshi, M.L. Desward, T. Dams and Hans G. Hirsch.

SECTION II

Subnational

JIN HWAN PARK

The Work of Agricultural Economists at Community, Village and Local Governmental Levels — Accomplishments and Challenges

1 INTRODUCTION

Traditional rural Korea has shown a rapid progress in recent years. Physical environments in 3,500 villages have been improved dramatically, while the living standard of farm people has been improved materially. But above all, the work ethic of farmers is far better than before. Most people in Korea agree that the rapid progress of rural life is due to the Saemaul (New Village) Movement which is loosely understood as a movement for a "better living".

The Movement was intended to build up a better "work ethic" among farmers. It was intended to build up a work ethic not by lectures or preaching but by inducing farmers' participation in various action-taking programmes.

As an agricultural economist, working in the Presidential Office, I have been closely involved with the Saemaul (New Village) Movement. For the last eight years most of my time has been spent in training village leaders, local officials and social élite groups to enhance the Movement on a national scale, and I have visited around 4,000 villages to meet villagers and local officials.

This paper summarizes my experience of bringing agrarian changes in Korea, with special reference to the Saemaul Movement which has been the integrated rural development programme since 1971.

While I was teaching at University I came to the conclusion that a good work ethic among farmers, such as the self-help spirit, diligence, and co-operation, is the vital factor for reducing development cost and for accelerating rural modernization. Because of very limited physical resources, human capital is the main resource for the development of Korea. Reviewing the changes in the human capital of Korea for the last three decades it can be said that the level of technological knowledge among Korean people has been improved significantly, and it has been the basic factor for the economic developments in the 1960s and 1970s. Comparatively speaking, however, the work ethic of the people was not being developed at the same rate.

147

Political disorders and hyper-inflations which prevailed right after the end of World War II were hardly conducive to building up people's work ethic. The Korean War (1950–53) was the most critical factor demolishing such work ethic as honesty in business transactions, penny saving habits, co-operation for a common goal. The rapid economic developments in the 1960s brought severe tensions between the haves and the have-nots. Some of the persons who got a windfall gain out of the economic growth did not know how to use their fortunes and this tended to create jealousies among persons who did not profit as much from the rapid changes.

In the process of rapid urban industrialization of the economy, the young farm operators became reluctant to stay on the farm. A feeling of "growth shock" prevailed among farm people. During election seasons, politicians tended to get votes by making unrealistic political promises to the local people. Farmers, on the other hand, increasingly came to rely on the government's budget. Without a strong self-help spirit of farmers, the rural sector became too costly for the national development. People talked often about the urgent need for a self-help spirit of farmers, but solutions were not easy.

2   "CEMENT" FOR RURAL WORK ETHIC DEVELOPMENT

In 1971 the Korean economy had an excess supply of cement, and the government made a decision to dispose of the surplus cement by distributing it freely to rural villages. Around 300 bags of cement were distributed to each village evenly, on condition that the cement should not be divided individually but be used for common village projects. On the average, there are about 80 farmers in a village unit. Hence, the 300 bags of cement means 4 bags of cement per farmer (about $4.00).

The responses of farmers in the first years' programme were far greater than the policy makers had expected. In most cases villagers added their own capital goods and labour to the distributed cement in order to accomplish selected projects. In many cases the contribution of the villagers' capital goods and labour was unbelievably large and the accomplished projects were so remarkable that many villagers remain ever proud of their own accomplishments.

Overall, the first year's results showed that, out of 35,000 villages, about 16,000 villages responded very actively. Hence, for the second year programme (1972), the government provided 500 bags of cement with one ton of steel to those 16,000 villages which responded more actively in the first year.

Taking into account the variation in the degree of participation in the self-help programmes, the 35,000 villages were classified into three categories; basic villages in which the degree of participation was rather low, self-helping villages and self-standing villages. Government assistance was given mainly to the self-helping or to the self-standing villages.

This was to stimulate the emergence of a self-help spirit in the basic villages. In order to get government assistance the villages must help themselves.

One of the key factors affecting the response of farmers to self-help programmes in basic villages is the changes in neighbouring villages. Observing their neighbours in self-standing villages who were making visible progress in a programme of self-help, the farmers in the do-nothing villages came to feel envy and frustration. In 1973 about one third of the 35,000 villages belonged to the basic villages. Since then, the number of basic villages has become only a negligible proportion of the total, and around two thirds of all villages belong to the self-standing category.

About twenty kinds of projects were undertaken under the Saemaul Movement and most of them were intended to improve the living environment of the villager. A few of them will be introduced in this paper.

Village road improvement
Village roads connected to the local public road are often narrow and winding without bridges, and vehicles are unable to reach villages. Most of the 35,000 villages improved their village roads by widening and straightening them so that vehicles could reach villages easily. Small bridges were constructed with their own resources. In 1971, the total number of bridges in all the rural villages in the country was around 50,000. In 1976, the total number was 100,000, which indicates that about 50,000 bridges were additionally constructed in the last few years under the Saemaul Movement. Presently, vehicles can reach any of the 35,000 villages, except those located in the islands.

The improvement of inner village roads involved more complex and difficult tasks than the village access roads. Taking for example a typical village in Korea, about 100 farm houses have clustered irregularly over many years and village roads connecting farm houses are often too narrow and winding to use oxcarts, push-cars, motor tillers, and vehicles. Thus, traditional in-village roads became a critically restricting factor for introducing labour saving machinery and equipment. To widen and straighten village roads many farmers in the village had to sacrifice part of their housing sites and often even part of their houses. The Government paid no compensation for the properties so sacrificed. The decisions concerning whose properties and how much should be taken away had to be made by the villagers themselves. Almost every night villagers got together to discuss and reach an agreement.

In the traditional rural Korea decision on village affairs used to be often made by men alone excluding the women's voices. This tradition was changed entirely in the process of carrying out Saemaul projects. For example, because the village road developments affected every household, women as well as men participated in the meetings. Evidently, they have learnt that the active participation of women is an essential factor for the successful execution of any Saemaul project. Consequently villagers have elected a woman leader in addition to the male village leader. In most villages housewives have organized a women's association to carry out the Saemaul programmes and women's activities in rural life have increased remarkably. To raise the association's fund housewives put a rice saving jar in the kitchen and a spoonful of rice was deposited at each meal. Once every month the rice in the jar was collected. The raised funds were then utilized for various programmes, such as group cooking facilities, the operation of a co-operative consumers' store, a children's playground, etc.

Replacement of rice-straw thatched roofs
In 1971, over 80 per cent of the 2.5 million farmhouses had rice-straw thatched roofs. By 1978, almost 100 per cent of the roofs were of cement-made tiles or materials other than rice-straw. Because of the roof changes the physical appearance of rural villages has changed dramatically.

Due to the soft quality of rice straw, roofs have to be replaced annually in the winter season, and it takes a large amount of labour input. As the cement-made tiles and slates become increasingly available, farmers have come to recognize that the annual replacement of rice straw for roofing is uneconomical.

The development of village access roads and in-village roads reduced the transportation cost of roof materials which have to be brought in from urban or other areas. It became possible to buy a truck load of ready made tiles or to bring in cement and sand to the village by trucks from far distances. In many cases cement tiles were made co-operatively at the village by using tile-making moulds, while roof changes were done co-operatively by villagers. They have learned the effectiveness of co-operation through such activities.

Running water supply
Traditionally most farm households depended on wells for drinking water. It was often insanitary and time consuming for housewives to bring water from wells located far away. Hence, the facilitation of a running water supply was an important Saemaul project.

Wherever possible, a small reservoir was constructed and drinking water supplied by pipe-line to individual households. By 1977 about one-third of the 35,000 villages had acquired such facilities. In those villages where the topography is not suitable for the construction of a reservoir, deep wells were dug and drinking water supplied through pipe-line to individual kitchens by a pump. This system is being adopted widely in rural areas due to the availability of electric power.

Rural electrification
In 1971 only about one-fourth of the 2.5 million farm households enjoyed electric light; the rest used traditional kerosene lamps. By 1978 rural electrification rose to 99 per cent. The cost of rural electrification is

paid for by farmers in cash and long term loans and partly by government subsidy.

The rapid increase in the availability of electric power at a farm level has induced a new demand for various electric goods for farm households, such as radio, television, electric irons, cooking facilities, refrigerators, etc. In order to purchase the newly available consumer goods farmers have to earn more income by increasing productivity in farming and/or by working on non-farm jobs. Also, farmers tend to put small amounts of cash on hand in savings accounts in the agricultural credit institute to accumulate enough money to buy electric goods.

High yielding varieties
The national average rice yield has increased drastically in recent years; it has increased from 3.3 tons to 4.8 tons in polished rice per hectare in the period 1970 to 1977. The number of farmers producing over 7 tons of polished rice per hectare has increased rapidly. The nationwide dissemination of newly developed high yielding varieties was the most important factor for increasing farm income and for achieving self-sufficiency in rice. In the period 1969 to 1972 Korea had imported 0.7 million tons of rice per year on average. No rice has been imported after 1976 and the excess supply of rice is being held increasingly by the government.

From the group activities for improving living environments farmers have learned "how to work co-operatively", and the experiences were used in production activities. It is very common for 10 to 30 farmers to make a team to work jointly in rice production. A young knowledgeable person is elected as the team leader, and following the team leader's guidance the rice seedbed is made in one location for all members instead of individual seedbeds scattered in many localities and the selection of variety and application of inputs for growing healthy seedlings are carried out jointly. The transplanting, application of fertilizers and insecticides, weeding, irrigation, harvesting work, etc., are done jointly. Thus, the joint work system has enhanced the adoption of newly available technologies for the entire village within a short time period.

Farm income and rural saving
Farm income has increased rapidly in the period 1970 to 1978, and after 1974 the average farm income reached the same level as that of urban wages and salaries. The national averages of farm incomes for the last nine years are shown in Table 1. Average farm income increased from $1,025 in 1971 to $3,681 in 1978.

Up until the 1970s very few farmers in Korea had saving accounts in credit institutes. In the period 1971 to 1978 the number of farmers with savings accounts in the primary agricultural co-operative, which is the credit institute for farmers, has increased rapidly, and the deposit per member farmer has increased from 4,300 Won ($12) in 1971 to 245,300 Won ($507) in 1978.

As farmers' savings through the agricultural credit institute has

TABLE 1   *National average of farm income, 1970–78*

Year	Annual income per farm[1]	In US dollars
	(1,000 Won)	
1970	256	828
1971	356	1,025
1972	429	1,075
1973	481	1,209
1974	674	1,393
1975	873	1,804
1976	1,156	2,389
1977	1,433	2,961
1978	1,782	3,681

[1] average of 1,300 record keeping farms

increased rapidly, it has become the major source of funds for farm credit. In the middle of the 1960s about 70 per cent of the funds for agricultural sector credit was provided by public funds, namely the government budgetary fund and by borrowing from the central bank. Toward the latter part of the 1970s the proportion of public funds in the farm credit supply was reduced to about 20 per cent. This indicates that farmers are generating the greater part of the farm credit funds.

Village hall and social functions
In carrying out Saemaul programmes villagers had to find a place to hold meetings, especially during the winter season. They started to build village halls from the second year of the Movement. Currently, most of the 35,000 villages have a village hall where village affairs and production technologies are discussed and various ceremonies are performed.

It is very common for a group cooking facility to be attached to the village hall. In order to save the time of housewives for cooking individually in the peak session, meals are prepared for all the families in the village hall using the group cooking facilities and the cost is shared later. Also, a store selling consumer goods is operated by the women's association to save the time and expense of frequent individual shopping trips to the local market.

In most village halls we can find charts showing basic statistics of the village life. We can even find the average farm income data of the villagers. The yields of major crops are reported in terms of kilograms. In many cases we can see the future development plans of the village.

3   LEARNING BY DOING

At the initial stage of the Saemaul Movement most action programmes were focused mainly on improving the living environment of rural villages. One reason was that the improvement of the living environment was desperately needed. Another reason was that it was much easier to induce a full participation of all villagers for programmes intended to improve the physical conditions of village life than for some other programmes.

By improving the living environment by their own decisions and co-operative efforts, farmers have learned what the self-help spirit is. In accomplishing a series of Saemaul projects farmers have learned that the fatalistic attitude to traditional peasant life can be broken by the Saemaul spirit of hard work, self-help, and co-operation.

From the experience of putting aside a spoonful of rice at each meal preparation, farmers have learned that poverty can be overcome by penny saving. By participating in numerous meetings for village programmes, farmers have learned the democratic process of decision-making. They have learned the importance of good leadership and also the difficulties of finding a good leader. Above all, they have learned the critical role of women in carrying out self-help programmes.

The development of grassroot democracy at village level has affected the attitudes and decision-making process of local administrators. In the course of the Saemaul Movement, farmers' complaints against the local administration have been reduced significantly and a feeling of mutual understanding between local officials and farmers has been improved remarkably. Also, the development of grassroots democracy at village level has affected the political parties and those politicians who had obtained votes from farmers by offering unfeasible promises in the past.

As Saemaul projects were accomplished one by one, the sense of frustration among villagers was reduced and pride and a sense of dedication among the tillers of the soil have increased. Farmers put in more and better inputs to increase soil fertility for more and better crops and livestock. Love of the soil has led the tillers of centuries old land to love their own community and nation as well.

4   TRAINING OF VILLAGE LEADERS

For the successful accomplishment of the Saemaul programmes, three factors were important: well qualified village leaders, the active participation of villagers, and appropriate guidance and a minimum amount of material assistance from the local government.

At about the same time as the cement distribution in 1971, the training of village leaders was undertaken in various institutes. The Saemaul Leaders Training Institute in Suwon is the one most well-known for its uniqueness in curriculum and its effectiveness. The following description highlights the more important aspects of the training programmes offered at this Institute.

In January 1972, 150 male village leaders (one from each county district) were enrolled for the first time at the Institute as trainees. It was a two week training programme and the local administration office recommended the leaders who should attend. At an early stage of training, male village leaders emphasized the need for similar training programmes for women leaders. Thus, in each term, around 150 male leaders and 70 women leaders were trained during the last seven years.

The trainees arrive at the Institute in the afternoon of Sunday for each term. After registration a set of uniform, cap and shoes are provided. The trainees are divided into subgroups and a team of 10–15 persons stay in one room. Each team elects a leader who takes care of the team members. The blankets, bedclothes, pillows, shoes, slippers, desks, chairs, etc., must be kept neatly. This is considered an important part of the training.

At six o'clock in the morning all the trainees come out to the ground to line up for physical exercise, which includes jogging two kilometres.

The training curriculum mainly consists of the presentation of successful farmers' case stories. About fifteen case stories are presented during each training term, and they have played an important role for the success of the Saemaul Movement in Korea. No text books are used in the training programme. The afternoon sessions are used mainly for sports, field trips, and video programmes. The evening is devoted to panel discussions. On the Monday evening the team members of each room select a chairman and a reporter for panel discussions. They select one topic and panel discussions continue on the topic throughout the training period. The reporter takes notes to make a summary chart to present to all trainees in the final evening. The contents of the presented charts are printed in book form and trainees take it as the most important reference to use for villagers after they return home.

For women trainees, the programme lasts one week instead of two. For a housewife to leave her home for a week to have training is not an easy decision and training programmes were an entirely new experience for housewives.

A common request of village leaders was that local officials, such as the district administration chief, the manager of agricultural co-operatives, and the district police chief should take the same training. This request was accepted in the Institute and most of the local officials were trained with village leaders under the same curriculum.

Then the local officials had a common view that high ranking officials in the central government should also have the same training. This request was also accepted by the Institute, and almost all the high ranking officials including cabinet ministers entered the Institute for one week training programmes. Their dominant reaction was that it was a most valuable experience for them to share the same training programme and live together with the remarkable village leaders for a week. Soon it was extended to university professors, businessmen, journalists, leaders of religious groups, judges, congressmen, television producers, comedians and so on. The officials and members of the social élite were deeply moved by listening to the various case stories of successful farmers.

The training programme of the Institute in Suwon has had many impacts; it has contributed greatly to an effective implementation of the integrated rural development programmes; it has also helped to extend the Movement from the rural to the non-farm sectors to create a better work ethic among the Korean people; it has finally contributed towards making the government clean.

5 CONCLUSION

1 In the early stage of the Saemaul Movement the local administration played a crucial role in inducing villagers to improve the living environments of their respective village districts. As the living environment improved significantly, however, the roles of local administration are being replaced by agricultural co-operatives at primary level to provide better services to villagers in credit and marketing.

2 The factors which are not mentioned explicitly in the paper but which have performed crucial roles for the successful accomplishments of the New Village Movement in Korea can be listed as follows:

The land redistribution programmes carried out in the period 1950 to 1955 have contributed to retaining a relatively homogeneous rural Korea.

The political leader's determination to enhance agricultural development and his well awareness of rural life should not be discounted.

Rapid growth of the industrial sector of the Korean economy in the 1960s has stimulated farmers to move for self-help programmes.

A national consensus was attained among officials, intellectuals, mass communicators, city people, etc., to help the faster progress of rural people.

DISCUSSION OPENING – ARDRON B. LEWIS

What Dr Park is saying in his paper is that Korean farmers are first of all human beings. They may be aware of improved methods of farming, but they may not choose these methods unless they see a reason to use them. Many farmers are living close together in the villages, but they may not co-operate with one another for their common good unless they feel good about one another and take pride in their home village. The farmers may not exert themselves very much if they lack courage. They will try to help themselves and help one another if they do not feel helpless against the large natural and market forces which are always arrayed against them, and if they do not feel bound and held down by their poverty.

It has been the objective of the Saemaul Movement (New Village Movement), which is described by Dr Park in his paper, to provide villagers with courage and confidence in themselves and in one another, and to develop among themselves a spirit of self-reliance and of co-operation for the common good.

Dr Park has described how this movement began in a very concrete way – no pun intended! – in 1971 with a distribution of cement to the villages, and how this was followed up the next year with a distribution of still more cement, plus some steel, to those villages which had done the best with the previous year's free cement.

At this point I became curious to know more about how the villagers had used the cement which they received and the form in which the steel was distributed and how the villagers made use of that.

At any rate, as Dr Park makes clear, the Saemaul Movement has expanded in many different directions since 1972, until by now almost all the 35,000 farming villages in Korea have accomplished enough to be considered "self-standing", that is, self-reliant villages. Village roads have been improved, even the roads within the closely settled village itself. Villagers have developed skills in making decisions on these and other matters co-operatively and, contrary to previous custom in Korea, the women as well as the men have taken part in making these decisions. Farmers and housewives as well have formed the habit of working co-operatively wherever an advantage is to be gained by this. Improvement of the village itself, as well as of the life going on within it, has been diverse and quite remarkable, as Dr Park reports.

What will concern and interest most of us the most, I suspect, will be the degree to which the method used in the Saemaul Movement in Korea can be adapted to and made use of in other countries, and I suggest that it would be profitable for us to discuss Dr Park's excellent paper with him and among ourselves at least in part from that viewpoint.

Dr Park has said that three factors have been most important for the success of the programme in Korea. These were well qualified village leaders; active participation of the villagers; and appropriate guidance and a little material help from local government. Leaders have not only been selected but they have also been given training in programmes especially developed for the purpose. Finally, not only the village leaders, but also officials much higher up in the government hierarchy, as well as public figures with an interest in village improvement, have undergone the same training.

As you read Dr Park's paper, some of you may have felt that the methods used in the Saemaul Movement in Korea would be difficult to apply in the farming villages of your own nation. I think it is important to realize that in Korea the social relationships between people are largely Confucian in origin and this leads to a respect for authority and a disposition to accept leadership and a certain orderliness in dealing with common affairs. It also means that persons who are chosen for positions of leadership will take their responsibilities very seriously and their neighbours will expect this of them. Nevertheless, even if some changes have to be made in the methods if the objectives of the Saemaul Programme are to be reached in another country, there is surely much food for thought here for us all. Because farmers are human beings everywhere no doubt they will respond in very positive and very economic ways to a strengthening of their working morale and what Dr Park has called their work ethic.

As an agricultural economist Dr Park has had much to do with the conception and the management of the Saemaul Movement, and he would have some valuable comments to add, I feel sure, on how agricultural economists have contributed and can contribute to the success of such a programme.

GENERAL DISCUSSION –RAPPORTEUR: ROGER G. MAULDON

Two points were raised in the general discussion. Dr Park's paper represented an interesting case study as part of the growing literature on the creation of physical infrastructure in the rural communities of developing countries. However, the role of the agricultural economist, as such, had not been made clear. Another speaker agreed with Dr Park's approach, claiming that high powered models were not needed to get development going in rural communities but that such communities needed guidance in order to recognize their own problems. He wondered if any factors, such as population pressure, threatened the success of the Saemaul movement.

In reply, Dr Park stated that in his experience field priorities lay in leadership training and that agricultural economists had to operate on a broad basis. Regarding the effect of population pressure, he felt that this encouraged rather than threatened the movement. Ten years ago the opportunity cost of village labour in Korea was low, but today the buoyant demand for labour outside the village made it less easy to encourage labour into voluntary community development work.

Participants in the discussion included Deryke G.R. Belshaw and Edward Karpoff.

Y.T. WANG

The Roles of Farmers' Associations and Agricultural Development Programmes in Taiwan

Taiwan is a subtropical island located in the West Pacific and bisected by the Tropic of Cancer. Its total area is 13,890 square miles, about one-eighteenth the size of the Province of Alberta. Roughly two-thirds of the island is mountainous terrain, leaving only 24 per cent of the land or approximately 2.2 million acres for farming.

And yet within this small area now live nearly 17 million people, almost as many as the total population of Canada excluding Toronto and Montreal. Because of heavy population pressure, Taiwan's agriculture is characterized by a small farming scale, with the farms averaging about one hectare, or 2.5 acres. With about six members and one hectare of land per farm family, farm operations in Taiwan has been labour-intensive. Three, sometimes four, crops are often grown each year on the same piece of land.

In the early 1950s when our economy was about to grow under the first Four-Year Economic Development Plan, agriculture was the dominant sector, over 50 per cent of the civilian population were rural people and farm workers accounted for 55 per cent of the total labour force. Agricultural production provided more than 35 per cent of the domestic product.

Because of its predominant economic and social importance, the agricultural sector has always been accorded full attention in our economic development. Even at present when industry has replaced agriculture as the major economic sector, the welfare of the rural people has never been overlooked. My paper today will first make a brief description of Taiwan's agricultural development programmes and then, in greater detail, examine the role of the farmers' association in Taiwan.

1 AGRICULTURAL DEVELOPMENT PROGRAMMES IN TAIWAN

Since the economy of Taiwan is predominantly agricultural, the Government realized very early in its course of economic development that the agricultural sector is not only a source of food but also a source of investment capital and raw materials required by the industrial sector. Moreover, industry depends on the export of agricultural products for needed equipment and supplies and looks to the rural population for an outlet for its manufactures. Consequently, the Government made clear at the very beginning its policy to "develop industry with agriculture and support agriculture with industry", and proceeded with its economic development with due emphasis on both agriculture and industry.

After seven years of recovery from the ravages of World War II, Taiwan's agriculture had by 1953 restored its prewar production levels and laid the foundation for further development. Since 1953 Taiwan has entered the period of planned development and carried out a series of economic development plans.

The first and second four-year plans (1953 to 1960) emphasized increases in the production of rice and other crops to reduce imports and raise self-sufficiency in food supply.

During the third and fourth plans (1961 to 1968), the production of export crops and industrial raw materials was stressed instead.

Rapid industrial growth since the mid-sixties has drawn more and more farm labour to urban areas. Therefore, the fifth and sixth four-year plans (1969 to 1976) and the subsequent first six-year plan focused on farm mechanization, improvement in farm marketing and the promotion of foreign trade. In the meantime, a nine-point programme for accelerating agricultural and rural development was put into effect in 1972. It calls for increased investment in rural infrastructure, regional resource planning and improvement in farm income by lowering production cost.

The agricultural development plan follows the basic guidelines of and constitutes an integral part of the national development plan. Its policy objectives are flexible and change with changing situations.

The highest government agency in charge of agricultural matters in Taiwan is the Ministry of Economic Affairs. Earlier the Sino-American Joint Commission on Rural Reconstruction (JCRR) played a very important role. On 15 March 1979 this commission was replaced by the Council for Agricultural Planning and Development which may be regarded as an agricultural administrative agency. Actually, the JCRR assisted in formulating policies and programmes and provided technical and financial assistance for their implementation. At the provincial level, the agencies concerned with agriculture are the Department of Agriculture and Forestry, the Food Bureau, and the Water Conservancy Bureau. At the local level, each county government has a reconstruction division and each township a reconstruction section to take charge of agricultural production activities. In addition to government agencies, farmers' associations have played an active role in implementing the agricultural programme.

In general, the sectoral programmes and supporting measures for agricultural development were drafted by provincial agricultural agencies. All agricultural programmes reflect general economic policy, trends in production and marketing, and the government's financial position. Annual production goals are set up tentatively in each development plan but are adjusted each year to meet the changing conditions of the market both at home and abroad. Apart from annual revision, these goals also have to be broken down into regional goals. For this purpose, provincial and county production conferences are held at the beginning of each year. The participants include representatives from local agricultural offices, local extension services, banking institutions, food processing industries and other public and private organizations. At such meetings, participants express their opinions and make suggestions regarding overall annual plans and regional goals. The central planning agency also sends representatives to these annual production conferences. Such two-way communication has contributed greatly to the smooth and successful implementation of agricultural programmes.

To achieve the production goals, detailed projects are developed for irrigation improvement, distribution of chemical fertilizers, demonstration of improved cultural methods, pest control, storage and processing, provision of rice production loans, extension of improved rice varieties, etc.

Such projects covering one or more items are implemented by the agencies and organizations concerned. Many of the field projects are carried out by the county and township governments or farmers' associations under the supervision of provincial agencies.

I would like to emphasize that the agricultural development plans of Taiwan have great flexibility. The government does not force farmers to plant certain crops or to raise certain animals. It passes on relevant information, disseminates technical know-how, and gives economic incentives to encourage and induce farmers to work towards goals set by national agricultural programmes. But each farmer makes his own decision in the allocation of his limited land, labour, and capital resources.

2 FARMERS' ASSOCIATIONS IN TAIWAN

From the very beginning, the role of Taiwan's agricultural development of institutional improvement and farmers' organization has been recognized. Prior institutional adjustments are essential to obtain the desired results because they give farmers more inputs and improve their way of doing things. Thirty years of experience have led us to believe that projects for increasing agricultural production and improving the general well-being of rural communities can be successfully executed only by the farmers themselves; our policies and programmes have been formulated accordingly.

There are a number of farmers' organizations in Taiwan, but the largest and most outstanding is the farmers' association. Other major farmers' organizations include the irrigation association, the fishermen's association, and specialized agricultural co-operatives. The farmers' associations in Taiwan are a federated system of co-operative organizations which render credit, purchasing, marketing and agricultural extension services to their members. An understanding of the farmers' associations will give us an idea of how the rural community in Taiwan is organized for mutual benefit.

The farmers' association in Taiwan is a rather unique one, and it is more than a multi-purpose co-operative society, as is generally known in many parts of the world. In Taiwan, farmers' associations are organized on three levels: township, county and provincial. Each corresponds to a level of local government. Under the Provincial Farmers' Association, there are now 20 county and city associations and 273 township associations. Each township association serves on the average 2,400 farm households.

Furthermore, farm households of each village within a township area are also organized into a small "agricultural unit". On the average, there are about 15 units to each association and about 180 members per unit. The small agricultural unit is organized to serve as a bridge between a township farmers' association and its members for disseminating useful information on agricultural improvement and for election purposes. Therefore, the farmers' association in Taiwan is not only an agency to serve its members in practically all aspects of social and economic life, but also a grass-roots organization to train the farm people in parliamentary practices as well as in self-help activities.

3   THE ROLE OF FARMERS' ASSOCIATIONS

During the past years, the farmers' association has rendered a variety of services both to the farmers and to the government. Although its role may have varied with the emphasis of development, it has been an essential instrument for carrying out various rural reconstruction programmes. The following is a brief description of the major functions that the farmers' association has performed.

1   *Assisting government to work out agricultural development plans*
Agricultural experience in the postwar period indicates that no development plan can be effectively carried out without the active participation of the local people. It is also noted that the local people cannot fully participate unless they are sufficiently organized and trained to put forth a united effort. In this respect, the farmers' association in Taiwan can offer a unique example.

The farmers' association in Taiwan serves in the capacity of partner with the government. With a three-tiered organization to correspond with the levels of civil administration, the farmers' association acts as a channel to make government plans and policies known to all the farmers. By the same token, the farmers can express their views about government plans or make their problems known to the government. This two-way communication system has helped make government agricultural plans meet the felt needs of the farmers. As I mentioned earlier, annual production targets are not decided by the overall planners; they are the result of close consultations between local governments and farmers' organizations, whose opinions reflect farmers' wishes.

In Taiwan, many agricultural programmes have been carried out with the active participation of the farmers' association. In the case of land reform, the farmers' associations were entrusted with the task of collecting land purchase prices in kind from the farm operators and paying the land bond in kind to the landowners on behalf of the government during the ten-year period from 1953 to 1962. In recent years, the farmers' associations have played an active role in realizing contract production for some cash crops under the Accelerated Rural Development Programme. In addition, the farmers' associations handle other government entrusted services such as the distribution of fertilizer, the collection of rice and other farm products from the farmers and the processing of these products for the government.

2   Facilitating agricultural extension

Newly developed agricultural practices and expertise must be diffused and put to use in actual farming operations. This is usually done by means of the agricultural extension system, which serves as a bridge between agricultural research at the experimental stations and adoption of new farming techniques at the farm level.

One of the major services that a farmers' association performs is farm extension. In each township association there is an agricultural extension section with an average of six extension workers. Among all the farm extension activities the farm discussion groups have been the most successful, influential and unique in several respects. As each farm adviser often had more farm families to care for and more subjects to teach than he could handle, farm extension authorities began in 1957 to encourage the establishment of farm discussion groups in every agriculture unit of the township farmers' association. Owing to the farmers' keen interest, the number and membership of discussion groups have increased rapidly. At present, there are 6,415 farm discussion groups.

A farm discussion group is composed of approximately twenty farmers. They meet once a month to study, discuss and carry on agricultural production activities and receive instruction and advice from township advisers. Subjects for the discussion groups usually include crop production techniques, family farm management, problems relating to joint operations, joint marketing and procurement, mutual assistance and co-operative service, and training in citizenship.

In addition, the farmers' associations help organize 4–H clubs for farm boys and home economics clubs for farm women. The 4–H club teaches the youngsters the rudiments of farming, under the guidance of local leaders and 4–H advisers. Under the home economics programme, farm women are given new knowledge on nutrition and new cooking methods.

It should also be mentioned that the agricultural extension service performed by the farmers' associations is closely co-ordinated with other activities of the associations and other agencies concerned. In the technical aspect, the specialists at the various District Agricultural Improvement Stations play a very important role. They do research and field experiments and supply new techniques and cultural methods.

3 Providing supply and marketing services
In the process of agricultural development, it is essential to provide farmers with adequate inputs of production and convenient outlets for their outputs. The farmers' associations in Taiwan have also played an active role in these respects. In the supply business, the distribution of chemical fertilizer has been most important.

Under the rice production programme, the Food Bureau of the Taiwan Provincial Government is responsible for the procurement and allocation of chemical fertilizer. But actual distribution is handled by the township farmers' associations as they are conveniently located and well-equipped with warehousing facilities.

To meet the needs for crop and livestock production, the farmers' associations have made considerable efforts to develop self-initiated purchasing and supply services during recent years. The supply of feedstuffs, pesticides, seeds, breeding stocks, farm implements, etc. has increased year by year.

The marketing service is to eliminate the undue profiteering by middlemen. As the agricultural industry has become more commercialized in recent years, the role of the farmers' associations in the marketing of farm products has become more important. The farmers' associations in Taiwan now handle about 30 per cent of the farm products marketed by the farmers. The co-operative marketing of hogs is one of the most successful activities of the farmers' associations. In the major cities, the hogs supplied by farmers' associations account for about 35 per cent of the total number marketed. Increasing volumes of vegetables, eggs and fruits have also been co-operatively marketed through the associations in recent years.

4 Supplying farm credit
Modern farm inputs mean to some extent higher production costs for the farmers, which in turn become a heavier financial burden. To relieve this financial constraint, farm credit is needed.

Before the implementation of land reform in 1952, approximately 50 per cent of farm credit had been furnished by the landlords. After the land reform, landlords ceased making advances to farmers and other credit sources had to be sought. Since then the credit departments of township farmers' associations have supplied the lion's share. Such credit departments are like rural banks and are operated on a co-operative basis. They accept savings deposits from and extend loans to members. They promote farm production and free the farmer from exploitation by the usurer.

The expansion of credit services of farmers' associations since 1953 has greatly assisted the small and low-income farmers in obtaining input factors. The loans extended by farmers' associations are more effective and compatible with the farmers' needs because extension services often go along with them. Most of the loans extended are for production purposes. The lending funds of the farmers' associations come mainly from the savings deposits of their members. Borrowings from the government and banks make up the seasonal shortage.

The farmers' associations in Taiwan are generally recognized as very effective in financing agricultural production. Because they have an intimate knowledge of the farmers' needs and are capable of linking the farmers' borrowings with extension services, they are in a position to render credit service directly to the farmers. At present, about 80 per cent of agricultural production loans made to the farmers in Taiwan are handled by the farmers' associations and over 90 per cent of the farmers can get loans from their associations to meet their financial needs. Since farmers usually feel more at ease discussing their financial problems with staff members of the farmers' association than with bankers, some of the loans provided by the government and banks are also channelled through the farmers' associations. This has contributed greatly to the successful implementation of agricultural development programmes.

5   Training farm leaders

Although they are organized primarily for social and economic development purposes in rural areas, the farmers' associations offer the best opportunity for training local leaders in parliamentary procedures and in self-help activities.

Good leaders are made, not born. But before they are made, they must be found. And before they are found, we must know how to look for them. By means of election, the farmers' associations find potential leaders in rural communities in a democratic way, and get them interested and trained in programmes for the good of their communities. It is now no surprise to find magistrates, mayors and provincial assemblymen who were formerly elected officers of the farmers' associations.

4   CONCLUSIONS

The postwar economic experience of Taiwan indicates that the agricultural development process involves not only a close relationship between inputs and outputs but also various human and institutional factors. Agricultural development calls for detailed planning and, most important, practical actions. Therefore, co-ordination among various agencies and economic activities becomes indispensable for ensuring the success of a development programme. In other words, concerted effort is an invisible ingredient which is essential to putting many visible ingredients together to achieve satisfactory performance and policy goals.

The ultimate aim of agricultural development is to increase production and improve the welfare of the farm people. Farmers' active participation, besides sophisticated planning, is therefore a "must" to guarantee successful agricultural development.

Taiwan's agricultural development adopts a "package" approach, although the term had not been coined when Taiwan started its development planning. This approach calls for simultaneous improvement in many aspects — institutional, technological, financial and organizational. Farmers are given various incentives, modern inputs, new technology, and, more important, a system which can deliver these things to the farmers efficiently.

Finally, before I conclude my report, I would like to say a few words about the transferability of the Taiwan experience. We all know that no two areas have the same social and economic conditions and that to transfer an institution from one area to another is a difficult and complex process. Nevertheless, if the will to develop is strong, the Taiwan experience may serve as a useful reference to countries which have similar basic conditions and face similar problems as Taiwan.

DISCUSSION OPENING – PAUL G.P. HILL

Dr Wang's factual account of the policies underlying Taiwan's remarkable agrarian development and the part which farmers' associations played in achieving it is appreciated. What is particularly intriguing is Taiwan's approach to development, whether made explicit, like reliance on economic incentives, or implicit, like the apparent harmony at all levels which is taken for granted. To open the discussion I should like to refer to Taiwan's approach to development, to events which may have contributed to increased farmer participation in decision-making, and finally to revert as Dr Wang did to the question of transferability.

Taiwan's success is due in part to the early identification by government of the potential contribution of agriculture to national development and to the systematic creation of institutional arrangements and economic incentives which harmonize farmer and national interests. Remarkable progress has been achieved through an approach which provides positive roles for government and farmers, and where farmers' associations provide a two way communication vehicle for implementing development plans and programmes. Are there no conflicts of interest between government's need for revenue, urban consumers' need for cheap food and farmers' desire for higher incomes, which cannot be equitably resolved using the Taiwanese approach? Was one essential element to successful rural development in this instance the existence of a thriving industrial demand for food, raw materials and workers which enabled possible tensions to be relieved?

Secondly, it has been stated that concerted effort is essential to achieve satisfactory performance. How is this invisible ingredient acquired? Is an early egalitarian land reform programme a pre-condition for wholehearted participation by all farmers? In addition to achieving a more equal distribution of assets, does such a programme also hasten the decline of traditional local leadership patterns dominated by landlords and open the way for greater representativeness of participants in local decision-making bodies?

Finally, transferability is like the medieval search for the elixir of life. Transplants are clinically difficult even between identical twins as Dr Wang indicates. What would be of particular value would be some appreciation of how and why farmers' associations started, what evolutionary stages they went through, and what parallel circumstances facilitated their growth such as land reform and industrial off-farm markets. It is the guidance from experience rather than the association blueprint which, with luck, may be transferred in a timely way to facilitate development elsewhere.

GENERAL DISCUSSION – RAPPORTEUR: ROGER G. MAULDON

The first speaker referred to the structure of farms in Taiwan as typified by small farms with many workers and family members. He considered that it was likely that farmer associations would act to reinforce that structure rather than change it. Dr Wang replied by saying that there were many conflicts of interest in farmer associations, and many arguments over production targets. This required getting people together and working out compromises. Land reform had paved the way for the formation of the associations since the landlord no longer stood in the way of change. Labour now is flowing off farms, and farm labour shortages have been developing.

Another speaker felt that it would be useful to identify the sociological variables which made the formation of the associations possible. If this were done it might help other countries to innovate a similar movement. He also asked if the smallness of farms and absence of fences between them enabled farmers to co-operate in the use of facilities. Dr Wang said that smallness of farms was not important. The greatest problem was developing an adequate water supply. Many small machines were now privately owned on farms and rented out to other farmers, but machine usage has made the scheduling of water supply a critical factor.

In reply to a question about the average number of years of schooling attained by most farmers in Taiwan and the percentage of illiteracy among farm families, Dr Wang said that illiteracy was virtually non-existent. Schooling is compulsory through the 9th grade. Most Taiwanese children now take two further years' training at either a technical school or an agricultural vocational school.

Participants in the discussion included Christian Jorgensen, Mario J. Ponce and Harold C. Love.

P. LIZARDO DE LAS CASAS

Central Planning, National Policies and Local Rural Development Programmes: The Planning Process in Latin America and the Caribbean*

During the last International Conference of Agricultural Economists held in Nairobi, Kenya in 1976, a discussion group was organized which focused on the conceptualization of rural development. The ideas were abstracted from the experiences of and illustrated by participants from different countries.

In broad terms, it could be said that the discussion pointed out two different approaches to rural development. One could be labelled the "single level" approach. In this case rural development is carried out through autonomous projects. Throughout most of Latin America and the Caribbean, it is fairly common to find rural development projects of one type or another. However, these are isolated projects, and their administrators frequently work toward different objectives and under different assumptions without any general strategy to guide them or any reference to each other's activities. Many of these projects are generally based on the support provided by international organizations. The recent interest of these organizations in the small farmer, the rural poor, etc. has pushed the countries in this direction. These projects may be thought of in terms of horizontal integration but they lack vertical linkages to national policy.

A second or "multi-level" approach was also identified. This refers to the rural development projects integrated with sectoral and national policies, an important aspect of national development strategies. The complexity and diversity of local situations and the tendency to simplify or specialize sectoral administrative responsibilities at the national level require a strategy, policies and priorities that consider the need for careful co-ordination between the many national agencies responsible for different aspects of rural development. Without this vertical link, rural development project designers might define priorities which conflict with the interests of national decision-makers.

This second approach has also been tested in some countries in Latin America and the Caribbean. Because of the need for a strong commit-

* The views expressed in this paper are those of the author and do not necessarily represent the views of IICA.

167

ment to rural development policies at the national level, these efforts should be analysed in the context of the evolution of the planning process in these countries. Planning systems with units at national and regional levels were legally created in several of the Latin American and Caribbean countries during the sixties. By mid-1978, 73 per cent of the Latin American and Caribbean countries reported having agricultural planning systems, although only nine indicated having regional planning offices. The lack of a regional and local dimension to planning has been identified as "planning without implementation".

To many, planning in most of the Latin American and the Caribbean countries is no more than an academic and technocratic exercise removed from the reality it is to affect. In order to move away from the formalistic task of plan preparation towards a more operational focus, several international organizations are supporting a more "pragmatic approach". To assure feasible, sound projects instead of aggregated national plans,[1] early inclinations of countries towards a "multi-level" approach are being reoriented to a "single level" approach with the help of financial international organizations.

These organizations have been funding the already well known if somewhat ad hoc "project preparation courses" through universities and public and private institutions in Latin America and Caribbean. "Proyectistas" (project specialists) are "trained" as a result in very short periods. Unfortunately, this situation has originated what is known as "implementation without planning".

Paradoxically, both situations – "planning without implementation" and "implementation without planning" – can be found at the same time in several Latin American and Caribbean countries. This has been referred to as the "planning crisis". Is this so-called "crisis" of a purely technical nature? This could perhaps be implied by what has been said thus far. Moreover, there are those that claim that planning is only associated with certain political systems and is not applicable to others.

In general, most opinions about this "crisis" reflect different views on the importance and role of planning in the countries' social and economic development process. The common characteristic of all these opinions is the noted separation between the way in which planners generate their products and the real processes of policy analysis and decision-making adopted by governments.

Without actually ignoring existing instabilities and deficiencies of the planning organizations of Latin American and the Caribbean countries, it may be said that most opinions against the use of planning are based on apparent rather than real reasons. The results of the studies[2] conducted by the Latin American and Caribbean Agricultural Planning and Policy Analysis Project (PROPLAN) of the Inter-American Institute of Agricultural Sciences (IICA) support this statement.

The concepts elaborated, as well as the empirical results obtained by PROPLAN–IICA studies, show that planning may be adapted to any political system. Its efficiency is based on an essential comprehensive coherence which includes: internal coherence among planners (national, regional and local planners); internal coherence among decision-makers themselves; coherence between the evolution of the political process and that of the socio-economic process; coherence between alternative policies proposed by planning technicians and the government's doctrinal position; as well as coherence between planners' proposals and the actual socio-economic situation.

Thus, the problem is not just one of imbalance between local planners who ignore central planners and central planners who ignore local planners. It can be shown that this is just one aspect of a more complex problem. Planners are not the only nor the more important actors of the planning process. The responsibility of planners is not only a matter of preparing plans or programmes; their task involves much more. This paper briefly presents a comprehensive view of the planning process, and goes into the essence of a planner's task.

This conference would seem to be an appropriate forum at which to discuss this topic. The PROPLAN–IICA studies indicate that 72 per cent of the Latin American and Caribbean countries identify the Sectoral Planning Units (SPU) as the co-ordinating agencies of their agricultural planning systems. The studies also show that at least 60 per cent of the technicians working in the SPUs of the Latin American and Caribbean countries are either agronomists with some training in economics or economists with some training in agriculture. Only about 10 per cent of all personnel working in SPUs have an MS or PhD degree while 15 per cent do not even have a BS degree. A problem common to the whole area identified at the three regional seminars recently held by PROP-LAN–IICA for planners from twenty-four Latin American and Caribbean countries, was that there are no serious training efforts in agricultural planning nor are the applied research activities useful to the work underway on the problem-areas being faced. Therefore, there is an interesting challenge to economists that requires a clear understanding of the planning process.

THE PLANNING PROCESS

A socio-economic system is present in every society and can be conceived of as the technical and social relationships which produce goods and services, their exchange and use, as well as the distribution of generated wealth. These actions take up time and space and are highly interdependent. This socio-economic system is the thrust behind every society (Figure 1).

The socio-economic system evolves in a certain way which demands a specific political system in order to provide for specific services. This allows the socio-economic system to move in the desired direction. The political system can be conceived of as different political groups or parties differentiated on ideological grounds, together with three specialized branches: legislative, electoral and executive (Figure 2).

SOCIO–ECONOMIC SYSTEM

PRODUCTION   EXCHANGE   CONSUMPTION
PROCESS   PROCESS   PROCESS

DISTRIBUTION PROCESS
(Based on types of property
of means of production)

Fig. 1

POLITICAL SYSTEM

POLITICAL PARTIES

LEGISLATIVE   ELECTORAL
BRANCH   BRANCH

EXECUTIVE BRANCH

Fig. 2

The political system of a country is responsible for deciding on policies which will affect the socio-economic process of that country in order to attain certain objectives. This decision-making process, in general terms, is guided by the existing ideological position and the socio-economic situation, as presented by various interest groups (Figure 3).

SOCIO–ECONOMIC SYSTEM

Socio-economic
situation viewed   policies
by various interest
groups

POLITICAL SYSTEM

Fig. 3

The decision-making process is usually complex and involves a number of conflicting interests as well as many sources of influence of both national and international origin. Although government programmes frequently reflect the more ambitious and long range doctrinal position of the political parties or groups in power, the question of handling specific problems and daily matters tends to generate decisions which may take precedence although they may frequently be in conflict with medium and long term doctrinal positions.

Therefore, planning should be seen as a process for rationalizing governmental action in order to regulate and accelerate the countries' economic and social development. This serves as a basis for presenting three complementary views of the planning process:

the planning process as a continuous policy-producing process.

the planning process as the integrator of two processes: policy analysis and decision-making.

the planning process as characterized by the formulation, implementation and control of policies.

The planning process as a continuous policy-producing process
The agricultural planning process can be defined as a continuous policy-producing process[3] with goals to accelerate agricultural development within a desired framework of regional and national development. The essential characteristic of this policy-producing process is to bring integral coherence to decision-making on agricultural policies, and is conditioned by the political position of the government (doctrinal position) and by the problems arising from socio-economic realities.

The planning process is conditioned by the historical evolution of each country's socio-economic and political[4] processes. In every development process the socio-economic viability of the planners' products is the determinant in the last instance, for directing the desired transformation of the socio-economic process. However, a lack of coherence between the government's political position and the socio-economic reality can give political viability a dominant role in the short run over the socio-economic viability. This implies that the work of the planners will be of significance only when it is politically acceptable.

The planning process as the integrator of two processes: policy analysis and decision-making
Governments are forms of expression of the political system created to perform technical-administrative functions. Here, they are referred to as the political-administrative system. Governmental actions take form when decisions are made on policies in different fields and at different administrative levels. Thus, any government decision at the national level related to agriculture, must be made tangible at regional levels and in concrete areas. The multisectoral inter-connections of the socio-economic process that is to be affected must always be taken into due consideration.

The decision-making elements and the executor elements are the two important groups of the political-administrative system. The first participates in the planning process by making decisions that will affect the

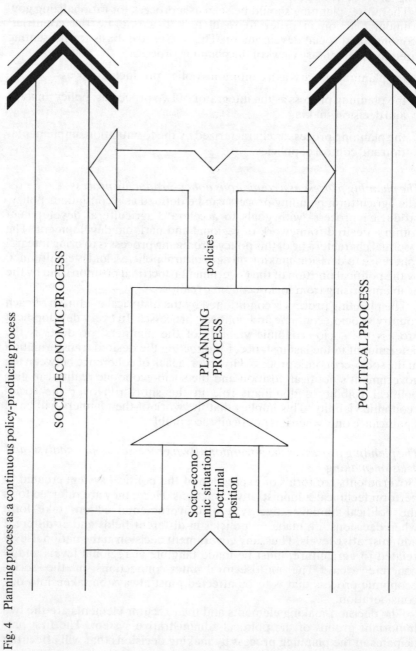

Fig. 4   Planning process as a continuous policy-producing process

socio-economic system; it includes the president, ministers, vice-ministers, national directors of specific areas (research, extension, agrarian reform, marketing, credit, etc.) regional directors, etc. The executor elements are the specialized technicians that are responsible for administering and proposing specific technical directives for carrying out the approved policy measures and who, at the same time, support the decisions made on actions specific to their fields of technical specialization. The actions of these executor elements do not constitute part of the planning process but are supported by the elements of the planning system.

The political-administrative systems in most Latin American and Caribbean countries have created technical advisory groups for different fields of specialization and at the different administrative levels. These groups are called planning units. The integration of these units at a technical level to ensure coherent products, has been defined as the planning system which advises the decision-making elements on the policies to be adopted in order to regulate and accelerate a country's economic and social development.

Since planning has been conceptualized as a process for rationalizing governmental action to promote socio-economic development, the structural element of the planning process can then be defined as the *planning system* and the *political-administrative system*. Both systems are furnished with quantitative and qualitative information from the *socio-economic system* through various participative mechanisms or through their relationships with the pertinent socio-economic agents and their organizations. Similarly, the planning and the political-administrative systems exchange information; the political-administrative system transmits its doctrinal position while the planning system provides policy alternatives for purposes of decision-making. Each system in turn, relates to the socio-economic system; the political-administrative system transmits the decisions taken in the form of adopted policies while the planning system provides the technical bases and the implications of these decisions.

Both the planning and the political-administrative systems are essentially characterized by the processes they generate. Thus, they should be characterized by the very essence of the structural elements of the planning process, rather than by the apparent aspects of those elements. Hence, reference to the planning system is in terms of the policy analysis process,[5] whereas when referring to the political-administrative system, one refers to its decision-making process.[6]

The planning process as characterized by formulation, implementation and control of policies

The planning process is also characterized by the activities that its essential elements develop in an integrated manner, to produce effective policies and policy measures for the desired transformation of the socio-economic system. The agricultural planning process is defined as the formulation, implementation and control of policies oriented towards

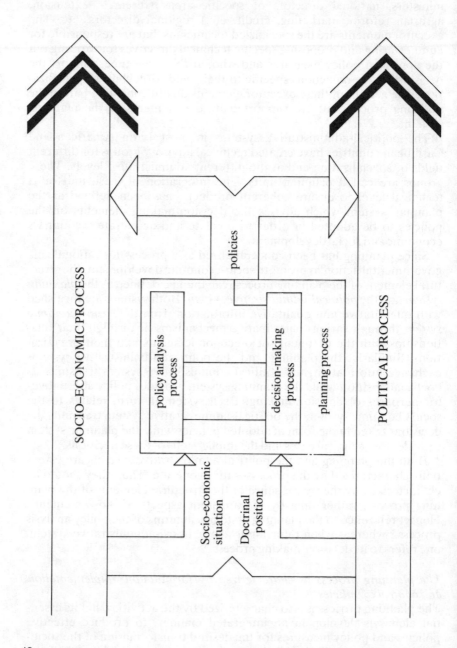

Fig. 5

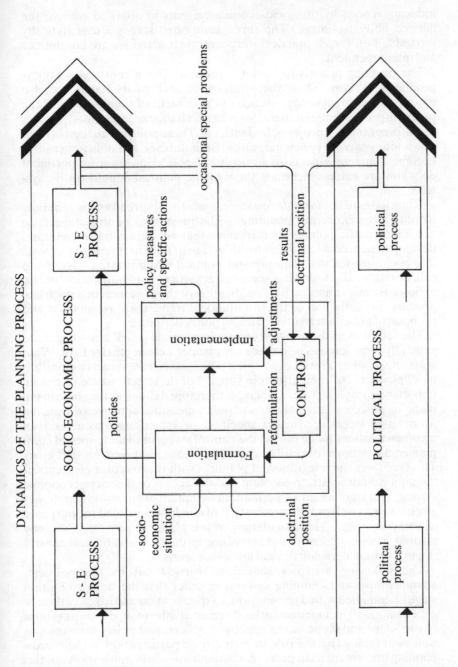

Fig 6

DYNAMICS OF THE PLANNING PROCESS

inducing actions by the socio-economic agents in order to achieve the desired objective-image. The three mentioned stages are analytically separable but, for all practical purposes, their activities are continuous and interdependent.

The planning process has been conceived of as a continuous policy-producing process. Thus, the products of each of its stages are also policies. This refers to the essence of the content of the products of the planning process and not to the form in which they are presented, such as plans, programmes, projects, budgets, etc. These policies are then broken down into concrete policy measures. Both policies and policy measures become concrete aspects of agricultural policy[7] as soon as pertinent decisions are made concerning them by the political-administrative system.

Knowledge of the *formulation stage* is most widespread and is generally identified by the term "planning". The main goal of this stage is to generate specific policies or directions that accelerate the agricultural development process. In order for this stage to fulfil its intended purpose, it is necessary for the planning and political-administrative systems to collaborate in the following series of activities: i) identification of the socio-economic situation; ii) identification of the government's doctrinal position; iii) definition of the orientational framework; iv) analysis and proposal of policy alternatives; and, v) policy definition.

The activities of the *implementation stage* are less well known and are generally considered to be outside the planner's conceptual sphere. What is actually done as a result of adopted policies is not the direct responsibility of planners but their efforts in support of those actions are of crucial importance. Implementation, here, is therefore defined as the stage in the planning process where policies and policy measures approved during the formulation stages are further specified, or are adjusted as a result of recommendations made during the control stage, or include special complementary actions for resolving specific occasional problems that arise. This facilitates the integration of planners with the executor elements of the political-administrative system and the agents of the socio-economic system. This stage assures a permanent definition of agricultural policy at given levels as well as the specification of conditions needed for purposes of carrying it out. The articulation of the planning process is thereby assured, bringing content and relevance to the formulation and control stages at national, regional, local and other levels.

The following activities should be carried out by the political-administrative and planning systems in order that the implementation stage be complied with: i) promotion, ii) specification and iii) direction.

"Promotion" includes activities directed at informing different groups of the intent and scope of the approved policies and policy measures, as well as of their expected role to assure their participation in the corresponding implementation process. Dissemination and motivation are this group's primary activities.

"Specification" is directed at implementing the policies and policy measures approved during the formulation stage, along with the adjustments outlined during the control stage, and those complementary actions designed to deal with specific occasional problems that arise. They determine what is necessary for the successful application of the approved directives and decisions. This presupposes a viability analysis as a complement to the other two stages. Necessary for its realization are: i) the disaggregation into specific tasks; ii) their organization in terms of the activities of the socio-economic system; and, iii) the assignment of institutional responsibility and allocation of resources. It will then be possible to define detailed work programmes for the public sector and operative mechanisms for applying the policy measures.

"Direction" refers to a set of activities of crucial importance, although not generally recognized as such, since they provide continuity to the entire planning process. They are always present and their products are inputs not only for other activities of the implementation stage, but for the formulation and control stages as well. These activities help avoid deviations that may occur because of technical deficiencies or because of a lack of political foresight when specific occasional problems may generate pressures causing inconsistent decisions to be made. This set of activities includes the following: i) analysis and advice on measures to correct specific occasional problems; ii) co-ordination of executor elements; and, iii) technical support to other planning units.

The activities of the *control stage* are not seen as a simple matter of auditing but as a feedback stage of the planning process through which changes generated by the evolution of socio-economic and political activities are fed back into the planning process.

In order to fulfil its responsibilities in the planning process for the development of the agricultural sector, the control stage must constantly evaluate and review the policies and policy measures formulated within the context of the sector's evolution (socio-economic and political processes). The results of this continuous evaluation and review are communicated to the decision-making elements of the political-administrative system. To this end, the control process contemplates: i) measuring the results of the evolution of the socio-economic and political processes, as well as the achievements of the political-administrative system; ii) policy evaluation and review; and iii) definition of corrective measures.

THE PLANNING SYSTEM: POLICY ANALYSIS PROCESS

The planning system is conceived of as the technical elements of the planning process with the aim of constantly advising the political-administrative system, proposing alternative policies and policy measures that are consistent with both the government's doctrinal position and the existing socio-economic situation. The primary task of the planning system is to generate a policy analysis process that provides integral coherence to its products.

"Sectoral Planning", no matter how closely related to a productive sector, as in the case of agricultural planning, should be considered within a context of the pertinent technical and social relationships of the participating socio-economic agents and within the multisectoral context of its actions at national, regional, and local levels.

The agricultural planning systems in Latin American and Caribbean countries are defined as an integration of planning units within the limits of the agricultural sector, *per se*. However, PROPLAN–IICA studies identified a fairly high degree of relevance attributed to planning units not directly related or functionally identified with the agricultural sector but which influence policy alternatives for the sector.

Planning units of relevance within the policy analysis process of the Agricultural Sector in Latin America and the Caribbean

	National Planning Units	Agricultural Sectoral Planning Units	Agricultural Sub-sectoral Planning Units	Non-agricultural Sectoral/Sub-sectoral Units	Regional Planning Units
Number of countries	21	21	17	14	9
%	100	100	81	67	43

Even though the planning units from other than the agricultural sector are so important, they are not considered an integral part of the formal agricultural planning system. Therefore, the definition of planning systems should not be restricted to sectoral administrative limits but should take into consideration all those units that participate in generating policy alternatives for the entire socio-economic process of the sector.

The figures show the importance of the planning units from other sectors as advisors to decision-makers in the agricultural sector. However, their effect is limited, if they are not part of the agricultural planning system, as in the case of many Latin American and Caribbean sectoral planning systems. Also significant is the lack of importance of regional planning in almost 60 per cent of the countries.

The above indicates an important weakness in the advisory functions of the sectoral planning systems in the decision-making process concerning agricultural policy, since regional planning is essential for the conceptualization of sectoral planning for two fundamental reasons: it is a means of operationalizing the planning process which must be multisectoral in nature in order for agricultural development to be integrated and harmonious from both national and regional viewpoints. Regional planning is therefore a way to integrate both aspects: to operationalize the process and to assure intra and intersectoral consistency.

Thus, the efficiency of the planning system depends on the degree of the integral coherence accorded by the policy analysis process to its products. This is described as: i) formal coherence or internal consistency; and, ii) an adequate correlation with the evolution of the political process and the socio-economic process.

The formal coherence or internal consistency is based on the technical capability (human and information resources) to generate the pertinent policy analysis process. This situation should be studied at the level of planning units, both individually and as integral components of the planning systems.

In the planning unit, formal coherence refers principally to the consistency which should exist between policies defined within their corresponding area of action at the three stages of the planning process (formulation, implementation, and control). This is mainly concerned with the temporal dimension (long, medium and short term policies) of each policy area.

For the planning system, formal coherence means the consistency which should exist among different policy areas (structural or developmental policies such as: agrarian reform and settlement, productive and natural resources, research, extension, etc; and stabilizing policies or those to deal with occasional special problems such as: prices, credit, subsidies and incentives, salaries, taxes, etc.) and different spatial levels (national, regional, local, etc.) within their multi-sectoral and sectoral dimensions, as well as for the three stages of planning.

Socio-economic and political coherence refers to the need to assure the appropriateness of alternative policies and policy measures submitted by planning system elements, as applied to existing possibilities for national development, from both the socio-economic and political points of view. The appropriateness of the planning system's products, as applied to the evolving socio-economic process (in terms of the socio-economic situation) will determine its socio-economic viability. The appropriateness of the planning system's products, as applied to the evolving political process (in terms of the government's doctrinal position) will determine its political viability. The planning system must be in constant contact with the agents of the socio-economic system and with the decision-making and executor elements of the political-administrative system. This requires that the planning system have a flexible and comprehensive information system, the products of which are adapted to each stage of the planning process and to each administrative level of the planning system.

There are three steps to the policy analysis process; i) collection and systematization of information; ii) drawing up alternatives; and iii) discussion of the results. These steps or phases essentially characterize the participation of the planning system in the formulation, implementation and control stages.

The "collection and systematization of information" requires a specification of the needed information based on the theoretical framework of the sector's development (socio-economic and political processes), its organization into categories, an estimation of its parameters and relationships, as well as its organization within the given theoretical framework.

"Drawing up alternatives" refers to the use of the information based on an analytical scheme[8] in order to simulate the reaction of the socio-ecomomic agents and the executor elements of the political-administrative system to the alternative policies, policy measures and specific actions being studied.

"Discussion of results" refers to the process of consultation concerning suggested alternatives, to be carried out internally by the planning system's elements (national, regional and local) as well as with the executor elements of the political-administrative system and representatives of designated strategic groups of the socio-economic system.

In this manner, planning units could generate alternative policies and policy measures with at least some degree of participation of other planning units, of the elements of the political-administrative system and strategic agents of the socio-economic system.

RELEVANT ASPECTS OF A PLANNING UNIT'S STRATEGY FOR INFLUENCING THE DECISION–MAKING PROCESS

In general it was noticed that planning units in Latin America and the Caribbean play an important role during the formulation stage of agricultural policies, especially in the areas of structural or developmental policies and to a lesser degree in stabilization policies. Planning units are only slightly involved in control activities, in other words, in designing and defining corrective measures and adjustments to adopted policies. Implementation activities are the least developed of all. Therefore, the promotion, specification and guidance efforts undertaken by the planning units, in an attempt to improve relationships with the decision-making and executor elements of the political-administrative system, as well as to provide support to the rest of the agricultural planning units, have not been adequately taken into account.

Consequently, it may be said that the planning units in Latin America and the Caribbean have not developed the formulation, implementation and control stages consistently, in an integrated manner as a continuous and permanent advisory service to the decision-making and executor elements of the political-administrative system and as support to other planning units.

The majority of Latin American and Caribbean countries recognize the existence of agricultural planning systems, but most of them have had trouble defining them. Also noted was that the set of agricultural policies covered was only partial, with emphasis on developmental or structural and national-sectoral policies. Less attention was placed on regional-sectoral policies. An inadequate relationship between planning units was also detected; their relationship with the socio-economic agents is completely absent.

Three weaknesses have been identified as the most crucial to the performance of planning units at different administrative levels (national, regional and local) in order to fulfil their role as permanent advisors to the political-administrative system in the decision-making process in most of the Latin American and Caribbean countries. There is a clear need to *improve the relationships between the planning units and the political-administrative system* in two ways: by increasing planning unit policy measure implementation activities, fostering improved relationships with the decision-making elements, mainly with the executors of the political-administrative system; and increased political support. There is urgent need for the *development and operation of mechanisms to facilitate the participation of strategic socio-economic groups in the planning process*. The relevance of *strengthening the agricultural planning system* together with *increasing the technical capability of the planning units* in the policy analysis process are necessary conditions to assure integral coherence of the planning products.

In short, adequate technical capability and planning units well organized in fulfilling activities pertaining to the formulation, specification, adjustment and readjustment of policies and policy measures, as well as their implied relationships with the political-administrative system, strategic groups of the socio-economic system and the rest of the planning system elements at all administrative levels are an integral part of the planning units' strategy for providing efficient advisory services to the political-administrative system in their decision-making process.

Since economics is a predominant discipline involved in planning in Latin America and the Caribbean, we, as economists have an essential role to play. We serve as teachers, training potential planners or upgrading the skills of those already active in the field. As researchers, we try to develop the tools necessary to improve the policy analysis process. As advisors to planners, we help them to perform as permanent advisors to the country's decision-makers. We also serve as planners ourselves.

In order to solve problems facing planners in Latin America and the Caribbean we must understand the dimensions planning is taking in these countries and their needs at the present time. There is an increasing demand for support in the area of policy analysis, not only for the formulation stage of the planning process but also during the implementation and control stages. There is also a need for information systems that would allow this policy analysis process to be carried out at different stages and at different administrative levels of the planning process (national-multisectoral, national-sectoral, regional-multi-sectoral, regional-sectoral, etc.). These areas are being considered as the bases for the development and operation of planning systems which assure the integral coherence of planning products already mentioned.

In several Latin American and Caribbean countries a more flexible, more comprehensive and less capital intensive technology than that being generated presently at universities and research centres is being demanded. This is the challenge we have to face if we want to have an active role in rural change during the eighties.

182   *P. Lizardo de las Casas*

NOTES

[1] As opposed to the needed interaction of plan formulation and project analysis discussed by Tinbergen (*Development planning*, New York, McGraw-Hill, 1967), Dasgupta, Sen and Marglin (*Guidelines for project evaluation*, New York, United Nations, 1972), Little and Mirrless (*Project appraisal and planning for developing countries*, New York, Basic Books, 1974) among others. Little and Mirrless put this in a nutshell in their twin statements that "plans require projects" and "projects require plans".

[2] The documents published so far based on PROPLAN–IICA studies are the following:

Documento PROPLAN 1 Marco conceptual del Proceso de Planificación Agrario en América Latina y el Caribe: una visión integral de los procesos de análisis de políticas y de toma de decisiones en el Sector Agrario. San José, Costa Rica, 1978. (Version available in English.)

Documento PROPLAN 2 Análisis del Funcionamiento de las Unidades de Planificación Sectorial en el Proceso de Planificación Agrario en América Latina y el Caribe: su participación en el proceso de análisis de políticas y de toma de decisiones en el Sector Agrario. San José, Costa Rica, Febrero 1979. (Version available in English.)

Documento PROPLAN 3 El Proceso de Análisis de Políticas en el Sector Agropecuario de Costa Rica. San José, Costa Rica, Febrero 1979.

Documento PROPLAN 4 El Sistema de Planificación Agrario en Bolivia. La Paz, Bolivia, Febrero 1979.

Documento PROPLAN 5 La Etapa de Formulación del Proceso de Planificación Agrícola en Venezuela, Caracas, Venezuela, Febrero 1979.

Documento PROPLAN 6 La Etapa de Instrumentación de la Ejecución del Proceso de Planificación Agrícola en Honduras. Tegucigalpa, Honduras, Febrero 1979.

Documento PROPLAN 7 La Etapa de Control del Proceso de Planificación Agrario en el Perú. Lima, Perú, Febrero 1979.

Documento PROPLAN 8 Seminario Regional sobre Planificación Agrícola y Análisis de Políticas en América Latina y el Caribe: Zona Norte (América Central, Haití, México, Panamá, y República Dominicana). San José, Costa Rica, Junio 1979.

Documento PROPLAN 9 Seminario Regional sobre Planificación Agraria y Análisis de Políticas en América Latina y el Caribe: Zona Andina y Sur (América del Sur) Lima, Perú, Junio 1979.

PROPLAN Document 10 Regional Seminar on Agricultural Planning and Policy Analysis in Latin America and the Caribbean – Antillean Zone – (Barbados, Guyana, Jamaica, Suriname, Trinidad & Tobago). Kingston, Jamaica, June 1979.

[3] "Policies" are understood as the group of aspects defined by the Public Sector as needed to produce a desired effect in the socio-economic process. Footnote [7] discusses this in some detail.

[4] Understood as the generator of the governments' doctrinal position usually expressing general guidelines and objectives that represent the objective-image desired for the socio-economic system and constitute the essential political input for the planning process.

[5] The process of the transformation of fundamental inputs of the planning system (socio-economic situation and the government's doctrinal position) into its products (policy alternatives) characterized as response functions of the socio-economic agents that establish the bases for the social benefits and costs of each alternative.

[6] The process of transforming fundamental inputs of the political-administrative system

(group problems and policy alternatives) into its products (adopted policies) that give form and content to the transformation of the socio-economic reality.

[7] "Agricultural policy" refers to the role assigned by the government to the agricultural sector in its efforts to direct the national development process. It is a set of general proposals in the form of objectives reflecting the government's doctrinal position (a simplification of the structural characteristics of the agricultural sector and its relationships within the objective-image of the desired society) and the strategy for achieving them. The interpretation of these general proposals into explicit directives should guide the performance of the agents of the agricultural sector, as well as those related to it.

"Policies" are specific orientations that define the direction of the different fields of action which the government employs to manage and regulate the agricultural development process. These orientations refer specifically to the relationship between the political-administrative system and the economic agents of the sector in each of the fields of action employed by the government for implementing agricultural policy. Literature on economic policy refers to policies as "instruments of economic policy" and are defined as the means used by the government to achieve its goals. They are generally grouped in two larger classes (analytical level). The first has been given a number of different names such as quantitative or stabilization policies, or policies for special problems. The second class identifies the qualitative, developmental or structural policies. Their existence in planning must be acknowledged and must not be overlooked if decisions are to be consistent. Otherwise they may indirectly neutralize or invalidate some of the decisions taken. Spatial and temporal levels are also considered in order to assure policy consistency.

"Policy measures" are concrete decisions made within the framework of policies adopted by the political-administrative system. They involve actions that affect the performance of the economic agents of the sector and are directed toward operationalizing the "policies". These "policy measures" generally refer to "specific actions" to be carried out by the executor centres of the political-administrative system.

[8] de las Casas, P. Lizardo. A theoretical and applied approach towards the formulation of alternative agricultural sector policies in support of the Peruvian agricultural planning process. PhD dissertation, Iowa State University, 1977. (This study develops a system for policy analysis which provides the basis for an ex-ante comprehensive social benefit-cost analysis of single policies or combinations thereof.)

DISCUSSION OPENING – WERNER KIENE

On behalf of all of us I would like to thank Dr de las Casas for a very comprehensive description of the planning process and its problems in Latin American and Caribbean countries (LAC). His paper is based on the interesting, and to my view, valid observation that dissatisfaction with the planning approaches of the sixties and early seventies has led to an increasing reliance on so-called "single-level" or integrated rural development projects that are often isolated from the bulk of the countries' overall development policies and strategies. He believes that while we had "planning without implementation" in that earlier era we now have a lot of "implementation without planning"; and to make things worse we now have more of both of these deficiencies than ever before. His recommendation seems to be that we should not throw out the child with the bathwater but should continue with developing more realistic and more coherent and efficient approaches to national and sectoral planning. Although he does not say so explicitly in his paper, I believe, or at least I hope, that he does not advocate a return to the past but that he appreciates the complementarities that exist between the horizontal (or single level) approach and the vertical (or multi-level) approach to rural development planning.

In his paper Dr de las Casas emphasises that planning may successfully be adapted to any political system and he then proceeds to describe three complementary views of the planning process that may help in rationalizing government action *vis-à-vis* the country's economic and social development. All three views of the planning process rely on a close and continuous interaction between the socio-economic system and the political system. Planners are viewed as agents that interpret and, to some extent, facilitate this interaction and in the process produce coherent policies; link these policies to actual decision making; implement the policies; and monitor their impact on development objectives.

In the – unfortunately too brief – final section of his paper de las Casas compares this idealistic view of planning with the reality of planning in LAC. It might be worthwhile to summarize again his findings:

1   Planning units in LAC do play an important role in the policy formulation stage. They do some work on the monitoring side, but they do very little, and in de las Casas' view too little, in terms of implementation.

2   Planning units cover only a small portion of direct or indirect agricultural policies.

3   Emphasis is placed on policies at the national level but not enough attention is paid to policies at the regional level.

4   Interaction between planning units is inadequate.

5   Interaction between planning units and socio-economic agents is completely absent.

Given these weaknesses in the present LAC planning scene, de las Casas suggests the following key measures:

(a) improve the relationship between the planning units and the political administrative system;

(b) facilitate the participation of strategic socio-economic groups in the planning process; and

(c) strengthen the agricultural planning system through improved and expanded training of planners.

I believe that particularly his two latter recommendations should be of interest to us here and I wish he had expanded on them more. How should one go about getting more and more meaningful participation from strategic socio-economic groups? Who determines which group is strategic and which is not?

I would like to know whether de las Casas determined the input/output relationships of different types of planning approaches. In other words, what evidence do we have that the more complex planning approaches he advocates are, firstly, feasible and, secondly, produce better results than the less complex ones? Let me also raise another issue that needs to be analysed in greater depth: Dr de las Casas pleads for more training; but he does not tell us what kind of training and what kind of a planner is needed. In one West African country we have repeatedly argued for more training that would foster greater creativity in policy formulation. However, a survey of policy makers and administrators indicated that they were more interested in people who could make sense out of a 200 page World Bank project proposal and condense it into half a page of plain English.

Related to that issue I would like to get Dr de las Casas' ideas on how agricultural economists who are engaged in planning can make more important contributions to the directions of the planning process. I have the feeling that a lot of planners are optimizing within a given set of options which are often sub-optimal to begin with. How can the creative genius of rural social scientists be released to broaden the number of meaningful choices that are up for discussion? Universities certainly play a role in that respect; but it seems limited, since they are often not asked to participate in the direct policy formulation process. I feel that economists tend to be happy with assuming that their task is limited to take objectives as given and then find algorithms to achieve these objectives with limited resources. We need to realise that the real choices are made in the process of defining objectives; but it seems that planners in general and agricultural economists in particular have not been able to be part of that crucial process. I would like to close by asking Dr de las Casas to expand a bit on his ideas on:

How planners should get more involved in implementation?
How one could effectively integrate single-level projects into multi-level planning?
How single-level projects could serve as a means for interaction between planners and the socio-economic system?
How he proposes that LAC countries move towards the ideal planning approach he painted in his paper. It is one thing to know where you want to be and another one to know how to get there.

GENERAL DISCUSSION – RAPPORTEUR: KWAKU ANDAH

A participant asked the speaker why he did not consider cultural anthropology as a background of planning. Cultural anthropology is important because it is a part of the cradle in which economists need to develop their profession. The economist needs to be aware of the fact that sociology is part of the needs of planning.

Another speaker congratulated the author of the paper for his excellent analysis of the topic and confirmed that the paper was very relevant to Panama but wondered if copies were available in Spanish.

A concerned participant mentioned that deficiency in data is very important as a problem in planning, especially in developing countries. Without improving basic data one cannot do justice to planning. Furthermore, planners should get involved with implementation of plans and with the beneficiaries of the plans.

Another contributor pointed out that there was some inconsistency in the paper. This arose from the fact that the speaker mentioned that capitalised technology was expensive whilst at the same time advocating it.

In his reply Dr de las Casas reminded the participants that he had not mentioned in detail cultural anthropology in his discussion though he realised that it is an interesting and perhaps relevant point to the issue under debate. He stipulated that when one wants to talk about cultural anthropology it is accepted that it plays an important role. Nevertheless, when it comes to planning, the agricultural economist has a restricted role to play and should not pretend to be an anthropologist.

The crux of the planners' task is policy preparation as well as data analysis. If this statement is accepted then one may come to the conclusion that even our text books are incomplete and also that planners have done very little. We should then ask ourselves what information planners need to be good advisors for the development process.

The speaker felt that it was incorrect that he was suggesting or advocating elaborate planning process. He was actually advocating selective participation. However, because the dynamics of the process is of such magnitude planners cannot always cope with it. The type of planner needed for development will differ from country to country. Planning is not mechanistic. Planners must understand what politicians want and should not participate in decision making.

HERBERT C. KRIESEL

The Need to Co-ordinate Central and Local Rural Development Planning and Administration

It was almost universally accepted early in the postwar period, especially for newly independent nations, that there should be national economic planning. While respectable growth rates occurred generally in the 1950s and 1960s, some have said in spite of planning, it was realized in the late 1960s to early 1970s that the human condition was not being improved in line with earlier expectations or the potential. In earlier years, especially, plans were not followed by effective implementation. But even conceptually, most plans have not meaningfully provided for development of the rural sector.

An earlier approach to rural development was conducted under the label of "Community Development" (CD), applied in up to fifty developing countries before being abruptly terminated in the early 1960s. It did not bring material improvements, especially increased food production, and countries and donors opted for more direct efforts to introduce improved agricultural technologies. In many situations it was recognized that broader supportive efforts were needed fully to exploit available technologies. The term "rural development" (RD) has been increasingly used to describe these broader efforts and to address problems of employment and income inequities.

In this paper it is accepted that more effective national planning is needed. Some limitations of planning will be considered, CD will be briefly analysed and an attempt will be made to conceptualize rural development. Then the kinds of co-ordination in planning and administration to promote RD will be considered with indications of development purposes to be served. The challenging role for agricultural economists in this endeavour will become evident.

EARLY PLANNING EXPERIENCES

From the earliest post World War II development assistance efforts, it was accepted by people of most ideological persuasions that national governments should play a larger role in promoting development than was the case when the present advanced industrial societies were in their early stages of development. In several of the latter instances, in fact, substantial economic development occurred before national governments were established (Hicks, 1969). If the role of government was to be so relatively large, it followed that there should be some master design – a plan – for deployment of resources. This was not only encouraged but was often made a precondition for assistance by some of the early bi- and multi-lateral donors.

Planning for rural development is different in some important respects from planning for overall economic (and social) development. But it will be instructive to reflect briefly on the overall economic planning effort.

Economic planning has been condemned because even where there have been respectable growth rates, there have been little if any improvements in conditions for major, poorer population components. This has brought a challenge to the objectives of planning. Among the first to do this was Mahbub Ul Haq who has proposed that development goals be defined in terms of progressive reduction and eventual elimination of malnutrition, disease, illiteracy, squalor, unemployment, and inequalities" (Haq, 1976, p. 35).

But merely reformulating targets will be to little avail unless there is a change in approach to planning and an expansion in meaningful research to support it. Some useful insights on how the approach to planning might be changed emerged from a significant conference in 1969 arranged by the Institute for Development Studies of the University of Sussex. Among his comments in that conference, Colin Leys (1972) observed:

> In short, the rationalistic/economistic model of planning must be replaced by an analysis which (1) somehow provides general ideas which will yield prescriptions for action in any particular case; . . . and (2) is capable of handling all relevant social processes and structures, and does not consign them to a limbo of unanalyses "constraints" or "obstacles" which, in practice, make the model inapplicable to most LDC situations.

Reinforcing Leys' position here are the observations of Ilchman and Bhargava (1971): "The viable modernized state which would have as a major activity economic development requires conscious and rational investments in social, political, and administrative infrastructure as well." They assert that economic planners and development strategists have under emphasized these areas partly because the economic thought many of them employ was formulated at a place and time when these conditions (it was thought, at least) could be subsumed.

ECONOMIC PLANNING AND RURAL DEVELOPMENT – EVOLUTION

Early planning efforts were distinctive in two important respects: (1) they were oriented to large scale usually urban based industry and (2) they gave little attention to rural areas. To the extent agriculture was considered, the focus was on commodities suitable for export or for domestic manufacture. This usually excluded indigenously used foods.

After the CD programmes were operational for a time in the 1950s, economic planners though still emphasizing urban large scale industry were becoming somewhat more sympathetic to agricultural and rural development. However, as will be discussed below, some disharmony emerged as between agriculturalists and CD personnel and the latter with their diffuse field efforts, did not engender from the centre the planning policies and resource flows supportive of directly productive endeavours.

In the 1960s economic planners' attention was directed more to agriculture and rural areas by two developments: (1) the release and distribution of substantially improved wheat and rice suitable to large areas in Asia; and (2) realization that improved food productivity was needed in all countries to meet rising market demands and to avoid hunger. Introducing the new technologies demonstrated the manifest shortcomings of price policies in many countries and some adjustments were made. Economists' documentations, moreover, of high returns to investments in agricultural research and extension gained considerable respect and some increased relative support for agricultural development. In many countries, agricultural economists were posted to newly formed planning offices in ministries of agriculture where they helped bring more sophistication to planning activities, particularly project preparation and analyses. However, their focus was almost entirely on the strictly economic, especially on commodities in concert with guidelines from central planning offices. A major activity for many was establishing subsectoral government outlays and monitoring these. In many instances they were not given an opportunity to contribute on price and tax policy issues. They were required to take as given the existing asset distribution among farmers and rural institutions though on the latter there were opportunities to advise on operational structures and procedures. Issues of employment generation and equity in economic benefits were addressed all too infrequently.

THE COMMUNITY DEVELOPMENT APPROACH

As a backdrop against which to consider planning and administrative measures for rural development, it is appropriate to reflect on the CD programmes of two decades ago. The term CD itself presents a definitional problem. Holdcroft (1978) defined CD as "a process, method, program, institution, and/or movement which: a) involved people on a community basis in the solution of their common problems, b) teaches and insists upon the use of democratic processes in the joint solution of community problems, and c) activates and/or facilitates the transfer of technology to the people of a community for more effective solution of their common problems".

The CD approach to modernizing rural areas was formulated first in India in the early 1950s with support of both the US foreign assistance agency and the Ford Foundation. The objectives were to promote political and social harmony as well as economic growth in the Cold War environment. The constructive ideals of Gandhi were blended with social change concepts from outside India. Central to its implementation was the posting of government village level workers (VLW) (as change agents) in villages. The VLW representing all "nation-building" departments was expected to "combine the functions of a missionary, organizer, technician, and patron. (The programs') vision of development included the improvement of everything: social harmony, economic production, education, health, and recreation" (Khan, 1978).

Following installation of the programme in India in 1952 the concept was rather rapidly adopted in other countries. During the 1950s the US assistance agencies were active in rural development in thirty countries, involving at the peak effort in 1950, 105 community development advisers. Programmes in an additional thirty countries were supported by United Nations agencies which functioned in a similar manner.

Within country programmes several shortcomings have been noted including: (1) the relatively heavy emphasis on "welfare" activities as compared with directly productive programmes and a particular inability to solve food production problems; (2) functional department dissatisfactions emerged over field representation by generalist VLWs; agricultural specialist agencies became particularly concerned and comparable tensions emerged in donor organizations: (3) central government planning units, oriented narrowly to economic growth objectives, became increasingly unsympathetic to broad-purpose CD field activities; (4) some national leaders became disappointed over failure of CD to promote harmony among its rural citizenry and encourage broad cross-section participation in the development process.

Conceptually it would appear that the CD programme encompassed many of the features of comprehensive societal development articulated by social scientists, to be discussed further below, quite likely more than is true on a comparable basis for many current RD programmes. But partly for lack of appreciation for inputs required and serious deficiencies in both vertical and horizontal co-ordination with respect to both planning and administration, support for the approach faded in the 1960s as fast or faster than it formed in the 1950s. From 1959 to 1960 the number of countries receiving US support for CD was reduced from 25 to 19 and the number of advisers from 105 to 68. By 1963 the Community Development Division had been eliminated at the US agency's Washington headquarters and any remnant efforts in LDCs country offices had been merged into "rural development offices" (Holdcroft, 1978).

GENESIS OF RURAL DEVELOPMENT

There are two, not entirely separate, origins for RD as currently used with respect to LDCs. The first grew out of the realization that to introduce new agricultural technologies many supportive activities and a range of government inputs were required. The term "integrated rural development" came to be used to describe the concerted efforts although it was not always clear just what was being "integrated."

The concurrent stem for the term was the broadening realization that a large proportion of the world's poorest reside in rural areas. It was reasoned that more broadly conceived plans and programmes could assist these people as well as contribute to a solution of the food problem. RD was adopted as a convenient term to describe the broader efforts though in many instances, judging from programme content, it is a mere synonym for agricultural development.

WHAT IS RURAL DEVELOPMENT?

Few terms in developmentalists' jargon vary so much among individuals and institutions as is true of RD. Many presentations on rural development are made without defining terms. Where definitions are made, they are variously framed as: (1) goals; (2) processes, or (3) government interventions (especially, programmes/projects). For the purpose of this paper it will be useful to have a formulation of the process. First, let us reflect on a few existing definitions.

1 Rural development is a strategy designed to improve the economic and social life of a specific group of people – the rural poor (World Bank, 1975).[1]
2 Rural development "seeks to involve a process of transformation from traditionally oriented rural cultures toward an acceptance and reliance on science and technology" (Ensminger, 1974).
3 ". . . RD is defined as improving living standards of the mass of low income population residing in rural areas and making the process self-sustaining" (Uma Lele, 1975).

A characteristic of many "definitions" of rural development or discussions on the subject is the prominent – sometimes exclusive – role accorded government for bringing it about. The role of governments will, of course, vary with forms of societies and strategies chosen for given forms. But in all societies, individuals ultimately play the major role. To accord government a virtually exclusive role in the RD process *per se*, particularly in the long run, appears inconsistent with the principle of self-reliant development.

RURAL DEVELOPMENT IN THE CONTEXT OF SOCIETY

In concerning ourselves about rural development we are focusing on a portion of a society which is not self-governing. To understand and articulate the meaning of the rural development process, an overall conceptualization of society is needed. In this context, a useful one is that given by macro-sociologist Edward Shils: "A society – a human society – is a differentiated and co-ordinated system of the institutionalized and freely adoptive actions of individuals, self reproductive through time and taking place within a territory which has meaning to those who reside in it" (Shils, 1975). Shils asserts that every society may be interpreted as a centre and periphery. The centre embodies a Central Value System (CVS) (i.e., values observed and espoused by those in authority) and a Central Institutional System (CIS) which is legitimated by the CVS and is composed of the following:

	Sub-system	Purpose
1	Polity:	to cope with power, stability, order and justice.
2	Economy:	to provide sustenance, shelter, and commerce.
3	Cultural:	to provide instructional and sacred knowledge, aesthetic expression, reception, and moral judgement.
4	Kinship or Family:	to provide affection, convenience, genetic continuity, sexual gratification.
5	Status:	to articulate value orientations.

Central authority, consensus and territorial boundaries are the main factors that establish and maintain a society.

In many developing nations the rural component of society, usually highly differentiated, constitutes a major part of the periphery, though usually less in a population than a territorial sense. Both the CVS and the CIS remain relatively weak in such a nation and face considerable strength at lineage, ethnic, and local subcentres. Enhancement in the administrative system and the national economic system would provide opportunities for political processes to generate greater consensus between the centre and the periphery and thereby lead to enhanced stature of the centre both institutionally and culturally and greater overall integration. This is a major challenge to statesmen, politicians, and political scientists.[2]

Conceptualizing the process of rural development is made difficult by the all-encompassing macro phenomena involved. The single discipline most nearly adequate to the task appears to be macro-sociology. But in terms of research or programme prescriptions RD should be viewed as a subject matter calling for multidisciplinary efforts. Disciplines with inputs, among others, are political science, economics, anthropology, sociology, history, and some behavioural and management sciences. A formulation is needed that will be meaningful to development planners and other practitioners, designers of comprehensive information systems and researchers. It is desirable to have at least a workable preliminary version which, against the conceptualization of society above, will be suggestive of the interdependencies that should concern us.

The concept must be people-oriented. The population focus must be on agricultural areas and rural non-farm areas containing towns or villages of less than some minimum number. Within these guidelines rural development can be said to entail an investment or accumulation process (including some in adjacent non-rural areas) such that there are increases in capabilities of individuals and of social, political, and economic institutions. These enhancements permit more efficiently supplying greater material and other want-satisfying opportunities and powers in which the population may share more equitably.

This formulation, no doubt, will satisfy few people. The author hopes that it can be improved through multidisciplinary interactions. It implies coverage of the appropriate population, that modernization or increased productivity must occur in many population components and institutions of society and that in formulating strategies, plans, and research a number of social science disciplines must be involved.

RATIONALE FOR CO–ORDINATION

The importance of vertical co-ordination in governments' efforts to plan and promote rural development can be supported by considering:

1 The complex, interdependent nature of societies and the rural development process with involvement of most governments from the centre to the most distant points of the periphery.
2 Examples of successful co-ordination.
3 Examples of adverse consequences of insufficient co-ordination.

These points will be discussed briefly in sequence. Some specific economic considerations will be presented below.

The complex, interdependent nature of society says much on an *a priori* basis for the need for careful co-ordination among intervention efforts. Given that development is a gradual process of accretions to (investments in) the several components of society – economic, political, social, cultural, etc. – it follows that there should be some balance to approximate optimum benefits. It is crucial in the economic area that on a national basis at least there be sufficient emphasis on directly productive areas that returns to investments can maintain all those made and enable accretions to the economic and other components. This means in most cases identifying comparative advantages in agriculture (products) and rural non-farm (products and services) areas as nuclei for sustained rural development. In both planning and implementation, government actions can do much to influence or promote co-ordinative investments. In a broad sense, the process of rural development will contribute to integration of the total society.

There have been few instances of well co-ordinated planning and administration for rural development among developing countries. The Republic of Korea's Saemaul Undong (New Village Programme) is a relatively effective, nationwide effort. This activity, commenced in 1970, is premised in large part on village level proposals, largely in local infrastructure and in training, but there is effective horizontal co-ordination among villages by county governments; provincial offices provide the link between local and centre levels and co-ordinate horizontally on the province level. There are national incentive prices for agriculture; the Ministry of Home Affairs gives major direction and co-ordination at the centre; the president gives leadership and general support (Asian Productivity Organization, 1978). The People's Republic of China is also generally credited with an effective rural transformation.

Each observer familiar with developing country conditions could cite impressive consequences of incompatabilities between central and local planning and/or administration pertaining to aspects of RD. Saleh and Goolsby (1977) identified approximately 600 institutional disincentives just to agricultural production. Serious repercussions also occur with respect to marketing, nutrition, research, etc. The production and service sectors of rural non-farm sectors, long under-recognized in the rural development process also offer consequences of incompatabilities (Chuta and Liedholm, 1979).

NATURE OF CO–ORDINATION REQUIRED

The co-ordination requirements differ somewhat as between planning and administration for rural development. Hence the two areas will be considered separately. While the title focus is on vertical co-ordination central with local – there are some horizontal aspects that should also be considered.

A. PLANNING

At the central level

1   Interactions between planners and researchers, on the one hand, and government and party leadership as well as spokesmen from the society at large, on the other, regarding general directions of the society's development and of the rural component in this context.

2   Co-ordination between national planning agencies (or ministries) and planning units of specialized ministries or departments, preferably with involvement of appropriate university disciplines to promote understanding of premises and intended direction for rural development.

3   Co-ordination between planning units of specialized departments and national leadership of any association/groups on content of plans which through communications to membership will help build local sup-

port for national thrusts.

4   Negotiations with foreign assistance agencies, particularly on capital aid, to assure compatability with domestic realities in terms of nature, volume, time profile of pay-offs, maintenance costs, and efforts on motivations to generate capital by indigenous means, private and public, including "in place" types.

Vertical

5   Co-ordination between the central planning agency and its field offices. This should help maximize use of local insights (government and private individuals) regarding balance of measures/investments among different functional areas and among the immediately productive, deferred productive, and welfare measures.

6   Co-ordination between planning units of specialist departments and their field offices. This presumes horizontal interaction with client personnel and is a crucial step in introducing realism as to what plans should stipulate in terms of policies and resource flows to induce farmers and small scale non-farm entities to increase their capital formation and productivity. Insights should also be produced on the nature of infrastructural support and the annual rate at which they should be augmented.

7   Co-ordination between the central planning agency and its field offices to assure close monitoring and rigorous ongoing and final evaluations of programmes/projects with timely feedback for altering plans /policies/programmes or for preparing plans for a subsequent period.

Horizontal

8   Co-ordination between planners at central and lower levels with counterpart administrative leadership to assure plan workability and obtain commitments from administrative personnel to effectively carry out the plans.

9   Co-ordination between planning authorities and counterpart budgetary personnel at all levels to assure adequate and timely resource support.

B. ADMINISTRATION

At the central level

1   The administrative leadership of government with advice of planners should assure adoption of development policies, both those which are explicit and those implicit in administrative procedures which are consistent with development plan objectives and, as they are articulated, with programmes and projects. These will range from simple procedures governing issuance of a business permit for a new small non-farm firm (to lessen entry problems) to price policy for the country's major food product (to assure incentives for enhancing capital accumulations and productivity). It is not sufficiently appreciated that adjusting policies can

be an economical means to help promote development.

2   Co-ordination between headquarters departments and their respective field offices to translate plans into meaningful programmes/projects with subsequent continuous interactions during implementation. This stage particularly affords opportunities for reflecting sensitivities regarding effects of projects and accompanying policies on individual/group incentives for increasing capital formation and productivity.

3   Co-ordination of the centre and lower echelons with educational/training institutions to help assure availability of proper skills among both government and nongovernment personnel.

4   Co-ordination between field offices of central government and provincial or local government offices as needed for collaborative or courtesy purposes. Usually local government staffs have greater empathy with villagers. These local officials often can reflect critical sensitivities of villagers on revenue raising measures or development projects. Moreover, if adequately informed on national plans and programmes, they can help instill local support for them, convey the impression that the intent of government programmes is to activate and assist, not to replace local efforts. Specifically, this means shaping programmes/projects so as not to inhibit and hopefully to stimulate usually unappreciated capacity of peasants to increase capital formation and productivity. This applies to both private endeavours and public efforts in economic, social, political, and cultural infrastructure or institutions.

5   Co-ordination among government agencies to give each employee a perspective as to his role in the total development effort and to develop a personnel system with individual rewards and penalties which will help generate an efficient, sensitive, and responsive bureaucracy.

KNOWLEDGE BASE FOR CO–ORDINATION OF RURAL DEVELOPMENT PLANNING AND ADMINISTRATION

A precondition for improving rural development planning in particular countries and the centre – local co-ordination of planning and administration is expanded knowledge regarding: (1) The nature of the rural development process in perspective of the total society, with a particular focus on problems and opportunities, (2) The nature of the private and public administrative systems and styles of administration with a focus on ways to improve their effectiveness and efficiency in the context of that society's values, and (3) alternative approaches for choosing strategies and formulating plans.

In support of all three items, introduction of a development-oriented information system is merited (Bonnen, 1976).

The rural development process should be construed as a broad subject matter calling for multi-disciplinary research, the outcome of which should be prescriptive in nature. Hettne (1978) can be endorsed: "The effort to correct the biases and imbalances which exist in the field of development research is a most important way of supporting the process of development. This . . . will necessitate *indigenous* research on the problem of underdevelopment, thereby facilitating the emergence of strategies adopted to varying resource endowments and value systems in particular countries". In addition, inquiries on development processes of given societies can be enriched by pragmatically considering historical experiences of other societies (Knutsson, 1978).

Choosing rural development strategies on which to base plans calls for models of some nature. Broader models are needed for work on rural development than have been utilized in economic areas. Meriting consideration for the purpose is the General Systems Simulation Approach (Rossmiller, 1978). Any formal modelling technique chosen will require substantial time to develop and operationalize. Meanwhile, use of relatively simple approaches would help create an awareness of interrelatedness often not manifested in current practices.

The purposes of rural development are too important to continue fragmentary, unco-ordinated thrusts at portions of the total complex of problems. Whether there will be broader, better co-ordinated efforts to promote rural development depends largely upon whether the political will exists. Pressures arising from the desperate human condition are likely, sooner or later to bring this about where it is now lacking. The social scientists with others in the research community and planners should coalesce in their efforts to serve decision makers better. Agricultural economists can expect (and be expected) to carry a major role in this, due to the importance of agriculture in rural development and the strong tradition of the profession's involvement with problem-oriented research.

NOTES

[1] In an address at the 1978 joint conference of the American Agricultural Economics Association and the Canadian Agricultural Economics Society, Dr W. David Hopper a vice president of the World Bank, expressed dissatisfaction with the Bank's conceptualizations and encouraged agricultural economists to contribute toward a better one.

[2] In many countries one of the most under-used researchers available among social scientists are the political scientists.

REFERENCES

Asian Productivity Organization (1978) "Rural Development Strategies in Selected Asian Countries" (Report of a Multi-Country Study Mission), Tokyo.

Bonnen, James T. "Improving Information on Agriculture and Rural Life", *American Journal of Agricultural Economics*, Vol. 57, No. 5, pp. 753–63.

Chuta, Enyinna and Carl E. Liedholm (forthcoming in 1979) "Rural Off Farm Employment – A Review of the State of the Art", Michigan State University, East Lansing.

Ensminger, Douglas (1974) "Rural Development: What is it? (Its Contribution to Nation Building)", Paper presented at East-West Centre's Conference on Integrated Com-

198   *Herbert C. Kriesel*

munication for Rural Development, Honolulu.
Haq, Mahbub Ul (1976) *The Poverty Curtain – Choices For the Third World*, Columbus Press, New York.
Hettne, Bjorn (1978) "Current Issues in Development Theory", Swedish Agency for Research Co-operation with Developing Countries, Stockholm.
Hicks, John (1969) *A Theory of Economic History*, Oxford, London.
Holdcroft, Lane E. (1978) "The Rise and Fall of Community Development in Developing Countries, 1950–65"; A Critical Analysis and an Annotated Bibliography, Rural Development Paper No. 2, Michigan State University, East Lansing.
Ilchman, Warren F. and Rarrindra C. Bhargava (1971) "Balanced Thought and Economic Growth", *Frontiers of Development Administration*, Fred W. Riggs (ed.), Duke University Press.
Khan, Akhter Hameed (1978) "Ten Decades of Rural Development: Lessons from India", Rural Development Paper No. 1, Michigan State University, East Lansing.
Knutsson, Karl E. (1978) Statement Opening a Conference on Emerging Trends in Development Theory, Bjorn Hettne and Peter Wallensteen (eds), Swedish Agency for Research Co-operation with Developing Countries, Stockholm.
Lele, Uma (1975) *The Design of Rural Development-Lessons from America*, John Hopkins, Baltimore.
Leys, Colin (1972) "A New Conception of Planning" in Faber, Mike and Dudley Seers, *The Crisis in Planning*, Volume I, Sussex Press, Edinburgh.
Rossmiller, George E. (ed.) (1978) *Agricultural Sector Planning – A General System Simulation Approach*, Michigan State University, East Lansing.
Saleh, Abdullah, and O. Halbert Goolsby (1971) "Institutional Disincentives to Agricultural Production in Developing Countries" in *Foreign Agriculture* (Supp.) US Department of Agriculture, Washington.
Shils, Edward (1975) *Center and Periphery – Essays in Macrosociology*, The University of Chicago Press, Chicago.
World Bank (1975) "Rural Development", Sector Policy Paper, Washington.

GENERAL DISCUSSION – RAPPORTEUR: GUNNER G.H. HÖKAS

As there was no official opener present the discussion was started by Bo L. Andersson. He stated that there were limited resources and a shortage of planners. Therefore we have to accept central planning. However there were also problems in connection with central planning. Individual incentives may be reduced. Central planning was not accepted by all politicians and there can be conflicts between central planning and political ideas.

Another speaker stated that central planning was of importance in order to initiate economic development. Central Planning ought to be continuous, and plans and results ought to be compared continuously. There was a need for more adequate concepts. It was of great importance to separate macro and micro planning. Planning at the macro level ought to be of a more comprehensive nature and should provide scope for detailed planning at the micro level. Information was needed as a basis for central planning. The more detailed the central planning, the larger the need for information. Detailed information was costly and difficult to handle. Therefore it was important to balance central and individual (local) planning in an appropriate way. Co-ordination between different levels in the hierarchy of planners was of great importance.

Two speakers, from Indonesia and an African country respectively, gave some short comments. It was stated that we have to learn from experience. We are working with individuals. It was also said that marketing must be given more attention in planning. Also, we have to give more consideration to the problems of the poor. Co-ordination is more of an art than a science and consequently multi-disciplinary research was necessary.

Participants in the discussion included Bo L. Andersson and Deryke G.R. Belshaw.

TÚLIO BARBOSA*

The Farm/Non-farm Interface with Special Reference to Rural Brazil

INTRODUCTION

This paper reviews the interface of the farm and non-farm sectors in Brazil, and the extent to which this interface has facilitated or impeded agricultural development both in the aggregate and within certain regions of the country. The farm and non-farm sectors are interrelated through a number of markets. In this paper agricultural output, purchased inputs, labour, capital and land markets are specifically discussed. Recent changes in the manner in which the sectors interface, especially as related to government policies, and their effect on the development process, are presented.

In order to understand the farm/non-farm interface in Brazil, it is essential to keep in mind that various market imperfections exist – some of them induced by government policies – which prevent the equalization of factor prices and real income in each sector in each region.

As suggested by Schuh[15], as an economy develops the agricultural sector tends to experience a relative decline in farm income. This is a result of the particular shifts in the demand and supply relationships that are imposed on the agricultural sector during the development process. Consequently, markets tend to be in disequilibria as development occurs.

BACKGROUND: THE DEVELOPMENT STRATEGY[1]

Until the 1920s agricultural exports (mainly coffee) represented the most dynamic sector in the Brazilian economy. Between 1920 and 1928 the annual growth rate for agricultural export products was 9 per cent while that of agricultural production in general was 4.5 per cent and of industrial production only 3.9 per cent. Economic expansion, based on the growth of agricultural exports, lost its dynamism with the onset of the

* The author is indebted to Robert L. Thompson, Aércio S. Cunha, Marshall A. Martin, Antonio L. Bandeira, Geraldo S.C. Barros, Evonir B. Oliveira and Silvio Sant'Ana for helpful comments. The usual disclaimer applies.

1929/33 World Depression which severely reduced Brazilian exports, particularly coffee.

In the 1930s industrial production began to replace agricultural exports as the dynamic sector in the economy. The total recovery of the Brazilian economy from the Depression was not achieved until the 1940s, but then further expansion of the economy was prevented when World War II cut off trade routes. During the war period, the difficulties in obtaining foreign goods resulted in an unsatisfied domestic demand and stimulated an import-substitution effort, particularly for industrial goods.

The import-substitution process, however, had a timid beginning. At first, because of import difficulties, it was based primarily on the more intensive utilization of the existing production capacity. Later, after the war was over, incentives for industrialization were given second priority relative to policies intended to alleviate internal inflation. The exchange rate was significantly overvalued throughout most of the postwar period. This tended to encourage imports and discourage exports.

It was not until the 1950s that an explicit industrial development policy was formulated. However, the existing tariff system did not provide effective protection for the domestic industry and the overvalued exchange rate gave an implicit subsidy to imports. Initially the import-substitution development strategy was largely an effort to reduce the balance of payments difficulties that Brazil was facing rather than to encourage industrial development as a dynamic source of growth in the Brazilian economy.

In the mid-1950s Brazil's industrial development policy was based on: (1) import-substitution, protected by tariffs on imports and foreign exchange subsidies for the importation of capital goods; (2) a foreign exchange policy, which acted as a mechanism for the transfer of resources from the agricultural sector to the industrial sector; (3) an inflow of foreign capital, which was given incentives for direct investment, and (4) inflation, which in so far as it provided a mechanism for resource transfer from the private sector to the public sector and an income transfer from labour to the entrepreneurial class.

The result was an accelerated rate of growth in the period 1957 to 1961. While the industrial sector grew at an annual rate of 12 per cent, the agricultural output grew at only 4.9 per cent. This generated a series of distortions in the 1960s: (1) oversized plants, with idle capacity and a high unit cost of production; (2) a low level of investment in social services, and (3) a high rate of inflation, which finally led to a slow-down in growth and a recession. In 1963 industrial production declined 0.5 per cent and the gross national product grew only 1.6 per cent, which implied a decrease in per caput income, since the population grew 3 per cent. The rate of inflation reached 81 per cent in 1963 and 92 per cent in 1964. From 1964 to 1967 the government adopted stringent policies to check inflation.

It was not until 1968 that recovery began. Again, difficulties with the balance of payments dictated the industrial development strategy. With minor exceptions, import-substitution was no longer the dynamic centre of industrial development. An expansion of exports became the primary policy objective. A system of flexible exchange rates was introduced and fiscal incentives for exports were granted.

The period 1968 to 1973 was characterized by a high level of economic activity. The annual rate of growth of the gross national product was over 10 per cent and, due to favourable international market conditions, coupled with fiscal incentives, the rate of growth of agricultural export production was increasing. At the same time, the rate of inflation was declining. This period came to be known as the "Brazilian economic miracle". However, by late 1973 the world oil crisis shocked the whole system, raising the external prices of imported goods relative to those of exported goods. As a results, new difficulties with the balance of payments emerged, coupled with rising rates of inflation and concern regarding an adequate food supply for the domestic market *vis-á-vis* the need to increase the export of agricultural products. This is the situation currently faced in Brazil.

The discussion thus far of Brazil's development strategy, which emphasized the industrial sector, does not adequately account for the role played by the agricultural sector in Brazil's total economic development process. As will be seen below, the particular set of development policies pursued in both the farm and non-farm sectors has exacerbated the relative income problem in the agricultural sector while at the same time giving it a rather unique regional dimension. The result is that the bulk of the poverty in Brazil is concentrated in its agricultural sector, especially in the Northeast, and most of the agricultural sector has not shared in the post-World War II development of the economy on a scale anywhere near that of the non-farm sector.[2]

THE AGRICULTURAL SECTOR IN THE DEVELOPMENT PROCESS
AND THE PRESENT FARM/NON–FARM INTERFACE[3]

Despite all efforts directed towards the expansion of the industrial sector – based fundamentally on a policy of import-substitution – the agricultural sector still accounts for a substantial share of employment (44.3 per cent in 1970) and exports (61.2 per cent in 1976) but accounts for only 14.6 per cent of the national income (in 1970).

From 1920 to the present, the agricultural sector has provided a substantial part of the resources required for industrialization through the transfer of the agricultural surplus[4] to the industrial sector. Growth in agricultural production came largely from the expansion of the agricultural frontier and use of the readily available labour supply and not from government sponsored investment in modern agricultural practices, except in the case of the state of São Paulo.[5]

The agricultural sector has been the major source of labour for the non-farm sector, even though the observed transfer of labour has not been sufficient to diminish the gap in labour income per caput between the two sectors.

It is becoming apparent that the possibilities for extracting surplus from agriculture and the transfer of labour to the non-farm sector are gradually being exhausted. This is due, in part, to the past low levels of public investment, especially in agricultural research, rural education, rural extension, and basis infrastructure. As a consequence of inadequate levels of public investment in the agricultural sector, the possibilities of increasing agricultural productivity in the short run are reduced and thus limit the amount of the agricultural surplus and labour available for transfer.[6]

Efforts to increase agricultural exports to help improve the balance of payments via special incentives such as subsidized credit, coupled with favourable international prices, have led to a reallocation of resources from food production (for domestic consumption) to the export sector. This reallocation of resources coupled with the policy of protection of urban consumers (through price controls) has led to the present situation, i.e., the rate of growth in food production – aggravated by adverse weather conditions – is declining or not growing and thus cannot satisfy the domestic and foreign markets at constant or declining real prices.

This has helped fuel the current rate of inflation. However, it should be remembered that food price increases have contributed only in part to the current high rate of inflation. Credit policies, wage increases, and fiscal policies have also contributed.

One of the key policy issues Brazil faces today is to determine the extent to which it can increase agricultural production via further technological advances.

In the following sections the current farm/non-farm interface is examined. Some of the major forces which are likely to favour or to hamper the agricultural process in the future are identified.

PRODUCT MARKET

1 *The subsistence sector*
The domestic food supply is basically provided by small producers (small landowners, sharecroppers, and renters). Available data show that in 1970, 79 per cent of the cassava, 73 per cent of the edible beans, 64 per cent of the corn and 44 per cent of the rice production were supplied by producers with an area less than 50 hectares. It should also be noted that 83 per cent of all producers in Brazil may be classified as small producers (less than 50 hectares). Even though these small producers are located in all parts of the country, the major concentration is found in the Northeastern region, a poverty stricken and drought prone area of Brazil.

Given the importance of small producers as a source of food for domestic consumption, the linkage between the small producers and the non-farm sector is extremely important. On the one hand, they demand relatively few inputs produced by the non-farm sector. Moreover, a considerable share of their production is consumed on the farm where it is produced in order to guarantee the family subsistence. Studies have shown, however, that small producers are price responsive.[5] But their ability to increase production in response to a product price increase is limited, given their low resource base (land) and limited access to credit. Without adequate resources, it is difficult for them to satisfy both their consumption needs and still to have resources available to purchase current inputs. Furthermore, the use of new inputs and new technologies is often perceived as a very high risk undertaking.[21]

Given these conditions, which prevail throughout most of the subsistence agricultural sector, and which are aggravated in the Northeast by climatic uncertainties, it is very likely that price incentives alone will not suffice to mobilize a larger share of production for the market. A considerable portion of the food products (e.g. edible beans, corn, cassava) which enters the market for the urban food supply is the residual of production minus farm family consumption.

To reverse this situation efforts should be directed towards: (1) the development and diffusion of land saving technology with low yield risk, and (2) access to institutional credit for small producers. This policy prescription, however, needs some qualifications. First, assuming that suitable technological packages and funds for credit are available, the problem still remains of how to provide credit to a large number of small farmers scattered throughout the country. Secondly, it is doubtful whether the existing market infrastructure (especially in the Northeast) will be sufficient to handle efficiently the expected increased output and transfer the corresponding gains to producers and consumers. Thirdly, as pointed out by Schuh,[15] if both of these policies are pursued, those small producers with entrepreneurial talents will realize significant income gains and will experience internal growth. Those who do not have such entrepreneurial potential will be expelled from the sector, and their problems will have to be handled by other means. Fourthly, there remains the problem of how to produce and distribute suitable technology and provide access to credit for small producers who do not own land, such as sharecroppers and renters.

In the short run it seems plausible that, given adequate incentives, medium-sized farmers can expand corn, edible beans, rice, and cassava production. The rates of return on investments of such a policy may be high. However, this policy prescription does not imply neglecting the subsistence farm sector. Given the present state of the subsistence sector – as characterized by relatively low income levels and involving a considerable fraction of the population – the opportunity to make it an important market for output of the growing industrial sector, both for agricultural inputs and for consumer goods, should not be overlooked.

2   The agricultural export sector

While the domestic food supply is mainly produced by a large number of small producers, the production of export products, such as coffee, cocoa, sugarcane and more recently soybeans, comes primarily from large producers. This sector enjoys a close interrelationship with the non-farm sector, through product, input, capital and foreign exchange markets.

Because of its importance as a foreign exchange earner, it has been relatively more favoured in terms of public investments in research and infrastructures as well as by credit and fiscal policies. Although penalized by overvalued exchange rates, favourable international prices in recent years have encouraged a transfer of resources from food to export production, especially from edible beans and corn to soybeans in the southeastern and southern regions.

This development has contributed to a relatively higher rate of increase in the price of domestically consumed foods. This has become an important source of pressure for modernization of the food producing sector, which in the Brazilian context means a higher rate of use of land-saving technologies. This may seem contradictory since Brazil still has a large land frontier. However, the increasing cost of bringing new land into production, the large distances from these areas to the major urban centres, and inadequate storage facilities, make it cheaper to increase productivity on the old lands rather than on the new ones.

3   Beef cattle: a special case

So far the discussion has been dichotomized in terms of food crops versus export crops. However, it should be noted that beef cattle production is also an important enterprise in Brazil. It is characterized as a land extensive activity and has expanded over time. Beef cattle production provides a secure and profitable form of savings under inflationary conditions and provides a high degree of liquidity relative to other assets.

The expansion of beef cattle production has been observed in both old (Northeast) and new areas (West and North). In the former, it has aggravated the food supply problem since cultivated areas have been transformed into pasture. This is particularly evident in the Northeast where areas cleared and cultivated by sharecroppers and small renters are often planted to grass as a partial land rental payment. Consequently, subsistence crops production, has tended to move into new areas in the agricultural frontier, reproducing the same type of structure found in the old areas.[7]

LABOUR MARKET

Imperfections in the labour market in Brazil are regarded as a major reason for the low income level of a large portion of the Brazilian population.[15,17]

Available data indicate[17] that agricultural incomes were substantially lower in 1970 than those in the non-farm sector, but also that they experienced a relative decline during the preceding decades. From 1960 to 1970 the average income per member of the labour force in the agricultural sector increased by 14 per cent while in the non-farm sector it increased by 38 per cent. In reality, the average income per member of the labour force in agriculture declined by 17 per cent as a proportion of the national average over the decade. In 1970 income was more equally distributed in the agricultural sector than in the non-farm sector. Schuh and Singh[17] suggest that the basic problem in the agricultural sector is not so much the distribution of income within the sector, but the absolute poverty of people in the agricultural sector relative to the non-farm sector.

The data also reveal that the labour market has experienced a structural transformation of some significance in recent years. The relative role of agriculture as a source of employment has decreased and all regions have experienced an upward movement in their rural/urban wage structure. However, persistent wage differentials for different categories of farm workers among the regions, and for rural/urban wages, imply that sufficient structural adjustments are not occurring in the labour market.

A widely accepted hypothesis[15] is that the low level of skills and education of the workers in the agricultural sector is a major barrier to their mobility from farm to urban employment or even to agricultural employment in other regions. This hypothesis is supported by empirical evidence which reveals that out migrants tend to be the healthier, the younger and the better educated.

It must also be noted that agricultural workers generally are not "pure" wage employees. This is particularly true in the Northeast and East where a substantial share of the labour force is composed of sharecroppers, small renters, squatters, and small landowners who derive part of their income from the cultivation of a small plot of land which they own or which is under some type of contractual arrangement. This creates additional institutional relationships (to landlords, for instance) which tend to retain the worker in that geographic location or occupation.

In the last decade some distortions in the wage/capital price ratio have been induced by government policies. The wage/capital price ratio was distorted through the simultaneous application of two policies: subsidized credit (at substantially negative real rates of interest) for acquisition of farm machinery and the extension of minimum wage and social security benefits to farm workers financed by a payroll tax. The result was a rapid rural-urban migration. The agricultural sector of the southern region, in general and in São Paulo, in particular, has experienced a rapid rate of modernization[16] involving an increase in the capital/labour ratio through the adoption of labour-saving technologies (mechanization).

Estimates provided by Martin[8] indicate that in the period 1950/70 the economically active labour force in São Paulo, which alone accounted for 22 per cent of Brazil's economically active labour force in 1970, increased 86 per cent, for an annual growth rate of 3 per cent. The agricultural labour force declined by 12 per cent in the same period at an annual growth rate of -0.7 per cent. In fact, the absolute number of agricultural workers in São Paulo has been declining in recent years due to both the mechanization of existing crops and a change in the crop mix towards less labour-intensive crops.

Unemployed rural workers tend to move to large cities or to the outskirts of urban areas where many of them cannot find employment – partly because of the type of industrialization pursued. However, since not all agricultural practices can be mechanized at the present time – particularly harvesting, – a new class of urban-based itinerant workers has emerged (known in Brazil as "volantes" or "boias frias"). Most are former agricultural workers who were displaced by mechanization.[18 & 20]

In areas such as the poverty-stricken Northeast, the agricultural sector has remained a major source of employment. However, real agricultural income per caput in the Northeast has not risen. Increases in incomes per caput are only possible if there are some major structural transformations (e.g. changes in the crop mix which are highly dependent upon improved technology for arid areas, successful adjustments to adverse climatic conditions, etc.). Otherwise there will continue to be a large migration from the agricultural sector to the non-farm sector in the Northeast and South and to the farm sector in the South.

The perceived probability of finding high-paying jobs elsewhere encourages outmigration from the Northeast. In reality, the perceived probability of finding a better paying job seldom materializes. In general, the migrants are absorbed in low-paying occupations in the service sector, often as construction workers, or they simply do not find a job. It appears that potential migrants are receiving inadequate information on the availability of jobs in non-traditional areas, other than in São Paulo and Rio de Janeiro.

The heart of the question is that the solution to poverty problems through the labour market is highly dependent upon the availability of alternative employment opportunities and a massive programme of public investment in human capital in rural Brazil to provide potential migrants with saleable skills, particularly for the next generation. This could contribute to the long run reduction of labour market imperfections in Brazil.

The policy question Brazil faces now seems to be how to increase in the short run income per caput while maximizing agricultural employment with the current land base. It appears that there is little room for adjustments in the short run.

The only hope of achieving income parity, especially in the Northeast given its land/labour ratio, is through the provision of off-farm employment opportunities in the agricultural regions. This calls for a policy which has been virtually ignored in Brazil: incentives for the development of rural non-farm activities.[24]

Available data show that small farmers in Brazil are tending to become part-time farmers. For example, it is estimated that at least 20 per cent of the family income is generated in off-farm employment in the eastern and southern regions. One study based on a large sample, covering seven states, showed that off-farm employment was as important as the sale of farm products (38 per cent each) as a source of family income for small farmers.

The spectrum of rural non-farm activities is widespread and diverse. They include construction, commerce, service, processing, and manufacturing. The public policy priorities for non-farm activities should be based on their labour absorbing capability. It appears that agro-industries for the processing of regionally produced agricultural goods such as fruits, cassava, etc. should rank high on the list of priorities.

Another policy question is related to the potential for using land reform to expand employment in agricultural areas. Brazil has had no formal nor large experience with land reform. *Ex-ante* evaluation studies[3] have shown that in certain areas (such as in the Northeast) and under some specific schemes (such as subdivision of large land holdings) such a policy can have a positive effect on labour absorption. However, these studies did not provide good estimates of costs and other adjustments required or implied by land reform. This issue merits additional empirical research.

Along the same lines there also exists the alternative of resettling farmers in new areas (controlled colonization).[5] Brazil's past and present colonization efforts, however, have not been very successful.[4]

CAPITAL MARKET

1   *Capital transfer and economic policy*
Historically, as mentioned at the beginning of this paper, the agricultural sector has performed an important role in transferring the agricultural surplus to the industrial sector, particularly from coffee production. Currently, the persistence of a policy of an overvalued exchange rate has also been a mechanism through which capital has been transferred from the agricultural export sector to the non-farm sector by implicitly taxing all exports of which agriculture contributes the largest share.

From a regional point of view, it is important to mention that, according to estimates provided by Martin,[8] from about 1950 until 1961 the Northeast, and in fact the entire country outside the state of São Paulo, experienced net capital outflows as a result of shifts in the terms of trade. In the 1950s approximately one to two per cent of the gross product of the Northeast was transferred to the rest of Brazil, particularly into the state of São Paulo. Beginning in 1962, the resource flow through the terms of trade was reversed. In the period 1962 through 1973 there was a net inflow into the Northeast of approximately 2 per cent of the Northeast's gross product, and the flow became larger towards the end of the period. The factors associated with the reversal in the terms of trade were: (1) massive devaluation of the cruzeiro; (2) tariff reform and (3) increase in international commodity prices. It is useful to note that the government developed other programmes for the Northeast starting in the 1960s. Various development agencies (SUDENE, Banco do Nordeste and CEPLAC) began to invest substantial sums of money in industrial, agricultural, and general infrastructural projects in the Northeast. Special tax incentives were also provided to encourage investment in the Northeast.

2 Agricultural credit market

Recently the agricultural credit market has been an effective channel for transferring income or wealth from the non-farm to the farm sector through subsidized interest rates. The problem is that this income transfer has largely benefited the large landowners. This has contributed to the aggravation of the income distribution problem within the agricultural sector since it discriminates against the small producers. It was observed that most of the credit has been directed to agricultural export products and to beef cattle. The rationale has been that large producers can make better use of the credit, given their lower marginal propensity to consume and higher rate of capital accumulation. In addition, costs of delivering credit are lower and risks are smaller from a lender's point of view. No doubt a credit policy which favours large producers provides a greater response in terms of increased production in a relatively short period of time. However, this must be weighed against the distortions it imposes in terms of income redistribution and reallocation of resources such as (1) shifts to capital-intensive crops which reduce labour employment and (2) shifts in the locational pattern of production, which lead to artificial comparative advantages.

Subsidized credit and fiscal incentive policies have also generated income transfer to the farm sector through investment by large industrial and commercial interests, both multi-national and national. Given these policies, these firms are buying large land holdings in newly opened areas. Forestry and/or beef cattle are the main production activities. The occupation of new areas, under this system, is likely to reproduce there the same land tenure and modes of production found in many old areas.

Even though these policies have caused resource reallocation in Brazil in many instances, the application of price support, and input price subsidies (e.g. on fertilizer) have helped to minimize some of the undesirable effects.

Given its importance as a source of the domestic food supply, credit policies can no longer afford to ignore the small farm sector. Thus, it is expected that in the near future new credit policy guidelines will be announced. According to government authorities, it is expected that small and medium sized farmers will be the priority recipients of subsidized credit and large landowners will have to pay interest rates closer to market interest rates. Again, it is necessary to weigh the expected gains against the implied adjustments associated with this change in credit policy. The question is one of determining the appropriate credit mix.

If the new guidelines in fact materialize there remains the problem of finding an efficient means of delivering credit plus technical assistance to a very large number of small farmers scattered over various parts of the country.

In addition to the provision of credit it is necessary to adopt an insurance policy which will absorb most of the risk faced by the small producers. There is some limited pilot experience in which credit and crop insurance have been provided through a scheme of "pre-planted purchase of production" by government agencies.

Finally, a comment should be made with respect to inflation and the land market. Inflation and the expectation that it will continue at high rates in the future has led to a transfer of capital into the farm sector. Land is being purchased not strictly for production purpose but as a hedge against further inflation. This is socially undesirable since it does not increase production. Moreover, because of land price increases it reduces the opportunities for the landless and the unemployed to purchase land for production purposes.

CONCLUDING COMMENTS AND POLICY GUIDELINES

This brief description of the development strategy pursued by Brazil in the last few decades as well as of the role played by the agricultural sector in the development process provides several insights into the interface between the farm and non-farm sectors. Government policies directed towards the farm and non-farm sectors have had a major influence in determining the pattern of resource allocation, both inter-sectoral and inter-regional.

The consequences of this particular set of policies resulted in a double squeeze on agriculture.[15] Relative agricultural prices were kept low by means of price and trade policies, thereby encouraging resources to leave the sector. At the same time Brazil's industrial development policies reduced employment opportunities in that sector.

The basic policy guidelines for the problems Brazil faces today should include the following: (1) extend the modernization process throughout the agricultural sector, taking explicit account of the large number of subsistence farmers; (2) develop a coherent policy which simultaneously increases agricultural exports and food production for domestic consumption; (3) increase agricultural income per caput in the short run while maximizing agricultural employment with the current land base and (4) in the long run, tackle the poverty problems in the agricultural sector by improving the quality of the labour force and eliminating existing market imperfections.

NOTES

[1] For details see: Almeida[1], Villela,[22] Pastore[12] and Weisskoff.[23]

[2] For an insightful discussion on this point see Schuh.[15]

[3] For a thorough treatment on the role of the agricultural sector in the development process see: Schuh,[14] Schuh,[15] Schuh,[16] Paiva,[11] Martin,[8] and Lopes & Schuh.[7]

[4] See Nicholls.[10]

[5] See Schuh,[16] Martin,[8] and Seixas Neto.[19]

[6] Empirical studies have shown that investments in agricultural research, extension and rural education in Brazil offer relatively high rates of return. Ayer & Schuh,[2] Monteiro,[9] and Patrick & Kehrberg.[13]

[7] See Dias[6] for an insightful discussion about the occupation of new areas in the frontier.

REFERENCES

[1] Almeida, J. *Industrialização e Emprego no Brasil*. IPEA/INPES. Relatório de Pesquisa No. 24, 1974.

[2] Ayer, H. and Schuh, G.E. "Social Rates of Return and Other Aspects of Agricultural Research: The Case of Cotton Research in São Paulo, Brazil". *American Journal of Agricultural Economics*, Vol. 54, No. 4, November 1972, p. 557–69.

[3] Barbosa, T. *A Normative Analysis of Land Reform Measures in the Priority Area of Rio de Janeiro, Brazil*, unpublished PhD thesis, Purdue University, 1973.

[4] Castro, M.C. *Colonização Dirigida no Brasil: Considerações Criticas sobre o Sistema de Implantação de Projectos*. FIPE/USP, 1976.

[5] Cruz, T.A., Barbosa, T., Oliveira, E.B. and Teixeira, J.A. "Resposta dos Pequenos Agricultores a Estimulos de Preço". *Rev. Ceres*, 25(142): 554–572, Nov/Dec. 1978.

[6] Dias, G.L.S. *Mercado de Capital, Adoção de Tecnologia e o Ciclo de Vida*. Seminário do Projecto "Alternatives de Desenvolvimento para Grupos de Baixa Renda na Agricultura Brasileira". Fortalexa, 1976.

[7] Lopes, M.R. and Schuh, G.E. *A Molilização de Recursos da Agricultura: Uma Análise de Política para o Brasil*. CFP. Coleção Análise e Pesquisa, Vol. 8, 1979.

[8] Martin, M.A. *Modernization of Brazilian Agriculture: An Analysis of Unbalanced Development*, unpublished PhD thesis, Purdue University, 1976.

[9] Monteiro, A. *Avaliação Econômica da Pesquisa e Extensqo Agricola: O Caso do Cacau no Brasil*, unpublished MS thesis, Universidade Federal de Viçosa, 1975.

[10] Nicholls, W.H. "An 'Agricultural Surplus' as a Factor in Economic Development". *The Journal of Political Economy*, February 1973, 71(1), p. 1–29.

[11] Paiva, R.M., Schattan, S., Freitas, C.F.T. *Brazil's Agricultural Sector*, XV International Conference of Agricultural Economists, São Paulo, 1973.

[12] Pastore, A.C., Barros, J.R.M., Kadota., "A Teoria de Paridade do Poder de Compra, Minidesvalorizaçóes e o Equilíbrio da Balança Comercial Brasileira". *Pesquisa e Planejamento Econômico*. Vol. 6, No. 2, ag. 1976, p. 287–312.

[13] Patrick, G.F. and Kehrberg, E.W. "Costs and Returns to Education in Five Agricultural Areas in Eastern Brazil", *American Journal of Agricultural Economics*, Vol. 55, No. 2, May 1973, p. 145–153.

[14] Schuh, G.E. *O Desenvolvimento da Agricultura no Brasil*; Rio de Janeiro, APEC, 1971.

[15] Schuh, G.E. *The Income Problem in Brazilian Agriculture*. Seminário de Pesquisa "Alternativas de Desenvolvimento para Grupos de Baixa Renda na Agricultura Brasileira". Piracicaba, 1974.

[16] Schuh, G.E. *The Modernization of Brazilian Agriculture: An Interpretation*. Conference on Growth, Productivity and Equity Issues in Brazilian Agriculture, The Ohio State University, January 1975.

[17] Schuh, G.E. and Sing, R.D. *The Labor Market in Brazil: Existing Imperfections and Future Possibilities in the Context of Country's Poverty with Special Reference to the Role of Education*, Department of Agricultural Economics, Purdue University, mimeo., 1977.

[18] Secretaria de Economia e Planejamento. *Trabalho Volante na Agricultura Paulista*. Governo do Estado de São Paulo. Série Estudos e Pesquisas 25, 1978.

[19] Seixas Neto, A. "O Processo de Mudança Tecnológica na Agricultura Paulista", unpublished MS thesis, Universidade Federal de Viçosa, 1976.

[20] Universidade Estadual Paulista Júlio De Mesquita Filho. *Mão-de-Obra Volante na Agricultura*. 111 Reunião Nacional, 1977.

[21] Valdés, A., Scobie, G.M., Dillon, J.L. *Economics and the Design of Small-Farmer Technology*. Iowa University Press, Ames, 1979.

[22] Villela, A.V. and Suzigan, W. *Polïtica do Governo e Crescimento da Economïca Brasileira, 1889/1945*. Série Monográfica No. 10, IPEA/INPES, 1973.

[23] Weisskoff, R. "Vinte e Cinco Anos de Substituição de Importações no Brasil: 1948/72". *Pesquisa e Planejamento Econômico*, Vol. 8, No. 1, April 1978, p. 1–32.

[24] World Bank. *Rural Enterprise and Nonfarm Employment*, A World Bank Paper, January 1978.

DISCUSSION OPENING – TOM W. CARROLL

Professor Barbosa's paper is a broad brush picture of how governmental policy and trends in the larger economy can affect the development of the agricultural sector. Although most of the discussion is specifically related to Brazil, many of the issues and policies that are discussed are relevant to development strategies being formulated in other countries.

In the opening background section of the paper, Brazil's general development strategy over the past few decades is summarized as being oriented to industrial development with a shift in the late '60s from import substitution to export generation. It is noted, however, that in spite of this industrial emphasis, agricultural exports in 1976 still accounted for over 60 per cent of the total value of exports.

The farm/non-farm interface is characterized in terms of six "markets". These are the agricultural product market (including both domestic food and foreign agricultural exports), the factor input market, the labour market, the capital market, the land market and the foreign exchange market.

The Brazilian farm sector is heterogeneous, comprising at least four important subsectors: (1) large commercial enterprises primarily oriented toward the export crops of coffee, cotton, sugar cane, cocoa and, more recently, soybeans; (2) large scale beef cattle enterprises; (3) small to medium size, advantaged commercial farms located in the foodsheds of the urban centres and having a high percentage of owner-operators, with increasing levels of non-farm income; (4) small disadvantaged subsistence farms having a high percentage of sharecroppers, small renters and squatters, many of which are located in the Northeast.

Professor Barbosa's paper focuses on the nature of the interaction between the farm sector and non-farm sector at the extremes, namely, the strong interaction in the case of the large commercial farms and the weak interaction in the case of the small subsistence farms. This imbalance of interaction at the extremes contributes to the problems of efficiency in food production and equity in terms of farmers' access to productive resources.

With respect to the product market, there has been a shift of production away from basic food crops to export crops and livestock products as a result of the strong linkages between these products and the non-farm sector through the product, input, capital and foreign exchange markets. As a result, food production apparently is no longer keeping pace with the general population increase, thus contributing to the general inflation problem. Although research has shown small farm operators to be responsive to rising food prices, the supply response is constrained by the availability of low risk technology oriented to food crops as well as access to institutional credits. Because of high transportations costs, the availability of land on the frontier does not appear to be an important factor in supply response.

With respect to the labour market, it appears that labour is being both pushed and pulled out of the agricultural sector. In the large commercial farming areas, hired labour is being pushed out as a result of two government policies: highly subsidized credit for the purchase of farm machinery and the extension of the minimum wage and social security benefits to farm workers. Farm operators have shifted the crop mix to less labour-intensive crops. On the other hand, the higher incomes in the urban areas and the more affluent agricultural areas are pulling people off the subsistence farms in the Northeast where there has been no appreciable increase in real income. The actual probabilities of finding jobs, however, are much lower than reported back to the farming areas, resulting in high unemployment among migrants with low job skills. Thus the tough policy question in the Northeast is how to increase income per caput. The paper suggests consideration of programmes to promote the development of rural non-farm industries, particularly agro-processing industries, to provide off-farm income opportunities. Also, land reform in the Northeast should now be given serious consideration for the purpose of absorbing labour in the region. Resettlement schemes have not worked well in Brazil.

The paper also calls for a massive programme of public investment in human capital now resident in rural areas. The dilemma, of course, is how to design formal and non-farm education programmes that serve the needs of those remaining in agriculture as well as those migrating into the urban industrial sector. It would seem that basic training in literacy and mathematics and science skills oriented to the agricultural sector, with which the residents are already familiar, would serve both needs.

With respect to capital markets, it is noted that historically there has been a transfer from the agricultural sector to the industrial sector through explicit taxes and implicit taxes on agricultural exports. The implicit tax resulted from overvalued exchange rates. More recently, a subsidized agricultural credit market has opened up the transfer of capital from the non-farm sector to the large commercial farm sector. The problem, however, is that the channels of credit have bypassed the small farmers who produce basic food crops. It is argued that subsidized credit backed by an insurance scheme should be made available to the small farmer with the large farmer paying commercial rates.

With respect to the land market, Brazil, with its high rates of inflation, has not escaped the problem of the investment of non-farm capital in agricultural land, resulting in an increase in land values. This investment has had little effect on agricultural production and blocks access of the landless and underemployed to productive resources.

I hope that this short paper could form the basis for a longer monograph in which the observations are supported by data on the Brazilian situation. Nevertheless, even the short paper provides many leads for the discussion to follow. I have two specific questions to lead off:

First, I am puzzled by the statement that "the possibilities for extracting surplus from agriculture are gradually being exhausted", because I have seen no indication that Brazil intends to abandon support for the agricultural export sector still comprising some 60 per cent of total export. Secondly, is it correct to conclude, as I have done, that there are relatively fewer problems at the farm/non-farm interface for the small to medium size commercial farmers operating in the foodsheds of the urban centres?

GENERAL DISCUSSION – RAPPORTEUR: HERNAN ELIZALDE

The discussion initally revolved around the transfer of agricultural surplus to the industrial sector, particularly in the case of the agricultural export subsector. This did not make feasible the improvement of the socio-economic conditions in the rural areas.

Next, several of the solutions presented by the author to rural poverty problems were commented on, particularly for the Northeast region. Firstly, the proposition to deliver subsidized credit to small and medium size farmers was questioned in relation to the feasibility of supplying credit to such a large number of farms and the high cost involved in a programme of this nature.

The alternative of providing public incentives for the development of non-farm activities in the rural sector was also discussed in the sense of forcing the market allocation of resources.

Finally, efforts to develop appropriate technologies for small farmers as well as the selective use of land reform in order to improve rural conditions were also commented upon.

In reply, Professor Barbosa stated that he believed that although expensive subsidized credit was necessary in order to increase the supply of urgently needed food, he felt that the promotion of non-farm activities, especially home industries, would counteract previous policies which emphasized the industrialization of the urban sector.

Participants in the discussion included M. Igben, Louis F. Herrmann, Ralph Lattimore, Howard Osborn and Alberto Valdes.

JUDITH HEYER

Rural Development Programmes and Impoverishment: Some Experiences in Tropical Africa

I am very grateful for this opportunity to air some problems with external intervention in rural development in tropical Africa that have been concerning me recently. These problems are not new to those working in rural development in Africa in different capacities. What is worrying is that despite considerable evidence and even public recognition of these problems, programmes continue to be pursued as if the problems did not exist.

It seems to me important that we agricultural economists involved in rural development in Africa stop to think more seriously about what it is that we are doing. I think we need to recognize that not only may we not be achieving as much as we would like, but we may also be doing considerable damage. An analysis of external intervention in rural development in tropical Africa raises the question, for me, of whether rural development intervention can succeed in alleviating poverty. It raises the possibility that rural development intervention cannot provide a solution. However, I do not think we yet have grounds for serious pessimism. We do not yet have evidence that rural development can succeed. I believe that if we face up to the problems we may yet be able to devise different sorts of strategies that can succeed both in raising production and incomes in the aggregate and in raising the incomes of the rural poor. This requires a different approach, however, from that currently being pursued by the majority of those involved in rural development intervention. In the first place it requires a different analysis. If we begin with an analysis of interest group conflicts and then devise and analyse strategies with these in mind, we will be able to explore the possibility of following rural development strategies that take account of conflicts through a process of bargaining, compromise and explicit concession to groups that normally lose out. The challenge is to try to face up to conflicts of interest and to see if we can develop a more successful strategy from that. I would expect such an attempt to result in some programmes in which interests strongly represented at present are still satisfied but those normally left out are also catered for. In other situations, I would expect there to be more fundamental conflicts, in which case the only

215

solution would be a bargained solution in which a share of the gains went to the underprivileged but only at the expense of those accustomed to appropriating all of the gains to themselves. Until there is a serious attempt to see what is possible through an approach based on conflict analysis, I think we can remain optimistic, or at the very least agnostic. Only when such an attempt is shown to have failed will there be real grounds for pessimism.

A group of us who had been working in East Africa and West Africa met at a workshop in 1977 with some of the following questions in mind. Why does external intervention fail again and again? In what sense does it fail? Is there any solution? The workshop has been followed up in a book to be published next year.[1] We are concerned about the adverse effects of external intervention in rural development in Africa, defining external intervention as intervention from outside the rural areas, usually by government or international agencies. We are concerned with what many of us see as an experience of repeated failure, either a failure to alleviate poverty among lower income groups, or an outright failure to achieve even the primary goals of the programmes and projects. Some of the experiences with which we are dealing can only be explained as examples of gross ineptitude involving failure by almost any criterion. In other cases, the failures represent conflicts between different interest groups, with the poor often the losers as a result of "rural development". The conclusions that emerge from our examination of the record in different East and West African countries over the past few decades are depressing, suggesting that there may be fundamental contradictions in the process of rural development. Some of us are now questioning whether there can be a rural development solution that alleviates poverty at all.

REPETITION OF GROSS FAILURE IN LARGE SCALE PROJECTS

One of the things that comes across very clearly is that mistakes of a very simple and fundamental kind have been repeated, in different contexts, time and time again in Africa over the past few decades, and that such mistakes are still being repeated on a large scale in the 1970s.

The mistakes that concern us, because they are still being repeated, are very fundamental mistakes, such as those now familiar as a result of the groundnuts scheme in Tanganyika after the second world war. I use this example deliberately because it is so well known. It has often been said that the groundnuts scheme was an expensive lesson, but that it served at least to ensure that such basic mistakes would not be repeated. Apparently this is not so. Very similar mistakes are continuing to be made even in the 1970s.

Coulson[2] summarizes mistakes for which the groundnuts scheme is famous as: inadequate surveys of soil and rainfall conditions; untried mechanical equipment; inadequate provision for spare parts and maintenance; insufficient attention paid to known groundnuts disease problems; inadequate investigation of headquarters' water supplies; and finally an inability to accept failure until well over a year after it was obvious to all technicians in the field. The groundnuts scheme provides us with an example that is all the more disturbing because, in Coulson's words, "The most experienced agricultural officers in Tanganyika were involved in this project, and yet, of these seven reasons for failure, five were agricultural considerations of a most elementary kind".

Coulson's paper suggests that equally basic mistakes were behind the failure of Tanzanian settlement schemes tried between 1964 and 1966, the Tanzanian State farms programme launched in 1969, and even *ujamaa*. Other examples include Kenya settlement schemes of the early 1960s, some of which failed on very fundamental technical grounds; the 1965 Senegal River irrigation development described by Adams;[3] and Ghanaian State farms in the early 1960s reviewed by Beckman.[4] Forrest[5] suggests a record of repetition of failure in Nigeria comparable to Coulson's account of what happened in Tanzania. In Nigeria, the record starts with the Niger Agricultural Project "which managed to replicate the disastrous experience of the Tanganyika groundnuts schemes though on a smaller scale", and it continues through settlement schemes and mechanized food farms in the 1950s, farm settlements in the 1960s, and now through the huge programme of irrigation development of the 1970s. The 1970s irrigation programme provides us with striking evidence that large scale projects are still being pursued on the basis of grossly miscalculated initial assumptions. Wallace[6] summarizes the problems of the Kano River Project in Northern Nigeria in its early stages in 1976/77, as follows:

> Firstly there is an acute shortage of manpower in Nigeria in irrigation, second there is a lack of commitment of Nigerian and expatriate salaried staff to rural employment, thirdly the government has a shortfall of necessary inputs which means that the provision of vital services and inputs cannot be guaranteed. Even if the inputs are available the government sector is plagued with inefficiencies in areas such as transportation, close supervision of distribution of inputs and the provision of tractor services. Finally, the problems facing any bureaucracy in a changing situation are that it is a relatively inflexible institution, capable of responding only slowly to change.

Thus, tractors do not plough on time; irrigation water supply is erratic, lack of spare parts causes delays in repairing pumps, vehicles and tractors, which are also affected by shortages of petrol and diesel; there are limited supplies of fertilizer; and there are major shortages of both unskilled labour and managerial staff for the project. Much of this could be a description of what went wrong with the groundnuts scheme. What is new is the underestimation of shortages of labour and managerial resources. Over-optimistic projections of labour availability are all too familiar to those working on rural development in Africa. They commonly arise from assumptions that labour is plentiful and will always be forthcoming for the family farm or at the "going wage" however low this may be. In the planning of the Kano River Project, the analysis of labour availability was based on mistaken assumptions, that had already been seriously challenged at the time the project was being designed. As so often happens, relevant evidence available locally was ignored by those responsible for the project design.

Why do such fundamental mistakes continue to be made? Why do those involved fail to learn from past experience? If it is not possible to do any better, why do such large schemes continue to be supported? One explanation of the repetition of mistakes lies in the hurried planning of large scale projects. Forrest gives an interesting example, the Anchau scheme in Nigeria, started in 1937 where "thorough preliminary work" and "integrated effort over a period of ten years" was thought to have made for a relatively successful large scale settlement project. The thorough and lengthy process of investigation and development may well have contributed to the project's success, although it is not clear that it was the only important factor, but one wonders whether the project would have appeared justified if the costs involved in such a process of planning and preparation had been included in an evaluation.

Another possible explanation for the repetition of failure lies in the career structures of those involved. Project planning tends to be in the hands of relatively young and inexperienced personnel who may not have been sufficiently exposed to the lessons of past experience. One might ask: why not? The lessons are not difficult to pass on. Moreover, this explanation does not apply to the groundnuts scheme where the complaint was precisely that such fundamental mistakes had been made by "the most experienced technical officers" in the colonial agricultural service at the time.

What seems more likely is that the explanation lies in the impossibility of designing a successful large scale project in the conditions that exist in much of rural tropical Africa at present. Large scale intervention has to be planned in the presence of too many unknowns. Furthermore, it is being undertaken in situations in which large scale projects are inappropriate. The cost of obtaining information on the basis of which one could plan with confidence is often prohibitive and the time involved is often considered too long. Moreover, these large scale interventions require large inputs of managerial and organisational resources that are scarce, they require support from well developed marketing and other institutions, and they make substantial demands on imported or locally produced inputs that are both expensive and scarce. Large scale agricultural projects are not usually of sufficiently high priority to warrant the diversion of scarce resources to the extent necessary to make them a success. However, there are alternatives that are much less expensive. There is enough experience in tropical Africa of rapid and successful growth of marketed output from small producers already operating. This provides us with a real alternative to the large scale projects that appear to have been so repeatedly unsuccessful in rural African conditions.

Large scale projects continue to be supported nevertheless. Those responsible prefer large scale projects because they are visible, relatively self-contained, they can be implemented in conditions in which participants can be controlled, and they provide relatively secure mechanisms for the extraction of surpluses and the generation of financial flows which ensure the repayment of the loans involved. The alternatives are much harder to define, they involve more difficult relationships with existing institutions and groups of producers, and they make both the extraction of surpluses and the generation of financial returns unsure.

CONFLICTS OF INTEREST, RURAL POVERTY AND THE RURAL FOOD PROBLEM

The evidence of gross failure in large scale schemes which appear to be doing so little to alleviate poverty and may indeed be increasing it is disturbing. Equally disturbing is the growing body of evidence suggesting that external intervention in rural development in tropical Africa is exacerbating poverty and famine more generally. Not only do the patently unsuccessful projects not succeed on their own terms, but these and many apparently much more successful interventions are having secondary effects that increase poverty and famine over a wider front. One of the commonest ways in which this occurs is through a decrease in the availability of food in the rural areas affected. Thus, the promotion of large scale capitalist rice farming in northern Ghana which is designed to improve the food situation in the towns, displaces traditional rural food production and encourages what food there is to flow out through newly developed marketing channels to urban areas. Serious rural food shortages and famine that are reported from this area for the first time are linked to these developments. Large scale irrigated wheat production in Nigeria does not appear likely to be very successful in meeting the urban wheat demand, but it alters income earning opportunities in the rural areas in such a way that rural food suppliers are threatened. Less radical interventions like the introduction of credit, fertilizers, or new crop varieties to existing rural producers accentuate the trends towards increasing poverty and food deprivation less obviously than in the case of the more radical interventions; but these trends are no less severe for being less obvious. The records of colonial governments that have often been accused of an excessive preoccupation with local food supplies may look good when compared with the widespread neglect of the basic food needs of the rural poor in tropical Africa today.

There is a naive view, still dominant in the African context, that rural development is in the interests of everyone concerned. This view is represented by statements such as "We are all interested in the common fight against rural poverty . . ." and "Rural development is our highest priority because the rural areas are where the majority of the poor live".

There is an assumption that development that raises income in an area raises the income of everyone in the area, certainly the incomes of the majority, and usually the incomes of the poor. Rural development projects are located in areas where there is widespread poverty in the belief that they will benefit large numbers of poor people simply by virtue of the fact that they are located in areas where large numbers of poor live. Thus, highland cash crop developments are justified on the grounds that two-thirds of the population live in highland areas when it is clear that only a very small proportion of people in those areas is at all likely to benefit. A credit project involving only a handful of farmers is justified on the grounds that it is in an area of great poverty. Similar arguments are put forward in support of fertilizer projects. There is astonishingly little recognition in rural development interventions in Africa of the possibility of differential impact among those living in the areas in which the interventions are located. A simple trickle-down analysis may be behind such lack of recognition, but there is enough evidence now for this analysis to be taken for granted no longer. The possibility of conflicts of interest involving a deterioration in the position of the very poor has to be considered more explicitly than it often is at the moment. To ignore conflicts of interest can be extremely damaging; it can encourage the wrong sorts of interventions; it can give a false impression that poverty is being tackled through rural development; and it can make it easier for intervention that is against the interests of the poor.

The fact that rural development interventions have differential impacts on different sections of the African rural population is hardly surprising. Heyer, Roberts and Williams[7] point out that *"the rural development problem"* tends to be seen in very general terms as *one* problem with essentially one solution. The solution is to get rural producers more involved in market production, by which is meant specifically production for urban and international markets. Thus, rural development programmes focus on the production of wheat or rice for the urban market, or the production of tea, cocoa or coffee for export, but seldom on augmenting the production of food for consumption within the rural areas concerned. It is assumed that subsistence consumption will take care of itself, either because production for the market can be grafted on to subsistence production without affecting it adversely, as appears to have been possible in Ghana and Nigeria earlier in the twentieth century, (although Berry[8] has an alternative view on this) or because the increase in marketing output will more than compensate, enabling producers to satisfy their subsistence needs at a more generous level through the market, as is often assumed in East Africa. All of this ignores the fact that while rural producers may gain in the aggregate, substantial groups may lose out. Aggregate increases in, say, wheat production may represent substantial increases in aggregate incomes which will more than enable rural producers to maintain consumption levels in the aggregate. However, these increases are likely to represent losses for some groups and disproportionate gains for others. It seems that as often as not the poor lose when production for the market replaces local food production without any parallel development to counter adverse effects on the local food situation in tropical African conditions at present.

There are many indirect effects of increasing participation in market exchange that tend to get ignored in the practice of rural development. One of the more obvious is the effect on the redistribution of assets, particularly land. Land concentration is often associated with intervention in rural development as one might expect. It appears to be occurring as a result of the Mumias sugar development in Kenya;[9] in northern Ghana;[10] and in central Kenya as a result of the growth of marketed output in the 1960s and 1970s.[11] Less well recognized is the fact that the development and restructuring of produce markets resulting in substantial changes in the size and direction of produce flows can be very damaging to some groups in the rural population. This has been the case in northern Ghana. It also seems likely in the case of the Kano River Project, and it has long been recognized as a danger in areas of smallholder cash crop development in Africa. The adverse effects of changes of market opportunities are beginning to be recognized more widely, as is clear from the work of Sen and others on famine,[12] but it is seldom explicitly discussed in connection with the planning and implementation of rural development interventions.

Failure to look even cursorily at the secondary effects can be responsible for the neglect of serious problems that could often be tackled if acknowledged. The displacement of local food production could be countered at least to some extent by giving support to local food production as well as production for the market. Marketing developments that encourage the flow of locally required food out of an area could be accompanied by the provision of additional storage and finance and if necessary also more direct short term measures such as physical controls over the movement of produce to ensure that enough food remains in the area at reasonable prices. This used to be common practice in colonial times, and although it may have exacerbated the problems of the food-deficit areas it is a measure that is worth considering in the short term at least. When it is the erosion of purchasing power that makes it less and less possible for the rural poor to purchase food at times of shortage the solutions required may be more fundamental. Nevertheless, there is often a lot that can be done by tackling basic food problems directly.

One might ask why so little attention is given to the rural food position these days. There has been a big change in this respect since colonial times when the complaint was that the authorities' preoccupation with food security was detrimental to important sections of the rural population. Williams[13] argues that the neglect nowadays has to do with the involvement of international capital and national urban interests preoccupied with the problem of extracting food for the urban population and exports to maintain foreign exchange earnings. For urban groups it is a question of getting the necessary food and foreign exchange in the cheapest possible way. In addition, they have an interest in the extraction of a surplus from the rural population. The surplus is threatened by policies directed towards improving the rural food position. Market participation is necessary both for the extraction of the surplus and to generate the cash flows that will enable loan finance to be repaid. Finally, market dependence is seen as a goal in itself, enabling government and other outside agencies to gain control over potentially independent rural populations whose interests will conflict at times with the interests of those seeking increased control. It is difficult to explain the current widespread neglect of rural food problems without some such argument.

THE "DELIVERY SYSTEM PROBLEM"

The new strategies for rural development rely crucially on "delivery systems" for the distribution of new technology inputs and credit. Co-operatives, government bureaucracies, parastatal institutions and even private organizations are suddenly expected to play a very much bigger part without the additional resources that might enable them to develop the capacity to handle the increased demands. Often, radical reorganization is also required. It is sometimes argued that inefficiencies are inevitable at early stages of development, that delivery systems will improve as time passes, but there is as yet little to suggest that this happening. Indeed the persistence of difficulties despite increased allocations of resources raises questions as to whether such organizations as presently constituted are able to perform the new roles expected of them. The ability of government bureaucracies to administer small farm credit is seriously in doubt, for example. The ability of co-operatives to function democratically without more radical reorganization than appears at present contemplated is also open to question.

In addition to the straightforward inefficiencies that prevent delivery systems from distributing credit, inputs and technology in sufficient quantity, there are difficulties in getting these systems to operate without a persistent bias in favour of the élite. Some of these problems are well illustrated in the case of co-operatives which continue to be encouraged despite what many would regard as a very poor record, at least as far as democratic participation is concerned. Co-operatives appear to be efficient only if heavily controlled and supervised from above, in which case they lose their resemblance to co-operatives in the sense in which the term is generally understood. Those that survive, heavily controlled from above, often with strong government support, are used to further the interests of dominant groups in the rural population. King[14] provides us with some interesting examples from northern Nigeria. Co-operatives that had become moribund were resuscitated in 1973 in the area King studied. He looked at six neighbouring villages and found that the effects of an apparently uniform policy of co-operative development were very different in each case. In every case, a locally dominant group was able to appropriate the gains available through the government supported co-operative movement, but the groups that were able to appropriate the gains and the ways in which they did so were different. Despite similar experiences in other parts of tropical Africa, co-operatives still appear to be regarded as a superior form of organisation in the context of rural development interventions.

The administration of farm credit is another example that illustrates some of the general problems of delivery systems. It appears difficult to disburse enough farm credit and even more difficult to enforce repayment once the credit has been disbursed. Furthermore, there seems to be little that can be done to counter the bias in favour of the local élite where the distribution of credit is concerned. Kenya[15] provides us with an example of credit programmes continually underspent, gross repayment problems, and what credit does get to farmers going to upper income groups, even in the small farm areas. The distribution of inputs provides us with another example of a delivery system in difficulty. Inputs arrive late or not at all. There are endless reports of bias, again in favour of upper income groups. The position is not much different with extension services.

Delivery system problems are particularly serious in a strategy that relies heavily on modern technology and purchased inputs. The reliance on purchased inputs has been particularly noticeable in recent years as more international agencies have become involved in African rural development. It can be argued that a strategy that relies heavily on purchased inputs is particularly inappropriate in tropical Africa. It certainly poses problems in a continent in which delivery systems are so relatively undeveloped.

What may be more fundamental however is the association of the systems with what is essentially a paternalist approach to rural development. Rural development interventions tend to be based on the view that those outside the rural areas know best what can and should be done. As Heyer, Roberts and Williams[16] put it, "rural development is something that is done to rural inhabitants". This can be seen in phrases such as "the need to develop the rural population" which implies that rural people are the *objects* of development. "The need to elicit rural participation" may really mean the need to get the rural population to do what the agencies want them to do, sometimes against their own interests. There is little recognition of the development that has been undertaken by rural producers themselves, often in the face of opposition from those who think they know better, trying to promote a different kind of development. There is now ample evidence of the ability of rural producers to respond to opportunities from which they stand to gain. There is also evidence of peasant resistance to changes which threaten rural standards of living even though the changes are being made in the name of rural development. Cowen[17] gives a convincing account of initiatives taken by rural producers coming into opposition with authorities promoting rural development of a different kind. Producers growing sun-dried tea come up against opposition from officials defending the official policy of support for the controlled development of factory processed tea, the financing of which is threatened by sun-dried tea production. Producers press for veterinary measures to protect exotic cattle at a time when the veterinary department refuses to support them. Another longstanding grievance in Kenya is producers' insistence on giving priority to food crops rather than cotton in areas in which official policy is in favour of cotton. Barnett[18] describes how tenants in the Gezira evade water use regulations to get better returns on scarce water resources. Coulson's account of agricultural development in Tanzania[19] is full of examples of rural producers coming up against official policy that runs directly against their interests. In many such cases it is clear that policy was based on quite false premises. Finally, Adams[20] provides us with a particularly interesting account of peasant resistance to change which is perceived to be against their interests in the Senegal River Valley. The particular interest of her account derives from the fact that the peasant association involved was unusually conscious of the conflicts which it articulated very clearly at each stage. In one of the exchanges with officials of SAED, the Senegal River Valley development authority, the peasant speaker is reported as follows:

> They had begun work before ever hearing of SAED interest in the area, and from what they had heard of SAED's activities in the Delta, it seemed that SAED-run co-operatives were not free to choose what crops they wanted to grow, and had to organise their work according to SAED specifications, which meant contracting debts for equipment, and having to grow more and more cash-crops; this was also the plight of peasants in the co-operatives of the groundnut areas.

And at a later meeting the peasant association chairman said:

> We don't reject SAED; we want to be free to say what we want to buy, and to keep our own accounts. We don't need much fertilizer, because the soil is good. It's not old soil. SAED would say, take 20 sacks, 30 sacks – then we're in debt. We don't want that.

The peasant association clearly understood what was involved in being taken over by SAED and it resisted strongly.

The idea that rural development might be initiated jointly with the rural population, or even that it might follow the lead given by the rural population acting as independent agents conscious of their own interests, is still far from being accepted in tropical Africa at present. Where the notion of partnership is suggested the rural population is always the subordinate "partner". Yet very real conflicts of interest are at stake, and the interests of different groups in the rural population are suppressed at present in most rural development strategies.

RURAL DEVELOPMENT EVALUATIONS

Fundamental conflict of interest questions are seldom, if ever, raised in the evaluations of rural development that are undertaken, often extremely carefully. This is because the evaluations tend to be undertaken within too narrow a frame of reference. The evaluations can and do show up the cases of gross failure, where the intervention fails by its own criteria. What they do not show up is the failure to alleviate poverty, and the aggravation of poverty where this occurs. These are questions beyond the terms of reference of most evaluations. We are suggesting that these questions should be brought to the fore. Both the design and the evaluation of rural development interventions must be based, at least partly, on analyses of conflicts of interest, paying particular attention to the position of the really poor. If rural development programmes cannot be shown to be alleviating poverty in the rural areas, one should ask (1) exactly what they are achieving and (2) whether this is something with which those responsible would want to continue to be associated.

NOTES AND REFERENCES

[1] *Rural Development in Tropical Africa*, edited by J. Heyer, P. Roberts and G. Williams, forthcoming from Macmillan, 1980. Many of the ideas in this paper have been developed in discussion with co-editors and authors of this book, although none of them shares responsibility for this particular paper.

[2] A. Coulson "Agricultural Policies in Mainland Tanzania 1946–76", *Review of African Political Economy*, 1978, and forthcoming in the Heyer, Roberts and Williams 1980 volume.

[3] A. Adams "The Senegal River Valley: What Kind of Change?" *Review of African Political Economy*, 1978, and forthcoming in the 1980 volume.

[4] B. Beckman "The Agrarian Basis of the Post-Colonial State, Ghana 1951–78", forthcoming in the 1980 volume.

[5] T. Forrest "Agricultural Policies in Nigeria 1910–78", forthcoming in the 1980 volume.

[6] T. Wallace, "Development Through Irrigation: An Overview of the Kano River Project, Nigeria", forthcoming in the 1980 volume.

[7] H. Heyer, P. Roberts and G. Williams "Rural Development", forthcoming in the 1980 volume.

[8] S. Berry *Cocoa, Custom and Socio-Economic Change in Rural Western Nigeria*, 1975.

[9] G. Holtman and A. Hazlewood *Aid and Inequality in Kenya*, 1976, p. 156.

[10] A. Shepherd "Agrarian Change in Northern Ghana: Public Investment, Capitalist Farming and Famine", forthcoming in the 1980 volume.

[11] J. Heyer, "Agricultural Development Policy in Kenya from the Colonial Period to 1975", forthcoming in the 1980 volume, among others.

[12] A.K. Sen "Starvation and Exchange Entitlements: A General Approach and its Application to the Bengal Famine", *Cambridge Journal of Economics*, March 1977, and forthcoming monograph, *Poverty and Famines: An Essay on Entitlement and Deprivation*, Oxford University Press.

[13] A. Williams "The World Bank and the Peasant Problem", forthcoming in the 1980 volume.

[14] R. King "Co-operative Policy and Village Development in Northern Nigeria", forthcoming in the 1980 volume.

[15] Heyer op. cit.

[16] Heyer, Roberts and Williams op. cit.

[17] M.P. Cowen "Commodity Production in Kenya's Central Province", forthcoming in the 1980 volume.

[18] T. Barnett "The Gezira Scheme Black Box or Pandora's Box", forthcoming in the 1980 volume.

[19] Coulson op. cit.

[20] Adams op. cit.

DISCUSSION OPENING – WILSON NGUYO

Rural development programmes have come to be a regular activity of virtually all governments and many non-governmental agencies in developing countries. Such programmes are viewed as a vehicle for alleviating rural poverty among subsistence rural communities. Dr Heyer's paper is therefore very timely and treats a subject that is very dear to the hearts of many, especially in our association.

The author has had considerable experience in the area of rural development and her word cannot be taken lightly. It is therefore all the more disturbing to note that, after reviewing rural development programmes for a period spanning several decades over a good number of countries in both East and West Africa, she comes to the conclusion that not only have large scale projects been failures, on the basis of nearly all criteria, but rural development programmes in general have actually led to a reduction in the incomes of the poorest while disproportionately benefiting those better off who need help least, thus widening the already wide income disparities. Even more disturbing is the worsening food situation.

Dr Heyer identifies a number of factors which have contributed to the failure of both large scale projects and rural development programmes in general. I shall not go into the details of these except to note that many are fairly elementary and avoidable but so far experience shows that the same mistakes continue to be repeated. The inevitable conclusion one arrives at is that the rural population would have been better off without any development programmes.

I have a few observations to make on Dr Heyer's analysis.

1   I would argue that Dr Heyer has been too ambitious in preparing this paper. She has covered too long a span of time, too extensive a region and too many programmes and projects to be able to give an in depth evaluation of such programmes and projects. She has therefore tended to overgeneralize her analysis and her conclusions.

I would agree with her that many projects were failures. But I would argue that some projects were successful, either on the basis of some or all criteria. I would also agree with her that it is enlightening to point out the failures and the causes of such failures. But I would argue that a mention of successes and lessons to be drawn from them would give a more balanced picture.

What I am saying, in short, is that Dr Heyer has given an unduly pessimistic view. Let me illustrate my point by referring to one project – The Land Settlement Programme started in 1960 in Kenya. The objectives of the programme were:

(a) To increase the agricultural productivity of the land involved through more intensive farming. It was expected to achieve a 50 per cent increase in productivity in each of the schemes at maturity in four years.

Results: Some schemes met the targets and a few even exceeded the targets. But the majority failed. The authorites concerned have drawn usefully on the experience so gained to help the less successful schemes and individual holders.

(b) To increase employment on the land involved and therefore ease unemployment in the country. It was expected that the land would support twice as many people after settlement as it supported before settlement.

Result: Some 40,000 families, the majority of whom were landless and unemployed were settled in the programme. It is doubtful that the population supported on the land was doubled and, indeed, the programme did not make a significant contribution to the unemployment problem. But the equity aspect of it was most appropriate.

(c) To effect a rapid and orderly transfer of land from foreign ownership to indigenous ownership. Kenya was at the point of attaining independence and this was indeed the most important reason.

Result: This objective was attained. As a result, a desirable degree of political stability prevailed, thus creating a good climate for a vigorous economic activity, both in the rural and the urban sectors.

In conclusion, the settlement programme could not be described as an unqualified failure.

2   Judging by the currently prevailing mood in the developing countries and, indeed, the world as a whole, rural development projects will continue to be undertaken. The question is what contribution can we, as agricultural economists, make to minimise repetition of past mistakes and to bring about greater success in future? This is a very difficult question seeing how little success we have achieved in the past. I have one or two observations to make.

(a) First, government leaders are in a hurry to undertake programmes. They want to be seen to be doing something to solve the problems afflicting their peoples. Economists are often accused of taking too long to arrive at meaningful advice on the possible outcomes of alternative courses of action in rural development. They have also been accused of giving rather theoretical, operationally imprecise reports which cannot be put into operation without considerable reorganization.

If we want to be effective, we must meet the challenges implied in these statements rather than take defensive positions.

(b) If we as agricultural economists want dramatic changes in the performance of rural development programmes, it is unlikely that we shall get them on the basis of marginal improvements in the conventional design and implementation techniques we have so far been using. We must come up with new approaches. In this connection I find suggestions made by Niels Roling, Fred Chege and Joe Ascroft interesting. These individuals were based at the University of Nairobi Institute of Development Studies and did considerable empirical work on rural development programmes in Kenya, especially on the Kenya Special Rural Development Programme. They were especially concerned with the problem of equity. They suggest what they refer to as "a feasible alternative route to equitable rural development". They suggested the essential features of such a development strategy as:

1. Vigorous continuation of the development of welfare services which are available to all, such as roads, water, electricity, health services, schools, recreational facilities, etc.
2. Vigorous development of agricultural innovation packages especially adapted to small farms, combined with strict control of preemptive production by big companies or large farms using such innovations.
3. Rechannelling of extension, credit and marketing services to those small-holders who lag behind in development so as to enable them to adopt the innovation packages. (The "progressive" farmer will forge ahead anyway with less assistance.)
4. Strong emphasis on group extension over individual extension methods to increase coverage of scarce government resources so as to enable inclusion of small farmers.
5. Support of the elements listed above by
     (a) imposition of a ceiling on land ownership and redistribution of excess land.
     (b) the vigorous promotion of contraceptive methods, and
     (c) the development of rural industries.

Time does not allow going into detailed discussion of these issues. Neither can one guarantee that such a strategy will definitely lead to success if adopted. But I hope it does stimulate thoughts into possible innovations in rural development planning.

Finally, I would like to re-emphasize three or four points mentioned above:

(a) Concentration of extension resources on the "forgotten" farmer is likely to pay off more in the long run since he has, in comparison with the "progressive" farmer, a greater unexploited potential than the farmer who is already farming relatively efficiently.
(b) Innovations must be presented in packages that present a favourable mix of inputs and services. Otherwise, the problem of a limiting factor or bottleneck will continue to frustrate efforts to improve the performance of rural development programmes.

(c) Education is one of the most powerful weapons against rural poverty. Universal education, up to a reasonable level of literacy, available to all is likely to have a substantial pay-off.

(d) Rural development programmes must be based on empirical results if maximum results are to be achieved with limited human and material resources. Training in agricultural economics must take this into account.

GENERAL DISCUSSION – RAPPORTEUR: A. SEN

The discussion was opened with many participants observing that the author was too critical. It was argued that many large scale projects were indeed successful. The author had referred to the groundnuts scheme for a large part of her discussion. This was too old an example and indeed was so heavily dominated by political factors as to have been known to be a failure even before it started. There were examples of successes, such as the Gezira scheme, and not all projects ignore local resources.

The discussion then went on to conceptual points. It was suggested that there was a confusion in identifying failure with the failure of certain groups to gain. Could we really afford to concentrate on special groups? Where there not always trade-offs? Should we not give proper emphasis to comparative advantage rather than protect local agriculture? What did the author mean by "large scale" – plantations or large investment? The former presented problems but these should not be confused with rural development involving the latter.

On the question of actual implementation, two types of points were raised. First, it was asked who was to blame? Large scale projects are usually preceded by feasibility studies – the failures must be at the design stage. Local personnel are generally ignored and, later, blamed for not being competent. Could we not have more interaction with local administrators as a substitute for consultation with farmers? The heterogeneity, which the author admits, means that we should have a longer time frame, i.e. give the projects a chance before declaring them failures, especially because data gaps make evaluation difficult. Secondly, some participants felt that the author was not sufficiently aware of the adaptibility of African farmers – although they are distrustful of strangers, they would not be so stupid as to destroy their base of subsistence.

In the midst of this critical response one participant felt obliged to support the author. Most models were biased by neoclassical assumptions which were not very suitable to underdeveloped countries. The author had made a start by appreciating conflicts of interest. What was needed was greater emphasis of political questions and dialectic between politics and economics.

In reply, the author apologized for not being able to discuss individual questions because of a shortage of time. On the accusation of being too critical, she said that there was no intention of being despairing but she did want to make a strong plea against complacence. True, everything had not failed in every way. Success or failure depended on the criteria one chose. This was at the heart of the disagreements that the discussion revealed. She had chosen to focus on the increasing incidence of poverty and famine. This is now well documented although possibly Kenya suffers less than other African countries.

ULF RENBORG

Energy Analysis of Agriculture
Biology or Economics – a survey of approaches, problems and traps

BACKGROUND: AGRICULTURE IN THE NATIONAL ENERGY SYSTEM

The successive rises in crude oil prices since 1973 and the increased awareness of the risks associated with nuclear power stations – so dramatically emphasized by the Harrisburg incident this spring – have brought the energy supply question to the forefront of economic and political discussions.

This debate is difficult to survey and it is confusing. One reason is that so many questions are at the same time brought into the discussion. Here are some common examples: Economize with finite energy sources! Lower economic growth to save energy! Lower use of nuclear energy to protect man from radiation risks! Lower use of fossil energy sources to protect environment from sulphuric acid fall-out! The claims show a mixture of legitimate requirements, half-truths and mistakes and are often incompatible. Another reason for confusion, even in the educated part of the debate, is the wide differences in background among participants. Of specific interest for this author is that certain science writers[1] and economists come to such different conclusions as to what is meant by a desirable development of energy use in society.

This paper aims at shedding at least some light on this question as it shows up in an analysis of agriculture in the national energy system.

Figure 1 gives a simple picture of agriculture in the national energy system. From this is seen that agriculture uses energy and produces/can produce biomass for the energy system. These are the two roles that agriculture can play in the energy system of a nation.

Figure 2 indicates that agriculture's role in the national energy system varies from country to country. Investigations show that agriculture in industrialized country situations – (1) and (2) – consumes a share of total support energy smaller than its contribution to GNP. In this situation energy saving within agriculture is thus of minor national interest although possibly of some importance within agriculture itself. On the other hand agriculture *can* play an important role as producer of energy

231

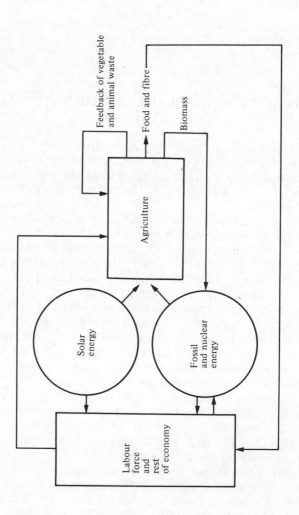

FIG. 1   *Agriculture in the national energy system*

FIG. 2   *Agriculture in four national situations*

	Small acreage of land per caput	Large acreage of land per caput. Ample water supply
Agriculture small part of the economy	(1) Energy saving and biomass production not feasible in agriculture	(2) Biomass production feasible in agriculture
Agriculture large part of the economy	(3) Energy saving feasible in agriculture	(4) Energy saving and biomass production feasible in agriculture

Complicating factor: national supply of fossil energy resources

resources as biomass. This reaches major importance for the nation only when large acreages of land per capita are available. Situation (2) has potentials in boreal temperate zones – USSR, Canada, Scandinavia. In developing countries situations – (3) and (4) – energy saving is important in agriculture where it takes the form of labour intensive production and efficient use of wastes for fuel in situation (3). Biomass production has potentials in situation (4), of which Brazil is a possible example.

A meaningful analysis of agriculture in a country's energy system can only be made against the goals guiding the political decisions in each country. Appropriate goal dimensions are economic growth, low vulnerability of fuel supply, environmental control and solidarity with future generations and developing countries. Countries with different weights in these dimensions and in different situations as of Figure 2 will come up with quite different pictures of agriculture's role in the national energy system. One reason for differences in approaches to analysis of the energy system by science writers and economists may well be the differences in attitudes to these various goals.

ORIGIN OF ENERGY ANALYSIS (EA)

Economists and engineers have well established methods to analyse energy systems like national energy supply schemes, power plants, industrial energy supply plans etc. Investment calculations, input–output studies, studies of price and income elasticities of supply and demand have long been used for these purposes.

In the beginning of the 1970s the effectiveness of these methods were questioned by a group of mainly natural scientists and ecologists.[1] They observed that the processes of industrialization characteristic for economic growth of nations are using increasing amounts of energy and that this energy above all comes from finite resources like fossil fuels (oil, natural gas, coal) and uranium. They also pointed out that the world's crude oil deposits would be rapidly emptied if the industrialization process went on as they observed. This means, they pointed out, that the prosperity of today's industrialized countries have a shaky foundation, not to speak of the prosperity of future generations and that of underdeveloped countries. To this can be added the more and more apparent risks of nuclear power stations. Man's future energy source has therefore to become – and rapidly become, they claim – based on renewable energy sources like direct use of solar energy, or energy from waterpower, wind and production of biomass.

From various scientists in this group were developed alternative methods for analysis of energy systems. An important early contribution came from the ecologist Howard T. Odum (1971). He analysed the energy requirements to build and run energy systems based on finite energy sources and developed a specific language – with flow charts and symbols – by which to analyse these systems. Energy systems have also early been treated by Chapman (1974). Other authors analysed the total energy content – from primary products to final products – in various capital good, cars, buildings, etc. Early contributions in this field was made by Hannon (1972), Makhijani and Lichtenberg (1972) and Berry and Fels (1973). Early studies of energy flow through agriculture have been made by Pimentel et al (1973), Leach and Slesser (1973). An early and important forerunner with thoughts related on thermodynamics and economics is Georgescu-Roegen (1971). He summarizes his criticism of economic analysis in two long articles in *Ecologist* (1975). In 1974 and 1975 at two meetings arranged by IFIAS, The International Federation of Institutes for Advanced Studies, a set of common recommendations for Energy Analysis, here called EA, were formulated (IFIAS, 1974 and 1975). It is clear from these two later documents that EA is a young field of science which is not yet a well-defined discipline. Its practitioners are physicists, biologists and ecologists. It studies "societal use of a single aggregate resource, energy". It traces quantitatively "the changes in the thermodynamic potentials of materials as they pass through successive process stages". One of its goals is to "indicate where reductions in the energy requirements for total processes could be made". These are looked upon as "the pressure points for technological change". Energy is thought of as being provided by fuels or by renewable sources such as solar, fluid or hydro power generation *and also* as the flow of thermodynamic potential associated with the material flows in a process (IFIAS report 9, 1975, pp. 3–4).

It is this EA we are going to study here. We concentrate on EA of agriculture. The reason for economists to do so is twofold. Analysis of energy problems with EA has met serious attention in political circles and official documents (Webb and Pearce, 1975). EA challenges the economic analysis of energy questions.

ELEMENTS OF ENERGY ANALYSIS OF AGRICULTURE

Energy

In EA all inputs into a production process (e.g. wheat or milk production), an energy system (e.g. production of biomass and energy delivery from it) or a sector (e.g. agriculture) are measured as Gross Energy Requirement, GER. For any input GER is the total energy required in all parts of the chain of production processes from primary products (oil, ore, etc.) to the final input as used in the system studied. GER is counted as the free energy of combustion of natural energy sources corresponding to all energy inputs required (IFIAS 1974 and 1975). It is therefore also possible to say that the energy requirement of an input is a direct measure of the withdrawal from the global stock of finite natural energy resources it represents (Nielsen and Rasmussen 1977). Energy inputs from water and nuclear power stations are counted as the corresponding amounts of natural energy resources.

Solar radiation is a natural flux resource from which a flow of energy occurs over extended periods of time. The potential of all energy flux source refers to the maximum average rate of supply of free energy (IFIAS, 1974).

In most EA of agriculture the input and use of solar energy is not counted (for example Pimentel et al, 1973, Leach 1976, Nielsen and Rasmussen 1977). There are three reasons given for this by energy analysts. The first is that EA deals with the use of finite, mostly fossil, energy resources. Solar energy is not, it is said, a technically useful source of energy (Leach 1976). The second is that including solar energy in the study would make it "little more than a study of photosynthetic conversions of solar energy to food energy, and could say nothing about the effects on fuel usage of changes in methods of producing food" (Leach 1976). The third reason is that solar radiation is available in a constant flow for use or non-use, and thus can be treated as a fixed resource.

The third objection to including solar energy does have a meaning in EA of an acre of a specific crop or cropping system (Pimentel et al 1973) and parts of Leach's (1976) cropping budgets calculated per acre. In cases where the whole agricultural sector is analysed none of the objections are valid. This is due to the fact that direct substitution between solar energy and direct energy inputs from finite sources exist, for example in roughage and grain drying in wet and cold climates. Similar substitutions are also possible in choices between low fertilizer inputs on a large acreage or high fertilizer inputs on a smaller acreage to produce a given amount of grain. How solar radiation should be treated in EA of agriculture is obviously determined by the way in which the system under study is specified. It cannot be determined without such a specification.

Factors of production

In cases where energy from solar radiation is not included in EA of agriculture – and these are the majority of cases – *land* is not included as a

factor of production in EA. This is also true for the minerals and other primary products, other than fossil fuels and uranium deposits, usually included in land in socio-economic considerations. Phosphate and potassium for fertilizers, iron ore, bauxite limestone and clay, and other basic resources included in buildings, and machines have thus no value in EA. Nor has the alternative value of land for other use. Land is thus in EA counted in its role as deliverer of finite fossil fuel and uranium resources.
Capital is, as we understand what has been said earlier, only counted as the energy input it represents. Webb and Pearce (1975) have pointed out that in doing so EA does not separate energy inputs into durable capital and into productive inputs for direct use. In doing so EA misses a fundamental characteristic of the meaning of capital, namely that "capital generates a flow of goods in excess of the original value of the capital" (Webb and Pearce 1975, p. 320).

Human *labour* is in EA of agriculture either not counted as an input at all (Leach 1976, Nielsen and Rasmussen 1977, Slesser 1978) or as the metabolizable energy in food (Pimentel et al 1973) or as number of hours of labour (Renborg, Uhlin et al 1975). This situation is confusing and can be traced back to the conventions adopted by IFIAS in 1974 (IFIAS 1974, pp. 46–50). The IFIAS's workshop of 1974 did not solve this problem. It agreed that "the figure of real interest is how much in the way of energy sources was consumed to furnish the life support system of the man that works on the process. . . . However, once this approach is accepted a further problem arises. Does one include in the energy for the life support of the worker, only food, or also his family, house, car, etc?" (IFIAS 1974, p. 46). After calculating through a series of agricultural examples the workshop concluded that energy inputs associated with labour – according to their viewpoints – were of negligible size as compared to other energy inputs in developed and industrial economies but of importance – and as a matter of fact often the only energy inputs – in primitive and low intensive agriculture. Thus the following convention was adopted:

> Where the analysis refers to developed or industrial economies it is not necessary to consider the energy for life-support of manpower. Where the analysis considers low intensity agriculture manpower considerations play an important role in the calculations. (IFIAS 1974, p. 50).

This convention is fatal on two accounts, irrespective of how much energy is associated with labour inputs. First, any comparison of energy use between systems with different intensities simply does not make sense. This can be seen in Leach (1976) where these kinds of comparisons are made on page 8. To be able to make a reasonable analysis of this material Leach consequently has to introduce labour as a factor of production counted in hours on page 9. Second, any comparison over time including a change in technology of the common type which replaces capital for labour requires some way of allocating energy to the diminishing labour input. Pimentel et al (1973) has realized this and made such an allocation. However, by only counting the food input the real nature, also in energy terms, of structural change in agriculture does not show up in their analysis.[2]

It is not possible for this author to come to any other conclusion than that EA has to adopt a new convention regarding the treatment of energy requirement for labour. Approximately the following might be considered: Input of human labour should be accounted for by counting the Gross Energy Requirement necessary to furnish the total life support system – food, family, house, etc. – of the man that works on the process.

Energy flow through agriculture
EA can result in pictures of the energy flow through agriculture like the one in Figure 3.

This figure indicates that the flow registered adds features not included in EA conventions. By including solar radiation substitution of fertilizers for land over time is shown. Human labour has been drastically substituted by help energy and imported feed. Indications of waste products, mainly straw, back to the field and of the stream of feed to animal production raises questions as to the efficient use of these products. The same is true for manure and wasted heat, produced by animals. This enrichment of the picture stems from the aim of the EA in this case, to identify points in the agricultural system where research efforts could bring possible improvements. For this use it is less fatal that the output of the system is measured only in energy units. This is very daring, considering differences in protein content per energy unit of various products and in protein quality, for example between vegetable and animal products. EAs of agriculture also seldom push the analysis so far. Either the analysis only covers the input side (for example Nielsen and Rasmussen 1977) or give the products in energy *and* protein units (like Leach 1976).

Energy units or costs?
As we can see from what has been already said EA is a calculation of the technical flow of resources through a system or a production process. The selection of the energy unit to aggregate inputs and outputs includes a distrust of prices formed in a market economy as reliable decision variables by the builders of the EA. Thus for example Slesser says 1975: "Energy analysts believe that it makes sense to measure the cost of things done, not in money, which is after all nothing more than a highly sophisticated value judgement, but in terms of the thermodynamic potentials". Hannon 1975, says that "in the long run we must adopt energy as a standard of value and perhaps even afford legal rights". (Citations after Webb and Pearce 1975.)

Webb and Pearce (1975), also point out that cost calculations – with shadow prices – are in economics also possible without market determined prices. Mäler (1977) points out that it may very well be that today's prices of fossil energy resources underestimate the importance and thus

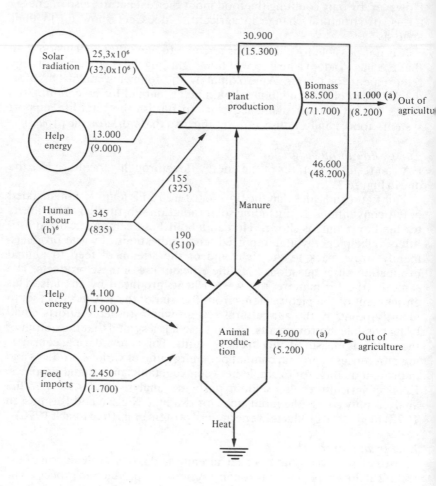

a) food products for human consumption

FIG. 3   *Energy flow through Swedish agriculture 1956 and 1972 (KWh)*

the value future generations will place on these resources if saved for their use. This does not, however, exclude expressing energy flows in cost terms better adjusted to more realistic social costs of fossil fuels. The economists' point here is that EA does not offer a better weighting system.

This can be seen in Figure 3 where energy in solar radiation fossil fuel, electricity, feed inputs with certainly different value in production are measured in the same energy units. It is even more obvious on the output side where vegetable and animal food for human consumption is also measured in energy units.

Criteria of optimality
EA can mainly be used to describe the flow of (finite) energy resources through a system. However, the majority of EA studies include comparisons of energy use between productive processes or production systems. These comparisons indicate prescriptive claims in EA. In the comparisons processes are usually *ranked* according to some measure of output per unit of energy input. This implies that some kind of optimality criterion is visualized in EA and that this includes selection of alternative production processes or systems so as to minimize the use of finite energy resources.

A common ranking measure is the energy ratio (Er) where – in its simplest form – the output of a process or system in energy terms (Eo) is expressed per unit of Gross Energy Requirement (Ei) of the process or system, i.e. $Er = Eo/Ei$. In studies of the food system Eo generally is expressed as the nutritive energy content of edible food for humans (Leach 1976) or metabolisable energy (Pimentel et al 1973, Slesser, Lewis and Edwardson 1977). Energy ratios are often supplemented (Leach 1976) or substituted (Slesser, Lewis and Edwardson 1977) by ratios showing the produced weight of crude protein per unit of GER.

We understand from this that the ranking criterion is a sheer technical entity. This means that it does not contain any other consumer preference than saving finite energy. As Webb and Pearce (1975) point out this "introduces the idea that energy as a constraint on economic activity is more important than any other constraint" and that selection of policies with low energy input could very well mean that policies with high total resource costs were selected.

As we have seen earlier, EA rejects the price mechanism of the market system to act as signals for supply and demand of energy. With the ranking criterion chosen EA does not replace this system with any signal system of comparable sensitivity. It is also obvious that both Ei and Eo are non-homogeneous entities. Energy sources like oil, natural gas, coal and biomass have values for man in other relative proportions than their energy content. Buildings, machinery and cars also have values in other proportions than the Gross Energy Requirements for their production. The energy content of outputs like wheat and potatoes, beans and fish, meat and eggs also have vastly different relative values in human consumption than their relative nutritive energy values.

Important to note is that energy ratios do not account for the meaning of time in production and consumption. This is closely related to the treatment in EA of optimal use of finite resources, which requires a final section of its own. Our conclusion so far is that EA does not offer an optimality criterion more powerful than other available techniques to allocate scarce resources.

Fossil fuel, biomass and the optimal use of finite resources
Both as user of energy and as potential producer of biomass agriculture has a clear interest in how scarce fossil fuel really is and what is meant by an optimal use of this scarce – and in some time-perspective obviously finite – resource. EA practitioners mean that "economics has no real mechanism for coping with resource depletion" (Leach 1976, p. 4). When we turn to EA for help in economizing with the finite energy resource the only simple answer is: as fossil fuel is a finite energy source the best thing is to use as small an input as possible of it to make it last as long as possible.

As has been pointed out by among others Beckerman (1974) and Webb and Pearce (1975) this answer does not take into account at least four important circumstances.

The first is that all historical experience shows that estimations of current reserves of finite resources have been underestimations. This is the consequence of the fact that calculations of available reserves are based on current prices and that intensified prospecting and lower grade deposits become profitable when scarcity raises prices.

The second is that two important feed-back mechanisms start when supply cannot meet demand. The price will rise and make producers and consumers adjust their demand by decreasing energy consumption and substituting labour for energy. Also the technological development is redirected which in the long run means that the new technique is less energy-consuming than the old.

The third circumstance is that intergenerational comparisons of the utility of energy resources and of welfare are extremely complicated. Beckerman (1974) illustrates this by asking the following question: What is best . . . "that ten million families become better off during one hundred years in the future or that one hundred families become better off during the coming ten million years? How much of the former are we prepared to give up for a very uncertain chance to the latter?" (translated from the Swedish edition). In shorter time perspectives economic theory offers a well developed system for intertemporal addition of inputs and outputs which give more satisfactory results than EA when comparing investments in alternative energy systems.

The fourth point is also put forward by Beckerman (1974) when he asks: "If the finite energy sources will one day be depleted are we then really facing a catastrophe?" Man will then most probably develop new ways of life of a type we cannot imagine today. In earlier situations of this type agriculture replaced the hunter-gatherer culture.

NOTES

[1] I.e. Odum, Pimentel, Slesser, Leach.

[2] Pimentel et al. (1973) associated labour inputs with that part of total food intake which is assumed to be metabolized during working time. This means that the production does not need to pay – in energy terms – for food requirements outside working hours. Nor is it necessary to account for food requirements during childhood and old age, not to mention energy in clothing, housing and private transportation.

This means that Pimentel et al. in their EA hire a naked slave at 18 years of age and dismiss him at 65 and only guarantee his food for his working hours. The consequences of the accounting method are obviously absurd.

SELECTED BIBLIOGRAPHY

Beckerman, W. 1974 *Two Cheers for the Affluent Society*, (Swedish edition 1975).

Bergman, L. and Carling, A. 1977 ((Energiskatten och ekonomisk utveckling", *Ekonomisk Debatt*, Vol. 5, No. 7.

Berry, R.S. and Fels, M.F. 1973 "The Energy Cost of Automobiles. Science and Public Affairs", in *Bulletin of the Atomic Sci*.

Chapman, P.F. 1974 "Energy Costs: A review of methods", *Energy Policy*, Vol. 2, p. 91.

Georgescu-Roegen, N. 1971 "The Entrophy Law and the Economic Problem", Distinguished Lecture Series No. 1, Dept. of Economics, University of Alabama.

Georgescu-Roegen, N. 1975 "Energy and Economist Myths, Part 1", *Ecologist*, Vol. 5, No. 5; "Part 2", *Ecologist*, Vol. 5, No. 7.

Hannon, B.M. 1972 "Bottles, Cans, Energy", *Environment*, Vol. 14, No. 2.

Hannon, B.M. 1975 "Energy conservation and the consumer", *Sci*, Vol. 189.

International Federation of Institutes for Advanced Studies (IFIAS), 1974 "Energy Analysis", Report No. 6.

International Federation of Institutes for Advanced Studies (IFIAS), 1975 "Energy Analysis and Economics", Report No. 9.

Leach, G. 1976 *Energy and food production*, Guildford, Surrey.

Mäler, K.G. 1977 "Varför energipolitik", *Economisk Debatt*, Vol. 5, No. 7.

Makhijani, A.B. and Lichtenberg, A.I. 1972 "Energy and wellbeing", *Environment*, Vol. 14, No. 5.

Nielsen, A.H. and Rasmussen, S. 1977 "En kartlaegning af den primaere jordbrugssektors energiforbrug", Økonomisk Institut, Verterinaer- og landbohøjskolen, Köpenhamn.

Odum, H.T. 1971 *Environment, Power and Society*, Wiley.

Pimentel, D. et al, 1973 "Food Production and the Energy Crisis", *Science*, Vol. 182, p. 443.

Renborg, U. Uhlin, H.E. et al. 1974 "Resursflöden i svenskt jord- och skogsbruk 1956 o 1976 med tonvikt på energiströmmar", Rapp 64, inst för ekonomi o statistik, Lantbrukshögskolan.

Slesser, M. 1975 "Accounting for energy", *Nature*, Vol. 254.

Slesser, M. 1978 "Energy Analysis: Its Utility and Limits", IIASA Research Memo, RM-78-46.

Slesser, M., Lewis, C. and Edwardson, N. 1977 "Energy systems analysis for food policy", *Food Policy*, May 1977.

Webb, M. and Pearce, D. 1975 "The economics of energy analysis", *Energy Pol*, 1975.

DISCUSSION OPENING – STEWART H. LANE

May I begin by complimenting Professor Renborg on his interesting, important and timely paper. I am sure that the availability of energy and how the limited supplies of it should be allocated are matters of vital concern to all countries represented at this Conference.

In opening the discussion on this paper I should make it clear that I cannot claim any expertise in addressing the issues relating to the conservation and use of energy. However, Renborg's paper has raised a number of questions which I believe agricultural economists will need to give much more attention to in the immediate future. But first let me summarize very briefly what appeared to me to be the main thrust of his paper.

He described the approach used by the biologists (Energy Analysis) in determining the optimum use of energy resources in a society, especially as it relates to the agricultural sector. In the context of their analysis energy refers to the use of finite resources, mainly fossil fuels.

He contrasts this approach with the traditional one used by economists and draws attention to the limitations of the EA approach. He notes especially its disregard of the implications which restriction of energy use will have on the combination of factor inputs (land, labour and capital) and thus on economic efficiency and points out that the fundamental differences in these two approaches result in very different, often conflicting, energy policy recommendations.

Some of the major differences in these two approaches would appear to the following:

Firstly, EA views saving finite energy as the most important economic activity. Thus the rate of utilization of finite energy is the sole criterion by which one measures the desirability of any production process or energy policy. Economic analysis, on the other hand, tends to rely on the price mechanism as the regulator of economic activity. It assumes that consumer preferences operating through the market mechanism will result in the best allocation of resources.

Secondly, EA appears to attach little significance to the concept of time preference. For it the decision rule for energy use is simple and straightforward – "use as little as possible so as to make it last as long as possible". In contrast, Economics converts future income flows to present values. These discounted values are then used as the basis for evaluating alternative resource use patterns.

Thirdly, EA assumes there is little possibility, or at least attaches little significance to the possibility, of developing new and alternative sources of energy. Indeed the significance of a major existing resource (coal) is often minimized because of its deleterious environmental effects. This assumption leads biologists to recommend the substitution of labour intensive production systems for more mechanized systems.

I suspect that economists as a group are less pessimistic than the biologists concerning the possibilities of developing alternative energy sources whether it be nuclear, solar or other forms we are not yet aware of.

In the foregoing brief listing of the main features of the EA and economic approaches for evaluating energy use I have no doubt exaggerated the differences between them. However, I have done so deliberately on the assumption that by so doing, and by presenting them as a dichotomy, it will help to bring the key issues into sharper focus.

My reading of Renborg's paper leads me to wonder whether either the biologist's or the economist's approach is the right one, or whether a middle ground would not be preferable. It is a well known fact that North America uses a disproportionate share of the world's energy resources in relation to its population and to its developed energy resources. Irrespective of whether we can afford to purchase our energy needs at world market prices we are being told that unless we reduce or at least limit our consumption of the available energy supply, our share of OPEC energy supplies will be further curtailed. This suggests to me that factors other than purely market forces are important considerations in determining the allocation and rate of utilization of fossil fuels today.

Similarly, within our national economies we need to examine the criteria which should be used to allocate energy among alternative uses. Can we rely on the interplay of market forces and the price mechanism to do this job or should other criteria be used? For example, in our food system the major share of the energy used is consumed in the food processing and distribution sectors – not in primary production. Should governments intervene to ensure that primary producers receive preferred access to the limited supplies? Should preference be given to grain producers relative to livestock producers because of their greater efficiency in energy conversion?

Agricultural economists will need to address a host of issues related to energy utilization and conservation in the years ahead. It seems safe to assume that energy related issues will be a dominant factor affecting the future pattern of rural change.

GENERAL DISCUSSION – RAPPORTEUR: KWAKU ANDAH

The first speaker felt that the paper had guided the audience to an analysis of the future use of energy but asked if the speaker had included horse power in his analysis. He felt that horse power was very important in energy analysis and if the speaker had not taken account of it then his energy input and output ratio would be incomplete.

Another speaker reminded participants that energy analysis was a special case of the material balance approach and should be considered merely as a tool of analysis. It should not be forgotten that the crucial aspect of energy was that we need energy to adjust ourselves to the catastrophe of energy systems. Professor Renborg was then asked what suggestion he had for the future use of energy with special reference to the ecologist and economist.

The final speaker thanked Professor Renborg for a most helpful paper but felt that agricultural economists (or economists in general) should spend much more time and care in discussing their points of view and the relevance of their skills with other (physical and biological) scientists who appear better able to communicate with each other than with social scientists. In addition to developing an analytical approach to energy problems in agriculture, an approach which can be refined within the profession, was it felt that, as a profession, agricultural economists pay sufficient attention to communicating with other scientists concerned with the energy problem?

In reply, Professor Renborg reiterated that he had only attempted to elaborate what ecologists had been saying and to relate these with the economists' role in solving these problems. He agreed that other considerations like economic and ecologic factors were all important factors in energy analysis. Since individual people have different attitudes one was bound to have different levels of appreciation as to how various factors are involved in energy analysis. He agreed with the discussion opener that market prices today do not adequately take into account the utility for future generations.

Turning to floor contributors, the speaker agreed that horse power was important but note should be taken of the fact that horse power is decreasing in importance in recent years. It is not good analysis to consider production alone but account should also be taken of food processing.

He assured the audience that whenever development takes place we always experience decreasing resources of our energy. In so far as the energy problem is concerned, the speaker stated that attempts *are* being made by agricultural economists not only to communicate with other scientists but also to develop a multi-disciplinary research approach to solving some of the problems of energy.

Participants in the discussion included: Adolf A. Weber, David Torgerson and David A.G. Green.

SECTION III

National

C.H. SHAH

Accomplishments, Present Status and Future Opportunities for Agricultural Economists in the Planning Processes in Less Developed Economies

Planning involves evolving development strategies that reflect political and economic aspirations of the nation. At the same time, to be realistic the strategies have to be based on an understanding of the economic behaviour of the people. Besides, their implementation requires knowledge and understanding of administration. Evolving strategies that satisfy all these requirements is a major challenge. In underdeveloped economies where stagnation preceded the recent planning these challenges were real and formidable. Economists, administrators and policy-makers joined in facing the new challenges of economic planning. Agricultural economists interacted with all of them. Since agriculture constituted a major sector of the developing nations, the agricultural economists were called upon to have a major share in handling the problems of planning.

Our endeavour in this paper is to highlight one aspect of the contribution of agricultural economists to the evolvement of planning strategies. We shall discuss mainly the influence of economic theory and empirical findings pertaining to understanding the working of the agricultural sector, in shaping the planning strategies. Agricultural economists were almost at the centre of this process.[1]

1 ACCOMPLISHMENTS

Contributions of agricultural economists in the planning processes of centrally planned economies and market economies varied. The contributions to planning in market economies can be divided into three distinct phases. In the initial stages emphasis was on institutional reforms, followed by a search for new and better sources of growth. Employment and poverty have engaged the greater attention of agricultural economists in the recent past. While distribution has been an underlying objective, growth has remained a primary concern of the market economies. Attempts to integrate the two have recently been intensified.

Institutional reforms: first phase

Economic planning followed the political freedom attained in the post-war period by many of the developing nations. Though emphasis on growth in planning resulted from the gap between developed and undeveloped nations, the desire of the latter to collapse decades into years in attaining higher economic level (an element of idealism following political aspirations), led to an emphasis on a distribution aspect as well. Agriculture in these nations provided a major source of income to a large section of the community and land occupied a pivotal position in agriculture. "Agrarian Unrest in South-East Asia" reflects the political yearnings of developing nations in the early stages of planning. The early contributions from agricultural economists came therefore in terms of institutional reforms. The "land reforms vs. agrarian reforms" – a definition feud was settled in favour of the latter – and the term "agrarian reform" was defined broadly to include all institutional reforms pertaining to agriculture.

Linked with agrarian reforms was co-operation. In many countries property rights in land were relics of the past alien imperialist governments. Other institutions (e.g., credit and marketing) were built around the then prevailing land-related institutional arrangements. The first step was to remove old interests in land rights which evoked unanimous response. A second logical step was taken to pass on the rights to the tillers. The removal of conventional agents in credit and marketing institutions required replacement and co-operatives were suggested as healthy alternatives, since in principle they permitted wide and equal participation by members.

Theory and empiricism: second phase

Agricultural economics acquired vigour from both theory and empirical studies. Economic theory pertaining to both statics and dynamics – the latter relating to growth – had an impact on thought development in agricultural economics.

A.   Impact of Efficiency Consideration. The neoclassical theory of markets in the context of economic statics influenced thinking regarding issues in agricultural planning. The major consideration pertained to efficiency in operation of markets. The functioning of the markets for produce, credit and land was brought under theoretical scrutiny. How efficiently or inefficiently the existing markets functioned within given institutions, was the major thrust of the scrutiny. It was believed that removal of inefficiency would make a direct contribution to growth, as it would save resources and would increase production with resources then available to the community. This search for efficiency came at a time when planning agencies were looking for a 'spark plug' effect to provide initial momentum to the engine of growth, so that the economy may move on the path of progress, in other words a take-off or threshold stage may be attained.

While land reforms continued to be a favoured component of planning for political reasons, they have remained until this day an "unfinished task". When they came under scrutiny through application of efficiency criteria, they ceased to enjoy prime importance in the armoury of the planning agency. The agricultural economists provided lukewarm support to the programme. They were not sure about the trade-off the land reforms involved between gain in distribution and loss in efficiency. The history of the debate regarding tenancy (mainly share tenancy) and production efficiency is known. The debate on grounds of theory and empirical evidence is still inconclusive. A similar position obtained regarding the relationship between scale of operation and production efficiency (i.e. size of farm and productivity input).

Institutional reforms regarding credit and marketing had from the start an emphasis on the distributional aspect; "remove exploitation by intermediaries and let the benefit of 'labour' go to the producer" was the main argument supporting reforms. It was the slow progress of reforms that later invoked theoretical investigation. Thinking on this topic drifted in favour of the existing arrangement being efficient, under constraints of "high-risk high-cost" caused by lack of communication. Hence, changing the institutional form alone was regarded as a weak alternative for improving efficiency or for even substantial distributional gain. In practice, with co-operativisation of credit and marketing, only the power structure of local politics changed. This was a new situation and tackling it was outside the competence of agricultural economists.

While scrutiny of the efficiency of operation of marketing institutions led to less firm conclusions, the accumulating empirical evidence heavily discounted the initial assumption of non-rational economic behaviour of individual producers. Studies relating to allocation of land to alternative uses, response of crop production and sales to prices and incomes revealed a surprising consistency of the individual producer's response. Instances of this type of empirical finding can be multiplied by similar findings regarding savings, borrowing and investments. Such findings nearly baffled the policy-makers as they minimized the role of policy interventions. If the economy was in low gear, despite high economic efficiency, how was development to be planned? Obviously, the pace of growth had to be quickened, but intervention was likely to upset the old equilibrium and a temporary reversal of growth was regarded a major political risk.

B.   *Growth Theory Impact*. Three major strands of growth theory that made an impact on thinking pertaining to agriculture found a way into planning. They pertain to the role of physical capital, food and human capital in aiding development.

Role of capital
Initially, the importance of investment in physical capital was emphasized by growth theories. The contributions of the Harrod-Domar model, Lewis's *Theory of Growth*, Joan Robinson's *Accumulation of Capital*, and Hicks's *Capital and Growth*, emphasized the role of capital in growth.

Under the influence of the prevailing growth theories, the role of capital came to be accepted as decisive for agriculture as well. Massive investments in agriculture in the form of gigantic irrigation dams and fertilizer factories – Damodar Valley Corporation (DVC) and Bhakhra Dam and Nangal Fertilizer Factory – were developed in India with "the biggest in Asia" label and belong to this period. The public sector investment came to be accepted readily in the field of agriculture as the contrast between the scale of investment in the public sector and that by individual farmers was obvious.

The agricultural economists in India played a critical role with regard to public investment in agriculture. Their conviction arose not from capital-output-ratio related theory alone; it was rooted in a social versus private benefits (and costs) perspective. If policy makers had been guided by direct-return criteria, few gigantic irrigation dams would have been constructed. Immense indirect social benefits made these investments economically feasible. What initially was an approach has now developed into a discipline and with several refinements has found national and international acceptance for non-market investment decisions. While the logic of massive investments was convincing, the programme faced rough weather owing to the long gestation period of large capital projects. Since in agriculture the decision regarding utilization of new irrigation facilities rested finally with the tiny producer, the total gestation period was much longer than the technological one.

The massive investment operation met opposition from the wage-goods theory which can be traced to Ricardo. The theory acquired new meaning when a wage-goods multiplier extension was developed. Lewis's dual economy model and its extension, particularly by Rani and Fei, came up with a strategy involving intersectoral transfer of labour. Transfer of labour involved transfer of food and if the two did not match, a wage goods gap would develop. In substance, these theoretical developments emphasized the primacy of agriculture. Since immediate expansion of agricultural production would require climbing up the Ricardian cliff of diminishing returns, international transfer of food as a catalyst was commended for the intervening period.

Micro-level planning
Agricultural economists perceived a stellar role of the individual producer as a decision-maker in regard to the use of inputs and levels and composition of outputs. Even if market prices provided general guidance for decision-making, increased access to an expanding resource base and to new knowledge about better methods of production would improve production efficiency. The agricultural extension services were introduced with this objective from the start of the planning process. However, their contribution during early years was limited.

A new slant on agriculture in growth theory, strengthened the search for sources that would yield immediate results for raising farm production and micro-level planning came to be emphasized in this context. Its logic was simple: to help the producer it was necessary to identify the problems as close to him as possible. In agriculture the production problems are more location specific. To improve access of the individual producer to resources, the resource base had to expand at the local level. Further, the potential for growth could be better identified and more quickly exploited if local knowledge were brought in as an ingredient of planning. It would be easier to identify at micro-level the unemployed persons who were presumed to be in large number in agriculture and who could be brought into the production activity by a planning strategy.

In the context of micro-level planning in India, a district, and below it a block, was accepted as a unit of planning. While district level planning was adopted as a general strategy, intensive efforts were made in a few selected districts. This strategy was known as the Intensive Agricultural District Programme (IADP). The ideal of helping the individual producer to plan his production was central to IADP. Farm budgeting was accepted as a tool and was extensively used for the purpose of production planning. Agricultural economists, particularly in the agricultural universities, extension agencies and agricultural scientists played important roles in IADP. From farm budgeting to linear programming was one more step. But linear programming being a more complex tool, its use did not spread beyond the experimental stage.

Food
Food shortage was inherited as a war time legacy by most of the developing nations. Bad years aggravated it, good years provided relief. Management of food, however, was done with a sense of apology. Policy makers in the context of food would emphasize food production policy to be the planning plank and food management as a short term relief measure. With the emphasis on the role of wage-goods in the growth process, food acquired a "growth-good" label and food management the respectability of an "investment" activity. Internationally "Development Through Food" came to be accepted as a part of a planning strategy. Unutilized labour together with additional food would produce capital, which in turn would move the wheel of the economy ever faster. Agricultural economists once again came out of the side-wing. The history of food management in India bears witness to the significant contribution agricultural economists made in developing the "art" of food management in terms of procurement, distribution and price fixation. Food policy generated controversies also. In the context of the efficiency criterion any long term intervention in market operations was regarded by market economy-oriented agricultural economists as a violation of basic economic tenets resulting not only in loss of efficiency in the short run, but also in damage to long run growth prospects. The controversy regarding food market intervention has not died down but the market efficiency view has gained a measure of acceptance. The food management which should have received orientation to serve growth could not wholly shake off its wartime legacy of protecting consumers from the

crushing inflationary burden. Nevertheless, both micro-level planning and food management have survived as components of planning strategy. Their contents have even expanded. "Food for work" explicitly links employment and growth with food management.

Dual economy models generated new enthusiasm for empirical research mainly for the measurement of unemployment. Attempts to explain the nature, composition and extent of rural unemployment however, have met only partial success. Views have varied from an absence of unemployment to an existence of a vast pool of unemployed labour. The magnitude of the problem and the complexities of the task have been continuously examined and nation-wide data, collected over more than a decade, have given an increasing pile of quantitative information. While measurement of unemployment and under-employment has engaged the major attention of agricultural economists, the policy prescriptions they came up with to combat the problem were of a general character. Specific policies directed towards increasing employment range widely. They include redistribution of land, encouragement of traditional village crafts and a guaranteed employment scheme. Diversification of occupations was recommended at the individual producer's level by adding to cultivation, animal husbandry, poultry, fishery and (now) farm forests.[2] The varied nature of these prescriptions and their tenuous link with development theory reflect the present state of thinking.

The primordial role assigned to agriculture in the post World War II period differed from its physiocratic origins. Agriculture is not regarded as the source of "surplus", but is considered an instrument of growth which provides food as an input. Where wage-goods theories, Lewis's model and its extensions left off, Leontief's inter-industry input–output model took up. It emphasized that just as expansion of industries depended on supplies from agriculture, expansion of agriculture itself depended on supplies from industries. Thus, growth is a product of inter-sectoral resource flows. Both these theories made efforts to increase agricultural production, a "respectable" activity. The new respectability of agriculture changed its postwar label of "Achilles' heel" to that of "Engine of Growth". Label-changing, however, did not ease the task; the Ricardian wrinkle stayed with it nevertheless. The diminishing marginal product was more than a brake. It cranked down the "engine of growth" to a dead stop in a conceptual framework. Theory did not go beyond it. The appeal had to be made to history, past experiences and current developments in fields other than economics. At this stage came the contribution of *Transforming Traditional Agriculture*.

Human capital

The thought development reflected in *Transforming Traditional Agriculture* has a history. While endeavours to develop a framework of growth theory were underway, economists were reaching out to capture even scattered potentials for growth by exploiting "increasing returns" as a counter to diminishing returns. Firstly, Libenstenian construct led to the "wage goods" multiplier. Later, a major contribution came in the form of a "Human Capital" concept. The amazing capacity of adaptation to face challenges continuously was demonstrated to be the characteristic of this newly "uncovered" form of capital. Empirically, its high pay-off was demonstrated earlier through staggering returns to technological research. It was decided that education, research and technological change provided a way to the modernization of agriculture. They would facilitate a higher rate of absorption of material investment. Indeed, a breakthrough in the theoretical conceptualization was achieved. The contribution came almost simultaneously and independently in agricultural economics and in general economics in development theory. Sraffa's contribution in value theory together with its reinterpretation and a survey of growth theory by Hahn and Matthews, bear witness to the contribution in growth theory itself. Acceptance of the importance of education, purchased inputs that embodied higher level technology (viaz., fertilizers and seeds), and increased investment in technological research in agriculture as a part of planning strategy, is recognition of the new theoretical breakthrough.

What became the fate of the past theories and the strategies based on them, perhaps would have been the fate of the new theoretical development also. A happy coincidence occurred, however. A technological breakthrough in high yielding varieties of rice and wheat ushered in what has now come to be known as the "green revolution". Was it a revolution? What happened to its potency which seemed to lay buried under the heap of empirical evidence, showing growth rate to be no greater than the two decades old trend in the sub-continent of India? The early empirical evidence could not reverse the thought of the contribution of theory nor did it dissuade the policy maker from adopting a planning strategy based on new technology in agriculture. Agricultural economists in national planning agencies responded quickly to the new developments. They examined, ahead of time, second and third generation problems. They evolved strategies for speedier distribution of inputs and credit. They discovered a kink also: what if the green revolution turned red?

2   GROWTH AND DISTRIBUTION

A patient journey back into the experience of growth through the analysis of consumption data uncovered "mass poverty" underneath economic growth. What could be the explanation? Those who uncovered the fact were agricultural economists and those who raised the question loudly were the development economists. Empirical agricultural economists responded to the problem differently. They identified "the poor" as being landless, or a tiller cultivating a small plot of land, or any one of the two not finding enough employment.

As an immediate response to the "newly" discovered situation of mass poverty, the agricultural economists particularly favoured the bi-modal planning strategy. It meant that growth strategy was to be supplemented by special programmes for reaching the target groups. The Rural Works Programme provided employment to the unemployed in India around this time. The scope of the supplementary strategies was expanded by adding special agencies like "Small Farmers Development Agencies", and "Marginal Farmers and Agricultural Labourers Development Agency", "Guaranteed Employment Scheme", and special extension services for tribals. The Regional Rural Banks strengthened the financing of agriculture in less developed areas where poverty was believed to be widespread. Some of these programmes were initiated a little before the "target group" strategies became a part of "bi-modal" planning. Since target groups varied, so also were the strategies to reach them; bi-modal planning in practice assumed a multi-modal form.

The empiricism of agricultural economists became engaged in exploring the nature of association between growth and income distribution. The available empirical evidence came up with sharply contrasted indications. Calorie-based real income levels used for dividing the poor from the rest suggested an enlargement of the pool of the poor over time. An equally powerful indicator, viz., the expectation of life at birth, suggested a dramatic welfare improvement of all classes in the community. "P Quali" of the Overseas Development Council (ODC) and the calorie-gap indicator of the Food and Agricultural Organization of the United Nations (FAO) have taken the debate regarding the association of growth with income distribution to the international level. A theoretical integration of growth and income distribution has been attempted by John Mellor. Taking clues from consumption behaviour and working back to the production processes, he suggests that growth with its income effect will have a built-in element related to employment. The improved incomes will raise demand for products which have greater employment content, especially so in the matter of agricultural produce. Economists are currently re-examining demand theory. They have opened new "boxes". They ask how should the "quality" of consumer goods be measured? An even more basic question is raised: how can economic "good" be defined? If goods are to be defined – as they should be – in terms of their characteristics, we would be taking a journey back to "utility".

Agricultural economists are examining empirically issues relative to the characteristics of food. Is the demand for food by consumers nutrition-related or taste-related, and if both, what degree of emphasis is on nutrition and on taste at various income levels? This inquiry is in an embryonic stage. Its findings may add a wrinkle to the major inquiry regarding association between growth and equality. Tastes in a dynamic context are not unchanging, and what is more important, interpersonal effects on demand (i.e. on the consumption side), may be greater and faster than on the production side. In other words, the poor may emulate the food tastes of their rich neighbours in preference to nutrition or calorie-content much before the desired level of the latter is reached.

Such emulation of the technology of the rich farmer by the poor one is likely to be much slower.

Demography and dynamics of rural development
The tidal wave phenomenon of population expansion in the post World War II period has brought back demography into the fold of economics. While increased life expectancy is a clear sign of improved health, it adds mouths to be fed. Is the recent population expansion an exogenous phenomenon and is it transitory? Is it growth-related and likely to damage growth prospects themselves? Is population expansion linked with improved nutrition? Can policy intervention succeed in limiting population growth so that economic growth can continue unhindered? In this multiple question inquiry economists have participated more than demographers. Their major finding is that children are positive goods (in terms of numbers) at low incomes especially in rural areas. This finding brings the agricultural economists into the arena; they would want to examine in a more comprehensive context the rural dynamics that would take account of demographic behaviour. The inverse relationship between acceptance of fertility control and income levels with its attendant undesirable effects on economic growth and employment has once again spurred the search for an effective policy intervention instrument. The most malleable human capital, with its growth-aiding character, is found contributing positively to fertility control also.

All related issues that have been raised in the wake of demographic inquiries cannot be put back into Pandora's box. The vital question that challenges the intellect of practising economists and agricultural economists pertains to the time lag involved in beneficial effects that may put the economy back on the rails for its speedier journey to growth with equity. Agricultural economists not adequately equipped with knowledge of demographic techniques are waiting for findings to crystalize so as to include them in the calculus of rural dynamics. Witness, for instance, the finding of inverse relationship between property holding (mainly land) and family size: does it represent a "life-cycle" phenomenon? Is it related to a non-economic (mainly social) phenomenon of changing family structure? In both these cases, the phenomenon would vitiate the traditional income distribution measurement and hence, throw doubt on the observed inverse association between growth and income distribution. While economic theory is grappling with the new question of the relation of growth with equity, the agricultural economists in their role *vis-à-vis* the planning agency take a cautious route of multi-modal planning strategy.

Regional income distribution
Connected with the "Green Revolution" was the problem of regional income distribution. In fact, the problem of spatial distribution of income in the rural sector is also linked with the public sector investments in location-specific projects like irrigation dams. The steep differentiation

in adoption of promising technology embodied in the Green Revolution only brought the problem of regional income distribution to the fore demanding immediate attention. In the multi-modal planning strategy the backward area development programmes are included to aid the tribals and other weaker sections. These programmes are also location based. The problem not yet adequately attended to, even at the research level, pertains to mobility of labour over regions and its impact on inter-income-class and inter-regional income distribution. Regional science that embodies location theories takes account largely of the movement of labour from rural to urban areas and its attendant problems. Rural-rural and rural-urban migration would raise different sets of problems. The planning strategy has remained silent in attacking the problem of labour mobility in general. Since the mobility of labour from one rural area to another has become sizeable, we shall soon find attention turned to this problem. Until then, it remains a "dark continent" of agricultural economics.

3 PRESENT STATUS AND FUTURE CHALLENGE

Agriculture was the major sector of many developing nations that accepted planning as a major strategy for economic development, and it still continues to be so in many of them. The importance of agriculture in the economy led to pressing demands on the role agricultural economists were required to play. It went beyond filling the details in the framework evolved by others. In fact, at all stages, a major content to the planning was contributed by agricultural economists. Even at a stage where theorists faced a near impasse, the breakthrough came from leading agriculture economists and it made a lasting impact on the planning processes. The present status of agricultural economists is that of an equal partner in the process of planning.

The bi-modal or multi-modal planning strategies now adopted do not resolve, they only contain the biggest current challenge to planning as a strategy of development within the market economy. The understanding of inter-relationships between growth and distribution in (relatively) free economies is not yet within our grasp. Expedience of alternatives can buy time, but not for long. This then constitutes the biggest challenge. Agricultural economists being nearer the complexities of the new situation, as these are more sharply manifested in the rural areas, are expected to shed light to show the way. In their endeavour they need the co-operation of other colleagues in the economic profession trained in theory and techniques of planning.

NOTES

[1] While much of the discussion is general in character, experience of India provides the background. While what happened inside the planning commission, and how the decisions

were taken on most vital issues, are important to evaluate the effectiveness of agricultural economists, we can judge their effectiveness in terms of the final decisions that went into planning documents and follow the process in terms of the thinking that influenced the shape of the issues. I have preferred the latter of the two approaches. By the very nature of the issues raised, the discussion here relates to the contribution of planning in the context of the market economies.

² The latest Five Year Plan of India has an emphasis on the employment generation. A switch in the policy favours traditional crafts in the industrial sector and auxiliary activities in the agricultural sector.

REFERENCES

Government of India: Five Year Plans (latest for 1978–83), New Delhi, India.

Mellor, John W. *The New Economics of Growth*, Ithaca, New York, Cornell University Press, 1976.

Schultz, T.W. *Transforming Traditional Agriculture*, New Haven, Connecticut, Yale University, 1964.

Shah, C.H. (ed.) *Agricultural Development of India: Policy and Problems*, Bombay, India, Orient Longman, 1978.

DISCUSSION OPENING – SUDHIN K. MUKHOPADHYAY

There are two points to note at the beginning: (1) The paper is concerned largely with the subject of *agricultural economics* as a discipline and the performance of economists dealing with the subject, rather than a given set of "agricultural economists" as such; (2) It is the response of agricultural economists as a whole to the emerging problems of planning for economic development which is dealt with in the paper, rather than exclusively that of those working in any national planning agency. The broad setting is India.

Accomplishments

The author distinguishes between three broad phases in the accomplishments of agricultural economists in the context of planning for national development: (1) institutional reforms, (2) growth, and (3) distribution. Spillover between phases is not ruled out, however.

(1) Institutional reforms: the contribution of the agricultural economist is traced to the post World War II period when many nations in their postcolonial attempts at economic development were faced with the institutional bottlenecks of land tenure and property rights in agriculture. The agricultural economist moved to highlight the need for reforms in the existing land, credit and marketing institutions. However, doubts were soon raised about the likely benefits from land reforms without loss of economic efficiency. The answer was indeterminate and so the planning machinery was left without any effective policy guidance. Agrarian reforms, therefore, in spite of the early initiative of the agricultural economist, remain largely an unfinished task.

(2) Growth: a related question that came up before planners concerned

with the problem of speeding up agricultural growth was: how far was the existing operation of factor and product markets in agriculture rational? Substantial attention was spent, often with the tools of neoclassical theory, on this problem of efficiency in farmer behaviour in production and sale. A surprising degree of consistency and rationality in this behaviour was revealed, implying that little could be recovered from anticipated inefficiency in operations and channelled into growth.

Faced with the pressing policy need for growth, agricultural economists interacted generously with growth theorists. On the theoretical scaffoldings of Harrod-Domar, Joan Robinson, Hicks, and others, agricultural economists put forth the case for massive public investments in agriculture. The dual economy models (Lewis, Ranis-Fei, etc,) brought to the fore the problem of intersectoral transfer of labour and wage goods. The role of farmers' knowledge and the extension worker was stressed, and agricultural economists, now hand in hand with growth theorists, came to highlight the prime need for micro-level planning in agriculture – an activity location-specific in character. Policy planners responded favourably (e.g., IADP), although not without controversies regarding the consequent uneven distribution of the results of such planning. The agricultural economists also concerned themselves with the problem of food management. "Food for Growth" and "Food for Work" came to link food management with growth and employment.

Investment in physical capital, extension, micro planning and food management could hardly alter the tendency of agriculture to display the "Ricardian diminishing marginal product" and assuage the discomfort of the agricultural economist, when a twin development occurred, one in theory and another on the farm: the theory of human capital demonstrated remarkable ability to explain growth or lack of it in terms of investment in education, research and purchased inputs representing higher technology in agriculture, while the new HYV seeds almost dramatised the reality of technological change in agriculture. Inevitably, serious questions were asked about the extent, nature and possible consequences of this "revolution", and agricultural economists got busy exploring them.

(3) Distribution: three major elements have been pointed out in the response of the agricultural economist to the observed disparity in the distribution of the fruits of development: (a) use of bi- or multi-modal planning and supplementing growth strategy with special programmes to reach poverty afflicted target groups or regions; (b) adoption of micro-level location-specific programmes to reduce spatial gaps in the levels of technology; (c) seeking more effective policy instruments with the help of the new economic-demographic theory of household behaviour.

Present status and future challenge
The response of the agricultural economist to the call for economic development through planning has so far been prompt and positive, and his contribution substantial in steering the course of many developing

economies. This has given him well earned status no less effective than the economic theorist.

The challenge now appears in the form of the crying need to harmonize considerations of growth with those of distribution. The agricultural economist's answer of multi-modal planning may still leave much to be desired. He has to join hands with the economic theorist and the planner in facing this challenge.

Suggested issues for discussion

1 The agricultural economist may be assumed to perform the dual role of an advisor to the policy planner in dealing with short term exigencies, as well as that of a social scientist providing long term guidelines for socio-economic development. Dr Shah's paper seems to be dealing mainly with the first role of short term policy advisor; what is the accomplishment of the agricultural economist in indicating the long-run course for development?

2 The somewhat non-committal role of the agricultural economist with respect to institutional reforms mentioned in the paper leads one to ask some further questions. Does this reflect the view of the agricultural economist that the current institutional pattern is optimal? Or does it suggest the relative difficulty in influencing institutional changes in the absence of technological progress?

3 The relationship between technological progress and institutional change as perceived by the agricultural economist has been ignored in the paper. How far can one be assumed to be inducing the other? What in the agricultural economist's view is the prime mover? Can the agricultural economist follow the dichotomy of concentrating on institutional changes at some time and place and technological progress at another?

4 In the light of the seed–fertilizer revolution, how far has the past record of the agricultural economist been characterized by his interaction with other agricultural and relevant scientists and the farmer in the field? Should increased and sustained collaboration of the agricultural economist, at the micro level, with the farmer, the policy-maker, the agronomist, the breeder, the agricultural meteorologist, the extension worker and others be considered useful for the future (especially as illustrated by the international agricultural research agencies). Can that be expected to facilitate the emergence of models to deal more effectively with the baffling challenges of the future course of agricultural development?

GENERAL DISCUSSION – RAPPORTEUR: PAUL WEBSTER

In the discussion it was suggested that the paper had perhaps underestimated the contribution of agricultural economists to planning at the state or regional level. In reply Dr Shah reminded the audience that he had been asked mainly to concentrate on contributions at the national level and that he fully appreciated what could be done at other levels. But it was also suggested that a possible difficulty arose in the development of programmes for the alleviation of poverty since many of the relevant policy-makers came from groups (e.g. industrialists and large farmers) who had little interest in changing the *status quo*. It was recognised that agricultural economists had a continuing role in the analysis of structural change. The link between technological change and the necessity for institutional change was also recognised. Some planners were advocating, for instance, the formation of unions for small farmers.

Participants in the discussion included A.S. Kahlon and Ali Mohammad.

KEITH CAMPBELL*

The Risks of New Technology and their Agricultural Implications

It is a feature of many forms of modern technology that they involve risks to the lives of those who use them and in some instances put the lives of wider sections of the community in jeopardy. It is not that industrial processes long in use, not to mention day-to-day social activities, do not involve inherent risks to human life and limb,[1] but the public in latter days appears to have become peculiarly sensitive to the risks associated with new technology. This concern (together with rising anxiety about technological unemployment) has spawned an increasing volume of literature advocating social control of technology.[2]

The change in public perceptions of certain classes of risks seems to have occurred largely as a result of the recent rising tide of interest in environmental issues. Public controversy about nuclear power generation, about the dispersed effects of insecticides and about the potential carcinogenic properties of foodstuffs have helped to fire what may eventually come to be regarded as an unduly exaggerated concern about safety and environmental protection. Anti-pollution regulations necessarily imply significant costs both in benefits foregone and in costs of administration. Accordingly, because of resource limitations, the more stringent environmental legislation can only be contemplated in more affluent societies. For that reason, an internationally uniform approach to environmental hazards is a Utopian conception.

IMPLICATIONS FOR AGRICULTURE

These shifts in community attitudes have come to have serious repercussions on agricultural policy in that governmental responses to the changing attitudes and the resultant bans and limitations are beginning to constitute significant restraints on rural production potential and technological advances. To date, in most countries, agricultural scientists and administrators have endeavoured to accommodate themselves to changing public sentiment.[3] But, given the important counterproductive effects

* Read by G.J.W. Longworth in the absence of the author.

of latter-day environmental constraints, it is perhaps time that concerned agricultural professionals played a more active role in bringing home to the public the costs to society of excessive controls in the rural arena, however well intentioned those controls may be.

The purpose of this paper is not to outline in detail the nature and extent of the newer constraints on agricultural progress. Suffice it to say that they include, *inter alia*, (1) restrictions on the use of fungicides, insecticides and weedicides, (2) overzealous resort to quarantine controls, (3) prohibitions on the use of feed additives, (4) controls on residues and effluents of agricultural origin, and (5) controls over genetic advances involving recombinant DNA.[4] The paper is concerned rather to discuss some of the issues associated with framing public policy in respect of research and production activities where the community has certain perceptions of the possible dangers to their safety or well-being which may flow from the practice of them. The issues will be illustrated principally by reference to agricultural chemicals, though the observations also apply to a large extent to the other facets of agricultural technology mentioned above.

Though the scientific, engineering and medical professions have given some attention to the social issues involved, they have been relatively neglected by economists and agricultural economists in particular. The overwhelming mass of economic literature in the area of risk is concerned with the production decisions of risk-liable individuals and the degree to which they can mitigate their risks by resort to insurance, futures markets and diversification. This is especially true of the literature in agricultural economics. Such theoretical framework as exists offers few insights as to how governments, whether socialist or capitalist, democratic or authoritarian, can come to grips, in a policy context, with the attitudes about risks formed by the electorate – attitudes which may simultaneously be irrational, inconsistent and inaccurate (in the sense of being out of line with objectively established probabilities) and which may be swayed quite erratically by irresponsible treatment of the subject in newspapers or electronic media. David Hopper has sagely remarked that, in a governmental context, "truth is determined by a majority of voters, not by the test of the laws of proof".[5]

PROBLEMS OF LATENCY AND UNCERTAINTY

It might be well to begin with a catalogue of some of the characteristics of the so-called "toxic" or hazardous substances which find their way into latter-day agricultural research and practice.[6] First, unlike various compounds of arsenic, lead and mercury, as well as nicotine sulphate, which have been used in farming practice for many decades and whose toxicity is well known, it has taken time for the toxic effects of many of the agents used in latter-day pest control to become evident. The latency and the uncertainty about their effects make risk assessment difficult if not impossible and enhance public apprehension about them and related substances. It may be decades before persons exposed to a particular chemical may show adverse effects. Thus there may be occupational exposure to a chemical without knowledge of its toxic properties – a very different situation to that of voluntary occupational exposure in full knowledge of the attendant risks. There is also the problem of possible exposure of third parties as a result of air or water pollution.

The facts that the carcinogenic, teratogenic and other adverse effects of some agricultural chemicals has been established, coupled with the growing recognition of the environmental causes of cancer, have increased public concern about these and other substances. The problem is exacerbated to the extent that this concern is reflected in statutory form, as in the Delaney clause in the United States which requires the banning of all substances suspected of being carcinogenic.

Testing procedures required by national legislation, such as the US Insecticide, Fungicide and Rodenticide Act, as a prerequisite for the registration of agricultural chemicals, raise all sorts of perplexing scientific questions. First, an insecticide may be deemed suspect by virtue of its chemical structure rather than as a result of tests. Second, in view of the impossibility of tests on human subjects, the required toxicity tests are conducted on animal populations. This raises serious questions as to the validity of inferences made about effects on man from tests on other mammals. The position is further complicated by claims that some lines of laboratory animals are cancer-prone and the fact that progressive refinements in instrumentation are, in effect, changing the criteria used in the tests.

Then there is disagreement about the dosage rates required. It is frequently charged that animals under test are given massive doses far beyond any level that would be liable to occur in real life. Of the same genre is the so-called "threshold controversy". This has to do with the question whether the human organism can tolerate exposure to a hazardous substance up to a certain level without adverse effect; or whether, on the contrary, liability to damage is linearly related to the degree of exposure, even where minute quantities are involved.

Quite understandably, problems connected with the latent and uncertain effects of chemicals give rise to disagreements between scientists, particularly when some are more anxious to attain public notoriety than concerned about following the statistical and other procedures necessary to establish reliable scientific knowledge.[7] Such scientific controversy, whether mischievous or genuine, helps to fire public unrest and apprehension, provides excellent fuel for agitators who revel in scientific uncertainty and represents a very questionable basis for sound governmental regulation. As Paul Portney has observed "it is difficult to legislate that which scientists appear to understand imperfectly. . . ."[8] The stage is set for extreme governmental regulation which takes no account of costs and benefits but bans outright the production or use of substances which may potentially be of great value to the world but are under a cloud because of scientific uncertainty about the precise extent of their effects on man.

THE PUBLIC ACCEPTABILITY OF RISKS

In recent years, scientists and engineers have devoted considerable attention to the assessment of risks associated with emerging technology and have speculated about the public's willingness to accept such risks.[9] The fundamental philosophical question concerns inconsistencies in the public's willingness to accept risks of differing magnitudes – why people are willing unflinchingly to use automobiles in increasing numbers and accept without question the generation of electricity from coal where the risk of death or incapacitation is relatively high and yet baulk or protest vehemently at new technology when the risks associated with it are significantly less. Doubtless fear of the unknown is partly involved, but that is by no means the sole explanation.

One point to be made is that it is the public's perception of a risk rather than the actual statistical assessment that is important from a policy point of view. The public's perception of a hazard is mainly determined by its severity and to a much more minor extent by its frequency. The 150 people who die each day on United States roads have little or no local or international news value, whereas the plane crash at Chicago on May 26 involving the death of 273 people was flashed to the world's capitals immediately. Propinquity also affects risk perception. A farmer living adjacent to a cotton grower who sprays his crop regularly by plane is likely to be much more concerned about pollution than someone 50 miles away. Furthermore, people are prepared to accept higher risks if they are self-imposed especially if their latency period is likely to be long (e.g. smoking). Such persons are likely to be far less tolerant of some hazard with a statistically lower risk, if they are subjected to it involuntarily.

Attempts have been made to determine the acceptability of various risks by establishing a subjective relationship between the risk and the monetary benefit to be derived from accepting it.[10] It is postulated that the risk of death from an act of God such as a flood or an earthquake (estimated at about one death per year per million people) is of no consequence to the average individual. A risk of one in 100,000 may call for warnings and, where the risk is one in 10,000, the public may be willing to accept limited public expenditure to reduce it. It is asserted that when the risk rises to the order of one in 1,000 per year, the public finds it unacceptable and demands public action to do something really tangible about it.[11] To give perspective, the normal death rate from disease in the United States is about one death per year per 100 people.

Such attempts to establish what might be called thresholds for political action have recently been criticized by Lord Rothschild, partly on the grounds that the duration of the risk is unspecified (which is not altogether true), but more particularly on grounds that the probabilities cited lack any statistical basis.[12] He argues that in any case both citizens and politicians who may be involved in decision-making have little or no real appreciation of what a statistically defined risk implies whether it be expressed in probability terms or in terms of deaths per year. Rothschild, for his part, arbitrarily suggests that the risk of being killed in a car accident in Great Britain (one in 7,500 in 1974) can be taken as the threshold for people's concern about risks.

IS OBJECTIVE RISK ASSESSMENT OF VALUE IN PUBLIC DECISION–MAKING?

All this raises the more fundamental question of whether attempts to give greater precision to risk liability are going to lead to more rational political decisions. It may well be that in areas involving environmental protection, where uncertainties are great and where conflicts in value systems are of an extreme order, anything approaching rational political action is particularly difficult to achieve. Lord Ashby who presided over a UK Royal Commission on Environmental Pollution between 1970 and 1973 had, no doubt, genuine grounds for his observation that "There is copious literature on decision theory under conditions of uncertainty, but most of it deals only with very simple problems and I do not think it is of much use to those who have to make complex policy decisions".[13] He asserts incidentally that decisions involving a hazard to human health are comparatively easy as compared with decisions about the environment. This would seem to imply the zero-risk approach to human health hazards, but it is hard to accept that they should not be subject to some economic calculus, even though any sane person would accept that human life is on a different ethical plane to that of flora and fauna.

Ashby is prone to argue that, irrespective of the objective inputs of scientists and economists and the more subjective representations of affected parties and more broadly based pressure groups, the political decision-maker depends ultimately on hunch or intuitive judgement.[14] The politician, he says, is influenced by his value system and the relative weights he attached to particular beliefs. Perhaps much more attention needs to be directed to the factors affecting politicians' judgements and the whole processes of rational decision-making in this area,[15] because the scope for non-rational representations and decisions is greater than normal.

Again Rothschild, as might be expected of a scientist, has, in his Dimbleby lecture, criticized this stated dependency on politicians' judgements.[16] He thinks that there should be greater reliance on hard information, though he accepts that this is very difficult to achieve in practice. I believe he is saying that researchers and others should not be diverted from the task of assembling hard economic and scientific facts by the illogicality and emotionalism that currently surrounds decisions involving environmental risks.

What contribution can economists make by way of providing hard information which may assist in ensuring better environmental decisions, particularly those affecting agriculture? I concur with the view stated earlier that work on decision theory as such, at least in the short run, is likely to contribute little to public decision-making in the difficult area which is the subject of the present discussion. I believe the economist's immediate contribution potentially lies in two principal areas: (1) in defining the limits of public intervention and (2) in the area of cost-benefit analysis.

THE CASE FOR REGULATION

Economic literature dealing with environmental problems and with the problem of externalities in general, particularly in so far as it impinges on policy issues, is prone to come down heavily in terms of the "polluter pays" principle. Portney has recently examined the usefulness of the market solution as an alternative to government regulation of toxic hazardous substances.[17] A market solution would involve, among a number of other things (1) the use of wage premiums for workers who voluntarily accept hazardous jobs and (2) the associated incentive to employers to supply protective clothing or equipment in lieu of paying wage premiums. It can be argued that through a competitive market, benefits and costs are balanced through individual decisions and the market itself determines the optimal amount of risks. Portney however concludes that information at all levels is too imperfect for a market solution to be applied in this instance. As he says, "the necessary conditions for labour, land, or product markets to balance automatically the benefits and costs of exposures to toxic substances are not descriptive of the real world".[18]

At the other extreme, lies the possibility of a government's intervening to ban completely the manufacture or use not only of known but also of potentially toxic substances. Potentially toxic ones may be defined, for instance, as those shown to induce cancer or other serious disease in laboratory animals. Such a blanket policy is also unsatisfactory and unwise from the standpoint of public welfare. Though it may eliminate the risk of death or illness arising from exposure to the chemicals in question, it may deprive the public of very significant benefits. Such extreme policies ignore the fact that the risks incurred through the use of different chemicals may vary greatly, and imply that the benefits that may arise from even limited exposure to all such chemicals are always less than the costs. Assuming that all risks are equal implies that less than optimal decisions will be made.

There is therefore a case for public intervention somewhere between the two extremes. The difficulty is to find wise and prudent benchmarks which may help in setting the limits of government intervention. In areas where human life is in jeopardy there is a propensity for governments to introduce coercive measures, such as bans, but even when the state does not go that far, paternalism and detailed regulation is frequently the order of the day. The tendency too often seems to be to treat all users (including both farmers and employees in an agricultural context) as morons devoid of any capacity to look after their own interests, insteady of relying on educational processes to encourage wise and careful use of the more dangerous agricultural aids. Issues of economic and personal freedom typically receive scant regard.

To illustrate the extremes to which recent pesticide control legislation may go, let me cite some of the provisions of the 1978 Act now in force in the State in which I reside. That legislation requires that "a person shall not before . . . using . . . a registered pesticide . . . fail to read, or to have read to him, the instruction contained on any label . . . affixed to its container" and provides a penalty of $500 in default.[19] A farmer is liable to a similar fine if he wilfully or carelessly disregards the instruction or if he should "wilfully and without reasonable cause of anything likely to cause a risk of injury by a pesticide to himself. . . ." Although the Departments of Agriculture of the various Australian States frequently make differing recommendations as to the appropriate dosages of pesticides that should be used against a specific pest, this legislation makes it a punishable offence to use the pesticide at a rate different to that recommended by a specific Department of Agriculture. Moreover some chemicals are licensed for designated uses only and farmers are liable to prosecution if they use them against other plant or animal species. Such specificity may restrict opportunities for economic substitution and is rarely justifiable on scientific, health or efficiency grounds.

Another difficulty about much current control legislation is the variety and inconsistency of the criteria laid down in the relevant statutes. They are typically vague and tend to give virtually unlimited discretion to the appropriate administrator. The Australian legislation cited above, for instance, requires that bans be instituted where the administrator "*thinks* [my italics] that (a) the interest of public safety or the safety of any individual: or (b) the protection of the environment from unintended harm that might be caused by the pesticide, so requires".[20] The United States legislation is more clearcut in that it defines the use of a pesticide as constituting an "imminent hazard" when "a situation . . . exists when the continued use of a pesticide . . . could be likely to result in unreasonable adverse effects on the environment or will involve unreasonable hazard to the survival of species declared endangered by the Secretary of the Interior. . . ."[21] Unlike the Australian case, the US administrator must publish reasons for denial of registration of a pesticide and this usually involves some assessment of risks relative to the benefits. But US environmental statutes as a whole are highly inconsistent as regards the need to take account of benefit and cost comparisons.[22]

BENEFIT–COST ASSESSMENTS

From the economist's standpoint, the use of benefit–cost analysis is a necessary condition for intelligent decision-making in this as in many other areas of public policy. In the broadest sense, using such a mode of analysis simply represents the application of ordinary commonsense. It is when the procedure is used more precisely and the attempt made to reduce all benefits and costs to a common monetary measure, that the technique becomes a target for criticism and economists are subjected to unjustified denigration by scientists and politicians. Ashby even goes so far as to describe economists who endeavour to convert into monetary terms noncommensurable effects, such as aesthetic attributes or the saving of human life, as being morally wrong, not in the commonly used sense but in the sense of being overbearingly presumptuous.[23] All the same, however, he is at pains to explain that attempts to quantify what he calls "fragile values" are not illogical. It would be hard for him as a distinguished scientist to claim otherwise, strongly committed as he was in his earlier days to Kelvin's doctrine that, without measurement, knowledge is meagre and unsatisfactory.

It has to be stressed that pollution control itself is costly. If a society devotes its scarce resources of labour, capital, administrative and technical skills to checking and controlling environmental pollution, these resources are not available to be used to produce other goods and services desired, and sometimes desperately needed by society. As indicated earlier, the opportunity costs of these measures are probably of more vital relevance to developing countries than affluent countries. But even in the latter countries, the economic justification of automobile emission controls is coming increasingly under scrutiny as the price of oil rises.

In an agricultural context, the cost is not simply the production currently lost and the increased costs incurred in producing current foodstuffs as a result of the banning of efficacious pesticides. It also involves the future production that may not come into existence as a consequence of the powerful disincentives for investment in research and development brought to bear on chemical companies as a result of complicated and costly hurdles that have to be surmounted before new pesticides can be registered in some countries. It is extremely doubtful whether those groups who have been most vocal about the need for controls over DNA research have any real understanding of the opportunities for increased food production this research may open up in agriculture alone not to mention its potential benefits in other areas of human endeavour.

Despite the disinclination of many to discuss the economic value of human life, it is clear that the harder a government works at trying to reduce the loss of human lives, the higher the marginal cost of control for each extra life saved. To abbreviate a hypothetical example of Myrick Freeman, it might cost $10 million to reduce the annual death rate from a certain form of pollution from 50 to 25 lives a year; it may cost an additional $90 million to reduce it to zero.[24] Clearly governments have to make decisions as to whether the community should forego the benefits of $90 million invested in other directions in order to save every life from this specific form of pollution. Traffic engineers make these kinds of decisions every week of the year, though admittedly not in such explicit form. Exactly the same logic should apply in the area of environmental controls.

Costs and benefits are therefore important data in making policy choices though many environmental scientists wish they were not. Whether noncommensurable forms of benefit are quantified in some way by economists or whether their assessment is left to the politicians, it is impossible to avoid trade-offs between economic costs and the benefits which some people deem to be unquantifiable. There is reason to believe that in many areas of environmental control affecting agriculture "massive and certain costs are being expended to achieve small and uncertain benefits",[25] and that, as a result, a substantial misallocation of resources occurs. Greater resort to benefit-cost analysis, however crude the data and however great the problems of placing values on noncommensurables, could not do other than improve agricultural prospects in the short and longer run.

A FINAL COMMENT

As a contributor to the London *Observer* recently stated, "all technology has its risks and . . . those risks are the price society pays for the overwhelming benefit of such new technology".[26] Though admittedly large sections of the public remain to be convinced of the essential truth of this axiom, it is incumbent upon agricultural administrators to use their best endeavours to ensure that the "overwhelming benefits" which the rural industries and the public at large stand to gain from modern technology are not lost through inept, inefficient or unnecessarily restrictive legislation and regulation.

At the same time, it would be absurd to underestimate the difficulties that confront modern governments in attempting to come to grips with community reactions to risks associated with such recent technology, both in agriculture and other sectors of the economy. Today even trade unions and local government bodies are instituting bans on substances the use of which national governments after more thorough investigation have not deemed it wise to ban.

If indeed "truth is determined by a majority of voters", the application of science for the betterment of the human race is going to be greatly constrained until the public adopts a more rational approach to technological advances and their attendant risks. Unless a change of heart occurs soon (and that implies an educational task of massive proportions) it is likely to be in agriculture that the adverse consequences of societal risk aversion will first make themselves manifest. I believe that a resolution of the issues discussed in this paper is a necessary precondition if the agricultural industries are to be able to feed the world at all adequately after the turn of the century.

NOTES AND REFERENCES

[1] For a wide ranging catalogue of estimates of voluntary and involuntary risks, see T.A. Kletz "What Risks Should We Run?", *New Scientist*, Vol. 74 (12 May 1977), pp. 320–1.

[2] See, for instance, David Elliott and Ruth Elliott *The Control of Technology*, (London, Wykeham, 1976).

[3] This phenomenon is doubtless due as much to the low status of agriculture in the scentific and political worlds, as to the latter-day pressure of the environmentalists. On the undervaluation of agriculture, see Theodore W. Schultz "On Economics and Politics of Agriculture" in Theodore W. Schultz (ed.) *Distortions of Agricultural Incentives* (Bloomington, Indiana University Press, 1978), pp. 10–13.

[4] For a more detailed discussion, see Keith Campbell *Food for the Future* (Lincoln, University of Nebraska Press, 1979), pp. 75–81.

[5] W. David Hopper "Distortions from Government Prohibitions" in Theodore W. Schultz (ed.), op. cit., p. 72.

[6] For a fuller discussion of these characteristics see Paul R. Portney "Toxic Substance Policy and the Protection of Human Health" in Paul R. Portney *Current Issues in U.S. Environmental Policy* (Baltimore, John Hopkins Press for Resources for the Future, 1978), pp. 110–11 and Talbot Page "A Generic View of Toxic Chemicals and Similar Risks", *Ecology Law Quarterly*, Vol. 7, No. 2 (1978), pp. 207–44.

[7] See John Ziman *Reliable Knowledge* (Oxford, Oxford University Press, 1978), especially pp. 137–42.

[8] Paul R. Portney, op. cit., p. 111.

[9] See, for example, William D. Rowe *An Anatomy of Risk* (New York, John Wiley and Sons, 1977); William W. Lowrance *Of Acceptable Risk* (Los Altos, William Kaufmann Inc., 1976); Robert W. Kates *Risk Assessment of Environmental Hazard* (New York, John Wiley and Sons, 1978); and Council for Science and Society *The Acceptability of Risks* (London, Barry Rose, 1977).

[10] cf. C. Starr et al. "Philosophical Basis for Risk Analysis" in J.M. Hollander and M.K. Simmons (eds), *Annual Review of Energy*, Vol. 1 (Palo Alto, Annual Reviews Inc., 1976), p. 630.

[11] Eric Ashby *Reconciling Man with the Environment* (London, Oxford University Press, 1978), p. 72.

[12] Lord Rothschild "Risk", *The Listener*, 30 November 1978, p. 716.

[13] Ashby op. cit., p. 73.

[14] Ibid., p. 76.

[15] See Lord Ashby "Protection of the Environment – The Human Dimension", *Proceedings of the Royal Society of Medicine*, Vol. 69 (October 1976), pp. 721–30.

[16] Rothschild op. cit., p. 717.

[17] Portney op. cit., pp. 112–14.

[18] Ibid., p. 118.

[19] New South Wales Pesticides Act 1978, No. 57.

[20] Ibid.

[21] US Federal Insecticide, Fungicide and Rodenticide Act Public Law 92–516 (1972) as amended.

[22] Portney op. cit., pp. 129–33.

[23] Ashby op. cit., pp. 52–3.

[24] A. Myrick Freeman "Air and Water Pollution Policy" in Portney op. cit., p. 20.

[25] Ibid., p. 21.

[26] *The Observer* (London), 8 April 1979.

DISCUSSION OPENING – STEFAN TANGERMANN

On many of these points Professor Campbell takes the risk of running counter to current fashions. We ought to be grateful that he has not shied away from dealing with such a touchy issue, and he has done this in a very stimulating and sometimes even provocative way, combining economic reasoning with political insights.

In discussing this paper we are not faced with the difficulty of not knowing which issues to address but rather the problem of deciding which of the many thought-provoking points to leave out. The paper covered two areas:

1　Evaluation of, and views on, current environmental policies;
2　Consequences for economic analysis.

I would suggest we leave out the first area, though its discussion is tempting, otherwise we might end up banging our value judgements on each other's heads.

With respect to the second area (consequences for economic analysis) I suggest we discuss the following four questions:

1　With respect to effects of new technology, do we really deal with *risks* in the sense of known negative events with a given random distribution or are we rather faced with uncertainty? If the latter, can we as economists help anyhow?

2　How can we find out more about people's willingness to take risks? Most related examples in the paper (such as smoking or car driving) refer to people's willingness to accept certain risks of their own individual activities with also individual benefits for them. But what about risks of public activities or other people's operations?

3　Should we as economists really claim (or should I rather say "pretend") that we could make good cost-benefit analyses of environmental policies? Everybody would agree that we should not only consider the benefits of environmental policies but also their costs. In this general sense nobody would oppose Professor Campbell's quest for CBAs but when it comes to empirical analysis we should make sure that we do not raise too high expectations. For example, how to value human health and life or the environment and how to obtain sufficient information about costs in terms of output lost?

4　To what degree is it the right or the obligation of the economist to try and persuade the general public that its current excitement over environmental risks is exaggerated? Or do we simply have to conclude that what some call a current fashion and what others see as the emergence of a new consciousness reflects a shift in values which we as economists have to take into account rather than trying to change?

GENERAL DISCUSSION – RAPPORTEUR: PAUL WEBSTER

It was suggested during the discussion that at least as important as the risks referred to in the paper were risks of natural hazards and uncertainties concerned with newer technologies in developing countries. A second discussant felt that the paper had been overly pessimistic in regard to the possibility of the analysis of risks. There were various approaches that might be fruitful that had yet to be followed up. Finally it was pointed out that the area was one of genuine public concern and that despite the methodological difficulties agricultural economists could and should be making significant contributions to the debate.

Participants in the discussion included Syed M. Ahsan, Jim Johnston and John W. Longworth.

ZHAN WU

The Development of Socialist
Agriculture in China

1 ESTABLISHMENT OF SOCIALIST AGRICULTURE

As agriculture in old China was under the multiple oppression of imperialism, feudalism and bureaucrat capitalism, it was very backward and of a
semi-feudal and semi-colonial nature. Feudal land owership subjected
the peasants to ruthless exploitation, the land rent usually accounted for
more than 50, even 80 per cent of the crops harvested; the reactionary
government extorted heavy taxes and duties; the imperialists carried out
economic plunder and aggressive wars caused serious damages. All these
factors combined to ruin the rural economy and make it impossible for
the peasants to earn enough for decent food and clothing despite their
incessant toil. Such is the fundamental cause for the stagnation of China's
agricultural production over long years.

Under the leadership of the Communist Party of China, the broad
masses of the toiling peasants were mobilized and relied upon to carry out
land reform, thus putting an end to feudal exploitation and domination in
the rural areas. By the end of 1952, land reform was in the main completed throughout the country. Those peasants who used to have no land
or little land and who constituted 60 or 70 per cent of the rural population
obtained over 46 million hectares of cultivated land without compensation and were exempted from paying 35 million tons of food grains
annually as land rent. They also acquired large numbers of draught
animals, farm implements and other means of production. In this way, the
peasants' enthusiasm was aroused and agricultural production rapidly
restored and developed. By 1952, food grains, cotton and other major
agricultural crops had attained or surpassed their record levels in the
pre-liberation years.

However, individual economy was still predominant in China's vast
rural areas, with each family constituting a separate productive unit.
Their productivity was low, their ability to combat natural disasters was
weak, and a number of peasants still encountered difficulties both in
production and livelihood. This kind of small-peasant economy was very
fragile, it tended to breed class differentiation, and could not adapt itself

273

to the requirements of socialist industrialization. In order to change this situation, the Chinese Communist Party formulated its strategy on the agricultural problem. The first step was to bring about agricultural collectivization, and the second step was to realize mechanization and electrification of agriculture on this basis. In this manner, the peasants' enthusiasm released by the land reform could be guided in time to go along the path of socialism.

The policies in effecting China's agricultural collectivization were as follows. Through various concrete and appropriate forms of transition, the peasants were actively and prudently guided to change their zeal for individual economy into enthusiasm for mutal aid and co-operation. In the course of collectivization, the peasants were educated through patient persuasion and demonstration of typical examples. On the principles of voluntary participation and mutual benefit, they first organized themselves into mutual-aid teams, and gradually developed into agricultural producers' co-operatives of the elementary and advanced type. Agricultural co-operation was thus completed by 1957. In 1958, rural people's communes were formed by uniting the agricultural producers' co-operatives. The ownership of the people's commune at present is still collective ownership by the labouring peasants. In the commune, a three-level ownership is instituted, that is, ownership at the commune level, ownership at the production brigade level and ownership at the production team level, with the production team as the basic accounting unit. This form of organization corresponds well to the level of agricultural productive forces in China and the managerial ability of Chinese peasants. It also enables a commune or a production brigade to concentrate necessary manpower or resources in farmland capital construction on a scale much larger than ever before and to set up its own factories and enterprises.

While a socialist agriculture based on collective ownership was established, more than 2,000 state farms and livestock farms were set up, which were owned by the whole people. Although what they produce constitutes a small percentage in Chinese socialist agriculture, yet they play a meaningful role in improving China's overall agricultural layout, providing agricultural commodities and giving a demonstration to the Chinese peasants.

2 SPEEDING UP THE DEVELOPMENT OF SOCIALIST AGRICULTURE

The establishment of a socialist agriculture not only made it possible for the Chinese peasantry to take the road of common prosperity through getting organized, but also guaranteed sufficient supplies of food grains and raw materials as well as an expanding internal market for the development of industry, thus facilitating the socialist industrialization of the country. Furthermore, hundreds of millions of commune members are enabled with the support of the state to tap fully the advantages of the collective economy of the people's commune to speed up the construction of socialist agriculture and provide conditions for agricultural modernization.

China has a relatively small cultivated area, averaging 0.12 hectares per person. Hence, while doing everything possible to facilitate land reclamation, the main measure for increasing agricultural production at present is to go in for farmland capital construction in a big way and raise the per-unit-area yield of crops. Specifically, the purpose of such farmland capital construction is to build fields giving a high and stable yield despite drought or excessive rainfall, its emphasis is on soil improvement and water conservancy, and its method is to carry out a comprehensive management of mountains, water resources, fields, forests and roads. This means primarily the transformation of the soil of cultivated land and the construction of various water conservancy projects so as to increase resistance to drought and excessive rainfall, improve soil fertility and ensure a high and stable yield.

In the light of China's specific circumstances, stress is laid on farmland capital construction, on the principle of "working according to local conditions and for practical results"; overall planning and integration of large, medium-sized and small projects is practised. Generally speaking, the central or provincial government is in charge of overall planning and technical guidance of projects covering whole river basins, and implements key projects, as well as rendering material and financial assistance to communes and brigades. Medium-sized projects are usually undertaken jointly by several counties or communes. Small projects and field works are jointly carried out by several brigades or production teams, or by the related production team alone. In this way, full play is given to governments at various levels as well as the people's communes so that big, medium-sized and small projects form an integrated network in stimulating the development of the farmland capital construction and achieving quick economic results.

As a result of the above principles and measures, farmland capital construction has made steady progress in China. Since the beginning of the 1970s, nearly 100 million people have engaged in this work each winter season; on top of this, about 28 million people work in farmland capital construction all the year round. Displaying the *Dazhai* spirit of "self-reliance and hard work", they have made remarkable achievements, by using simple tools. By August 1978 more than 81,000 big and medium-sized reservoirs had been completed throughout the country, increasing the total irrigated area from 16 million hectares in 1959 to 47 million hectares in 1978. Of the 22 million hectares of land susceptible to waterlogging, 13 million hectares had initially been improved. 6.7 million of the 26 million hectares of sloping land had been terraced. In the course of farmland capital construction, over 80,000 small hydro-electric power stations had been built. These farmland works have played their part in resisting serious drought and flood which have occurred in China during the past few years and ensured the steady development of China's agricultural production. Consequently, despite the unusually serious drought of last year, gratifying increases were recorded in China's agricultural production.

Although farmland capital construction has in a certain degree transformed basic conditions for agricultural production, it remains essential for the development of agricultural production to institute technical reforms and apply science to farming in accordance with local conditions. That is what is meant by implementing, in an all-round way, the "Eight Point Charter for Agriculture" formulated by Comrade Mao Zedong. In other words, while going in for water conservancy and soil improvement, it is important to apply more fertilizer, use improved seeds, control diseases and insect pests, reform cultivation patterns and adopt all effective measures in a comprehensive way, in order to raise crop yields by a large margin.

Application of more fertilizer is an effective way to raise yields. While trying to increase the amount of organic manure applied, grow more green manure crops and use plant residues as fertilizer, China is making every effort to ensure the application of more chemical fertilizer so as to add to the total amount of fertilizer available for the fields. In developing her chemical fertilizer industry, China builds medium-sized and small chemical fertilizer plants along with big modern plants with a view to rapidly increasing the supply of chemical fertilizer. By the end of 1978, the average amount of chemical fertilizer applied in China reached 367.5 kilogrammes per hectare, a fact that had significantly helped to increase agricultural production.

Farm mechanization is one of the key links in the modernization of agriculture in China. In the past 20 years and more, our agricultural machinery industry has started from scratch and developed rapidly. During the eleven years from 1966 to 1976, the number of big and medium-sized tractors in China has increased at an annual rate of 20.3 per cent, while walking tractors increased by 46.4 per cent each year. In 1978, 46 per cent of the total cultivated area was ploughed by machine, with 141 HP per 100 ha.

In the process of farm mechanization the Chinese Government stresses the importance of working in accordance with the actual conditions. Mechanization must correspond with and promote the reforms of cropping systems and cultivation techniques. Agricultural machinery must gradually achieve standardization, serialization, and universality. Power machinery and working machinery should be in proper proportion and form complete sets working in unison. Tractor stations are of two types: one is owned and run by the commune, i.e. the commune or brigade buys tractors and may get state credit when it is short of funds. The other kind of tractor station is owned and run by the state, which sets up tractor stations to serve communes and brigades at appropriate charges. Of the two types, the former is predominant.

At present, our country is increasing investments in focal areas in a planned and gradual way to supply complete sets of advanced agricultural machinery to state farms, communes and brigades producing a large percentage of commercial products, enabling them to serve as models in agricultural production. In this way, mechanization can be realized step by step.

The modernization of agriculture requires development of scientific research and education in agriculture to train large numbers of qualified agro-technicians, scientists and management specialists. By 1978, integrated or special scientific research organizations had been set up at national, provincial and county levels. In education, there are now 45 agricultural universities and colleges and 234 specialized agricultural schools. As early as 1958, a network of scientific research and experimentation began to emerge, which covered units at county, commune, brigade and production team levels.

People's communes have their own stations for giving guidance in science and technology, some of which have experimental farms attached to them. Brigades and teams run scientific research groups, each with its experimental plots, which demonstrate and extend advanced science and technology under the guidance of research organizations at higher levels. Improved varieties are dominant in the cultivation of rice, wheat, corn and cotton throughout the country. Much work has been done in pest control.

In order to accelerate the modernization and rapid development of agriculture, emphasis has been laid on the development of enterprises at commune and brigade levels.

By the end of 1978, 80 to 90 per cent of China's communes and brigades have set up a total of more than 1.4 million various enterprises, whose output value makes up 31 per cent of the total income of the communes, brigades and teams. This has transformed the economic structure of the commune, and strengthened its collective economy.

The commune/brigade-run enterprises serve agricultural production and the people's daily life, as well as the requirements of large industry and exports. Falling under many kinds and varieties, they generally make use of local resources, by going in for cultivation and breeding, farm and sideline produce processing, mining, building agro-machinery, transport and so on, according to local conditions. In terms of output value, industrial enterprises make up the greater part. Urban industrial enterprises often transfer to them the production of some products and parts which can be best handled by commune- and brigade-run enterprises, supplying them with the necessary equipment and techniques. The state will gradually incorporate commune- and brigade-run enterprises into overall planning at different levels through signing contracts with them for sales, production and purchases. Communes and brigades are allowed to sell some of their products themselves. Joint enterprises can also be run by communes and brigades if necessary.

The development of commune- and brigade-run enterprises had given a great push to the development of a socialist countryside. Firstly, it provides agricultural production with funds, techniques and equipment. Modernization of China's agriculture requires enormous financial resources and equipment. Apart from state investments and proceeds from agricultural production, the income of commune- and brigade-run enterprises plays an important role in the accumulation of funds. In 1977, for example, funds coming from the profits of commune- and brigade-run enterprises for farmland capital construction and purchase of farm machinery were equal to 60 per cent of state investments in agriculture. Secondly, commune- and brigade-run enterprises, being located in the countryside, link up agriculture closely with industry, enabling industry to play its leading role and serve agriculture better. Thirdly, commune members engaged in these enterprises are both workers and peasants, working at the enterprises most of the time but helping in the fields during busy seasons. This helps to narrow the gap between workers and peasants. Fourthly, the fact that industries processing grain, oilseeds, cotton, fruits, poultry and aquatic products come to be located in the countryside reduces transportation costs, promotes comprehensive use of agricultural and sideline products and rationalizes production generally. Fifthly, the development of commune- and brigade-run enterprises provides employment for the manpower released by mechanization, avoiding the unchecked expansion of big cities and facilitating the emergence of medium-sized and small towns. All this, as Comrade Mao Zedong pointed out, "Our great and brilliant hope lies here."

3 ACHIEVEMENTS, PROBLEMS AND PROSPECTS

Under the leadership of the Communist Party, China's hundreds of millions of peasants have made remarkable achievements in the socialist construction of agriculture through their hard work. From 1949 to 1978, the nation's total output of food crops increased by 1.6 times, that of cotton by over 3.5 times, and the production of other crops, forestry, animal husbandry and fishery also increased by various degrees. All this has helped to solve basically the problem of feeding and clothing China's 800 million people. Yet on the whole, China's agriculture is still backward compared with advanced countries, as demonstrated by her underdeveloped means of production and science and technology, and low labour productivity, management level and income per caput. For nearly thirty years, China's agriculture traversed a tortuous path. During the first eight years after liberation, it developed fairly fast and the nation's grain output registered an average progressive increase of 7 per cent a year. But it slowed down in the following years. Worse still, during the Cultural Revolution, due to the sabotage of Lin Biao and the "gang of four", China's agriculture kept a low pace of development and saw unbalanced progress in different areas.

Over twenty years' practice in agriculture have convinced us: first, like other economic undertakings, political stability is indispensable to the development of agricultural production. Second, in developing agriculture objective economic laws must be observed. Agriculture is the foundation of China's national economy – this must find its full expression in the country's allocation of investments for capital construction, in the scale and speed of development of industrial enterprises serving agriculture, and in agricultural credit and in agricultural scientific research and education. Agriculture, forestry, animal husbandry, fishery and sideline occupations should be well co-ordinated and develop in a proportionate way; they should gradually change from self-sufficient production to specialized production on a regional basis. As the current commune system having a "three-level ownership with the production team as the basic accounting unit" is basically in conformity with agricultural productivity, we should stabilize it and fully respect the autonomy of the production team. As the basic accounting unit in the commune, the production team should have the right to decide what to cultivate according to local conditions, what measures to take to increase production, what method of management to adopt and how to distribute its products and cash income. Third, it is essential to give full play to the initiatives of the central government, local authorities, communes and commune members themselves. Being a socialist country with a planned economy, China must co-ordinate the efforts of all sides in the course of modernizing its agriculture, and pay particular attention to tapping the initiatives of the people's communes at all three levels of ownership and of the commune members for doing a good job in agriculture.

On the basis of the experience summarized, Premier Hua put forward at the Second Session of the Fifth National People's Congress a policy of concentrating our efforts within these three years on earnestly doing a good job in readjusting, restructuring, consolidating and improving our economy. In adjustment, we uphold the guiding principle of taking agriculture as the foundation of our economy and concentrate our efforts on raising agricultural production. Government investment in agriculture has increased from 10.7 per cent in the 1978 economic plan to 14 per cent in 1979. Purchasing prices for farm and sideline products have also been raised by over 20 per cent. Agricultural taxes have been remitted or reduced in poor areas. Continued efforts will be made further to implement various economic policies, conscientiously to carry out the principle of distributing income according to one's work, to restructure managerial systems in agriculture, and to respect the autonomy of enterprises, so as to further boost the enthusiasm of the enterprises, commune members and managerial personnel.

In modernizing China's agriculture, we are confronted with many important problems and tasks, for instance, economic structure and management of modernized agriculture, application of modern agricultural science and technologies and their economic results, agricultural specialization on a regional basis and implementation of the distribution of "to each according to his work". These problems can not be solved both in theory and in practice without the participation of agricultural economists.

However, sabotaged by Lin Biao and the "gang of four" in the last decade, research work in the theories and personnel training of agricultural economics practically came to a standstill. Following the smashing of the gang of four, the Party and Government adopted immediate measures in this field. The research institute of agriculture economics was set up under the auspices of the Chinese Academy of Social Sciences, while the research institute of agricultural economics of the Chinese Academy of Agricultural Sciences was restored. Departments of agricultural economics in the institutions of higher learning have one after another begun to enrol new students and post-graduates. Thus research work in agro-economics is rapidly being restored and expanded. In order to strengthen studies in the theories of agricultural economics and to promote the exchanges of research results and relevant data, a Chinese Society of Agricultural Economics has been established. To speed up China's agricultural modernization, it is not only necessary to sum up its own experience, but also to learn from advanced experience and theories of science from other countries. As an agricultural economist, I eagerly hope to strengthen academic exchanges with my colleagues of foreign countries, and I will do my share in promoting mutual understanding among peoples of all countries and in safeguarding world peace.

DISCUSSION OPENING – B. STAVIS

I wish to express my thanks, and I am sure the thanks of all members of the Association, to Mr Zhan Wu for coming here and for presenting such a clear and concise overview of China's experiences over the past three decades. Our general concern about the human condition makes us all most interested in what has been happening to the fifth of humanity in China. Our academic concern makes us especially interested in the results of one of the major distinctive rural development programmes in human history – a programme based on revolution, land reform, a collective ownership of the means of production, and mass consciousness in a concerted effort to achieve both growth and equity.

Zhan Wu's paper highlights one particular factor, namely the importance of political stability. Implicit in this statement is an acknowledgement that agriculture has done well in years of political order, and has suffered in years and places of political turmoil. A full understanding of agricultural and rural development will require an understanding of political policies and processes at the central and local levels.

To meet Glenn Johnson's strict deadline, Zhan Wu sent in his paper many months ago; and after he sent it in, China's State Statistical Bureau published a set of statistics which permit a clearer description of agricultural performance (Table 1). The figures show a long term growth rate in grain production from the mid-1950s to the late 1970s of about 2.2 per cent per year. Population has grown at about 1.9 per cent per year, so grain production per caput has grown at 0.3 per cent per year. If popula-

TABLE 1 *Agricultural production indicators*

	1953	1957	1977	1978
Population (million)	595.5	656.6	948	959
annual growth rate		1.89%		
Grain and soya (million tons)	166.3	195.0	282.7	304.7
grain/capita (kg)	(279)	(297)	(298)	(317)
average		(288)	(307)	
annual growth rate		0.3%		
Cotton (million tons)	1.174	1.64	2.049	2.167
cotton/capita (kg)	(1.97)	(2.50)	(2.16)	(2.26)
TOTAL Value Ag. (billion yuan)	53.7		134.0	145.9
ag. value/cap (Y)	(81.7)		(141.4)	(152.1)

Sources: 1953, 1957, State Statistical Bureau, *Ten Great Years*, 1959. 1977, 1978, State Statistical Bureau, "Communique of China's 1978 National Economic Plan," *Peking Review*, No. 27, 6 July 1979, p. 38.

tion growth can be reduced, obviously per caput production can be greater. Grain production has been close to 300 kg/per caput, a relatively high level compared to other countries in Asia – roughly 30–40 per cent above India. It is enough to supply a generally adequate grain diet on average, but does not provide much surplus for local crop failures, or for a meat diet. Cotton production per caput has remained fairly constant, fluctuating with weather and other factors. The total value of agricultural output per caput has gone up dramatically as the rural economy has diversified into high value products. However, we do not know the costs of production and the net revenue from agriculture. It is entirely possible that the net revenues from agriculture have been stagnant. I hope Mr Zhan Wu can comment on the problem of rising costs of production.

China's government budget figures have also been released after the paper was completed, and these figures highlight the complex combinations of policies which are needed. The total rural budget will be about 24 billion yen. However, total investments in industry are almost 60 billion, and national defence takes 20 billion – a lot, but less than expenditure on agriculture. There are other expenditures for culture, science, technology, education, and public health. In short there is a wide range of policies which must be carried out simultaneously.

As Mr Zhan Wu has hinted, a full understanding of rural development in China will require great sensitivity to regional differences. It appears that regions with good infrastructure, with water resources and with access to industrial supplies and urban markets have been growing rapidly. However in some areas, such as North China, this growth has been from a poor beginning and the standard of living in such regions is still not high and may be vulnerable to the vagaries of nature. This, combined with internal transport and procurement problems, accounts for continued substantial grain imports. These regions have been growing rapidly because of labour intensive public works, but also because of conventional technology. They have been supplied with large amounts of modern inputs, including chemical fertilizer (of which China is now the world's third largest producer) and modern means of water control, including low lift pumps and tube wells. Machinery has been widespread, particularly for ploughing. Mr Zhan Wu has noted that 46 per cent of China's cultivated area is machine ploughed. I hope he will comment further on the impact of such extensive tractorization on cropping patterns and on employment.

At the same time mountainous areas in general appear not to have shared in this growth. They had previously been poor and some of them remain poor or have deteriorated over the last decades. This problem has been particularly severe in the Upper Yellow River plateau. In this region, erosion has been a serious problem for centuries and it seems to be increasing. The total amount of silt in the Yellow River has increased from 1.3 to 1.6 billion tons per year over the past 25 years. This appears to be due to a policy of forcing these areas to be self sufficient in food, even if they are not well suited for grain production. They have been unable to

specialize in animal husbandry and in forestry products, which would
have been more stable ecologically. At the same time there have been
major constraints on out-migration from these areas, so that population
pressures remain high. The problem of how to develop poor mountainous
areas remains a problem in China as in other countries.

The collective ownership system in China has presumably had a major
impact on equity. It is for this reason that we have not heard this morning
about small farmers who cannot get credit or about landless labourers
being forced to migrate. I would, however, note that there are few
consumption or income surveys available from China, which could allow
empirical confirmation of the equity impact of Chinese policies.

At the same time the Chinese experience has shown some of the
difficulties in managing collective agriculture. Pressure for egalitarian
wages has been strong, and this has meant weak individual incentives for
planning; arbitrary bureaucratic commandism has been a constant problem. In the last few years there have been new examples of commandism,
in which production teams have been forced to adopt a costly triple
cropping pattern.

The problem of who controls the managers is a political problem which
was identified by Greek philosophers over 2000 years ago, and it has not
yet been settled and is probably a problem without final solution. In the
past decade the Chinese have made some remarkable experiments with
mass participation, training, ideological consciousness and face to face
criticism and self criticism as a way of controlling the controllers. It now
appears that this system has not worked adequately, except when strong
willed local leaders were present.

The Chinese are now accepting much more conventional approaches,
namely reinforcing the property rights of collective units and encouraging
voluntary negotiations of contracts between production units. They are
trying to end the bureaucratic command of targets and other economic
relationships. The Chinese are contemplating competition between suppliers, and are requiring more rigid accounting of profit and loss and more
market interactions to ensure efficiency. These modes of interaction
seem particularly important as the economy grows more complicated and
as enterprise and regional specialization become more important.

I hope that over the years to come we can find out the most important
question, namely, how do people feel subjectively. Do they feel they have
a good balance between individual, family, village and national rights and
obligations? Do they feel they are participating in creating their own
future? Has socialism reduced the problem of alienation that otherwise
seems an unavoidable part of modernization?

To return to Mr Zhan Wu's point on political stability, I wonder if
bureaucrats will easily give up control of the economy to market forces. I
wonder if everyone in China agrees with the definition of socialism that
emphasizes economic efficiency? Is not some political struggle likely in
the future?

These are not the kind of questions that the speaker or anyone here can answer in a few minutes. Rather, the answers will gradually emerge after years of normal scholarly exchange, which we are all pleased to have initiated today.

GENERAL DISCUSSION – RAPPORTEUR: SHEILA DICKINSON

In response to questions about methods of price determination Mr Wu explained that for the main commodities prices were fixed by government through a price control bureau. For some unimportant commodities local authorities could decide the prices. At rural fairs, however, prices could be negotiated between buyer and seller.

It was suggested that the reward system was important and also that the effect of distributing to each according to his work was similar to that now introduced in Eastern Europe. Mr Wu had not studied the latter point. He explained, however, that although food grain was distributed partly according to basic needs it was also partly distributed according to the work contribution, as was the whole of the cash distribution.

A discussant asked what were the two most important human factors in raising productivity and how they were incorporated in the production process. In response it was suggested that a good job had to be done in ideological terms and good democracy practised. In addition attention must be paid to the national economic interests involved and this was now being currently discussed. The most important point was the principle of "to each according to his work". When this had been followed enthusiasm was high, productivity and output rose and costs were reduced. There was a great difference where the principle was not accurately observed and egalitarianism was practised. Control over production costs was, however, a weak link and in certain areas costs had risen because of an increase in physical inputs.

The nature of individual enterprises at local level was also queried. Mr Wu explained that the enterprises described in his paper were owned by communes, production brigades or production teams and their autonomy had to be respected. Private enterprises referred only to household sidelines. In reply to a question about the adoption of mathematical economics, Mr Wu explained that this was a new subject which they were just beginning to learn to use.

The importance of stability was emphasized. It was suggested that this and other material reasons for China's agricultural development might not be available elsewhere, and the question was raised whether Chinese experience could be replicated in other developing countries. It was also pointed out that increased mechanization, with an increased requirement for capital and reduced requirement for labour, implied more specialization and the emergence of new kinds of organization and might lead to a clash between the aims of employment and growth.

Participants in the discussion included Walton J. Anderson, Ichiro Kaneda, Raphael S.J. Shen, I. Fendru and Benedict Stavis.

FERENC FEKETE

Accomplishments of and Challenges for Agricultural Economists Working at the National Level of Centrally Managed Economies*

To undertake an account concerning the activity of agricultural economists working at national level in the CME means also to face the old but straight challenge thrown out by the French reasoner Chamfort almost 200 years ago to the corps of economists with his ironic words: "The economists are like operating surgeons who dispose of sharp dissectors but their operating scalpel is notched and therefore they brilliantly carry out a necrotomy but they torture flesh". This paper endeavours to prove that agricultural economists working at the national level in CME performed already resultful activities so far and they are ready also in the future to do much for the end that they and other people active in the sphere of economics should be acknowledged and kept in evidence not as "necrotomists" but as calculating, planning, constructing, developing, competent masters of their profession.

1 HISTORICAL AND IDEOLOGICAL BACKGROUND

The roots of the ideology characteristic for agricultural economists working in the national institutions of the CME can be dated back to the outset of the organized movement of the working class and to the emergence of the Marxist theory of socialism. The ideological seeds of socialist agriculture were sown by the Communist Manifesto speaking about the "improvement of the soil generally in accordance with a common plan" as well as about "farming on collective account". Marx and Engels declare in the Manifesto about a school of socialist literature that it

---

* On the basis of practical considerations, the author accepts the term "centrally managed economies" (CME) and means thereby the European countries belonging to the CMEA. Corresponding to the previously established List of Agenda of the Conference, the attention of the author is focused on the activities of agricultural economists working in national organizations and in governmental institutions. His exposition is mostly based upon the situation prevailing in Hungary but he endeavours also to outline the general historico-theoretical characteristics as well as experience gained in other countries, mainly in the Soviet Union.

285

"disserted with great acuteness the contradictions in the conditions of modern production. It laid bare the hypocritical apologies of economists".

The role of Lenin was determinant in the construction of the theoretical model of socialist agriculture and in the establishment of its first practical types. Among his words far-reachingly written about agrarian subjects which embrace a long period of time, one must first of all refer to the Agrarian Theses formulated in 1920 and to his respective articles published in 1923 about co-operative subjects. Socialist agriculture was established in the Soviet Union about one and a half decades after the October Revolution. In Hungary this process began in 1948 and was finished in 1961. The organization of socialist agriculture was established earlier in Bulgaria, at the same time in Czechoslovakia, while a short time later in the GDR and in Rumania than it had been in Hungary.

The major characteristics of the socialist system of agriculture can be summarized as follows: collective ownership of land and of the other important means of production; the organization of large-scale collective agricultural enterprises in the form of co-operative and state farms and more recently in the form of inter-firm organizations; the application of farming systems based upon a concerted enterprise plan; the same of up-to-date technologies and scientifically founded production techniques in the large-scale farms under collective ownership; the getting nearer of the incomes and living conditions of farm people to those of industrial workers i.e. to the income level and living standards of the urban population.

Socialist agriculture was established and is further developing as a result of processes accompanied by multifarious social, economic, cultural and human problems. The requirement that agricultural production should grow in the course of the socialist transformation period (including the years 1958–61) stood in the focus of the agricultural economists' attention in Hungary. It was also an important objective in the period of socialist transformation that the evolving large-scale farm organization should result in the substantial and systematic increase of agricultural production. Today it is already proven that this task was accomplished. In the course of the last 25 years the net value of agricultural production increased by 1.2 per cent yearly in Hungary and the annual increase amounted to 1.6 per cent in the recent 5 years. Simultaneously, mainly in the course of the last decade, the personal incomes of labourers of the socialist large-scale farm enterprises increased more rapidly than the social average did and the amount of personal income per caput in agriculture practically equalled that of people working in other branches of the national economy.

The interrelations existing between economy and policy which were intensively examined by Lenin have a particular importance in the socio-economic system of socialism and, we may add, in each modern social system as well as also in the activity itself of agricultural economists. According to his conclusions "policy is the concentrated expression of economy" on the one hand and "policy has a primacy against economy" on the other. These general principles mean in the practice of economists' activities at the national level first of all that the socialist state deliberately formulates and sets the major economic objectives and also develops the relevant conditions for their implementation within the planned management of the national economy. The above quoted principles represent at the same time the "political approach" to economic problems which is nothing else than a firm effort to set out from the public interests of the whole population and to concert the interests of the diverse social groups.[1]

Veritable milestones were represented in the agriculture of the Soviet Union and of the European people's democratic states as well as in the agricultural economic activity at national level by Party and state decisions made between autumn 1953 and spring 1957 and by the changes which started following them. The nature of these changes is symbolized by the XXth Congress of the CPSU. Mr Machewicz, former minister of agriculture, said at this Congress: ". . . up to recent times the economic categories were quite carelessly treated in the activity of agricultural agencies and experts . . . the recommended agrotechnical and other techniques were not evaluated under the aspect of economic efficiency . . . no economically justified remarks were set up against the plans of crop structure or against the diverse recommended agrotechniques which were mechanically prescribed by the central institutions although in several cases they were inadequate for the farms".

In the Soviet Union and in the other CME the route passed since 1956 can partly be marked by the accomplishments of the agricultural economists: like the new system of agricultural planning, and the increasing role of farm planning, the reorganization of the machine and tractor stations of the state and the selling of the big machines to the kolkhozes (co-operative farms), the gradual elimination of the compulsory delivery of agricultural produce and the increased role of purchasing (producer) prices, the progress of the system of labour remuneration and the significant increase of the personal incomes of the agricultural labourers, mainly of the kolkhoz (co-operative farm) members (including also the income originated in their home plot farms).

The decision taken in the political and professional leading bodies of the CME statutorily and systematically deal with the development tasks of socialist agriculture and with the duties of agricultural economists. Under this aspect we may lay particular stress on the Programme of the CP in this Soviet Union, on the resolutions of the XXIIIrd, XXIVth and XXVth Congresses of the Party, as well as on the decisions made at the plenary sessions of the Central Committee of the CPSU, and at the plenum in November 1978 among them. In Hungary the Central Committee of the HSWP discussed at its session of March 1978 an item of agenda having the title "The situation of agriculture and food industry and the tasks of their further development" and adopted a detailed resolution thereon. At the General Assembly of the Hungarian Academy of Sciences the 1978 plenary session took place under the title "The development of agriculture and food industry and the tasks of the sciences". In its resolution the Academy invites the representatives of each discipline "to take part in the construction of an optimum organizational framework in order to promote the more efficient use of the resources and . . . to assist in answering those great economic questions which will emerge before the future development of agricultural production".

2 ACHIEVEMENTS, POSSIBILITIES – NATIONAL ECONOMIC PLANNING AND CENTRAL MANAGEMENT

National economic planning can look back to a past longer than half a century in the Soviet Union and longer than three decades in the other European CME. In the course of this period abundant experience cumulated in both the theory and practice of national economic planning as well as the activity of agricultural economists progressed. In addition to the general determinant characteristics, also the particular conditions, state of development and the fundamental economic political trends of the diverse countries are reflected in the national economic planning of the CME. Considerable changes resulted in the practice of national economic planning in Hungary by the reform of economic management elaborated in 1966 and introduced in 1968.

An important element, i.e. one of the starting point of national economic planning, is represented by the assessment of domestic needs, of the demand in the country and in the world market. Facts indicate that in close connection with national consumption habits characteristic exporter and importer countries can appear in respect of certain commodities. Thus, e.g., Hungary is a beef exporting country where at the same time beef consumption is relatively small. It is well known that Hungary carries on an extensive international trade and therefore when developing agriculture it is very important for the country to reckon with the changes in the world economic situation which exert an impact upon the CMEA as well as also upon the capitalist world market.

In recent years the overemphasized orientation of planning towards production and mainly towards the recent organization of production became apparent in the practice of Hungarian national economic planning; but also in other CMEA countries. The so called "problem oriented" approach began in planning what was called systems approach or complex planning in the Soviet Union. This approach relates to the category of social planning, to intersectoral problems (arising, e.g., between production and domestic commerce), to technical development, etc. In Hungary, agriculture, food industry and farm machine, fertilizer, etc. industries are taken together as a unit in the development plans of "production blocks". Block-building and a "problem oriented" approach mean the application of new complementary aspects in national economic planning.

National economic planning and the central (state) economic management form an organic unity. Therefore significant changes were effected in Hungary by the reform of economic management (the so called economic mechanism) also in the national economic planning. This reform was a continuation of the same economic-political tendency which was expressed in the abolition of the compulsory delivery of agricultural produce to the state implemented ten years ago, in the earlier initiated easing of the inflexibilities of national economic planning and of the central direction over economy.

The reform endeavoured to replace – by means of stopping the administrative "breaking down" (specification) of detailed production plans constructed at national level to the production units – with planned assessment and operation of economic regulators (prices, credit conditions, taxes, rate of exchange of foreign currencies, etc.). The mostly bureaucratic system of the fully centralized distribution of the material resources was replaced by the methods of commodity turnover and by the centrally influenced (controlled) market. The major investments and the establishment of new firms and large-scale enterprises represent, of course, the subject of central governmental decisions also in the future. The role of prices in orienting and encouraging the economic decisions of the producers and consumers are emphasized by the reform of economic management (direction).

The reasons for the existence and the positive effects of the reform of economic management are indicated also by the increase of agricultural production. Compared to the average of the preceding five years it increased by 20 per cent in the years 1971–75. (A 15–16 per cent increase was envisaged in the national economic plan.) The increase of national income (by 35 per cent) and of industrial production (by 37 per cent) was also more rapid than envisaged for the same period; real wages per earner increased by 18 per cent.

Today in Hungary agricultural economists acting in diverse positions of the national economic planning and central management over the economy operate under the conditions of the so called intensive phase of economic progress. In this phase the tripartite watch words of efficiency, quality and competitiveness formulate the most important requirements. These requirements are to be satisfied under conditions becoming ever more exacting since (a) the acreage suitable for agricultural production of the country is constantly diminishing; (b) the number of agricultural earners radically diminishes and particular measures are needed for the good performance of labour peaks; (c) up-to-date large-scale agricultural production is still young and costly; (d) agrarian protectionism regained its strength all over the world again and competition become keener in the markets abroad. Under such severe conditions – as it was emphasized also in the resolutions of the Central Committee of the HSWP – the export orientation of agricultural production as well as the rentability of the exports are to be increased and the efficiency and structure of the production activities must be improved. In spite of the fact that compared to the past the growth rate of investments decreased, the planners reckon in the long term development plans with the annual 4–5 per cent increase of large-scale agricultural production.

The plenary session of the Central Committee of the CPSU held in July 1978 declared necessary the development of agricultural planning and the consolidation of the inter-sectoral relations of the agro-industrial complex. The importance of the correct economic foundation of the five-year plan of purchasing and of the development of the agricultural price system were also emphasized. The making of concrete governmental decisions was envisaged for the improvement of the realization (marketing) system of agricultural produce and of stimulation of the enterprises. Soviet agricultural economists working at diverse posts of national economic planning and management are performing responsible tasks nowadays in the preparation of the plan for the years 1981–85 and of the long term socio-economic development plan for 1990.

3   PROBLEMS, URGENT TASKS – PRICING

Pricing and price planning represent an organic part of the system of national planning while price policy does the same in the sets of economic policy. National economic plans and prices can also be considered in the CME as interlinking means for the central management of the economy.

In the sphere of pricing, economists working at the national level construct by means of calculations and models so called price centres (calculated prices). In quantitative respect each price centre is determined by the amount of net income surpassing costs in the calculation i.e. by the distribution of net social income among the diverse branches (products) of the economy. The types of calculated prices are distinguished by the principles accordingly to which the co-ordination of inputs (costs) and net incomes is performed. The price centres, the calculated price-types, are created through great simplifications and therefore their weaknesses are first of all the following: (a) they do not reckon with the fact that the application of a new price necessarily alters the produced and consumed quantity of the diverse products and thereby the quantity of inputs per unit output of the respective produce also changes; (b) calculated prices do not express those economic political preferences which deliberately deflect prices from the inputs; (c) they do not reflect the demand supply relations of the diverse products. Because of these and other (political, social, etc.) reasons calculated prices are considered only the starting point in price planning.

Prices in practice play their parts well when they are assessed under the combined impact of production costs, the value-judgements of the markets (users) and state (social) preferences. The enforcement of this triple requirement in price policy is not a simple task and it cannot be solved without compromises and contradictions. In the CME there asserts a mixed price mechanism itself i.e. centrally fixed or maximized prices,

prices moving between established limits, centrally guaranteed (minimum) prices and "free" market prices exist simultaneously. The reform of economic management in Hungary increased this latter sphere of prices. At the same time about 60 per cent of the purchasing of agricultural products is performed by the state and/or by the co-operatives at centrally fixed prices.

Agricultural economists of the CME are of the opinion that the most important economic condition for a planned increase of agricultural production is the establishment of a producers' price level which covers the costs of production and maintains also a net income rate suitable for the producer enterprises. Producers' prices play a key role in the indication of social interests and of needs (demands) to the producers. The role and the scope of the diverse subsidies (subventions, donations for investments and operation) are very large in Hungary rendering thereby the economic overlook and the efficient stimulation of the producing enterprises more difficult.

In most of the CME there is a great difficulty caused by the fact that a particular gap, a certain kind of reversed two-level phenomenon exists between the producers' and consumers' prices of agricultural products. This gap is bridged over by the sophisticated system of dotations granted by the state for the processing industries and for the retaining sector (commerce). Great importance is attributed to the stability of consumers' prices from the aspect of the planned development of people's living standards. Simultaneously with the consideration of this principle, consumers' prices of agricultural products should better reflect the costs of production and relations between consumers' and producers' prices should become more pronounced. This requirement was distinctly formulated in the professional circles of economists earlier and unambiguously expressed in economic-political measures recently taken. Also the consolidation of the connection between the domestic price system and world market prices became the question of the day in Hungary.

The adequate co-ordination of the orienting and income distributing functions of prices present a sophisticated task also for the economists of the CME. The scientific foundation and the planned development of the territorially differentiated system of agricultural producer (purchasing) prices sets a particular task for the Soviet agricultural economists. In the territory of the Soviet Union there are 73 price zones for the purchasing of milk and 62 ones for cattle on foot. There are 27 price zones for wheat in the territory of the USSR.

4 PROSPECTS AND LONG TERM CHALLENGES – AGRARIAN ORGANIZATION AND DECISION–MAKING MECHANISM

While the main supporting pillars of the socialist agrarian system invariably remain the state farms (sovkhozes) and the co-operative farms (kolkhozes), new types of agricultural organizations also emerge and gain ground in the agriculture of almost each CME.

At present or as they formulate "in the new implementation stage of the co-operative plan of Lenin" agricultural inter-firm organizations and agro-industrial unions are gaining ground at a very rapid rate in the Soviet Union. All kolkhozes and more than half of sovkhozes take part in these organizations. The total number of agricultural inter-firm organizations was 7,000 at the beginning of 1977 and 1,200 agro-industrial unions operated among them. At the beginning of 1978 the number of these inter-firm organizations amounted to 7,800. An important task is for agricultural economists working in the Ministry of Agriculture and in the other national institutions to survey the activities and experiences of these inter-firm organizations. The activity of agricultural economists is directly motivated also by the fact that the operation of the new agricultural and agro-industrial organizations is related with the development of the central management of agriculture. The elaboration of the basic theoretical principles of the so called automated system of national economic and sectoral management is also of great importance. At the plenary session of the Central Committee of the CPSU held in July 1978 critical conclusions were drawn in the statement that the Gosplan and the Ministry of Agriculture "could not become so far such centres which are able to control and co-ordinate the activities related to the specialization and concentration of agricultural production".

The system of agro-industrial complexes (APK) in formation represent the new organizational basis of large-scale socialist agriculture in Bulgaria. The specialization and concentration of production rapidly develops in the GDR. The so called organizations for co-operation in crop growing – in co-operation with the agro-chemical centres – represent the new type of specialized agricultural enterprise and at the end of 1975 they cultivated already 88 per cent of the total agricultural area in the GDR.

At the beginning of the 1970s, production systems came into existence in Hungary as the new organizations of agricultural inter-firm co-operation. Already 67 production systems were active at the end of 1977 and 86 per cent of the state farms as well as 78 per cent of the farmers' co-operatives were co-operating in these systems. Four production systems are operated in large-scale corn production; there exists certain division of function among them but their competition is not fully eliminated. The production system implements general collaboration in respect of the supply of production means, the elaboration and continuous development of production technology, the organization of marketing and professional training for one or more organically interlinked lines of agricultural production. Co-ordinating and extension services are performed by the so called system master or gestor farm. Partner farms are joined to the former. Farms may voluntarily join the system most suitable for them; each large-scale agricultural enterprise is allowed, of course, to be a member of several production systems at the same time. The partner farms can establish the system centre in the form of their joint venture.

The production systems, however, can operate also as simple associations and the functions of the system centre are performed in this case by the separated section of a larger state farm or farmers' co-operative.

The partner farms pay for the services of the system centre a fee in cash or in kind which consists of the base fee and of a contracted part of the increase of yield. Within the economic concerns of the system centre and the partner farms also contrasting tendencies can be observed. The former is mainly interested in the quantitative increase of yields while the latter is interested in the increase of the enterprise's income.

With an experimental character four agro-industrial unions were established in Hungary in 1976. These organizations are created with the co-operation of agricultural producing enterprises, food industrial firms and agro-commercial agencies for the complex utilization of resources in a given zone.

All the aforesaid facts well indicate that a number of particular agricultural economic problems originate in the new organizational formations of socialist agriculture.

The development problems of the decision-making mechanism energetically take up the attention of agricultural economists in the CME. Herbert A. Simon, the 1978 winner of the Nobel prize in economics, states that instead of procedural rationality substantive rationality prevailed in the economic decisions. Starting out from this standpoint he intensively studies the applicability of operations research, programming and simulation as the apparatus of technical procedures for economic decision-making. The attention of Marxist economists covers also the social and political dimensions of the economic decision making mechanism. At the XIVth Conference of the IAAE they treated in detail the democratic character of planning and the consolidation of the democratization of economic decisions made at national level.

One of the most important sources of the vitality of the socialist system of agriculture is represented by its "multisectorality" and by its richness in respect of the types and diverse sizes of the enterprises. Even in these days the household farms of the co-operative (kolkhoz) members and the relatively small-scale agricultural production carried out by workers and employees – partly as their hobby – represent an organic complementing of the activities of the large-scale collective agricultural organizations managed as enterprises.

It was already earlier obvious for the agricultural economists of the CME that the members of kolkhozes (farmers' co-operatives) are not only labourers but also co-owners and even associate undertakers in the one and same person. The principle of consolidating co-operative democratization remains in prominence, but also the problem of enterprise democratization of the state-owned enterprises comes into the focus of attention in the recent period. Socialist democracy in the firm or enterprise should and can be studied also under a national economic aspect. The agricultural economists of the CME are to consolidate the essential character of socialist property and to promote the assertion of this essen-

294 *Ferenc Fekete*

tial character in economic decisions made in the decisive spheres of increasing the collective owner's role as worker in the utilization of production means and of surplus produce as well as selecting, consistently with principles, the determinant factors of personal incomes.

From the lessons of the past, agricultural economists may draw the direct conclusion that they should assume commitment and they are to be resolute for action. Let us express this with the words of Goethe: "Who has the case at heart should take a stand for it otherwise he does not merit to exert any influence anywhere."

REFERENCES

Balassa, Ákos *A magyar népgazdaság tervezésének alapjai* (The bases of national economic planning in Hungary), Közgazdasági és Jogi Könyvkiadó, Budapest 1979.
Erdei, Ferenc "An Idea and its Realization", *The New Hungarian Quarterly*, Budapest 1968, No. 30.
Erdei, Ferenc A XX. Kongresszus utmutatása az agrárgazdasági és üzemszervezési munka számára (Guidance provided by the XXth Congress for agricultural economics and farm management), Agrárgazdasági és Üzemszervezési Közlemények, Budapest 1956, No. 1.
Essays on Economic Policy and Planning in Hungary (ed. by István Friss) Corvina Kiadó, Budapest 1978.
Fekete, Ferenc, Heady, Earl O., Holdren, Bob R. *Economics of Co-operative Farming*, Sijthoff, Leyden, Akadémiai Kiadó, Budapest 1976.
Friss, I. "Ten Years of Economic Reform in Hungary", *Acta Oeconomica*, Budapest 1978, No. 1–2.
K. Marx F. *Engels Collected Works*, Progress Publishers, Moscow 1976, Vol. 6.
Lenin Selected Works, Progress Publishers, Moscow 1967, Vol. 3.
Magyar Tudomány, 1978, No. 6.
Mezshozjajsztvennaja kooperacija i agropromüslennaja intyegracija v szel'szkom hozjajsztve, Kolosz Izdatyelsztvo, Moszkva 1978.
Politicseszkaja Ekonomija, Ucsebnyik 2, Politizdat, Moszkva 1976.
Öri, J. "Pricing of Agricultural Products and Foodstuff in Hungary", *Acta Oeconomica*, Budapest 1976, No. 1.
Schulze, H.G., Trutzschler, A. "Zur Kombination der Produktion landwirtschaftlicher Erzeugnisse und ihrer Be- und Verarbeitung beim Übergang zur industriemässigen Produktion in der Landwirtschaft der DDR" (To the combination of agricultural production and of processing agricultural products in course of the transition to industrial production in the agriculture of the GDR), *Wirtschaftswissenschaft*, Berlin 1976, No. 6.
Simon, H.A. "On how to decide what to do", *Economic Impact*, Washington DC 1979, No. 3.
Szabó, K. "Factory Democracy and Political Economy", *Acta Oeconomica*, Budapest 1974, No. 1.
Voproszü Ekonomiki, Moszkva 1979, No. 2.

DISCUSSION OPENING – ROBERT L. THOMPSON

I have read Dr Fekete's paper with considerable interest and find it quite informative. We have too little professional dialogue between agricultural economists working in different economic systems. While our respective points of departure in terms of social objectives and the distribution of ownership of factors of production may differ, all are ultimately concerned with increasing the efficiency of resource allocation to achieve the respective objectives. Dr Fekete's survey of the accomplishments of and challenges for agricultural economists working at the national level in centrally planned economies makes a useful contribution to this dialogue.

In my comments I attempt to review briefly what I interpret to be the principal issues raised in Dr Fekete's paper and suggest several other questions which he does not specifically treat. The comments are organized in four areas of research and analysis in which I think agricultural economists can potentially play a very important role at the national level in the centrally planned economies: (1) Price determination; (2) Demand analysis and projection; (3) Marketing and transportation and (4) Production planning and projection. These are discussed in turn.

Price determination
I concur with Dr Fekete that one of the greatest challenges for agricultural economists in centrally planned economies lies in the area of price determination. In an economy where both prices and target quantities are centrally planned there exists a great challenge to ensure consistency of the production plans in all sectors with demand for their respective outputs, whether as inputs for further processing or as final consumption or export. The ultimate measure of planning success is whether or not there exists excess supply or excess demand at the administered price. While economists in centrally planned economies have made important contributions to the development and application of input-output analysis for this purpose, the data requirements are enormous. Moreover, in agricultural production which is characterized by climatic risk, it is inevitable that realized production will not equal planned use. Observed disequilibria and bottlenecks in centrally planned economies provide prima facie evidence that planning in practice still leaves much to be desired. The move towards greater reliance on less rigid planning with some market determination of price in some eastern European countries suggests an official recognition of the inevitability of planning failures at least in the agricultural sector.

In recent years more use has been made of linear programming models in central planning. Some years ago Oscar Lange demonstrated that theoretically a centrally planned economy organized according to shadow prices would achieve the same efficient allocation of resources as an otherwise identical market economy. By implication, if there were not data constraints or limitations on computer capacity, one could construct an immense mathematical programming model of the economy and use the resulting shadow prices as the administered prices in the economy. Agricultural economists in centrally planned economies have made progress in building some aggregate linear programming models, as evidence in Professor Csaki's paper, also presented at this conference. These can provide a useful input into price determination in centrally planned economies; however in the real world we have several data constraints and measurement problems. The correspondence between large quantitative models and reality usually leaves much to be desired in both centrally planned and market economies. While much more research is probably merited in this area, it may have limited payoff until better data and improved supply and demand forecasting techniques are available.

Demand analysis and projection

In the planning process and in making pricing decisions in centrally planned economies, agricultural economists have to project the change in quantity demanded in response to changes in prices and income. My review of the literature suggests that demand analysis is a weakly developed area of agricultural economic research in centrally planned economies, but one in which much more work is needed.

Demand analysis poses particular problems for at least two reasons. First, under administered consumer prices there is very little variation in price. This makes it difficult, if not impossible, for regression techniques to measure the effect of price change on quantity demanded. Second, and more important, since there exists nonprice rationing, the observed price quantity points do not lie on the demand functions. Therefore, the analyst must resort to recent developments in disequilibrium econometrics. Not surprisingly, this field was pioneered by a Hungarian economist, Kornai, but there is also work done by many others outside the centrally planned economies, such as Chambers and Just in the United States.

Marketing and transportation

The agricultural product distribution and marketing system is a third area in which agricultural economists could make an important contribution in centrally planned economies. Casual observation suggests that bottleneck and inefficiencies abound, and heavy subsidization is required. While linear programming transportation models are employed to improve efficiency in some parts of the transportation system, such as railcar allocation, much wider application of the available techniques could be made.

Closely related to the marketing issues is the problem of determination of the spatial pattern of prices, as well as the consistency between internal and world market prices. As a result of a product pricing strategy in some countries, which attempts to remove economic rent associated with differences in land quality and environment, a spatial pattern of production results, which at times is not only at odds with the factor endowments but which also places additional strains on the transportation system. Agricultural economists in centrally planned economies need to provide analysis of the social costs of following present pricing policies to planners.

Production

Agricultural economists working at the national level in centrally planned economies have made their greatest contributions in agricultural production and farm management analysis. Useful applications of mathematical programming have been made in annual enterprise planning and in selecting the optimum machinery complement for state or collective farms. Farm management simulation games are now being effectively used in training farm managers (for example, by Csaki). While advances have been made in this area, more work is nevertheless needed. Recent developments in multigoal programming can permit the analyst to maximize more than one objective, subject to whatever constraints exist, to determine an optimum farm plan. Moreover, given the relatively large variance in crop yields due to climatic variability, use of stochastic programming needs to be made to define optimum farm plans in a risky environment.

For purposes of investment planning at the national level, more research is needed on both economies of scale and appropriate technology in agriculture. Closely related to this is the question of optimum energy intensity of agricultural production. An energy-intensive agricultural development strategy may have been appropriate while the CMEA countries were energy self-sufficient. But now with the energy crunch agricultural economists need to determine the optimum future energy intensity of agricultural production. More generally, their input is needed in determining agricultural research priorities, as well as in assessing the ecological effects of technological change in agriculture.

At the aggregate level agricultural economists need to improve production forecasting techniques and produce regular forecasts of supplies of agricultural products. This may require close collaboration with agricultural meteorologists to improve short-run forecasting performance. Nevertheless, this could be a very high pay-off endeavour for agricultural economists; one which is essential in a centrally planned economy in which market prices do not function to signal needed changes in demand and in foreign trade.

GENERAL DISCUSSION – RAPPORTEUR: SHEILA DICKINSON

In discussion attention was drawn to the problem of determining prices in trade between CMEA and non-CMEA countries and it was suggested that this topic should be included in the next IAAE Conference. With the introduction of free price determination in the CMEs it was also suggested that differences from the free market economies were diminishing.

In response, Dr Fekete recalled that prices were not just arbitrarily determined but were the concrete realisation of socio-economic realities. Conditions in Hungary differed from those in other CMEs and because of the importance of trade to Hungary they tried to create close links between domestic and world prices. Producer and consumer prices might be closely linked; but they might differ. He could not in any event accept the suggestion that the Hungarian economy was a market economy since 60 per cent of agricultural produce was marketed at fixed prices and only 14 per cent at free prices.

Questions were asked about the co-ordination of the profit method with the Marxist theory of value and about the welfare function of a socialist system. Dr Fekete explained that the profit sharing arrangements amounted simply to a distribution of any surplus to workers in proportion to their direct wages. A socialist system did not work for the sake of profit but in response to the needs of society.

Dr Fekete added that questions of demand had not commanded much interest in the CMEs for some time but a group was now working on income and price elasticities of demand and on nutritional aspects. His paper had not covered questions of marketing and transport or of economies of scale and technology, since these were micro-economic questions, but they received considerable attention. They were particularly interested in the most efficient method of production and optimum farm size. In addition they had applied a range of existing technologies imported from countries where relative input prices were different and they were now trying to adjust these technologies to their own conditions.

Participants in the discussion included Ichiro Kaneda and Adolf A. Weber.

HARTWIG DE HAEN

The Use of Quantitative Sector Analysis in Agricultural Policy: Potentials and Limitations

1 INTRODUCTION

The use and application of quantitative models in the process of agricultural decision-making has always been controversial. In spite of methodological progress, models have been criticized as lacking an empirical foundation and excluding relevant facts which may not easily be pressed into the formal structure of mathematical models although they are offered up to policy makers as the complete basis for rational decisions.[1] On the other hand, there is a growing demand by agricultural policy agencies in many countries to evaluate costs and benefits of alternative policy measures quantitatively.

In order to promote the discussion of this issue, four questions will be analysed in this paper: (1) Do we need quantitative models and what can they contribute to the decision-making process? (2) What are the theoretical requirements on which models should be based? (3) What is the state of the art of model building and application? (4) How can quantitative sector analysis be better integrated into the policy process?

2 QUANTITATIVE MODELS AND THE PROCESS OF AGRICULTURAL POLICY DECISION–MAKING

2.1 What are the determinants of agricultural policy?

Ideally policy conclusions derived from model calculations could be directly transformed into policy action. However, such a one-to-one relationship would not only require that economic models could predict future developments accurately. It would also assume a complete congruency between the domain of competence of economic theory and the range of responsibilities of practical policy. This congruency, however, does not exist: economic efficiency and growth are only a subset of the goals of agricultural policy. A deeper understanding of their respective impact and mutual interdependence is needed in order to improve the relevance and application of models as planning and policy analysis tools.

299

Several theories have attempted "to explain" policies within the political economy, as were dealt with in the 1976 IAAE Conference on "Decision-Making and Agriculture".[2] Yet a lack of empiricial knowledge and widely accepted theories about agricultural policy processes remains. There is, however, agreement that governments typically do not "articulate a single-valued long-run policy and immediately adopt it. Instead they formulate a broad general concept of long-run goals and move in their direction, away from structures existing at the moment, through a succession of short-run improvisations upon which agreement can be obtained".[3]

Two conclusions for the economist and model builder follow from this. One is the notion that the policy process is a stepwise and iterative procedure in which information collection and analysis precede decisions and actions in which goals and instruments are frequently, in the course of time, revised.

The other conclusion is that economic analysis can only have a limited relevance for practical policy. The desire of a government to stay in office, the attempt to reach agreement between interest groups, preference for the avoidance of any kinds of short-run bottlenecks and institutional resistance to change are other policy determinants.

Those groups negatively affected by a policy will tend to prevent its full application by organized political action. Success of these groups is more likely when they are small with a comparatively high burden per head and when the groups positively affected are large and the benefits are relatively dispersed.[4] This paradigm may explain why many developed countries, with low levels of food expenditures in consumer budgets and well organized farmers' unions, have maintained high levels of farm support and many developing countries, with high levels of food expenditures and few organized farm groups, have neglected farm support and emphasized more consumer oriented policies. The prevalence of national over international interests in the absence of external political or economic pressure is another aspect of this political process. The stabilization of agricultural prices within the EC at the cost of destabilizing prices on international markets may exemplify this tendency.

Although the significance of the elements in the preference function of different countries may vary, an increased material well-being, a more equitable distribution of income, a more ecologically sound pattern of growth, and an increased awareness of the impact of domestic policy on international relations are all goals which must enter as elements in the decision process. This alone would justify the development of new quantitative models which would incorporate these elements in the analysis and describe the impact of alternative policy instruments on them.

2.2 The potential role of quantitative models in the policy process
The stepwise and iterative process of policy decision making has been frequently described as a sequence of the following phases:[5]

1   goal definition and problem perception,

2   analysis and diagnosis of past development,
3   analysis and projection of policy effects,
4   discussion and evaluation of policy alternatives within and outside
the decision making bodies,
5   decision,
6   execution and control.

Ideally, model development and implementation should occur in close
co-ordination with the preparation of policy decisions. In phase 1, the
problem – discrepancy between desired and observed states of the system
– is defined based on an observation of the facts and a knowledge of stated
goals. The co-ordination would ideally continue through the following
three phases, to each of which corresponds a distinct model type (consistency and explanatory modes to phase 2, simulation models to phase 3,
and policy decision models to phase 4).

What is the potential role of quantitative models in the policy process?
Simply speaking, their role is to take into account complex interactions
between real world events and policy measures and reduce these interactions to a limited number of performance indicators which clarify the
effects to alternative policy instruments. Models can thus help to detect
conflicts, i.e. undesired side-effects, inconsistencies between instruments
and goals etc., which are potentially foreseeable on the basis of given data
and assumptions but which of themselves are too complex to be envisaged
and quantified without models. One example is the annual decision on
intervention prices made by the European Council of Ministers, when the
long run allocation effects are usually neglected in favour of short run
income effects. Another example is the domain of rural development
policies in many developing countries. Many of the investments, such as
rural infrastructure, small farmers' programmes etc. in this area, may not
be effective or even be made ineffective by counteracting macro policies,
i.e. policies of reduced interest/wage ratios, low food prices etc. Quantitative models are clearly needed which can be used to evaluate the mutual
interactions of policies at the micro and macro level.

3   PROBLEMS OF FORMALIZING GOAL–INSTRU-MENTS–SYSTEMS IN ECONOMIC POLICY

The following aspects of quantitative modelling for economic policy
deserve more consideration in empirical research. They represent pre-conditions for a closer interaction between quantitative modelling and
policy making. Such aspects include: (1) analysis of goals and problems;
and (b) analysis of the relationship between explanation, forecasting and
controllability of a system's development.

(a)   Goal and problem analysis
Two issues need to be discussed in the context of goals and problem
analysis: the delineation of model boundaries and model structure and

the specification of performance indicators. A positive relationship between the number of goals incorporated and the richness of structure
given to a quantitative model clearly exists. In order to broaden the range
of policy goals in an analysis one needs to endogenize more real world
phenomena, e.g. to explain policy effects on income distribution, market
stability, employment, inflation etc. While some attempts have been
successful within the boundaries of sector models, others have had to
incorporate the explicit consideration of national or even international
markets. The larger the share of the agricultural sector in total resources,
consumption or production of a country and the less realistic the assumption of zero or infinite elasticities of intersectoral supply and demand, the
more important is the construction of a full national model. The analysis
of intersectoral resource flows and foreign trade in developing countries,
for example, is hardly possible with an isolated agricultural sector model.

Similar considerations apply to the boundaries between national models and the rest of the world. Usually, the "small country hypothesis" of
infinitely elastic world supply and demand is made. For countries with
large world market shares this is unrealistic and their trade policies have
then to be analysed under explicit consideration of the demand and
supply behaviour of the rest of the world. Increasing research effort is
indeed moving in this direction of linking national and global models.
Yet, the delineation of necessary boundaries and of optimal complexity
of models remains an unresolved issue.

A second aspect of goal analysis, the specification of performance
indicators, will only be briefly discussed here. Two fundamentally different approaches are conceivable. One approach is to define a set of
unweighted performance indicators, to simulate their development
through time under alternative assumptions, and to present the
decision-makers with the full range of policy alternatives. General System Simulation Models fall into this category. The other much more
ambitious approach is to specify a policy preference function and to
generate through the model an "optimal" policy. Most optimizing policy
models are still restricted to a single hypothetical objective, such as
maximum growth or least cost resource allocation, possibly expanded by
some lexicographic ordering of constraints.[6]

Empirical estimates of governments' (multi-valued) "revealed preferences"[7] and their use in practical planning are still problematic if not
impossible. Governments frequently update even their most vaguely
defined goals which has the effect that the use of an objective function
derived from past trends could lead to the neglect of some or all of the
determinants discussed earlier.

(b)   Explanation, forecasting and control
A review of the models which have been applied to agricultural sector
analysis and planning reveals three issues which require further discussion: (i) explanatory power of models; (ii) time horizon and dynamic
behaviour; and (iii) controllability of model development.

(i) The "explanation" of relevant world phenomena is a precondition for useful forecasting because it provides the positive basis for any normative policy decision. This precondition, however, is often neglected. In the place of an empirically validated theory one often finds *a priori* fixations of parameters and/or output variables which, although fixed by assumption only, are "buried" in the computer programmes and have not been properly documented so that they may be understood and manipulated by the user. Models of this type produce only limited "surprises" and represent hardly more than a book keeping device. In order to evaluate the level of goal attainment of alternative policies, however, the output variables have to be widely endogenized, i.e. causally related to level and time path of exogenous variables. While pure econometric models mostly fulfil the requirement of endogeneity, many General Systems Simulation and Programming Models, both of which often contain a more or less overseeable number of switching rules and restrictions, do not. Misled interpretations and premature or false policy conclusions may be the result. In addition to ex-post validation tests, the effects of such restrictions on the model output and the model's remaining structural degrees of freedom have to be carefully documented by sensitivity runs and earmarking of pre-specified variables. As models have become more complex and various kinds of parameter (guess) estimation are frequently used − e.g. where so called General Systems Simulation is involved − a comprehensive documentation has become more difficult. However, this should not lead model builders into the temptation to be dishonest and suppress essential information about *a priori* fixations of model behaviour. It is not unlikely that competition for public reputation and funding further support such dishonesty.

(ii) The time horizon of projections, limited by the decreasing confidence in parameter forecasts, has to be consistent with the expected duration of policy effects. Although no definite rules can be given here, an important characteristic of a model should be its ability to detect conflicts between short-run and long-run goal achievements. To give an example, farm support policies via price and investment subsidies in the EC are justified because of their income raising effect in the short run. A useful quantitative model should not only project the income effects but also indicate the related economic costs of resource malallocation in the long-run.

Both comparative-static and dynamic models are used to compute the changes of allocation patterns through time. What is usually of interest to policy makers is not a hypothetical final state or equilibrium growth path but the structure of disequilibria and the direction of time paths of development.[8] Dynamic systems' simulations do potentially fulfil such requirements.

(iii) Finally, the usefulness of such dynamic forecasts is very much determined by the controllability of the system's performance. Many models contain no, or an insufficiently specified, policy component linking the state of the system's model to instrument variables. To give an example, there exists an increasing number of regional simulation models which may yield a good ex-post time-series tracking. Yet, such models are often useless for regional planning because instruments such as investment subsidies or labour market policies etc. are not explicitly included. This increases the surplus of officially declared goals compared to the number of instruments which is typical for agricultural policy in many countries. A broadening of the set of goals (e.g. improved personal income distribution or better ecological balance) is often not accompanied by the introduction of appropriate new instruments. It is a mostly neglected task of the analyst and model builder to detect such inconsistencies and propose alternative goal-instrument systems. Not only do such systems have to have as many goals as instruments, but the structure of the models developed has to ensure that the output variables are indeed controllable.[9]

So far, the theoretical potential of quantitative sector models has been discussed. The following part of the paper will be devoted to a discussion of the state of the art and limitations of available models.

4   THE STATE OF APPLICABILITY OF MODELS IN PRACTICAL POLICY DECISIONS

In spite of a growing number of quantitative sector models reflecting some of the theoretical issues discussed above there is more and more concern about the credibility of such models among decision-makers.[10] Unfortunately, policy makers seldom clarify the reasons for their hesitation to make more use of the models. Presumably, these reasons have to be seen in the following three domains: (1) lack of clarity concerning structure, empirical basis and policy relevance of existing models; (2) uncertainty with respect to the empirical performance of available models; and (3) inappropriate implementation of model building and model use in the policy process.

A comprehensive survey and evaluation of models is impossible here.[11] Instead, the following section will exemplify how the discussion of the state of modelling could be systematized.

4.1   *Classification of models according to structure, methodology, and decision-making problems*
With the exception of some recent empirical applications of optimal control which have limited policy relevance,[12] none of the known sector models can be classified as policy decision models in the sense that they yield an optimal policy set on the basis of empirically validated relationships between policies and system development. Theoretically, optimal control models do have such properties. Yet, further structural richness and empirical foundation will be needed before a direct policy use can be recommended.

Most sectoral optimization models, i.e. linear single or multi-period programming models, lack an empirical component. Although frequently interpreted as policy instruments to "optimize" the projected future development, they assume an unrealistic identity between expected individual behaviour and optimal sectoral performance. Rather than providing policy recommendations directly, the equation system of sectoral programming models can be seen to be useful in the following four areas of application:[13] (a) as an input–output system to check data consistency; (b) as a test for sensitivity with respect to short-term yield or price fluctuations; (c) as a comparative analysis of equilibria under alternative exogenous conditions to determine new policy goals and targets; and (d) as a computation of shadow price systems for given or hypothetical allocation patterns through space and over time.

An increasing number of models can be classified as non-optimizing forecasting models. Given assumptions about exogenous variables, they project time paths of future sectoral development without necessarily yielding an "optimal" path. Many of these system models follow a building-bloc structure, i.e. they are bloc-recursive with dynamically linked components.[14] Typically, for instance, resource capacities and supply are assumed to depend on past prices and incomes, and market clearing is achieved through domestic consumption, foreign trade and, if short-run projections are intended, by stock manipulation. The building-bloc approach has several advantages for policy application, namely: flexibility in the choice of data bases, equation structure, and estimation techniques; possibility to use individual components separately; and lower level of complexity which facilitates communication with policy-makers.

The general systems simulation approach has increased modelling potential. Many relevant aspects of policy, however, remain poorly represented in the structure of most sector models, although separate analyses are often available. They include, for instance, components representing: (a) endogenous resource (land, intermediate inputs, labour) transfers between farm size groups and/or regions; (b) marketing and processing; (c) determinants of price or income instability; (d) ecological effects of intensive agricultural production.

Referring to the broader problem domain of agricultural policy more deficiencies of current quantitative analysis become evident. One is the dominance of aspects of allocation and growth over those of distribution. There are hardly any models which describe endogenously the impact of various policies on functional and personal income distribution in agriculture. The other is the neglect of interdisciplinary linkages. This criticism applies, for instance, to the hypotheses on farmers' investment and production behaviour under risk and uncertainty or to assumptions with respect to co-operation and participation in regional development projects. In both cases, there are important contributions of psychology and sociology which need more consideration in quantitative models. A third aspect is the almost complete neglect of costs of policy implementation in quantitative models. Policy instruments, such as EC-market orders,

investment subsidies or promotion of rural development require considerable inputs of personnel and material. To neglect their opportunity
costs would mean to overestimate the competitive position of the respective policy. Yet, the incorporation in formal models is an extremely
difficult task.

In this final section, a discussion of the state of the explanatory and
predictive capacity of models in the agricultural sector seems most
appropriate.

4.2   State of empirical performance of agricultural sector models
The crucial questions model users ask are: which parts of the "real world"
can be realistically modelled? How accurate are the forecasts? Which
areas need more attention?

Given the great number of empirical models, these questions can only
be tentatively answered here. A difficulty common to many empirical
studies is the lack of an ex-post validation test for a sufficiently long
period beyond the sample period. This is a serious deficiency which may
cause a credibility gap to develop especially for general system models,
whose behaviour is partially constrained by flexibility constraints or
switching rules.

Explanatory and forecasting models of consumer demand have a fairly
long tradition in the form of individual agricultural commodity models.
Especially when the commodity under study has little interdependence to
other consumer goods they have yielded high levels of accuracy. If larger
sets of interrelated commodities are included, the specification of complete demand systems, however, becomes necessary. Good empirical
applications including forecasts and policy evaluations have been presented in recent yers. Complete demand systems have the advantage of a
sound theoretical basis and consistency with respect to total income
expenditure. In spite of remaining methodological and empirical difficulties, such as insufficient degrees of freedom in estimation, inappropriate
choice of functional form, problems with separability requirements, and
lack of household surveys, this research area is in a good state of applicability.[15] Of course, when long-run, rather than short- or medium-run,
forecasts are intended, problems of constancy of preference structures
and parameters etc., also arise.

Explanation and forecasting of supply involves many more unresolved
problems. In analogy to the demand side, the substitutability of commodities in production and supply is at the core of the modelling problems. To compare available models it is necessary to analyse their data
base and to evaluate how the approaches account for: (a) consistency of
common factor use; (b) aggregation errors; (c) irreversibility of supply
due to asset fixity; and (d) technical progress.

The major disadvantage of commodity-specific direct supply models is
certainly the neglect of competition among enterprises for fixed
resources. Moreover, there is hardly any *a priori* information to be used
on the parameters so that several of them are statistically insignificant.

Simultaneous estimates of equation systems, on the other hand, require rather restrictive parameter constraints and functional forms.

Other models are based explicitly on the determinants of resource allocation and production. On the one end is the diverse group of pragmatic models, mostly disaggregated into yield functions and resource allocation components, where the allocation of resources (land more often than capital or labour) is either achieved by simple rules (e.g. productivity ranking) or by proportional scaling of output levels, or the consistency of demand and supply of resources is not considered at all. While models of this type lack a sound theoretical basis, they provide full flexibility with respect to estimation procedures and model structure discussed earlier.

Another type of model explicitly assumes behavioural rules (e.g. constrained profit maximization on farms) to simulate the allocation, production, and supply process. One type are linear production models (e.g. linear programming), eventually recursively linked through dynamic feed-back functions. These recursive decision models have a better theoretical basis than the first type described immediately above.[16] Unfortunately, in the past the parameters in these models have not often enough been econometrically estimated, which has made confirmation of their results difficult. Moreover, because they need to assume linearity, unrealistic discontinuities in enterprise substitution have frequently arisen. Another type are supply functions derived from duality theory, which have some nice theoretical properties (e.g. linear estimation procedures) but which do not allow definition of the underlying technological specifications.

More recently, we have proposed a general nonlinear production model which combines the econometric parameter estimation and the behavioural hypothesis of an ex-ante optimizing resource allocation on the farms in one iterative approach.[17] The structural form involves a standard nonlinear maximum likelihood parameter estimation in which the numerical evaluation of the function itself is performed through a nonlinear optimization routine. Initial results, received from a 14-commodity model for EC-member countries indicates quite a good explanatory and forecasting capability.

In spite of recent improvements, the state of applicability of agricultural resource allocation and supply models for policy purposes is less favourable than that for the demand models. The lack of data, the complexities of intertemporal, interregional, and intercommodity relationships, and the theoretical deficiencies of models which attempt to explain farmers' goals and behaviour have kept a series of questions unanswered.

Finally, a few comments about the simulation of agricultural prices (ratios and levels) will be made. So far, most quantitative sector studies have avoided endogenous price generation. This is justified in so far as prices are mainly policy determined by foreign trade and market intervention measures or, in the absence of national policies, by international markets. If national markets are separated from world markets by quotas, if international trade does not exist due to differences in preference, high transportation costs, etc. or if world prices are to be explained themselves, an endogenous determination of prices becomes necessary.[18] The unpredicted price boom of the early 1970s and the increasing number of efforts to link national and global models have considerably raised an interest in this area. However, more ex-ante validation tests of available algorithms are required.

It seems justified at this point to suggest that the rapid increase in the number of quantitative sector models in recent years has to a large extent served academic interest and has only brought slow progress with respect to policy relevance and empirical performance.

An important reason for the remaining credibility gap may be the fact that most modelling projects are initiated by academic institutions alone and not in direct co-ordination with policy-making bodies. Policy alternatives analysed with the help of these models are often highly hypothetical. Co-operation with policy-makers often starts only when the model development is completed and when published results happen to raise the interest of decision-makers.

5 THE IMPLEMENTATION PROBLEM: HOW CAN CO–OPERATION BETWEEN DECISION–MAKERS AND RESEARCHERS BE IMPROVED?

The following aspects are considered as requirements for model implementation, necessary to co-ordinate quantitative agricultural sector modelling and the preparation of policy decisions more effectively.

(a) Short time intervals between problem perception and availability of results.
A period of five to seven years, which is needed to build up comprehensive information systems and sector models, would certainly be too long to be of any use for the preparation of most decisions. Hence, a quantitative system of models has to be permanently available.

(b) Need for flexible modelling systems adjustable to real world problems
The nature and complexity of policy problems change frequently. A unique, homogeneous model, e.g. a large scale sectoral linear programming model, lacks the flexibility necessary to accommodate such change. More flexible are separable building-bloc systems in which variable sets of components with consistent data bases and hypotheses can be assembled according to policy needs. Congruence between the phases of the policy process (information and diagnosis, projection, decision) and the respective model types is an important characteristic of a system, if it is to be of practical use.

(c)   Competence and objectivity in defining policy alternatives
In order to insure that policy alternatives are discussed before decisions
are made, two points need to be considered. First, model builders and
users should be competent technicians and knowledgeable in the area of
agricultural policy formation, understanding both the quantitative and
qualitative external effects involved. Second, researchers should be
institutionally situated such that they are in close contact with policy-
makers, such as working attached to a branch of the Ministry of Agriculture, and sufficiently yet independent of the policy-maker that even
"unpopular policies" (i.e. trade liberalization, agrarian reforms, reduced
farm support, etc.) will at least be considered in the analytical phase and
brought to the attention of administrative bodies.

(d)   Open indication of potential for social conflicts
Any execution of policies causes conflicts of interest between groups
within a society (producers and consumers, tax payers and farmers, those
emphasizing environmental goals and those who pursue mainly income
goals etc.) or between societies (e.g. EC-member countries' conflicting
interests in certain joint decisions on agricultural prices). Insofar as
performance indicators for conflicting goals can be endogenized in models, their levels of attainment should be clearly documented. Provided the
models have a sound empirical and theoretical basis and confidence
intervals are indicated for the forecasts, this documentation removes
potential conflicts into the pre-decision phases of the policy process. Yet,
if they are not carefully specified and if unqualified predictions are
published, such documentation could increase, rather than decrease, the
potential for conflict.

(e)   Availability of frequently updated data banks
Realistic policy analysis requires a data base which is up to date and
adjusted to the needs of quantitative models. While the actuality and
availability of data systems depends on sample intervals and the efficiency of data processing systems, the completeness and appropriateness
of data banks is more often the institutional problem of feedback between
data suppliers and users.

6   SUMMARY AND CONCLUSION

Considering the number and diversity of quantitative agricultural models, this review could not possibly provide a complete critique. The
growing need for these models had not been fully matched by growth in
our potential to meet the need. More work is needed.
   Certainly, the benefits of quantitative models, which require considerable resources, cannot be measured only in terms of their direct use in the
policy process – on this scale they still score poorly – they must also be
seen as an educational tool for researchers and administrators, and as a

medium for public argument of policy alternatives. Yet, the ultimate purpose of building models remains to develop usable policy aids able to predict future developments as accurately as possible.

Progress in this respect requires improvements of the empirical foundation and the implementation of models. The progress of computer science in recent years has brought about an increasing potential to construct complex models, in many cases clearly ahead of the empirical basis. In order to reduce the credibility gap of models, the concepts of explanation, parameter estimation and validation have to receive more attention, especially when general systems simulation models are used. Moreover, since policy domains change frequently and since model development is a costly and time consuming process which requires frequent revisions and updating, there is a clear need for closer coordination between quantitative sector analysis and practical policymaking.

NOTES

[1] See, e.g., the critique discussed in Faber, M. and Seers D. (eds) *The Crisis of Planning* Vol. 1, London 1972. The planning needs of practical agricultural policy is clearly illustrated in Willer, H. "Agrarpolitische Planung und politisch-administrative Praxis", *Berichte über Landwirtschaft* Bd. 55 (1977), H. 2, p. 177–213.

[2] Dams, T. and Hunt K.E. (eds) *Decision-making and Agriculture*, Oxford Agricultural Economics Institute, Oxford 1972.

[3] Heady, E.O. *Agricultural Policy under Economic Development*, Ames, Iowa 1962, p. 361.

[4] This hypothesis has been formulated by B. Frey, *Moderne Politische Ökonomie*, München 1977, p. 16.

[5] See, e.g., Johnson, G.L. "Contributions of Economists to a Rational Decision-Making Process in the field of Agricultural Policy" in Dams, T. and Hunt, K.E. (eds), op. cit., p. 25–46.

[6] This concept was originally introduced by Encarnacion, J. "A note on Lexicographic Preferences", *Econometrica*, Vol. 32 (1964), p. 215–17. An application is exemplified in Mahler, K.G. "Optimal Price Policy for Agriculture at Production Capacity Restriction" in Gulbrandson, O. and Lindbeck, A. *The Economics of the Agricultural Sector*, Stockholm 1973.

[7] An application is demonstrated by Chenery, H.B. and Bruno, M. "Development Alternatives in an Open Economy: The Case of Israel", *Economic Journal*, Vol. 42 (1962), p. 79–103.

[8] A good illustration emphasizing the characteristics of disequilibria is given by Heidhues, T. "Change: A permanent phenomenon in agriculture", *European Review of Agricultural Economics*, Vol. 3 (1976), issue 2/3, pp. 151–62.

[9] The concept of controllability of systems models is discussed in Manetsch, T. and Park, G. *System Analysis and Simulation with Applications to Economic and Social Systems*, East Lansing 1974, ch. 9.

[10] See, e.g., Johnson, G.L. op. cit.

[11] Comprehensive surveys of quantitative models for agriculture are contained in Levis, A.H. and Quance, L. (eds) "System Theory Applications to Agricultural Modelling", US Department of Agriculture, Washington DC, 1978 and in Neunteufel, M. "The State of the Art in Modelling of Food and Agriculture Systems", International Institute for Applied Systems Analysis, RM 77–27, Laxenburg, Austria 1977.

[12] Recent applications can be found in Rausser, G.C. and Hochmann, E. *Dynamic*

Agricultural Systems: Economic Prediction and Control, Amsterdam 1978 and van Kaick, B. "Dynamische Aspekte agrarpolitischer Entscheidungsregeln", PhD Diss. Göttingen 1977.

[13] Moreover, interpreted as a hypothesis about farmers' real allocation behaviour, programming models can be components within explanatory models of economic development (e.g. recursive linear programming). Such models, however, cannot be interpreted as policy optimization models.

[14] Such models are frequently referred to as General Systems Simulation Models. See, e.g., Rossmiller, E. (ed.), *Agricultural Sector Planning. A General System Simulation Approach*, East Lansing 1978.

[15] Examples are George, P.S. and King, G.A. "Consumer Demand for Food Commodities in the United States with Projections for 1980", University of California, Giannini Foundation Monograph No. 26, Davis 1971 and Radhakrishna, R. and Murty, K.N. "Food Demand Model for India", mimeograph, Sardar Patel Institute Ahmedabad, India 1978.

[16] A sample of applications is contained in Day, R.H. and Cigino A. (eds) *Modelling Economic Change*, The Recursive Programming Approach, Amsterdam 1978.

[17] Frohberg, K., H. de Haen, M. Keyzer, S. Tangermann "Towards an Agricultural Sector Model of the European Community: Model Structure and Preliminary Results", *Second European Conference of Agricultural Economists*, Dijon/France Sept. 1978.

[18] Methodological aspects are discussed in Heinen, D. "Price Determination Processes for Agricultural Sector Models", *American Journal of Agricultural Economics*, Vol. 59 (1977), No. 1, pp. 126–32.

CSABA CSAKI

National Agricultural Sector Models for Centrally Planned Economies

Because food production is one of the most decentralized activities of mankind and nations are the largest units in which agricultural problems appear in their full complexity, the study of national food and agricultural systems has always been under focus of research in food and agriculture. At IIASA[1] to study the world's food and agricultural problems, consistent national agricultural policy models are going to be constructed and linked. In this paper the first results of IIASA's modelling work on centrally planned food and agriculture systems are summarized.

1 OBJECTIVES AND MAJOR ASSUMPTIONS IN THE MODELLING OF CENTRALLY PLANNED FOOD AND AGRICULTURE SYSTEMS

In the CMEA[2] member countries, agricultural policy and policy goals are determined according to the central plans of the countries. The basic figures of production and consumption are fixed by the national plan and realized by a co-ordinated system of sectoral (industry, agriculture, etc.), regional, local (country, city, etc.) and enterprise plans. Therefore, the major policy goals in agriculture are to ensure a level of consumption to satisfy industrial needs in agricultural products as determined by the national plan. Thus the government's agricultural aims are the following:

the satisfactory growth of food production by increased efficiency and productivity in agriculture;
a certain degree of self-sufficiency of the country in agricultural products;
optimization of foreign exchange earnings from agriculture;
the improvement of living and working conditions of the population.

From the above mentioned policy objectives in each country in a given period of time only few and not by any means all are emphasized. The methods for realization of these policy objectives often differ. Though agricultural policies of the individual countries are not unified, we intend

312

to model the European centrally planned economies on the basis of a *common model structure*. We believe that the similarity of major agricultural policy objectives, and the fact that the food and agricultural sector is an integral part of the centrally planned national economy, fully justifies our approach.

Using the experiences gained from former agricultural modelling work in socialist countries and the results of methodological research on the general structure and linkage of national sector models,[3] we aimed at the development of a relatively new model structure for centrally planned food and agriculture systems. This structure

should incorporate the basic features of the CMEA member countries' economy,

should be suitable to incorporate the specific features of the individual CMEA countries,

should be consistent and comparable with other parts of IIASA's Food and Agricultural model system

should be detailed enough to be used as an experimental tool for investigations connected with the development of food and agriculture, and

would hopefully contribute to the further development of techniques applicable in the planning and management of food and agriculture.

2   THE GENERAL MODEL STRUCTURE

The basic characteristics of the IIASA model for centrally planned food and agriculture systems is determined by the main objective of this modelling effort. Our main goal is not straightforward optimization, but to make a tool that offers opportunities for a better understanding of the dynamic behaviour of the centrally planned agricultural systems and the interactions of their elements, so that the model can also be used for mid- and long-range projections. Unlike the normative agricultural models that have been developed, this model has a *descriptive character*. It reflects the present operation of the centrally planned food production systems and, therefore, the present decision-making practices and economic management of the government are described. At the same time, various normative elements, such as government decisions and published plan targets influencing the projected operation of the system, are also considered.

In the model we try to endogenize a large part of the economic environment and the most important factors of food production. Food and agriculture is modelled as a disaggregated part of an economic system closed at the national as well as at the international level. Therefore our model has the following features:

the food consumption sphere is incorporated;
the non-food production sectors of the economy are represented by

Csaba Csaki

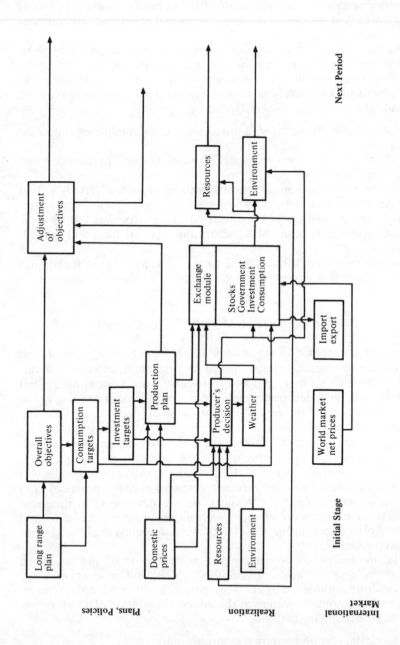

FIG. 1   General structure of the model. The detailed mathematical structure of the model is described in[1].

assuming that they produce only one aggregated commodity;
the economic, technical, biological, and human aspects of food production are covered;
both the production of agricultural raw materials and food processing are modelled;
under "other" agricultural production and food processing, all products not individually represented are aggregated; and
financial equilibrium is maintained.

The structure of the model is outlined in Figure 1. The overall methodology used by the model is a *simulation technique*. For the description of subsystems, suitable techniques, e.g. linear and nonlinear programming, econometric methods, are employed. The *model is dynamic*, with a one-year time increment. Subperiods within the year are not considered. The time horizon of the analysis is 15–20 years. Random effects of weather and animal disease conditions can also be considered.

Long-range government objectives such as the growth of the whole economy, the growth rate of food production and consumption, a given relation of consumption to accumulation, and a given positive balance of payments in food and agriculture are considered exogenously as they are determined by the long-range development plan of the national economy. The model is focused on the development of food and agriculture (production structure, investments) and its interaction with the rest of the economy. The major steps of the solution can be described as follows:

1   As a first step the overall growth targets are settled for a given year based on long-range objectives and results of the previous period. After setting targets for gross and net production the planned consumption and accumulation funds are calculated, determining the targets for consumption of individual commodities and investment funds in food and agriculture as well as in the rest of the economy.

2   Next a detailed plan for food and agriculture is determined considering available resources and minimum required production of certain commodities.

3   As a third step the behaviour of producers (state and co-operative farms, private producers) is described and the random effects on the final output of food and agriculture as well as the rest of the economy are calculated. In the model both direct and indirect instruments of government can be handled to realize the production targets of the central planners. According to the government's economic management system (more or less decentralization) in a given country the producer's decision model and relations between government and producers might be modelled in various ways.

4   The Exchange Module compares supply and demand. Here export and import figures, final private consumption and investments are calculated satisfying the balance of trade equilibrium constraint. The model can be linked with other IIASA national models through this model part. To express the reaction of a centrally planned economy to changing world

market conditions a special equilibrium type of model has been developed.

5   As the final results for a given year are obtained, overall government objectives and policy instruments (prices, tax rates, etc.) are adjusted based on the analysis of the performance of the whole system. The available resources and some of the model parameters are also updated.

3   A PROTOTYPE MODEL: HUNGARIAN AGRICULTURAL MODEL (HAM)

As a first step in the realization of IIASA's objectives in the modelling of centrally planned agricultural systems, the Hungarian Agricultural Model has been developed as a prototype for the modelling of CMEA countries. This work is a joint undertaking of IIASA and three institutions in Hungary.[4]

HAM structure has been developed according to the general principles summarized above. Figure 2 shows the structure of the final version of the model. HAM is in fact a system of interconnected models. Two spheres are differentiated within the system. The economic management and planning submodel describes the decision-making and control activities of the government. The submodel of real sphere covers the whole national economy, including the disaggregated food production sector. The major blocks of the latter submodel are related to production, consumption and trade as well as updating available resource and model parameters. In Hungary the overall targets of food and agriculture are realized mostly using indirect economic means (price, tax, subsidies), therefore HAM represents a *decentralized version* of our general model structure, where producer's decisions play quite an important role.

HAM-1
HAM is the first system simulation model to describe the Hungarian food and agriculture sector. The former modelling works offered many useful experiences but in several cases HAM applies entirely new approaches and the development of HAM requires the analysis of several possible alternative methodological solutions. Therefore, to avoid the difficulties of immediately working with a large scale system, we have decided to develop first a more aggregated, relatively simplified model version (HAM-1).[5]

Hungarian food and agriculture is described in HAM-1 on a relatively high level of aggregation. The Hungarian food and agriculture is represented by 5 agricultural and 4 processed food commodities, the 10th commodity is related to the rest of the economy. Practically all the model commodities represent a relatively wide range of products. On the whole, approximately the whole Hungarian food and agriculture and the national economy as well are covered. Therefore the computed results of

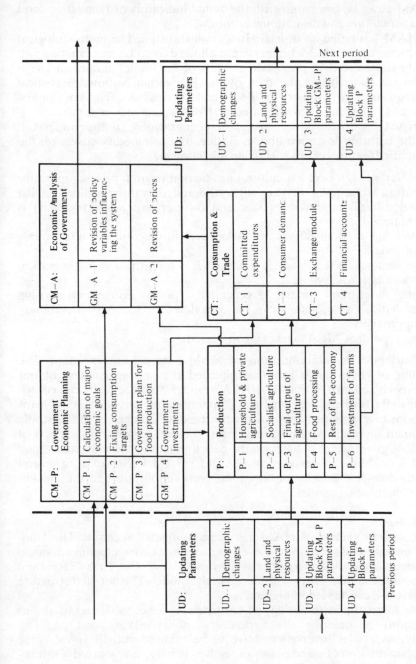

FIG. 2 Schematic structure of the second version of the Hungarian Agricultural Model

HAM-1 can be compared with the actual indicators of Hungarian food and agriculture and the national economy.

HAM-1 is based on official Hungarian statistics. The methodological character of the HAM-1 experiment allowed us to be less exacting and sophisticated in data preparation. Most of the model parameters have been calculated using the data of the Hungarian National Statistical Bureau and the Ministry of Food and Agriculture. The consumers' demand system has been estimated at IIASA based on time series.

HAM-1 is structured according to our general model outline and has all of the features described above. Besides the commodity coverage, the simplified features of HAM-1 mean the following:

> different sectors of agricultural production (state farms, co-operative farms, household plots) are not considered, only the so-called socialist agricultural production (state and co-operative farms together) is modelled,
> weather random effects on agricultural production are not directly included,
> in some cases (e.g. savings function) less sophisticated mathematical formulation is applied,
> the description of the government's policy instrument revising activities (e.g. pricing) can be considered as the first preliminary approach,
> no separate CMEA market is considered.

During 1978 numerous runs of HAM-1 have been executed. The results of these investigations supported the appropriateness of our approach and proved that the IIASA's model structure really can contribute to the further development of planning techniques and is suitable for various investigations connected with the development of the centrally planned food and agriculture systems. (Figure 3 shows the impacts of various government policies on the development of the Hungarian food and agriculture as forecasted by HAM-1.) HAM-1 also led us to several methodological conclusions that are very important for the further refinement of the model.

HAM-2
The second version of HAM has been completed recently. The Hungarian food and agriculture as well as economic management system are modelled in HAM-2 in a rather disaggregated way. There are 45 food and agriculture commodities considered in the model. The detailed structure of HAM-2 can be seen in Figure 2.

As far as the methodology of the model is concerned, first of all our attempts to describe the agricultural policy-making and planning activities of the government have to be pointed out. In HAM-2 the implementation of given policy objectives is fully endogenized. Government plan targets on food and agriculture are determined by a linear programming model assuming that central planners want to maximize

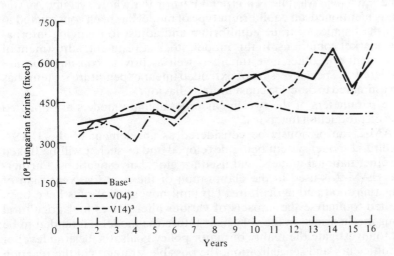

FIG. 3   GNP in food and agriculture as projected by HAM-1

[1] Basic Variant expresses the present operation of Hungarian food and agriculture.
[2] Variant 4: world market prices are used as domestic producer prices using 1 US\$ = 30 Hung. Ft. exchange rate.
[3] Variant 14: instead of 100% only 70% is the required level of self-sufficiency from food and agricultural commodities.

foreign exchange earnings from food and agriculture beside a given level of self-sufficiency. The adjustment of overall objectives and policy instruments is modelled by heuristic routines. This is one of the first attempts at a mathematical description of the pricing mechanism in a centrally planned economy.

The food and agricultural production is modelled according to producing sectors. The socialist agriculture (state and co-operative forms) is modelled by a linear programming model, the behaviour of private and household farms is described by supply functions and a separated model block is related to the food processing. A simulation type of model is constructed to describe the investment decisions of producing firms. The output of the non-food producing part of the economy is calculated by a Cobb-Douglas type function.

The Exchange Module is a crucial part of the whole system. As was already mentioned, an equilibrium type of model has been constructed to reach the balance of trade equilibrium and adjust to changing international market conditions. In this model, stock adjustment, adjustment of government and other investment as well as private consumption are considered. A special version of extended linear expenditure systems has been estimated to describe consumers' behaviour.

The parameters of the two linear programming models are updated based on production functions.

HAM-2 can obviously be considered as an element of the IIASA agricultural model system being developed and as such it will be linked with other national models, and used for global investigations. Furthermore HAM-2 is used in the elaboration of the next five year plan of Hungarian food and agriculture. Up until now several runs have been executed to analyse the impacts of various alternatives for agricultural pricing mechanisms. In the very near future the model is intended to be used to investigate the reality of major policy goals, the desired level of self-sufficiency and specialization, the possible strategies of the reaction of the domestic to the world market and changes in export and import structure.

4 AGGREGATED CMEA MODEL

Based on IIASA's model structure and experiences gained by the Hungarian Agricultural Model, an aggreated CMEA model has also been constructed at IIASA. The CMEA model first of all is designed to represent the European centrally planned countries within IIASA's aggregated model system.[6] Therefore our main objective is to develop a model which realistically describes the aggregated behaviour of this group of countries on the international market of agricultural commodities. The model is not for the study of problems of the agricultural development of the CMEA countries in detail. But besides its aggregated character it hopefully will be useful for investigations related to the overall problems of agricultural development of these countries. Based on the model, first of all:

the realization of major targets on growth of agricultural production and their main alternatives,
the key factors and conditions of realization,
the interaction of agricultural and industrial development (more or less investment in agriculture),
the feasibility of certain overall targets (consumption versus investment) can be investigated.

The CMEA model which actually covers the European CMEA member countries (Bulgaria, Czechoslovakia, GDR, Poland, Hungary, USSR, Romania) has a structure consistent with other elements of the aggregated model system including the same commodity coverage. Figure 4 shows the general structure of the model.

In the model, similarly to the general structure and HAM, we assume that long-range government objectives are taken as exogenous variables. We also assume that central decisions on the production structure of agriculture are transferred directly to producing enterprises. Therefore a producer's decision model is not included and deviation from targets at the national level is not considered. The production plan of the government is modelled using a non-linear optimization model including constraints on available resources and minimum required production of certain commodities. In the objective function either the net national product of food and agriculture or foreign exchange earnings from the food sector are maximized. The parameters of the production model have been estimated based on FAO data.

The Exchange Model is solved similarly to the Hungarian Agricultural Model. The development of private consumption is modelled based on past trends and considering overall objectives on changes in the food consumption structure.

In the model three types of prices are distinguished: producer prices, consumer prices and international prices. The domestic prices are expressed in roubles. The initial prices have been calculated as weighted average of the individual country prices using the inter-CMEA exchange rates as published in Hungary. The domestic prices are not modified during the simulation run.

As further steps in IIASA modelling work on centrally planned food and agriculture systems the Polish and Bulgarian agricultural models will be developed. In the case of Poland the special role of private farms and in the case of Bulgaria the higher level of centralization in the management of agriculture, represent new features and obviously require special solutions.

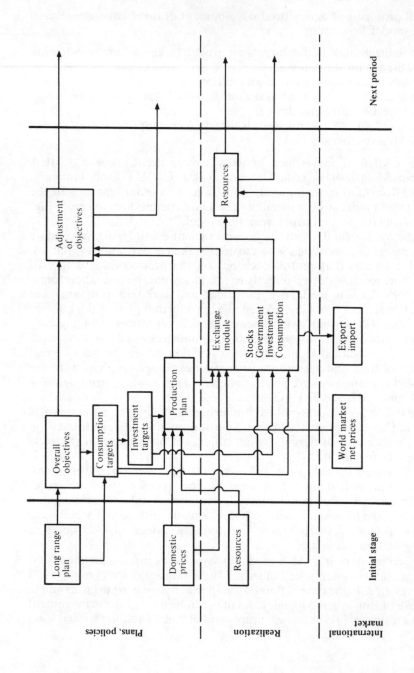

FIG. 4 General structure of the CMEA model

NOTES

[1] International Institute for Applied Systems Analysis, Laxenburg, Austria.
[2] CMEA = Council for Mutual Economic Assistance.
[3] Primarily Prof. Ferenc Rabar's and Michiel Keyzer's works[5,6,7] and [9].
[4] Research Institute for National Planning at the National Planning Bureau, Research Institute for Agricultural Economics of the Ministry of Food and Agriculture, and Department of Agricultural Economics at the K. Marx University of Economic Sciences.
[5] The experiences with HAM-1 are discussed in detail in[2].
[6] First aggregated version of IIASA's food and agriculture model system. The commodity coverage of the study includes: wheat, rice, coarse grain, bovine and ovine meats, dairy products, other animal products, protein feeds, other food, non-food agriculture, non-agriculture.

REFERENCES

[1] Csaki, C., Jonas, A., Meszaros S., "Modelling of Centrally Planned Food and Agricultural Systems: A Framework for a National Policy Model for the Hungarian Food and Agricultural Sector", IIASA, RM-78-11.
[2] Csaki, C. "First Version of the Hungarian Agricultural Model" (HAM-1), IIASA, RM-78-38.
[3] de Haen, H. Schrader, J.V. Tangermann, S. "Modelling the EC Agricultural Sector: Problem assessment, policy scenarios and model outline", IIASA, RM-78-23.
[4] Heady, E.O. Srivestana, U.K. (eds): *Spatial Sector Programming Models in Agriculture*, Iowa State University Press, Ames, 1975.
[5] Keyzer, M.A. "Linking National Models of Food and Agriculture – An Introduction", IIASA, RM-77-2.
[6] Keyzer, M.A. "Analysis of a National Model with Domestic Price Policies and Quota on International Trade", IIASA, RM-77-19.
[7] Keyzer, M.A. "International Trade Policies in Models of Barter Exchange", IIASA, RM-77-51.
[8] Parikh, K.S. "A Framework for an Agricultural Policy Model for India", IIASA, RM-77-59.
[9] Rabar, F. "Food and Agriculture Programme Annual Report of IIASA, 1977.
[10] Rosmiller, G.E. (ed.) *Agricultural Sector Planning – A General System Simulation Approach*, Michigan State University, 1978.

DISCUSSION OPENING – MOHINDER S. MUDAHAR

Introduction

This paper describes national agricultural sector models for centrally planned economies in general and the Hungarian agricultural sector model in particular. It is part of a large modelling effort at IIASA to build global models for the food and agricultural sector. The main purpose is to provide insights to the planners about the development process of the agricultural sector and to provide guidelines for them to formulate agricultural policies which are effective and consistent with national goals.

Professor Csaki has presented us interesting and very complicated agricultural sector models in a very limited time and space. The paper summarizes four different but closely related agricultural sector models. These are (a) the general model structure for centrally planned

economies, (b) the aggregated Hungarian agricultural sector model
(HAM I), (c) the disaggregated Hungarian agricultural sector model
(HAM II), and (d) aggregated CMEA (Council for Mutual Economic
Assistance) model. My knowledge of decision-making in centrally planned economies is rather limited, and the information provided in the
paper about the specifics of the models is rather scanty. As a result, I have
decided in favour of raising some general issues for discussion and asking
some important questions for clarification. I have divided my opening
comments into three categories, namely, methodology, empirical
analysis, and relevance of the results for policymakers.

Methodology
I commend Professor Csaki on his ability to develop comprehensive
agricultural sector models which incorporate three major modelling
approaches, namely, system simulation approach, mathematical programming approach, and econometric approach. However, I have not
been able to determine which model components use which of these
approaches, how these various methodologies used in different model
components are made consistent and linked with each other, or the basis
for choosing each of these alternative approaches.

From the macro point of view, the objective (or set of objectives) and
constraints for the models are specified exogenously. It is not very clear,
however, what the optimality criterion is to determine the allocation of
physical resources to achieve these objectives at the regional and/or
national levels.

From the micro point of view, one component of these models deals
with the "producer or farmer's decision". However, it is not clear how the
farmers make the production decisions with respect to various farm
activities, allocation of resources, and what their decision criterion is. For
example, in "market-oriented" economies farmers may maximize profit
and/or minimize cost and/or minimize risk subject to different
behavioural and resource constraints.

The model is dynamic with a one-period time increment. Sub-periods
within a year are not considered. Since agriculture is seasonal in nature,
the models do oversimplify the agricultural sector and thus cannot realistically address very interesting policy issues dealing with seasonal allocation of physical resources and scheduling of marketing, storage, and
transportation activities for inputs and outputs.

Empirical analysis
The paper does not deal with the empirical aspects of these models. I wish
that Professor Csaki had chosen instead just one model and provided us
with more detail on the methodological and empirical aspects of that
model. Since the models reported in the paper are not empiricially tested
– except a prototype model for Hungary – it is rather difficult to discuss
the associated data needs, estimation of these models, and interpretation
of the results. To what extent these models would track the real history of

the agricultural sector in Hungary or for that matter in any other centrally planned country is a question which can only be answered (a) by comparing model results with actual time series of various variables in the agricultural sector and (b) by subjecting the model results to various validation tests. Professor Csaki has indicated that the empirical results obtained from HAM I support the appropriateness of these models for planning purposes. However, these empirical results and the basis for this conclusion are not reported in the paper.

Relevance for policy-makers
The models do incorporate producer prices, consumer prices, and international prices for inputs and outputs into various model components. However, it is not clear what the roles of these prices and the shadow prices derived from programming models are. Also, what are the flexibility and constraints imposed in the model to determine consumer and producer prices?

What are the other policy instruments incorporated in these models and how do they influence the working of the model structure such that they could provide insights with respect to the implications of various policy instruments and thus be relevant to the policy-makers to achieve the stated goals?

Finally, in all fairness, I fully sympathize with Professor Csaki in the sense that it is very difficult to present these complex models in a limited space. However, the answers to these questions would, I believe, be quite informative for our professional colleagues from the so-called "market-oriented" developed and developing countries.

A.W. SMITH and RHONDA L. SMITH

The Impact of Changing Economic Conditions on the Australian Agricultural Sector

SECTION 1

In 1945 agriculture was a leading sector in the Australian economy. Since then the rural sector has declined in relative importance and has become increasingly dependent on other sectors of the economy. This trend is likely to continue. However, the last eight years have been a period of marked changes for Australian agriculture. Most agricultural commodities have experienced at least one full cycle of price boom and slump; the OPEC oil price rise of 1973 drastically changed fuel costs; high rates of inflation have exerted strong pressure on costs, and agriculture has had to "withstand" the development of minerals as a major new export industry during this period. It is not surprising that production has increased more slowly during the 1970s than during the previous two decades. There have also been pronounced changes in the product mix, resulting from, at various stages over the 1970s, wheat quotas, low sheep and wool prices, and low cattle prices.

During the commodity boom of 1973–74 the rural sector added to Australia's inflationary problems, whereas subsequent low beef prices helped lower the inflation rate. Owing to their inability to adjust their product price, farmers suffer a loss of competitive advantage at home when export prices rise more slowly than the inflation rate, and a loss of international competitiveness when Australia's inflation rate exceeds that of her trading partners. The traditional response to a cost-price squeeze has been to raise productivity through investment. By the 1970s many farmers were unwilling or unable to undertake such investment (both real and money farm incomes fell after 1973–74). Instead they allowed their capital to deteriorate and reduced factor input. By the late 1960s government agricultural policy aimed to make the rural sector responsive to changing market conditions and the emphasis was on structural adjustment. However, it can be argued that the rural sector suffered considerable pressure due to government measures to pursue national policy goals.

Gregory (1976) argues that the growth of the mineral industry relative to the rest of the economy had drastic implications for the rural sector because it resulted in higher costs for the entire economy due to competition for resources. This thesis has attracted considerable attention, centring on three aspects. Firstly, Gregory ignores any income effects of the investment which generates the increase in mining exports (Snape 1978). Secondly, the quantitative conclusions drawn by Gregory depend crucially on the supply elasticities used. Although available data are inadequate, Gregory did not allow sufficiently for the reduction in elasticities when moving from individual products to total agriculture. Thirdly, some of the assumptions employed restrict the generality of the analysis. In particular Gregory assumes that no policy adjustments other than exchange rate or tariff adjustment are used by the government. This is relevant to any policy application of the thesis.

A number of policy options are available to a government confronted by a large increase in exports. For example, increased exports remove the balance of payments constraint to growth so higher rates of growth should be attainable. To achieve these, imported capital and labour are required. Both use foreign reserves. Thus the level of foreign reserves need not increase, and adjustment problems outlined by Gregory need not occur. The conventional wisdom seems to be that the current structural problems, especially of the rural and labour-intensive manufacturing sectors, are basically a result of the mining boom of the late 1960s and 1970s. However, it is obvious that any structural problems are exacerbated by a recession. The economic development of recent years suggests an alternative view of the mineral boom. This development removed the balance of payments constraints on government policies. The additional export revenue provided an opportunity to introduce government policies while ignoring their balance of payments implications, and perhaps accentuating any emerging structural problems.

SECTION 2

The theoretical basis, structure and operation of the Institute Multi-Purpose Model (IMP) is described in Brain (1977). The model consists of eight modules, viz. main, demography, finance, energy-transport, industrial activity, international, Australian States, and agriculture. The prime role of the main module is to collect micro data obtained from the other modules and to translate these into traditional macro aggregates. The key inputs from the agricultural module into the other modules are farm product and income, rural exports, and agricultural commodity prices. From the main module, the agricultural module derives the exchange rate, general price level and wage levels. Data for real gross non-farm product and commodity consumption are also provided. Population data are obtained from the demography module.

The agricultural module distinguishes ten product groups, viz. wheat, other grains, sugar cane, other crops, wool, cattle, sheep, dairy, pigs and other livestock. For each product group the module includes equations for supply, average price received by farmers and, for the "homogeneous" product groups, stocks are treated as exogenous, and exports are derived as the residual from the total supply/total utilization identity. Supply and farmers price for total crops, total livestock and total agriculture are obtained by summation, or weighted averages as appropriate; gross value of production can then be calculated. To derive farm income, equations are estimated for a few aggregative groupings of costs; other minor items (such as farm interest taxes, stock valuation adjustment and farm income of companies) are treated as exogenous.

The equations in the agricultural module are estimated for the sample period 1948–49 to 1976–77 (or 1975–76 where data for the more recent year were unavailable). A full specification of the equations is given in Smith and Smith (1976).

Supply

$$SP_{it} = f(SP_{it-1}, FP_{it-1}, (FP_i/FP_j)_{t-1}, Y_{it}, I_{it-1}, X_{it-1})$$

where SP is planned supply of an agricultural commodity, FP is price, Y is a measure of technological progress, I is stocks of the commodity, X is exports of the commodity, i and j indicate different agricultural commodities and the subscripts t and t-l refer to current and previous farm years respectively.

Actual supply depends on planned supply (incorporating deliberate production changes where possible) and weather. By manipulation, the unobservable planned supply variable can be eliminated. The supply equation for a given product group will consist of the relevant variables from the general specification together with any factors specific to the product group. The lags specified above may not be relevant for cattle due to the longer production period.

The supply of wheat, other grains and sugar either adjusts within one production period or past supply has no influence on current supply. The partial adjustment approach was valid only for wool and pigs; for the remaining groups inclusion of lagged supply indicates only that farmers are guided in their production decisions by supply in previous periods.

As disaggregated time series of cost data for agricultural commodity groups are unavailable, price or relative price is used as a proxy for profitability in the supply equations. Only sugar supply (which is subject to quotas) is not directly affected by any price variable. There are strong interrelationships between the supply of wheat, wool, cattle and sheep and the prices of these four products. The joint production of wool and sheep meat tends to distort some of the price responses. For example, the negative wool/total meat price coefficient in the wool supply equation indicates a dominant short-run meat supply effect.

Following Powell and Guren (1966), indexes of deviations from trend yields or trends of animal deaths were used as indicators of weather conditions. These measures are related to basic weather factors in a non linear way and thus have a non linear effect on actual supply, in accordance with *a priori* expectations. A weather variable was found to influence the supply of all commodity groups except cattle and sheep meat. The failure to identify a significant weather effect on cattle supply may be due to data problems, and for sheep, to the problems of joint production.

Meaningful stocks data are unavailable for the composite groups. An inverse relationship between own stocks and supply was found only for wheat. The non-significance of this variable may be explained by wholesalers rather than growers holding stocks. Exports directly affect the supply of sheep meat, cattle and sugar. The supply equations indicate that any marked short-term increase in meat exports is achieved by slaughtering earlier, thus depleting future supplies.

Some specific factors affected supply decisions in particular product groups. Non transferable wheat quotas (operative May 1969 until 1973–74) reduced wheat production, encouraged diversification into other grains and reduced farmers' ability to switch between sheep and wheat. Supply decisions concerning pigs and other livestock are influenced by real income per caput. A time trend was included in the wheat, other grains and sugar equations; fertilizer usage affects wheat and sugar supply but was not relevant to other product groups.

Farmers' Price

$$FP_{it} = f(SA_{it}, (FP_i/FP_j)_t, FP_{it-1}, X_i, XP_{it}, I_{it}, DP_t, W_t)$$

where X is the volume of exports, XP is the export price index, DP is real gross non-farm product per caput and W is weather. The prices of all commodity groups except wheat, are influenced directly or indirectly by supply. Only meat prices are influenced by own stocks, and the farmers' prices of wool, sugar and wheat and cattle are determined primarily internationally rather than by domestic availability. Export prices help explain farmers' prices for these commodities and for sheep, pigs and whole milk. Quantity exported affects the farmers' price of wool, sugar, wheat, cattle and sheep meat. Every commodity group price equation includes a price variable of some sort. The results also support the hypothesis that the prices of commodities which compete for the same resources are interrelated. Weather affects other grains, sugar, other crops and cattle prices. It appears that the effect of weather on price tends to be via quality changes with crop prices being depressed by poorer quality crops, while cattle prices increase as meat of a given quality becomes more expensive.

Consumption. To avoid duplication of effort, it was decided to relate the consumption or apparent domestic utilisation of the various agricultural product groups to the relevant consumption categories estimated in the main module of the IMP model.

$$C_{it} = f(PCE_t, DP_t, TS_{it}, (FP_i/FP_j)_t, C_{it-1})$$

A.W. Smith and Rhonda L. Smith

where C is the quantity of commodity i consumed in Australia, PCE is real personal consumption expenditure on the consumption category which includes commodity i, and TS is total supplies of commodity i. For wheat, wheat products, seed and stockfeed utilisation are distinguished. The consumption equations display a wide disparity in terms of variables included. Price effects were detected only in the consumption of meats. An income effect was identified in all consumption equations, except that for wheat products. It was not possible to construct a satisfactory equation for wheat for stockfeed, and this variable was treated as exogenous.

Costs. From the constant price data calculated for gross value of rural production at factor cost and the constant price data for gross farm product at market prices, a measure of production inputs at 1966–67 prices can be derived. However, stock valuation adjustment and net indirect taxes cannot be eliminated from the constant price data.

$$TPIA_t = f(SP_t, W_t)$$

where TPIA is the value of production inputs (in constant dollars). It was found, however, that unfavourable weather conditions did not significantly alter factor inputs, possibly due to the unsatisfactory nature of the variable.

$$PPIA_t = f(FP_t, PE_t, SA_t)$$

where PPIA is the price of production inputs, PE is the general price level and SA is actual supply. The value of production inputs at current prices can be calculated by multiplying the quantity of inputs by their price. Gross farm product at current or constant market prices can then be determined via an identity. Unfortunately no constant price data are available for other cost items. Consequently equations for depreciation and wages, net rent and interest paid have to be specified with the dependent variables in current prices.

$$WRI_t = f(SP_t, TPIA_t, WAGE_t)$$

where WRI is the value of wages, net rent and interest at current prices and WAGE is the general wage level. Depreciation allowances for the primary sector are determined in the main module and allowances for the farm sector account for over 97.5 per cent of these.

$$FADP_t = f(DPA)_t$$

where FADP and DPA are depreciation in the agricultural and primary sectors respectively. The regression results for the cost equations conformed to the above specification.

SECTION 3

Four sensitivity analyses are reported in this section. In the first scenario, the rate of inflation, as measured by both the Consumer Price Index and the implicit gross non-farm product deflator, was assumed to increase by one percentage point per annum. Reference has been made above to the lack of suitable cost data and the consequent necessity to use price variables rather than profitability variables in the supply equations. Accordingly, it is not surprising that the major effects of the increased rate of inflation are felt through increased farm costs. After ten years the price of production inputs are 7.7 per cent higher than in the base run, whilst the increase for wages, net rent and interest paid is 8.3 per cent higher. The higher rate of inflation could lead to a decline in the "real" prices of at least some food items (whether this happens or not will depend on the causes of the higher rate of inflation, and how it pervades the economic system). If this occurs, the model suggests that domestic consumption of beef and veal will increase slightly, leading to a slight increase in beef and veal production. Offsetting this will be a slight decline in wool and sheep meat production. The net result is a very small increase in the gross value of farm production. However, the influence of increased farm costs dominates, so that after ten years of higher inflation farm income declines by 10 per cent compared with the control solution.

In the second scenario, a hypothetical devaluation of 10 per cent is assumed to take place at the beginning of Year 1. If export prices are set in world markets, the immediate effect is to increase the export price of farm products in Australian dollars (refer below for further comment on this aspect). The higher export prices lead to higher farm prices. The effect is least on the price of other crops, as few commodities in this product group are exported, and greatest for wool and cattle and sheep meat, reflecting the importance of the overseas markets in determining prices, and the absence of home pricing schemes. Initially there is no effect on supply – this is a reflection of the basically pre-determined nature of supply. But even after a number of years, the effect on supply is minimal, with total agricultural supply (in quantity terms) increasing by only 0.5 per cent. Consequently the changes in the gross value of production of each product group closely reflect the changes in the farmers price for that product group. The increase in the total gross value of farm production over a number of years is just under 10 per cent, a fraction less than the percentage devaluation assumed.

The quantity of production inputs used increases slightly (by about 0.5 per cent) reflecting the small increase in the quantity of agricultural production. The price of production inputs is influenced by both the implicit gross non-farm product deflator and by farm prices. Thus the price of production inputs exhibits little change in the first two years, but then increases and eventually reaches a level about 8 per cent higher than in the control solution. Wages, net rent and interest paid also increase, reflecting the higher wage levels after the devaluation. However, each item of costs increases by less than the gross value of farm production. Consequently farm income increases proportionately more than the gross value of farm production. Even so, the effect on farm income is greatest in Year 2, when it is 18 per cent greater than in the control solution. The effect of rising costs then gradually erodes some of the benefits, but ten years after the devaluation farm income is still over 12 per cent greater than in the control solution. The effects of the devaluation on the quantities exported are quite small, reflecting the small effects of the devaluation on the quantities produced. However, the value of agricultural exports increases markedly, reflecting the higher prices (in Australian currency) caused by the devaluation.

Obviously the effects of exchange rate changes on Australian agriculture depend to a large degree on whether the Australian export prices change to the full extent of the change in the exchange rate. It is generally accepted that wool is the only agricultural commodity of which Australia is a dominant supplier. Assuming that only 50 per cent of the exchange rate change "flows on" to the Australian wool price, there will be very little effect on the supply responses. However, the increases after ten years in gross value of farm production and farm income as a result of a 10 per cent devaluation are reduced by under 1 and over 1 percentage point respectively.

The third scenario considers a sustained increase in the volume of mineral exports. The macro economic implications of this and the following scenario are considered in Brain and Gray (1977). The increase in mining exports, compared to the control solution, results in a revaluation of the exchange rate, little change in real gross non-farm product and a small increase in personal consumption (in this analysis the importation of extra capital and labour was not considered). Over a ten year period the exchange rate is revalued by 5 per cent (compared to the control solution). This leads to lower farmer prices than would otherwise prevail. The increased consumption expenditure encourages a small (about 1 per cent) expansion in cattle production; other supply responses are negligible. After ten years of extra mineral exports, the gross value of farm production is about 3 per cent lower than in the control solution. Farm costs change only slightly so farm income declines by 8 per cent.

The fourth scenario considers a sustained increase in the prices of mineral exports, the price increases giving the same improvement in exports as resulted from the increased quantity of mineral exports considered in the previous scenario. The improved terms of trade for minerals leads to a faster rate of revaluation of the exchange rate, a very slight fall in real gross non-farm product, and larger increases in personal consumption. After ten years the exchange rate is 7 per cent higher than in the control solution. This leads to lower farmer prices than would otherwise prevail. The increased consumption expenditure encourages both sheep and cattle production to expand by about 2 per cent. After ten years of higher mineral prices, the gross value of farm production is 5 per cent lower than in the control solution. Again, prices hardly change so farm costs change only slightly. Consequently farm income declines by 13 per cent.

SECTION 4

The sensitivity analyses reported in the previous section reveal that the Australian agricultural sector is very sensitive to changes in both the exchange rate and the rate of inflation. Australia revalued against most currencies by considerable amounts between December 1972 and September 1974 and during most of the 1970s Australia also experienced rapid inflation. It is not surprising then that there arose considerable concern that Australian farmers were suffering severe reductions in their overseas competitiveness. Miller (1976) states: "After adjustment for changes in input prices and exchange rates, $100 earned by the Australian grain grower in the late 1960s is now worth only $50. For the North American grain producer, his $100 is now worth $70." A comparison between the index of prices paid by farmers in Australia and the United States over the decade to 1977 shows that while Australian prices paid rose slightly faster before 1970, between 1970 and 1974 the position was reversed. However, after 1974 Australian prices paid rose much faster so that while the Australian index was about 2 per cent less than that of the US in 1974, by 1977 it was nearly 24 per cent higher. Exchange rate adjustments more than offset the advantage gained by Australian farmers due to a slower rate of inflation between 1972 and 1974. However, while Australian prices paid continued to rise much faster than those of US farmers, in 1976 and 1977 exchange rate movements improved the relative position of Australian farmers.

The apparent decline in the competitive position of the Australian farmer over the period from 1967 does not represent a reversal of trend. How, then, were Australian farmers able to continue producing? The critical variable is relative farm income. Australian and US farm income, both at current value and at constant 1967 prices (that is, deflated by consumer prices), was compared. Although the ratio fluctuated, it displayed no statistically significant trend. This suggests that the indexes of prices paid and prices received by farmers do not satisfactorily indicate what is happening. Maybe the weighting of the components of the index of prices paid is no longer representative, at least for the Australian producer. Farmers may have offset the effects of rising input prices either by cutting back on those inputs or by producing more efficiently. Even a reweighted index may fail to satisfactorily account for changes in resource usage if farmers significantly alter their usage of items which are not or cannot be fully included in the index of prices paid.

Surely any productivity gains available to Australian producers will also be available to American producers. Thus, differential productivity gains seem an unlikely explanation of the relative movements in the ratio of prices paid and received by farmers. However, as the level of farm technology has been consistently higher in the US, further increases are relatively more difficult to achieve. This suggests that any productivity gains by Australian farmers are a catching up process.

The other possibility and perhaps the most likely one, is that Australian farmers are more easily able to switch between products in response to changing market conditions than the more highly specialised American farmers. Australian farmers produce basically three commodities: wheat, wool and meat, and few if any farmers produce only one commodity. Thus, if wheat prices rise farmers may increase their acreage of wheat and cut back on the number of livestock carried. American farmers lack this flexibility partly due to climatic conditions and also as sheep play a much less significant role in US agriculture. This reduces flexibility by removing the option to switch between meat and wool production as market conditions change.

SECTION 5

Econometric models can be used to project key economic variables, as in Section 3 of this paper. However, these projections are only conditional statements indicating what would happen if the variables followed a specified trend or pattern. There are some limitations to the usefulness of the projections due to the structure of the model. For example, it is not disaggregated by region and consequently regional effects cannot be ascertained.

No projected profitability variables are available for the simulated events. A major explanatory variable in supply equations should be relative profitability. However, as already stated, no product disaggregated time series of cost data are available. Consequently it has been necessary to use price or relative price variables instead. During the 1960s when inflation was only moderate, prices were usually reasonable proxies for profitability. However, in recent years the rate of inflation has increased markedly. Further there have been substantial disparities in the rate of increase in the prices of the various agricultural inputs. This has altered the relative profitability of different agricultural products. Under these circumstances prices are not a satisfactory proxy for profits. Inability to adequately account for profitability changes means that simulations with the existing model can yield clearly implausible results. For example, with relatively stable product prices, failure to take account of rapidly rising costs results in a prediction of stable or increased product supply, rather than a contraction of supply. A project to develop suitable cost data for each product group was initiated by the authors in 1976 and preliminary results are now becoming available.

Australian farmers are heavily dependent on the overseas market. At present the agricultural module treats variables associated with the overseas sector as exogenous and the supply of exports is the excess of Australian supply over demand. A project is currently underway to model overseas influences on Australian agriculture to enable more useful projections of market demand and a better understanding of the impact of export quantities and prices.

CONCLUSION

This paper has explored the impact on the Australian economy of certain events affecting the agricultural sector, using an econometric model. Despite the limitations and difficulties mentioned, this approach enables a better understanding of the flow-on effects associated with the events analysed. It enables a critical evaluation of the conventional wisdom regarding these events, and should directly aid the development of more appropriate policies to deal effectively with undesirable aspects of these events should they occur in the future.

REFERENCES

Brain, P.J. (1977) "The Institute Multi-Purpose Model: An Outline", *Australian Economic Review*, 3rd Quarter, pp. 47–64.
Brain, P.J. and Gray, B.S. "The Australian Manufacturing Sector and the Economy – 1990", paper presented to the Conference on Trade, Growth and Structural Change in an Open Economy, Salamander Bay, Australia, November 1977.
Gregory, R.G. (1976) "Some Implications of the Growth of the Mining Sector", *Australian Journal of Agricultural Economics*, 20(2), pp. 71–91.
Miller, G. (1976) "Intersectoral Competition and Rural Prosperity", *Australian Economic Review*, 4th Quarter, pp. 29–38.
Powell, A.A. and Guren, F.H. (1966) "Problems in Aggregate Agricultural Supply Analysis", *Review of Marketing and Agricultural Economics*, Vol. 34, Nos. 3 and 4, September and December.
Smith, A.W. and Smith, Rhonda, L. (1976) "A Model of the Australian Farm Sector: A Progress Report", *Economic Record*, pp. 462–482.
Snape, R.H. (1977) "Effects of Mineral Development on the Economy", *Australian Journal of Agricultural Economics*, 21(3).

SELECTED EQUATIONS FROM THE AGRICULTURAL MODULE

(A full listing of the model is available from the authors upon request)

The figures in brackets under the coefficients are standard errors. R2 denotes the coefficient of determination adjusted for degrees of freedom ($\bar{R}^2$), DW denotes the Durbin-Watson statistic and m denotes the m-statistic.

Supply – Wheat SCWT $M (1968/71 Prices)
SCWT = $-1179.598 - 0.0117\text{IWF(T-1)} + 4.2250\text{WWTY} + 5.3732\text{TIME} + 9.4005\text{WFER} +$
            (0.0079)   (0.783)   (3.742)   (2.695)
28.4051FPWT(T-2)/FPCC(T-2) − 0.7934WTQU
(14.896)   (0.400)
        $R^2 = 0.851$ DW = 1.43   m = 1.087 $v = 21$

Supply – Other Grains SCOG $M (1968/71 Prices)
SCOG = $-197.505 + 6.7235\text{TIME}$
                (0.419)
+ 35.8353FPOG(T-1)/FPWT(T-1)
(22.835)
+ 2.7844WOGY − 1.1622WWTY + 0.2897WTQU
(0.537)   (0.481)   (0.103)
        $R^2 = 0.955$ DW = 1.85   m = 1.07 $v = 22$

Supply – Wool SCWL $M (1968/71 Prices)
SCWL = $252.261 - 0.7798\text{WSLD} + 0.7340\text{SCWL(T-1)} - 9.8195\text{FPWL(T-1)/FPCS(T-1)}$
                  (0.218)   (0.085)   (7.444)
        $R^2 = 0.911$ DW = 2.01   m = 0.116 $v = 24$

Supply – Cattle SCCC $M (1968/71 Prices)
SCCC = $-80.6600 + 1.1122\text{SCCC(T-1)} - 0.3955\text{XQCC(T-1)} + 0.2217\text{XQCC(T-3)} +$
                  (0.240)   (0.230)   (0.114)
184.7825FPCC(T-3)/FPSL(T-3) − 169.7823FPCC(T-1)/FPWT(T-1) +
(115.510)   (62.079)
166.6513FPCC(T-3)/FPWT(T-3)
(102.475)
        $R^2 = 0.955$ DW = 2.69   m = 2.24 $v = 21$

Supply – Sheep and Lambs SCSL $M (1968/71 Prices)
SCSL = $-14.738 + 0.7793\text{SCSL(T-1)} - 0.2351\text{XQSL(T-1)} + 0.0802\text{WTQU}$
                (0.136)   (0.067)   (0.080)
+ 47.5619FPWT(T-1)/FPWL(T-1) + 67.7043FPCC/FPWL
(8.391)   (10.463)
        $R^2 = 0.945$ DW = 1.94   m = 0.47 $v = 22$

Farmers' Price – Wheat FPWT (1968/71 = 1000)
FPWT = $23.9275 + 0.0710\text{FPWL(T-1)} + 0.0316\text{XQWT} + 7.0157\text{XPCL}$
                  (0.063)   (0.013)   (0.777)
        $R^2 = 0.870$ DW = 1.46   m = 1.20 $v = 24$

Farmers' Price – Other Grains FPOG (1968/71 = 1000)
FPOG = $615.111 + 0.563\text{FPWT} - 4.195\text{WOGY}$
                  (0.086)   (1.729)
− 403.968FPOG(T-1)/FPWL(T-1) + 0.624FPOG(T-1)
(103.155)   (0.108)
        $R^2 = 0.911$ DW = 1.78   m = 0.20 $v = 23$

Farmers' Price – Wool FPWL (1968/71 = 1000)
FPWL = $24.803 + 13.5791\text{XPWL} - 0.1674\text{XQWL}$
                (0.371)   (0.126)
        $R^2 = 0.983$ DW = 2.18   m = 0.53 $v = 25$

Farmers' Price – Cattle FPCC (1968/71 = 1000)
FPCC = $389.720 + 0.5118\text{WSLD} - 5.8391\text{IFBV(T-1)/IFML(T-1)} - 1.1831\text{SCCC} +$
                  (0.360)   (4.057)   (0.141)
1.4238XVCC + 7.2360XPMT
(0.494)   (0.855)
        $R^2 = 0.961$ DW = 0.92   m = 3.45 $v = 22$

Farmers' Price – Sheep and Lambs FPSL (1968/71 = 1000)
FPSL = $1155.834 - 13.4411\text{IFML(T-1)} - 12.8657\text{SCSL} + 0.3393\text{FPCC} + 2.0961\text{XQSL} -$
                    (6.081)   (1.706)   (0.240)   (0.900)
62.6982FPWL/FPCC + 162.5449FPWL/FPWT + 12.1283XPMT
(38.091)   (89.109)   (1.543)
        $R^2 = 0.941$ DW = 2.03   m = 0.55 $v = 20$

List of other variables used in the above equations

FPCS	Farmers Price – Cattle and Sheep	Index 1968/71 = 1000
IFBV	Stocks – Frozen Meat in cold stores – Beef + Veal	Th. Tonnes
IFML	Stocks – Frozen Meat in cold stores – Mutton + Lamb	Th. Tonnes
IWF	Stocks – Wheat + Flour	Th. Tonnes
TIME	Time	Number 1948/49 = 1
XQCC	Exports – Quantity – Beef and Veal	Th. Tonnes
XQSL	Exports – Quantity – Mutton and Lamb	Th. Tonnes
XQWL	Exports – Quantity – Wool	Mill. Kg.
XQWT	Exports – Quantity – Wheat and Flour Years Ended Nov. 30	Th. Tonnes
XVCC	Exports – Real value – Beef and Veal	$M 1959/60 Prices
WFER	Wheat – Fertiliser per Hectare	Kg. per hectare
WOGY	Weather-deviations from trend–Other Grains Yield	Index Base 100
WSLD	Weather-deviations from trend–Sheep deaths	Index Base 100
WTQU	Wheat Quotas (Reciprocal of quota in tonnes* 1000000)	Number
WWTY	Weather-deviations from Trend–Wheat Yield	Index Base 100
XPCL	Export Price Index – Cereals	Index 1959/60 = 100
XPMT	Export Price Index – Meat	Index 1959/60 = 100
XPWL	Export Price Index – Wool	Index 1959/60 = 100

DISCUSSION

The authors replied to the various points raised in the discussion* as follows:

In our model, export prices are exogenous. However, export quantities, which are determined from the supply/utilisation identity, are endogenous, depending on both output and apparent domestic utilisation.

We feel that our inability to detect the influence of weather conditions on cattle and sheep output is due to the lack of adequate measures of weather conditions. Our measures of weather conditions are product specific, and it is for these two product groups that we have had the greatest problems in deriving satisfactory measures.

The lack of suitable cost data has been commented on in our paper. We believe this has its greatest effect on specific products. The aggregate farm income estimates should be reasonable. However, estimates of the net income (or revenue) of each of the product groups cannot be made.

The estimation period ends at the financial year 1976/77 (i.e. July 1976 to June 1977). This was the latest generally available data at the time the paper was written.

* No report of the discussion was, unfortunately, received by the editor.

MICHAL KISIEL

Links of Polish Agriculture with the World Economy

The aim of this paper is to present the evolution, range and directions of links of Polish agriculture with foreign countries and their significance for the development of this sector and of the national economy as a whole. The problems in the paper were limited to ties connecting agriculture with the world economy:

in the sphere of material outlays for development of agricultural production (imports of production means of agricultural and industrial origin for the needs of agriculture),

in the sphere of exchange of non-material goods which make up the concept of scientific and technical co-operation with foreign countries,

and in the sphere of agricultural produce distribution (exports of agricultural products and their derivatives). Considering the fact that the development of Polish agriculture has been implemented on the basis of national resources and reserves, without the share of foreign capital, problems of capital links of agriculture with foreign countries were left out in the paper.

I

Poland is a country in which the use of import links with the world economy for developing the rate of growth of agricultural production and for social and technical reconstruction of individual agriculture, dominating in our country, is of a growing range. However, so far, this process has not brought a higher dependence of that economic sector upon foreign countries, which has the effect of several conditions.

Firstly, it is noteworthy that the implementation of a long-range industrialization programme, aiming at acceleration of the rate of economic growth and at reshaping the general social and economic structure of the country, required a concentration of financial and material means for the purposes of developing high-priority sectors of economy. It meant necessary reduction, particularly at the time of intensive industrialization, of accumulation possibilities of agriculture as the initially leading economic

338

sector. It also meant that the stream of working and fixed production means, directed to agriculture, was out of proportion small in relation to the contribution of agriculture to the creation of social product and gross national product. Although in the postwar period the investment outlays for agriculture kept increasing systematically,[1] it was only in the seventies, when the share of agriculture in creating GNP dropped from about 30 per cent in 1960 to about 11 per cent in 1975, that relations of the compared shares have reversed.

Secondly, for most of the postwar period, the inadequacy of the material structure of national product for the required structure of its final division, typical for developing countries, accounted for the fact that any investment activity was associated with a considerable growth of demand for imports. In view of high income and production elasticity of the demand for imports of production means, the granting of priority to industrial development was tantamount to admittance of industrial priority in supply of imported goods.

Thirdly, in the postwar period, the export volume kept increasing systematically, the foreign currency inflow, however, was incomparably low in relation to rapidly growing import needs. That circumstance strongly affected the inter-sector proportions of division of imported goods. In general, the priority of industry was more conspicuous in foreign trade than in the intersector and inter-branch structure of investment outlays.

Fourthly, with increasing production capacity of heavy industry, it was possible to raise outlays for production lines manufacturing production means for sectors and branches turning out consumption goods, agriculture and food industry included. In a relatively short time there were created – practically from the beginning, the industries of fertilizer, fodder, building materials, in co-operation with other countries there were developed some branches of machine industry, and that of agricultural transportation means, there were expanded and modernized branches of food industry, etc.

The above mentioned circumstances, only a few of them, determined both the degree of dependence of Polish agriculture upon foreign supplies, and the model of import links of this sector of material production with foreign countries. The fact that the supply of agriculture with fixed and working production means depended mainly on deliveries of domestic industry, the branches of which work partly or fully on imported raw materials, accounts for the significance acquired primarily by all connections of intermediary character. With the introduced up-to-date technologies and advancing mechanization processes there is growing, in particular, the indirect dependence of agriculture upon foreign supplies of raw materials for the liquid fuel industry, raw materials for fertilizer production,[2] as well as upon imports of licences for agriculture as such and for servicing branches.

The range of changes occurring in the field of direct import links of agriculture with foreign countries is synthetically characterized by the data concerning the share of agriculture in total Polish imports. In the years 1957–72, after the intensive industrialization was completed, the share of agriculture in the final division of imported goods was stable and did not exceed 3 per cent. In the division of imported production means for the whole sphere of material production, on the other hand, the share of agriculture was somewhat higher, within the limits of 4 per cent. Simultaneously, the share of these imports reported for that period in the total material costs of the agricultural sector ranged from 1.7 to 2.7 per cent, and in the value of material outlays from outside agriculture the share was on the level of 7 per cent.[3] Let us add that the latter category of outlays was the most dynamically growing item in total outlays for agriculture, which increased from about 24 per cent in 1957 to about 38 per cent in 1975.

The awareness of limitations occurring in the field of production and imports of investment goods, of the demographic pressure,[4] and of the demand pressure on the food market, accounted for the fact that the strategy of agricultural development assumed in the fifties did not allow radical changes of agrarian structure (with the share of peasant farming reaching 80 per cent). The strategy was oriented more on production maximization per unit of arable land than on increase of labour productivity. Therefore, in the agrarian policy particular attention was attached to increasing the stream of production means to allow a more intensive use of production factors functioning in agriculture, i.e. manpower and land. The mentioned preferences were fully reflected in the material structure of imports implemented for the needs of agriculture. With the share of industrial production means reaching 90 to 93 per cent, in the import structure came to the fore the supplies of working assets directly influencing the increase of crops, such as fertilizers and pesticides. In the sixties, when the domestic fertilizer industry was being created, those products made up to 16 per cent of the value of total chemical imports, and over 70 per cent of the value of production means imported for agriculture.

Till the end of the sixties imports of production means of agricultural derivation did not play a major role in shaping the level of outlays for agricultural production, and they were not of great significance in agricultural-food imports either (share was of the order of 24 per cent). The volume of those imports was determined by cereal imports, implemented mainly for the needs of exports of products of animal derivation.

The ever growing scale of tasks in feeding the population, with fast increasing and changing production needs of agriculture, accounted for the fact that in the new development strategy, adopted in early seventies, the import links of agriculture with foreign countries gained more significance. It concerned indirect and direct links in the same degree. Now already, the wider opening of the economy and agriculture to world markets showing, among others, in the considerable expansion of imports of production means of agricultural derivation (traditional cereal-fodder imports included), is reflected in the level of outlays for agricultural production and in acceleration of dynamics of production growth.

Thus, in the years 1971–75 the mean annual rate of growth of agricultural production amounted to about 3.7 per cent, whereas in the years 1966–70 it was on the level of 1.8 per cent. Continuation of this strategy in the next coming ten to twelve years depends, however, on the advance in developing export links and in possibilities of compensating the balance of trade.

II

The dependence of the process of structural changes of the national economy on the inflow of investment goods from outside caused the expansion of export connections to become a matter of high priority in the postwar development of Poland. Considering that agriculture had, and still has, a significant share in the material structure of social product and of GNP, great expectations for increase of foreign currency incomes were linked with the development of exports of raw processed agricultural products.[5]

Though in the postwar 25 years, from 1950 to 1975, the rate of growth of agricultural production achieved in Poland was fairly high, of the order of 3 per cent, which allowed a gradual expansion of agricultural-food exports, the latter never reached the extent adequate to the production potential of Polish agriculture. The available evaluations of the degree of involvement of agriculture in export production show that in the early seventies, i.e. at the time of the fastest growth of agricultural production, agricultural exports, together with those of other branches, constituted less than 10 per cent, with direct agricultural exports about 2 per cent of the total production of this sector.[6]

Focusing attention for the time being only on domestic factors, the dynamic increase of national food consumption should be considered as the main reason for the weak export links of agriculture. Under the circumstances of maintained high income elasticity of demand for food[7] and high dynamics of incomes, the principle of priority in supplying the domestic food market was adopted in Poland. It meant a weakening of dynamics of agricultural exports and of foreign currency incomes but, at the most difficult periods, it effectively counteracted the menace of lowering the rate of growth of real wages. Moreover, also important for shaping of these exports' volume were the fluctuations in the level of agricultural production, difficulties in adjusting the rate of growth of plant production to the desired rate of growth of animal production, and a relatively slow rate of modernization and expansion of production capacities in the food industry.

Polish postwar exports of agricultural food products are a continuation of ties of agriculture with foreign countries established in previous periods. Though their share in the total exports of the country gradually declines, with the growing volume, it has been for years a vital item of total foreign currency income.

During the two decades from 1950 to 1969, with the decreasing share of agriculture in the product designated for satisfying the final demand, agricultural-food exports provided 16 to 17 per cent of total foreign currency incomes, and only in the seventies did this drop to about 10 per cent (in 1977).

As it appears from the comparison of foreign currency incomes from exports of agricultural-food commodities with expenses for their imports, till the mid-seventies agriculture, as one of several sectors and branches of the national economy, was a surplus sector, which participated, in a large measure, in financing imports of investment goods and raw materials needed for the country's development. In this respect, an essential role was played, in particular, by surpluses in trade of those commodities obtained in exports directed to West European and North American markets. Though the markets of those countries absorbed less than 30 to 35 per cent of the total agricultural-food exports from Poland, still their share in total exports to those countries exceeded, as a rule, 50 per cent. This meant, of course, the possibility of a greater influx to the country of investment goods of the highest technical and economic parameters, and of the latest technical achievements. We can say that the agriculture and food industry, though relatively slightly involved in export production, by supplying the country with foreign currencies performed essential functions in the process of modernization of the national economy, and, at the same time, contributed in this way to creating bases for its own social and technical reconstruction.

III

For many years Polish agrarian policy has attached great importance to the development of scientific and technical co-operation with the world. The significance of this co-operation is growing constantly with the development of agriculture, and the achieved effects can be compared with results obtained through the exchange of material goods. Staff and financial aspects, which do not allow to develop all lines of research necessary for agricultural advance, also speak in favour of this co-operation. Many technical, production, economic and organizational problems have been scientifically elaborated and tested in other countries. A part of these solutions is being gradually adjusted to Polish conditions and introduced in practice. On the other hand, Poland shares its experience in many fields, such as veterinary medicine, seed production, sugar industry, with other countries.

The range and directions of the undertaken scientific and technical co-operation are indirectly characterized by the fact that, apart from bilateral contacts, Poland is a member of over 20 international agricultural organizations, besides COMECON and UN specialized agencies (FAO, ECE, IMO, etc.).

While fully appreciating the significance of other organizations, it should be emphasized that especially convenient conditions for international scientific and technical co-operation were created within COMECON. Besides exchanging the results of research, carried on separately in single countries, common scientific works are taken up, among others, in growing new varieties of cultivated plants, in animal rearing, in fighting pests, weeds and insects, in organization and mechanization of production processes, in economics and organization of agriculture, and many other fields. Moreover, the co-operation covers mutual consultations, scientific training, and production practice.

IV

As it appears from Polish experience, the expansion of multilateral links of agriculture with the world economy provides for a country, which starts accelerated development, a prerequisite determining the rate of changes of the entire economy and of agriculture as such.

Theoretically speaking, the development of those links must not be limited to operations aiming merely at the adjustment, through trade, of the material structure of accumulated domestic means to the needs of the investment programme. In the case of the necessary maintenance of high employment in agriculture per unit area, as it was in Poland, it may be advisable to start with imports of production means which stimulate land yield, including means serving the valorization of manpower reserves for export production purposes. In practice, however, freedom of action in both cases is limited, and often rendered impossible, by outside conditions.

It should be stated that the postwar economic development of Poland proceeded in exceptional and unique circumstances. The basic part of Polish trade, effected within COMECON, was excluded from the influence of economic fluctuations. At the same time, up to the early seventies, it was a period of favourable trends of business on the world agricultural market. Relatively wide sale possibilities for products of animal derivation were available. The relation of world prices for products of animal derivation developed, in general, favourably to the prices for cereals and fodder. There also dominated periods of relative stabilization of economic conditions of purchase of production means and of sale of final products.

Phenomena occurring in the present decade, such as the advancing growth of the degree of self-sufficiency of traditional food importers, combined with deterioration of economic conditions of raw material purchasing for food production, periodical shortages of raw materials for purchase, etc., bring about the fact that, in view of low elasticity of agricultural production, the adjustment to unexpectedly changing outside conditions becomes most complex, even for countries of average development level. This is confirmed, among others, by difficulties encountered recently by Poland, in spite of attempts of adjustment, in locating agricultural-food exports, for financing purchases of cereals and fodder, and for compensating the trade balance in these commodities. In this respect, Poland is not an isolated case. Therefore, the above mentioned circumstances speak in favour of the thesis that efforts aiming at settling the situation on world markets should be accompanied by steps towards expansion of less conflicting mutual links, among others, scientific and technical co-operation, which bring results similar to those of business connections. The aptness of this thesis is confirmed, among others, by the experience of co-operation within the group of COMECON countries.

NOTES

[1] In 1961–75 this mean annual rate ranged from 8 to 14 per cent.

[2] In covering the demand for raw materials of those industrial branches, the supplies from the USSR are, in particular, of essential significance. They cover almost in full the demand for crude oil and natural gas, the basic raw material for production of nitrogen fertilizers, and a part of demand for potassium chloride. The demand for phosphorites, on the other hand, is covered mainly by North African countries.

[3] A. Woś "Links of agriculture with national economy", PWRiL Warsaw 1975, p. 132.

[4] The rate of population increase in the fifties and sixties amounted to about 1.8 per cent, and decreased to 1 per cent only in the seventies. In the years 1950–78 the number of population increased from 25 to 35.0 million persons.

[5] Taking into account the fact that an ever bigger part of total agricultural product is industrially processed (44 per cent in 1975), 90 per cent of which is in the food industry, where the value of agricultural raw materials exceeds 50 per cent of material costs and 40 per cent of the total production value of this sector; the analysis of links has been limited to the agriculture and food industry.

[6] Compare A. Woś, op. cit., p. 143.

[7] The shaping of the level of income elasticity of food demand was essentially influenced by the low food consumption level at the starting point, a high population birth rate (of the order of 1.8 per cent), persistent differences in the consumption level of non-agricultural population, as well as the relatively slow supply increase of domestic market with wanted consumption articles of industrial derivation.

[8] For the sake of comparison, in 1957 this share amounted to about 41 per cent, while in 1975 it decreased to 25 per cent.

DISCUSSION OPENING – J.KLATZMAN

First of all I must point out that it was only yesterday that I was asked to introduce the discussion on this paper. I have certainly had time to read it thoroughly, but not to let my thoughts develop.

My aim is to raise some questions likely to provoke discussion, but I should like to begin with two remarks.

First, I appreciate the fact that M. Kisiel did not confine his analysis to exchanges of goods, but also included trade in non-material goods, namely scientific and technical co-operation. This is a factor of basic importance in international trade, but one which one sometimes tends to forget.

My second remark concerns a point which was not included in the presentation, but which is included in the text. M. Kisiel recalls the need to give priority to industrialization, at the expense of agriculture, in the early stages of economic development. I do not dispute the principle of giving priority to industrial development. But I think that if agriculture is too much neglected this may slow down industrial progress.

On the main theme, one cannot but be struck by the complexity of interrelationships which planners have to take into account. To give but one example, one can say that the importance of raw materials for fertilizer manufacture is aimed at increasing agricultural production, so as to increase exports of food products, which procure the means to purchase industrial goods abroad. Thus one imports raw materials to manufacture fertilizer to increase imports of industrial machinery.

One wonders to what extent a planned economy can build a mathematical model of such interrelationships for rational decision-making.

But there are cases where the decision is purely political. When, for example, it is decided to increase domestic food supply at the expense of exports, no economic model can provide the means to decide how far in this direction it is desirable to go.

It also emerges from M. Kisiel's paper that, in spite of close trade links within COMECON, trade with the rest of the world is continually expanding. The Polish economy is increasingly closely linked with the world economy. She thus runs the risk of suffering the consequences of the current economic crisis and the growing instability the experts are predicting. Agriculture is involved in these interdependencies. But I think it is impossible to study in isolation the possible effects on Polish agriculture of its international trade links. The problem has to be analysed within the framework of a global study in a (quantitative or qualitative) model in which agriculture and even the agro-industrial complex appear as part of the national economy.

ANTONIO BRANDÃO

Alternative Agricultural Development Models Commonly Advocated in Latin America*

1 INTRODUCTION

Industrialization via Import Substitution is an important characteristic of the process of economic development experienced by most countries in Latin America. This style of development has had far reaching consequences for the economies of these countries, not only because of its emphasis on industry but also, and more importantly, because of the adjustment problems caused by the speed of the changes. Agriculture has been deeply affected by this pattern of development. The incentives designed to promote industrialization have had in many cases undesirable consequences for resource allocation and for the sectoral distribution of income.

This set of events has been submitted to various analyses. Development economists with interest in the problems of agriculture have given alternative interpretations of these facts and, in consequence, alternative policies were recommended. It is the purpose of this paper to review these models in order to evaluate the state of knowledge on the causes of poverty and backwardness in Latin American agriculture. Three models are the object of the study. I have called them Structuralist, Neoclassical and Marxist respectively since they can be better understood in the context of the general approach to economic development advocated by each of these "schools". The paper is concerned with a simplified view of these models. Most of the details are left out in an attempt to provide an overview of them. This, one must acknowledge, does not give full justice to various contributions to the literature. Despite this general level at which the analysis has been carried out it broadly illustrates the main ideas involved and policies proposed.

Each of the following three sections is dedicated to the presentation of a model. Section 5 summarizes and presents some concluding comments.

* Helpful comments and suggestions on an earlier draft were received from Raul José Ekerman and Luiz Gonçalves Ávila.

2   THE STRUCTURALIST MODEL

The core of the structuralist thought is associated with the work of economists of the Economic Commission for Latin America. Their work furnished the theoretical foundations for Import Substitution Industrialization. Among these, the most influential (and controversial) has probably been Raul Prebisch's "demonstration" of a secular tendency for the terms of trade to decline against the low income-primary exporter countries.[1] Prebisch has been criticized both at the theoretical and empirical levels[2] but, despite this, his demonstration is a basic piece in the Structuralist thought. However, other factors are also important to justify the emphasis on import substitution: the balance-of-payments problems faced by most Latin American countries and the external economies created by industry[3] are two of the most significant.

The Structuralists have also an explanation for the chronic inflationary process experienced by the region. This explanation is largely based on inelasticities of the supply of goods and services in a period within which the economy is faced with an increasing demand that also experiences changes in its composition.[4] The inelasticity of the supply of agricultural products plays an important role in this process since food is a significant part of the expenses of consumers in low-income countries.

Viewed in this context, agriculture's role in the model is, in essence, to provide food and raw materials for the non-farm sector of the economy. Production of foreign exchange appears as a residual goal, since import substitution industrialization was intended to protect the domestic markets from the "evils" of international markets.[5] Thus, the concern with agriculture is primarily a concern with the supply of cheap food and raw materials for the urban sector in order to facilitate the growth of industry.

Backwardness and poverty in agriculture were a direct consequence – in the structuralist view – of the land-tenure system existing in the region.[6] This structure was characterized by the "latifúndio–minifúndio" complex. Backwardness and poverty were the outcomes of this dichotomous system. The "latifundiários" were not directly interested in agriculture for they held land as a protection from inflation and the infinitely elastic supply of labour to them would take away the incentives for the modernization of their production systems. In the "minifúndios", on the other hand, the scarcity of land would impede modernization (by making it unprofitable).[7]

The policy prescription for the development of agriculture was land-reform. By correcting the above sources of inefficiency, a land-reform programme would modernize agriculture, and therefore allow the sector properly to fulfil its food supply function.

Two final comments are in order. The first is that there has never been a comprehensive study of technological alternatives for agriculture in the structuralist's analysis. By now, it is generally accepted that a major difference between agricultural technology and industrial technology is that the former is locational specific and that mere transfers of it are destined to fail. Thus, even though land reform appears as an element of modernization, the central question of the existence and adaptability of technologies has never been seriously tackled. The second point that deserves some thought is the following: in the context of a model of import substitution industrialization, there is a large area of conflict between price policies designed at stimulating agriculture and industrial growth. Land reform then appears as a policy instrument logically consistent with the general model that "could" modernize agriculture given the rate at which industrialization should be carried out.

3   THE NEOCLASSICAL MODEL[8]

Although some of the earlier writers in the tradition of Neoclassical Economic Theory would possibly disagree with industrialization in itself,[9] modern neoclassical economists however, are much more concerned with the high social costs of the import substitution industrialization route to development as followed by countries in Latin America. These costs have taken various different forms, the most important being the squeeze of the export sector caused mainly by the maintenance of overvalued exchange rates; the inefficiency of the import competing sector in view of the high tariff structure intended to protect it, and, finally, the anti-employment bias introduced by a factor price-policy of subsidizing capital. This critical view has lead to agricultural development models markedly different from the one in the preceding section. To review the main pieces of this analysis, we first look at its theoretical underpinnings.

T.W. Schultz's book[10] is a benchmark for the theory of Agricultural Development. It has provided an important link between the neoclassical economic theory and the behaviour of economic agents in agriculture. Backwardness is, thus, interpreted in the context of rational choice; low returns to factors – in particular, human and physical capital – provide weak economic incentives to modernization; agriculture is trapped in a low level equilibrium.[11] Schultz's analysis has had the merit to encourage the use of rational behaviour in the explanation of backwardness. This was, indeed, the central part of the research performed by neoclassical development economists in Latin America. Variables related to profitability became very important to account for the observed low levels of modernization.

Overvalued exchange rates have persisted during most of the import substitution period in Latin America. This has been especially true for the years following World War II and up to the end of the 1960s. This in turn plays a twofold role in the model: from one hand it is viewed as an implicit tax that reduces the rentability of exports and thus is equivalent to a leftward shift of the supply function; on the other hand, this tax, together with measures like the "confisco cambial", is utilized to transfer part of the agricultural surplus to the urban sector in order to finance the growth of the latter. The magnitude of the distortion in the allocation of resources has been estimated in the case of Brazil. For example, Lopes[12] found that a 10 per cent decrease in the price of agricultural products would lead to a reduction in the use of labour, capital and land by 18, 27 and 10 per cent respectively.

Discrimination has taken other forms, too. On the input side, high tariffs on modern inputs like fertilizers, machinery etc. have contributed to increase their domestic prices. Cheap food policies have also imposed costs to agriculture. Usually they have taken the forms of fixing prices below equilibrium and imposing export quotas and other quantitative restrictions.[13]

Another important element in the general diagnosis of poverty made by neoclassical economists is the functioning of the labour market. It is observed that incomes in agriculture usually lag behind incomes in the non-farm sector, and this is attributable to frictions (imperfections) in the labour market, which do not allow it to perform its equilibrating function. Among the various imperfections, the following are usually mentioned: low levels of education; the fixed asset nature of agricultural labour, small chances of productive employment in the urban sector, and the high costs of migration. Despite the high rate of rural–urban migration observed in the last two decades in Latin America, it is argued that this has not been enough to close the sectorial income gap, and, that in consequence, investments to eliminate these imperfections are an essential part of any policy directed towards elimination of poverty.[14] Implicit in this is the argument that elimination of the distortions in factor prices will increase labour absorption substantially in the economy as a whole and in the urban sector in particular.[15]

Another important element incorporated by neoclassical economists to explain the low level of use of modern technology was the question of the existence of such a technology. Two distinct factors – an empirical observation and a theoretical advance – contributed to such analysis. The first one was the recognition of the failure of programmes elaborated to transfer US technology to low-income countries. This failure was credited to the specificity with respect to location of agricultural technology. The second factor that drove forward the process of incorporation of technology was an advance of theory. Technical change used to be introduced in economic models by means of a shift parameter in the production function. Although useful for certain theoretical applications, this approach was not adequate for empirical analysis. An operational characterization of technology was obtained with the "sources of growth" type model in which the Fisherian concept of capital plays the central role. In this approach, growth is a result of investment in sources of income streams (capital); maximum growth is obtained by investing in the cheapest sources of income streams.[16] It was again T.W. Schultz who provided the theoretical link to emphasize the role of new production technology. In a word, technology is a source of income streams and, according to him, the unique way to break the low level equilibrium of traditional agriculture.[17]

Another important step toward the effective incorporation of technology as a policy variable is the Hyami-Ruttan's "induced development model".[18] By relating the rate and the bias of technical change to factor scarcity (and factor prices), they have made technology an endogenous variable and, as such, possible of being affected by economic policy.

This set of knowledge has been extensively utilized by economists to emphasize the importance of research institutions intended to create and adapt production technology to each country or region. Estimates of the rates of return to research have been made, and the values encountered were usually very high.[19] That, in turn, gave further support to those advocating investment in research. The natural follow up of this process was the concern with research priorities, an idea which opens the way for interesting research.[20]

In short, the neoclassical explanation of rural backwardness in Latin America is based on orthodox theory. The low returns in agriculture are a consequence of the economic policies designed to promote industrialization at the rate experienced in the region; low incomes – low as compared to incomes in other sectors – are rooted in the imperfections in the labour market and in the anti-employment bias in factor-price policy, and, finally, disregard of research activities has also contributed to such a low level of modernization.

The policy recommendations made have been a natural consequence of the diagnosis. Devaluation of the exchange rate, decrease in trade barriers, especially quantitative restriction to trade flows, and lowering tariffs are the usual proportions for trade policy. Elimination of the distortions in factor policy; increasing the opportunities of access to education, and lowering information costs for potential migrants are the conventional prescriptions with respect to the functioning of the labour market. Finally, financing of research activities is an essential part of neoclassical policy prescriptions.

A word is in order with respect to the role of land reform in the neoclassical analysis. Land reform is not an essential part of their analysis. Sporadic references to land reform exist, but in general, they are not enthusiastic in favour of an overall land reform programme. Localized reforms are sometimes proposed as a means of correcting inefficiency or to improve income distribution. However, on an overall basis, fiscal and price policies are the usual instruments to cope with production and distribution problems.

The above considerations should be sufficient to give the reader a pictorial view of this model. It is noticeable that it has covered a wide variety of aspects of reality. It has broadened both our theoretical knowledge of the problem and our empirical knowledge of the region.

4   A MARXIST MODEL

By now, scientific Marxist interpretations of the Latin American underdevelopment are common among researchers. By this it is to be understood those models or analyses of the problem focusing on the "production relations" as the basic social relation and on the logical-historical method, to use Meek's terminology.[21] A distinctive feature of the Marxist interpretation is the relationship established between the development of the world capitalistic economy and the phenomenon of underdevelopment. As Alain de Janvry[22] puts it:

> ... underdevelopment cannot be treated apart from development if backward areas or countries are related by the market to the advanced areas or countries. In fact, within the world capitalist system, a theory of underdevelopment and rural poverty needs to be a theory of economic space which can explain how the contradictions of development in certain areas transform, in other areas, traditional societies into underdeveloped ones.

It is this functional relation between development and underdevelopment that is at the centre of the Marxist analysis. This is, indeed, what distinguishes these authors from the structuralists with their dual interpretation of the phenomenon of underdevelopment in which the expansion of the modern sector will eventually transform the backward sector into a modern sector. This, as showed above, does not necessarily occur in the Marxist analysis.[23]

Agricultural poverty is a resultant of a set of contradictions in the system. To explain the causal relations that ultimately account for the underdevelopment of agriculture, the model presented by Alain de Janvry is utilized.[24] Two fundamental concepts are those of marginality and periphery.

> The periphery is that portion of economic space which is characterized by backward technology with consequent low levels of remuneration of the labour force and/or by advanced technology with little capacity to absorb the mass of population into the modern sector. These excess human masses created by the very process of economic growth are the "marginals.[25]

The transformation of Latin America into a peripheral region is a result of colonization and free trade. Free trade – according to the model – has both prevented the rise of national industry (and of a national bourgeoisie) and provided the basis for a class alliance between the internal élites of landlords and foreign (British) capital. This process of transformation was further accentuated by the problems with the balance of payments experienced by most countries after the second industrial revolution in the twentieth century. In spite of the import-substitution policies intended to improve the performance of the industrial sector, the "coercive" decline in the terms of trade[26] after 1930 imposed a new constraint to the continuation of growth. The possibility of continued growth is now dependent on the ability of nations to transfer the costs associated with this decline in the terms of trade to labour.[27] This, in turn, decreases the profitability of mass-consumption industries and thus redirects new investments to sophisticated consumption goods industries that will satisfy the demand from the upper classes. Consequently, distributive policies to increase the purchasing power of low-income groups do not benefit industry and therefore the process of growth may continue without any changes in the distribution of income.[28]

What are the effects of this "unequal exchange", in the Agricultural Sector? Continued growth of industry requires low wages and overvalued exchange rates. These, in turn, contribute to the decline of the internal terms of trade against agriculture. The particular structure of the land tenure in the region, the "latifúndio–minifúndio" complex, allows a further transfer of these costs to workers in agriculture. The mechanism by which this transference occurs is the reduction of wages to below subsistence levels in view of the presence of the subsistence sector. That is, agricultural wages will be set at a level equal to the subsistence wage minus the net value of production in the "minifúndio". As the working of this mechanism illustrates, a functional relation is established between "latifúndio" and "minifúndio" and this is consistent with and – even more – necessary for, the growth of the economy as a whole.

Land reform and rural development projects are analysed in the context of this interpretation. The economic objective of redistribution to increase market size is dismissed in view of the arguments above. Land reforms, in general, have two goals: (i) increase production to keep urban wages low and alleviate the balance-of-payments problems and, (ii) a distributive goal which amounts essentially to a "bribe" of potentially revolutionary peasants for the maintenance of the *status quo*. This latter objective is also an integral part of rural development projects. However, the production goal of these is much more limited in scope. The target is the increase of food production in the "minifúndios" so that a larger share of subsistence needs can be attended to by "home production". As a consequence, the market wage rate for the commercial agricultural sector can be further depressed, and growth further stimulated.

The effectiveness of the rural development projects in counteracting the exploitation of labour in agriculture depends, once more, on the nature of the class alliances in society. In regions where the traditional alliances between landlords, national industrial capital and foreign capital persist, rural development projects will be of only limited scope. The maximum effects will be obtained in the societies in which the rupture of the traditional alliances was complete, as in the case of Cuba, and the earlier period of the revolution in Peru.

This is the essence of De Janvry's model of rural poverty. It illustrates important aspects of the Marxist analysis, and, as far as I know, it is the unique integrated Marxist interpretation of rural poverty in Latin America. The model is similar in at least one aspect to the structuralist's. They both share the same Prebischan view of international markets. In both cases the decline in the term of trade is the instrument of exploitation utilized by rich countries to extract a surplus from the poor countries. However, De Janvry's model goes a step further, and uses a similar argument to explain internal exploitation which finally ends up explaining poverty in agriculture. What is interesting is that the neoclassical model has also pointed out the discrimination suffered by agriculture during the process of industrialization, and, despite the difference in terminology; the two analyses are fairly similar as regards to the interpretation of the low levels of modernization.[29] Note, however, that the implications of this discrimination are quite different whenever one looks at the labour market. In particular, it is very hard to explain the decrease of the wage rate to below subsistence levels with any static choice framework which has been the usual goal of neoclassical analysis.[30]

5 SUMMARY AND CONCLUSIONS

In the preceding sections, an analysis of three agricultural development models has been presented. The three models studied were called Structuralist, Neoclassical and Marxist in view of their relation with these "schools". To understand the alternative explanations of backwardness and poverty in Latin American agriculture was the main object of the research performed.

Instead of reviewing all previous analyses it is interesting to concentrate here on one of the most controversial themes in any discussion of agricultural development: land reform. As we have seen, according to structuralists' view land reform is an instrument to increase agricultural production and promote income distribution. In the Marxist view, land reform plays a similar role, except that the analysis is usually qualified and couched in terms of the historical conditioners of the process in each country. Neoclassical analysis pays very little attention to land reform questions as an integral part of the model. In order to increase production or to promote income distribution other instruments are suggested.

However, the question of how effective land reform is to satisfy the goals of increasing production and redistributing income as compared to other means of attaining these goals has not been fully investigated. This is unfortunate because studies of this nature are possibly one of the most effective contributions that the professional economist can give to the land reform debate. Land reform is in itself a problem that goes beyond the limited framework available to us as professionals, but unfortunately we have not yet provided the elements for a broader discussion of this question.

NOTES

[1] Prebisch (1950).
[2] Baer (1962); Flanders (1964); Johnson (1967); Brandão (1978).
[3] This argument is explicitly stated in Singer (1950).
[4] Grunwald (1967).
[5] Brazil is an interesting example that illustrates this type of concern of policy makers with

agriculture. See, for example, Smith (1969); and Homem de Melo (1979).

[6] Grunwald (1967); Prebisch (1968) and Baer (1968).

[7] Baer (1968); Furtado (1972).

[8] My understanding of neoclassical analysis has been influenced, in various ways, by my work with G.E. Schuh. Two interesting references are Schuh (1968) and Schuh (January 1973).

[9] Viner (1958).

[10] Schultz (1965).

[11] Schultz, op. cit.

[12] Lopes (1977); Alves and Pastore (1978).

[13] Leff (1969); Alves and Pastore, op. cit.

[14] It should be emphasized, that the problem of poverty in Latin America is, in essence, a problem of rural poverty. For some evidence with respect to Brazil see Schuh (August 1973) and his references.

[15] For a critical view and some evidence of role of factor prices, see Baer (1976).

[16] Friedman (1962).

[17] Schultz (1965).

[18] Hyami-Ruttan (1971).

[19] Grilliches (1958); Ayer and Schuh (1972).

[20] Castro and Schuh (1977).

[21] Meek (1967).

[22] De Janvry (1975), p. 490.

[23] See Oliveira, Francisco (1977) for critique of the structuralist's dual interpretation.

[24] De Janvry (1975).

[25] De Janvry, op. cit., p. 491.

[26] De Janvry, p. 492. No specific references are provided for this.

[27] That is, since unskilled labour is immobile and capital mobile internationally the adjustment costs of this "unequal exchange" should be borne by the labour force.

[28] This, however, does not happen in the central economies since mass consumption is an important component of aggregate demand.

[29] De Janvry, op. cit., p. 494 and footnote 8.

[30] Dynamic optimization techniques might, possibly, generate solutions of this nature depending on the assumption made with respect to the depreciation of the stock of labour.

REFERENCES

Alves, Elizeu Roberto de A. and Pastore, Affonso Celso "Import Substitution and Implicit Taxation of Agriculture in Brazil", *American Journal of Agricultural Economics*, Vol. 60, No. 5, Dec. 1978.

Ayer, H.W. and Schuh, G.E. "Social Rates of Return and Other Aspects of Agricultrual Research: The Case of Cotton Research in Brazil", *American Journal of Agricultural Economics*, Vol. 54, No. 5, November 1974.

Baer, Werner "The Economic of Presbisch and ECLA", *Economic Development and Cultural Change*, Vol. X, January 1962.

Baer, Werner "A Controvérsia Sobre a Inflação na América Latina: Uma Pesquisa", *Revista de Ciências Económicas*, Vol. 1, 1968.

Baer, Werner "Tecnologia, Emprego e Desenvolvimento: Resultados Empirícos", *Pesquisa e Planejamento Económico*, Vol. 6, No. 1, April 1976.

Brandão, Antonio Salazar P. "New Perspectives on the Terms of Trade and the Gains from Trade", PhD thesis, Purdue University, May 1978.

Castro, J.P. Ramalho de and Schuh, G.E. "An Empirical Test of an Economic Model for Establishing Research Priorities: a Brazil Case Study", in Arndt, T.M., Dalrymple, D.G. and Ruttan, V.W. (eds) *Resource Allocation and Productivity in National and International Agricultural Research*, University of Minnesota Press, Minneapolis, 1977.

De Janvry, Alain "The Political Economy of Rural Development in Latin America: An Interpretation", *American Journal of Agricultural Economics*, Vol. 57, No. 3, August 1975.

Flanders, June M. "Prebisch on Protectionism: An Evaluation", *The Economic Journal*, No. 2, June 1964.
Friedman, Milton. *Price Theory, A Provisional Text*, Aldine Publishing Co., Chicago 1962.
Furtado, Celso, Formacâo Económica da América Latina Lia, Editor S.A., Rio de Janeiro, 1969.
Furtado, Celso, Análise do "Models" Brasileiro, Curlização Brasileira, Rio de Janeiro, 1972.
Grilliches, Zvi "Research Costs and Social Return: Hybrid Corn and Related Innovations", *Journal of Political Economy*, Vol. 55, October 1958.
Grunwald, Joseph, "Estabilidade de Preços e Desenvolvimento Segundo a Escola "Estruturalista": O caso chileno", in Hirschman, Albert O. *Monetarismo x Estruturalismo*: Um Estudo Sobre a América Latina, Lidador, Rio de Janeiro, 1967.
Homem de Melo, Fernando, B. "A Política Económica e o Setor Agrícola no Após-Guerra", *Revista Brasileira de Economia*, Vol. 33, No. 1, January/March 1979.
Hyami, Y. and Ruttan, V.W. *Agricultural Development: An International Perspective*, The John Hopkins Press, Baltimore 1971.
Johnson, Harry G. *Economic Policies Towards Less Developed Countries*, The Brookings Institution, Washington, DC 1967.
Leff, N. "The Exportable Surplus Approach to Foreign Trade in Underdeveloped Countries", *Economic Development and Cultural Change*, Vol. 17, 1969.
Lopes, Mauro de R. "The Mobilization of Resources from Agriculture: A Policy Analysis for Brazil", Phd thesis, Purdue University, 1977.
Meek, Ronald L. *Economics and Ideology and Other Essays: Studies in the Development of Economic Thought*, Chapman and Hall Ltd., London 1967, Chapter 6.
Oliveira, Francisco de. "A Economia Brasileira: Crítica à Razão Dualista", in Seleções CEBRAP 1, 1977.
Prebisch, Raul, "The Economic Development of Latin America and its Principal Problems", United Nations, Department of Economic Affairs, Lake Success, New York 1950.
Prebisch, Raul, "Dinâmica do Desenvolvimento Latino Americano", Editora Fundo de Cultura S.A., Rio de Janeiro 1968.
Schuh, G.E. "Effects of Some General Economic Policies on Agricultural Development", *American Journal of Agricultural Economics*, Vol. 50, No. 5, December 1968.
Schuh, G.E. "Lecture Notes on Agricultural Development" (draft), Purdue University, January 1973.
Schuh, G.E. "The Income Problem in Brazilian Agriculture", paper prepared for the EAPA/SUPLAN of the Ministry of Agriculture, August-September 1973.
Schuh, G.E. "Imperfections in the Labor Market and Policy for the Rural Poor in Brazil", Presented as Normation Document at the Conference on Problem of Rural Poverty in Brazil, August 1976.
Schultz, T.W. *Transforming Traditional Agriculture*, Yale University Press, New Haven, 1965.
Singer, H.W. "The Distribution of Gains Between Investing and Borrowing Countries", *The American Economic Review*, Vol. 40, May 1950.
Smith, Gordon "Brazilian Agricultural Policy, 1954–1967", in Ellis, Howard (ed.) *The Economy of Brazil*, University of California Press, 1969.
Viner, Jacob "International Trade and Development – Lectures Presented at Universidade do Brasil, 1953 (6th lecture). Reprinted in Agarwala, A.N. and Singh, S.P. (eds) *The Economics of Underdevelopment*, Oxford University Press, New York, 1958.

DISCUSSION OPENING – R. HOFFMANN

The paper tries to cover a very wide range of questions, with an emphasis on the problem of agricultural poverty; considering three "models", the structuralist, the neoclassical and the Marxist.

I will consider mainly the neoclassical and the Marxist approaches, since it seems to me that today the debate, at least in Brazil, is between these two approaches.

Let me first stress that any development model must take into account the relationships between the agricultural and the urban sector and also international relationships.

The "induced development model" of Hyami and Ruttan is mentioned as one where technology is an endogenous variable. Hyami and Ruttan illustrated their model by comparing the patterns of agricultural development in the United States and in Japan. In the United States, land was abundant, labour was scarce, and a technology was developed in which machines substituted for labour. The model really does give a contribution to the understanding of the different patterns of development in the United States and Japan. But what happens when one tries to understand what happened in Brazil in comparison with the United States? Land is also abundant in Brazil, but labour is cheap. Machinery production did not develop there. These problems are not covered in the "induced development model". One must look for the explanation in the history of the countries, remembering, for example, that in the same period when the Homestead Act was established in the United States, in Brazil, the "Land Law" of 1859 (in order to maintain a supply of labour to the big landowners) established a relatively high minimum price for selling public land and stated that the government would use this income to subsidize the immigration of workers.

Let me consider the problem of income distribution in Brazil and the differences between what can be labelled a neoclassical and a Marxist approach to the problem. I want to stress that there are really many different "neoclassical" and many different "Marxist" approaches. The more conservative neoclassical approach may not even consider a high degree of inequality in the size distribution of income as a problem.

It seems that it is well established by now, that after 1960 – during a period of more than ten years – the size distribution of income in Brazil showed an increasing inequality. The Gini index increased from around 0.50 in 1960 to 0.57 in 1970. That is indeed a striking increase.

Some economists of the neoclassical tradition considered this increase in inequality as a "natural" result of market processes. The basic wage is low because supply of labour is abundant and qualified labour gets relatively higher wages because it is scarce. Some salaries are also high because "managerial capacity" is scarce.

In some sense, a Marxist would agree that inequalities in income are "natural" in a capitalist economy; meaning that inequality is an intrinsic characteristic of the system. But he would point out the political aspects related to the class struggle in the process. After 1967 the government persecuted and put in prison many workers' leaders, labour unions were closed, etc. That destroyed the bargaining power of the workers. In my opinion this was clearly important for the type of "development model" of Brazil some years later.

I think that it is misleading to consider the distribution of income in the rural sector as an isolated problem. There are some processes, such as agrarian reform, that are essentially rural; but it also has important impacts on the other sectors. Agrarian reform will mean a less unequal distribution of income in the rural sector and, because of the decrease in the supply of *free* labour, will mean a less unequal distribution of income also in the urban sector. In consequence, production of wage-goods must increase and that will have further consequence on the distribution of income and demand for agricultural products. *Not* implementing agrarian reform is also a political decision. In 1967 an agrarian reform law was approved, partly as a consequence of some "public opinion" pressure created by the wide discussion of the problem in the years before. Fundamentally this law was never implemented.

So, one characteristic of the Marxist approach is to integrate economic, social and political aspects of the process of development. I feel, therefore, that it is difficult to define a Marxist *model* of development.

GENERAL DISCUSSION – RAPPORTEUR: P.A. LABBE REYES

It was generally agreed, that due to the fact that the Latin American countries have to benefit from their agricultural product export potentialities, the structural model, as well as De Janvry's arguments, were not relevant. In this region, neoclassical and Marxist models appear to be more applicable, mainly because of their similarities in relation to export potentialities. Some comments were also made about the importance of the terms of trade and the current underestimation of exchange rates applying to the food industry. This argument was supported with Brazilian experience on these topics.

It was further stated that under the Marxist model different emphases were given in Latin America, Asia and Africa, not only to dependency, but to the ways of production. Until recently, a lot of emphasis was given in Latin America to dependency, especially for historical reasons, but some researchers are now emphasising more the ways of production, as always was done in the case of Asia and Africa.

Finally, there was some kind of consensus of opinion among the commentators from the floor, as to the inadequacy of the Marxist model to provide explanations at a Latin American national level – it being a necessity for the area that all the countries work together towards improvements in the existing terms of trade.

Participants in the discussion included Rafael Posada, Alberto Valdés, Howard Osborn and Deryke G.R. Belshaw.

KENNETH H. PARSONS

The Challenge of Agrarian Reform

I

This is an attempt to characterize the agrarian reforms of this century and to identity a few central reform issues in rural development policy, in ways which can support a division of labour among the different professional disciplines.

Until the last two or three decades agrarian reforms were usually referred to as land reforms, and were directed principally to the distribution of land to smallholders. The more comprehensive term agrarian reform now in common use reflects a recognition of both the reciprocal involvement of agriculture with other sectors of an interdependent economy and the necessity for the reformation of the service infrastructure as well as systems of tenure if agricultural development is to be supported. In the early stages of agricultural development the holding of land is the principal dimension of both opportunity and power. But in an interdependent economy a land reform programme which reduces the power of landlords may actually leave both the real opportunities of cultivators and the power of landlords unaffected, if the landlord continues to control the access to credit, marketing, and education.

II

Any agrarian reform programme which is followed through sufficiently to achieve an enduring degree of reformation or reconstruction must be a complex set of activities, pursued with vigour. Otherwise the efforts peter out engulfed in frustration. Something of the dimensions of the character of the transformations through agrarian reform is suggested by the fact that the recent reform programmes which most of us are likely to recall have occurred as parts of much more comprehensive happenings.

The first major reform programme of the century began in Mexico in 1910. Here a revolution erupted out of the frustration and despair of the poor. At the base of the struggle was a system of haciendas superimposed

358

upon the native people by the descendants of the conquistadors. The proprietors of these haciendas were not, for the most part, interested in either the development of agriculture or the welfare of the peons who worked the land. Rather, these establishments were the means to political power and high social status. The revolution did not become a systematic land reform programme until the struggle had gone on for years. The idea of the ejido commune had roots in both native and Spanish traditions.

Another set of early land reform programmes was in Eastern Europe, which followed in the wake of the disintegration of the Austro-Hungarian and Ottoman Empires after World War I. Here the large landholdings, many of them owned by foreigners, were dismembered and distributed to small farmers and this became a region of smallholders. But the area was again swept by revolution and reform after World War II, this time under the auspices of Marxian ideas – an extension of the Communist revolution in Russia. This agrarian reform was directed not only against large landholdings but against the idea of private ownership of land itself.

In both Asia and the Middle East the disintegration of colonial empires after World War II created a situation where the nations again became independent. All through this region, virtually all the land previously owned by foreigners was returned to native owners. If the governments moved fast enough the land was often declared public domain and distributed by governments to their own people in some sort of land reform; if not, occupancy was resumed under native tenures.

In the partition of territory between India and Pakistan the split occurred along religious lines. Once the territory had been stabilized, India initiated an agrarian reform programme under which the land vacated by fleeing Muslims became available for settlement by non-Muslim refugees from Pakistan. This created an opportunity in India for embarking upon an agrarian reform programme under which the refugees were organized into co-operative farms. Following independence, the first major move by India was the elimination of the Zamindari interests in the areas where the British arrangements for revenue collection had matured into property rights based on limited liability for tax collectors but on unlimited exposure of tenants to the extraction of revenues. Again an alien arrangement was eliminated by a resurgence of the pride and the power of self-government. Subsequently, attempts to limit the size of holding in the Ryotwari areas were less successful.

Much the same thing happened in Egypt: with the withdrawal of the British, a revolution overthrew the king. The first and major programme of the revolution was a land reform based upon the confiscation of all lands owned by the royal family and the requisition of all lands above a ceiling of 200 acres owned by everyone else, if used for growing annual crops. This assumption by the government of the ownership of something like 10 per cent of the Delta land, and especially the best land, then served as the basis of an agrarian reform programme which instituted a system of co-operative farms. The central principle in the programme was the allotment of the land as their own to former labourers on these lands, in

ways which subordinated the tenure of the land to the technical requirements of irrigation and possibilities of large scale mechanization.

The real success story in land reform of the postwar era is that of Japan.
Here the reform was about as simple as can be imagined: it was a change
in the status of tenants, who already enjoyed substantial rights of occupancy, into fee simple owners of the land they were already farming. To
be sure, this was done with the strong support of an army of occupation,
but the ideas had already been threshed out by the Japanese over a
quarter-century of discussion and legislation. Also, the land was sold to
the tenants at nominal prices as a part of the wartime arrangements for
price and rent controls. This meant that the tenants were able to pay for
the land in a year or two – while the authority of the army of occupation
still prevailed. This gave the farmers the secure status of fee simple
ownership, unencumbered by debts, which they could now protect with a
secure citizenship. Later, the Japanese government compensated the
landlords somewhat for their losses of wealth for land taken by near *de
facto* confiscation.

The outcome is a nation of small farmers, where title to farmland is
dependent upon the continuous occupancy and use of the land in farming,
with most farm families becoming part-time farmers. There is now again
much concern among agricultural economists about the need for better
economies of scale. In the meantime, the productivity of 1 hectare
owner-operated farms is impressive. This productivity is rooted in the
security of expectations of assured ownership implemented with appropriate technology and, perhaps most important of all, in the demonstrated
productivity of security of expectations and freedom.

In Latin America, there was something of a surge of land reform
programmes in the 1950s and 1960s. They arose from somewhat the
same roots as in Mexico, in conflicts between the haves and the have-nots
– established by the superimposition of an alien form of landholding upon
a native people. Also, the holdings of élite groups were sanctioned by
state law and authority, with the poor lacking such secure rights – even the
capacity of citizenship – except in a few countries. As a consequence, the
powers of government were used in agriculture mainly to serve the
interests of the élite; as a result, an initial inequality was deepened,
becoming a major impediment to development.

Cuba is, of course, a celebrated case, where an agrarian reform confis-
cated all large holdings, most of them foreign-owned. Much progress has
been made in eliminating illiteracy and improving the physical condition
of the poor. But hundreds of thousands of middle class professionals and
entrepreneurs fled the country. The interpretation of this Cuban experience has become so deeply involved in ideological controversy that a
dependable understanding is lacking.

The occurrence of agrarian reform programmes in this century is to be
explained in part by the hope aroused by the establishment of the United
Nations and the demonstrated wartime productivity of technology. For a
few years it seemed possible that the ancient scourge of poverty might be

lifted. This remains to be done. In my understanding, these agrarian reform programmes have not been central to the interests of agricultural economics, as a craft. A part of this indifference may be attributed to an attitude that the rural poor are the problem of someone else. Also, for some decades we have been preoccupied with the problems of introducing technology and the conditions of efficient production. When agrarian reforms are approached from this perspective, the stock answer has been: let us first increase the size of the pie and decide later how to divide it up. This is the road to relief which distributes income, not reform which reconstructs opportunities. But the real reason for the lack of concern has been, I suspect, that the mainstream of thinking in the craft simply does not understand the significance of conflicts of interests or power or the history of institutions, and has no way to analyse them. Meanwhile, this has left such controversial issues to the revolutionaries, who are much more adept at destroying an old order than in creating a new one.

III

As I have sought to identify a few key issues in agrarian reforms, three points of emphasis seem strategic: (1) agrarian reforms usually entail the reconstruction of agriculture as systems of farming; (2) such reforms, if effective, also reconstruct the encompassing public and economic order; and (3) the ways in which these two aspects of economies are harnessed together set the terms and conditions for the participation in the agricultural economy by farm people.

Of these three points of emphasis, the reconstruction of systems of farming is closest to the long-time concerns of agricultural economists. As with other aspects of agrarian reform, an historical interpretation helps one see changes in systems of farming in global perspective. All our ancestors who survived by cultivating the soil seem to have devised similar systems of subsistence agriculture. These subsistence economies were characteristically based upon the exploitation of natural fertility, with as much allowance for resting or fallowing as the immediate needs for land use permitted. The use of land was achieved by the authoritative allocation of land use opportunities to families who cleared the land and put it to use. Under such arrangements survival depended upon the efforts of a family.

The large reaches of subsistence agriculture are now found mostly in tropical Africa, but there are millions of people all over the world whose most dependable means of even partial survival is still the practice of subsistence agriculture. Almost all these people are being pressed down into a deepening poverty because of the declining capacity of such economies, due to increases in population and the deterioration of soil and vegetation.

Such conditions provide the base line for needed programmes of rural development directed to the mitigation of rural poverty, and this need holds the prospect of an unprecedented flood of reforms or agrarian revolutions in the poorer countries of the world. But a deepening poverty due to the deterioration of subsistence agriculture has not, as a general rule, evoked agrarian reforms during this century. Rather, such reforms have been directed toward situations in which political and economic developments have resulted in a pathological or distorted reconstruction of agriculture – one which has seemed unjust to people who thought about it, to both intellectuals and peasants.

Over large areas of the less developed world a kind of extractive feudalism developed which was basically a rent-collecting operation, one which neither energized the production processes nor enhanced the welfare of the peasant people – as in much of Asia. In the western hemisphere, the practitioners of traditional agriculture were pushed aside by outsiders and continued to survive, if at all, mostly by their ancient ways but with few resources. Where agriculture was developed under colonial administration, subsistence agriculture was either pushed aside to make room for a cash export crop, as in the cocoa-growing regions, or barred from an area in order to make room for enclaves of European agriculture. In none of these approaches was traditional agriculture energized and transformed, as happened in Western Europe where the modernization of peasant economies was achieved, with the production of indigenous crops for nearby urban markets serving as the engine of growth.

IV

The reconstruction of systems of farming as production organizations requires attention to the size of farms and the general pattern of organization – as individual, co-operative, or collective farms – and the modes of participation by farm people.

Although the size of farm has long been near the centre of concern of agricultural economists, it does not seem that the size of the land allotment per caput has been deeply influenced by considerations of an optimum size of farm. Rather, the size of allotment of land per farm both individually and collectively has been limited by the available land.

Other considerations have operated where land has been allotted to individuals. In most of the old world tenants have historically acquired some sort of equitable claim to the land they cultivate. Thus land reform programmes have assigned land to tenants, even to the exclusion of poorer casual labourers. In Latin America, where workers on haciendas were not tenants, the land distribution programmes seem to have favoured the resident labour force as against the casual labourers – as happened in Chile.

The issue of the kind of general organization of farming, collective versus individual, seems to have been decided mostly on ideological grounds. The case is clear where reforms were conducted under the aegis of Marxian doctrine, in pursuit of large scale organization to exploit technology and the determined avoidance of private economic power. Also, over much of the remainder of the developing world, there is a deep intellectual quest for an agrarian socialism as a middle way, between the colonial capitalist regimes which they have observed firsthand and the Marxian route of collectivization.

V

We have argued that the primary focus of agrarian reforms has been on the reformation of antecedent orders. Orders, in our conception of things, are basically ordered systems of human arrangements. Such systems develop over centuries and are so complex and fundamental to the lives of individuals that their invention as a system is beyond both the ingenuity of man and the adaptive capacity of peasant people. Viewed genetically, the encompassing order is first of all a social order, constructed of working rules which channel human conduct and sanctioned by whatever power is vested in the heads of tribes, families, or communities.

Both the sanctions and the rules become differentiated in development. For economists the critical differentiations are those which create nation-states and the correlative systems of national political economy through the use of state sanctions. The superimposition of the sovereign powers of alien governments, and the use of state powers for private purposes, has been the major source of the kinds of derangements of the antecedent order which have evoked agrarian reforms in this century. It seems to follow by implication that it may have been possible to modernize the antecedent orders by the power of the state to create a more equitable system of political economy by gradual means. Such a vast undertaking could be, and should be in our view, a fruitful ground for professional collaboration of lawyers, anthropologists, political scientists, and agricultural economists, if economists have sufficient will and insight to extend the scope of their analysis to embrace agricultural economies as systems of human organization as well as mechanical systems for the transformation of resources into commodities.

The essential role which economists must perform in such reformations is to transform the key insights of economics into operational definitions which serve to select and strengthen those social procedures which lead to investments, the better use of resources, the needed degree of market specialization, and which elicit willing participation and much more. Such operational definitions may be suggested by, but cannot be read off of, the agricultural economies of the United States, Canada, or any other country. Among the general problems here are those of conceptualizing the meaning of land beyond being a gift of nature to include capacity-expanding investments in land, without introducing an unendurable degree of insecurity to people on the land. Similarly, the transmission of land by descent alone needs to be broadened to permit land users which give support to better utilization of land; correlatively, the birthright claims to land need to be subject to a statute of limitations after a lapse of a generation or so. Such would be only a beginning. But in the absence of professional understanding of such issues, alien concepts of property and contract have been introduced which deprived people of their once secure status, engendering disorder but without energizing the traditional economies.

One of the major changes which a system of economy undergoes as it develops is that it becomes more depersonalized; I see no way in which a developing agriculture can escape this fate. Such a change is particularly important in the selective differentiation and establishment of economic institutions. An observation of Professor Commons in his analyses of developmental changes in the English common law is pertinent here: "There were two circumstances which prevented the primitive common law from enforcing the assignment or negotiability of contracts, namely the concept of property as tangible objects [held for one's own personal use] and the concept of contract as a personal relation."[1] All contracts were at one time considered to be as personable and nonsaleable as promises to marry are today. In an interdependent market economy, property is not merely a physical object, but, more strategically, a system of social arrangement sanctioned by the state.

The role of the state in all this is critical, for the basic structure of a modern system of national economy is, or is made up of, the working rules for associated activities which the state sanctions. Although the working rules which are sanctioned need to be derived mostly from the experience of the people, if they are to make sense to those who occupy and operate the system, the selectivity and refinement of such rules, as well as the extent of importation from other cultures, is a function of the operative ideology of those who control the use of the power of government.

This is why the agrarian reforms under the auspices of a Marxian ideology in this century are such remarkable experiences in the reformation of agricultural economies. Given the Marxian condemnation of private economic power, the predilection for an order created by command and obedience with the effect that the wills of those who man the powers of state should prevail from top to bottom, the outcome is a collective system of economy in which private property is limited essentially to the ownership of homes and bonds, with limited zones of individual or private discretion outside the home. Such arrangements lead to a concentration of both economic and political power at the top. Only the moral power of a largely passive resistance remained to implement the wills of peasant people, who feared such changes. This was, however, sufficient to secure concessions in many countries which permitted them to have their own homes and gardens as a condition of their willing participation.

In contrast, where the use of the power of government is informed by ideas basic to the western liberal tradition, an economic order is created which accords wide scope for discretionary conduct by individuals and results not only in a structure of private property, but also in the creation of zones of secure opportunity for owners of farmland. These variations are consequences of differences in the conception of whose will is to be effective on what.

VI

The ways in which farm people participate in an economic system are specified and limited by interrelation between agriculture as a system of production and the encompassing public and economic order. We have already commented somewhat on the modes of participation. Here I would only add one or two remarks – one from Professor Commons who was among the wisest of men regarding the nature of a democratic, political economy in an age of economic power. I refer to his definition of an institution: an institution, he noted, is "collective action in control, liberation and expansion of individual action."[2] In fact, there is no way to liberate and expand individual action without appropriate social controls. The trick is to figure out ways in which the working rules encourage and support the willing and energetic participation of people. All over the industrial world there is now a search for new forms of group organization which enlist the sustained, willing, and energetic participation of workers, including experiments with shared management. The fundamental problem seems to be that, in a purely technological approach to development in agriculture and elsewhere, the logic of technology treats people as a part of the machinery.

VII

The most insistent question put to me by Glenn Johnson in his invitation to write this paper was: "What can and cannot be contributed by economists to practical decisions about agrarian reforms?" I hope the above remarks have some relevance to this question. Here I add only a comment or two.

If the practical decisions are to be those of implementing policy decisions made by someone else – politicians, generals, whomever – economists have much to do: for every project there is a need for cost-benefit analysis, with shadow pricing, linear programming, and much more. Also, insofar as the reform established systems of farming and marketing, there will be serious questions about such issues as the efficiency of operations and the character of demand. However, if the practical decisions are about the formation of agrarian reform policies – whether there should be a reform, or what should be the nature, objectives, and content of such reforms – I do not see that the mainstream of agricultural economics as currently practised by the craft has much to offer beyond specifying conditions which need to be met in the design of institutions and studying the "effects" of agrarian reforms which got started somehow.

It is not that agricultural economics should embrace the analysis of all aspects of agrarian reform policy. Rather, what is needed are formulations that permit joining of issues in a fundamental way with other disciplines. One central problem is that of social valuations in public policy. Fundamentally, such values as justice, freedom, equality, and security, even the public itself, are the meaning of social procedures, not something to be picked up and moved about, or to be understood more than a little, by the substantive approach to valuation by welfare economics. The matrix of social valuation is social organization. Such value possibilities are a function of the whole system of human arrangements – as epitomized in the phrase, a free society.

Thus it seems to me that if agricultural economists are to deal professionally, and not merely as eminently sensible people, with the central issues of the formation of agrarian reform policies, agricultural economics needs to be humanized into a social science and toughened up into a political economy of agricultural development.

NOTES

[1] John R. Commons *Legal Foundations of Capitalism*, Madison, University of Wisconsin Press, 1959, pp. 246–7.
[2] John R. Commons *Institutional Economics*, 1934 and 1959, p. 73.

DISCUSSION OPENING – CLARK EDWARDS

Professor Parsons has provided us with a solid conceptual paper on agrarian reform, including insights into what can and cannot be contributed by economists and other professionals to practical decisions. Parsons defines agrarian reform in its broadest sense which recognizes the interrelation of the agricultural and nonagricultural sectors, and which involves reformation of a social and political, as well as an economic, order.

Parsons begins his paper by reviewing a number of important facts. He traces a history of agrarian reform with which he is thoroughly familiar; a history which runs to all corners of the world and which covers all of this century. The historical section of his paper, which recounts success stories as well as dismal failures, is largely in terms of an older and narrower definition of agrarian reform: he uses the phrase "land reform" to make this clear.

Parsons then turns from facts to the theories and logic needed to understand the case studies he has recounted. He generalizes from history in order to understand and explain what has been happening. He explains how agrarian reform restructures not only systems of farming but also the public and economic order. Among the theoretical problems are those of conceptualizing the meaning of land, beyond being a gift of nature, to include capacity-expanding investments. Attention is given to size of farm, to alternative patterns of agricultural organization, and to institutional arrangements for linking agriculture to the non-farm sector through factor and product markets. Parsons draws upon economic theory to explain the levels of output and the distributions of income that follow from neoclassical markets, Keynsian policies, Marxist conceptualizations, and institutional economics. He stresses, however, that we must go beyond economics if our theories are to be useful in explaining and predicting the consequences of alternative reformations.

Facts and theories are important parts of Parson's paper, but he passes over these topics quickly in order to use his scarce time to concentrate on what he considers to be a more important set of issues: conflicting values. Parsons admits that agrarian reform can grow out of purely economic issues, such as a deepening of poverty due to the deterioration of subsistence agriculture. However, says Parsons, agrarian reform is more likely to come from other sources: a change in the political power base, a pathological derangement of the social system, or some ideological ground. Reformation changes the social order and the way of life; some persons will gain while others lose their social status and their inheritances. Property, says Parsons, is a social arrangement; therefore land reform is social reform. The operative ideology of those who control the power of government comes into conflict with the moral power of the wills of peasant people. Parsons speaks of the need for individual values and choices, and he notes the contrasting need for these to be constrained by social values and controls. A central problem in agrarian reform is that of social valuation. Economists have a tradition of providing prescriptions which enable us to move efficiently towards given ends. They also have a tradition of contributing to value theory, of clarifying values, and of helping to judge ends.

There is a further aspect of agrarian reform lurking in the paper. He did not discuss it explicitly, but you could see it in the flash of his eyes as he presented it. And you can find it in the choice of language used when he makes certain points in the written version. The further ingredient is this: agrarian reform is an emotional issue. Those involved tend not to be logical or neutral. They are revolutionaries dealing with frustrations and despair. The revolutions involve deep conflict between the wealthy and powerful on the one hand and the desperate on the other. All reforms involve a change in the way of life of members of the society; some reforms go so far as to involve bloodshed.

From his incisive tour of the facts, theories, values, and emotions involved in the history of agrarian reform during this century, Parsons draws two conclusions about a role for agricultural economists.

1 Agricultural economists can make practical contributions to the implementation of decisions made by someone else; by a politician, for example, or a general. Agricultural economists can be helpful in providing descriptions, explanations, and prescriptions which are based on

cost/benefit analyses and on linear programming. Parsons appears to be saying that such contributions are useful and necessary, so far as they go. But he is clearly saying that they do not go far enough. This brings us to his second conclusion.

2   We need to build institutions which help to resolve social conflict, and to promote such fundamental values as justice, freedom, equality, and security. We need formulations of alternative agrarian reforms which join issues in a fundamental way with other disciplines, and which not only help to build needed institutions and to choose effective means but also help to judge ends.

GENERAL DISCUSSION – RAPPORTEUR: GARY CARLSON

There were comments from the floor respecting the difficulty of taking sides and supporting certain value systems; it was felt that as professional agricultural economists we must recognize that we are part of the élite and associated with the élite.

One speaker said that Indonesia urgently needed land reform but did not really know where to start and how to begin. He would have liked Professor Parsons to provide more direction on this aspect.

The comment was also made that the social ostracism an agricultural economist may encounter upon researching land reform came from two sides: the landowner class which does not want the matter studied at all, and the extreme left which does not want it studied objectively (and at times is unwilling to allow the public to have information on the economic effects of the violent approach it advocates). It was fortunate that there were many people who did not fall into either of these sides.

Two questions were asked:

1   How can agricultural economists help the government initiate land and agricultural reform?

2   How can we as agricultural economists do justice to help solve agricultural reform problems by taking sides in our deliberations without being accused of being political?

Professor Parsons responded by saying that taking sides means or involves: (a) supporting the agrarian reform that reflects the needs and aspirations of the people we are seeking to assist; and (b) developing conceptual models of society (its values and rules) against which agricultural economists can conduct economic analyses, etc.

Participants in the discussion included John D. Strasma and Mr. Mubyarto.

PER PINSTRUP-ANDERSEN

Economic Theory Needed in Studying the Economics of Getting Poorer While Redistributing

The topic on which I was invited to speak is of considerable magnitude and I have found it impossible to cover all the relevant aspects in this short paper. Instead, I shall try to identify and discuss only a few of these aspects in the hope – but without the illusion – that I have selected the issues of greatest interest and importance to agricultural economists who, at some future point in time, may find themselves studying "the economics of getting poorer while redistributing".

Let me begin by defining the terms and establishing the boundaries of the paper. Glenn Johnson, in his invitation, states that "we (the developed countries) are commonly told that we are exhausting the world's fossil fuel, land, water and mineral resources, while polluting the air and destroying natural beauty. This implies a reduction in total real income. We are also being told (and in some cases being forced) to redistribute to the less developed countries". Johnson further states that this paper should not investigate the empirical truth of the above but rather suggest what conceptual and theoretical issues are important for studying the economics of getting poorer while redistributing.

In line with the above, I shall define the term "getting poorer" as a situation where non-renewable resources are being depleted and/or the quality of our environment is being reduced at such rates that overall growth rates may slow down and eventually become negative. Thus, I am defining the relative term "poorer" in terms of the non-renewable resource base and the quality of the environment rather than the existing growth rate *per se*. Defined this way, society may become poorer even though short run income growth rates are positive. However, such a situation may eventually lead to negative income growth. Thus, the critical issues become those related to the substitution of non-renewable resources, externalities related to the quality of the environment and resource allocation, and distribution of incomes between current and future generations.

I shall assume that more income (both current and future income) is preferred to less, both for developed countries as such and groups within these countries. This assumption is made to avoid dealing with the small

369

minorities that advocate a lower income for its own sake (the romantic view of the simple life). Thus, as the developed countries get poorer, in a resource and environmental sense as stated above, with the resulting squeeze on real incomes, the primary concerns of governments and groups within society will focus on counteracting the negative income effect by maintaining acceptable growth rates in real incomes or at least avoiding large decreases in real incomes both for current and future generations. This will naturally lead to severe conflicts among groups and the relative economic and political power may come to play an increasing role in the distribution of incomes within a given country.

The increasing importance of the relative power in determining the income distributions is likely to have severe implications for the current efforts to assist developing countries in gaining additional material well-being. While the motives for transfers from developed to developing countries are varied, a squeeze on developed countries' income growth will undoubtedly have negative effects on these transfers unless the bargaining power of the developing countries is increased.

The issues mentioned above have been singled out for further analysis in the remainder of this paper. Selected parts of the existing economic theory of most specific relevance to the issues of getting poorer – with primary emphasis on intra-national distribution – will be discussed first. Then follows a discussion of the international distribution of incomes with specific reference to transfers to developing countries in a situation of falling real incomes in developed countries. The next section deals with the economics of the use of scarce non-renewable resources and the paper terminates with a discussion of the challenge to agricultural economists.

ECONOMIC THEORY OF "GETTING POORER"

The prospects of negative economic growth and related causes and consequences have been discussed throughout the economics literature. No exhaustive review of the relevant literature will be attempted here.

Existing economic theory on the subject is logically divided into that focusing on overall reductions in real incomes due to resource scarcity, population growth, excess savings and/or political and organizational disorder and that which focuses on the deterioration of incomes by specific groups in society, i.e. the distributional aspects.

Classical economists including Smith, Ricardo, Malthus and Mill believed that the development process of industrial countries would reach a point of stagnation – a long run equilibrium – while Marx argued that the capitalist system would in fact collapse. Malthus, however, believed that the long run equilibrium would be an unhappy one.

Malthus' theory of population and production growth is well known. Since it was first published, the Malthusian theory has been cited extensively in connection with short term food shortages. Likewise, during periods of high growth rates in food production, a number of authors have argued that the theory was not supported by empirical evidence. The Malthusion theory is, of course, focused on the longer run development and should not be "proved" or "disproved" on the basis of short term fluctuations in population growth or food production. Recent developments have shown that food production can be expanded at relatively high rates. At the same time, experience from most developed and some developing countries have shown that the population growth rates can be reduced severely and that net population growth rates close to or equal to zero are entirely possible irrespective of political system. It is equally clear that unless the high population growth rates in many developing countries are severely reduced within a reasonable time frame, growth rates in food production will not be able to keep the pace. Thus, the primary utility of the Malthusian viewpoint is that it serves as a reminder of what would happen if the relevant issues are neglected or ignored.

While Malthus was concerned with population growth and the inability of the agricultural land to meet the increases in food requirements, a somewhat similar argument regarding non-renewable resources has gained strong support during the last ten to fifteen years. The basic argument is that: (1) the amount of non-renewable resources is finite, (2) a continuation of the use trends of recent years will result in the depletion of many of these resources within the not too distant future, and (3) that such depletion will result in drastic reductions in real incomes of current as well as future generations. This argument was highlighted by the Club of Rome[7] and has been discussed by a number of authors including[3,16]. Closely associated with this argument is the concern that a continuation of current production and consumption trends will lead to widespread pollution and destruction of the environment, some of which being irreversible. Hirsch[5] goes a step further and argues that increased consumption by individuals will result in externalities with a negative effect on the utility obtained from the consumption. These externalities imply that the utility associated with expanded consumption of a particular good depends on how large a proportion of society participates in the consumption expansions. As consumption increases and an increasing proportion of the population gets access to high consumption levels, externalities will impose constraints on the growth of real incomes. Highway congestions and air pollution associated with more widespread ownership and use of automobiles is but one example of what Hirsch argues will lead to what he calls "social limits to growth".

Among other theories related to "getting poorer", although not in a resource and environment sense but in the sense of stagnation and possibly negative income growth, the most widely accepted up through history has undoubtedly been that related to excess savings and the resulting demand deficits as mentioned above. The basic theory is that the capitalist development process will lead to excess savings and accumulation of capital which in turn will constrain demand and thereby make it impossible to find sufficient investment opportunities. The basics (but not necessarily the finer points) of this theory was shared by a number of economists with very different philosophical backgrounds, e.g. Keynes, Marx and Hobson. However, the prescriptions for a cure to the problem varied greatly among these economists. Keynes' answer to the problem was to use government spending to assure the proper balance between savings and demand. Marx, on the other hand, believed that the problem could not be solved under the capitalist system while Hobson prescribed measures to equalize the distribution of incomes and thereby reduce savings. While Keynesian economics has played an important role in Western societies, it is important to remember that negative income growth induced by resource scarcity and pollution may require quite different curative or adaptive measures. I shall return to this issue at a later point in the paper.

Let us now move to the theory related to the relative or absolute deterioration of the incomes of specific groups. Here economic thought has placed the primary emphasis on the distribution between labour and capital. Classical economists including Ricardo and Mill argued that the wage ratio would decline in the course of development within capitalist societies. Furthermore, the expected decline in the wage ratio was a key element in the Marxian theory of the collapse of capitalism.

Results from empirical studies, particularly those by Bowley, Douglas and others did not support the theory of declining wage ratios but rather pointed towards a more or less constant wage ratio. Recent empirical studies for developed countries show a clear trend of increasing wage ratios.[1,9] Thus, on the basis of data from the main OECD countries, Paldam concludes that the wage ratio in these countries has increased by an average of about 20 percentage points during the period 1947–75.[9] The increasing wage ratios may be explained at least partially by the increasing political and economic power of labour through organized union efforts and participation in the political process. The importance of the greater power of labour is further illustrated by the reaction of the wage ratio to the price shocks for imported raw materials which occurred around 1950 and again during the period 1972–74. While the reaction in 1950 was a fall in the wage ratio such a reaction did not occur during 1972–74. On the contrary, the wage ratio increased considerably during that period in most of the OECD countries.[9] While the comparison is somewhat crude, it nevertheless supports the hypothesis that the increasing power of labour was successful in avoiding sharing the loss associated with the worsening of the terms of trade during the period 1972–74.

The increasing power of labour together with expanded unemployment compensation schemes and related social programmes in developed countries may have severe implications for the distribution of incomes in a situation of potential or actual decreases in real incomes in general. Without the threat of severe reductions in personal incomes of members who might become unemployed, organized labour is likely to use its power to avoid decreases in real incomes in situations of general real income decreases, even if it implies increasing unemployment and further reductions in production and incomes in general. Likewise, capital owners will use their power to avoid taking part in the income decreases through adjustments in production, employment and investment. The public sector, on the other hand, will be faced with increasing demands for unemployment compensation and larger social programme outlays, demands that in the final analysis must be met mainly through taxes.

In countries where a considerable proportion of the production must compete in international markets, whether through export or competition from imported goods, such a development may be self-perpetuating. In such cases the increasing unemployment and the resulting reductions in production and expansions in the demand for public funds may lead to direct public subsidy to production or public ownership of production facilities. Indications of such a development are seen in some countries, e.g. Sweden, where industrial facilities, although as yet to a very limited extent, are being taken over by the public to maintain employment opportunities.

Distortions in the labour market caused by excessive wage demands as discussed above, may result in large and increasing gaps between social and private costs of labour. This, in turn, will bias the path of technological innovation in favour of labour saving technology in societies where resource allocation decisions are made on the basis of relative private costs of resources. Examples of such biases are plentiful both for agricultural and industrial technology. In fact, the majority of publicly as well as privately funded research and development aimed at technological progress in market oriented developed countries is likely to suffer from this bias. The paradox is that public as well as private funds are spent to promote labour saving technology which in turn increases the demand for public funds for unemployment compensation and related social programmes. In situations of large and increasing gaps between social and private labour costs, the costs to society of ignoring the social labour cost in planning the future technology development path may be high.

Another critical question regarding the distribution of incomes within countries experiencing economic slowdown or negative growth rates is how the poor will be affected. Reduction of poverty in most industrial societies has come about primarily through proportional or differential growth. Actual redistribution of existing wealth and incomes has not played a major role. However, in order to continue to reduce poverty in a situation of constant or falling real incomes, such redistribution must occur. Unless the poor possess considerably more political power than what is presently apparent, actual redistribution will probably not occur to any significant extent. Hence, the poor will most likely have to carry their share of the burden of falling real incomes.

Up to this point we have discussed the implications for the distribution of income within the individual developed country. Let us now turn to the implications for transfers from developed to developing countries.

TRANSFERS TO DEVELOPING COUNTRIES

Existing inequalities in the international distribution of incomes have resulted in demands for transfers from developed to developing countries. The legitimacy of such demands is recognized by many national governments and international institutions. The motives of developed countries behind current transfers are varied and covers a large spectrum from purely military and security motives through economic motives to purely moral desires to diminish human suffering.

Depletion of non-renewable resources influences the magnitude of transfers in two ways. First, to the extent that developing countries control the critical resources, the potential power of these countries to increase resource prices and thus expand the transfers will increase. Whether such potential power is actually used will depend on a number of factors including the geographical and political concentration of the individual resource, the ability of the resource owners to agree on price and supply control, their wishes to actually exploit the power and the availability of substitutes. Recent experience regarding oil prices illustrates the potential for transferring resources from developed to developing countries. Even if complete compensation were given to oil importing developing countries, the additional oil revenues obtained by the OPEC countries would be very large indeed.

Secondly, the negative impact on real incomes in developed countries brought about by the depletion of non-renewable resources or contamination of the environment will tend to reduce transfers to developing countries *ceteris paribus*. Such reductions will come about as a direct result of the earlier mentioned attempts by the various internal groups to avoid reduced real incomes. The classical argument that it is easier to redistribute through growth than through transfers of existing incomes and wealth is, of course, as valid among countries as among groups within a given country. The perceived sacrifice of foreign assistance is likely to be considerably greater in a situation of negative than in a situation of positive growth in real income.

The magnitude of transfers will depend on the bargaining power of the developing countries. Strong desires on the part of the developed countries to maintain security, peaceful coexistence and markets for their products may be exploited by developing countries as bargaining power. The composition of the transfers is also likely to be altered. More aid tying can be expected for the purpose of assisting domestic production. Transfer of surplus labour (in the form of commodities and to a much lesser extent as technical assistance), excess productive capacity and surplus commodities will be attempted. Such tendencies are not new. The tendency has traditionally been to use surplus commodities and resources in foreign assistance where possible. However, there will be a much stronger desire to do so in a situation of economic slowdown. Pressure from groups and segments in economic distress for tying of aid and orientation of trade in such a way as to assist these groups and segments will be increasingly powerful as the economic slowdown becomes more severe.

The question as to who are the actual beneficiaries of transfers is likely to be much more carefully scrutinized. Due to the greater perceived sacrifice of foreign assistance in times of economic slowdown, transfers believed primarily to benefit high income groups are likely to be rejected unless they meet urgent security or economic goals. This might imply that voluntary concessions in trade relationships with developing countries and other types of transfers where the impact on the low income groups is not readily shown may be even more limited than in the past, while direct welfare type assistance programmes may take over a larger proportion of the total assistance. Voluntary trade concessions may also be reduced as a means to protect domestic production. Assistance measures with a clear benefit to the donor countries, particularly in the short run, will be promoted more than currently.

NON–RENEWABLE RESOURCES AND INTERTEMPORAL DISTRIBUTION

Some of the implications of getting poorer for (1) the distribution of income between labour and capital and (2) transfers to developing countries were discussed in the previous sections. This section focuses on some of the issues related to the depletion of non-renewable resources with primary emphasis on the intertemporal distribution. As in previous sections, the analysis will be very brief.

As a result of the drastic price increases for oil and certain other non-renewable resources, the interest for economic analysis related to the optimal depletion of scarce non-renewable resources has increased considerably. Some of the key issues dealt with in these analyses are (1) how to specify optimal distribution of income between generations, (2) the most efficient allocative mechanisms for the depletion of non-renewable resources including the obvious question: Will free market conditions lead to depletion rates that will meet the requirements of an optimal intertemporal income distribution? and (3) uncertainties regarding (a) the magnitudes of the stocks of non-renewable resources, and (b) the economic and technical feasibility of developing substitutes.

The interest for intertemporal income distribution is not new. It is an integral part of the theory of optimal capital accumulation. It does, however, take on new dimensions in the light of planning for the depletion of scarce non-renewable resources.

Traditional growth theory was, at least implicitly, concerned with the question of how the burden of capital accumulation and of raising the standard of civilization was to be shared between generations. The depletion of non-renewable resources, on the other hand, must face the question of what proportion of the foundation for future generations' incomes can justifiably be used by the current generation. Rawls[11] concludes that a classical utilitarian approach "leads in the wrong direction for questions of justice between generations. The utilitarian doctrine may direct us to demand heavy sacrifices of the poorer generations for the sake of greater advantages for later ones that are far better off". Instead, in questions of equity and savings among generations, Rawls proposes a principle "given by the balance between what a typical person feels it is reasonable to ask of his parents and what this same person is prepared to do for his children".[11]

While Rawls proposes the max-min principle (improving the position of the poorest) for intragenerational income distribution he concludes that this principle is inapplicable to intergenerational distribution because it would imply no saving at all. The max-min principle requires that consumption per person be constant through time. Therefore, the principle can only be applied after a certain capital stock has been developed that is big enough to support a decent standard of living.[14] In fact, the principle implies economic stagnation, i.e. zero growth, at whatever level it is initially applied. Solow concludes that the principle "seems to be a reasonable criterion for intertemporal planning decisions" if the above mentioned capital stock has been developed and technical progress is limited.[14]

In addition to the desired intertemporal income distribution, the optimal rate of depletion depends on the elasticity of substitution between non-renewable resources and other capital resources. This elasticity, in turn, depends on the nature of technical change and the possibilities of substitution of man-made factors of production (capital) for non-renewable resources. A number of attempts have been made to determine the optimal rate of depletion and the optimal growth path under various assumptions regarding the market structure and the elasticity of substitution. One of the more serious problems noted in some of these studies, e.g.,[15] is that reliance on the competitive market price formation may lead to long run instability because the time horizon influencing the price formation is too short. Inability to foresee sufficiently far into the future may result in too high depletion rates and too low prices. This, in turn, might imply underinvestment in the development of substitutes, too slow technical change and severe interruptions in the development process.

THE CHALLENGE TO THE AGRICULTURAL ECONOMIST

A situation of "getting poorer while redistributing" poses some interesting and difficult challenges to economists and agricultural economists. A few of the areas of research where such challenges appear to exist are mentioned below.

The increasing importance of the power of individual groups in society and the related social conflicts in a situation of "getting poorer" is an area where innovative theoretical and empirical work could have a high payoff. The increasing power of labour in the face of economic slowdown caused by severe scarcity of non-renewable resources and pollution of the environment may lead to self-perpetuating decrease in employment and real incomes and unacceptable expansions in the demand for public expenditures. The final result may be increasing public ownership of productive resources. There is an urgent need for economic analysis related to the increasing gap between private and social costs of labour to assist public policy aimed at the reduction of private labour costs to equate social labour costs through subsidies, regulation of the power of labour or in some other way. Work is needed to determine the implications of the gap for the technological development path and technical change. Severe distortions in the labour market leading to biased technological development may be excessively costly to society. My hypothesis is that the distortions will increase in importance under falling real incomes.

Economic analysis is also required to guide the technological development path on the basis of long run social costs of non-renewable resources and pollution of the environment. To the extent that future effects of externalities are ignored or underestimated, long run social costs may greatly exceed short run private costs. To the extent that the latter are used for allocative decisions, significant misallocation may occur. Furthermore, the magnitude of investment in efforts to develop viable substitutes for non-renewable resources at any given time may not be optimal. This relates closely to the need for more work on the optimal depletion rate of non-renewable resources. This issue is too important to be left to sensation and doomsday writers. However, unless we get a better foundation for intertemporal distributional issues, efforts to determine optimal depletion rates for resources for which no acceptable substitutes seem to be available will continue to be very subjective exercises.

The question of negative externalities for the individual, associated with economic growth – the "social limits to growth" – deserves some additional theoretical and empirical work. In the context of this paper such work might focus on the magnitude of change in the external effects associated with falling real incomes. If the negative external effect at the margin is large, it might be expected that the net effect of marginal reductions in the incomes of individuals on their utility would be small. Part of the postulated drop in real incomes, such as additional pollution, will, of course, show up through external effects.

Regarding transfers to developing countries there may be a need for additional work to show how trade concessions and other elements of the "new economic order" affect low income groups in developing countries.

Let me conclude by restating that, in line with the request, this paper was based on the premise that developed countries would "get poorer" due to increasing scarcity of non-renewable resources and negative externalities such as pollution of the environment. No attempts were made to assess whether in fact the premise is likely to be true.

378　　　　　　　*Per Pinstrup-Andersen*

REFERENCES

[1] Atkinson, A.B. *The Economics of Inequality*, Clarendon Press, Oxford 1975.
[2] Boulding, Kenneth E. "Marxism and the Future of Capitalism", *National Forum*, Vol. LXIX, No. 1., 1979, pp. 18–22.
[3] Brown, Lester R. *The Twenty Ninth Day*, W.W. Norton and Company, New York 1978.
[4] Galbraith, John Kenneth *Economics and the Public Purpose*, Houghton Mifflin Company, Boston 1973.
[5] Hirsch, Fred *Social Limits to Growth*, Harvard University Press, Cambridge, Mass. 1976.
[6] Jolly, Richard "International Dimensions", Chapter VIII of Hollis Chenery, et al. *Redistribution with Growth*, Oxford University Press, 1974.
[7] Meadows, Donella H. et al. *The Limits to Growth*, Universe Books, New York 1972.
[8] Mill, J.S. *Principles of Political Economy*, Ashley 1923.
[9] Paldam, Martin "Towards the Wage-Earner State", *International Journal of Social Economics*, Vol. 6, No. 1, March 1979, pp. 45–62.
[10] Pincus, John *Trade, Aid and Development*, McGraw-Hill Book Company, New York 1967.
[11] Rawls, J. *A Theory of Justice*. Harvard University Press, Cambridge 1971.
[12] Schultz, Theodore W. "Is Modern Agriculture Consistent with a Stable Environment?" *The Future of Agriculture*, Oxford Agr. Econ. Inst. and IAAS, 1974, pp. 235–42.
[13] Schultz, Theodore W. "Conflicts over Changes in Scarcity: An Economic Approach", *American Journal of Agricultural Economics*, Vol. 56, No. 5, December 1974, pp. 998–1004.
[14] Solow, R.M. "Intergenerational Equity and Exhaustible Resources", *The Review of Economic Studies*, Symposium 1974, pp. 29–45.
[15] Stiglitz, Joseph "Growth with Exhaustible Natural Resources: The Competitive Economy", *The Review of Economic Studies*, Symposium 1974, pp. 139–52.
[16] Ward, Barbara and René Dubos *Only One Earth*, W.W. Norton and Company, New York 1972.

DISCUSSION OPENING – SECONDO TARDITI

Many issues have already been raised by Pinstrup-Andersen on "the theory needed to study the economics of getting poorer while redistributing" so that only two more points will be raised in this opening discussion: the first adds one dimension to the paper's approach on the "redistributing" side, while the second point deals with a somewhat wider dimension on the concept of "getting poorer".

"Redistributing", as a consequence of getting poorer, has been deeply analysed in its intertemporal, international and intranational dimension, the latter mainly focused on income distribution between labour and capital, following the major emphasis given to this problem in economic thought.

Quoting Professor Michael Lipton of the Institute of Development Studies at Sussex: "The most important class conflict in the poorest countries in the world today is not between labour and capital, nor is it between foreign and national interests. It is between the rural classes and the urban classes". As agricultural economists we cannot miss the opportunity of looking at the problem by this approach. Under conditions of low and negative rates of development in real income, the rural population will be affected in contrasting ways. From one side the low income elasticity of demand for food will reduce the negative effects on agricultural prices, supply and employment, while on the other side, lower development rates will reduce non-agricultural and urban absorption of rural manpower, fostering labour pressure on agricultural land and worsening the income distribution in the country between land owners and landless workers. Existing social tensions in rural areas will increase, particularly where land property is unevenly distributed and landless workers earn very low incomes, determining forced changes in income distribution and in institutional organisation.

A much larger demand for agricultural land, water and fertilizers will explode if we really are compelled to shift from a non-renewable resource system to a renewable resource system, for example producing automotive fuel from alcoholic fermentation of sugar or starchy roots. In such conditions a strong movement back to the land from urban areas is much more probable and the urban–rural power relations could be deeply affected. Obviously agricultural economists are deeply involved in the analysis of such consequences.

A second point which could be usefully brought into discussion deals with the definition of "getting poorer" which has been specified in the paper in the dimensions of real income, of environment, and of non-renewable resources. The "social welfare" parameter in a certain way summarises these three dimensions and moreover adds some aspects of the concept of utility which help to explore a wider range of the meaning of "getting poorer". Through this parameter we could try to examine the subject of this paper in the opposite direction: how redistributing could improve or worsen the process of "getting poorer", coming perhaps to the conclusion that income redistribution very often fosters social welfare and could be a major tool for fighting the "getting poorer" trend, as may seem evident in the field of food and agriculture.

Agricultural resources on earth are far from being fully exploited. The Wageningen members of the team which built up the "Model of International Relations in Agriculture" estimated for 1965 that on the basis of a detailed inventory of soil characteristics, rainfall, temperature and sunshine, according to natural restrictions to the growth of agricultural crops, the earth is capable of producing thirty times the amount of food actually produced. Obviously it is not so easy to increase agricultural production to the theoretical maximum, but hunger and malnutrition which affect such a large share of mankind is mainly attributable to a lack of purchasing power, which would be largely increased by a more equitable international and intranational income distribution, bringing a swift increase in social welfare. On a welfare basis, redistributing in most cases will then involve "getting richer" or "getting less poor".

Theoretical problems arise in quantifying the broad range of variables included in the social welfare function concept, starting with the interpersonal comparability of utility functions, which could be solved as Pigou's work demonstrates or could sterilize economists' effort through useless quibbles.

One major point is that real income is only one dimension of welfare and a measure of other basic human needs should be worked out. To integrate the usual parameters of real income per caput, the Overseas Development Department Council has devised a new indicator, "The Physical Quality of Life Index", weighting three social indicators: infant mortality, life expectancy and literacy; but more comprehensive and effectual parameters could be worked out for specific economic policy purposes.

To what extent a decreasing marginal utility function is in the short run a sufficient condition to guarantee that income redistribution will increase social welfare and to what extent income redistribution will hinder sufficient savings so as to threaten future economic development, are open problems for discussion and work.

The outcome of such theoretical work could improve our knowledge of different facets of human welfare, beyond that of material acquisitiveness, and help policy makers to prevent forced income redistributions both international and intranational through economic blackmailing or through open revolutions.

GENERAL DISCUSSION – RAPPORTEUR: GARY CARLSON

The assumption of "getting poorer" as non-renewable resources were depleted was questioned as being an incorrect assumption to begin with. The paper was criticized for linking together several humanitarian issues – perhaps it is more a question of reallocation of resources among countries. Much more economic research was needed on this topic.

The point was made that redistribution of wealth from rich to poor countries and labour's struggle for higher wages were not only separate topics, but problem areas irrespective of depleting non-renewable resources – there were more fundamental constraints affecting these matters.

Finally the question was posed: what effect could the existence of domestic and/or international reserve funds have on income distribution, given the assumptions used in the paper?

Participants in the discussion included P.J. van Blokland, H.L. Chawla and Ulf Renborg.

J.A. MACMILLAN and G.R. WINTER

Income Improvement versus Efficiency in Canadian Rural Development Programmes *

INTRODUCTION

The purpose of this paper is to review the relative emphasis on income improvement (income redistribution) versus efficiency in Canadian rural development programmes. Revisions are suggested based on the available data which point to the achievement of income improvement and the overlapping of rural development with stabilization programmes.

Canadian Rural Development programme expenditures increased substantially through 1961–76 in response to problems of rural poverty. Under Agricultural and Rural Development Agreements (ARDA) $62 million was spent in the 1961–66 period[1] and $1.1 billion during 1969–76.[2]

In contrast to the situation of relative price stability in the 1960s, recent price increases have been substantially greater than input price increases. The resulting escalation in farm land prices has contributed to large increments in the net worth position of Canadian farmers. Available data indicate average farm family income is greater than average non-farm family income for the first time in several decades. If the increments in amortized value of land assets are included then the average annual income differential in favour of farm families is even greater.

It is our tentative hypothesis that recent increases in total farm family income relative to total non-farm family income warrant a decreasing emphasis on income improvement relative to productivity criteria in Canadian rural development programmes. For example, land clearing and farm management training programmes may be inferior to the drainage programmes with respect to productivity but preferred with respect to income distribution effects.[3] The income distribution effects of community pasture programmes may be substantial but the projects in British Columbia did not provide a return greater than costs.[4] A decreasing emphasis on income improvement in Canadian rural development programmes would imply that community pasture, land clearing and farm management training programmes be carefully reviewed to determine

* The helpful contributions by R. Barichello are acknowledged.

whether or not programme changes could be made to meet a "normal" rate of return on investment criteria. If such projects could not be made profitable they should not be implemented. The hypothesis is necessarily tentative because complete income data required for farm and non-farm income comparisons are not available.[5]

The hypothesis is elaborated below with respect to:

1   Indicators of Canadian rural development.
2   Brief review of Canadian rural development programmes and
3   Suggested revisions in future Canadian rural development policies and programmes.

INDICATORS OF CANADIAN RURAL DEVELOPMENT

The direction of Canadian rural development expenditures in response to rural poverty requires elaboration. From an international perspective, Canada's farmers are well off. According to Hayami and Ruttan, Canada ranked fourth among thirteen developed countries in terms of agricultural value added per worker.[6] Nevertheless policymakers responded to the low relative income of farm operators and the large proportion of small farm operators with sales of farm products less than $2,500. During 1961–71, non-farm labour income per employee rose by 87 per cent ($3,865 to $7,232). In contrast, 1960–70 net farm income per farm operator increased by only 54 per cent ($2,514 to $3,863). Complete income data for farm and non-farm families are not available prior to 1971 and will not be available again until the 1981 census; which prevents a more precise comparison of trends in farm versus non-farm incomes.

Indicators of Canadian rural development (Table 1) summarize information on population and income by urbanization, farm versus non-farm income, distribution of low family income by urbanization, average income of farm operators by economic class and agricultural product and input prices.

Farm population and labour force components are about 5 per cent of the respective Canadian totals. In 1971, average farm family income was $3,000 below the Canadian average. It was highest in British Columbia and lowest in Saskatchewan. Net farm income per farm operator divided by non-farm labour income per worker has increased substantially (from 0.53 in 1971 to 1.10 in 1976). The largest decrease in the proportion of low income families across urbanizations occurred for farm families resident on farms 1971–73 (Section D). Low income families spent 62 per cent or more of their income on food, shelter and clothing.

The 1971 cross-classification of total farm operator income by economic class of farm indicates that 28 per cent of farm operators with total income below $2,000 were spread across all economic size classes. It is likely the impact of the 1970–75 fourfold increase in average net farm income per farm operator will also be spread across all size classes and substantially reduce the number of low income farm operators in all

TABLE 1   *Indicators of Canadian rural development*

A. Population and Income by Urbanization, 1971

	Population ('000)	Average Family Income ($)
Rural: Farm	1419.8	6610
Non-farm	3737.7	7428
Canada	21568.0	9600

Source: Ronald D'Costa, *Socio-demographic Characteristics of the Population by Community Size: A Comparative Study* (Ottawa: Canadian Council on Rural Development, 1977), Table A–2.

B. Range of Provincial Family Income, 1971

Highest:	Rural Farm – British Columbia	($8767)
	Rural Non-farm – British Columbia	($8940)
Lowest:	Rural Farm – Saskatchewan	($5037)
	Rural Non-farm – Newfoundland	($4952)

Source: D'Costa, *Characteristics of the Population*, Table XIII.

C. Farm Versus Non-farm Income Comparisons

	Net farm income per census farm operator/ non-farm labour income per non-farm worker
1971	0.53
1976	1.10

	Net farm income per census farm operator
1970	$ 3863
1975	$14730

	Non-farm labour income per non-farm worker
1971	$ 7232
1976	$13541

Source: Net farm income per farm operator calculated by net farm income (Statistics Canada, *Net Farm Income*, Catalogue 21–202) divided by the number of census farms. Non-farm labour income per employee calculated by labour income (Statistics Canada, *Estimates of Labour Income*, Catalogue 72–005 (Ottawa: Ministry of Supply and Services) divided by the number of employees (Statistics Canada, *Estimates of Employees by Province and Industry*, Catalogue 72–513 (Ottawa: Ministry of Supply and Services).

TABLE 1   *Indicators of Canadian rural development (continued)*

D. Low Family Income Distribution by Urbanization

	Per cent of low income families by urbanization	
	1971	1973
Rural areas	27.2	17.3
Farm-resident	35.2	21.8
-nonresident	16.8	12.8
Canada	18.3	13.4

Highest provincial percentage of low income families:
Newfoundland	34.3	23.7 Newfoundland

Lowest provincial percentage of low income families:
Ontario	13.5	8.9 British Columbia

Source: Statistics Canada, Office of the Senior Advisor on Integration, *Perspective Canada II* (Ottawa: Ministry of Supply and Services, 1977), 164.

E. Distribution of Total Income of Farm Operators by Economic Class, Canada, 1971

Economic Class ($)	Operators (no.)	Total Income (no. <$2000)	Average Income ($)
2500	107095	31995	4676
2500–4999	62955	20610	3899
5000–9000	82115	25045	4215
10000 +	113190	24285	6760
	365355	101935	4932

Source: Statistics Canada, *Basic Socio-economic Characteristics of Farm Operators*, Catalogue 96–712 (Ottawa: Ministry of Supply and Services, 1977), 1–2.

G. Agricultural Product and Input Prices (1961 = 100)

	1971	1974
Index of Farm Prices of Agricultural Products	117.2	229.6
Grains	100.9	295.5
Livestock	127.3	201.5
Input Price Index	135.9	193.4
Hired Labour	179.2	255.5
Farmland	176.9	270.8

Source: Statistics Canada, *Index Numbers of Farm Prices of Agricultural Products (1961 = 100)*, Catalogue 62–003 and *Prices and Price Indexes*, Catalogue no. 62–002 (Ottawa: Ministry of Supply and Services).

classes. The price indices indicate that the largest 1971–74 increases occurred for grains and land. Since 1974 input prices have risen more rapidly than product prices.

Net government expenditures on agriculture are estimated to be greater than net farm income in British Columbia. Net government expenditures on assistance programmes for BC agriculture totalled $108 million in 1976.[7] These provincial estimates are illustrative of the magnitude of government involvement. Comparable estimates are not available for other provinces.

BRIEF REVIEW OF CANADIAN RURAL DEVELOPMENT PROGRAMMES

The evolution of Canadian rural development programmes incorporated changes in the definition of goals and perceived problems relating to rural poverty. Throughout 1961–76 income improvement for small farmers was emphasized and the adopted measures were to increase the resources available such as land, water, credit and farm management skills. At the same time mobility assistance was made available for farm families preferring to move to non-farm jobs and industrial assistance was provided to stimulate the location of industry in low income rural areas.

During the 1970s policy implementation shifted to reducing the instability in farm income associated with commodity price cycles by means of joint farmer and government payments into stabilization funds. Government payments under federal and provincial stabilization and subsidy programmes are substantially greater than rural development programme expenditures. The impacts of these programmes on income improvement of small farmers and rural communities are similar to the impacts of rural development programmes.[8] In many cases redistribution is a goal of stabilization programmes implemented by ceilings on payments to large farmers..

The political debates about the Canadian Agricultural and Rural Development Agreements (ARDA) focused on the land use and resource base adjustment required to increase income of small farmers versus programmes to stimulate off-farm migration.[9] The intent of the resource adjustment programmes was to increase the production capabilities of small farmers by drainage, irrigation, land clearing, farm management assistance and other resource investments.

The Fund for Rural Economic Development (FRED) established in 1966 was labelled as a comprehensive approach to rural development. It was recognized that in addition to natural resource stocks, human capital and public infrastructure are an important stimulus to rural development. For example, a total of $85 million was allocated over 1976–77 to the Interlake Area of Manitoba ($27.3 million for adult education, $26.7 million for schools and education, $29.4 million for resource improvement and $1.7 million for administration). The FRED plans were comprehensive only in relation to the natural resource focus of ARDA. In the Interlake area of Manitoba the FRED expenditures were $5 million out of the total local, provincial and federal expenditure of $47 million.[10] A truly comprehensive plan would involve programming total government expenditures of the entire $47 million to jointly achieve developmental and other public objectives.

Industrial and infrastructure assistance to rural regions has been provided by the Area Development Agency initiated in 1963. Legislation was passed in 1969 giving the Department of Regional Economic Expansion (DREE) the responsibility for co-ordinating regional development planning in Canada. DREE became responsible for ARDA, FRED, industrial incentives, and local government infrastructure grants through special Area Agreements.

According to Agriculture Canada, rural development and income security goals include: increased producer bargaining power, stability of producer returns, viable farm units and rural community development.[11] In the definition of goals it is clear that the rural development goal includes commodity payments to farmers and is primarily directed to the income improvement goal and not economic efficiency. A lack of emphasis by Agriculture Canada on rural development programming other than commodity payments to farmers is indicated. From 1970/71 to 1975/76 $1.8 billion in direct payments to farmers were made including $1.0 billion to dairy farmers.[12] In contrast, Agriculture Canada spent $22.6 million on the Small Farm Development programme. The intent of the programme (terminated in 1979) was to develop low income farms into viable units by farm management counselling, credit assistance to farm purchasers and retirement assistance to sellers. Furthermore, none of the research expenditures are allocated to the rural development goal area.

The current trend in public expenditure is towards increasing federal and provincial commodity income stabilization programmes and natural resource investments. In addition to the stabilization programmes outlined above the 1977–84 ARDA programme in British Columbia funded by DREE includes a commitment of $60 million to be spent primarily on the beef sector in four programme areas: (1) Research, planning, training and market promotion ($4.95 million); (2) Co-ordinated resource management (range improvement, $19.8 million); (3) Primary resource development (irrigation and drainage, $15 million); (4) Support services and community development ($20.95 million).

The agreement provides for local, provincial and federal participation in the planning process, but a formal plan and evaluation criteria have yet to be formulated. The regional development planning under DREE, from a national perspective, is focusing on sectoral agreements – agriculture, industry and tourism for provincial regional units.

SUGGESTED REVISIONS IN CANADIAN RURAL DEVELOP-
MENT POLICIES AND PROGRAMMES

Major expenditures by Agriculture Canada have been directed to the rural development goal of income improvement. In the 1970/71 to 1975/76 period $1.8 billion direct payments to farmers were made including $1.0 billion to dairy farmers. Major expenditures have also been made by DREE directed to both income and efficiency goals. In the 1969–76 period $1.1 billion was spent on a wide variety of rural development projects. It is likely that the nearly $3 billion spent by Agriculture Canada and DREE in the early seventies to achieve rural development goals had a small impact relative to increasing the economic efficiency of production in rural areas but had a substantial impact on the income improvement goal. It is our suggestion that available income data indicates a re-allocation of rural expenditures to the efficiency goal would improve the effectiveness of public expenditure on Canadian rural development.

The following general hypotheses are provided to assist in achieving increased economic efficiency in Canadian rural and agricultural development:

1   Most provinces in Canada have delineated rural regions (non-metropolitan areas with significant agricultural production). Urban centres in these regions provide public services to the farm population. Efficiency in the provision of services such as schools, health, transportation, sewer and water could be improved by rural development programmes.

2   Investments in human capital and entrepreneurship, such as general education and farm financial management skill training, have a high pay-off relative to public and private costs. Public funds are warranted if the economic benefits which occur to the rural region and the nation are greater than the costs.

3   Natural resource investments in drainage, irrigation, land clearing, community pastures, etc. depending on the region, may or may not have a high return in relation to total costs. From a public expenditure viewpoint the magnitude of public good externalities associated with positive production interdependencies between farmers in a watershed, irrigation district or community pasture is a critical justification for public expenditures. Furthermore if group benefits exist the institution of user charges to cover costs would promote further economic efficiency.

4   Global assessments of the regional relative profitability of public expenditures on alternative major programme areas are required including: industrial incentives, tourism, forestry, public infrastructure (transportation, schools, etc.) versus investments in agriculture. The research technology exists for impact analyses of rural area and agricultural development programmes on a regional basis requiring a very small percentage of total programme expenditures.[13] It is essential for administrators to view the results of such studies as information

useful in indicating ways of improving their programmes and not as an assessment of success or failure. If rural development programmes cannot be made efficient then such programmes may duplicate the impact of agricultural income stabilization programmes and become redundant in the 1980s.

5 Provinces such as British Columbia and Quebec[14] which have in the past focused on self-sufficiency criteria for commodities such as beef which forms a large proportion of provincial imports could modify those agricultural policies to focus on the productivity of public investments in specific agricultural areas.

NOTES AND REFERENCES

[1] Helen Buckley and Eva Tihanyi *Canadian Policies for Rural Adjustment*, Ottawa, Economic Council of Canada, 1967, p. 98.

[2] Marcel Lessard "Notes for an Address to a Seminar on the Future of Rural Development Sponsored by the Canadian Council on Rural Development", Ottawa, 31 March 1976, p. 8. The $1.1 billion includes other rural development programmes in addition to ARDA.

[3] F.L. Tung, J.A. MacMillan and C.F. Framingham "A Dynamic Regional Model for Evaluating Resource Development Programs", *AJAF* 58:3, August 1976, pp. 403–14.

[4] Richard R. Barichello, *An Economic and Distributive Evaluation of Community Pasture Programs*, Vancouver, Department of Agricultural Economics, University of British Columbia, 1978.

[5] For a detailed discussion of the problems involved in Canadian farm and non-farm comparisons see D. McClatchty and C. Campbell "An Approach to Identifying and Locating the Low Income Farmer", *Canadian Farm Economics*, 10:2, April 1975, pp. 1–11; J.A. Gellner and G.L. Brinkman *Relative Rates of Resource Returns on Ontario Government Farms from 1971 to 1974: A Comparison with Nonfarm Businesses*, Guelph, School of Agricultural Economics and Extension Education, University of Guelph, 1977: Paul Shaw "Canadian Farm and Non-Farm Family Incomes", *AJAE*, to be published November 1979.

[6] Yujiro Hayami and Vernon W. Ruttan *Agricultural Development*, Baltimore, The Johns Hopkins Press, 1971, p. 73.

[7] Select Standing Committee on Agriculture *Government Aid Programs in British Columbia*, Victoria, Province of British Columbia, 1979.

[8] J.A. MacMillan, D.F. Kraft and D. Ford "Impacts of Agricultural Stabilization Programs on the Development of Rural Communities", *CAES Workshop Proceedings*, March 1976, pp. 169–77.

[9] T.N. Brewis *Regional Economic Policies in Canada* Toronto, Macmillan Company, 1969, p. 105.

[10] James A. MacMillan, Chang-mei Qu and C.F. Framingham *Manitoba Interlake Area: A Regional Development Evaluation*, Des Moines, University of Iowa State Press, 1975, p. 21.

[11] Agriculture Canada *Orientation of Canadian Agriculture: A Task Force Report*, Vol. II: *Domestic Policies and External Factors which have Influenced the Development of Canadian Agriculture*, Ottawa, Agriculture Canada, 1977, p. 33.

[12] Ibid., p. 44.

[13] See E.W. Tyrchniegicz et al. "The Abandonment of Uneconomic Branch Lines and Unremunerative Grain Rates: Effects on Agriculture and Regional Development", *The Logistics and Transportation Review*, 14:4, 1978, pp. 411–30: J.A. MacMillan and J.D. Graham, "Rural Development Planning a Science?" *AJAE*, 60:5, December 1978, pp. 945–49; N. Brown and J.A. MacMillan, "Recreational Program Development Impacts: A Dynamic Regional Analysis", *AJAE*, 59:4, November 1977, pp. 750–4.

[14] Francois Dagenais "The Development of a Food and Agriculture Policy in Quebec", *AJAE*, 60:5, November 1978, pp. 1045–50.

SECTION IV

Supra-National

THE W.K. KELLOGG FOUNDATION LECTURE

ERIC M. OJALA

Accomplishments and Opportunities of Agricultural Economists Working in International Agencies

This is the first time that international agricultural economists have been invited to give an account of themselves to the profession, as represented by this Conference. I have to declare at once that I am biased after twenty-five years in service with international agencies, mostly with the Food and Agriculture Organization of the United Nations (FAO). I have, however, supplemented my experience and judgement by inviting opinions from agricultural economists in other international agencies. I am most grateful for their contributions, but accept full responsibility for my interpretation.

OBJECTIVES

For most agricultural economists, the goals of their work are set in the framework of national policies and of individual farm or firm objectives.

For international agencies, the objectives of nations and enterprises are still basic elements, but the role of agriculture is focused more sharply on the needs of mankind, and the emphasis is on international co-operation and regional or world-wide action. This is illustrated in the Preamble to the Constitution of FAO:

> The Nations accepting this Constitution, being determined to promote the common welfare by furthering separate and collective action on their part for the purposes of
> - raising levels of nutrition and standards of living of the peoples under their respective jurisdictions,
> - securing improvements in the efficiency of the production and distribution of all food and agricultural products,
> - bettering the condition of rural populations,
> - and thus contributing toward an expanding world economy,
> thereby establish the Food and Agricultural Organisation of the United Nations . . . through which the members will report to one another on the measures taken and the progress achieved in the fields of action set forth above.

391

It is in the framework of these objectives – and their counterpart in other bodies – that the achievements and opportunities of agricultural economists working with international agencies have to be assessed.

INTERNATIONAL AGENCIES EMPLOYING AGRICULTURAL ECONOMISTS

FAO was preceded by the International Institute of Agriculture (IIA) started in 1905 in Rome on the initiative of an American, David Lubin. The human misery in farming which Lubin saw in many lands in the economic depression of the 1890s fired his determination to work for some effective international machinery for agriculture. The IIA functioned usefully for forty years, mainly in Europe, through statistical and scientific information services, before being absorbed into FAO in 1945.

After the establishment of FAO, the United Nations, created in 1946, soon set up regional economic commissions – in Europe, Latin America, Asia and (much later) in Africa and the Near East. All these regional commissions established agriculture divisions as joint units with FAO. They were staffed by FAO and UN agricultural economists, who set to work, with their national counterparts, on the economic problems of agricultural development in their respective regions.

In 1946 the World Bank came into being, but only over the last five years has it become a major source of international financing for agricultural and rural development. Regional development banks were subsequently set up by the governments of Latin America, Asia, Africa and the Near East, and agricultural lending has always been an important part of their activities.

The year 1961 saw the birth of the World Food Programme (WFP), sponsored jointly by FAO and the United Nations. This agency performed the miracle of converting an international liability – food surpluses – into an international resource for development. Its activities now commit over 300 million dollars of aid annually, mostly to the food and agricultural sector of food deficit countries.

The only international financing agency committed solely to the agricultural sector came into being in 1977, as one of the more tangible results of the 1974 World Food Conference. This is the International Fund for Agricultural Development (IFAD) which has a large component of funding by oil exporting countries. Its purpose is to combat hunger, and it is therefore focusing on projects to bring small farmers and landless workers into the development process.

At the other end of the relative income scale, the OECD (Organization for Economic Co-operation and Development) whose members are all developed countries, has an important Food and Agriculture Directorate. Because agriculture is one of the more troublesome sectors in the relationships among these countries, the agricultural economists of OECD have been particularly active in the analysis of agricultural policy.

Less comprehensive in their geographical coverage are the regional groupings of governments which have committed themselves to varying degrees of co-operation in development. Most notable are the European Community in Western Europe and the COMECON in Eastern Europe, but there are a growing number of such regional groupings among developing countries, particularly in Latin America and South East Asia.[1] In Africa such attempts have been less successful. Because of the rigidity of its national structure, and the proportion of population involved, agriculture poses special problems in the implementation of regional economic integration policies.

A potential if not actual international workplace for agricultural economists is the World Food Council, set up by the UN to co-ordinate intergovernmental efforts to solve the world food problem.

International and about to become inter-governmental is IFPRI, the International Food Policy Research Institute based in Washington, DC, a very recent establishment, where agricultural economists are developing a programme of world-wide studies in the many facets of food policy.

One of the most promising international initiatives for world agricultural development in recent times has occurred in research in the developing regions on food production, an area long neglected by scientists. I refer to the Consultative Group on International Agricultural Research (CGIAR), an international body of donors sponsored by FAO, the World Bank and the United Nations Development Programme, established in 1971. CGIAR now supports nine regional research centres[2] investigating methods for raising yield and quality of basic food crops, improving livestock production, combating major diseases and pests, and generally trying to intensify and spread the "green revolution". Most, if not all of these centres, have engaged agricultural economic staff, to study the farming systems in which food is produced and identify the economic and social obstacles to the adoption of research results. The aggregate budget in 1979 amounts to 103 million dollars.

The international trade agencies, UNCTAD and GATT, employ a few agricultural economists, as do the specialized commodity bodies, such as the International Wheat Council, the International Sugar Organization, the International Coffee Organization and the International Cocoa Council.

The largest group of international agricultural economists (around 200) is almost certainly to be found in the FAO, which is the only global agency charged with comprehensive responsibility for food and agriculture. Agricultural economists account for about 20 per cent of the regular professional staff, with many more at work in the field service. The World Bank employs another large group. Of some 500 professional staff working in agriculture and rural development in the Bank, about 150 are agricultural economists. The numbers in these and other agencies include some economists who can be described as "agricultural" by the nature of their work, rather than by specific training.

ACCOMPLISHMENTS

Training – in addition to individual qualities – may help to explain the
relatively high representation of "true" agricultural economists among
senior administrative posts in some big agencies. In the World Bank, for
instance, three of the six Regional Vice-Presidents are experienced
agricultural economists, and so are two of the six Project Directors. In the
Asian Development Bank the Director of Agricultural Projects is an
agricultural economist. In FAO the Deputy Director General was for
many years an agricultural economist, and the heads of the operational
and investment wings are currently agricultural economists. There are no
doubt other instances in other agencies. The positions held by members
of the profession in international agencies are surely acceptable as one
indicator of "accomplishment".

Beyond this, it is difficult to separate the achievements of the agency
staff from those of the member governments and of the agency itself. In
practice, in most inter-governmental agencies there is a constant dialogue
between staff and delegates, and between international and national
professional staff, which contributes to the decisions of the governing
bodies. It is the agency as a unit which makes achievements. In FAO the
position of the secretariat is relatively strong, because the Constitution
gives to the permanent head, the Director General, the prerogative of
proposing the agency's programme of work and budget to the member
governments, for their consideration and adoption. In bodies such as the
European Community, the secretariat's position is much stronger,
because the Community can make decisions binding on its members.

Member governments expect the staff of an international agency to
propose to them possible lines of international policies and actions in
pursuit of the agency's objectives. An agency with an inactive staff will
have few achievements, although it may pass many resolutions.

In this spirit I propose to look for the main achievements of international agencies to which agricultural economic staff contributed significantly. I have to be selective and have put main emphasis on global
international co-operation. The fields I have chosen are: international
information on food and agriculture; international food policy and international commodity policy; and national and international approaches to
agricultural policy.

International information
The assembly, analysis and dissemination of information about food and
agriculture on a world basis has been a charter responsibility of FAO
from the beginning. In 1946 FAO prepared its first World Food Survey.
Others followed, and the fourth was published in 1977. In 1948 began the
regular publication of the FAO statistical yearbooks on world agricultural production and trade, on forestry and fisheries, and the annual
analytical report on The State of Food and Agriculture. Starting in 1950,
FAO sponsored a world programme of censuses of agriculture every ten

years, which have successively improved the reliability and comparability of national agricultural statistics. The agricultural economists, statisticians and nutritionists of the Organization have collaborated closely, especially in more recent years, to solve the problems of standardization, consistency and interpretation that have to be overcome before a vast array of national data can be meaningful in studies of the performance of the world's agricultural sector. FAO's statistical data bank is now available on computer tapes, and these have gained acceptance as the starting point for global studies by national agencies such as the United States Department of Agriculture, and by other international agencies, including the World Bank.

The significance of the FAO information services over the years can hardly be over-stated. By documenting current problems and identifying trends, the FAO Secretariat alerted the nations to the urgency of new or larger action on behalf of the world's needy farmers and hungry peoples. In many cases, governments responded by intensifying the agricultural impact of existing development institutions or starting new ones to meet new needs, e.g. WFP, IFAD, World Food Council. The wide educational impact of the UN World Food Conference in 1974 was largely due to the universal acceptance of the FAO documentation on which it was based. Agricultural economists usually have the influential information function in all international agencies with an agricultural wing.

International food policy
It was in this area that the FAO staff launched, in 1946, their first great international policy initiative. I refer to Lord Boyd Orr's proposal as FAO Director General, for a World Food Bank. This proposal failed. It called for too much international co-operation in food policy before the nations had gained experience in co-operating on practical issues in this sphere. Nevertheless it was an historic concept and some of the functions envisaged for the World Food Board were later assumed, in part, by other agencies.

Thus, after refusing to create the World Board to stabilize prices by buffer stock schemes, and to hold a world food reserve against famine, the governments of the day subsequently negotiated successive international wheat agreements under which prices were stabilized by stocks held in North America which – for nearly twenty years – effectively constituted a world food reserve against famine.

When this system broke down in the 1970s and the world ran out of grain stocks, the agricultural economists of FAO devised the concept of an international undertaking on world food security. This approach was based on the idea of an internationally co-ordinated network of national grain stocks, not excluding some international food reserve if the food trading nations could agree to establish it, the whole adding up, through the organized exchange of information on stock levels and targets, to an informal international food security system. The programme was supported by the FAO governing bodies and the World Food Conference, and a special inter-governmental Committee on World Food Security has been established to oversee its implementation. The system is far from complete, but it has been launched, and various approaches to further progress are being widely explored.

Boyd Orr's concept of an international institution to finance the transfer of food surpluses to needy people had to wait fifteen years. First preliminary was to overcome the concern of food trading nations that such transfers would harm the flow of normal trade. In 1955 FAO set up a consultative machinery in Washington to monitor all such transactions, against guidelines contained in the agreed Principles of Surplus Disposal. The drafting, negotiation and general acceptance of these Principles by governments constitute a major achievement in the realm of international food policy. The consultative machinery is still working satisfactorily, serviced by agricultural economists.

Next came acceptance of the concept that food could be used as capital for development in food deficit countries with a high degree of under employment. The theoretical basis for this acceptance was developed in a path breaking piece of research led by one of the most distinguished of FAO agricultural economists, Dr Mordecai Ezekiel. The study was published by FAO in 1955 under the title "Use of Agricultural Surpluses to Finance Economic Development in Underdeveloped Countries – a Pilot Study in India".

Thus, when in 1960 the United Nations General Assembly requested FAO to study the feasibility and acceptability of an arrangement to mobilize and dispense food surpluses through the United Nations system, the Director General was able to submit a positive report. He invited outside agricultural and development economists to assist him in the study, and his report[3] was drafted by staff agricultural economists. It was this report which focused the goodwill of the United States Government and led, in the same year 1961, to the establishment of the World Food Programme. It is a more modest institution than that envisaged by Boyd Orr, but it had the virtue of being created. It has worked, and channels an increasing proportion of total food aid into development uses.

International commodity studies
In this area there has been more achievement in documentation of issues than in international policy. Thanks to the persistent efforts of international agricultural commodity economists in a number of organizations, no interested person can claim ignorance of the basic workings of any of the important agricultural commodity markets. This is a worthwhile achievement, providing a basis for both national and international policy making, including the negotiation of a number of useful international commodity agreements.

In addition, distinctive contributions of FAO have been its programme of successive long term commodity projections and analyses of the factors shaping supply and demand, and the initiation of informal types of international commodity arrangements for products such as tea, jute and hard fibres, on which governments were unwilling to make formal commitments.

National agricultural policy analysis and advice
International agricultural marketing economists, most of them with FAO, quickly adapted to the environment of the developing world. Their contribution, through reports, manuals, technical assistance and active promotion, to the improvement of marketing systems, often linked with credit, processing and supply networks, has been impressive, as evidenced in two papers presented to this Conference. In agrarian reform FAO, UN and ILO have given notable leadership, and were actively promoting rural development programmes in many developing countries long before this concept became fashionable.

When national economic planning was spreading in newly independent countries in the 1950s, international agricultural economists worked closely with national economists towards more systematic approaches to planned development of the food and agricultural sector. This work was first focused in the UN regional economic commissions, where FAO and UN economists collaborated fruitfully. More recently, scores of agricultural economists of different specializations have been engaged by FAO to assist governments, on request, to improve their planning for the agricultural sector.

The major recent achievement of the agricultural staff of the World Bank, in response to a new overall policy orientation of the institution, has been the enormous absolute and relative expansion of the Bank's lending for agriculture. The proportion of loans for agriculture has risen from 12 per cent of its total operations in 1970 to a likely 33 per cent in 1979. Along with expansion has gone a major shift in emphasis from resources to people. The Bank's agricultural staff have succeeded, in a relatively short time, in converting rural development from a concept into an investment strategy for the world's biggest financing institution. This reorientation of the Bank's approach to agriculture, bearing in mind the influence of the Bank on other agencies, as well as the magnitude of its own efforts, is one of the most hopeful recent changes in favour of the world's rural poor, assuming that the new types of projects achieve their goals.

In the context of national policy, nutrition is another area where international agencies have contributed to a new thinking. In the 1970s vigorous leadership from FAO has transformed the international approach to nutrition improvement from one of protein or other dietary supplements to national food policy and planning. The same approach is also being developed in the World Bank, and sponsored by the World Food Council.

The successive reviews of agricultural policies undertaken by the OECD secretariat are among the more objective and creative works of international agricultural economists, bearing in mind the sensitivities of developed country governments in this area. In the face of such difficulties, this secretariat has managed over the years to make a positive contribution to national agricultural policy thinking. In many respects the agricultural policies of industrialized countries are as backward looking and as trade restricting as ever, but at least there is now more open debate on alternatives. FAO analyses of agricultural adjustment in developed countries have also stimulated discussion of more rational approaches to agricultural policy.

International framework for national policies
This may seem a rather high-sounding concept, but the Common Agricultural Policy of the European Community demonstrates what a forceful reality it can be under some conditions. In fact, in all regional integration schemes one of the aims must be to arrive, sooner or later, at some common framework for national policies in agriculture, as in some other sectors.

The European Community has gone furthest in this direction and a paper on the achievements of its agricultural economists would have been of great interest to this Conference. The structure of the Community entails for its staff an involvement in international decision-making, in implementation of the Treaty of Rome, which is beyond that open to the staff of most other international bodies. A key aspect of the challenge to its agricultural economists is how to implement a common agricultural policy in the absence of a common economic policy.

Nevertheless, it is easier to conceive of an international framework for national policies at the regional level, where the governments concerned are inclined to set their course to secure advantages for their own farmers, usually at some cost to farmers in other countries.

The idea of a *global* framework for national policies is a much more difficult one, involving as it does a sharing of the burdens of adjustment, in the search for a larger total good. I see the FAO Principles of Surplus Disposal as an effective instance of an informal international framework for national policies, in the sensitive but narrow field of food aid. In the wider area of agricultural policies, a mild beginning has been made, which in my view rates as an accomplishment – one in which agricultural economists play a major role.

During the latter 1960s the Director General of FAO mobilized the knowledge of the Organization to prepare the Indicative World Plan for Agricultural Development, a major analysis of longer-run issues and options in world food supplies, agricultural development and commodity trade.

Governmental discussion of the Indicative World Plan focused on the harmful effects on developing exporting countries of the agricultural policies of the developed countries. In response to this discussion, FAO prepared a programme for international agricultural adjustment in favour of the developing world. Eleven guidelines for national policies were drafted and accepted by FAO member governments, designed to promote a gradual shift of world agricultural production, consumption and trade expansion towards the developing countries. The secretariat is required to report progress in terms of the agreed guidelines every two years, for review by the FAO Conference. This is the only broad consensus approach to international action in this difficult area. It is a voluntary programme, without "teeth". But how else, except through information, education, opinion-building and mutual persuasion can international co-operation advance? Beginnings are all-important – and it is a beginning which can be built on progressively. The work of OECD in analysing the external effects of the agricultural policies of the developed countries is an important element in this global strategy.

OPPORTUNITIES AHEAD

The above accomplishments are illustrative only. I have not been able to do justice to the work of agricultural economists in all the agencies, especially the regional ones. But even if the list could be completed, I suspect that the result would still be a thin stream of real achievements in international co-operation per decade. If this result has been relatively small so has the input, in terms of the proportion of national income which governments have been willing to contribute towards international co-operation.

Moreover, international co-operation in agriculture is not determined by the vision and output of international agricultural economists. Indeed, it is not their function to publish research papers and articles.[4] Their role is rather to keep in touch with research done elsewhere and distil its conclusions in terms of policy options relevant to the changing concerns of governments. In any case, a staff position paper or policy document of the highest professional standard does not move governments when they have no will to move. Even when governments are not averse to common action, a staff position paper has to demonstrate not only professional quality but also a fine tuning to the potential political consensus if international action is to result. I always found the latter requirement to be the most stimulating challenge, as an international civil servant.

For whatever reason, the international accomplishments of the past have not been enough. Millions more people will have to die of hunger or hunger-induced disease before the answers are found. The problems that the FAO and other agencies were established to deal with are still rampant. Thus, 15 per cent of mankind, according to FAO, still exist in constant hunger, and the rate of increase in world food production is now slower than in earlier decades since the war. Some 500 million agricultural producers live in absolute or relative poverty, according to the World Bank. More and more of world trade in important temperate zone agricultural products consists of subsidized exports from the highest cost countries, which displace exports from lower cost suppliers. Although the developed countries produce more cereals than they need or can sell, they are still unable to construct a rational world food reserve. And despite their costly income support programmes, most of their farmers have incomes well below the average of urban incomes.

If the international agencies did not exist they would have to be invented to establish means through which governments could discuss and solve these problems of food, agriculture and rural change in which they all have a vital interest.

There are several types of service which international agencies can provide to member governments: technical assistance; investment or aid flows; policy analysis; forum for international policy formulation; information. Agricultural economists have a part to play in all these, through the various institutions mentioned earlier.

Technical assistance
With the rising complement of well-trained national agricultural staff in the larger developing countries, the scope for the individual resident foreign advisor is likely to diminish. The demand is increasing for higher specialized consultants for short periods. FAO, for instance, experiences a continuing demand from governments for consultants to undertake perspective studies of agricultural development. This work is led by agricultural economists and mobilizes FAO's technical competence as well as all the concerned national units. The visiting team helps the national staff to determine how to mobilize the domestic resources and institutions to achieve the national agricultural development objectives, with optimum effectiveness. Implementation rests with the national authorities. The emphasis in this and other technical assistance, will be increasingly on multidisciplinary approaches, including bilateral contributions.

Investment
If world agriculture is to fulfil its role to feed humanity adequately, the current rate of increase in food production in developing countries needs to be accelerated by about 40 per cent overall. The total international financial flow to agriculture is well below the estimated requirement for this acceleration. The twin scourges of humanity – hunger and poverty – now reside mainly in the rural areas of developing countries. Hence the type as well as the rate of agricultural development is crucial. So far the WFP, the World Bank and the IFAD have adopted the rural development approach, which should become widespread among development agencies. To support this approach IDA should be adequately replenished to supply funds for concessional lending to agricultural and rural development. Adequate investment outside agriculture is also essential to enlarge demand for food and other farm products. The role of agricultural economists in helping to promote the optimal development use of the available international resources, in effective projects and programmes, is a crucial one.

Policy analysis
Governments seldom accept advice from international agencies on what their development policies should be, and the agencies do not offer it – except perhaps the IMF and the World Bank. Nevertheless governments often request international agencies to review progress in important policy areas, from agrarian reform to price policies.

International agencies are particularly well qualified to undertake such policy analyses, because of the experience of their staff with a wide range of conditions and approaches in many countries, and their objectivity. In my view the slow progress of agriculture in developing countries is a failure of policy. This highlights the importance of such analyses. International agencies including FAO, have probably not done enough of this work or not with the right sense of priorities. Budget stringency is only partly to blame. Some topics which cry out for more analyses by international agencies and agricultural economists are: the linkages backwards and forwards between agricultural and non-agricultural development in developing countries, case studies of rural development projects; food and agricultural price policies in developing countries; incentives and disincentives for farmers at village level in developing countries; agricultural support policies in industrialized countries and the impact on farmers, consumers, taxpayers and trade; the experience with agriculture in regional economic integration schemes, in both developed and developing country groupings.

Some of the most sensitive of these areas have been rather neglected by national agricultural economists. Have they become reconciled to national policies which seem at first sight to be indefensible on economic and social criteria? Analyses by national and international agricultural economists could be mutually supporting, especially as regards national policies which unduly diminish trade.

International policies
In this type of international action the agencies provide the forum, and in many cases the working documents, for negotiation among governments. International staff work on specific proposals is ruled out until the respective governing body has requested it. But there are a number of areas where beginnings have been made by governments, which are open for further development. Some are mentioned below.

World food security
With the growing dependence of developing countries on imports, it is not acceptable for supplies of the world's major food grain – wheat – to be rationed by price in times of relative shortage, which are bound to recur. High priority therefore attaches to the negotiation of an international wheat arrangement with price ranges, food aid commitments and stock management provisions. Until an international reserve is established, food deficit countries should continue to receive assistance to acquire and manage their own reserves in the framework of their food and agricul-

tural policies. An effective world food security system should be a minimum expectation in this age.

International commodity policy
Agricultural trade remains the source of major fluctuations in the economies of many countries. The introduction of international frameworks for the more orderly management of commodity markets is likely to be extended. The possibility of having one framework for many commodities is being debated. In any case, the international agencies concerned have a constructive task to identify commodity problems, analyse alternative solutions in terms of the interest of producers, consumers and world development, and facilitate the process of compromise in negotiations. Objective studies of comparative costs of production and opportunity costs in different countries could help to orient the negotiated sharing of managed markets among producers.

World fertilizer policy
The FAO Commission on Fertilizers should move further towards a world fertilizer policy, involving governments, industry and development agencies. Farmers, especially in developing countries, should have adequate and regular access at reasonable prices to fertilizers, on which the success of the "green revolution" depends. Elements of the policy should include more orderly expansion of production in line with demand; more self-sufficiency in developing countries where appropriate; more economic research on fertilizer use and alternative plant nutrients; and an international fertilizer aid scheme.

More information about world agricultural performance
The FAO data base, holding no secrets, should become accessible on computer terminals to all member governments. The main gaps are data about rural people, rural welfare, rural institutions and these should be progressively filled. The food information system of FAO should be improved and strengthened. Remote sensing by satellite will offer the technical possibility of regular monitoring of the world's grain crops. Such information should become a multilateral service.

The basic agricultural data of FAO and other agencies should be progressively integrated with the economic and social data of the relevant agencies, so that international data for agriculture can be set in the world economy as a whole.

Above all, information is a potent force for change, even policy change. It must become a much stronger force for international co-operation for world development. For this, the statistical and other information needs to be presented in a policy framework. Not just statistical yearbooks, but also derived statistical series with development impact. Fortunately, the universal agreement of Governments in FAO on goals and guidelines for a better adjusted world agricultural development, and the decision to monitor progress towards them, provides such a policy framework. It is valid not only for FAO, but also for other agencies with a policy role including the World Bank, the IMF, UNCTAD, the inter-governmental commodity bodies, OECD, EC, and COMECON.

The current FAO perspective study of world food and agricultural trends up to 2000 is another instance of a policy framework for presenting information about the global performance of agriculture, in the evolution of a new international economic order.

Our President in his opening address drew attention to the scope for world-wide action if needed rural change is to be achieved on a broad human front. The current levels of international co-operation are not adequate to permit the world's agricultural resources to be mobilized in time to match the needs – let alone the hopes – of mankind. The alternative to more co-operation will surely be a world food disaster beyond anything so far experienced. The main weaknesses are in the realms of policy, national and international. Valid ideas that exist are not being implemented decisively, and there is a dearth of new ideas with development and convergent force. The opportunities before international agricultural economists are indeed clamouring.

As I said at Minsk some years ago[5] agricultural economists cannot themselves take the development decisions that will change the world. But whether working in national or international environments they can, through research, analysis, creative imagination and communication, illuminate the choices, and inform the opinion to which policy decision makers respond.

NOTES

[1] Central American Common Market, Caribbean Common Market, Andean Group, Latin American Free Trade Association, Latin American Economic System, Association of South East Asian Nations (ASEAN).

[2] e.g. IRRI, Philippines; CIMMYT, Mexico; CIAT, Colombia; IITA, Nigeria; ICRISAT, India; ILRAD, Kenya.

[3] "Development through Food – A Strategy for Surplus Utilization," FAO, Rome 1961.

[4] But see "FAO Studies in Agricultural Economics and Statistics 1952–1977"; FAO, Rome 1979, for an historical selection of published FAO staff papers.

[5] Ojala, E.M. "The Agricultural Economist and World Agriculture", *14th International Conference of Agricultural Economists*, Oxford 1971.

DISCUSSION OPENING – ELMER L. MENZIE

The paper by Dr. Ojala does an excellent job of describing the location and activities of agricultural economists within a number of international organizations. The FAO, employing about 200 agricultural economists, and the World Bank with 150, obviously are the dominant agencies both in terms of their international role and in the employment of agricultural economists.

Basic to Ojala's evaluation is the statement of the objectives of the

FAO as given in the Preamble to its Constitution. These include:

1   raising levels of nutrition and standards of living,
2   improving efficiency of production and distribution of foods,
3   improving conditions of rural populations,
4   contributing toward an expanding world economy.

Attainment of these objectives is used as a measure of accomplishment of agricultural economists working in the various international agencies.

Dr. Ojala examines the activities of organizations such as the FAO, the World Bank, the Asian Development Bank, the OECD, and the International Food Policy Research Institute. A number of examples are cited: the development of information and communications systems; work on international food policy including surplus disposal guidelines, the world food security plan and international commodity schemes; the implementation of improved World Bank lending practices focusing on agriculture and rural development. The fact that agricultural economists, in many cases, hold positions of influence in the international organizations is taken as some evidence that they are providing valuable contributions.

I do not wish to belittle the contributions of agricultural economists but I do find it a bit difficult to conclude from the evidence presented that they have made a major contribution to the objectives as stated. The focus is largely on the contribution of the agencies and it is extremely difficult to extrapolate from that to conclusions about individuals or groups. However, I am more concerned about the lack of evidence to demonstrate that the objectives are in fact being attained. At least some evidence seems to suggest that development progress in the past twenty years, in terms of the FAO objectives, has been extremely slow and not always positive.

If the results have indeed been small, as suggested even by Dr. Ojala, part of the problem undoubtedly lies in the general climate in which agricultural economists operate. In the First Elmhirst Memorial Lecture in 1976, Professor Schultz stated: "Most of the high priests of national and international policies, whether they speak for the first, second or third world, are at heart contemptuous of economics".[1] Professor Schultz further noted a significant tendency for economists to become "yes-men" and not to question the objectives of their respective governments or agencies. He stated, "Needless to say, agricultural economists are not renowned for their critical evaluation of the economic effects of various political institutions on agriculture".[2] This position is supported also by Charles Capstick in stating that: ". . . apart from occasional examples, policy decisions have not been greatly influenced by studies which analyse existing policies and go on to volunteer assessments of the economic consequences of feasible alternative policy options".[3] Professor Thimm in a paper at this conference states "there is no evidence teaching of agricultural economics has influenced any major agricultural policy decision in Europe".[4] These conclusions seem to me to be rather harsh but certainly suggest the existence of a real problem for the profession.

Dr. Ojala attributes the slow progress in developing countries to "a failure of policy". By the same token he states, "... international co-operation in agriculture is not determined by the vision and output of international agricultural economists".

Part of the lack of progress may be also that the inputs are too small and/or too widely dispersed in international agencies. Certainly the world-wide distribution of economists in the FAO would suggest that a fairly limited impact might be expected, even with a staff of 200. If there is a low level of acceptance, is this at least partly due to a failure of economists to understand the problems fully? Are the basic assumptions regarding the requirements for development correct? Are agricultural economists adequately trained for a role of leadership, including an adequate understanding of the political process necessary to establish a high level of acceptance? I also suspect a major contributing factor lies in agricultural economists' relatively poor record of communication.

While work must continue by agricultural economists in policy analyses, data development and various other important activities outlined by Ojala, a real challenge lies in increasing the level of credibility and acceptance. This is obviously a problem for all agricultural economists and not just those in international agencies. Surely it is worthy of considerable effort on the part of the profession to assess the situation accurately and to institute any corrective measures considered desirable and appropriate.

NOTES

[1] Schultz, Theordore W. "On Economics, Agriculture, and the Political Economy", *Proceedings, Sixteenth International Conference of Agricultural Economists*, 1976, p. 16.
[2] Ibid., p. 17.
[3] Capstick, Charles W. "Agricultural Policy and the Contribution of Agricultural Economics Research and Analysis", *Proceedings, Sixteenth International Conference of Agricultural Economists*, 1976, p. 49.
[4] P. 594.

GENERAL DISCUSSION – RAPPORTEUR: WILLIAM V. LACEY

In the general discussion it was asked if Dr Ojala would comment upon the response that has occurred within FAO following the post-Pearson reports. It was felt that part of the problem within the international agencies was the fact that they were administered by non-agricultural personnel. Had the quantity and quality of work prepared by agency staff been affected by short duration contract schemes? The belief was expressed that the competence and initiative shown by field staff within these agencies is commensurate with their preparedness or otherwise to be outspoken in their views.

Dr Ojala in reply re-emphasized his view that agricultural economists should attempt to influence policy, while recognizing that the policy decisions were finally taken by others. The comment made that the failure of agricultural economists to stimulate sufficent progress indicates a failure of the profession as a whole, might be correct; but in his paper he had been asked to present achievements, limited though they might be. The essential objective of international agencies was international co-operation to solve problems, and he reaffirmed his opinion that at this level, agricultural economists had made a real contribution to progress. This might not always be apparent to outsiders, since it was proper to attribute achievement to an agency as a whole, rather than to particular groups of staff. However, he had conceded that progress proceeds at too slow a pace, and he would not absolve agricultural economists of blame. He accepted that economists can tend to become "yes men", but considered this to be more likely at the national than the international level. He believed that the agricultural economist had a responsibility to present facts and alternatives to the policy-makers, so that the possibilities for better policy decisions did not pass by default.

Dr Ojala did not consider that it would be suitable for him to comment on the post-Pearson developments in the field organization of FAO, as three years had passed since his personal involvement with the agency. His impression was that any serious difficulties encountered in the field were not due to the system as such but rather to particular people in particular country situations.

Participants in the discussion included Deryke G.R. Belshaw and Elmer L. Menzie.

VICTOR NAZARENKO

Accomplishments and Challenges for the Future for Agricultural Economists Working in COMECON

The development of agricultural production, its transition to the machine stage, significant structural and socio-economic changes in agriculture pose new serious problems for agricultural economists in the CMEA countries. It stands to reason that the research areas depend on the specific economic and production problems confronted by each country. However, the common features of the socio-economic structure in agriculture in the CMEA countries, attainment of more or less the same level of agricultural development, simultaneous and identical changes in the farming sector, formation of the national agro-industrial complexes – all this predetermines the similarity of many researches undertaken in the field of agricultural economics. One should accentuate here the importance of the uniform and identical ideological Marxist principles underlying the science of agricultural economics in the CMEA countries.

Time does not permit reviewing all of the research areas in agricultural economics that hold interest and promise, except in brief summary.

One of the major research problems attracting the attention of agricultural economists in practically all CMEA countries is the formation of the national agro-industrial complexes and perfection of economic and organizational relations therein. Nowadays, industrialization of agricultural production, processing of an ever greater portion of farm products, establishment of stronger bonds between farm supplies manufactures, farming, food industry and other sectors of economy stimulate the formation of large national complexes which produce one single end product, i.e. foodstuffs. Changes are taking place in the very mode of food production. Agro-industrial sectors of the economy have been formed in place of relatively isolated industries. All these facts direct the attention of economists to the associated problems, such as analysis of interindustrial relations, their organizational and economic forms, price system within the agro-industrial complex, the level of profitability (efficiency) in separate branches, more rational distribution of capital investment and manpower in the complex, with a view to reducing food production costs, increasing food supply and improving food quality so as to meet the more exacting demands of today. This is closely related to such complicated problems as the optimal forms of management for the agro-industrial complex at the national level.

As is known, most of the CMEA countries have set up special departments to cater for the agriculture and food industry. The search for optimal forms of management at the state level is still continued in a number of countries as exemplified by the recent changes effected in the agro-industrial complex management in Bulgaria. Such multidisciplinary studies in many states involve not only agricultural economists, but also general economists, experts in industry, prices, management and political economy. This particular problem area, in view of its intricate nature and multidisciplinary aspects, will definitely continue to be among the most important in the years to come.

The interrelations between industries present a great scientific and practical interest not only at the national level but also at the level of regions, associations (firms) and individual enterprises. In recent years, this area of research has acquired specific significance, particularly in the Soviet Union and some East European countries. It incorporates analysis of the performance of the existing agro-industrial associations and enterprises particularly those operating in the field of wine production, horticulture and some sectors of animal husbandry. They have introduced a continuous production line, practise uniform principles of management on the interindustrial basis, and the entire production is geared to a concrete end product. Here the economists deal with such complicated and important problems as distribution of profits, capital investment, labour remuneration, organization and planning of production and forms of labour payment. Legislative aspects are no less significant, since these associations represent new forms of business operations and require formulation and adoption of corresponding acts.

Similar significance is attached to inter-farm co-operation. The fact is that in most socialist countries agricultural production has been concentrated in large state and co-operative farms. This was the situation that prevailed at least some years ago. At present, however, the economically optimal size of agricultural operations is larger than can be supported by one farm, especially in the industrialized branches of agriculture. Therefore, production and economic considerations for concentrated and specialized production created a need for larger producing units to be set up in certain branches of agriculture. In actual practice this is achieved through the organization of higher-level co-operatives, the so-called second stage co-operatives which run within their framework large-scale business operations like feedlots, food processing plants, construction works and so on. These enterprises and co-operatives financially depend on the shares paid by the usual type of co-operative and are managed by a council of directors. In different forms this system has been introduced on a large scale in a number of countries, including the Soviet Union and GDR. Their development, clearly, poses many new problems for the economists to consider, e.g. principles and forms of inter-farm associations, their organizational structure, management, planning, investments and distribution of income, internal prices, etc. Extensive research work is carried out in this field in socialist countries and undoubtedly this research will be continued in future on a large scale.

One of the key problems encountered by agricultural economists in the Soviet Union and abroad lies in the studies of the most rational ways of agricultural intensification. All East European countries, to one extent or another, have switched to a capital-intensive production which requires sizable investments in this sector of the economy. Suffice it to say that in the Soviet Union investment in agriculture in the last two five-year plan periods exceeded 300 billion roubles. Every economist can appreciate the responsibility of the planning and agricultural authorities for the most efficient distribution and utilization of this investment. Naturally, it calls, above all, for a fundamental concept of agricultural intensification, based on the main principles of the farm policies in each country and planned targets drawn out for major farm products. Agricultural research institutions participate in the decision-making at different levels as far as it is connected with the central questions of planning agricultural development.

The objective of research on agricultural intensification is to assess, in terms of economics, the significance of such factors as mechanization and chemicalization of agriculture, land improvement, construction of livestock premises and other farm buildings. A very complicated problem in this field is to determine the economic efficiency of capital investments and inputs, the sequence of their application and proportions, influence on labour productivity and increase of production volume, and efficiency of agricultural enterprises. These problems are not of merely theoretical, scientific interest; they are very important for practical activities, determination of specific areas of capital investment and its realization in agriculture and related industries. To facilitate the solution of these problems, methods are being developed to evaluate the economic efficiency of investments and fixed production funds in agriculture and to analyse the effect of direct inputs upon the efficiency of the current production.

As mentioned earlier, these are viewed as the key problems of agricultural production planning. Agricultural development plans can be subdivided into long term (covering over five years), medium term (five years), short term (one year) and current (plans for individual farm activities). Traditionally, planning is based on the balance sheet method. At the present time an ever greater use is made of the so-called input–output tables which are more or less identical to those suggested by Leontiev. The important fact to note here is that substantial complication of the agricultural production structure and a steep increase in the capital investment impart an ever greater significance to long term planning covering several five-year periods. Such plans are developed in the form of programmes, and the method used is known as goal-oriented programming, for each programme is designed to attain a certain final goal. It should be mentioned also that a good deal of co-ordination work

Victor Nazarenko

is done. The co-ordination is effected in the framework of the five-year plans and is facilitated by a close coincidence of the plan periods in most socialist countries. Nowadays, co-ordination has been raised to a still higher level: development of long term goal-oriented programmes for the CMEA countries envisaging production of different farm products and a corresponding division of labour in agriculture and related industries. The recently held 33rd top-level conference for the CMEA members emphasized particularly the importance of such long term goal-oriented programmes. Their development enlists the active participation of agricultural economists. The role of economists, definitely, cannot be confined to the programme development alone: they should be actively involved further in the building up of the programmes and the development of economic mechanisms to ensure their implementation.

Division of labour in agriculture is one of the most important problems, not only within the CMEA as a whole. Division of labour, i.e. territorial and branch specialization of agriculture and its rational deployment has always been ranked among the top priority problems tackled by agricultural economists in all CMEA countries. The growing specialization and concentration of production, the strengthening of inter-farm and inter-industrial relations render these problems particularly important. Studies carried out in this respective field of research aim at the most effective utilization of natural and labour resources as well as capital investment that would assure attainment of the plan targets. The studies concern labour division at the level of the state, large and small administrative units and within enterprises. Optimal deployment presupposes maximal concentration of each agricultural activity in the areas where specific natural and economic conditions favour the development of a given activity, with due consideration for the natural constraints to agricultural production. This results in the formation of relatively homogeneous specialized zones producing a limited number of the final farm products.

The first and foremost task of economists here is to analyse, in economic terms, the natural and economic condition of production, production costs, productivity, relative profitability and labour efficiency in each zone, as well as to estimate the future economic effect that can be obtained from the redeployment of agricultural production. The intricate and diverse nature of these problems calls for a wide use of economical and mathematical modelling. Of course, optimization of the production deployment and specialization is not something constant. It is and will continue to be subject to changes due to the continually changing economic situation, manpower availability and alternative uses of natural resources. Therefore the work for deployment optimization usually integrates agricultural forecasts and predictions. They are made with full consideration of the expected volume of farm production, farm supplies, working force, technical and technological changes and furnish the basis both for long term planning of agriculture as a whole and for the production plans in respect to each type of product and location of each type of farm production at the level of the country and individual regions. A great significance is attached to the perspective development of transport facilities, the entire production infrastructure, economic relations and ties within the agro-industrial complex, as well as to the implications that the concentration and specialization of production may have for the ecological system.

The predicted pattern of agricultural production deployment and specialization results from the investigation of the future material and technical basis, changes in the productive forces, rate of urbanization and amount of labour available in the rural areas, the future capacity of the transportation facilities, the type of the food industry to be expected in the long run, the pressure of the environmental problems, etc. One of the principal objectives in this research is to ensure a rational deployment of industries with due regard for the future trends in scientific and technological progress and the full use of such irreplaceable factors of production as climatic conditions.

Such investigations, normally, include the following stages: formulation of the concept; elaboration of the deployment pattern or rather its alternative versions; choice of the version that would most adequately meet the constant requirements; development of the industry deployment prognosis, preparation of the materials and suggestions on the production deployment for the long term plan; clarification of the deployment pattern when the next five-year plan is under consideration. These stages are present, to one extent to another, in the agricultural economic research carried out by most socialist countries in the field of farm production deployment and specialization. As to the macro economic investigations, particularly noteworthy are the studies pertinent to the economic relations between the state and agriculture as a whole and separate agricultural enterprises.

Such relations are effected through production planning, farm supplies and purchase of farm products, as well as through prices, credits, finances, taxes, etc.

It should be also mentioned that the significance of each economic and administrative method and mechanism the state uses to exert its influence on agriculture varies from country to country. And this is only natural because the importance attached to each of these factors, their concrete contents, reflects the specific features characteristic of the economic life in each country. Nevertheless, among the various tools used by the governments in all countries to affect agriculture, there is one common factor and that is the effort of all state authorities to utilize the entire range of economic factors to stimulate the attainment of the state-defined targets in agriculture.

So, the task of agricultural economists here is to analyse the effectiveness of the economic levers, to investigate their economic and production effects, functioning and correspondence to the outlined targets; to study the profitability trends in individual branches and regions, the level of income received by the rural population. In the research dealing with economic mechanisms whereby the state can influence agricultural production prices are viewed as a most essential element. The price formation processes are studied in most socialist states, which can be explained by the fact that each farm keeps its own cost accounting of the farm products and the data are then summarized by the relevant statistical bodies.

The principle objective of research in the field of price formation is to study the main trends existing in the production costs and efficiency in respect of different products, often in different regions; to determine the most rational price level which would ensure expanded production in the given branch, duly accounting for the plan targets. The research results are used by the state to make decision as to the level of farm purchase prices.

So far as the micro economic studies are concerned, one should point to those which are devoted to the perfection of economic relations within agro-industrial enterprises, forms and methods of labour remuneration. These studies, as a rule, are aimed at increasing the general efficiency of enterprises, reducing and eliminating subsidies payable to them and their developing into financially self-sustained entities; at introducing such economic relations that would serve to cut down the cost price and save inputs in each field of production activity. In the economic literature these problems are referred to as the problems of internal cost accounting.

Research on labour remuneration normally includes such issues as the level of payment, differentiation of payment according to the workers' skill and qualification, forms of payment, labour norms, etc. This problem area, in addition to its micro economic significance (i.e. practical application of different forms of labour payment used to stimulate production) has a tremendous socio-economic importance, since at the present time all socialist countries are making efforts to bridge the gap between the living standards in town and countryside and to bring the rate of labour payment in rural localities closer to that in the urban centres. The problem of labour remuneration is very closely associated with the problem of labour productivity. The spectrum of scientific studies in this area is usually very wide. It includes first of all analysis of trends and alterations in the level of labour productivity in agriculture as a whole, in its separate branches and in separate regions and factorial analysis of causes inducing these alterations. They provide the basis for prognostic studies concerning the likely trends in labour productivity. The level of labour inputs and other inputs are defined and then used in the process of planning.

In addition to these problems of economics, agricultural economists have also to deal with the problems of rural sociology.

In brief summary, they are as follows. The first is the problem of migration and reproduction of manpower. The rapid rate of urbanization and industrialization, higher educational level of the people, including in rural areas, introduction of compulsory middle education in rural schools in a number of countries, a new generation of workers – all this brings to the foreground new social problems to be tackled by economists. Second, the very nature of labour in agriculture is undergoing radical changes. Although the natural differences between agriculture and other sectors of economy continue to exist, labour processes in agriculture are becoming more comparable to those in industry, which fact is conditioned by the changing quality of labour and the new relations between the workers and the means of production.

Third, another important fact to note here is the alteration in the very lifestyle of the rural people which is manifested not only in increased incomes but also in the new production and non-production infrastructure, new types of settlement, changes in the quality of life in the countryside.

Fourth, the range of social problems integrates all issues relating to the form of ownership in agriculture. These problems are many and depend largely on the social structure of agriculture in each country. They cover the relationship between private farmers in Poland, introduction of the known forms of co-operatives there, development of higher forms of co-operation in most socialist countries, rapprochement of the state and co-operative forms of property, the process experienced in most socialist countries.

These and many other fundamental problems make up the object of research in the field of agricultural economics in the CMEA countries. Of course they reflect only the main lines of research. The current and long term research programmes underway in each of these countries are more diversified and account for the development targets and conditions prevailing in agriculture in each respective country.

DISCUSSION OPENING – J.S. HILLMAN

Before addressing some points for discussion, I shall take a moment to put the major themes of Dr Nazarenko's paper into context from which I shall raise *questions* that constitute the thrust of my opening statement.

At the outset, I fear that Nazarenko has overdrawn the common features of socio-economic phenomena in CMEA countries, even that of ideological principles. Be that as it may, some major problems attracting the attention of agricultural economists in those countries are outlined rather clearly and we are indebted to him for that. These problems fall generally under the following topical headings:

1 Agro-industrial complexes; which include interrelationships between industries, between industries and firms, and between firms.
2 Intensification of production.
3 Planning of production, which includes the division of labour, cost analyses, and tasks preparatory to the prediction of patterns of production and employment.
4 Techniques to achieve state-defined targets in CMEA countries.
5 Macro economic studies.
6 Labour remunerations.

7   Agricultural and rural sociology problems, such as migration, manpower and rural environment.

Despite his commendable effort, Dr Nazarenko's presentation leaves us with large researchable gaps, and with questions which are relevant not only to agricultural economists working in COMECON but to those working in other countries as well. I now proceed to a partial list of these questions.

The first set of questions relates to trade and trade policies between CMEA countries, and between these countries and the world. What are the bases for trade and the actual movement of commodities between CMEA countries? It would be helpful, for example, to know more about the grain imports and utilization policies of these countries, particularly those of the USSR. Agricultural economists there might undertake studies which would relieve the world of some instability in grain markets if they were to tackle seriously the problems inherent in the transportation, storage and distribution of grain. I might add that the grain reserve problem is a unique one to be probed from that vantage point.

In this general vein, a second major question arises in relation to the consumption of certain products, particularly livestock and dairy products. Is there over-consumption because of the relatively low prices of these products to consumers? In this regard, I might point out that Dr Nazarenko's paper is quite devoid of mention of research on the demand side – all his attention seems to be given to resource, production, or supply problems.

A third set of questions involves the economic relationships between the "players" in the agro-industrial complex. On what basis do industries and farms share in income distribution? This is but another way of asking what are the methods for pricing inputs and outputs in the various systems. In passing, what is meant by the words "profit" and "profitability" used throughout the paper? How are wage differentials determined; or what determines who works where? What is the future of the agro-industrial complex – to assure increased efficiency or stagnation? Farm labour: how do you keep the rural worker happy given the wage differential between farm and factory?

My fourth question relates to the actual investigations already underway and to research capabilities. The paper mentions *many* studies that are being carried out, e.g. those on the division of labour; but little mention is made of any results. Moreover, in light of the voluminous number of research and other problem areas in COMECON raised by Dr Nazarenko, I pose the problem of the availability of personnel and other resources for the task.

Finally, the paper might have been more informative if Dr Nazarenko had told us the *aims* of COMECON, how it works, and at what stage are many of its activities (i.e. for talking or for action). This is of special interest due to the different problems which face the different countries.

Dr Nazarenko has made a beginning. It would be helpful to all if more light could be thrown on the topics he raised and the questions which I have asked here.

GENERAL DISCUSSION – RAPPORTEUR: WILFRED MWANGI

The questions from the floor were in line with those raised by the opener of the discussion. The questions were mainly on the role of agricultural economists in trade and trade policies, the basis for trade, over-consumption of livestock and dairy products, the method of pricing inputs and outputs, the concept of profit, wage differentials in regard to labour, freedom of workers, availability of research resources to agriculture, conservatism of economic policy in allocating resources to agriculture and finally the aims and activities of COMECON.

In his response to the questions raised by the opener as well as from the floor the author first explained that agricultural economists in the USSR are usually specialized according to the Ministries in which they work. In his paper therefore he was only dealing with the work of agricultural economists in the Ministry of Agriculture whose major concern was in agricultural production. He had not, therefore, discussed foreign trade which was the responsibility of Foreign Affairs.

Dr Nazarenko indicated that grain production in the Soviet Union is mainly in marginal areas and this leads to considerable fluctuation in production. It was noted however that in recent years grain production had increased by 75 per cent. Production will be increased further through the improvement of tillage systems as well as through increased fertilizer use. He refuted the contention that there was over-consumption in livestock and dairy products in COMECON. This might appear so because the system of calculation applied is different, say, from that applied by FAO. Meat prices, for example, might appear to be low just because, again, the pricing system is different. Further, the price formation system is difficult to explain because it is not only economic, but also other factors, such as social considerations, that are involved in its determination. However, regional as well as zonal pricing reflect costs of production. The economic policy pursued by COMECON in regard to agriculture was not conservative. Capital investment in agriculture which stood at 27 per cent of total capital investment in the economy reflected the highest priority to agriculture. The aims and activities of COMECON headquarters were not discussed in the paper because the author felt that the subject was different and complicated since COMECON was a supra-national organization.

Participants in the discussion included Edward F. Gillin and Maxwell S. Myers.

G. EDWARD SCHUH

Floating Exchange Rates, International Interdependence, and Agricultural Policy

The Bretton-Woods Conference of 1944 established rules that governed the economic relations among countries for almost thirty years. An essential element of these rules was a dependence on fixed exchange rates. The competitive devaluations of the 1930s, which many authorities believed responsible (at least in part) for plunging the industrialized countries into depression, strengthened a natural aversion to floating exchange rates. Relations among currencies were to be fixed and changes were to be made only under dire circumstances. Equilibrium in the external accounts of individual countries was to be maintained by the use of appropriate domestic macro economic policies. If a disequilibrium in the external accounts developed, the remedy was to be sought first by changes in domestic policy. Only after domestic policies had failed was there to be a realignment of exchange rates.

The Bretton-Woods regime came to an end for all intents and purposes in March 1973, when generalized floating exchange rates were established among the industrialized countries. We now have a mixed system in which exchange rates float relatively freely among some countries (albeit with a great deal of intervention), but in which many countries still keep their exchange rates tied to the dollar or to other reserve currencies.

Exchange rate arrangements are, of course, more diverse than just fixed or floating. At a minimum, one can identify at least five different exchange rate regimes: (1) countries pegged to a single regime, (2) countries pegged to some "basket" of currencies, (3) countries that float jointly, (4) countries that float independently, and (5) countries that change their currency values on the basis of a predetermined formula. To gain some perspective on the significance of flexible exchange rate regimes, the IMF estimates that for total trade among member countries, less than one-fifth of such trade takes place with pegged rates and more than four-fifths of it takes place under floating rate regimes.

The main thesis of my paper is that the nature of the exchange rate regime has important implications for both agriculture and agricultural policy. It affects the way that monetary and fiscal policy affect the agricultural sector, and at the same time influences the nature of external

416

shocks to which the sector is submitted. An important conclusion of my paper is that under a regime of floating exchange rates the trade and trade-competing sectors have to bear an important share of the adjustment to changing monetary and fiscal policy. Hence, if a country either imports or exports agricultural products, its agricultural sector may be subject to more instability under a regime of floating exchange rates than under a regime of fixed exchange rates. From these conclusions there are important implications about such things as stocks policy, adjustment policy, and domestic price policy.

I would like to divide my comments into four parts: (1) a discussion of flexible exchange rates and economic independence; (2) an analysis of macro economic policy with flexible exchange rates and an international capital market; (3) an analysis of macro economic policy and agriculture; and (4) a discussion of some of the implications for agricultural policy. My analysis tends to draw more on the export case than on the import case, but it is important to recognize that the issues are pertinent to both groups of countries.

FLEXIBLE EXCHANGE RATES AND ECONOMIC INDEPENDENCE

The conventional view of alternative exchange rate regimes has been that a system of flexible exchange rates would give individual countries more independence in their domestic macro stabilization policies. Moreover, an important assumption has been that greater stability in the domestic economy would be a logical consequence of such a system, for monetary and fiscal authorities would presumably be able to pursue policy measures more suited to the domestic situation, and would not have to impose adjustments on the domestic economy as a means to bring the foreign sector into equilibrium.

Those conclusions now seem overly sanguine. The problem is that such arguments largely neglect the capital accounts or the international capital markets. As I will attempt to show below, the international capital market can be an important means of linking one economy to another. Once they are linked by this means, a country has no more independence in its economic policy with flexible exchange rates than it has with fixed exchange rates, although it obviously gains an additional means of adjustment. With respect to the expected independence in policy making, it is worth noting that economic summits to co-ordinate economic policies have been much more frequent since exchange rates were freed than they were before.

Perhaps there was a time when international capital markets were not important. But that obviously is no longer the case. The Eurocurrency market, for example, is huge. Moreover, it is relatively easy to gain access to this market, and it is virtually free of regulation or intervention by national or international agencies. The availability of this large capital market deserves a great deal of credit for the success with which international money markets handled the gorge of petro-currencies associated with the OPEC-induced hikes in oil prices. It also has now become an important means by which the economic policies of one country impact on another.

This "open" capital market of Eurocurrencies is not the only dimension to the international capital market, however, nor the only indication that capital is highly mobile among countries. Private banks and consortiums of private banks in the United States and in European capitals have also contributed in an important way to financing the short term balance of payments problems that low-income countries have suffered in recent years. In addition, these same banks and consortia have played an increasingly larger role in financing longer term development programmes.

The consequence of a high degree of international mobility of capital is that the interest rate is no longer a completely endogenous variable subject to the control of domestic monetary and fiscal authorities. Rather, the interest rate now takes on a high degree of exogeneity for many countries, depending on the relative importance of the country in international capital markets. The real interest rate is determined in international markets, with arbitrage tending to equalize the interest rate throughout the world.[1] This integrated capital market influences the way that monetary and fiscal policy impacts on an economy and at the same time provides a linkage among the policies of various countries. The equalization of interest rates is also why the close integration of international monetary markets is viewed by many as a mixed blessing. Movements of capital in response to small interest rate differentials are frequently alleged to frustrate the domestic stabilization policies of monetary authorities. Other complaints have been quite common lately and are one of the reasons why some countries want to return to a regime of fixed exchange rates.

MACRO ECONOMIC POLICY WITH FLEXIBLE EXCHANGE RATES AND AN INTERNATIONAL CAPITAL MARKET

If the exchange rates are fixed and the international capital market is weak or non-existent, monetary policy will tend to have a rather broad effect on the domestic economy. To put it in its simplest form, a policy of monetary ease designed to stimulate the economy will lower interest rates, thereby stimulating the construction sector, investment, and consumption. A policy of monetary restraint, on the other hand, will raise interest rates, thereby choking off construction, investment, and consumption.

---

[1] Although real rates of interest will tend toward equality, nominal rates will differ to reflect inflationary premiums.

With flexible exchange rates and a well developed international capital market, the mechanism by which monetary policy operates is quite different. This difference is quite significant for agriculture if agricultural products are tradeables – either as exports or as imports. To illustrate what this difference is all about, let us suppose the authorities want to stimulate the economy, and assume again that they decide to do it through an expansion in the quantity of money. Monetary expansion will in the first instance put downward pressure on the rate of interest, other things being equal, and if capital is highly mobile there will be a capital outflow – an outflow that will continue until domestic and international interest rates are equalized if capital is sufficiently mobile. The consequence of the capital outflow is to bid up the price of foreign currency, which is to say that the value of the domestic currency would decline in international markets. The decline in the value of the domestic currency would make imports more expensive, while providing a stimulus to exports. The demand for domestic output would consequently increase, and adjustments in the trade sectors (and trade-competing sectors) would be the means whereby the authorities attain their stabilization objective.

The important point to note is that the channels through which the economy is stimulated are rather different than they would be if exchange rates were fixed and if capital were immobile, or if there were barriers to international flows of capital. An important effect of the monetary policy is through the trade sectors, whereas it would tend to be principally through the non-traded goods and services sectors if capital were not mobile. Although not directly pertinent to my paper, it is worth noting that this form of adjustment now constitutes one of the main threats to the maintenance of free international capital markets. The point is that governments are not likely to remain indifferent between whether their countries increase investment by lending abroad or by engaging in real capital formation at home. Under the present institutional arrangements, however, the attempt to stimulate capital formation at home is likely to lead to exports of capital.

Now, suppose as an alternative that the authorities want to restrain demand by pursuing a tight monetary policy or restraining the growth in the money supply. Upward pressure would be created on domestic interest rates, capital would flow in from abroad to bring about equalization, and the value of the domestic currency would rise in international markets. A rise in the value of the domestic currency would stimulate imports and reduce exports, other things being equal. The consequence would be to dampen down the economy – as policy-makers desire. But once again the effect of the policy would be realized through the trade sectors – through adjustments in the import and export sectors – and not through that part of the economy that is producing non-traded goods and services.

One should not conclude from this analysis that a system of relatively flexible exchange rates and a well developed international capital market is either better or worse than the previous system of fixed exchange rates and a poorly developed capital market. I frankly do not think we know

420   *G. Edward Schuh*

enough about how such a system works in practice to draw any firm conclusions. Moreover, I believe our current experience can be viewed largely as an exercise in trying to learn how such a system would in fact work. It would seem that the system of flexible exchange rates and relatively free international capital markets has served us quite well in our recent period of stress. However, the new system creates a quite different environment for agricultural policy, especially if trade in agricultural products is important. And that is what I want to turn to next.

MACRO ECONOMIC POLICY AND AGRICULTURE

An important implication of this analysis is that macro economic policy has a quite different effect on agriculture under the two exchange rate regimes. With fixed exchange rates the main effect of changes in monetary policy was transmitted to agriculture through the inter-sectoral labour market. Demand for agricultural output over the cycle was relatively stable and agricultural capital markets were relatively isolated from conditions in national monetary markets. Moreover, a major share of the capital for agricultural investment came from internal financing.

Tight money policies, however, almost inevitably lead to higher levels of unemployment. Out-migration from agriculture is quite sensitive to the level of unemployment. And the rate of out-migration has a great deal to do with the income of farm people. Hence shifts in monetary policy impacted on agriculture in large part through the labour market.

Under the new situation, the effect of macro economic policy is quite different, especially if agriculture is either an export sector or if agricultural products are imported in significant quantities. In the first place, demand for domestic agricultural resources will no longer be relatively stable. On the contrary, it will shift in response to changes in monetary policy, with the source of the shifts being either shifts in foreign demand or foreign supply (depending on whether an importer or exporter).

But there are other effects as well, especially if the international capital markets are well developed. Capital will flow back and forth from one country to another in response to shifts in monetary policy. Such shifts may make for a more efficient use of the world's resources. On the other hand, they may create serious stabilization problems for individual countries, as well as political difficulties.

Finally, asset values in agriculture – especially the value of land – will be sensitive to the exchange rate. This will be both a product-market and capital-market effect. But it also has important implications for further capital formation in agriculture.

IMPLICATIONS FOR AGRICULTURAL POLICY

One of the first implications is that world agriculture will tend to be more unstable in the new regime than it was in the past. Given that agricultural trade is important to a large number of countries, agriculture in individual countries can expect to experience larger shocks in the future due to shifts in monetary policy and exogenous shifts of capital. Moreover, for exporting countries, the effects of those shifts will be transmitted in such a way that they affect the demand for agricultural output. Hence, in the future we should expect to have a rather unstable demand for the agricultural output of individual countries, in marked contrast to the past, with the source of that instability coming from the foreign sector, even though those fluctuations of foreign demand are an indirect consequence of domestic monetary and fiscal policy.

It is also important to note that there can be important international flows of capital that have little to do with domestic monetary and fiscal policy, and that these can impose further exogenous shocks on agriculture. For example, a shift out of other currencies into dollars can cause the value of the dollar to rise, thereby reducing the foreign demand for US exports, other things being equal. Similarly, a shift out of dollars into other currencies, for whatever reason, can cause the value of the dollar to decline, thereby stimulating exports. These monetary shifts, whether motivated by speculative motives or more basic investment decisions, can be an important source of shocks to US agriculture as well as to the agriculture in other countries.

Central banks can sterilize both the external shocks and the induced changes in the exchange rate by an appropriate open market operation in the foreign exchange markets. There are limits to the amount of such interventions, however, since foreign exchange reserves are not typically unlimited. But when there are such interventions, of course, the system has moved away from flexibility and back towards a fixed exchange rate regime.

There are a number of implications that follow from this analysis. The first is that agriculture in the aggregate is not noted for its flexibility in adjusting to changing economic conditions, although as modernization takes place it may have more flexibility than it has under more traditional conditions. But the biological process inherent in agriculture clearly affects its responsiveness, and with sectors such as beef that have large inventory components accelerator effects can cause policy to be rather destabilizing. This raises doubts about monetary and fiscal policies that depend for their effectiveness on adjustments in sectors such as agriculture. Although agriculture is relatively unimportant in the total economy of many countries, it is sufficiently large that it could attenuate the effectiveness of monetary and fiscal policy.

Another implication for agriculture follows from the accelerator effects and the livestock sector. Recent experience of the US is again an interesting example. Shifts in grain prices, induced at least in part by shifts in exchange rates, are imposing shocks on both the beef and pork sectors – and at rather critical times in their production cycles. Managing these effects is quite a challenge to policy makers.

Another implication, of course, is that agricultural economists have another important reason for taking a greater interest in monetary and fiscal policy. Moreover, their perspective has to be somewhat different from what it has been in the past. Direct effects of such policies will probably be even less important than they have been in the past, with the indirect effect through fluctuations in exchange rates taking on added importance.

A corollary of this, of course, is that in a world of flexible exchange rates macro economic policy makers are *not* likely to leave as much autonomy to agricultural policy as they do in a world of fixed exchange rates. Rather, food and agricultural policy is likely to be woven much closer into the overall fabric of general economic policy.

The policy with respect to grain reserves also takes on a somewhat different perspective than it has had in the past. The presence of reserves or a reserve system could serve to blunt the effectiveness of monetary and fiscal policy. In a period of economic slack, when the government was increasing the money supply, the desired consequence would be that the increase in foreign demand that resulted from the decline in the exchange rate would lead to an increase in agricultural output and the demand for factors of production. But if stocks were released to meet this foreign demand, say because a relatively inelastic short-run supply caused food prices to rise in the face of this shift of demand, the effect could be to reduce the stimulus to factor demand. If the authorities had a target level for reserves, the reduction in stocks would eventually lead to an increased demand in order to rebuild them. But this would be only after a lag.

Grain reserve policy traditionally has been viewed in large part as a means of offsetting fluctuations in supply, especially domestic supply. In an economy with floating exchange rates, especially if the country should be an agricultural exporter, reserves may have multiple objectives. This new perspective needs to be introduced into our analyses of grain reserves.

Another issue has to do with domestic agricultural policies that attempt to fix agricultural prices. Clearly that will be much more difficult to do with a regime of floating exchange rates. A system of price bands, or price corridors, similar to what the US now uses, is likely to be the more common approach. It is interesting to note that our own domestic price policy took this approach starting with the 1973 farm legislation – the very year we shifted to a system of floating rates.

Finally, we seriously need to develop more effective positive adjustment policies to deal with the shifts in demand against domestic agricultural resources that are likely to occur in the future. The growing availability of off-farm employment for farm people in many countries provides an important adjustment mechanism. But that alone is not likely to be sufficient to handle the resource shifts expected under a system of flexible exchange rates.

CONCLUDING REMARKS

The days when agriculture in most countries could be analysed through the prism of a closed-economy model are long since over. It is not just that the volume of agricultural trade has grown so rapidly, or that individual countries have become more dependent on trade. The shift to floating exchange rates has changed the way that domestic monetary and fiscal policy impact on the sector, and also exposes the sector to a wider range of external shocks. And the growing integration of international capital markets had important implications for agriculture.

We have a great deal of sorting out to do before we fully understand the new circumstances in which we now find ourselves. At the same time, the need for new institutional arrangements is ever before us. Institutional innovation is needed for both our domestic economies, and for the relationships we have with other countries. Our challenges in the next decade are quite great.

REFERENCE

Schuh, G.E. "The New Macroeconomics of Agriculture," *American Journal of Agricultural Economics*, December 1976.

DISCUSSION OPENING – PETER RIEDER

Dr Schuh has written a very interesting paper on Floating Exchange Rates, International Interdependence, and Agricultural Policy. He has discussed the very complex interrelationships between capital markets and agriculture. The issues are specially important for countries, where the agricultural import or export is an essential part of the whole economy. This may be the case for the USA, Canada and some others. Looking at previous papers I found a controversy about the influence of changes in exchange rates in the USA. I refer to the articles of Mr. Schuh from 1974 and 1976 in the *AJAE* and to Kost's and Vellianitis' articles in *Agr. Econ. Research* in 1976, as well as a reply on that article.

Mr Schuh argues that macro economic policy or money policy has an important influence on agriculture. I understand his argument concerning the interrelationships between money policy, levels of unemployment, out-migration from agriculture and income of farm people. However, reasons other than exchange rate policy may be much more important as well in US agriculture as in other developed market economies.

The *main* conclusion of Dr Schuh's paper is that floating exchanges rates influence the international agricultural trade and that agriculture will tend to be more unstable in the future. He assumes an unstable foreign demand for agricultural products as a consequence of the changing value of the dollar (US). Looking at earlier papers, I could not find any empirical evidence for this hypothesis.

The main question remains, how big are the price elasticities of demand for exporting products? At the same time we have to take into consideration the import restrictions of the main importers. For instance, the European Community applies trade restrictions for some products. Furthermore, I do not know whether USSR imports are related to prices. Maybe our Russian colleagues can tell us something about their behaviour to world market prices.

I also wonder whether developing countries are in a position to buy agricultural goods in hard money. The oil exporting countries may be the exception.

In conclusion, the price elasticities for agricultural products may be low, due to the mentioned behaviour of the big importers. The agricultural trade has grown rapidly in the past. The main reason for this expansion seems to be the additional demand of several countries outside the western capital market. Short run changes in demand are more caused by weather or political conditions.

Finally, I would like to ask Dr Schuh if he were a decision-maker whether he would advocate fixed or floating exchange rates for stabilising the international agricultural trade.

GENERAL DISCUSSION – RAPPORTEUR: WILFRED MWANGI

The paper was recognized as raising very important and relevant economic considerations often overlooked by agricultural economists. It was felt, however, that it concentrated too much on the US and its relevance to other countries was questioned. Thus, it was suggested that more research should be done to get a better perspective of the relationship between the changes of the exchange rate and the impact on agricultural policy not only for one country but for the most important countries and commodities.

Attention was called to the impact of currency market uncertainties which result in fluctuating exchange rate, especially with respect to the Common Agricultural Policy of the EEC. For instance, the monetary compensatory amounts, which were created in response to changes in relative currency values within Europe, strengthen the pressures to bring about a revision of the CAP. This will have an important impact on the international trade of major agricultural products.

It was further felt that the author arrived at certain conclusions in the paper due to the assumptions he made depending on whether he was analysing the effects of fixed or floating exchange rates. For example, in analysing the effects of fixed exchange rates he assumed that capital was immobile or that there were barriers to international flows of capital. On the other hand, in analysing the effects of floating exchange rates he allowed for mobile capital. Thus the different effects which emerged from the analysis were not only due to the different exchange rate regimes but also, and perhaps mainly, due to the different assumptions about mobility of capital. The author further neglected the fact that national agricultural policy very often tends to compensate for changes in exchange rates by applying national instruments and other policy devices; also that imported inflation in a less inflationary country can be an alternative to floating exchange rate and this will affect agriculture.

Further questions were raised with regard to introduction of non-tariff barriers to trade, shift from currencies to real commodities, whether world agriculture was more stable, depreciation of agricultural commodities in terms of gold and the implication of exchange rate regimes to less developed countries in regard to resource use, their agricultural products and their debts to developed countries in general.

In response, Dr Schuh stressed the fact that he would want to depersonalize his paper, as the contents were no invention of his as the comments from the floor tended to imply. Nor did he want to advocate one or the other type of exchange regime. He contended that empirical evidence was not conclusive as to how the system operates. He regarded this as a continuing learning process especially in a floating exchange rate regime. In general he was in agreement with most of the observations. The study, he argued, was relevant to all countries. To illustrate this, as well as in responding on the impact of exchange rate to LDCs, he gave the example of the formation of OPEC due to depreciation of the dollar. On the whole he felt that the issues raised could only be answered as more empirical evidence was generated through further investigation.

Participants in the discussion included Ulrich Koester, Adolf A. Weber, Margaret Loseby, Michel Petit, Clark Edward, Howard Osborn and Caleb W.W. Wangia.

MARGARET LOSEBY and LORENZO VENZI

Floating Exchange Rates and International Trade in Agricultural Commodities

Eight years have now passed since the first official devaluation of the US dollar in terms of gold an event which, in retrospect, is regarded as having brought to an end the system of fixed exchange rates established by the Bretton-Woods Agreement in 1944. That system has been replaced by a situation in which the former "key currencies", the US dollar and the pound sterling have been allowed to float roughly in line with market forces, and other countries have declared their intention either to float independently, or to align their exchange rates either to a specific foreign currency, or to a composite index of foreign currency values. This new situation, though scarcely corresponding to the theoretical view of flexible exchange rates, due, amongst other things, to a significant degree of government intervention in currency markets, results, in fact, in considerable fluctuations in bilateral exchange rates. The controversy regarding the desirability of fluctuating as opposed to fixed exchange rates is linked primarily to the efficacy of each system in resolving balance of payments disequilibria. From this macro-economic viewpoint no general consensus of opinion has been reached and, for example, five different approaches to the question have been summarized by H.G. Johnson.[5] The scope of this paper, instead, is limited to the consideration of the effects which the change in the system of exchange rate regulation may have had on trade in agricultural commodities.

The subject is of obvious importance to those countries where agricultural exports constitute a large percentage of total exports. But a further consideration suggests that it is also relevant to a wider range of countries.

First, in the onslaught of events at the beginning of the 1970s the official dollar devaluation was accompanied by a rapid rise in commodity prices. It has been inferred that some of this rise was also due to the switching of speculative funds into commodity markets in view of the uncertainty reigning in the foreign exchange markets at that time. If this were so, continuing uncertainty in currency markets, implicit in the present system of fluctuating rates, could be expected to cause similar disturbances in the levels, both relative and absolute of commodity prices, which may not be without consequence for trade flows, and the

426

evolution of trends in production and consumption.

Secondly, movements in commodity prices are considered of fundamental importance in determining economic trends in industrialised countries. N. Kaldor[7] has pointed to the fact that violent movements in commodity prices have been followed by periods of economic recession, whether the movements have been downwards, as in the 1920s, or upwards, as in the early 1970s.

As regards price, it is well known that its upward trend has been far more rapid in the 1970s than in previous decades. The index for agricultural products has risen even faster than that for manufactures. The steepest rises took place in 1973 and 1974, corresponding with the second official devaluation of the US dollar in terms of gold. But the years 1973 and 1974 corresponded, too, with a rapid decline of world stocks in cereals. Given the coincidence in timing it is virtually impossible to estimate the relative contributions to the price increase of the effect of supply shortage and that of exchange rate uncertainty, causing speculative funds to be moved into commodity markets.

Similarly, as the rate of price increase slowed down (see FAO index for agricultural commodities), or went into reverse (UN World Export price index for food), in 1975 world cereal stocks increased and a possibly more secure outlet for speculative funds became available in the USA with the reopening of gold dealings for private investors.

It is, however, the variability of commodity prices rather than its directional trend which is in question in relation to the debate on fluctuating exchange rates. In this respect the values of the coefficients of variation calculated on indices of prices for exported commodities in principal exporting countries are of some interest. In all cases a greater degree of variability is indicated for the years after 1971.

If, however, as has been argued, uncertainty caused by exchange rate variability impedes the steady development of international trade, the effects of the changeover would be seen presumably, in a slower rate of growth of the volume of world trade, if not actually in a decline in the volume of trade.

In a theoretical analysis of the situation facing a single firm trading in conditions of uncertainty in the exchange markets W. Ethier[3] concludes that the level of trade will be reduced to the extent that the firm is uncertain as to how its revenue is dependent upon the future exchange rate, but that where it has knowledge of the dependence of its revenue on the future exchange rate, exchange uncertainty will influence the degree of foward cover rather than the level of trade. D.P. Baron,[1] on the other hand, again taking a theoretical approach at firm level, argues that "uncertainty regarding exchange rates has no effect on trade" owing to the operation of the forward exchange markets, although he qualifies his view to the extent that there may be imperfections, either in capital or foreign exchange markets.

Indices of volumes of world trade both in manufactures and in agricultural products belie the assertion that the uncertainty inherent in a system of fluctuating exchange rates would impede the continued expansion in world trade. Although the index of trade volumes in agricultural commodities lagged behind that for manufactures, both grew at a faster rate than during the 1960s. This was so for agricultural commodities despite the decline in the index of 1974 and 1975, which took it below the high levels reached in 1973, but no further.

The effects of variations in exchange rates, however, could be expected to be more obvious at a bilaterial level of trade flows, with a tendency for an exporter to increase his exports to those countries whose currencies had appreciated in relation to his own, and a tendency for exports to those countries against which his own currency is appreciating to experience a relative, if not absolute, decline.

At this level, more emphasis has recently been given to the interaction of agricultural policy and balance of payments, both in the USA and in the EEC, where a system of border taxes (MCAs) has been introduced to counteract possible effects on agricultural trade flows of exchange rate variations between member countries. G.E. Schuh[9] stressed the importance of the exchange rate variable in the agricultural policy of the USA and a lively debate ensued, in which other authors attempted to verify the proposition with different results[10] and suggesting[6] that other factors had interposed an influence on price, at least as important as that of the US exchange rate.

This paper concentrates on the bilateral trading aspects of exchange rate variability, but from the point of view of specific commodities, rather than from that of any single country. The objective is to attempt to assess the importance of exchange rate movements in commodity trade as one of the many influences operating in commodity markets.

2   BILATERAL TRADE IN AGRICULTURAL COMMODITIES: SOME PRELIMINARY CONSIDERATIONS

It may be useful, at this stage, briefly to outline a framework of reference within which to analyse the effects of an exchange rate variation between a single exporting and a single importing country.

In theory the depreciation of an exporting country currency (or the revaluation of an importing country currency) would reduce the cost of imports to the importer in terms of the importer's own currency; the gain to the exporter would ensue from an increased volume of exports sufficient to offset the fall in foreign currency receipts from his price decrease (in foreign currency terms).

This mechanism may be counteracted, however, by several factors all working, basically, to undermine the necessary conditions of price elasticity demand on this part of the importing country for the exports in question and elasticity of supply on the part of the exporter. These factors include the possibility of (i) an equivalent currency depreciation by a competing exporter and (ii) an appreciation of the currencies of other importing countries. The structure of the market can likewise influence the final outcome insofar as, (iii) the exporter has some control over his export prices and quantities which may be exerted with primary regard to an aspect of economic policy other than balance of payments. This may occur in the case of state trading agencies attempting to maintain a minimum export price level, or where the market is dominated by large private firms. Moreover, (iv) the importing country may exert control over the quantity of imports and use this control with primary regard to minimising the outlay of foreign exchange. Finally, as regards trade in agricultural commodities in particular, both export supply and import demand elasticity are heavily influenced by (v) seasonal variations in production, both in importing and in exporting countries, particularly where the product is consumed (vi) domestically in the exporting country, and where (vii) it is produced in the importing country.

The net results of these factors, operating either singly, or in combination, on the conditions of import demand elasticity and export supply elasticity may be to offset to some extent the potential effect of an exporting country's devaluation in its trading relations with a single importing country. Thus, for example, if exporting country A devalues with respect to importing country B by 10 per cent, but export prices increase by 12 per cent (for reasons ii, v, vii) the price advantage to country B is eliminated, and, depending on B's bilateral trading prospects with other competing exporters, there may be no reason to expect an increase in quantity flows of exports from A to B.

In fact, in a preliminary test of correlation between trade volumes and bilateral exchange rates for the period 1970–76 covering forty bilateral trade flows between main exporting and importing areas for six major commodities, only one-fifth of the correlation coefficients proved significant at the 0.05 level of probability.

Nevertheless, although the direct effects of an exchange rate variation may be difficult to trace, particularly at the aggregate level of national statistics, it is hard to imagine that at trading level it is totally irrelevant. Moreover, in the hypothetical example cited previously, given the possibility that B's exchange rate may fluctuate in relation to the currency of a competing exporter C the outcome of A–B trade may well be influenced by the movements of exchange rates B : C; the influence[1] may be felt both on the levels of A's negotiated price and on the volume flows. In this situation, the problem of establishing a methodology which would permit us to identify the effects of exchange rate movements becomes paramount. It is evident that it would be extremely difficult to construct an econometric model capable of incorporating all the relevant variables. Instead, in this paper we have chosen a more limited approach and in doing so we have ignored the possible effects on bilateral trade of the currency variations of competing exporters.

3 THE METHODOLOGY

The methodology used here was evolved by Kreinin[8] and applied by him
to exports and imports of industrial goods in the time period 1970–72 for
several major trading nations.

Kreinin's methodology for the investigation of the effects of exchange
rate variability on export flows permits us to identify a "pass through"
effect of exchange rate variations on export prices, i.e. the extent to which
an exporter country's depreciation (appreciation) is reflected in a fall
(rise) in its export price in terms of the importer's currency. The formula
for measuring the "pass through" effect is:

$$\alpha_i = 1 - \frac{{}_iP_x^k - [{}_cP_x^k - {}_cER^k + ({}_cP_d - {}_iP_d)]}{{}_iER^k} \tag{1}$$

where: k denotes the exporting country;
  i denotes the importing country;
  x relates to exports;
  c denotes an importing country used as "control";
  α_i is the "pass through" effect for importer i from exporter K;
  P denotes the percentage change in export prices;
  ER denotes the percentage change in exchange rates;
  P_d is a measure of the percentage increase in domestic prices;

The formula for measurement of the "pass through" effect may be
explained as follows. The increase in export price to an importing country
i (${}_iP_x^k$) whose currency appreciated (depreciated) with respect to the
exporter's currency, is compared with the increase in export price to an
importing country C (Control), whose currency remained stable, or relatively so with respect to the exporter's currency. The theoretical validity
of the "control country" approach and the desirable attributes of a
country selected as control are amply discussed in Kreinin's paper. The
basic idea is that the control country is used as a proxy for a situation that
would have emerged had there been no exchange rate variability.

The terms ${}_cER^k$ introduced into equation (1) makes allowance for the
situation where the control country's currency experienced some (smaller)
variation in terms of K's currency; the possible effects of differences in
internal rates of inflation in the i and c countries that might filter through
on to the level of prices agreed for import transactions is discounted by
$({}_cP_d - {}_cP_i)$.

The formula can likewise be applied in the case of an appreciation of
the exporter country's currency; in this case the "pass through" effect
would be interpreted as the extent to which the exporter currency
appreciation accounted for price increases to the i country.

[1] Yet a further complication arises if exporting agencies request payment in a third currency,
or if national governments place restrictions on the availability of certain foreign currencies
to their importers.

If we denote the expression $[_cP_x^k - _cER^k + (_cP_d - _iP_d)]$ in the numerator by $_cP_x^k adj$, formula (1) can then be restated as:

$$\alpha_i = 1 - \left(\frac{_iP_x^k - _cP_x^k adj}{_iER^k} \right) \qquad (2)$$

The expression in the bracket in formula (2) may be termed the "absorption" effect. If its value is less than one and positive, we have what will be termed a "moderate" pass through effect. In the case of an appreciating importing country currency, this may be interpreted as meaning that K's export prices have risen to the i country relatively to a situation where no appreciation had taken place, but that some of the rise has been offset by the "pass through" effect; the advantage to the importer of the effect of the appreciation has been "absorbed" by the relative increase in K's export prices to an extent measured by the "absorption" effect. In the case of a depreciating importing country the disadvantage of its depreciation has to some extent been "absorbed" by a relative decrease in K's export prices, relative to a situation of bilateral exchange rate stability.

Should, however, the "absorption" effect assume a positive value greater than one, it becomes evident that K's export prices have taken a path, contrary to expectations derived on the basis of the exchange rate variation. The export prices to an appreciating currency importer have risen by more than his currency appreciation, whereas they have fallen to a depreciating currency importer by more than his currency depreciation. This situation could conceivably arise if, for example, a depreciating importer's currency has depreciated less with that of a second exporter and is thus in a stronger position to bargain with the original exporter. Conversely, if the appreciation of an importing country's currency with the first exporter exceeds the rate of appreciation with a second importer, it may be willing to offer a higher price to the first exporter.

Finally, where the "absorption" effect assumes a negative value the overall movement in K's export price has reinforced the movement to be expected on the basis of the exchange rate variation. For an appreciating currency importing country, prices fell more than in a hypothetical situation of no bilateral currency variation, whereas for a depreciating currency importer they rose more. In each case, the "pass-through" effect to the importer was magnified rather than absorbed by the movement in K's export prices. This situation could arise if an exporter were anxious to secure receipts in an appreciating currency, or to avoid loss in a depreciating currency.

4 THE ANALYSIS OF THE EXCHANGE RATE EFFECTS ON TRADE

Although this model does not take account of multilateral variations in exchange rates between competing exporters, it has several advantages in an application to trade in agricultural commodities. In particular any effects on trade with the i country deriving from conditions of K country supply, notably seasonal variations in production, domestic consumption of the exported product and price control over exports, should also be reflected in trade with the control country, and should not therefore invalidate the analysis. Parallel conditions influencing the two importer markets can less safely be assumed not to influence the price differential and, where they exist and are of sufficient importance, may be expected to introduce a bias in specific markets.

4a *The data*

The six commodities eventually selected for more detailed investigation were: wheat and maize, commodities which are also produced in importing countries, and cotton, tea, cocoa and coffee, commodities which are not produced in the major importing countries. The original intention was to study trade flows from the three major exporting regions to each of their three major export markets (defined on the basis of 1976 trade statistics), but it has not been possible yet completely to fulfil this objective.

Trade with centrally planned economies has been excluded, as have trade flows with the EEC area for commodities subject to "intervention prices".

The 3 digit SITC level of disaggregation of commodity data obtained from UN statistics was used; for certain products a finer level of disaggregation would have been desirable, but extremely difficult to obtain, for exports by destination.

Bilateral currency rates of exchange were obtained by conversion through units of national currency per US dollar, as published by the IMF, taking, where possible, the period average rates at their national market to US par rates.

As a measure of the rates of internal inflation, national consumer price indices relating to food, derived from UN statistics were used for all commodities except cotton; for cotton the corresponding consumer price index (all items) was used.

Where data permitted, the calculations were made first for the four-year period 1973 to 1976 and subsequently, because of its peculiarity, for two sub-periods 1973–74 and 1975–76.

The percentage changes in prices, exchange rates and quantities were taken as the difference between the end-of-period and beginning-of-period values of each variable calculated as a percentage of the average annual value of the variable in the time period under consideration.

4b *The results*
The calculations were performed for three time periods: the four-year 1973–74 and 1975–76 and the two sub-periods 1973–74 and 1975–76. The subdivision of the four-year period was considered necessary because there is greater likelihood of the erosion of the "pass through" effect over a longer time period and because it seemed interesting to examine the period 1973–74 in isolation, given the unusual disturbances in the market in that period.

Altogether 38 combinations of importer – control countries were considered. Some difficulties were encountered in identifying appropriate control countries. A major requisite of the control country is that its exchange rate should be stable in terms of the exporter's currency. Because of the continuous fluctuation in exchange rates, it was rarely possible to use the same importer – control country combination for each of the three time-periods.

The detailed results for each trade flows are available separately on request.

In Tables 1, 2, and 3 the results are classified for each time period according to whether the "pass-through" effects were moderate, reinforced by price movements ("absorption" effect negative) or offset by contrary price movements ("absorption" effect positive and greater than 1). The breakdown is given for each commodity according to whether the importing country currency appreciated or depreciated.

Of the three possible outcomes for a depreciating currency importer, that where commodity price movement proved contrary to the exchange rate effect was the least unfavourable. The most unfavourable outcome was that where commodity price movement and exchange rate effect reinforced each other. Conversely, for an appreciating currency importer and situation of "price movement reinforce" was the most favourable and the least favourable was that where commodity price movement was contrary to the exchange rate effect. By "favourable" is meant that unit price of imports in domestic currency would be relatively lower, and thus less likely to cause inflationary pressure.

Table 1, refers to the four-year period, and depreciating importers are in the majority. It can be seen that the number of cases where a moderate pass through effect is detected is very small and apply only to depreciating importers, implying an unfavourable situation for them. Rows Bi and Cii of the table indicate situations where relative price movements have been upwards and unfavourable to the importers and clearly they predominate. Nevertheless almost one-third of the observations are contained in row Bii which indicates a relative fall in price to appreciating importer currencies. It is worth noting that the observations in line Bii represent more than half the appreciating importer countries and it may perhaps be inferred that the relative price reductions may mark a greater willingness of exporters to trade with such countries, as well as a fear of losing trade to competing exporters.

TABLE 1 *Results of estimates of "pass through" effects for 1973–76* (number of cases)

	Wh.	M	Co.	T	Cf.	Ct.	Total
A. *Moderate "pass through"*							
(i) depreciating importer	1	1	0	0	0	0	2
(ii) appreciating importer	0	0	0	0	0	0	0
B. *Price movement reinforced*							
(i) depreciating importer	5	1	0	1	0	1	8
(ii) appreciating importer	1	0	1	1	1	2	6
C. *Price movement contrary*							
(i) depreciating importer	0	1	1	0	1	0	3
(ii) appreciating importer	0	0	1	3	1	0	5
D. *Totals*							
(i) depreciating importer	6	3	1	1	1	1	13
(ii) appreciating importer	1	0	2	4	2	2	11

TABLE 2 *Results of estimates of "pass through" effects for 1973–74* (number of cases).

	Wh.	M	Co.	T	Cf.	Ct.	Total
A. *Moderate "pass through"*							
(i) depreciating importer	1	1	0	0	0	3	5
(ii) appreciating importer	0	0	0	0	0	0	0
B. *Price movement reinforced*							
(i) depreciating importer	0	1	0	0	0	0	1
(ii) appreciating importer	0	0	0	0	0	2	2
C. *Price movement contrary*							
(i) depreciating importer	3	0	0	0	0	0	3
(ii) appreciating importer	2	0	0	0	0	0	2
D. *Totals*							
(i) depreciating importer	4	2	0	0	0	3	9
(ii) appreciating importer	2	0	0	0	0	2	4

TABLE 3 *Results of estimates of "pass through" effect for 1975–76* (number of cases)

	Wh.	M	Co.	T	Cf.	Ct.	Total
A. *Moderate "pass through"*							
(i) depreciating importer	0	0	0	0	0	0	0
(ii) appreciating importer	1	0	1	1	1	2	6
B. *Price movement reinforced*							
(i) depreciating importer	2	2	0	2	0	1	7
(ii) appreciating importer	1	1	2	3	2	2	11
C. *Price movement contrary*							
(i) depreciating importer	0	0	0	0	0	0	0
(ii) appreciating importer	2	0	0	0	0	0	2
D. *Totals*							
(i) depreciating importer							
(ii) appreciating importer	4	1	3	4	3	4	19

Key: Wh. = Wheat; M. = Maize; Co. = Cocoa; T. = Tea; Cf. = Coffee; Ct. = Cotton.

Table 2, relating to the period 1973–74 shows a greater incidence of the moderate "pass-through" effect almost in half the cases. All, however, apply to depreciating currency importers and indicate that benefits of a relative price decrease have been offset by a currency depreciation. In this period, the appreciating importer countries are evenly divided between the extremes of a highly favourable situation and a highly unfavourable situation, with no case falling into the classification of a moderate pass-through effect.

The results for the period 1975–76 are shown in Table 3. This period was more tranquil than the other two, and therefore the results can be expected to be more meaningful. A moderate pass-through effect is shown for appreciating importer countries, and it covered one third of their group. The majority of appreciating currency importers fell into the category where price movement reinforced the "pass through" effect. Looking at this phenomenon from the point of view of the exporting country it would be necessary to examine the relative elasticity of demand for his exports before any conclusion could be drawn as to benefits ensuing in terms of foreign currency receipts. Whilst all cases of appreciating currency countries coincided with outcomes favourable to the importer, it is a striking fact that all cases for depreciating importers correspond with the most unfavourable of outcomes i.e. where price movements reinforced the exchange rate effect.

5 CONCLUSIONS

The method used here has allowed us to identify the direction of an actual change in export prices relative to a (simulated) situation of constant exchange rates and relate this to change in exchange rates in a bilateral trading situation.

The results obtained have permitted us to identify two types of situation in which price changes have assumed a direction coherent with the exchange rate variation where a moderate "pass-through" effect has resulted, and where price movements have reinforced the exchange rate effect. The majority of cases fell into these two categories (49 out of 58 in the three periods considered; 33 out of 39 in the two-year periods).

Analysis of the shorter time periods takes an added significance in the context of the controversy over the efficacy of the use of exchange rate policy in correcting balance of payments disequilibria. Even if one accepts that "given sufficient time for adjustment . . . all internationally traded goods will command the same price everywhere" (the "law of one price" as summarised in (8)) the price effect, through exchange rate variation, may be discernible in a relatively short time period.

The question here, however, has not been posed in terms of balance of payments, but rather an attempt has been made to shed light on the possible price effects of exchange rate variation on commodity trade. The evidence is not yet sufficient to indicate that the contribution of commodity trade to balance of payments could be altered by a policy of exchange rate manipulation. For this, further evidence of import and export elasticities of demand would be necessary. Moreover, as is well known, large sections of trade in agricultural commodities are subject to regulation which eliminates price advantage, and thus, by implication, any advantage deriving from exchange rate variation. Insofar as the price effects of exchange rate variation affect the internal rate of inflation, the results of our analysis reconfirm the advantages of appreciating currency importers.

Although the analysis suggests that exchange rate variations are "passed through" into commodity prices, it has not been possible to make direct comparisons with what might have been a comparable situation with fixed exchange rates and devaluation. One feasible answer could be that in anticipation of devaluation, price movements to strong currency countries would tend downwards and vice versa for weak currency countries (an effect corresponding with "Price movement reinforced" in the present exchange rate situation). It is possible that this would create greater price instability than the present system of floating exchange rates at times when currency realignment became necessary.

REFERENCES

[1] Baron, D.P. "Flexible exchange rates, forward markets and the level of trade"; *Amer. Ec. Rev.*, June 1976.
[2] Bredahl, M.E., Meyers, W.H., Collins, K.J. "The elasticity of foreign demand for U.S. agricultural products: the importance of price transmission elasticity"; *Amer. Journ. Agr. Ec.*, February 1979.
[3] Ethier, W. "International Trade and forward exchange market"; *Amer. Ec. Rev.*, June 1973.
[4] Johnson, D.G. "World Agriculture, commodity policy and price variability"; *Amer. Journ. Agr. Ec.*, December 1975.
[5] Johnson, H.G. "Elasticity, absorption, Keynesian multipler, Keynesian policy and monetary approaches to devaluation theory: a simple goemetric exposition"; *Amer. Ec. Rev.*, June 1976.
[6] Johnson, P.R., Grennes, T., Thursby, M. "Devaluation, foreign trade controls and domestic wheat prices"; *Amer. Journ. Agr. Ec.*, November 1977.
[7] Kaldor, N. "Inflation and recession in the world economy"; *Ec. Journ.*, December 1976.
[8] Kreinin, M.E. "The effect of exchange rate changes on prices and volume of trade"; *IMF Staff Papers*, July 1977.
[9] Schuh, G.E. "The exchange rate and US agriculture"; *Amer. Journ. Agr. Ec.*, February 1974.
[10] Vellianits Fidas, A. "The impact of devaluation on U.S. agricultural exports"; *Agr. Ec. Research*, July 1976.

DISCUSSION OPENING – KAZUSHI OHKAWA

Exchange rate variations are expected to change the relative prices of exportable and importable commodities and hence induce responses in their supply and demand. These changes in turn, are expected to restore an equilibrium in the balance of payments. Such simple expectations,

APPENDIX TABLE 1

Commodity	K Country	Importing Country	Control Country	"Absorption effect"[i] 1973–76	1973–74	1975–76
Wheat	USA	Japan	Korea	N F	N F	R,4.16
		Japan	India	N F	R,3.72	R,6.09
		India	Japan	D,–2.70	N F	N F
		Korea	Japan	D,0.56	D,1.16	N F
		Korea	Korea	N F	N F	R,–17.43
	Canada	Korea	Japan	D,0.56	D,1.16	N F
		Brasil	India	D,–2.46	N F	N F
		Brasil	Japan	D,–0.94	D,0.07	D,–1.13
		Japan	Algeria	D,–1.38	D,3.93	D,–2.15
	Australia	Egypt	Algeria	D,–2.57	D,2.00	N F
Maize	USA	Japan	Japan	R,–0.11	R,3.59	R,0.30
		Spain	Korea	D,0.26	N F	R,–3.43
		Spain	Japan	N F	N F	D,–1.08
		Korea	Korea	D,3.27	N F	D,–0.31
Cotton	USA	Japan	Spain	D,–1.14	D,–0.58	N F
		Korea	Japan	D,–2.29	D,0.71	N F
		Korea	Korea	N F	N F	R,0.36
		Italy	Japan	N F	D,0.03	N F
		Italy	Korea	N F	N F	R,–1.22
	Turkey	Switzerland	Germany	R,–83.93	D,0.67	D,–1.79
		USA	Switzerland	D,17.92	D,0.49	N F
		USA	Germany	N F	R,–10.30	R,0.92
Cocoa	Ivory Coast	USA	France	R,20.35	N A	R,–0.31
		USA	Netherlands	D,28.49	N A	R,0.31
		Netherlands	USA	N F	N A	R,–1.39
Coffee	Ivory Coast	USA	France	R,–3.16	N A	R,0.55
		USA	Netherlands	R,13.52	N A	R,–2.30
		Netherlands	France	R,1.78	N A	N F
Tea	Sri Lanka	Netherlands	USA	R,1.55	N A	R,–1.72
		USA	UK	R,1.49	N A	N F
		UK	USA	N F	N A	R,0.53
	India	USA	UK	N F	N A	R,–1.22
		UK	Netherlands	D,–1.82	N A	D,–2.77
		Netherlands	USA	R,1.58	N A	D,–1.08
		USA	Netherlands	N F	N A	R,–1.50

N F – Not Feasible: exchange rate variation of the control country exceeded that of i country;
N A – No Available: data 1973 not available;
R – i country's currency appreciating;
D – i country's currency depreciating;
i – "Absorption effect": see formula (2) in text.

however, are possible only if the exchange adjustments are reflected in the prices of tradable goods, instead of being interrupted by the effects of other factors related and unrelated. Accordingly, what we call "pass-through" effects and their measurements are at issue. This is an important but controversial issue at the aggregate level, pertaining to the relations of balance of payments and domestic prices and home inflation, particularly in the context of comparison between the conditional floating system and the fixed exchange rate system. On the other hand, it is also important for us to analyse specific features of commodity markets in international trade because each commodity (or group of similar commodities) has its own performance of supply and demand and hence price.

The Loseby-Venzi paper seems to have an intermediate nature between the aggregate and the commodity approach with taking up major agricultural commodities. Their measurements and major conclusion pertain to those commodities, but some discussion and speculative observations are tried in relation to the problem of the macro approach.

May I suggest that the problems left for further research may be fruitful if deeper scrutiny is carried out in a specific context of each major commodity, including the measurement of elasticities of export supply and import demand. In this connection there are just two points I wish to raise along this line, apart from measuring technique.

1   Do you identify any different features between the two groups: wheat, maize (products also produced in importing country), and cotton, cocoa, coffee and tea (products not produced in importing country)? This aspect pertains also to countries, DCs and LDCs.

2   In general, can we identify special features of agricultural commodities as compared to industrial goods? In addition to the seasonal variations you mentioned, I am tempted to wish to know more about the characteristics of agricultural commodities, particularly in measuring the pass-through effects. I am inclined to share a speculation that in the case of agricultural commodities the effects of the other factors may be greater. In saying this I do not intend to cast clouds on your major conclusion that the pass-through effects are discernible for agricultural commodities, even though the findings suggest diversification.

GENERAL DISCUSSION – RAPPORTEUR: ALBERT J. NYBERG

In discussion it was noted that before World War II there were free exchange rates and these were frequently determined by wholesale price index ratios. It was suggested that exchange rate changes would tend to cause changes in the price of manufactured products (where they or their components were traded) but the price of raw materials would not change.

An enquiry was also made as to the practical relevance of floating exchange rates for LDCs, as the effects are minimal in the short run.

In reply to the general discussion, Margaret Loseby indicated that in theory, arbitrage occurs in primary commodity markets in both place and time but in practice she felt that a one-world price did *not* exist. She agreed that in many LDC markets the effects and relevance were minimal.

Participants in the discussion included Ardron B. Lewis and Ali Mohammad.

STEFAN TANGERMANN

Policies of the European Community and Agricultural Trade with Developing Countries

1 INTRODUCTION

The Common Agricultural Policy (CAP) of the EC and policies of the EC *vis-à-vis* the Third World have at least one feature in common. Both belong to those policy domains in which policies on the Community level, as opposed to national policies of the member countries, play an important role. This is not to say that national policies are no longer significant in both areas. But it means that the Community has been surrendered the sole responsibility for a major subset of policy instruments, as in the case of agricultural policy, or that national policies have been complemented by an active and extended Community policy, as happened in the case of policies towards the Third World. This common feature, however, does not guarantee, and in fact has not always entailed, that policies in both domains are consistently co-ordinated and harmonized. It rather has become a conventional wisdom to state that the Common Agricultural Policy has done much harm to the Third World and is in notorious conflict with aid and trade policies of the Community.

The present paper makes an attempt at analysing the nature of this conflict. Limited space prohibits comprehensive coverage of even the major issues involved. Instead, a rather subjective choice of some specifically controversial points is made. In the following section the impact of the CAP on the Third World and analytical problems in evaluating it are discussed. Section 3 broadens the framework and deals with agricultural trade in the context of EC trade preferences for developing countries. In the final section some possible changes in EC policies are indicated. Throughout the paper the problems are mentioned, rather than investigated extensively. An earlier paper by the same author presents a slightly more detailed discussion and some statistical evidence (Tangermann, 1978).

440

2 THE COMMON AGRICULTURAL POLICY AND AGRICULTURAL TRADE WITH THE THIRD WORLD

The main objective of the CAP is to protect farmers in the member states from too high a pressure to adjust in the process of economic change. In practical terms this means that the CAP is orientated towards supporting European farmers' incomes. This domestic objective is pursued with instruments which have decisive external effects on the international level. Income support is brought about by price protection which necessarily affects trade in agricultural products. In this respect the CAP is not much different from agricultural policies in many other industrialized countries and their effects on agricultural trade of the Third World. The specific method of price support in the CAP, however, results in some peculiar consequences which deserve special attention.

Agricultural protectionism in industrialized countries and its significance for LDCs
The trade structure of most developing countries is characterized by a predominant share of raw materials in total exports. It seems logical to conclude from this that LDCs have a comparative advantage, indeed in many cases the exclusive potential, to produce raw materials. Any policy of industrialized countries which impedes trade in raw materials must, therefore, be detrimental to LDCs. Protectionism in agricultural trade falls under this heading. The CAP would, then, have to be considered particularly harmful, as it provides for comparatively high rates of protection (farm product prices in the EC are among the highest in the world) and because of its comprehensiveness (currently about 90 per cent of the value of agricultural production in the Community is covered by CAP market regimes).

The view that most developing countries have "natural" advantages in raw materials including agricultural commodities is, however, contrasted by the statement that agricultural protectionism in industrialized countries typically applies to temperate zone products in which few if any developing countries are competitive at all (Heidhues, 1977). Looked at from this angle, liberalization in agricultural trade would primarily benefit exporters among the industrialized countries, above all the highly competitive farming industry in North America.

These differing views indicate that the impact of agricultural policies in industrialized countries on the Third World can be evaluated only on the basis of an analysis which differentiates with respect to commodities and countries concerned. At least, commodities exported by LDCs (and those countries which export them) have to be distinguished from commodities imported by LDCs (and those countries which import them). On their export side the developing countries are certainly hurt by protectionism in industrialized countries. But even this statement is only partly useful, because it deals only with actual exports and neglects potential exports. However, any empirical investigation of these issues is extremely difficult.

An analysis of current trade flows does not provide the necessary information as lack of exports of certain products from developing countries could be explained as well by low competitiveness as by import restrictions in industrialized countries. Even the fact that a given developing country is currently importing a certain product on a large scale is not necessarily an argument against its potential export capacity, as recent developments in India's wheat economy may demonstrate.

A direct evaluation of comparative advantage on the basis of micro economic data is empirically difficult because of lack of reliable data for international comparison and theoretically questionable with respect to the underlying economic reasoning. Thus, one is left with the necessity to hypothesize about the changes in trade volumes which would take place in LDCs if world market prices would increase as a consequence of reduced protection in industrialized countries (see, for example, FAO, 1971, and Valdes, 1979). There is, however, by no means a consensus among researchers in the area of international trade as to the rate by which world market prices for agricultural commodities would increase if protectionism were abandoned (Johnson, 1973), and we know relatively little about the way in which the export volumes of developing countries would react to these price changes. Thus it is extremely hard to estimate quantitatively the welfare losses which individual exporting countries in the Third World have to bear as a consequence of the inward looking agricultural and trade policies of developed countries.

Equally difficult is an assessment of the way in which LDCs are affected on their import side. One line of argument is concerned with the impact of industrialized countries' policies on self-sufficiency in food in the Third World. Depressed world market prices, it is argued, provide weak incentives for output expansion in developing countries which, therefore, remain dependent on supplies from developed countries and exposed to the vagaries of the world market. This statement may be a correct description of actual developments, as some developing countries made relatively little efforts to increase their agricultural production. Yet, it is not necessarily a logical criticism of the behaviour of industrialized countries. If there had been stronger desires to expand own food output in these developing countries, there would have been policy instruments available to provide domestic producers with better incentives while still, as a nation, benefiting from low import prices.

Similar remarks apply to investigations which show that protectionism in industrialized countries places a foreign exchange burden on LDCs because it induces them to import more than they would have done otherwise (Valdes, 1979). If a country suffers from balance of payments problems, an increase in its import prices does certainly not help this country. The reduced volume of imports, as caused by higher world market prices, could as well have been reached by domestic measures. Rising import prices as such impose a loss rather than a benefit on an importer. Here again it has to be stressed that this result of economic reasoning does not necessarily explain reality where governments may hesitate to promote domestic agricultural expansion unless rising import prices force them to do so.

In terms of economic welfare the Third World gains from protectionism in those temperate zone products in which LDCs are net importers.[1] The size of this gain differs widely among countries and commodities. The overall amount of the gain for the Third World, however, will hardly be negligible. Consider for example the case of grains. On aggregate the developing countries import considerable amounts of grain. During the past decades the total volume of grain (net) imported by developing countries increased at high rates, indeed (Heidhues, 1977). Several countries in the Third World are heavily dependent on grain imports to sustain minimal levels of food supply and encounter major balance of payments problems. For these countries as for the developing countries on aggregate, policies of price support to grain farmers in industrialized countries, as implemented for example in the EC, must be beneficial. This applies not only to concessionary grain exports to these countries, effected as food aid and at least partly designed as surplus disposal in industrialized countries. The greater part of the benefits stems probably from comparatively low prices at which these countries can import grain commercially from the world market.

Of course it has to be noted that farm support policies in developed countries with their depressing effects on world market prices are by no means invented in order to help the Third World. While grain trade policies of the USA exhibit at least a certain amount of feeling of responsibility for world market developments, the EC grain policy lacks any sign of taking more into account than just domestic problems. But still it could be detrimental for the Third World on aggregate and rather disastrous for some individual developing countries if the EC would, according to many suggestions of its critics, lower its price support to grain farmers, which would result in decreased exports of soft wheat and increased imports of coarse grains and corresponding price rises on world grain markets. Importing countries currently are to a certain extent unintentional free riders on domestic farm support policies in industrialized countries. This fact, however, tends to become forgotten in international debates about the effects of protectionism in agricultural trade. In the GATT negotiations, for example, liberalization of trade in temperate zone agricultural products is essentially looked at as an issue to be discussed among industrialized countries. Developing countries in these negotiations are primarily seen in their role as exporters who would anyhow gain from decreasing protectionism in developed countries.

Destabilization: a specific feature of the Common Agricultural Policy
While it is hard to derive general conclusions about the overall effect of agricultural protectionism in the EC on the situation of developing countries, there is at least one aspect of the CAP which is obviously detrimental to the world food economy and has specifically negative consequences for developing countries. The combination of variable import levies/ex-

port restitutions at the border and fixed intervention prices internally shields EC markets for agricultural products against fluctuations on world markets. This means that the EC makes nearly no contribution to the stabilization of world markets for agricultural products. Instead of bearing a fair part of the burden of instability in the world food economy the EC rather exports a large share of its internal supply and demand fluctuations. Thus by granting stability to the domestic market the EC aggravates the problem of instability on world markets. An obvious example of this behaviour was the reaction of the EC to the boom on international food markets 1972–75 (Josling, 1977). In this respect the CAP compares unfavourably with agricultural policies in the USA which in the past bore a major part of the burden of instability (Heidhues and Hollstein, 1978).

Clearly the EC, neither as an importer nor as an exporter of agricultural commodities, has an interest in fluctuating world markets. The destabilizing effects of the CAP again have been unintended by-products of the preoccupation with stable domestic markets and of the inflexibility in adjusting a supranational policy to changing conditions in the environment. During the recent negotiations in the framework of GATT and about a new international grains agreement the EC has shown some signs of willingness to accept a more responsible role. But still one feels that the EC is not sufficiently prepared to make a significant contribution to the stabilization of the international food economy.

Theoretical economists obsessed with static welfare economics still argue about the international distribution of gains and losses from instability (Turnovsky, 1978), and empirical research on the effects of fluctuating world markets still has not reached a consistent conclusion as to whether export fluctuations do or do not hamper economic development (Stein, 1977). From a pragmatic point of view, however, one may state that neither producers nor consumers nor governments like instability as such and that the negative consequences of world market instability are the more felt by a country the worse the balance of payments situation of that country is and the less the opportunities of that country are to diversify its exports and imports. From this point of view developing countries with high shares of agricultural commodities in their export earnings or with urgent needs to import food are most heavily affected by world market instabilities as caused or aggravated, among others, by the behaviour of the EC (Johnson, 1975).

3 THE FRAMEWORK OF EC TRADE POLICIES *vis-à-vis* DEVELOPING COUNTRIES: A DOUBLE HIERARCHY OF CONCESSIONS

Agricultural trade relations between the Community and the Third World have to be seen in the context of overall EC trade policies *vis-à-vis* developing countries. While the CAP in general exhibits a high degree of protectionism, the Community has granted developing countries a whole array of trade concessions. This raises the question of consistency in EC policies. Without going into any detail some remarks on this issue seem in place. The main point to be made here is that the Community has established a complex system of trade preferences, which, however, have not been shaped according to the global needs of the Third World. Instead the trade concessions of the Community rather reflect the structure of EC interests with respect to domestic output composition and foreign policy relations.

The commodity structure of concessions
Variable levies are provided in the CAP for those products for which the most intense support is desired. These are in principle commodities which are produced in the Community in noticeable amounts and contribute significantly to farmers' incomes. *Ad valorem* duties are in cases combined with variable levies (e.g. beef). Mostly, however, duties are provided for those products which play only a minor role in EC agricultural production and which are not close substitutes for domestic products. Such commodities, finally, which are used in EC agriculture only as inputs and do not compete with domestic production, as is the case with feeding-stuffs like oilseeds, enter the Community with low or zero tariffs.

Concessions on trade with third countries are, according to this classification, less harmful to Community producers if they take the form of reductions in *ad valorem* duties, and most intense if they apply to variable duties. This said, it is not surprising to find that most concessions in agricultural trade which the EC has offered to developing countries concern reductions of or exemptions from *ad valorem* duties. Most of these concessions apply either to agricultural raw materials for manufacturing, which are treated by the Community like industrial products, or to products listed in Annex II of the Treaty of Rome which contains agricultural commodities which have low significance in the EC and are not covered by the CAP (Harris, 1975; Ritson, 1978). These concessions do no, or hardly any, harm to farmers in the Community and have the main effect of lowering prices for EC consumers.

An intermediate position is held by wine, fruit and vegetables. These products have considerable importance for farm incomes in specific parts of the EC and still are not afforded variable levies, mainly for technical reasons.[2] On the other hand Mediterranean and African countries have strong interests in these products. Major trade concessions in this area are restricted to Mediterranean and ACP countries. In part they are limited to certain months, restricted to specified quota and include obligations to observe minimum import prices. But still they are important achievements.

When it comes to leviable products concessions become sparse. This is the domain of major temperate zone products. The only two products of this group for which the EC has granted concessions are beef and sugar. Nevertheless these are probably the temperate zone products for which

developing countries are most competitive. With both products concessions are restricted to ACP countries.³ For beef they take the form of
exemptions from the fixed duty while additional variable levies remain
unaffected.⁴ Sugar, finally, is the only product for which exemptions from
variable levies – for a given maximum volume of imports – have been
granted. Furthermore in the case of sugar the Community guaranteed a
price comparable to domestic producer prices.

The country structure of concessions
The productwise hierarchy of EC trade concessions is paralleled by a
complex hierarchy of trade arrangements between the EC and specific
groups of third countries (Tulloch, 1975; Coffey, 1976; Tovias, 1977).
These country-specific trade concessions in part reflect a multiplicity of
European foreign policy interests, ranging from old colonial responsibilities to military–strategic considerations.

By ranking groups of EC trading partners according to increasing
degrees of preferential treatment, the following rough classification
emerges. Non-beneficiaries are those developed countries, mainly non-
European, who, being contracting parties to GATT, enjoy nothing more
than most-favoured-nation (MFN) tariff treatment. Worse off than these
countries are only non-GATT partners who are discriminated against,
mainly state trading countries. Countries in these groups have to bear the
full burden of EC agricultural protectionism.

Next to these categories come already those developing countries
which are subject to treatment under the EC Generalized System of
Preferences. While these countries have duty-free access to the Community market for industrial products, subject to effectively binding ceiling
limitations for "sensitive products", in the area of agricultural trade the
preferences are restricted to duty concessions for certain agricultural
goods. Though the list of agricultural goods covered has been successively
extended to include more products of specific interest for single
developed countries, it still applies mainly to products which are unimportant in international trade and have low significance for Community
producers and processors. It basically leaves out all products subject to
the CAP.⁵ In a sense significant for the attitude of the EC is that in 1974,
when the GSP schemes of the United Kingdom, Denmark and Ireland
were adapted to that of the Community, the slightly more liberal treatment of agricultural products in the schemes of the joining countries was
downward adjusted to the EC practice (Murray, 1977).

By far more intense are the trade preferences which the Community
provided in what became called its Global Mediterranean Policy. This
policy originated from the necessity to take into account old political and
economic links between France and the Maghreb countries, was
extended for reasons of equal treatment to other Mediterranean countries competing with Maghreb exports, and had to be still further diversified for the sake of avoiding political disequilibrium (Andersen, 1975).
This somewhat accidental development was consolidated and converted

into a deliberate policy of establishing closer political and economic relations with a region of major interest for the Community, when a new round of negotiations was initiated in 1975 under the notion of a global concept of Mediterranean policy. Preferences in agricultural trade offered to Mediterranean countries cover a considerably greater number of products than the GSP and are of specific significance in the area of fruit, vegetables and wine. The core products of the CAP, however, which are protected by variable levies, are essentially not affected.

It is hard to evaluate whether the African, Caribbean and Pacific (ACP) countries, which is the last group of developing countries to be mentioned here,[6] are treated better or worse than the Mediterranean countries in terms of trade concessions. Formally the preferences granted to ACP countries under the Lomé Convention range further. On the other hand the significance of and competitiveness in some products concerned is higher in Mediterranean countries so that ACP countries in some cases can make less use of the preferences. Nevertheless the ACP countries is the only group which is afforded concessions for central CAP products like beef and sugar. Furthermore the ACP countries are treated specifically as they are exempted from the general application of safeguard clauses in specific cases like beef. Apart from the preferential tariff treatment this latter privilege at times has caused specific trouble among discriminated developing countries.

The privileged treatment of the ACP countries has far reaching historical roots. Most of the ACP countries are former colonies of EC member countries. At the insistence of France special arrangements for colonies were guaranteed already in the Treaty of Rome which provided for the colonies the opportunity of association with the Community. After most colonies had become independent the Yaoundé Convention was signed in 1963 and renewed in 1969. A similar development took place when the United Kingdom entered the Community in 1973 and sought compensation for the less developed Commonwealth countries. This led finally to the Lomé Convention of 1975, which, in addition to trade concessions, covers aid, industrial co-operation and a scheme for stabilizing export earnings of ACP countries (STABEX).

Global versus discriminatory approaches
The trade and aid policy of the EC *vis-à-vis* the Third World is very much characterized by what could essentially be called a discriminatory philosophy. It is discriminating against products which in the EC are considered sensitive in economic and political terms; agricultural products covered by the CAP are a major case in point. It is discriminating in favour of countries which have had or which are hoped will establish close political and economic links with the Community. It is tempting to describe this approach as a policy which is governed more by the interests of the Community than by the interests of the beneficiaries.

On an abstract level this policy could be contrasted by an approach which is global in the sense that it embraces any developing countries

meeting a general set of criteria and covers all products which are significant from the point of view of the developing countries (McQueen, 1979).
Clearly such a design were preferable as an approach towards a world-
wide balanced political and economic development. One could argue that
a community of countries, devoted to the general principle of integration,
should more easily be able to adopt such a global approach than a single
nation.

But one has to question whether this is a realistic alternative. If the EC
had been denied the option to design its policy according to spheres of
interest, would the alternative outcome have been more favourable for
the Third World as a whole? The answer to this question is highly
speculative. Part of it might be provided by comparing the EC policy with
policies of other countries towards the Third World. Viewed from this
angle the record of the EC does not look altogether bad.

4   ASPIRATIONS OF THE THIRD WORLD AND POTENTIAL OF THE EC

It is not easy to find a balanced evaluation of EC policies *vis-à-vis* the
Third World. On the one hand the major endeavour of the Community to
devise an active and progressive policy towards those countries for which
it feels a specific responsibility has to be acknowledged. On the other
hand some EC policies have clearly been detrimental to individual
developing countries and the Third World as a whole.

In the specific field of agriculture, EC policies have exhibited positive
as well as negative aspects, as has been discussed above. From the point of
view of aspirations in the Third World many problems remain unsolved.
Beyond some of the rhetorics in current international negotiations there
are a number of concrete demands of developing countries concerning
agriculture which have to be seriously considered if the state of the world
food economy is to be prevented from deteriorating. These demands can
be roughly summarized in four points:

1   Increased and secure access of developing countries' agricultural
    exports to markets in developed countries, at stable and high
    prices;
2   Safe supply of food imported by developing countries, at stable
    prices;
3   Long run commitments to an adequate volume of food aid for
    countries with chronic food scarcities and a sufficient stock of food
    reserves for emergency relief;
4   Increasing flows of financial and technical aid for the development
    of agricultural production in the Third World.

The EC could certainly improve on its current record and make major
contributions to meeting these demands. With respect to Third World
exports the list of products subject to duty concessions has to be further

extended, ceilings have to be lifted and duty reductions to be increased. The list of products treated as "sensitive" will have to be reconsidered and serious efforts to extend concessions to leviable products covered by the CAP are necessary. What seems most important is that the use of safeguard clauses should be far more limited. Disruptive import restrictions in "emergency" cases are extremely harmful for the long run development of Third World's exports.

In terms of current CAP developments a reorientation of EC policies on sugar and beef markets is urgently needed. This should be very much in the self-interest of the Community, because financial costs on these markets are mounting. Furthermore current discussions about alleviating problems on EC milk and grain markets by imposing barriers on imports of oilseeds and grain substitutes should be finally turned down. It means not only cheating EC milk producers if expansionary effects of generous increases in price support for milk are counteracted by raising feed costs. Such import barriers would also hit developing countries' exports. Furthermore these discussions have a noticeably negative influence on the climate of international trade negotiations as they run counter to the interests of the USA and reveal a low degree of feeling committed to GATT rules on the side of EC agricultural policy-makers.

With respect to the desire for stable supplies of food for imports the interests of the EC as a major grain importer very much coincide with those of grain importing countries in the Third World. Thus in the negotiations in the framework of GATT and for a new international grains agreement the EC could have backed the stand of the developing countries. To be credible, however, the Community has to show a serious willingness to shoulder a greater share of the burden of stabilizing international grain markets. To this end the EC has to be prepared to make a major contribution to an internationally co-ordinated stock policy and to adjust the destabilizing nature of its own market policy.

With respect to food aid and development aid, finally, the first step of the EC should be to fully meet its international commitments with respect to the volume of aid given. Furthermore provisions should be made for steadily increasing this volume. Commitments to raising annually the volume of aid by at least the rate of increase in the overall budget of the Community may be considered. In food aid longer run commitments are necessary. In financial and technical aid a broader geographical distribution according to the needs of recipient countries should be envisaged.

What are the main restrictions limiting further EC efforts towards improving agricultural relations with the Third World? First, there is the currently unfavourable climate in the overall economy. For agricultural policy this means in the first place that high rates of unemployment impede outmigration of labour from agriculture and structural adjustment of the farming industry. Liberalization of agricultural trade which increases adjustment needs is a particularly difficult political task under these conditions. The difficulties are aggravated by the slump in population growth, as a considerable cut in demand expansion means that agricultural market policies will have to be adjusted for this reason already.

Second there is the intrinsic inflexibility of the CAP which makes any adjustment difficult. The agricultural policy of the Community represents a delicate balance of the national interests of the member countries. Any movement which changes this balance leads to a round of negotiations in which compensating package deals are decided. This situation explains in part why the CAP reacts so slowly to internal and external pressures and why it is so difficult to co-ordinate EC agricultural policies with other policy domains.

Third, the problems involved in further enlarging the Community have to be mentioned. Not only will the process of negotiating and preparing the access of Greece, Portugal and Spain absorb much political and administrative activity and detract attention from external developments. Economic structures and commodity interests of the three newcomers are similar to those in some developing countries. And clearly outsiders will see their demands considered by the Community far behind the needs of entering countries. New problems in agricultural trade of the Community with the Third World will emerge which have not been covered by this paper.

Finally, at a somewhat different level, the Community will find itself increasingly locked up in divergencies of interests between Mediterranean and ACP countries on the one hand and the rest of developing countries on the other. Every significant additional concession offered to the first group is criticized by the latter as aggravating the discriminatory approach of the EC. Any attempt at broadening the range of beneficiaries is increasingly opposed by the Mediterranean and ACP countries as it lowers their margin of preferences and erodes their current benefits. Developing a balanced approach of Community policies towards the Third World as a whole will be one of the major tasks ahead.

NOTES

[1] Strictly speaking this is not necessarily true for all importers. If the price increase on world markets, resulting from liberalization of agricultural trade, were high enough and supply and demand response in the country concerned strong enough to make the country switch from an import to a sufficiently large export position, even a currently importing country could benefit from an increase in world market prices. In practice, however, these cases may not be too important.

[2] In situations of extremely low import prices, however, otherwise fixed *ad valorem* duties for these products may be increased. Thus in practice the import regime for these products comes close to variable levies.

[3] In the case of sugar some other developing countries are included with minor quantities.

[4] Unless the exporting country charges an export tax. In this case the

variable levy can be reduced by up to 90 per cent.

[5] Main, and important, exceptions are some concessions in the area of processed fruit and vegetables.

[6] In addition to the preferential schemes quoted here, the Community has entered into a number of bilateral agreements, with individual developing countries, mainly in South-east Asia, covering particular products.

REFERENCES

Coffey, P. *The External Economic Relations of EC*, London 1976.

FAO, "A World Price Equilibrium Model", Rome 1971.

Harris, S. "The World Commodity Scene and the Common Agricultural Policy", Centre for European Agricultural Studies, Occasional Paper No. 1, Wye 1975.

Heidhues, T. "World Food: Interdependence of Farm and Trade Policies. Trade Policy Research Centre", International Issues Series, No. 3, London 1977.

Heidhues, T. and D. Hollstein "Anpassungsmethoden bestimmter Länder oder Ländergruppen an wechselnde Knappheitslagen auf den Weltgetreidemärkten", *Agrarwirtschaft*, Vol. 27 (1978), pp. 144–56.

Johnson, D.G. *World Agriculture in Disarray*, London 1973.

Johnson, D.G. "World Agriculture, Commodity Policy and Price Variability", *American Journal of Agricultural Economics*, Vol. 57 (1975), pp. 823–8.

Josling, T. "Agricultural Protection and Stabilization Policies: An Analysis of Current Neo-Mercantilist Practices". Paper presented at the Symposium on "International Trade and Agriculture", Tucson, Arizona, 17–20 April 1977.

McQueen, M. "Trade Preferences for Developing Countries versus Most Favoured Nation Tariff Reductions: An Appraisal of the EEC's Schemes", forthcoming in the *Journal of Agricultural Economics*.

Murray, T. *Trade Preferences for Developing Countries*, London 1977.

Ritson, C. (ed.) "The Lomé Convention and the Common Agricultural Policy", Commonwealth Economic Papers No. 12, London 1978.

Stein, L. "Export Instability and Development: A review of Some Recent Findings", *Banca Nazionale del Lavoro, Quarterly Review*, No. 122 (September 1977), pp. 279–90.

Tangermann, S. "The European Community and the Third World: Problems in Food and Agriculture", paper presented at a conference on "The European Community, the Third World and the United Nations", Ralph Bunch Institute on the United Nations, Graduate School of the City University of New York, 13–18 March 1978.

Tovias, A. *Trade Preferences in Mediterranean Diplomacy*, London 1977.

Tulloch, P. *The Politics of Preferences*, London 1975.

Turnovsky, S. "The Distribution of Welfare Gains from Price Stabilization: A Survey of Some Theoretical Issues", in S.G. Adams and S.A. Klein, *Stabilizing World Commodity Markets*, Lexington, Mass. 1978.

Valdes, A. "Trade Liberalization in Agricultural Commodities and the Potential Foreign Exchange Benefits to Developing Countries", report prepared at the request of FAO, Commodities and Trade Division. International Food Policy Research Institute, Washington February 1979.

DISCUSSION OPENING – BRUCE L. GREENSHIELDS

Professor Tangermann states that his paper is an attempt to analyse the nature of the conflict between the European Community's Common Agricultural Policy (CAP), which some argue harms the developing countries, and EC concessionary trade policies which purport to help the developing countries.

The conclusion one draws from reading his analysis is that there is no conflict between these two sets of policies. While there may be an apparent theoretical conflict between protectionist policies on the one hand and concessionary trade policies on the other hand, there is no conflict between the actual effects of the two sets of policies as implemented by the EC. This conclusion follows from Professor Tangermann's assertions that EC protectionism does not harm the developing countries – he even maintains that in some cases it benefits them – and that the EC's concessionary trade policies do not in general include agricultural commodities that are protected by the CAP, thereby causing no injury to EC agriculture.

I have no quarrel with his claims about the actual effects of EC concessionary trade policies, but I find the claims about the effects of the CAP to be an unconvincing apologia for EC protectionism. Professor Tangermann states that liberalization of the EC's agricultural trade would primarily benefit the more developed countries, especially those in North America. This, he says, is because EC protectionism applies mostly to temperate zone agricultural products. Yet I would argue (and this is a verifiable fact) that all of the products covered by the CAP are produced by developing countries, in many cases in significant quantities, and in other cases at least the potential for significant production exists. And more importantly, many temperate zone products substitute in consumption for tropical zone products. Thus policies which affect temperate zone products indirectly affect tropical zone products as well.

Professor Tangermann further asserts that developing countries which are net importers of temperate zone products *benefit* from EC protectionism because EC protectionist policies depress world prices of these commodities. That EC protectionist policies depress prices is a moot point, but if we accept for a moment that they do, I suggest that the gains in consumer surplus from lower world prices of these products could be offset by losses in producer surplus, depending on the demand and supply elasticities and degree of protection in the importing countries. In any case, Professor Tangermann provides no evidence that the net change in social welfare would necessarily be positive.

This same criticism applies to his argument that the developing countries which are net importers of temperate zone products are free riders on the CAP. He again is ignoring the supply side of the market in developing countries and the fact that increases in world commodity prices positively affect farmers' incomes even if the country was a net importer of temperate zone products during some historical period.

Professor Tangermann points out that destabilization of world commodity prices is a feature of the CAP that distinguishes it from protectionist policies of developed countries outside of the EC. But he then attempts to discount empirical evidence that world price instability necessarily hampers economic development in the developing countries. He states that theoretical economists *obsessed* with static welfare economics have not reached consistent conclusions on this issue. Yet he implicitly uses the same static welfare model to make his point that lower commodity prices increase welfare in developing countries which are net importers of temperate zone products.

Professor Tangermann further suggests that if developing countries had stronger desires to expand their own food production, they would use policy instruments that would enable them to benefit from low import prices, presumably without undermining producer incentives. I would be interested in what specific policy instruments he would recommend to accomplish this. I would also like to know why the burden of adjustment to EC protectionist policies falls on the developing countries, and why the developing countries are, as he implies, in a better position to use policy instruments than the EC. After all, the EC could also benefit in social welfare terms, using Professor Tangermann's line of reasoning, by importing commodities which are available on world markets at prices well below EC intervention prices.

GENERAL DISCUSSION – RAPPORTEUR: A.J. NYBERG

Two questions were asked in the general discussion and both were concerned with the impact of expanding the EC to include the Mediterranean countries and the relationship between the CAP and EC Policies.

In reply to the opener's remarks, Professor Tangermann felt his paper had been misinterpreted. He did *not* state there was no conflict between CAP and EC and conflicts with LDCs were apparent and obvious. He agreed the EC has not granted the concessions it should have. He reiterated he did *not* state that liberalization of trade policies would help LDCs; but indicated that other authors *have* made such a statement. He re-emphasized that producers in the EC will gain from protection – the producers' surplus will not be less if a country is a net importer.

In replying to the questions he apologized for the fact that the impact of EC enlargement was too big an issue to comment on. However, he indicated that support prices on (say) wine in Spain and Greece will necessarily be high, as high as in other EC countries, and production will certainly expand. The trade of third country producers will undoubtedly be hurt.

Participants in the discussion included Magid Slama and Roberto Pasca.

ALBERTO VALDES and AMMAR SIAMWALLA

Assessing Food Insecurity in LDCs – Roles of International Schemes in Relation to LDCs

There are districts in which the position of the rural population is that of a man standing permanently up to the neck in water, so that even a ripple is sufficient to drown him.

R.H. Tawney, *Land and Labour in China*

1 INTRODUCTION

The lack of food availability to poor consumers is a problem that can be analysed under three different time frames. The first type of problem is the chronic lack of food arising out of low productive capacity, and its existence and solution extend over many years. The second is the temporary shortages that arise from the year to year fluctuations in the harvest. Finally, there is the acute shortage of food that strikes a community, usually concurrently with some form of natural disaster such as earthquakes or storms which severely damage the normal channels of delivery of food to the area. The concern of this paper will be with the second type of problem. Food security is then defined as the capacity of LDCs to finance or have access to food supplies to meet per caput target consumption levels on a year by year basis. The choice of what constitutes target consumption levels in our opinion is the heart of a country's food policy. The working definition for target consumption adopted in this paper is the trend of consumption estimated from past data. Food security as defined here does not imply a shift of the consumption trend from what it would otherwise be, although it may increase the long run level of consumption by making more food available in poor harvest years. Food security could contribute indirectly to an increase of food consumption trend by assuring governments of grain supplies in crisis years and thus supporting the implementation of national food distribution schemes. However, we do not intend to examine this secondary effect.

Food security can be looked at from a world, national, village, and even a household level. This paper focuses on the national level. At that level, low supply could force consumption per caput to fall and thus may lead to social and economic disruptions. It also has an adverse impact on scarce foreign exchange and capital resources, causing the country to forego other needed imports or to cut back on investments designed to increase the long run food supply or future export revenues.

The paper is organized as follows. Part 2 presents a description, both institutional and quantitative, of the food security situation of a sample of LDCs. Part 3 discusses various international schemes and their merits in reducing food insecurity for the LDCs.

2   INTERNAL ASPECTS OF FOOD INSECURITY

Since the focus of this paper is the assessment of the role of international schemes in alleviating food insecurity, it is important to point out from the very beginning the limitations on any international scheme from the point of view of an LDC food consumer.

Any international scheme, as presently conceived, will have to be directed via the central government of the particular LDC that faces food insecurity. It usually ends also there when either the money or the actual food is handed over to the government. Since the same government will have then to convert the resources so obtained into food for the consumer, the problem of food insecurity as faced by the government of the LDC is much broader than that faced by the international agencies. It involves essentially the problem of collating the information on the status of food supplies within the country in order to determine the requirements of food procurement on the one hand, and distributing the food to the deficit areas on the other.

The problem of collating information on the state of the harvest is acute in many countries. The range of estimates in extreme cases can differ by a factor of two or three (Lele and Candler, 1978). Even when the range of estimates as a proportion of total production is more "reasonable", it may still be large as a proportion of required imports. The resulting failure of import planning has been responsible for the frequent run-up of prices at the lean pre-harvest periods, something that will not be observed if the import plan has been used on accurate information.

The problems outlined above refer largely to the estimation of national needs. There are many countries where data have to be disaggregated to the regional level. This is particularly necessary where there are poor transport facilities within the countries. It may be more efficient in some of these cases to have local stockpiles. There are many traditional institutions and behaviour patterns that guide farmers' production and marketing decisions, and that help these societies to cope with food insecurity problems independently of any international or, indeed, of any national schemes. One example is from Northeast Thailand, where farmers tend to refrain from marketing their rice until the coming of the next monsoon when they can make better judgements concerning the prospects of the next crop.

These are the problems *prior* to the decisions to procure food supplies to meet the shortfall. Once the incremental supply arrives, there is also the problem of distributing it to reach the region or the group that otherwise would be most affected by the supply shortfall. Where the shortfall is regional, transport bottlenecks may arise, particularly if the shortfall is severe or has been allowed to develop into an acute crisis so that the supply inflow has to be concentrated in a short period of time.

In many cases, governments face a more complex problem of designing a system that will direct the incremental supplies to the poorer segments of the population. The supply shortfall and the consequent high prices usually have more impact on the food consumption of the poor than on that of the better off. In the past, many countries, particularly in South Asia, have not been able for a variety of reasons to procure enough foreign supplies to neutralize the effect of the shortfall. A consequence of this inability is the development of a public distribution system and a dual-price scheme so that the poor at least would be insulated from the effects of high prices. The needs of such a programme then become the driving force behind the government's food security concern.

Different LDCs would face different subsets of this myriad of problems. Consideration of some of these problems is relevant for some of the international schemes; for instance, accurate production statistics are essential for the operation of a food insurance type scheme. In most cases, however, they point in the direction of increased *working* stocks, an area in which the international community can put in only a modest amount of resources even though it may be an extremely critical task facing the LDC governments.

Quantitative assessment of food insecurity at the national level
In most studies on food security, food has been identified solely with cereals. Although the share of cereals in total food consumption (measured in calorie equivalents) is very high on average, it ranges from 85 per cent in Afghanistan to only 16 per cent in Zaire. Cereals are clearly the dominant food staple in Asia, but in Africa and Latin America the role of non-cereals in consumption is very important and must be incorporated into any meaningful consumption equation. However, in terms of what most governments express as their main concern with respect to food security, the commodity groups "cereals" cover on average more than two-thirds of total calorie intake in most LDCs, and also account for the more politically sensitive commodities. Cereals, particularly wheat, dominate among traded food products. Thus, they serve as a good approximation by which to measure the variability of food consumption.

In this analysis consumption instability is measured around the long term trend, using the "coefficient of variation" as an indicator of variability. The observed variability in food consumption in a sample of LDCs ranges from a low of 3 to 4 per cent, such as in the Philippines and Peru, to a high of 20 to 25 per cent in Morocco and Algeria. High variability levels of 15 per cent or more are concentrated in North Africa and the Middle

East where cereals' share in food consumption is above 40 per cent. Over 67 per cent of the countries had an amazingly high degree of consumption variability – equal to or greater than 7 per cent (Valdes and Konandreas, 1978).

Food consumption variability can also be expressed as the probability of actual consumption falling below, for example, 95 per cent of trend consumption, given the level of actual imports. In fifty-one out of sixty-seven countries, a consumption shortfall below 95 per cent of trend occurred every five years. In most of the Arab countries, it occurred approximately once every two and a half years.

Some may assume that shortfalls in domestic production are the basic cause of food insecurity. This need not be the case if the country concerned has the capacity to vary its food import volume to compensate for the variability of production. However, its ability to do so could be limited by sudden increases in world prices for food imports and/or decreases in export revenues. When these events occur simultaneously (that is, domestic production shortfalls in a year of adverse world prices, such as happened for many Asian and African countries in 1973/74), the ability of many LDCs to meet target consumption levels is devastated.

An alternative to relying on imports could have been to release stocks. However, historically, for most LDCs stock level changes have not been sufficient to reduce consumption variability. In view of the arguments presented above, this reliance on imports was a rational strategy, except perhaps in a large country such as India. Therefore, we may analyse fluctuations in consumption as resulting from fluctuations in the levels of production and of imports.

Production variability
Production has been relatively stable in most large low income countries. These include Bangladesh, Egypt, India, Indonesia, and the Philippines. For these countries, the coefficient of variation of production is around or below 6 per cent. In contrast, in thirty-three out of the sixty-seven countries this figure is 10 per cent or more, and several Arab countries it is above 20 per cent. The probability of production falling below 95 per cent of trend in thirty out of sixty-seven countries is once every three years. For the operation of a food security system, the absolute magnitude of the shortfall is critical. A country such as India may have a relatively low level of instability (6.4 per cent), but a high value of absolute variability (6.6 million tons); in contrast, Morocco has relatively high instability (27.2 per cent), but an absolute variability only one-sixth that of India (1.2 million tons). Hence withdrawals from an international scheme could very well become dominated by the large countries, many of which have relatively low production variability.

Variability in the food import bill
In an effort to compensate for the variability in domestic production, countries may destabilize their food import bill beyond a desired level.

Fluctuations are aggravated by the world price instability of cereals. Historically, analysis for the time period 1961–76 clearly shows that, except for a few countries like Egypt, the variability of the import volume explains most of the variability of the food import bill. On average, only one-quarter of the variability of the import bill is explained by world price movements (Valdes and Konandreas, 1978).

The above analysis has two important qualifications. First, particularly before 1972, world grain prices were relatively stable. Second, a considerable portion of imports to developing countries had been through food aid. The quoted price of imports overestimates the true cost of food aid imports to recipient countries.

Foreign exchange constraints
Foreign exchange availability could be the most critical factor in determining whether or not a country can import enough to stabilize food consumption.

Table 1 presents the average ratio of the actual value of food imports to total export revenues (including services) and its maximum for the period 1965–76. This ratio indicates the pressure on foreign exchange supplies to finance actual food imports. To the extent that actual food imports are already subject to financial constraints, this ratio would underestimate the true pressure exerted by foreign exchange shortages. The results show that, except for three out of the twenty-four cases (Bangladesh, India, and

TABLE 1   *Ratio of food imports to total export revenue, 1965–76 except as noted (per cent)*

	Mean	Max.		Mean	Max.
Asia			*Sub-Sahara Africa*		
Bangladesha	88.4	119.4	Ghanad	3.7	5.4
Indiab	22.4	44.5	Nigeriad	1.9	2.5
Indonesia	9.5	19.9	Senegalb	12.2	17.8
Korea, Rep. of	13.5	21.4	Tanzaniad	5.5	22.2
Philippines	4.9	9.1	Upper Voltae	7.4	13.0
Sri Lanka	27.2	49.2	Zaireb	3.1	6.9
North Africa/Middle East			*Latin America*		
Algeriac	6.0	9.3	Brazil	3.9	8.5
Egyptd	14.0	27.0	Chile	5.3	13.9
Jordand	10.6	15.4	Colombia	2.8	4.9
Libyad	1.4	2.3	Guatemala	2.4	3.3
Morocco	7.0	13.4	Mexico	0.4	9.3
Syria	5.7	18.4	Peru	6.6	10.5

a 1973–76   b 1965–75   c 1966–76   d 1967–76   e 1968–75

Note: All food import values at commercial prices, including food aid.
Source: Valdes and Konandreas, 1978.

Sri Lanka), during 1965–76 the mean ratio was less than 15 per cent, which, in our opinion, does not indicate a severe constraint during normal years. However, this ratio reaches significantly higher levels in unfavourable years. In Table 1, one observes that for some countries with "low" average ratios such as Tanzania and Syria, exceptionally unfavourable years raise this ratio by a multiple of more than four. This ratio becomes intolerably high, particularly in Asia, and in Egypt, Tanzania, and Senegal. The ratio remains remarkably low even at its maximum values in a few countries such as Nigeria, Libya, and Colombia.

There is a common impression, implicit in most of the discussion about the food gap projections of developing countries, that the weight of the food import bill measured, for example, as a ratio of total export revenues is increasing. Thus, the use of an "average" ratio for the period 1965–76 might understate the true magnitude of the problem of financing food imports by not revealing an upward trend in this ratio. This is, in fact, the case for some LDCs such as Sri Lanka, Morocco, and Chile, but it should not be generalized to describe the situation of LDCs in general. In fact, for many LDCs export revenues have increased faster than the value of food imports. As we can see in Table 2, the situation is mixed, as the trend varies sharply according to the country in question.

3 INTERNATIONAL POLICY ALTERNATIVES

There are two different but related approaches, currently discussed, to the problem of food security. One addresses itself to the question of world food security, in particular, world price stabilization mechanisms. The other addresses issues of food security for a sub-system of the world, namely, food deficit developing countries. For the latter, trade is an option, which is less attractive the more prices fluctuate.

Greater price stability in the world market for food is an important

TABLE 2 *Food import bill/total export revenue ratio (per cent)*

	1965–67 average	1974–76 average
India	39.4	19.7
Indonesia	7.1	6.0
Republic of Korea	13.4	9.2
Philippines	6.7	4.4
Sri Lanka	21.1	40.4
Morocco	8.0	11.5
Brazil	9.4	4.9
Chile	3.2	10.5
Colombia	2.9	3.5

Note: All food import values at commercial prices, including food aid.

element for food security in LDCs, as its fluctuations may aggravate fluctuations in the food import bill resulting from production shortfalls in domestic markets. As mentioned earlier, however, historically for most countries it is the variability of import volume that explains most of the variability of the food import bill. Thus, world price stabilization schemes do not solve, but might alleviate the burden of consumption stabilization in LDCs. Moreover, of course in themselves these schemes do not address aspects of financing food imports.

Several international approaches are currently being discussed which could contribute to food security in LDCs. These approaches include: (a) greater reliance on the responsiveness of grain reserves systems; (b) financial approaches to alleviate the foreign exchange constraint, and (c) consumption adjustments in developed countries. Political support for each of these initiatives is still, however, quite uncertain.

Grain reserves
In some food deficit LDCs, progress has been made towards building food storage programmes, assisted by international organizations. Examples of such schemes are FAO's Food Security Assistance Scheme (FSAS), bilateral food aid programmes, and some country projects financed by the World Bank. The objective of these programmes is to help LDCs through technical assistance and financial support for the design of storage programmes and distribution infrastructure. Given the relatively small size of the programmes (total contributions to FSAS in 1978, for example, were only $27 million), it seems to us that efforts should go first to the often lacking infrastructure to support working stocks (intra-year) rather than to provide year to year reserves, apparently the thrust of some programmes as they exist now.

Reserve stocks are needed only to supplement imports, and not to provide year to year internal price stability through the use of large buffer stocks. As Reutlinger (1978) has shown, the price stability objective can be achieved at a relatively lower cost primarily through varying the level of imports. Thus, except in the case of large grain importers, attempts to build buffer stocks may place an unnecessarily heavy burden on LDCs.

This approach requires, however, that there are adequate stocks held elsewhere in the system. But, to the extent that variations in the demands placed on these stocks by different countries may cancel one another out, the world can economize on the total level of reserves required.

Leaving aside politically unrealistic suggestions for internationally owned and managed buffer stocks, proposals under the International Wheat Agreement (IWA) call for a nationally owned, internationally co-ordinated system of grain reserves. Undoubtedly grain reserves could be managed to reduce world price variability, but the collapse of the IWA negotiations in February 1979 confirms the suspicion that an agreement on price levels and on the size and cost sharing of the reserves that would consider simultaneously market realities and accommodate LDC requirements was most unlikely. If the abundant research on grain reserves is used for clarification, it appears that price stability and world food security *per se* do not have much to offer for the exporters. Their interest lies in getting the rest of the world to share the cost of maintaining their domestic price support programmes. Since the LDCs perceive that these price programmes will result in large stocks being held by the exporters in any case, they have little incentive to reach an agreement.

Some analysts argue that, although its tangible effect on stocks and price bands would have been questionable, a new agreement would have allowed an active periodic review of market conditions and national wheat policies by senior policy makers, thus avoiding a repeat of the 1972/73 situation. In this sense, the collapse of the wheat negotiations poses a threat to LDCs; this should strengthen the incentives for developing alternative policy instruments which are relevant to food security.

Trade policies in developed countries
It is well recognized today by researchers in the field that a large fraction of world market price variability in cereals – between a third and a half – resulted from national policies as more countries, particularly developed countries, insulated domestic prices from conditions in world markets. Thus, the need for a large stock of grain reserves required by the world food system is due more to government policy than to nature. In this sense, consumption adjustments represent a direct alternative to variations in stocks. However, as a result of domestic price stabilization objectives, little progress is envisaged as to what could become acceptable policy proposals for the required changes in the system of protection.

Alleviating the foreign exchange constraint
Variable food aid programmes and compensatory financing for commercial imports represent the two major groups of policies which have been discussed recently.

Under the *variable food aid programmes*, such as the grain insurance programme suggested by D.G. Johnson, the United States, alone or in co-operation with other donors, would "guarantee to each developing country that in any year in which grain production declines more than a given percentage below trend production that the shortfall in excess of that amount would be supplied" (Johnson, 1978). A substantial degree of internal price stability could be achieved at low cost for each developing country. The results by Johnson indicate that food security could be achieved by modifying the distribution pattern of food aid, without significant increases in the average amount of food aid given in the long run. However, donor countries would have to change their food aid policies with respect to the required store of grain, the management of the variable food aid component, and the political criteria for eligibility.

Additional commitments by donors could be made in a renegotiated Food Aid Convention, as part of the International Wheat Agreement. These could be grants or concessional loans, depending on the income level and foreign exchange capacity of the recipient countries. Calculations by Huddleston indicate that "whereas for the entire period 1970–75, food aid flows substantially exceeded the variable requirements of LDCs (to achieve stability in supplies), the 5.9 million ton food aid flow in 1974–75 fell short of the amount of compensation required by two million tons". The same study shows that historically, the donor countries "chose to use a substantial portion of their restricted supply for purposes other than meeting the variable food security requirement. . . ." (Huddleston, 1978).

Up to now, concessional food sales have been dependent upon erratic surpluses in donor countries, and hence can hardly be considered a dependable base for food security in LDCs. Unlike the pattern for food aid in the past, food aid should increase when prices are high. Thus, minimum quantity guarantees are essential to food security. Moreover, political considerations are so important for eligibility that LDCs are unlikely to feel secure if they have to rely only on food aid programmes that are passed on an annual basis by the legislature.

The previous discussion on variable food aid facilities is very much tied to the availability of food grain stocks in the developed exporting countries. This has a number of implications which adversely affect the political feasibility of such schemes: (a) the burden of aid is unevenly distributed among donor countries and rests overwhelmingly on the grain exporting countries; (b) negotiations on the issue of provision of food security to the developing countries would be confounded with other issues such as the size of stocks and their management with resultant expansion on the areas of disagreement. We do not wish to imply that the demand for stocks is unrelated to the existence of this facility. On the contrary, as will be seen below, the facility will definitely increase the demand for stocks. What we are saying is that the negotiations on the issues can be kept separate.

The *financial food facility* has the advantage of simplicity. It protects member countries against fluctuations in the cost of cereal imports by providing foreign exchange in years of above-trend food imports. It has an added advantage in that the financing is made available to the government which is thus directly helped in maintaining food prices by subsidies when the price of imported food has risen. Possible approaches include enlarging the scope of existing compensatory financing schemes such as the existing IMF facility or the STABEX scheme to include the cost of cereal imports on the one hand or setting up an altogether separate facility on the other.

Fluctuations of a country's food import bill may coincide with fluctuations in its export earnings, and thus a country should have no problem in financing food imports. Results of our computations indicate the extreme sensitivity of the expected withdrawals with respect to whether or not the facility is adjusted for export earnings and with respect to the country coverage.

Table 3 illustrates this sensitivity of our calculations with respect to the

TABLE 3   *Financial facility to cover all fluctuations in cereal imports of food deficit LDCs in US $ billions, constant 1976 (1965–76)*

		67 countries[1]	34 MSA countries[2]
A.	Sum of excess food imports		
	actual food imports	12.0	6.8
	consumption stabilizing imports*	22.9	13.2
B.	Sum of increase in compensatory financing for export earnings adjusting for variability in the cost of cereal imports		
	actual imports	2.9	3.0
	consumption stabilizing imports*	12.6	9.5

* Excludes major oil exporters as defined by IMF, namely, Algeria, Indonesia, Iran, Iraq, Libya, Nigeria, Saudi Arabia and Venezuela.
[2] Most seriously affected countries (MSA) as defined by FAO.
* Computed as imports required to achieve consumption at the trend level for the period 1965–76.

country coverage (columns 1 and 2) and to whether or not the facility is adjusted by export earnings (sections B and A respectively). This calculation covers 100 per cent of the above-trend food import bill; another possibility is to cover only a fraction of the excess import bill.

It is our belief that some form of subsidy is essential for this scheme, because many poor countries would not be in a position to contribute significantly to financing a self-sustaining fund. However, this does not imply that the facility should operate on a grant basis for all countries. It would require that the facility have the flexibility to distinguish among country situations, similar to that of the IMF's Trust Fund, and the World Bank's IDA loans. Also, a totally subsidized scheme may induce misuse, and hence it is of strategic importance to cover something less than the full adjustment, and to require the recipient to bear a proportion of the cost of participation in the facility.

The existence of this facility would tend to reduce the elasticity of LDC import demand with respect to the world price as well as to increase the variability of this demand. These two consequences would increase both the need for and the profitability of holding stocks. There is as yet no research that examines the issue of whether the increased profitability would by itself induce sufficient stock accumulation to match the need.

A limitation common to the variable food aid scheme and the food facility scheme (to the extent that the latter has a concessional element) is that both rest on the availability of accurate information on production shortfalls. Although many claim that this is an insurmountable problem, particularly for the poorest LDCs, we share the optimistic belief that the existence of such schemes will in itself induce greater effort at overcoming problems whose solution, after all, is not *technically* difficult.

464   *Alberto Valdes and Ammar Siamwalla*

Interesting as the question is, we have not, due to space limitations, explored here why such a facility should or should not be expanded to insure the entire import bill of the member LDCs.

REFERENCES

The following papers used as references were all presented at the *IFPRI—CIMMYT Conference on Food Security for Developing Countries*, El Batan, Mexico, November 1978, and are part of a forthcoming publication of proceedings.

Huddleston, Barbara, "Grain Reserves, Food Aid, and Food Insurance: How a Comprehensive Scheme Might Operate."
Johnson, D.G., "Grain Insurance, Reserves and Trade: Contributions to Food Security for IDCs."
Lele, Uma and Wilfred Candler, "Food Security: Some East African Considerations."
Reutlinger, Shlomo, "Policy Options for Attaining Food Security: Feasibility, Effectiveness and Costs."
Valdes, Alberto and Panos Konandreas, "Assessing Food Insecurity in Developing Countries," Table 2.

DISCUSSION OPENING – LAWRENCE WITT

My congratulations to Drs Valdes and Siamwalla on preparing a comprehensive and interesting paper, and doing so within the rigid space limitations urged by the programme committee. I have five points to make in opening this topic for discussion.

First, I wish to re-emphasize the limited focus specified by the authors on the first page. The paper deals with national level, food security problems causes by year-to-year fluctuations in the harvest. On the next page, the authors touch on but do not elaborate many problems that may arise in assessing the need for additional food supplies and in actually making such supplies available where most needed. But the rest of the paper concentrates on supra-national efforts to assist national governments. I suggest that other discussants should remember that the Conference Programme has in this session shifted to the latter level of analysis.

Second, I believe the authors should have been as critical of the data on variability in food consumption, cited on the third page of the paper, as they were earlier on production statistics. Many of the national consumption statistics are derived as a residual, by adding and subtracting imports and exports from production with certain standard adjustments for seed, waste and industrial use. Thus, consumption figures suffer from some of the same statistical deficiencies as do production figures. Close examination of year-by-year consumption figures for some countries, including some major developing countries, provide unbelievable variations in consumption per caput. When they suggest that two-thirds of the LDCs have a consumption variability exceeding seven per cent, I wonder whether they are identifying wide variations in consumption or serious inadequacies in available statistics.

While some consuming groups within a country may suffer from significant year-to-year variations in consumption, I am arguing that the ability of other groups to maintain more stable levels of consumption is not fully identified by the process by which national levels of consumption are estimated. These adjustments include private stocks carried into the next crop and marketing year, production and use of supplementary crops, etc. However, this comment does not deny the national need for supranational programmes to help offset harvest shortfalls; it does argue for caution in estimating the size of the deficiency, whether based on consumption or production statistics.

Third, I would have placed greater emphasis than did the authors on the increased variability in the supply of grain imposed by the trade policies of the developed countries and including the Soviet Union. A large part of the food crisis of 1973–74 came as a result of policies followed by Western Europe, Japan and the USSR to maintain grain prices and availabilities at pre-existing levels, or nearly so, thus imposing a greater variability in both prices and supplies available to consumers in the major exporting countries and the LDCs. And among the LDCs, there were many with prices, import policies and foreign exchange availabilities to maintain internal food grain supplies, thus further increasing the variabilities imposed on the others.

Several of the existing proposals to alleviate the variability in food supplies to the LDCs could have the same effect of exacerbating the variability in the residual grain supplies available in world markets.

Fourth, such policies impose great variability in prices and supplies on the domestic livestock producers in the exporting countries and could lead to pressures to subject exports to some form of allocation.

This leads to my fifth point. I doubt that programmes that attempt to insure food supplies to the LDCs, whether through variable food aid, foreign exchange assistance, or modest levels of grain reserves, are likely to solve the problem unless there are complementary actions on the part of the developed countries. When world production declines in a particular year, the developed countries too must conserve in the use of grain by reducing consumption, decreasing national stocks, turning to alternative foods and feeds and seeking to expand production in the next crop period.

I conclude that the topic under discussion is important to all of us. It cannot be resolved by the LDCs by themselves or by certain supranational programmes directed towards the LDCs as a group. When food crises threaten to arise, the equitable resolution of these problems requires adjustments in the bread, butter, meat and milk available in all the world. The authors mention but do not emphasize this point. I suggest that both trade and internal policies in the developed countries, including the socialist countries, need to recognize this also.

GENERAL DISCUSSION – RAPPORTEUR: WAYNE LAMBLE

The observation was made, with which the authors agreed, that many LDCs, especially in Africa, attempt to deal with the food insecurity problem with programmes to store grain and other foods and that this seems to be a very expensive approach.

Another speaker maintained that programmes to address the problem of food insecurity can have a negative (undesirable) affect on income distribution – especially for farmers, giving rice production in the Philippines as an example.

The point was also made that there might be a contradiction between a "cheap food policy" to deal with food insecurity problems and a "high price food policy" to encourage food production.

In their reply the authors of the paper agreed with the comments on data on food consumption variability, but noted that little is known about this important variable. They acknowledged the importance of trade policies on food instability.

They also noted the income loss in the Philippines due to continued high production of rice in spite of a relative disadvantage of doing so and a policy to distribute that loss primarily on the producer.

Finally they suggested that programmes to deal with food insecurity should be more target oriented towards cheap food distribution programmes.

TODOR POPOV

Scientific and Technical Collaboration between the CMEA Member Countries in the Sphere of Agriculture

The contemporary scientific technical revolution is considerably changing the productive forces of society; it reorganizes the material and technical basis of production, turns science into an immediate productive force, raises to a new level the nature of labour, accelerates the social division of labour both nationally and internationally, and enriches its forms.

In the conditions of this modern general scientific and technical revolution, international trade in agricultural products relying on geographic, soil, climatic and other differences, ceases to be the only form of international relations and connections between the different countries and regions of the world in the sphere of food and agriculture. The dimensions of scientific and technical connections and relations, industrial co-operation etc. are considerable. The processes of international economic, scientific and technical integration are intensifying. The role of international scientific and technical co-operation widens and rises. This co-operation turns into an integral and irrevocable part of international economic and political relations between the different countries, and is a primary prerequisite for their further development.

This is particularly true for the economic, scientific and technical relations of the country members of interstate organizations and unions, where the development of the international scientific and technical connections is based on the functioning of a system of economic laws unified in goals and character. The CMEA is an example of that.[1]

In its thirty years of existence the CMEA carries out a wide range of activities for co-ordinating the efforts of the member countries for the

[1] The Council for Mutual Economic Assistance (CMEA), the first international organization of the socialist countries, was created in January 1949. At present members of the CMEA are: The People's Republic of Bulgaria, The People's Democratic Republic of Vietnam, The German Democratic Republic, The People's Republic of Cuba, The Socialist Republic of Romania, The People's Republic of Mongolia, The People's Republic of Poland, The People's Republic of Hungary, The Socialist Republic of Czechoslovakia and The Union of the Soviet Socialist Republics. The Socialist Republic of Yugoslavia also participates in some of the activities.

467

building of the developed socialist society and for a better utilization of
their material and economic resources. International scientific and technical co-operation in the sphere of food and agriculture is an important
part of this activity.

1   GOALS AND TASKS

The strategic goal of the international scientific and technical collaboration between the CMEA member countries in the field of food and
agriculture is to contribute to the solution of the major economic task of
the branch – a most effective utilization of the available materials,
economic and labour resources and the production of a sufficient quantity
and quality of products for the entire satisfaction of the constantly rising
necessities of society.

At the different stages of the development of international socialist
economic integration of the socialist community as a whole and also on
the different levels of production in the particular branches and sub-
branches, this goal is being modified in separate concretely formulated
programmes and tasks. The progressive evolution in the development of
the socialist system and the changes in food and agriculture of the individual CMEA member countries naturally increases the tasks and the
problems connected with their solution. They demand an adequate
development and improvement of the forms of organization and management of the international, scientific and technical collaboration itself.

The thirty-year history of existence of the Council for Mutual
Economic Assistance clearly confirms this regularity.

Created as an alliance of sovereign members with equal rights, CMEA,
during the first years of its existence, started to study and investigate the
questions of general interest, connected mainly with the expansion of
foreign trade relations, between the CMEA member countries under
conditions of full respect of national interests, mutual benefit and aid. In
the very early period of CMEA's activity (1949–56) there appeared the
objective necessity of *a joint organization of scientific and technical collaboration and exchange of technical experience* between the member
countries for the solution of tasks of general interest (multilateral collaboration), or of interest only to a given pair of countries (bilateral collaboration).

The valuable experience gained in the organization of the international
scientific and technical collaboration and especially the first results of this
activity led to the creation (in 1956) of the standing commissions for
economic, scientific and technical collaboration in the separate branches
of the economy, including a Standing Commission for food and agriculture.

In 1971 on the basis of the considerable success achieved in the
development of the productive forces, and under the condition of wide
use of the achievements of the scientific and technical revolution and
increased effectivity of social production, there was elaborated and sanc-

tioned *a Complex Programme for the further improvement and intensification of collaboration and development of socialist economic integration of CMEA member countries.*[1] This Programme specified the trends and activities, connected with the further development of the Council and defined the tasks of its authorities (bodies) in all spheres and branches, including food and agriculture.

In 1978 the XXXII nd Session of CMEA ratified *long term comprehensive programmes for further development and improvement of collaboration* in several basic spheres of material production, including the agriculture and food industry, which represents a further development of the "Complex Programme". It is essentially a new stage in the intensification and expansion of economic, scientific and technical collaboration between the member countries.

The main goal of the long term programme for collaboration in the sphere of the agriculture and food industry above all, is to contribute to the intensive development of national agricultural production, as well as to the development of the food industry in the individual countries, with a view to the entire satisfaction of their necessities and provision of the necessary quantities of food and agricultural production for participation in the international markets.

The basic ways for the achievement of this goal are:

the increase of meat production, mainly on the basis of own fodder;

the intensification of the international division of labour through specialization of the countries, disposing of optimal natural conditions for the corresponding crops, (special attention is paid to specialization in sugar, fruit and vegetable production);

the creation and joint use of high-yielding varieties of plants and highly productive breeds of livestock, especially fit for cultivation and breeding and particularly applicable to industrial methods of production;

the elaboration and use of progressive methods and technologies of production in plant-growing, animal husbandry and processing industries;

the further intensification and wider use of specialization and co-operation of production of machines, equipment, chemical, transport and other means, necessary for agriculture;

the elaboration and use of new and more effective forms for economic, scientific, and technical collaboration, including methods for economic stimulation necessary for the better satisfaction of public necessities, etc.

Together with the concrete production, technical, scientific and other tasks, the long term comprehensive programme for further improvement and collaboration between the CMEA member countries in the field of the agriculture and food industry, as well as other longer term programmes, has the task to contribute to equalizing and bringing closer together the level of economic development of the CMEA member countries and especially of some backward ones and assisting the increase of their export resources.

2 FORMS OF ORGANIZATION

The basic forms of scientific and technical collaboration between the CMEA member countries in the field of the agriculture and food industry are those applied also in the other national economic branches or spheres of collaboration.

The beginning of the collaboration was set with the mutual exchange of documentation, projects and information, training of highly qualified specialists and executives for new specialities and types of production.

Though most elementary and "old" this form has not lost its importance even nowadays. A basic source of documentation and production experience is the USSR.

In the years of the last five-year period (1971–75) the USSR gave to the CMEA member countries 244 sets of technical documentation in the sphere of agricultural machine building, 172 patterns of new tractors and agricultural machines for testing in the conditions of every country. During the same period the USSR received from the CMEA member countries 160 sets of technical documentation and 122 patterns of machines for testing.[2]

During the same period the CMEA member countries organized the production of 15 designs of machines on the basis of Soviet technical documentation. Since 1975 work has been done on the production distribution of about 30 designs of machines on the basis of Soviet documentation.

During the period 1967–75 the State All-Union Scientific Research and Technological Institute for repair and exploitation of the machine-tractor equipment (USSR) gave documentation for 224 designs along the line of scientific and technical collaboration and received documentation for 205 designs.[3]

In the recent years the co-ordination of the themes of scientific research on the most important, perspective and interesting scientific and technical problems plays an essential role.

Since 1965 in the CMEA Standing Commissions on Agriculture there have been worked out 5-year plans for collaboration in the field of scientific and technical research in agriculture and forestry.[4]

In the period 1966–70, 26 problems and 86 themes were included in the Plan for Joint Scientific Research on the Problems of Agriculture,[5] and in the years of the last five-year plan (1971–75) the scientific research on 12 problems and 39 themes was co-ordinated.[6]

The Plan for Scientific and Technical Collaboration in Agriculture for the current five-year plan period included 17 problems and 39 themes. The Bulgarian scientific and research organizations co-ordinate the investigation of 6 problems, the Hungarian of 4, the GDR of 7, the Polish of 4, the Rumanian of 3, the Soviet Union of 15, the Czechoslovakian of 7.[7]

In the period 1976–80 in the Plan for Scientific and Technical Collaboration in the Food Industry are included 55 themes, and most of these are included in the Co-ordination Plan for multilateral integration activities. Through joint efforts much will be done on: the search of new sources for obtaining protein; raising the biological qualities of food products; improving the production technology of food products; elaboration of technological processes and equipment for the complex processing of oil seeds etc. A programme for co-ordination up to 1990 has been worked out in order to improve the co-ordination of food industry machine building, scientific research, design activities and the adoption of the production of some highly productive kinds of equipment for packing food products, pouring out food liquids etc. Till 1990 the researches in all remaining sub-branches of food industry machine building will be co-ordinated.[8]

In the sphere of standardization a programme for collaboration was sanctioned in the period 1976–80 on the following problems:

veterinarian sanitary methods and means for diagnosis and struggle against the most dangerous diseases of livestock in the production of milk, meat, eggs and wool on an industrial basis;

methods and principles of veterinarian sanitary investigation on meat and meat products, milk and milk products, eggs and honey.[9]

A list of the most important problems of economic, scientific and technical collaboration co-ordinated on a multilateral basis in the years of the next five-year plan (1981–85) has been sanctioned in order to use more effectively this form in the future activity of the Council. In this list also have been included the scientific and technical problems originating from the long term comprehensive programme for collaboration in the sphere of the agriculture and food industry.

The form of joint testing of newly created varieties and machines is widely used, especially in recent years.

International variety tests in the CMEA member countries have been carried out since 1959. During the period 1961–71, 773 varieties and hybrids have been tested and in 1972–73 alone 120. As a result of the international variety tests in the CMEA member countries over 160 varieties were allocated into districts.

In 1976 alone, 47 varieties of wheat were tested in the CMEA countries and Yugoslavia. Five Bulgarian varieties of mild winter wheat took the first five prizes in this test for high productivity – Kaliakra 2, Ogosta, Kremena, Rubin and Sadovo-super.[10]

In 1972–74 control tests of 70 types of broilers and 78 hybrids of hen-layers were carried out in the International Control-test Station for Comparative Tests of Poultry created in Czechoslovakia.[6]

Since 1959 in the framework of the CMEA Commission on Agriculture have been carried out international tests of machines for mechanization and automation of production in agriculture and forestry. The tests are carried out according to unified programmes and methods. Information from the national tests is being exchanged. International comparative tests of veterinarian preparations, manufactured in the CMEA countries have been carried out for fifteen years now.[11]

Joint international tests of chemical and biological means for plant protection are being organized. About 220 preparations were tested, 77 of which have been recommended for adoption in production.[12]

A comparatively new but quite widely used form are the Co-ordination Centres created after the approval of the "Complex Programme". Of the present existing 41 Co-ordination Centres, 7 are working on the problems of agriculture, 1 on the food industry and 1 on packing of agricultural and food products.

In the framework of the Co-ordination Centres such problems are being solved as:

elaboration and introduction of electronic computer techniques and mathematical methods in agriculture;

elaboration of demands for the new complex and other mineral fertilizers, methods for their effective use and study of their influence on soil fertility by their continuous application;

working out of theoretical bases of selection and seed production and new methods for the creation of high quality varieties and hybrids of agricultural crops;

elaboration of the basic biological problems in the field of animal husbandry;

mechanization, electrification and automation of production processes in plant growing and animal husbandry;

raising the nutritive value of existing food products and creation of new types of high quality ones;

elaboration of the basic biological problems in the field of animal husbandry;

creation of new kinds of pesticides, elaboration of biological and other methods for plant protection and complex investigation of the influence of the means for environment preservation, etc.

3 PRACTICAL RESULTS AND THEIR APPLICATION

The purely scientific results from the collaboration are the following:

raising the theoretical and methodological level of the research and design activity;

speeding up the process of investigation and projection;

economy of means through the use of common material and technical equipment, etc.

International scientific and technical collaboration of the CMEA member countries already gives real practical results.

There has been created an international system for scientific and technical information on agriculture and forestry, "Agroinform", which is a branch subsystem of the International System for Scientific and Technical Information of the CMEA member countries.

An exchange gene fund of original forms of wheat and barley has been created in the All-Union Selection Genetic Institute. As a result of the fulfilment of the joint programme and national plans for scientific research work in the collaborating establishments there were created over 50 new varieties of wheat and barley, a part of which is already divided into districts and adopted in production, including the Bulgarian varieties of winter wheat "Sadovo" 1, "Jubileina", Kaliakra 2, Ludogorka, Krasen, Zlatoklas.[13]

As a result of the scientific and technical collaboration in 1971–75 in the food industry there have been constructed and adopted in production about 80 new kinds of equipment for the food industry and there has been made up a technical documentation for the production of about 500 types of new foods, including 130 for children.

Adoption of the results from the joint research work on improvement of the preservation of sugar beet permitted the decrease of sugar losses from 40–50 per cent in comparison with the preservation in the traditional way. This is equal to an annual additional production in the CMEA countries of 300 thousand tonnes of sugar.

Joint investigations have been carried out on the complex use of molasses for the production of spirits, baker's and fodder goods and others with the utilization of the various residues. As a result the production of baker's goods could be doubled and fodder goods increased by 25 per cent. The economic effect will be over 15 million roubles per year.

At the present moment Bulgaria, the German Democratic Republic, Mongolia, the Soviet Union, Poland, Rumania, Hungary and Czechoslovakia are carrying out joint investigations on techniques and technology improvement of processing residues of animal origin.[14]

Especially good are the results from the created joint scientific production establishments. In the international "Agromash" establishment where are made machines for vegetable production, fruit growing and viticulture four countries participated (USSR, GDR, PRB, PRH) in the period 1971–75 alone. In this establishment was elaborated and organized the serial production of 22 new machines for mechanization of work in plant growing, which allowed every participating country to decrease, by 50–70 per cent, expenditures in comparison with the necessary ones in independent working out.[2] Complex machines for gathering tomatoes, for gathering and additional processing of root crops are adopted in production. Till now under the management of "Agromash" there have been elaborated machines with 50 designs and some 32 are under working out and testing.[3] Complete solution of the problems of complex mechanization of the production processes in cultivation and gathering of the basic vegetable crops is forthcoming.

During the period 1976–80 this establishment will be carrying out scientific investigations on 10 problems, 31 themes on the over all division of labour between the participants, 22 of these themes are connected with the construction of new machines and 9 with technological problems. Over 20 scientific research organizations are participating in this plan.[15]

4   ORGANIZATIONAL AND ECONOMIC PROBLEMS

Organization and management of international scientific and technical collaboration among the CMEA member countries is built on a planned basis, regulated by a special legal and economic statute. Basic documents in this respect are the Organizational – Methodological, Economic and Legal Basis of Scientific and Technical Collaboration of CMEA member countries and different CMEA bodies' activities in this field.

All forms of international scientific and technical collaboration in the sphere of the agriculture and food industry depend on these conditions.

Organizational and economic conditions for international scientific and technical collaboration between the CMEA member countries regulate the rights and regulations of the countries and organizations participating in the various forms of collaboration. They clarify questions about:

their participation in the financial maintenance of the research, development and design activity;

the system, formation and amount of payment of the mutually consigned scientific and technical documentation and production experience;

the rights of property, the forms, dimensions and conditions for the use of the scientific and technical results obtained;

conditions for mutual supply and use of apparatus and the means for joint scientific and technical developments;

the rights and obligations of the individual countries for organizations in the management of the joint scientific and technical development and research work etc.

The experience piled up during the past thirty years contributed considerably to this system, to the precise nature of the common organizational, economic and law conditions for further development of scientific and technical collaboration in the sphere of agriculture.[16]

The continuous intensification of the general process of international social integration and the constantly expanding international socialist division of labour in the sphere of agricultural science and technique, however, set new and greater tasks along the line of further improvement of the processes of management of international scientific and technical collaboration.

REFERENCES

[1] "Kompleksna programa za po-natatushno zadulbochavane i usavarshen stvuvane na satrudnichestvoto i za razvitieto na sotsialisticheskata ikonomicheska intagratsia na stranite-chlenki na SIV", *Partizdat*, S. 1972, s. 106.

[2] Sinitsin, I. "Razvitie i uglublenie mezdunarodnogo sotsialisticheskogo razdelenie truda v oblasti traktornogo i selskohoziaistvennogo mashinostroenia", *Economicheskoe sotrudnichestvo stranchlenov SEV*, kn. 5, 1976.

[3] Seleznev, J. and Davidov, A. "Razvitie na satrudnichestvoto mezdu stranite-chlenki na SIV v proizvodstvoto na selskotopanska technika", *Mezdunarodno selskostopansko spisanie*, kn. 4, 1978.

[4] Ivchev, K. "Nauchno-tehnichesko satrudnichestvo mezdu stranite-chlenki na SIV", *Mezdunarodno selskostopansko spisanie*, kn. 6, 1976.

[5] Hadziiska, T. "Nauchno-technichesko satrudnichestvo mezdu stranite-chlenki na SIV v oblastta na selskoto stopanstvo", *Selskostopanska nauka*, kn. 3, 1974.

[6] Krustev, G. "Osnovnie itogi sotrudnichestva stran-chlenov SEV v oblasti proizvodstva selskohoziaistvennoi produktsii za 1971–1975 g. i puti ego uglublenia", *Economicheskoe sotrudnichestvo stran-chlenov SEV*, kn. 5, 1976.

[7] Aleksiev, A., Vikentiev, A., Miroshnichenko, B. "Sotsialisticheskaia integratsia i ee preimushchestva pered kapitalisticheskoi, izd", *Nauka*, M. 1975. s. 335.

[8] Tsvetanov, J. "Sotrudnichestvo stran-chlenov SEV v tehnicheskom prevooruzenii pishchevoi promishlenosti", *Economicheskoe sotrudnichestvo stran-chlenov SEV*, kn. 5, 1976.

[9] *Mezdunarodno selskostopansko spisanie*, kn. 5. 1976.

[10] Papazov, N. "Uchastie NRB v realizatsii planov sotrudnichestva stran-chlenov SEV v oblasti nauki i tehniki", *Economicheskoe sotrudnichestvo stran-chlenov SEV*, kn. 5, 1977.

[11] Krustev, G. "20 godini plodotvorno satrudnichestvo", *Mezdunarodno selskostopansko spisanie*, kn. 5, 1976.

[12] Shalamanov, S. "Dostizenia i perspektivi na satrudnichestvoto i sotsialisticheskata integratsia mezdu stranite-chlenki na SIV v selskoto stopanstvo", *Ikonomika na selskoto stopanstvo*, kn. 3, 1976.

[13] Sozinov, A., Sherbakov, V. and Shvedov, G. "Naucno-tehnichesko satrudnichestvo v oblastta na genetikata i selektsiata na rasteniata", *Mezdunarodno selskostopansko spisanie*, kn. 5, 1976.

[14] Buzdin, I. "Ratsionalnoto izpolzuvane na surovinite- vasna zadacha na satrudnichestvoto mezdu stranite-chlenki na SIV v oblastta na hranitelnata promishlenost", *Mezdunarodno selskostopansko spisanie*, kn. 4, 1978.

[15] Popov, S. "Agromash", *Sotsialisticheska ikonomicheska integratsia*, kn. 5, 1978.

[16] Popov, T. "The General Situation and Main Tendencies of Food & Agricultural Development in the European CMEA Member Countries (1960–1975 and up to 1980)", Vienna, IIASA, 1978, p. 193.

DISCUSSION OPENING – CHRISTA HAEBLER

The subject of the paper presented by Professor Popov is Scientific and Technical Collaboration. He restricted himself to the description of some experiences in the COMECON member countries and gave impressive figures concerning realized or planned research projects in the region. One must congratulate the COMECON on the given results. Nevertheless, given the fact that the international basis of COMECON makes the scientific collaboration relatively easy, I have been surprised that Professor Popov did not indicate more items especially interesting to agricultural economists. In his outstanding paper on "Accomplishments and Challenges for the Future for the Agricultural Economists working in COMECON", (page 407) Professor Nazarenko gave more detailed information on this subject, especially on the economic and research problems in centrally planned economies; but I feel we are still missing the discussion of some problem areas and possible or obvious frictions in the realisation of scientific collaboration and further technical collaboration.

Professor Popov mentioned briefly some questions of an organisational nature such as the existence of the Council for Mutual Economic Assistance and the participation of the member countries in the financing and the rights and obligations of the individual countries in the management. But he did not indicate details concerning, for example, the criteria guiding the collaboration of individual countries, with, to some extent, different basic economic and social situations – he mentioned some backward countries – towards the realisation of common goals. It would be interesting to know who determines the research subjects of common interest? How are priority lists fixed? How far the distribution of research work through specialization of countries or Institutes is going? How the decision-making according to Central Plan realization is organised? Of even more interest would be a deeper discussion of problems due to the nature of economic social research work. This conference has already given examples of problems to be dealt with in international collaboration. From my own experiences in a supra-national institution which is highly dependent on and using results coming out of scientific collaboration, I know that there are always problems to be solved. They exist in all kinds of research subjects: in the simplest ones, such as providing comparable figures, or in the more complex ones concerning economic modelling and sector forecasting. They must be even more severe in centrally planned economies with a common multinational model where they become a direct influencing part of the decision-making process at all levels. As examples I would like to mention only the following.

Time is one of the most important problems we are confronted with: on the one hand it needs time to get the results, on the other hand it takes time to get the results applied in the policy decision-making process or in the economic reality of farming. In most cases it is easier to solve the first indicated problem by a good organisation and management using highly developed teamwork. To take the second type of problem it may be worthwhile completing the economic analyses by an approach taking into account the results of research in politics and by elaborating alternative solutions.

Another sphere of problems concerns the flexibility of research against changing objectives in a changing economic and/or political environment. Those problems need an inter-disciplinary teamwork of highly qualified experts familiar with different approaches. According to C'saba Csaki's paper (page 312) in centrally planned economies with long term elaborated multinational plans, not only the handling of the feedback raises special problems but also the realistic estimates determining agricultural activity five years after the preparation period. I would be very grateful to Professor Popov if he would be so kind as to give us further information on this subject; how have the challenges been handled in the COMECON?

Without going into more detail I would nevertheless like to mention that scientific collaboration is a worldwide problem concerning both developed and developing countries. Because of another institutional framework or legal basis this type of collaboration has sometimes to solve more or other problems of organisation, financing and management challenging other problem areas. They will be different according to the degree of bilateral or multinational collaboration and to the uses of the research output. Because there is no direct link between Professor Popov's paper and those problems I prefer not to go into further details of this matter, especially since a discussion group is dealing more deeply with it.

So far as technical collaboration is concerned it is – to my understanding – above all the transfer of knowledge of all kinds to the potential users in the agricultural industry and the feedback from the farmer or the manager to the collaborating organisation. Professor Popov mentioned in his paper the international system for scientific and technical information on agriculture and forestry in the COMECON – the Agroinform. He also indicated the testing activities of seeds and other goods and the training of highly qualified specialist workers for new specialities and types of production. In other economies (even in Poland) the public and/or private extension services would play a big role not only in technical but also in socio-economic matters.

I would highly appreciate it if Professor Popov could complete his paper by more detailed co-ordinated information concerning the role of COMECON in training, consulting, financing and supporting technical assistance efforts.

GENERAL DISCUSSION – RAPPORTEUR: W. LAMBLE

Lack of time prevented further discussion and in response to the opener's remarks, Professor Popov replied as follows.

First of all he expressed his thanks to Mrs Haebler for her comments and for the opportunity to explain some aspects of his paper in more detail.

He drew attention to the fact that the paper had not its full title in the programme. The real title of this paper was "Scientific and Technical Collaboration between the CMEA Member Countries in the Sphere of Agriculture" and was to be an example of international collaboration in this field. His primary intention in writing this paper was only to give general information about CMEA activities and to show the first results in this field.

Bearing in mind a time scarcity he now intended to give a short answer in general terms only to those questions which are closely connected to the scentific and technical collaboration between the CMEA countries.

First, as is well known, most of the CMEA countries before World War II had less developed economies. As a result of this, even at the present time, they have a less favourable production structure *and lower* per caput GNP, GDP, net income, etc. The improvement of these indicators has been taken as a major criteria by developing the CMEA long term comprehensive programmes.

Second, the research subjects of common interest are determined by the CMEA Standing Commission for Science and Technology, and by the Standing Commission for Food and Agriculture. These commissions consist of representatives of the respective universities of the member countries.

Third, priorities in the international division of research between the various countries or institutes are fixed on the basis of several principles as follows:

existing scientific and research potential in various countries;
specialisation of a country's agricultural production within CMEA;
existing natural and economical resources in a given country;
demand for qualified specialists, etc.

Fourth, the financing of the international collaboration is solved in accordance with which subject is investigated, and with the expected benefit of the research. There are various possible solutions, for example:

every country or organisation participating in such research pays the same share of the total expenditure;
countries pay according to their national incomes;
the individual country pays in accordance with the extent to which results are utilised in that country.

Fifth, international scientific and technical collaboration between the CMEA is obviously not without any difficulties. The most important problems among them in the sphere of agricultural economics are:

the lack of a common data bank;
the relatively slow process of selecting top level scientists and organising the common research work;
the language gap between the scientists in the separate national research organisations;
organisational difficulties, when, for example, 10–15 organisations are involved, etc.

LOWELL S. HARDIN

Emerging Roles of Agricultural Economists Working in International Research Institutions such as IRRI and CIM-MYT

The International Rice Research Institute (IRRI), the first of the centres under discussion here, began its work in 1960. Today there are thirteen institutes and two associated centres in the global network (Table 1). Their programmes embrace the major crops and food animals in most of the ecological zones of the developing world.[1] These centres seek to help developing countries increase the quantity, quality, and stability of food production and thus contribute to general, widespread improvement in living standards. In pursuit of this objective, they do mission-oriented research and training while undertaking an array of catalytic initiatives to help evolve a global system for solving food production/consumption problems. This worldwide network extends from the farmer through his state and national institutions to regional and international research centres – as well as to scientific institutes and universities throughout the world. These inter-connections are sketched in the diagram on p. 480.

ORIGIN AND MISSION

The founders of the centres saw technological constraints on production as a serious barrier to agricultural and rural development in poor countries. They recognized that solutions to the problems addressed would likely call for structural and institutional changes also. But the case for focusing the power of modern production science on applied problems was and is a strong one. The technologically advanced nations, prime movers in the effort, have a real comparative advantage in this area. Under colonial regimes, research on food crops and animals had been neglected. The development assistance model in which the expatriate works alongside a counterpart in the developing country had been only moderately successful in producing research results. Further, work on food production technology is politically a less sensitive matter than is assistance directed to institutional and policy changes.

Coupled with the above was the growing belief, demonstrated by studies that were to follow, that there was underinvestment in agricultural

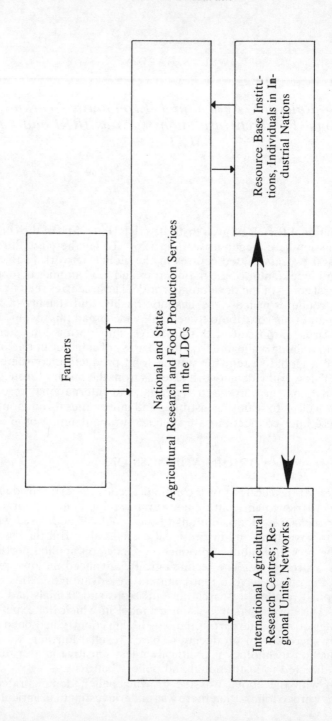

TABLE 1   *International Agricultural Research Centres, 1979*[1]

Centre Starting Date[2]	Principal Location	Major Programme	Senior Staff Posts Total	Senior Staff Posts Soc. Sci.	Core Operating Budget ($ million)
IRRI, 1960	Philippines	Rice	58	6	13.2
CIMMYT, 1966	Mexico	Wheat, maize	78	6	14.7
IITA, 1968	Nigeria	Systems, grains legumes, roots tubers	95	2	12.9
CIAT, 1968	Colombia	Forage-beef, field beans, cassava	61	4	12.5
WARDA, 1971	Liberia	Rice	n.a.	n.a.	2.1
CIP, 1972	Peru	Potatoes	29	3	7.2
ICRISAT, 1972	India	Sorghum, millet, dry-land systems	60	7	9.0
IBPGR, 1973	Italy	Genetic materials	n.a.	n.a.	2.7
ILRAD, 1974	Kenya	Trypanosoiasis theileriasis	51	0	7.6
ILCA, 1974	Ethiopia	L'st'le production systems	44	13	7.0
ICARDA, 1976	Syria	Crop, mixed farming systems	45	2	8.8
IFPRI	Washington	International food policy	20	20	2.0

[1] In addition to the 12 institutions listed, two more centres are associated with but not directly supported by the CGIAR: Asian Vegetable Research Development Centre, Taiwan, 1971; International Fertilizer Development Centre, US, 1975. IFPRI, while created in 1975, will become a full CGIAR member in 1980 as will a thirteenth centre, International Service for National Agricultural Research (ISNAR).

[2] Full designations of the centres are: International Rice Research Institute: International Centre for the Improvement of Maize and Wheat; International Institute of Tropical Agriculture; West African Rice Development Association; International Potato Centre; International Crops Research Institute for the Semi-Arid Tropics; International Board for Plant Genetic Resources; International Laboratory for Research on Animal Diseases; International Livestock Centre for Africa; International Centre for Agricultural Research in Dry Areas; International Food Policy Research Institute.

Sources: *Consultative Group on International Agricultural Research*, office of William Mashler, United Nations Development Programme, New York, 1976; *An Integrative Report*, Consultative Group on International Agricultural Research, CGIAR, World Bank, Washington, 19 September 1978; personal correspondence.

research as a contributor to growth. Fortunately the first two centres, IRRI and CIMMYT, scored spectacular successes in plant breeding and improving practices for growing wheat and rice. The rapid introduction and spread of the high-yielding varieties in high potential areas suggested that a similar approach with other important tropical food crops and animals could produce equally rewarding results. Thus, the network of centres that exists today owes much to the early track record of IRRI and CIMMYT.

By 1971 it was clear that growth of the four then existing institutes plus proposed expansion in coverage and number of centres would require substantially more funds than could be provided by the founding sponsors, the Rockefeller and Ford Foundations. To deal with this problem, a new institution was invented to monitor quality standards and organize the financing of the centres. A resolving principle behind this invention was to respect both the requirements of first class research and the political necessities of donors – and then to build bridges of voluntary association between them.[2]

The institution created, sponsored by FAO, UNDP, and the World Bank, was the Consultative Group for International Agricultural Research (CGIAR). This international consortium now has 29 donor members – 9 multinational organizations, 17 governments, and 3 private foundations. To monitor quality standards and to aid it in its judgments, the CGIAR formed its own Technical Advisory Committee composed of distinguished international agricultural scientists and research administrators. This year, CGIAR members have made bilateral grants totalling more than $100 million in support of the programmes of the ten centres and two related programmes in the network (ISNAR, the tenth centre, received funding for its organizational phase pointing toward a start in actual operation in 1980).

THE EVOLVING ROLE OF SOCIAL SCIENTISTS IN THE CENTRES

From the onset the scientific orientation of the centres has been on biological innovation as a means of improving production technology for particular crops and animals in tropical and subtropical environments. More recently, programmes of work have been broadened to include farming systems. Some centres have disciplinary departments. Others do not. However, all of these centres organize their scientists into problem-solving, interdisciplinary teams. Predominantly, team members are crop and animal scientists – breeders, agronomists, physiologists, soil scientists, entomologists, and agricultural engineers.

Managers and sponsors of the centres have adopted a straightforward working proposition: if a variety, practice or production system can be developed that in the eyes of the farmer is superior to what he is now using, it will be adopted. The technology will spread because it is better. But better must be defined in terms of the decision-making criteria employed by farm families – criteria that are not always understood and appreciated by scientists or by policy-makers.

The spread of high-yielding varities (HYVs) demonstrates that if the gains to be had are great, diffusion can be rapid. It is estimated that by 1976–77 HYVs of wheat and rice were grown on over 135 million hectares in developing nations in Asia, Near East, Africa and Latin America. Thus HYVs represented 44 per cent of the wheat and 34 per cent of the rice hectarage planted in these regions.[3] Few would argue that social scientists made major contributions to the biological research that produced the high-yielding varieties. What then is the role of the agricultural economists and social science colleagues in these biological research centres? As I hear centre economists speaking, they seek to help:

1 Identify and assess the factors constraining production increases;
2 Design improved research-training procedures as well as technologies that may lessen those constraints;
3 Predetermine the probable social and economic consequences of proposed technological changes.

Note that this formulation of objectives underlines *helping* to identify, to design, and to predetermine. The centres are involved in creative endeavours: inventing and designing; adapting plants, animals, chemicals, machines and equipment; fitting them into existing production systems or evolving new ones; bearing the risk that what they come up with may not work; hoping for a bit of serendipity to help them along. In these processes, the effective centre economist is a partner who symbiotically interacts with the physical and biological scientists. He applies his skills and tools in an effort to increase the payoff realized on the total investment in the centre. He comes to know and understand a great deal about soil–plant–moisture interrelationships, about agronomy, genetics, pests and pathogens. He does not hive himself off and independently pursue his personal, professional and scholarly interests. For he, too, is a member of a mission-oriented team.

COMMON PERCEPTIONS OF CENTRE ECONOMISTS

No two of the international agricultural centres are alike. There is a healthy degree of pluralism and experimentation in their organization and structure – even beyond that dictated by their separate missions and the environments within which they work. This is reflected in the professional mix of the staff, including the proportion budgeted for social scientists. Irrespective of their numbers, it is my understanding that centre economists tend to share several common viewpoints.[4]

First, they recognize that in exploring and capitalizing on their special opportunity to work intimately alongside first class biological scientists they have a comparative advantage. If one does not view such close association as an advantage, that person would probably find work on a centre staff unattractive.

Second, they participate in the process that creates technical advances of a biological, chemical or mechanical nature. They prefer to enter this process on an *ex ante* basis. Biophysical scientists seldom take kindly to social scientists who, absent at the design and implementation stage, come in for the evaluation to tell others what they did wrong. In appropriate ways social scientists become involved in the conception of changes that may result in advances. In doing so they too become accountable for the outcome.

Third, they view the constraints they seek to deal with to be of three broad types. Least tractable are the physical–environmental constraints (climatic extremes of cold and hot or wet and dry, infertile or toxic soils) most of which either are uncontrollable by man or require technologies for their removal that are presently uneconomic or still to be developed. More manageable are the physical and biological constraints (moisture limitations or excesses, diseases and insects) which are subject to at least partial removal or control if appropriate technology can be developed and applied. The third set of constraining factors is of a socio-economic character (timely availability of the correct inputs, management of irrigation systems, tenure arrangements, credit, incentives) largely institutional in character and subject to management and control by man.

While initiatives to cope with constraints of the first two types are often the primary province of the biophysical scientists, social scientists are expected to provide leadership in identifying and dealing with constraints of the third type.

Fourth, centre economists recognize that many of the problems being addressed transcend political boundaries and often require international co-operation and collaboration for successful resolution. Especially is this the case in addressing constraints of an institutional and policy character. It is the responsible citizens of their own countries, not the expatriates, who must ultimately make policy changes. Through collaborative projects, exchange of information, conferences, and networks of like-minded scientists resident and working in their own countries, attention can be focused on common problems. In this manner, consideration of policy changes can be catalyzed.

In centre efforts to link into Third World communities of like-minded scientists, the economists often face an even more difficult task than do the plant breeders or agronomists. Political sensitivity to institutional and policy matters is but one of the issues. Relative to the production scientists, interested economists are often in even shorter supply. Continuity of tenure of economists in ministry of agriculture research systems is often short, in part because alternative employment opportunities, inside and outside the country, are so attractive. Where there are nuclei of agricultural economists in universities, their links to agricultural research establishments are often tenuous. Therefore, special, innovative arrangements are frequently required to interest and bring together working groups within many LDCs as well as to link them to colleagues across national borders.

Fifth, centre economists judge that the odds are rather slim for achieving major breakthroughs of the type scored early on by CIMMYT and IRRI. Incremental gains rather than quantum jumps are anticipated. In order to achieve these incremental gains it is necessary to understand the behaviour of farm families, their circumstances, and their decision-making processes. To this end, the social scientists are involved in diagnosis, articulation of the right researchable questions from the farms and villages back to the scientists, and in interaction with centre management in decision-making on budgetary and resource allocation questions.

Sixth, the centre economists share the CGIAR's concern for the poor as reflected in statements such as the following.

> The recent advances in international agricultural research have not yet materially affected the substantial majority of farmers in the developing world who have limited resources. This has led to the conclusion that the Consultative Group must devote more of its effort toward the generation of technology suitable for the small farmer; that is, the resource-poor farmer with a limited access to the good land, purchased inputs, irrigation facilities, and the other elements on which the technological advances of the past decade, particularly in rice and wheat production, have depended.[5]

Most centre economists would agree that successful efforts to raise farmer incomes through technological innovation and incentive policies (e.g., the development and diffusion of HYVs) that increase total food production and productivity have resulted in mixed growth, welfare and equity consequences. There is a growing consensus that these efforts have tended to:

> Increase the total availability of food protein and energy – even where advances in cereal production technology proceeded more rapidly than with food legumes, vegetables and animals – thus reducing the overt or aggregate food "gap";
> Make possible, as some cushion of domestic production is generated, experiments with nutrition enhancing, employment generating programmes for the malnourished, such as food for work efforts now being undertaken in several states in India;
> Slow the rate of increase in food prices to consumers, thus lower income groups (rural and urban) who spend a high proportion of their total income on food grains or their equivalent, are principal beneficiaries (a positive distributional consequence);
> Modestly increase direct labour use per hectare, thus somewhat expand the demand for labour (generally reflected more in employment generation than in a rise in wage rates);
> Expand off-farm employment opportunities in situations where due to larger farm incomes demand is increased for local farm supply, marketing and agriculturally related non-farm businesses and services (as has been the case in the Punjab);
> Increase wage and income differentials between high potential and resource-poor areas (Appalachia effect);
> Widen the gap between the *absolute* levels of farm income of small holders and operators of larger units in areas where the innovations are technologically and economically superior to traditional practices. While farm size and farm tenure *per se* have not been a serious constraint on the adoption of improved high-yielding

varieties, there is typically a lag in adoption rates associated with farm size. Size remains a multiplier (of profits or losses);

Result in greater gains for land owners than for tenants or labourers due to the elastic supply of labour relative to the supply of land.

ISSUES AND IMPLICATIONS

In the discussion above I have commented briefly on the origin and mission of the centres, the perceived roles of the social scientists, some of the views thought to be held by the economists in the centres, as well as identifying some of the social and economic consequences of their work. Based on this background we now direct our attention to network-wide issues that may be of particular concern to economists. These we group under the general headings of clientele and priorities.

Clientele
With respect to clientele the most direct users of the economists' work are within the centres themselves – the biological scientists, the administrators and policy-makers. The expertise of well qualified social scientists certainly needs to be brought to bear on the centres' resource management and allocation process. This involves undertaking programme analysis and planning tasks. It also requires professional skill and sensitivity if one is not to be seen as making prejudicial judgements on the work of others. In one centre the social scientists report that almost one-half of their efforts are directed towards the what-to-do decisions bearing on resource allocation and use.

Outside of the centres, other economists, planners, developers and resource managers are direct or indirect users of the social scientists' product. Centre biologists distribute new seeds, suggest practices and techniques. By analogy, economists share procedures, techniques and processes, as well as findings from their studies and trials. These off-campus clientele groups include collaborators or prospective co-workers in other less technologically advanced countries, as well as colleagues in international agencies and academics who monitor and help interpret ongoing work.

Centres have not always seen a need for social science. Early on, the demands for the work of such staff members came more from certain donors than from management. As a result, the utility of the economist, more than that of the biological scientist, has been under test. All clientele groups appear increasingly to recognize, however, that social scientists are coming up with insights regarding constraints to, and consequences of, technological change that are not readily available from other sources.

Today, the question of serving both in-house and outside clientele groups is not at issue. What may be at issue are the questions of: (a) how many resources a specific centre should invest in social scientists relative to other disciplines and (b) what mix of social scientists to employ. Answers vary in accordance with the centre's mission. One centre, ILRAD, has no social scientists. At the other extreme, ILCA's 44-person senior research staff includes two social anthropologists, an economic geographer, and ten economists and agricultural economists. Typically the centres employ 40 to 60 senior scientists including three to five social scientists. If they are supported with technicians, enumerators and junior staff and trainees, this proportion of social scientists is probably about right. It seems probable, however, that in the future, greater use will be made of non-economic social scientists. This leads us to the matter of the social scientists' own priorities.

Some questions of priorities
Questions that could be addressed in this area are many. Is the focus to be on production – or on the larger set of production-consumption problems? If the latter, one plunges immediately into the socio-political as well as economic analysis of growth, equity and distributional issues. While many see biological centres as relatively ineffective instruments for reshaping skewed income distribution patterns, distributional and related poverty issues are central concerns.

From the research viewpoint it is yet to be demonstrated that one can invent improved technologies whose benefits are exclusively captured by the low-income, small, or resource-poor farmer. However, research and infrastructure investments can be tilted in the direction of the resource-poor, including efforts to develop improved technologies in areas environmentally disadvantaged. Such an orientation usually calls for *ex ante* analysis of the probable social as well as the economic consequences of the investments. Usual economic benefit-cost analyses based on efficiency criteria show up unfavourably when research addressed to resource-poor situations is compared with that directed to more favourable environments. Thus the centres are called upon to make estimates of the social as well as the economic consequences of their own work and of the investments of others.

In this connection IRRI's efforts to measure the trade-offs between economic efficiency and equity considerations are instructive. By their calculations potential net benefits to research (efficiency objective) would be maximized were they to allocate their South and Southeastern Asia efforts 40 per cent to irrigation, 26 per cent to rainfed, 12 per cent to deep water, 12 per cent to cold temperature, and 4 per cent to upland rice production regions. When the area devoted to rice culture and the numbers of producers (rather than the sole criterion of increasing total output) are factored in, the research resource allocation can change. Using the latter criteria rather than the efficiency objective only, IRRI is placing greater emphasis on upland, rain-fed and deep water rice than would likely be justified on the basis of total output alone.[6]

Another important question may be introduced by reflecting a moment on the centres' role in fostering institutional change. Ruttan[7] reasons that the demand for knowledge in economics and other social sciences is derived from a demand for more effective institutional performance. In the food production–consumption area, as some of the technical constraints are removed, institutional constraints emerge as increasingly significant. Knowledge leading to more effective institutions (defined to include both behaviour rules and decision-making units or organizations) results in lowered costs of institutional innovation and enhanced performance – just as advances in knowledge in biological sciences and agricultural technology reduce the costs of technological innovation.

The importance of induced institutional change is cited here as an illustration of a more general priorities issue. Much relatively basic work remains to be done more adequately to conceptualize and understand the process of institutional change and development. With respect to this and other problems, decisions have to be reached concerning how much attention centre researchers devote to relatively basic work on theory and methodology. Such work can be an important dimension of the scientist's continued professional growth. Without an opportunity for some staff members modestly to engage in realtively basic work, first class social science capacity may not develop. Therefore, while the centres are applied institutions, room needs to be left for modest involvement in relevant rather basic conceptual work of the type that springs from the real-world laboratory in which the centres are purposely located.

A third priorities question relates to the breadth of centres' and therefore necessarily the social scientists' programme of work. Do they engage a broad range of development problems or do they concentrate on selected commodities and the systems involved in their production and distribution? The ongoing debate on this issue is not to be resolved here. It is my view, however, that for high quality standards to be established and maintained, concentration of effort is required. The centres have resources, facilities, and non-political working environments superior to those available to most scientists in the newly developing countries. The intent is to create working conditions conducive to excellence. Undue diffusion of research and training efforts will surely undermine the reach for excellence that is within the grasp of the well programmed and managed centre.

CONCLUDING COMMENTS

The world now knows quite a bit about how to organize and operate a relatively successful, international agricultural research centre of the type we have been discussing. We also see productive and important roles for economists, anthropologists and sociologists as members of centre multidisciplinary research and training teams. What we are learning about multidisciplinary, problem-solving research processes is not the primary product of the institutes, but it is an important one. What we know far less about is how national or state research and extension programmes can better capitalize on the investment in the international centres.

In no sense was it intended that the international centres were to be or become substitutes for national programmes. As indicated in the diagram on the first page of this paper, farmers and villagers interact with their own local, state and national research and extension system. It is through the provision of materials to and the conduct of collaborative or technical assistance efforts with the national systems that the products of the centres' work reach rural people. Rarely are these products ready for direct consumption or use. At a minimum, local adaptation is usually required. Despite this sometimes tenuous linkage between the international centre and farmers, the work of the centres is evaluated in terms of the changes that occur in crop yields, food consumption, and human welfare. Thus the demands now being placed on national programmes – from inside their own countries and from outside entities such as the international centres – are enormous.

To help nations desiring such assistance a new international service is soon to be made available.[8] It is the CGIAR-sponsored International Service for National Agricultural Research (ISNAR). Its function will be to help countries strengthen their national research systems. Modest initial diagnostic help will be available on call. Beyond that point users will pay for the service provided drawing upon their own or upon donor funds.

This new service is being created in partial response to the pressures national programmes feel to develop more rapidly. It is also designed as a component of the CGIAR network designed systematically to draw on the work of the international centres while relieving them of some of the demands being placed on them for technical assistance.

Just what this development will mean to social scientists is unclear. Conceivably it could enhance opportunities for collaborative, field level informal R & D work now being pioneered by IRRI, CIMMYT, CIP, and ICRISAT.[9]

I conclude with comments on the role of national research and related programmes because they are crucial to the effectiveness of the international system that is evolving. And one of the weakest components of national systems often is their capacity for socio-economic analysis. My sense is that this situation is now being recognized in several countries. The organization of the international centres and the programmes of work of the social scientists there are not in themselves models for national systems to emulate. Next to the farmers themselves, professionals working in national programmes are the largest group of actors in the international network.[10] They, and this includes the social scientists, look to the centres to help them link to and learn from one another.

REFERENCES AND NOTES

[1] Consultative Group on International Agricultural Research "Report of the Review Committee", CGIAR Secretariat, World Bank, Washington 1977.

[2] McGeorge Bundy "The President's Review", Ford Foundation Annual Report, New York 1977.

[3] Dana G. Dalrymple "Development and Spread of High-Yielding Varieties of Wheat and Rice in the Less Developed Nations," USDA, Foreign Agricultural Economic Report No. 95, Washington 1978.

[4] Based upon helpful correspondence with former or present centre economists: Vernon W. Ruttan, Randolph Barker, and Robert W. Herdt, IRRI; Donald Winkelmann, CIMMYT; Fred Winch, IITA; Gustavo A. Nores, CIAT; Douglas Horton, CIP; James G. Ryan, ICRISAT; Hans E. Jahnke, ILCA; and David Nygaard, ICARDA. Their contributions are gratefully acknowledged.

[5] Consultative Group on International Agricultural Research "An Integrative Report", CGIAR Secretariat, World Bank, Washington 1978.

[6] See Randolph Barker's paper presented at this conference.

[7] V.W. Ruttan "New Rice Technology and Agricultural Development Policy" in "Economic Consequences of the New Rice Technology", IRRI, 1978. Also see Hans P. Binswanger and Vernon W. Ruttan *Induced Innovation*, Part IV, Johns Hopkins University Press, Baltimore and London, 1978.

[8] Consultative Group for International Agricultural Research "Report of the Task Force on International Assistance for Strengthening National Agricultural Research", CGIAR Secretariat, World Bank, Washington 1978.

[9] These centres are developing manuals for the conduct of agro-economic, farm-level collaborative research. Also see the paper by Derek Byerlee and colleagues, this conference.

[10] For an analysis of the future of the centres see Vernon W. Ruttan's "The International Agricultural Research Institute as a Source of Agricultural Development", *Agricultural Administration*, Vol. 5, No. 4., Reading October 1978.

DISCUSSION OPENING – JOHN W. LONGWORTH

Dr Hardin is to be congratulated upon a most clear and enthusiastic presentation. The major thrust of his paper is straightforward and I shall not waste time summarising his comments. Let me quickly turn to seeking highlights and controversial points for further discussion.

First Dr Hardin emphasized early in the paper that when these international centres were being set up the emphasis had always been on food production technology rather than institutional and policy change, the latter being a most difficult and sensitive area. Yet, as Hardin points out, the third set of constraining factors are socio-economic in nature. More often than not the removal of these constraints calls for institutional and policy change.

Second, in the light of the need for research in this sensitive area of institutional and policy change, there is a need to stress the training and educational role of the agricultural economists (and social scientists in general) at the international centres. At IRRI in particular, a strong working relationship seems to have developed with UP, Los Banos. The long term contribution to institutional and policy change via human capital formation should not be overlooked.

Third, Dr Hardin has stressed the need for a strong commitment to multi-disciplinary and applied work as a prerequisite for a successful input by a social scientist at an international centre. He is suggesting that "muddy boots" rather than "esoteric theory" is what is required. One might feel that few Agricultural Economics Departments in the United States have the capacity to produce this type of person. On the other hand, the traditional "Agricultural Science first – then Economics" approach to University training, which is the norm in Australia, might be expected to produce graduates more attuned to the needs of the international centres.

Fourth, a most important and fundamental issue raised in Dr Hardin's paper (and many others at this conference) is the issue of research priorities as between output efficiency and equity. What weight should research planners give to distributional issues as distinct from output increasing issues? This is undoubtedly one of the major questions facing people working at the international centres. Perhaps we should discuss it in the context of Dr Hardin's paper.

Fifth, another controversial aspect of Dr Hardin's paper concerns his view that 3 to 5 social scientists in a total staff of 40 to 60 is probably about the right proportion. Is there a case for more social scientists? Implicitly Hardin thinks there is! He suggests the importance of research to understand and reduce the socio-economic liaison to rural development. He stresses the need for a better understanding of institutional and policy change. He lists the wide range of social science skills required in addition to the skills normally expected of an agricultural economist. Despite recognizing the need for a greater social science input at the international centres, Dr Hardin still feels that with less than 10 per cent of the scientific staff trained in the social sciences, the mixture is about right! While those present could not be considered as disinterested in regard to this issue, it may be worthwhile discussing it further.

GENERAL DISCUSSION – RAPPORTEUR: EARL D. KELLOGG

Some concern was expressed regarding the proportion of staff at international centres being only 10 per cent since many of the important problems involved social science concerns. The reason for this was that the centres were originally focused on agricultural technology generation to increase yields. The early successes in some crops, drawn from worldwide research resources, tended to reinforce the technical agricultural research bias. Since the new international centre, IFPRI, had all social scientists, the proportion of social scientists at the present was over 10 per cent. As social scientists continue to contribute and problems become more focused on equity and consequent concerns, social scientist numbers will increase gradually. This trend is being reinforced by donors who want their contributions to be focused on the rural poor. Anthropology was mentioned as a discipline becoming more important in certain centres' work. The lack of social scientists in leadership roles in the centres was also discussed. At present, two social scientists are directors – Bill Gamble at IITA and John Mellor at IFPRI.

The importance of agricultural economists working with other agricultural scientists was emphasized, since problem definitions were being formulated that required mutual observation and diagnosis. Concern was expressed at the implication that applied research by agricultural economists in the centres was not being recognized by the profession. Since this research was so important, perhaps the profession ought to review the criteria used to give recognition. Some time is needed for centre agricultural economists to be involved in theoretical and methodological considerations to keep up to date in the profession. However, it appears that professional recognition and rewards are increasing for centre economists.

Comments were made that the paper had not given enough recognition to the considerable training going on at the centres. It was pointed out that 30 per cent of the budgets went into training activities. Although the centres do not grant degrees, many are located near universities with agricultural interests which provide opportunities for complementary activities. This close proximity, however, does raise problems of equity between centres' and universities' staff in terms of benefit and income levels.

Participants in the discussion included Ramesh C. Agrawal, John Timmons and Michel Petit.

RANDOLPH BARKER*

Establishing Priorities for Allocating Funds to Rice Research

There has been an increasing interest in recent years in the problems and procedures related to establishing priorities in agricultural research programmes. In developed countries this is a reflection of tighter budgets for research. In the developing countries the interest arises out of a growing recognition of the critical role played by research in the development process, as the severe limitations imposed by the lack of trained manpower as well as funds for research.

Agricultural research, particularly in the biological sciences, has the characteristic of a "public good" in that it is: (i) equally available to all, and (ii) it is impossible to exclude from utilization those who have not paid for it. The result is that investment in agricultural research is undertaken largely by the government rather than by the private sector. A number of recent studies have shown clear evidence of an under investment of public funds in research in the developing countries. This explains in part the rapid development of the network of international agricultural research centres. The creation of these centres has brought to the fore a number of important issues with respect to the allocation of research funds for agriculture. How much in total could or should the developed country donor agencies contribute to agricultural research? What types of research centres and activities should be supported? What should be the balance of support between national and international programmes; between focus on basic science and development of technology; between focus on current research problems and development of research capacity? How can national governments be encouraged to provide more support for research activities and for training research workers? The above questions are of concern to the international centres themselves who obtain their financial support from the Consultative Group on International Agricultural Research (CGIAR) and who have the dual role of engaging in research and facilitating the development of indigenous research capacity. Furthermore, the CGIAR, which is composed of representatives from the donor agencies, is warning of the

* Read by Robert Herdt in Professor Barker's absence.

possibility of a sharp slowdown in the growth of its own contribution (which now exceeds $100 million annually). Pressure is being brought on the individual research centres to improve their procedures for establishing priorities in the allocation of funds. In achieving this objective, an understanding of the interrelationship between the research in the international centres and in national programmes is of paramount importance.

In this paper we report the results of an exercise undertaken by one of the international centres, the International Rice Research Institute (IRRI), in an effort to clarify its own research priorities. Both the procedures followed and the results obtained should be of general interest to professional economists, research administrators and others concerned with agricultural policy.

The paper is divided into three sections. The first examines the structure of the research system. Methodologies for establishing priorities among rice research programmes are discussed in the second section. The third section presents the results of the analysis. This is followed by concluding remarks on the implication of these results for rice research in Asia.

THE ORGANIZATION OF RICE RESEARCH

A typology of rice research systems can be drawn which relates research skills and institutional organization to the stage of development of the system.[1] A research system passes through three stages of development: (i) *the low skilled system* dependent primarily on technical and engineering skills and characterized by widely diffused commodity oriented experiment stations, (ii) *the intermediate hierarchal system* with appreciable scientific skills and substantially economies to be gained by the concentration of these skills in leading institutions, (iii) *advanced scientific-based systems* characterized by a large supply of conceptual scientific skills and emphasis of the most highly regarded centres on research which does not have a direct technological objective.

Japan is perhaps the only country in Asia where the rice research system has passed through all three stages and can today be characterized as *advanced scientific-based*. The shift from the first to the second stage occurred in 1926 when the build-up of technical and scientific skills resulted in a major reorganization of agricultural research. The intermediate hierarchal system that emerged allowed Japan to capitalize on the development and dissemination of crossbred varieties.

Although the same scientific knowledge was potentially available to the experiment stations established throughout the tropics in the early part of the century, the scientific manpower needed to translate this knowledge into new technology did not emerge. Neither the pressures of population nor the priorities of the colonial administrations dictated the need for a major research effort to increase rice yields. Rice yields remained static. By mid-century an emerging food problem was becoming evident, but the belief was widespread that the *indica* varieties would not respond, like the *japonicas*, to conditions of intensive cultivation and heavy fertilization. The potential for altering the *indica* plant type through breeding was yet to be recognized.

The virtual disappearance of the arable land frontier in South and Southeast Asia after World War II hastened by the "population explosion" obviated the need for the development of modern technology to enable rice production to keep pace with rapidly growing demand. The dismantling of the colonial research network as the developing countries gained independence left tropical Asia with virtually no legacy of trained research manpower.

In the decade after World War II efforts to encourage agricultural development in the tropics still tended to ignore the potential of research in food crops. Extension received priority over research in part because it was felt that higher production could be achieved with existing technology, and in part because the benefits promised to be more immediate.

Beginning in 1954 the *extension model* was superseded and incorporated into a more comprehensive organizational structure for agricultural development patterned after the land grant universities in the United States.[2] The adoption and promotion of the *land grant model* was reflected in international aid agency funding of developing country research. This represented 40 to 50 per cent of the total investment in the 1950s and about one-third of the total in the mid-1960s. In research, export crops continued to be favoured over food grains. With one or two exceptions, such as India, the national research programmes of tropical Asia could continue to be categorized as *low skilled systems*. This lag in the development of research organization and scientific skills set the stage for the technological breakthrough that was to follow. The establishment of the International Rice Research Institute (IRRI) in 1962 as the "main station" in an international hierarchal system can be viewed as a temporary departure from the basic developing country research process.

The creation of IRRI and the other international centres for biological research has been referred to as the *"big science" model*.[3] After 1965 international aid funding for national research agencies declined as more and more funds were diverted to the establishment of the international agricultural research centres. The main criticism of this approach is that the new varieties tend to be limited primarily to farmers who can replicate the favourable environmental conditions (e.g. irrigation) and afford the costly inputs. Furthermore, analysis of returns on investment shows that returns in national programmes are very high. There is an observable high degree of complementarity between the work of the national institutions and international centres. A strong national programme can facilitate the spread of new technology by adapting the exotic materials to local conditions. This capacity becomes increasingly important as the easy gain in productivity in the more favourable environments is fully exploited. The establishment of the International Agricultural Development Service (IADS) in 1975, International Service for National Agricultural

Research (ISNAR) in 1978, whose main focus is on the strengthening of national research systems, reflects a growing recognition of the need to achieve an appropriate balance of international aid support between international and national programmes.

ALTERNATIVE METHODS OF ESTABLISHING RESEARCH PRIORITIES

Although the issue can be debated, there was undoubtedly more agreement among rice research workers in the early 1960s as to the best research strategy for increasing rice production than exists today. The lag in technology development created a gap, but experience with small grains elsewhere suggested the potential to be gained from developing a short-strawed fertilizer responsive variety. This objective having been achieved, however, the subsequent steps to increase production were less obvious. Thus, a little more than a decade after the establishment of IRRI, the appropriate allocation of research resources was a matter of considerable debate. Scientific and management staff alike showed increasing concern for the need to develop a clearer perception of research priorities.

Methods and procedures for evaluating agricultural research can be usefully divided into *ex post* studies and *ex ante* models.[4] We will discuss only the *ex ante* approaches. In degree of methodological sophistication, the *ex ante* models range from the simple scoring schemes to highly complex mathematical programming models. To a greater or lesser degree all such models depend upon the judgement of either the research or of knowledgeable individuals concerning the outcome of future events. While the results may be sensitive to these judgements, some of the most important findings are likely to hold under a wide range of sensitivity tests. Three *ex ante* approaches have been utilized by IRRI.

A wide range of models has been developed which attempts to examine the results of research in terms of expected impact on production and income distribution. One such approach employed by IRRI is closely related to the "gap and trend analysis" undertaken by the International Food Policy Research Institute (IFPRI).[5] The growing gap between projected demand for food and projected trend in supply reflects the need to achieve more rapid increase in production. A preliminary study was undertaken to determine the investments required in irrigation, fertilizer, and research to increase Asian rice supplies at a pace in keeping with projected demand.[6] A joint project is now being initiated by the ASEAN rice growing countries (Indonesia, Malaysia, Philippines and Thailand) in co-operation with IFPRI, IRRI, and the International Fertilizer Development Centre (IFDC) to investigate the supply, consumption, and trade dimensions of this problem in greater detail. This investigation looks on research as one alternative for shifting the supply function. It is concerned with the total research needs for rice, but not specifically with the allocation or research priorities within rice.

A number of studies have focused on the productivity and income distribution effects of the allocation of research funds among alternative problem areas or commodities. The scoring model has been employed to determine the relative research emphasis that should be given to specific problem areas.[7] Senior scientists were asked to rank the Institute's nine problem areas separately on the basis of twelve questions relating to research expectations. The results were weighed into a single ranking of problem areas. These rankings turned out to be highly comparable to the ranking according to budget allocation. The only significant discrepancy is in the lower rating by scientists of "machinery development and testing" and the higher rank by scientists given to "soil and crop management". The results are, of course, sensitive to the weightings given to the various questions (e.g. will the research increase the yield of rice?) A further difficulty is that even in an institute as small and homogeneous as IRRI, the average scientist is not and should not be expected to be concerned with the priorities of the entire institute.

In the analysis presented in this paper we have used a productivity approach to examine the benefits to be derived from research in different rice-growing environments – irrigated, rainfed, upland, and deep-water rice – in the main rice growing countries of South and Southeast Asia. Scientists believe that in large measure the research findings are environmental specific, and this is borne out by the fact that the new varieties have been adopted principally in the irrigated areas. Thus, we can assume that the four types of rice defined by the different environmental conditions are, from a production perspective, essentially different commodities.

This analysis of production potential in different rice growing environments has implicit implications for income distribution. Many of the rural poor in Asia are located in the unirrigated rice producing regions, particularly in Eastern India and Bangladesh. The initial success of the new rice technology in the irrigated environment has tended to widen the disparity between the irrigated and non-irrigated regions.

Theoretically, in order to maximize the productivity of research resources, expenditures should be allocated so that the increase in productivity from an additional amount of funds spent on research for each rice environment is equated. The analysis should take into account the hectares in the environment over which the new technology is suitable, the expected productivity gain, the farmer's cost involved in using the new technology or the reductions in costs achieved by the technology, the probability of success, and the time period from the start of research until the productivity gain is achieved. Given this information one may calculate the net present value of research for the ith type of rice environment as:

$$NVP_i = \sum_{t=t'}^{T} (1 + r)^{-t} \left[\sum_{m=m'}^{M} P(m)[(\Delta Q_{m,t} - \Delta C_{p,t})A_i] + \right.$$

$$\left[\sum_{n=n'}^{N} P(n)\Delta A_{n,t}(Q_i - C_i) \right] - \sum_{t=0}^{T'} (1 + r)^{-t} K_{i,t}$$

$$NVP_i \quad r \quad t \quad M \quad P(m) \quad \Delta Q_{m,t} \quad \Delta C_{p,t} \quad A_i$$

$$\Delta A_{n,t} \quad n \quad P(n) \quad Q_i \quad C_i \quad K_{i,t}$$

where:

NVP_i = net present value of potential new technology for environment i

r = social rate of time discount (interest rate)

t = time period

M = yield level

$P(m)$ = probability of success in achieving the production or yield increase

$\Delta Q_{m,t}$ = change in value of output made possible by the research in time period t

$\Delta C_{p,t}$ = cost to the farmer of using the technology in time period t

A_i = area over which the technology is successful

$\Delta A_{n,t}$ = new production area suitable for production made possible by research

n = cropping intensity level

$P(n)$ = probability of success in achieving the area change

Q_i = value of output per hectare in environment i

C_i = cost to the farmer of extending production to the new area in environment i

$K_{i,t}$ = capital investment for new technology environment i in time period t

Given this data for each type of environment, it would be optimal to allocate research resources to equate the net present value of potential new technology for each environment. This model has been used in carrying on the analyses in the following section.

ALLOCATION OF RESEARCH INPUTS TO RICE ENVIRON-MENTS

The analysis in this section includes the benefits derived from research in four rice growing environments – irrigated, rainfed, deep-water, and upland – in the main rice growing countries of South and Southeast Asia (see definitions of environments in footnotes of Table 1). We assume that the four types of rice defined by different environmental conditions are, from a production perspective, essentially different commodities. The analyses and results are discussed under three headings: (i) gross benefits, (ii) net benefits for irrigated vs. rainfed rice, (iii) contribution of research by country.

Gross benefits

A group of IRRI scientists estimated the anticipated increase in rice yield and cropping intensity that would be possible from "reasonable" research and extension inputs directed at each environment for South and Southeast Asia. It was assumed that these yields could be realized over a 20-year period. The probability of success, the direct cost of technology for each area, and the time required to achieve success were initially assumed to be identical for all environments. Thus, the objective of the exercise was to estimate the value of the potential increase in production in each area.

Increase in total production was assumed to be attributed to the gain in production from yield, cropping intensity, and new irrigation develop-

TABLE 1   *Estimated changes in yield and cropping intensity attainable in 20 years from reasonable research and extension efforts on rice and its cropping systems for specified rice environmental complexes in South and Southeast Asia, 1970s and 1990s*

Environmental[a] complexes	Yield (t/ha)			Rice cropping intensity			Upland cropping intensity		
	1970s (1)	1990s (2)	Change (3)	1970s (1)	1990s (2)	Change (3)	1970s (1)	1990s (2)	Change (3)
Irrigated	3.0	4.1	1.1	1.2	1.6	0.4	0.3	0.5	0.2
Shallow rainfed	1.8	2.6	0.8	0.7	1.0	0.3	0.4	0.5	0.1
Medium deep rainfed	1.0	1.8	0.8	0.8	0.9	0.1	0.3	0.5	0.2
Deep-water	1.0	1.5	0.5	0.9	1.0	0.1	0.3	0.4	0.1
Upland	1.0	1.5	0.5	0.8	0.8	0	0.5	0.8	0.3

a   For irrigated rice, water is added to the fields from canals, river diversions, pumps or tanks. For unirrigated rice the maximum water depths, tillering to flowering, are 5 to 15 cm for shallow rainfed, 15 to 100 cm for medium deep rainfed, 1 meter or more for deep-water. Most rainfed rice is grown in bunded paddy fields, but for upland rice, water is not impounded in paddy fields.

ment. Gains in yield and cropping intensity are shown in Table 1. Irrigated area was assumed to grow at 1.5 per cent per year. The gross area in rice increased by 3 million hectares due to the increase in the area double-cropped, but the area in rainfed rice declined by 6 million as land was converted from rainfed to irrigated area. Irrigated area thus grew by 9 million hectares.

The value of discounted benefits over the 20-year period are summarized in Table 2. The largest share of benefits, 56 per cent, is in the irrigated area, both because the area is expanding and because the absolute yield gain is larger for irrigated than for rainfed rice. The potential for increasing yields on shallow and medium rainfed areas was assumed to be equal (0.8 t/ha), but the shallow rainfed area is considerably larger than the medium deep rainfed. Rainfed rice accounts for 37 per cent of the total increase in benefits. Upland and deep-water rice account for only 3 and 4 per cent of the total benefits, both because the area is small and the potential for increase in yield is low.

Net benefits for irrigated vs. rainfed rice
We now take into account the cost of increasing production in the irrigated and in the rainfed land in order to compute a benefit–cost ratio and an internal rate of return on investment. The return to increased production in irrigated rice is divided between return on newly irrigated land and on land already irrigated (Table 3). Assumptions with respect to capital investment and annual costs for new irrigation, research and extension, fertilizer, and labour are shown in the paragraphs that follow.

Beginning in 1976 irrigation expands in South and Southeast Asia at a

TABLE 2 *Summary of discounted added benefits from research and extension due to yield increase and cropping intensity for specified environmental complexes in South and Southeast Asia, discounted to present value at 12% interest, 1970s to 1990s*

Environ- mental Complexes	Benefits (billion $) from				
	Increase	Rice cropping intensity	Upland cropping intensity	Total benefits	(%)
Irrigation	10.4	12.9	4.7	28.2	56
Shallow rainfed	5.2	7.4	1.8	14.4	29
Medium deep rainfed	2.3	0.6	1.0	3.9	8
Deep-water	0.9	0.3	0.2	1.4	3
Upland	1.1	0	1.0	2.1	4
Total	19.9	21.2	8.9	50.0	100

rate of 450,000 hectares annually for 20 years at which time there are 9 million hectares of newly irrigated land. The capital cost per hectare of irrigation is $1500 and the annual maintenance fee is $11. The stream of benefits from new irrigation begins 5 years after the investment and benefits are discounted up to the year 2010.

In the year 1976 the annual investment in research and extension on irrigated rice is assumed to be $40 million. It increases at a rate of approximately $3 million per year reaching $100 million in 1995. The investment in rainfed rice research is assumed to be $10 million in 1976 and to increase at approximately $5 million per year reaching $100 million in 1995. Beginning in 1981 yields increase by 55 kgs per year in irrigated land or a total of 1.1 tons/ha by 2000 and by 40 kgs per year on rainfed land or a total of 0.8 tons/ha by 2000. The stream of net benefits (return to rice less fertilizer and labour costs) remain constant after 2000 and is discounted to the year 2010.

Shifting from rainfed to irrigated rice raises the fertilizer nutrient (NPK) input by 60 kg/ha on the 9 million hectares of newly irrigated land by 1985. An additional 120 kg/ha NPK is required on all 36 million hectare of irrigated land, while 40 kg/ha NPK is added to 36 million hectare of rainfed land. The fertilizer costs approximately $150 per ton or $0.33/kg of NPK. Paddy is $0.10/kilo and the NPK to paddy price ratio is 3.3 Approximately half of the fertilizer is produced domestically in 12 new urea plants producing 500,000 tons of urea per year and costing $300 million per plant. One of the plants is charged to new irrigation, 8 to the

TABLE 3 *Annual discounted investment costs and net benefits, benefit–cost ratio and internal rate of return for alternative rice investments, 1970s to 1990s in South and Southeast Asia*

| | New irrigation[a] | Research and Extension | |
		Irrigated rice	Rainfed rice
Discounted investment costs	5800	2000	850
Discounted net benefits			
equal probability	5600	13500	11000
unequal probability[b]	5000	10100	5500
Benefit–cost ratio (12% interest)			
equal probability	1.0	6.7	12.9
unequal probability	1.9	5.0	6.5
Internal rate of return (%)			
equal probability	12	40	85
unequal probability	11	35	40

a Benefits from new irrigation include the yield increase due to research on new irrigated area.

b Assumed probability of achieving production gain from new irrigation = 100 per cent; from research/extension on irrigated rice = 75 per cent; from research/extension on rainfed rice = 50 per cent.

irrigated, and 3 to the rainfed area. The schedule for construction is 2 plants in 1980, 4 in 1985, 3 each in 1990 and 1995.

In both rainfed and irrigated areas labour is the main cost associated with increased production. Thirty days are required to produce an additional ton of paddy and labour is valued at $1 per day.

The results in Table 3 suggest that the benefit–cost ratio and internal rate of return is high for investment in research and extension on existing irrigated land, seemingly even higher on rainfed land. Why then do we find in the plans of many developing Asian economies increasing emphasis on irrigation investment and relatively little interest in research on rainfed rice? The answer is, in part, related to the fact that secondary benefits including employment impact are not incorporated in the benefit–cost analysis. Another important factor is the probability of success, the element that we have not yet incorporated in our model. Although the payoff is low, the greatest certainty is associated with increased productivity due to expansion of irrigated land. We assumed that the probability of success in achieving returns on a hectare of new irrigation comparable to that for existing is 100 per cent; the probability of achieving a 1.1 ton yield increase from investment in research for the irrigated environment is 75 per cent; the probability of achieving a 0.8 ton yield increase from investment in research on the rainfed environment is 50 per cent. Using these probabilities, we recalculate the benefits and costs and internal rates of return (Table 3). While the order of priority remains the same, the difference among alternatives is understandably much smaller.

Given these new calculations one might argue that with scarce scientific manpower, it makes better sense to concentrate these limited resources in irrigated rice. In the early 1960s, when the potential for increasing rice production even in the favourable tropical environments was uncertain, the argument seemed valid. However, to see this issue more clearly in the light of the situation existing today, we need to examine the potential benefits from irrigated and rainfed rice research and extension on a country by country bias.

Contribution of research by country
We sent questionnaires to a delegation of rice scientists from each country asking them for the information on the present area in irrigated, upland, deep-water, and rainfed rice (shallow, and medium deep) and for the present and potential yields in each of these categories. This unofficial data received from each of the countries was used to compute the potential benefits from research extension in each country following the procedure used previously. (Benefits due to cropping intensity were not considered.) The percentage share of the benefits attributable to each rice crop environment are summarized in Table 4.

The results indicate that the countries in Asia fall into two categories: those with high potential benefits from investment in rainfed rice research and those with high potential benefits from investment in irrigated rice research. Bangladesh, Burma, Thailand, and Nepal fall into the first category; Indonesia, Philippines, and Sri Lanka into the second. The exception is India, which shows a distribution of benefits similar to that for South and Southeast Asia. But if we were to divide India, which accounts for almost half of the total rice area, into regions we probably would observe the same biomodal distribution. Hence, the global priorities as seen by IRRI differ markedly from the priorities as seen by individual countries or regions.

IMPLICATIONS FOR RICE RESEARCH

The evolution of rice research systems in South and Southeast Asia has been accompanied by an extreme shortage of manpower and a chronic underinvestment in research funds. Developed countries have played an important role in establishing the system that exists today. However, this has involved an extended learning process as efforts to transfer first technology and then institutions to the developing countries did not solve the production problem. IRRIs initial success in increasing rice production has been criticized on the grounds that it failed to give adequate attention to the distribution problem.

The potential for increasing production on the non-irrigated areas is still in question. However, it now seems appropriate for social as well as economic reasons to concentrate more research resources on the more promising of the shallow rainfed areas. The success of such a research endeavour will depend much more than in the past on an understanding of the clientele that the research is designed to serve. To design appropri-

TABLE 4 *Estimated percentage contribution of research–extension to growth in rice production by specified environmental complexes for selected countries in South and Southeast Asia, 1970s to 1990s*

	SA	N	T	B	Bu	In	Ph	I	SL
Irrigated	52	20	22	23	25	45	75	76	79
Shallow rainfed	26	67	49		10	11	10	8	
Medium deep rainfed	12		24	22	72	26	1.5		9
Deep-water	5	–	4	4		4	0.5	6	–
Upland	5	13	1	10	3	15	12	8	4
Total	100	100	100	100	100	100	100	100	100
Implied annual growth in rice production	2.4	3.0	4.1	1.9	3.2	3.6	2.9	4.2	2.4

a Benefits are due to yield increase only.
Key: SA = South and Southeast Asia; N = Nepal; T = Thailand; B = Bangladesh; Bu = Burma; In = India; Ph = Philippines; I = Indonesia; SL = Sri Lanka.

ate research for rainfed farmers, it is necessary to understand their present farming system, and the factors that constrain their production. There are already attempts to experiment with this new *interactive model*. However, increasing rice production in the rainfed areas will require a major research investment and a new philosophy in place of the drive for high yield that pervades most experiment stations.

NOTES

[1] This typology is due to Evenson, developed in the context of developing country research generally, and not with specific reference to rice in Asia. Robert E. Evenson "Comparative Evidence on Returns to Investment in National and International Research Institutions", in *Resource Allocation and Productivity in National and International Research*, edited by Thomas M. Arndt, Dana G. Dalrymple, and Vernon W. Ruttan, pp. 237–64, Minneapolis, University of Minnesota Press, 1977.

[2] Esman discusses the postwar research and development phase in terms of four models, reflecting the particular emphasis of the period. These include: (i) the *extension model*, (ii) the *land grant model*, (iii) the *big science model*, and (iv) an *interactive model*, as yet in the formative stage in which the attempt is to provide appropriate technology to those farmers by-passed by the "green revolution," by strengthening the link between the farmer and the research worker. Milton J. Esman "Research and Development Organization", mimeo, International Studies, Cornell University, Ithaca, New York 1978.

[3] Ibid.

[4] Two useful review documents on this subject have been prepared at the request of the Technical Advisory Committee (TAC) of the Consultative Group on International Agricultural Research (CGIAR): (i) G. Edward Schuh and Helio Tollini "Cost and Benefits of Agricultural Research: State of the Art, and Implications for CGIAR", mimeo, Consultative Group on International Agricultural Research, Oct. 1978, and (ii) International Food Policy Research Institute "Criteria and Approaches to the Analysis of Priorities for International Agricultural Research," mimeo, Working Paper No. 1, Washington, DC Nov. 1978.

[5] International Food Policy Research Institute "Food Needs in the Developing Countries: Projections of Production and Consumption to 1990", Research Paper No. 3, Washington, DC Dec. 1977.

[6] Robert W. Herdt, Amanda Te, and Randolph Barker "The Prospects for Asian Rice Production," *Food Research Institute Studies* 16 (1977).

[7] The procedure and the productivity approach presented subsequently are described in detail in "IRRI Long Range Planning Committee Report," mimeo, Draft V, International Rice Research Institute, Los Baños, Philippines Sept. 1978.

GENERAL DISCUSSION – RAPPORTEUR: EARL D. KELLOGG

Since the indirect effects of increasing irrigated rice production are different from the indirect effects of increasing rainfed rice, the estimating procedure accounted for these differences through cropping intensity levels. The different adoption rates and equity impacts of increasing irrigated versus rainfed rice production were not included in the estimation procedures but could be incorporated when better data is available on which to base the estimates of the parameters. One reason for emphasizing the differences among countries was to encourage scientists in those countries to increase their own efforts to measure the probable returns to alternative investments in research on the various rice environments.

One question involved the reasons for a lack of communication between staff of International Agricultural Centres and National Research programmes. It was pointed out that, in some cases, individuals in both institutions did not *want* to communicate. In some cases, national research programmes decreased investments in some research areas because they were being emphasized by the international centre.

Participants in the discussion included Uma Lele and Indra Jit Singh.

SECTION V

Multi-national, Parestatal and State Trading Agencies

WILLIAM A. CROMARTY

Challenges for Agricultural Economists Working for Multi-national Firms

The fortunate characteristic of this topic is that it gives the author broad licence to comment on agricultural economists' activities. The difficulty of the topic is to confine the material to an area that is meaningful in terms of agrarian change and in particular as it relates to agricultural economists in multi-national firms. First, for purposes of this paper a multi-national firm is defined as an incorporated business having activities in more than one country. This does not necessarily mean having offices and processing facilities in more than one country, but it does require that international manufacturing or trading in agricultural commodities, or services, be carried on in two or more countries. Such activities may be firm to firm, firm to government, firm to state trading agencies, or the reverse of each of these. An agricultural economist is defined as an individual having a degree in agricultural economics.[1] This turns out to be a very restrictive definition since one is really interested in the functions performed in the agricultural economics area whether by economists or by others.

In accepting the invitation to present a paper on this particular topic, I realized that a considerable degree of self-analysis was involved. I also realized that it would be helpful to have an evaluation by other agricultural economists or senior management people employed by multi-national firms of what they perceive the challenges to be. To that end, I surveyed fifteen other firms, and twelve were gracious enough to reply to a questionnaire. The questions numbered seven and included:

(a) numbers of agricultural economists employed,
(b) how the numbers have grown over the years and why,
(c) is their function staff or operational,
(d) is there free movement from staff to operations,
(e) are problems primarily national or international in scope,
(f) what is the future of agricultural economists in your company,
(g) what changes in training are recommended.

These firms were all in the size category where annual sales currently range from an excess of $100 million to several billion dollars. A general summary of the answers follows, along with specific comments which may be more enlightening.

509

The average number of agricultural economists per corporation was six if one corporation is omitted. The range was zero to eleven. If one large corporation is included, the average increases to eleven.

The growth has been most rapid during the past decade. Since all corporations surveyed were involved with agricultural commodities or machinery, this growth, no doubt, reflects the increases in trade volume occurring during a similar period.

Most corporations (except for the one with many economists) reported that agricultural economics filled positions that were predominantly staff. These functions involved "information gathering and analyses" or as a "resource for the decision-makers." In those corporations where movement from staff functions to operations occurred, the results were deemed beneficial.

The freedom of movement from staff to operational or line positions varied. Several replies indicated agricultural economists were hired for staff positions and tended to stay in such positions even to the point of suggesting "dead-ending". Others indicated that mobility into operational functions depended primarily upon the "quality of the individual". Movement has become more pronounced in recent years. One company reported good results from moving people with training in areas other than economics, i.e., personnel, advertising, marketing, from operational positions into staff positions where the functions would normally be undertaken by agricultural countries. Of particular interest in this area was the response by a Japanese firm with headquarters in Tokyo, but having branch offices in many countries. Their activities involved manufacturing of agricultural commodities, marketing of the same, and trading on a world-wide basis in commodities. In accepting new employees, they ask all candidates to complete a written test. Those receiving the highest marks are then accepted into the firm. The interesting aspect is that, whereas, many of the resulting positions involve functions one might attribute to agricultural economists, the candidates come from all disciplines. They may have been graduates in law, engineering, electronics, literature, etc. No doubt the Japanese philosophy of remaining for a lifetime with the same firm has some distinct advantages when combined with this method of selecting candidates, since on-the-job training becomes a good investment. However, one must wonder if the significant successes reached by such firms is due to less emphasis on training in specific skills, in this case agricultural economics, and more emphasis in the blending of many disciplines as problem solving occurs.

It may appear redundant to ask if economists in multi-national companies work on national or international problems. All respondents answered that international problems were dealt with. However, several emphasized that this had become so only in recent years. The implicit deduction is that in previous years agricultural economists in a particular country worked on the national problems existing in that country while those economists in another country worked on the problems particular to that country.

There was unanimous agreement that use of agricultural economists in multi-national firms would increase. Perhaps it is natural, but the largest growth potential appeared to be with firms employing the greatest number of agricultural economists at present while little growth was expected where few economists are currently employed. There was particular stress here that growth involved the "availability of qualified people", that "as long as colleges attract and train good people, openings will be available", or "it depends on the calibre and expertise of the individual", or "there is a future for people who can do good in-house analytical work". Several respondents indicated that additions would be concentrated on those with advanced degrees.

The question regarding changes in training brought forth the greatest response in both variety and number of suggestions. Perhaps a direct quotation from a respondent can help focus on a pertinent area contained in most replies. "Most agricultural economists are unable to focus on practical objectives and the means of achieving them as opposed to stereotyped modeling where the emphasis is on the technique rather than on the answer needed." This was a common criticism of people entering the field. Suggestions on improving the situation included:

(a) "students need more case studies to show them approaches to decision making",
(b) "emphasis should be on problem solving, how to think it through, and then how to communicate it to others",
(c) "there should be work with business departments with, possibly, business internships, perhaps we need MBAs with emphasis in agriculture",
(d) "there is an over reliance on technical solutions and not a good enough grasp of the fundamentals of the problem" and "the cross fertilization between operations and staff is, therefore, desirable".

Criticism was fairly widespread regarding a lack of problem-solving abilities. Perhaps for this reason the tendency also existed to consider agricultural economists in multi-national firms as "information gatherers", "resources for decision-makers", and less as managers involved in decision-making. However, it is obvious that several agricultural economists in multi-national firms have risen to high level executive positions and are involved in major decisions of the corporations. One can easily attribute this to their own personal qualities of leadership, initiative, and opportunity.

Several suggestions were made on additional emphasis for specific formal courses. These included:

(a) agricultural policy, and especially the "politics of agriculture",
(b) business management, corporate finance, and accounting,
(c) emphasis on risk analysis, commodity theory, and price forecasting methodologies,
(d) communication skills,
(e) international finance and international trade,
(f) more emphasis on economics and less on mathematics.

Accompanying the suggestions were comments that the courses are available, but student selection suffers.

The above remarks concerning agricultural economists in multinational firms are undoubtedly biased because of the sample selection, it being comprised of 10 of the 12 respondents with headquarters in the USA. However, time and availability of potential respondents were limiting factors. There is also no reason to believe that results in other areas of the Western world would be different.[2] We should not treat lightly the Japanese approach. The intermingling of disciplines, acceptance of on-the-job training, limited turnover of personnel, and above all, the acceptance of the most highly qualified candidates regardless of training (accepting that a written examination can provide such a determination) would seem to go a long way toward solving many of the criticisms directed at training programmes in the Western world. When questioned as to how they tackled specific technical problems, the Japanese replied that they used outside consultants for limited time periods.

The above section deals with agricultural economists working in multi-national firms but says little about the challenges they face. The next section changes abruptly. Views on challenges are entirely those of the author and in no way reflect answers received by co-operating firms. The viewpoint is that of an agricultural economist with a multi-national firm working with senior level management and other agricultural economists in multi-national firms. The time span of such experience is twenty years, and the breadth of experience involves the major grains, livestock, sugar, coffee, and cocoa.

THE CHALLENGES FACED

A major difficulty involved in writing any paper is to decide from which framework one is going to operate. In this particular case, one could operate from an historical perspective and attempt to enumerate in chronological fashion the accomplishments of agricultural economists in multi-national firms over the past fifty years. Not only would the data requirements for this be a great obstacle but the results would turn out to be sterile and self laudatory for the profession. A second approach would be to be descriptive of the functions performed by agricultural economists. If such functions serve a useful purpose, and these are the only ones in which we are interested, then obviously problems arise, analyses are conducted, decisions are made, and some responsibility assumed. Since agricultural economists are primarily involved in this problem solving area, the challenges are great. The most important single challenge in this area is to become a "decision-maker" rather than a "data gatherer". There are notable exceptions in multi-national corporations, but generally agricultural economists are regarded as resource people who gather and analyse data and make recommendations to management regarding courses of action to be taken. This should not be regarded as an unimportant function, and there are certainly challenges faced in performing these functions adequately. However, the contribution to any multi-national firm is substantially greater if one operates at the end of the spectrum which includes decision-making, implementing decisions in an operational sense, and accepting the responsibility for them. Most major management decisions involve the acquisition and evaluation of information from several disciplines, e.g., finance, transportation, accounting, engineering, political environment, etc. The challenge to agriculture economists is to have some competence in such areas or at least to be capable of acquiring and evaluating information from such disciplines in a decision-making framework.

A recurrent problem and one where agricultural economists can make a significant contribution is in developing a "decision-making framework". Marschak wrote that, "knowledge is useful if it helps to make the best decisions".[3]

There are two aspects of this upon which to concentrate, namely, what constitutes relevant knowledge and what constitutes a good decision. Multi-national companies tend to be pragmatic in their approach to solving problems. This is understandable. However, this does not mean one should be pragmatic about information since this tends to concentrate too much on past decisions, known information and stable institutional factors. Such knowledge is useful and should be incorporated into the total body of knowledge, but it is not necessarily the most relevant. The most relevant knowledge may be information with great uncertainty as to its accuracy, that which deals with the nature of changing structures where subjective judgements are necessary, or new information not yet developed or available. The challenge for the agricultural economist who is primarily a "data gatherer" is related to these latter categories. When "facts" are unknown, "best current information" is of great help. Evaluation of changing structure requires creativity – the antithesis of "stereotyped modelling". Developing information is an art. One must be able to judge its relevance, its accuracy, its availability, and its cost.

The second aspect, or what constitutes a good decision, is a more difficult and complex problem. Problems in multi-national corporations are varied in nature, in importance, in ease of solution, and generally are of a continuing nature. Most have little time for formal definition, require decisions within time periods all too constrained, and many are settled on the basis of pragmatic information described above. Sometimes there are no alternatives. However, it is important to determine if alternative means of reaching solutions exist. For instance, if masses of data must be continually examined before a decision is reached, do you use computers to put the data in a more meaningful form; if faced with multi-office communication problems, do you change the technique of communication; or if a particular problem arises continually with repeated snap decisions, each treated independently, do you develop a decision process that can be "conditionally automated", i.e., if this occurs, then do this?

Again, these are the types of decisions that are relatively easy to handle. The relative ease is associated with the pragmatism of decision-making in multi-national corporations; namely, that internal policy dictates that profit maximization or cost minimization is the basic focus. It may be easy for those outside multi-national corporations to be critical of a goal which concentrates on monetary values but any other goal is often impossible, especially if one also believes in longevity of service.

But there are a group of problems where other values may have to be considered and certainly where less pragmatic approaches are necessary. This gets into the policy area or the strategy area. Usually associated with this area is a greater need to bear responsibility for one's actions and to develop mechanisms to make strategies operational. This point of separation is where many agricultural economists have either feared to tread or failed to tread. It is reflected in the responses of a majority of the companies that agricultural economists are not trained to be decision-makers. The decision-making implied here is in the area of "strategy", "policy", "normative analyses", or perhaps other terms. It involves competence in several disciplines, communicative abilities, personal attributes of creativity, initiative, ambition, etc., and certainly an ability to outline problems whether formally or informally, determine what information is necessary, reach a decision and bear the responsibility for its execution and results. The problems faced by multi-national corporations of this type, and where there is an expectation that training in agricultural economics can be helpful, include, but are certainly not limited to, the following, singly or jointly: commodity prices, income and expenses of related farm enterprises, commodity agreements, agricultural policy and its impact on all major groups affected, international exchange rates, inventory control, future markets, and in recent years an important group including government monetary and fiscal controls, controls imposed by government regulatory agencies, and controls imposed at the discretion of government administrators.

Solutions to these problems, even including the latter group, always have an element of pragmatism involved, but more often it involves heavy doses of normative analyses, i.e., what should be. Perhaps examples would help in clarification.

International commodity agreements have been upheld as instruments to provide price stability and subsequently income stability of producing groups. The basic mechanism for achieving this is generally export quotas for producing members, perhaps accompanied by buffer stocks. Academic and government economists may view such agreements favourably because of the welfare concepts involved. Yet, if trade volume, which is about to be restricted, is of major importance to a trading firm, what should the position be of that corporation's economist? Obviously, conflicts arise even though the same economic principles are used by all parties. Or what should the response be to a consuming corporation if such agreements increase prices? It is difficult to propose to management any solution which puts welfare concepts first at the expense of the corporation's potential profits.

Situations have arisen in which acreage restrictions, whether mandatory or voluntary, have resulted in smaller supplies and subsequently
higher prices. Again this may limit trade volume because of supply
shortages or competitively higher prices, or may result in consuming
corporations suffering substantial increases in ingredient costs. The
"goodness" or "badness" of such actions depends upon one's relationships to the market. Should corporation economists take academic
economists to task because their evaluation of potential results from
proposed policies differ sharply? Seldom do such policies permit Pareto-
better adjustment, where no involved party suffers injury.

A particular challenge facing agricultural economists in multi-national
corporations is that area of problems associated with government
policies, or more particularly how administrators administer legislation.
Reference here, by necessity, is confined to the USA, but affects other
countries and very often multi-national corporations.

One challenge presents itself in the formation of legislation or the
formation of policies by government agencies under existing legislation.
In many such instances, economists should be willing to drop pragmatism
in favour of principle. Yet there is a great reluctance to do so. The press
regards with great disfavour any attempts by corporations or trade groups
representing corporations to shape legislation for their benefit. Such
adverse publicity can be damaging to a corporation or to individuals
within a corporation, and, therefore, an input of most importance can be
lost to the formation of good legislation. Businesses, and economists
within them, should be willing to concentrate on economic principles and
to defend the "goodness" of such principles. They must also develop a
consistency of approach. Political positions of corporations cannot simply
be opportunistic with short run horizons, and the public interest must be
allowed for. If businesses develop a positive and consistent approach
toward legislative matter rather than an attitude of acquiescence to
legislation shaped without their involvement, there might be less necessity for regulatory agencies to dictate policies in the area of trade, pollution, safety and health, controls over food, etc. Businesses do have rights
and prerogatives which should be nurtured and protected in the shaping
of legislation. Agricultural economists with multi-national firms can do
much in this area if they have knowledge and a capability for decision-
making.

An associated area, but one of even more sensitivity, is the administering of legislation. Government power is inordinate. This, coupled with
the fact that when problems arise the problem statement is generally
defined by government personnel, can cause business serious difficulties.
Often business acquiesces to uneconomical demands by administrators
out of a sense of frustration, fear of retribution, or because there is a
feeling that yielding on lesser issues will result in a more co-operative
attitude by administrators on more important issues. None of these
reactions by business can be considered as desirable solutions to problems but again pragmatism may overrule principle. For instance, if gov-

ernment policies are a cause of inflation, then business endorsement of voluntary wage and price controls to restrict one's business is not only uneconomic, but is tacit admission that business is responsible for inflation. This example is even more illustrative when the courts have not decided whether or not such wage and price controls are constitutionally permissible. The power of the administrators in forcing compliance is fearful. If a multi-national company has two divisions, one of which is greatly reliant on government contracts, and one which operates on a small scale in the domestic consumer market, then the threat of withholding government contracts places pressure for absolute compliance on the smaller division, regardless of any economic principles one may wish to pursue. When executives of multi-national grain firms are summoned to the Executive Branch and asked to cancel sales made in all good faith one wonders in such cases at the normative nature of the problem statement, the information required to solve it, and the decision-making rules involved. Execution and responsibility are borne in any case.

Multi-national corporations who are critical of the manner in which programmes are administered can suffer severe consequences, even though the criticism can be justified on grounds of welfare and economic efficiency. If government staff regard themselves as dispensers of privileges, then criticizing them, especially publicly, can result in the withdrawal of such privileges, lack of co-operation by staff, and even litigation. This is no area for the faint-hearted. Yet it is an area in which multi-national companies find themselves, where the problems have strong economic connotations and where agricultural economists could play a role. It is not the bailiwick of the "data gatherer". It is the arena of the decision-maker. While the execution and the responsibility must be borne by the corporation, the decision-making step is the crucial one. If corporate policy dictates a pragmatic approach as against principles, then problem solutions may be simpler. The economists' input should help in deciding what the corporate policy should be.

It would be a simple matter to indicate specific problems which multi-national companies face, and for the pragmatic young people looking for a future with multi-national companies, this may appear useful. Problems of crop and livestock production, grain storage and transportation, trade policy, demand shifts, influence of climatic factors, inflation, government monetary and fiscal policies, energy, price forecasting, interest rates, are but a small sample. The list is not important because it is everchanging. The important factors are the knowledge to evaluate such problems as they arise and a decision-making capability to solve them.

If there is a central message in this challenge, it is for agricultural economists to lift themselves from the "data gathering" function to the "decision-making" function. For those who remain in the data area, there is a need to be more creative and less pragmatic toward data gathering and analyses. For those in the decision-making area, one must be able to help shape corporate policy, make decisions, and make decisions become operational. It requires a capability in several disciplines, or at a minimum an ability to evaluate information from other disciplines.

In the current era, multi-national corporations have been subjected to intense criticism by government agencies, the press, consumer groups, private economists, and others. Perhaps some of it is justified. On the other hand, there are few, if any, champions of the contributions they have made – contributions not matched by comparable public or state trading agencies. Future contributions, and they will be made, will depend upon the human element, upon well qualified, creative people with self initiative. There is a place for agricultural economists to be an important part of this group.

NOTES

[1] At least one respondent regarded an advanced degree as the definition pertinent to his answer.

[2] Other industry economists have reported on the role and training of agricultural economists in industry. See in particular, Kolmer, L.R., "Opportunities and Responsibilities of Agricultural Economists: A General View", *Amer. J. Agr. Econ*, 57 (1975), pp. 778–81. Sparks, W.R. "Preparing the Undergraduate for the World of Work: Perspective From The Grain Trade", *Amer. J. Agr. Econ*, 57 (1975), pp. 788–90. Luby, P.J. "Preparing the Undergraduate for the World of Work: Perspective From the Meat-Packing Industry", *Amer. J. Agr. Econ*, 57 (1975), pp. 791–5. Erikson, C.E. "The Role of the Agricultural Economist for Industry", *Amer. J. Agr. Econ.* 57 (1975) pp. 879–82. Brunthaver, C.G. "Agricultural Economics as an Aid in Management Decision Making", *Amer. J. Agr. Econ.* 57 (1975), pp. 889–91.

[3] Marschak, J. *Studies in Econometric Method*, Wiley, New York 1953, edited by T.C. Koopmans.

DISCUSSION OPENING – WILHELM HENRICHSMEYER

When I first read the topic of this paper I wondered which specific aspects of challenges for an agricultural economist working in multi-national firms might be discovered. Mr Cromarty must have felt this, when he writes in his first sentence that the topic gives him a broad licence to comment on agricultural economists' activities. He uses these opportunities widely in his paper to the benefit of this session, which might have been rather meagre if he had held narrowly to his topic.

In order to discover the challenges to agricultural economists working for multi-national firms Cromarty uses two kinds of approach: on the one hand he makes use of a questionnaire to a number of multi-national firms in the US; on the other hand he relies on his own judgement as an agricultural economist, who has broad and long standing experience from his work for multi-national firms. The results of the questionnaire inform us mainly about some facts, such as numbers of agricultural economists employed, their positions in staff and decision-making, etc. This information can be useful for agricultural economists looking for a job and as a background for teaching programmes, but there is not very much to discuss about it.

The results of the questionnaire with respect to the chances for agricultural economists are rather general, e.g. when it is summarized that openings will be available if the colleges attract good people, or that it depends on the personality of the individual. I suppose that the answers would not be very different if one had asked about the changes in any other profession or field.

In the same vein the proposed changes in the training of agricultural economists do mainly contain those points that most demanders for agricultural economists would put forward and – as I suppose – most teachers of agricultural economists all over the world are aiming for, such as to get a good grasp of the fundamentals of a problem or to have problem solving teaching instead of stereotyped modelling. The suggestions for new specific courses are so broad that they can hardly give a base for a discussion of teaching programmes.

So Cromarty can rightly conclude that there is no reason to believe that the results of the questionnaire would be different in other areas of the western world. I do not even suppose that managers of other kinds of firms or institutions would give significantly different answers. Possibly one might even have known most of the answers in advance.

The most informative and discussible points of the paper seem to me to be Cromarty's personal remarks and judgements about the activities and chances of agricultural economists in large business firms. He informs us in great detail about the functions of economists in the data gathering and in the decision-making areas as well as the educational and personal requirements for entering higher ranks. Many of the points will not be very new for most of us; but it is good to have these requirements expressed and confirmed by a person who has a long standing experience in the management of large firms.

The operational question for the profession of agricultural economists is, however, to translate these challenges into the training and research programmes of our universities. Therefore questions have to be answered of the following kind. How much of the scarce time of a student of agricultural economics should be devoted to the general background in economic theory, to analytical tools and to problem oriented applications? And with respect to the latter: should this be done in the form of case studies or by a more general policy analysis approach? These questions are beyond the scope of the paper, but might be taken up in the discussion.

A further question which Cromarty takes up deals with the conflicts of an economist between the specific goals of the firm he is working for and the general socio-economic goals of society. But these conflicts are not specific challenges to agricultural economists in multi-national firms. Usually the interests and goals of economic agents – whether they are private or public – will diverge from general "welfare-maximization", however this might be defined. Cromarty advocates a continuous and cautious way of pursuing long run goals. But even if they were doing so, nobody would expect that larger multi-national firms were striving for Pareto-like solutions. It will be a perpetual public task to limit and control the economic power of very large enterprises as well as of administrators of government agencies, to which Cromarty is referring in his paper. But this opens up a wide field of discussion which might be beyond the scope of this session.

GENERAL DISCUSSION – RAPPORTEUR: B.L. GREENSHIELDS

The role of agricultural economists in multi-national corporations (MNCs) was discussed, both from the perspective of the MNC and the economist. The MNC views the economist at the one extreme as window dressing and at the other as a key adviser to top management. The MNC requires a multi-lingual economist who can communicate the results of complicated analysis in simple language.

The agricultural economist views the MNC at one extreme as a dead end job of data collection and at the other as an opportunity to get into management. Professional rewards are few and authorship is usually not indicated on MNC reports prepared by economists. MNC create conflicts between economists, national interests and corporate interests.

The paper was criticized for the small sample of mostly US MNCs from which references were made. There was also a question as to the logic behind cross-fertilization improving economists' grasps of fundamentals. An alternative hypothesis was suggested that cross-fertilization would ensnare the economists in short run issues and impede in-depth, long range research.

Participants in the discussion included Adolf A. Weber, Clark Edwards, Chester W. Smith, James A. Akinwumi, Jim Johnston and Ben I.B. Warmenhoven.

HAROLD F. BJARNASON

Accomplishments of and Opportunities for Agricultural Economists in Parastatal Organizations

I have been asked to speak to you on the role of agricultural economists in parastatal organizations. All my experience in this area has been with the Canadian Wheat Board, so that my comments will be based entirely on my involvement with that organization.

The Canadian Wheat Board, defined in Canadian legislation as a "Crown" corporation, was established by the Government of Canada in 1935 to market Western Canadian grains in an orderly manner. At present, the Board has full responsibility for marketing Western Canadian wheat, oats and barley internationally. It also has sole responsibility for marketing these grains domestically to processors for human consumption (i.e., flour mills, malting companies, etc.), and is a standby supplier of grains to livestock feeders at (US) "corn competitive" prices.

In describing the role that agricultural economists have played and can play in an organization such as the Canadian Wheat Board, special attention must be given to that word in this year's IAAE theme "change." For change has characterized the national and international grain marketing system and has influenced the real and perceived need for economists, since the first batch of wheat was shipped abroad from the Canadian prairies in the 1880s. A very brief history of the evolution of the Canadian and international grain marketing systems can perhaps best illustrate this. A look ahead to probable developments in grain marketing structures and systems will say much about the need for input by agricultural economists in the future.

The Western Canadian grain growing area was quickly settled during the last part of the nineteenth century by the adventurous, the dispossessed and the downtrodden from scores of European countries. These settlers, arriving in large numbers, were armed for the most part with no more than simple and crude farm implements to do battle with heavy soils and unpredictable weather. Little time passed, however, before they found themselves in a continual and losing struggle with even harsher forces – the shippers and carriers of grain. The two major railway companies, which monopolized grain movements in their separate regions, granted monopoly rights to a small number of grain handling companies

520

or "syndicates" as they were called at the time. Syndicate owners then met daily in Winnipeg to set country prices, so that competing on the basis of price for a farmer's business became non-existent. Farmers' returns per bushel therefore remained at constantly low levels, even in the face of rising world prices. Syndicate profits, conversely, were allowed to fluctuate, depending on the world price, between moderate and exorbitant levels. Agricultural economics as a separate discipline did not, of course, even exist at the time, but the grain industry moguls did make good use, or rather, misuse, of the teachings of that great *laissez-faire* theorist, Adam Smith, to justify the workings of "free enterprise". Where farmers experienced injustice and exploitation, these corporate leaders saw immutable market forces at work, guiding the entire grains economy to its point of highest return. Instead of fostering the development of a healthy market economy, they used their market strength to meddle with market mechanisms, all the while protesting that their self-interest was allowing Smith's famous "invisible hand" to serve the highest interests of society.

Trapped in a world of back-breaking labour, poverty and broken dreams, prairie grain farmers showed little interest in the niceties of irrelevant economic theories. Instead they began to organize, to collect strength to stand up to and against the powerful transportation and marketing interests. They established farmer-owned grain companies and succeeded in forcing the federal government to regulate the activities of the grain companies and railroads. They were thereby able to put an end to the most blatant abuses, in that period, of the grain marketing system. And yet, control of their economic destinies remained largely out of their reach, as world demand and prices continued to fluctuate capriciously and without regard for the welfare of Western Canadian farmers.

During World War I, the grain marketing situation grew increasingly chaotic as the Allied Governments demanded all the excess grain that could be produced in the Canadian West. The Government, in response, was forced to resort to the establishment of a government grain marketing board, which was later restructured as the Canadian Wheat Board. Trading in futures at the Winnipeg Grain Exchange was suspended, and concepts such as the initial payment (a guaranteed minimum price) and the pooling of farmer funds for determining final payments were introduced.

Prairie farmers, who experienced a sustained period of high prices for the first time, under a marketing system they could view as a real marketing alternative, strongly supported continuation of the Wheat Board concept. Not so the federal legislators, however, who continued to view the production and marketing of Canadian grains in a world grain marketing system as the genius of Adam Smith in action. Direct involvement by economists at the time was limited or negligible, and then mainly to prepare theoretical justification for the *status quo*. The Canadian Wheat Board was therefore disbanded in July 1920.

Crop disasters, low prices and reduced marketing opportunities by the mid 1930s, however, finally forced the Canadian Government to consider radical changes in the Canadian grain marketing system. And yet, it remains ironic that passage of the Canadian Wheat Board Act in 1935 was due more, it seems, to personal differences that developed between Prime Minister Bennett and grain industry magnates, than it was to deeply felt economic principles. In any case the Canadian Wheat Board was set up with the objective of marketing "as much grain as possible, at the best price that can be obtained", and the Board has maintained responsibility for marketing the bulk of Western Canadian grain production since that time. Involvement of agricultural economists has increased only as world marketing structures, and consequently the Board's way of conducting its business, have changed.

Following the Second World War and up until the 1960s, the Canadian Wheat Board served mainly to provide initial payments to farmers, to pool funds received in addition to this for return to farmers, and to administer a quota system to bring grain into the marketing system in an orderly, programmed manner. Grain sales were made on an "in store Thunder Bay" basis, to a large number of private companies at the Wheat Board's asking price, and on the basis of international and domestic sales made by these companies to a large number of buyers in each importing nation. The Board exerted and desired little control over agency sales, by destination.

Crop failures in the early 1960s in the grain producing areas of the communist world's two giants, however, resulted in an abrupt and lasting change in the international market structure for grains, and as a result in the Canadian Wheat Board's involvement in international grain marketing. China and the Soviet Union, making all purchases through their central purchasing agencies, and dealing with all terms of trade, had no desire to arrange for imports of Canadian grains through middlemen. Instead they circumvented the Board's agency system and dealt directly with the Board on all terms of trade, including quantity, grade, shipping periods, port areas, prices, credit arrangements (if any), currencies to be used, and the host of other issues which must be negotiated in international transactions. The Board took the position then, which it has maintained to the present, that it will deal with grain buyers on the basis in which they wish to make their purchase of Canadian grains. As other communist countries came to the international market for grain therefore, Canadian Wheat Board involvement in negotiating contracts directly with foreign grain buyers increased.

But it was not only the presence of communist buyers that increased Board involvement in the international wheat market. Developing countries also became major actors in this area. Countries that had in the past been normally self-sufficient or even occasional exporters found that the productivity of their lands could not keep pace with rapid population growth, so they looked to world grain exporters to supply them with their deficit requirements. Most of these countries, having little or no tradition in grain buying and therefore no established trade, opted to establish government grain import agencies. Governments in most of these countries reasoned that their agencies would be able to provide longer term food security and greater bargaining power *vis-à-vis* exporters, than would the establishment of smaller and competing private import houses. Again in their dealings with Canada, the preference of the import agencies, on the whole, has been to negotiate all terms of trade directly with the Canadian Wheat Board. Purchases made by developing nations, incidentally, now account for over 50 per cent of the world wheat total.

Conditions have not remained static in the so-called open market economies either, as buying, which in most nations in the recent past was in the hands of a large number of firms, has become concentrated in the hands of a very small number. In Western Europe, for example, over 90 per cent of all wheat purchases made by our largest wheat customer on that continent, the United Kingdom, is now made by two firms. Foreign purchases of Canadian durum wheat for the 15 large semolina mills in Italy are made by one firm in Naples. The bulk of our barley sales to Italy are negotiated between the Wheat Board and one major buyer. Similarly, purchases of wheat and barley by Japan are made on a weekly tender basis by the Japanese Food Agency, which is part of that country's Department of Agriculture. In a relatively short period of time, therefore, the share of sales negotiated by the Wheat Board directly has increased from zero to over 80 per cent.

Concurrently, during this period of rapid structural change, the volume of world trade has grown substantially. The wheat trade has doubled over the past twenty years to a level in excess of 70 million tonnes, and the coarse grain trade has quadrupled, to over 80 million tonnes per annum at present.

Obviously, in the face of all this change and growth, a continuing level of high marketing performance has required a much higher level of technical and managerial expertise and training. In the last couple of decades therefore, agricultural economists have been taken on staff for the first time and have directly influenced the actual operations and policy decisions of the Canadian Wheat Board.

There is a great deal in an agricultural economist's training that will allow him to make valuable contributions to the efficient operation of a parastatal organization, and I will list some of them with specific reference to the Canadian Wheat Board. But I should also point out that to be effective, an agricultural economist must first secure rather extensive experience in the grains industry. Academics, for example, who have no practical experience in grain marketing often seem to reach invalid conclusions even with their highly honed academic tools, because they do not properly understand the nature of the product or the nature of competition in the industry. They assume, for example, homogeneity of a product such as wheat, when in fact wheat has many different end uses, all requiring different quality characteristics. They often ignore or downplay the psychological and political factors which can strongly influence price and purchasing decisions in a large number of countries; and conversely, they often overestimate the value of their econometric applications. Also, economists generally assume a competitive free trade international grain market, in which producers and consumers in all trading nations respond to international price movements. But that is in fact not at all descriptive of the international grain trade. I will say more on that later.

In an analytical sense, agricultural economists at the Wheat Board have engaged themselves in a very large and varied number of activities and project, including

pricing and marketing strategies to maximize farmers' returns. How much, for example, of which grains should be sold and to which individual markets? When should sales be timed and when should contracts be priced? How closely should the Board follow price movements in the US commodity markets? Are movements in these markets real or are they short term fluctuations not related to underlying market forces? What is happening to exchange rates, and what does that mean for Board pricing?

comparative economic systems. The United States is the dominant participant and the price leader in the world grain trade. An understanding of the American pricing system is therefore essential. Also of great importance is a good understanding of the planning systems of those major importing countries with communist governments. A firm grasp of the European Community's Common Agricultural Policy similarly is essential.

market analysis. The need for accurate and ongoing assessments of individual markets has increased greatly as the Board has become more directly involved in grain sales. A high level of expertise has therefore been developed within the Board constantly to keep abreast of changing supply and demand conditions for all grains in all major grain trading nations.

minimizing marketing costs. Board economists have participated in the development of policies to improve the efficiency and co-ordination of the movement of grain. This has resulted in a complete revamping of the grain logistics system, from farm level to terminal positions. The existing structure of the country elevator system, scattered as it is over very large areas, will continue to present challenges to analysts in the future.

forecasting market demand. We at the board have undertaken major studies to project world trade and the likely structure and needs of the Canadian grains industry in the long term. Our studies indicate continued growth in both the world wheat and feed grain trade. We expect, for example, to be able to export 30 million tonnes of grains and oilseeds from Canada by 1985, as compared with the 21.5 million tonne record level achieved in 1977–78. But we can accomplish this only if grain transportation and handling capacity in Western Canada is adequate to accommodate such a major increase in traffic. The Board, on the basis of these forecasts, has made proposals and provided incentives designed to encourage a significant increase in rail rolling stock and in West Coast terminal capacity. The Board has also encouraged farmers and agricultural scientists to prepare to increase agricultural productivity on the prairies so that farmers in Western Canada can take full advantage of this growth potential.

The agricultural economist in a parastatal organization is, therefore, always conducting his analyses from the industry perspective rather than the narrower one of a competitive firm. It is not the firm's short run profit–loss statement that concerns him so much as the industry's costs–benefits. Ventures that may be uneconomic for privately-owned firms (i.e., the construction of "surge" terminal elevator facilities to handle peak grain movements and minimize demurrage claims) are promoted because of the monetary gains provided to the entire agricultural community. Also, because of its monopoly position in an industrial sector, decisions and changes introduced by parastatal organizations directly affect all components of the industry. The agricultural economist's training will normally enable him to identify the major economic implications of proposed policy changes.

On a broader basis, the agricultural economists' role in the Wheat Board has included describing the structure of the world in which grain is traded, and on this basis, making recommendations about policies to maximize Canadian grain producers' welfare. The goal of the private exporter in the industry, for example, is to maximize short term profits. Margins are normally very small, so a private firm's returns can be maximized when its volume is maximized (i.e., increasing its share of the market). The Wheat Board, as a monopoly seller of Canadian wheat, however, has an entirely different objective – to maximize total returns to Canadian grain farmers, and in a world with very inelastic demand, this can be best achieved by increasing the world price.

Furthermore, agricultural economists experienced in Wheat Board operations quickly reject the widely held assumption that the free play of supply and demand forces internationally dictates the level of world prices. The fact is that consumers in almost all importing countries do not respond to international grain price fluctuations because grain prices in importing nations are usually set well above international levels (i.e., only about 5 per cent of all wheat exported internationally goes to countries where internal price levels are allowed to fluctuate directly with international levels). So consumers in these countries are in effect isolated from international price movements. When domestic production does not meet a country's needs, it imports grain to make up the difference. A country's import demand, in other words, is to a very large degree, a function of its domestic production and supplies. Even in developing countries, the politics of food is so important that most countries will sacrifice hard earned foreign exchange holdings to avoid the politically hazardous possibility of widespread hunger. Food imports in these countries, whether under commercial or aid programmes, largely reflect production shortfalls rather than changes in aggregate demand or financial considerations.

Since grain prices in most important nations are well above and fully insulated from exporters' selling price levels, farmers and governments in exporting countries such as Canada are in effect subsidizing grain buyers (normally governments) in grain importing countries. This has rather profound economic implications, particularly for international wheat agreements and other forms of exporter co-operation, because if this analysis is taken a step further it can be shown that international grain prices could in fact be set at much higher levels without disturbing trade levels. The level of subsidy would then simply fall. In contrast with most textbook examples of oligopolistic selling, in which price is raised above both unit and marginal costs of production, competition between exporting firms and agencies has often resulted in international grain prices at levels *below* unit and marginal costs.[1] Obviously, if exporting countries could agree on levels that would always cover production costs plus transportation and marketing costs to port areas, efficient grain producers in grain exporting nations would be justly allowed to thrive, while consumers in importing countries would have much improved year-to-year and long term supply security. Increasing world prices to such levels would reduce aggregate demand only marginally, if at all, but the transfer of income from exporters to importing countries as a result of restrictive import practices would be substantially reduced. This is the type of reaction that, in line with the theory of countervailing power, can be anticipated, for the exporting nations would be acting together to protect themselves from abuses on the import side.

In looking to the future, I would suggest that a high level of training in economics for all Wheat Board market analysts will be a vital ingredient in our continuing efforts to best serve Western Canadian grain farmers. Independent thinkers, well versed in the principles of economics, but not hidebound by the tidy models of yesteryear's sages, will hopefully be available to continue to describe and interpret the changing grain trade and to outline the implications for the Canadian grains industry. And analysts with imagination and initiative must continue to undertake economic research to develop policies and strategies that will improve the Canadian marketing system's performance.

There will always be frustration because most problems simply do not have solutions which please all grain industry participants. Also, the benefits of decisions made on the basis of economists' conclusions are almost always impossible to quantify. And yet, the grain industry is an exciting one, and is evolving at a rapid pace. Challenges continue to confront the agricultural economist at the Canadian Wheat Board as he faces a vast spectrum of issues, ranging from production and delivery problems on individual farms to commercial and political and sociological matters in a variety of foreign lands. The grain world will not get simpler, but can only become more complex as the world's population continues to increase, and as dependence on a very small number of grain exporting countries (notably in North America) grows. Greater marketing complexities will require greater imagination and freshness. Agricultural economists are well trained to provide that type of input.

NOTE

[1] It is encouraging to note that a few agricultural economists in North American universities have recently shown a willingness to grapple with some of these issues. The theory of oligopoly remains one of the least satisfying in the entire field of economics, so that a serious review of it, in particular as it applies to the international grain trade, would be welcome. Similarly, the formal general equilibrium neoclassical theory of international trade is not descriptive of the dynamics of price–quantity relationships in an oligopolistic–oligopsonistic (and highly regulated) world grain trade market and would benefit from attempts to introduce concepts of imperfect competition.

DISCUSSION OPENING – HANS G. HIRSCH

The late Henry C. Taylor, whom many of us admiringly call the father of agricultural economics, developed the case study method during his many years at Winconsin. Based on his judgement and insight – more than on statistical sampling – he created the concept of "the typical farm".

Bjarnason, who earned his doctor's degree at Winconsin and can thus be regarded as a Taylor disciple, has applied the case study method to "parastatal organizations". His experience has been with the Canadian Wheat Board; so he has given us a case study of that Board.

He has not given us a definition of "parastatal organization". The term has caused some bewilderment among some of my colleagues and bosses in Washington because we work on the principle of non-delegation of governmental regulatory functions to the private sector. By contrast, the parastatal organization, as it exists in British countries, in France, and perhaps also in some South American countries, may be regarded as a joint enterprise of the government and the private sector for some regulatory purpose. In Canada, the public and governmental nature of the marketing boards seems to predominate as against the private sector role in the parastatal organization. I invite Dr Bjarnason or some discussants to compare the Canadian Wheat Board with other marketing boards in Canada and with similar organizations in countries with British traditions, with the so-called interprofessional organizations in France, and with the Argentinian Grain Board.

The question of the representativeness of the Canadian Wheat Board for parastatal organizations as a class needed not have been raised if Dr Bjarnason had been asked to discuss the role of our profession in the Canadian Wheat Board – an assignment which would have been perfectly proper for a meeting of the IAAE in one of Canada's leading wheat provinces.

In presenting the history of the Canadian Wheat Board, Dr Bjarnason portrays the strategy of the communist world's two giants in their role as customers. These customers insisted on dealing directly with the Board and on avoiding the private sector grain trade. US relations with these two giants, in the absence of a National Grain Marketing Board, developed differently. In the arrangements for US grain exports to the Soviet Union, a dualism between Government and the private sector has emerged on the US side of trading: all terms of trade are typically worked out between the Soviet purchasing agency and US private trading companies. However, the US Government acts as an overseer. The five-year US–USSR Grain Agreement, which will enter into its fourth year next month, is the instrument of this oversight. It provides in essence that the Soviet Union will buy each year a minimum of six million tons of US grains, that it may buy up to eight million tons without consulting the US Government and that it will consult with the US Government if and when it wishes to buy in excess of eight million tons. The agreement also provides for periodic consultations between the two Governments.

Dr Bjarnason goes on to remind us that grain importing LDCs have also preferred state trading on their part. We in the United States have experienced this preference also and, as in the case of the Soviet Union, we have developed a kind of a dualism between the Government and the private sector for exporting to LDCs. The Government role is often played by the Commodity Credit Corporation, which extends credit either commercially or concessionally. Dr Bjarnason completes the picture by relating how we find either state-trading or monopsony-trading in some of the large, importing, developed countries.

I was surprised to hear that agricultural economists have been taken on the Canadian Wheat Board staff *for the first time* in the last couple of decades. I thought they had been there from the beginning. It seems that Dr Bjarnason is referring to fully academically trained agricultural economists, i.e. holders of PhD degrees.

For professionals so equipped and, at the same time, well familiar with the practical and technical aspects of wheat trading, he presents a challenge to improve our insight into the workings of a highly regulated oligopolistic–oligopsonistic world grain trade market. If I understand him correctly, he wants the profession to come to grips with newly refined measures of protection which separate importer-consumers from the exporter-suppliers. He would like to see the importer-consumer's payment reach the exporter-supplier without undue diversion and he reminds us of the inelastic nature of the demand for wheat.

It would have been enlightening, in this connection, to have at least a short exploration of the experience which we have gained in the pursuit of these policies. I am referring to the World Grains Arrangement signed in mid-1967 to take effect in mid-1968. It provided for prices which, with the knowledge of hindsight, turned out to be high. These prices acted as tremendous production incentives and in Canada they ultimately led to the so-called LIFT programme – lower inventories for tomorrow by a drastic curtailment in wheat acreage.

I should like to summarize my three principal discussion points:

(1) I am critical of the subjectivity with which Dr Bjarnason chose the Canadian Wheat Board as an organization representative of parastatal organizations in general and invite comparisons of the Canadian Wheat Board with other Canadian marketing boards and with marketing boards elsewhere during the discussion;

(2) I point out that we in the United States have developed a dualism between the Government and private trading companies in dealing with governmental customers in the communist part of the world and in the Third World; and

(3) as a cautious comment to Dr Bjarnason's postulate for higher international grain prices; I recall the production response to the relatively high prices that had been set in the International Grains Arrangement negotiated in 1967.

GENERAL DISCUSSION – RAPPORTEUR: B.L. GREENSHIELDS

It was felt that a drawback of the paper was that only the operation of the Canadian Wheat Board had been described by Harold Bjarnason and the role of agricultural economists in parastatal organizations in general was not covered. The structure of international grain markets was then discussed. It was noted that oligopoly on the sellers' side of the market fostered oligopsony on the buyers' side.

Harold Bjarnason and the discussion opener, Hans Hirsch, disagreed as to the causes of the increase in world grain production following the 1967 World Grains Arrangement. Among the causes cited were movement up the supply curve due to the increase in price, and outward shifts of the supply curve due to better-than-average weather and the introduction of high-yielding varieties.

In response to the question about how parastatal exporting organizations allocate supplies outside of the price mechanism, Harold Bjarnason replied that because of the lack of stocks and transportation system constraints, supplies were allocated first by bilateral agreements and residually by the price mechanism.

Participants in the discussion included W.E. Hamilton, Anthony E. Ikpi and Allan D. McLeod.

YVON PROULX*

Marketing Boards in Canada: Role, Impacts and Some Elements of Performance

There have been marketing boards in Canada since 1929. Such boards exist in all ten provinces. They have developed very rapidly over the last twenty years to the extent that their number increased from 66 to 105 and the share of farm cash receipts marketed through them has risen from 13 to 60 per cent (*Agriculture Canada*). Marketing boards regulate the production and/or marketing of almost all the major Canadian agricultural products, the main exception being beef cattle.

Despite these developments marketing boards are criticized by some farmers who dislike the constraints which are imposed on their freedom and are sometimes questioned by analysts who are concerned with some negative impacts which they appear to have (Forbes, Menzies) or lack of expected positive impacts (Loyns, Martin and Warley). This has not prevented the Canadian government, very recently, from providing the necessary approval for the implementation of a national chicken broiler marketing board, a board comparable in extent of power to those who are the centre of the "mounting wave of disaffection" noted by Martin and Warley.

Since there are probably few other countries in which the marketing of farm products is so extensively controlled by such type of mandatory agencies we believed that it might be useful, after a brief descriptive review of what these boards are, to attempt to summarize the impacts which have been identified thus far and to discuss briefly some elements of performance that may be pointed out at the present time. These are the three specific questions which I want to cover in this paper. I will obviously draw upon the studies already mentioned plus one which I conducted at Laval University with one colleague but which has not been published in English thus far (Proulx and St-Louis).

* The author is grateful to Dr R. St-Louis for his comments and to Dr W. Anderson for his assistance in editing this paper.

WHAT ARE MARKETING BOARDS?

Agriculture Canada in its annual marketing board statistics defines a marketing board as "a compulsory horizontal marketing organization for primary and processed natural products operating under government delegated authority. The compulsory features means that all farms producing a given product in a specified region are compelled by law to adhere to the regulations of a marketing plan. The horizontal aspect means that marketing boards control the output of all farms participating in the particular marketing boards scheme and that they aggregate the supply from all the farms up to a chosen or permitted level. Government authority through legislation is essential to achieve the required compulsion. The power of the boards utilizing this authority is generally wide enough to affect the form, time and place of sales and directly or indirectly, the prices" (Hiscocks).

These powers or functions of marketing boards are summarized in the same sources as follows: negotiating prices, designating specific sales agents, establishing marketing quotas, setting transportation allowances or other matters related to the marketing of specific agricultural commodities. To perform their functions, some marketing boards may collect levies from persons producing or marketing a product. The levies may be used for various purposes including equalization of returns to producers.

The description given above certainly gives a very good idea of what, in general, marketing boards are. It is important however to note that marketing boards are not all alike. They differ greatly among themselves on several fronts. Most marketing boards are provincial boards operating under provincial legislation, at least for those products which are produced and sold within the province. Federal legislation, the Agricultural Products Marketing Act, 1949, allows a provincial board to have its powers extended to include the regulation of interprovincial and export trade.

Beyond the provincial boards just mentioned there are five boards established under federal legislation: The Canadian Wheat Board which regulates or sells directly most of the grain produced in the Prairie Provinces, the Canadian Dairy Commission and three poultry boards which in conjunction with the provincial boards for these products operate national marketing plans for industrial milk, eggs, turkeys and chicken broilers.

Marketing boards differ also by the degree of producer control which is being exercised in their management. The Canadian Wheat Board and the Canadian Dairy Commission are controlled by government appointed officers. The national poultry boards are producer controlled agencies, as are most of the provincial boards.

Finally it may be useful to note that by grouping the categories of powers which are mostly exercised, Loyns has classified marketing boards into three main types. In order of increasing regulatory control, these are:

1   Negotiating agencies: mostly negotiate producer prices and other terms of sale (most fruit and vegetable boards).
2   Central selling agencies: sell on behalf of producers (some fruit and hog boards, Canadian Wheat Board).
3   Price and volume regulatory agencies: supply management and price setting (milk and poultry boards).

For the purpose of looking at the impacts of marketing boards to which I will now turn, I will group together the two first categories above and designate them as marketing boards who do not exercise supply management functions as opposed to boards who do.

IMPACTS OF MARKETING BOARDS

According to G. Hiscocks, marketing boards have been implemented to improve the bargaining power of producers and more specifically to achieve the following objectives:

1   to maintain or increase producers' income for a given product,
2   to stabilize producers' income,
3   to normalize the conditions of sale of a product (improve equity in producers' access and treatment in markets).

He adds that increasing income is by far the most important of these objectives and is generally expressed in terms of an increase in the unit price received by producers.

Given these objectives and my belief that supply management is a much more powerful device than bargaining I have chosen to organize this discussion of the hypothesized impacts of marketing boards in the following way.

1   MARKETING BOARDS WITHOUT SUPPLY MANAGEMENT

Impact on farm price level
Marketing boards which do not have as a target the adjustment of the volume of production in light of demand conditions but rather the promotion of a better balance of forces in negotiations on prices and other selling conditions should normally allow those who, without the board, would be in a weak bargaining position to obtain a better price. Such a price increase may also be the result of some other changes accompanying the implementation of a marketing board: decreases in marketing and transportation expenses associated with the rationalization of the marketing process, improvement and the timing of sales, improvement and/or standardization of product quality and a better approach to serve all the segments of given markets.

Support for this hypothesis has been found by Proulx and St-Louis in a comparison of producer prices of fruits and vegetables for which there have been marketing boards in operation in Ontario and British Columbia for quite a while with producer prices of the comparable relevant sectors in Quebec where there are no marketing boards.

This comparison was made by calculating the least-squares regression trend line of the farm prices of these products in these three provinces for the past twenty years. The rates of growth of the price obtained from this calculation showed that for the majority of the seven vegetable sectors retained for comparison, the price increased less rapidly in Quebec than in Ontario and British Columbia (Table 1).

The apple market was the only fruit market which could be studied on the same basis. Marketing boards were set up in 1969 in Ontario and 1972 in New Brunswick. The price in Ontario has increased much faster after its marketing board was implemented. It rose faster than in Quebec in both periods. In New Brunswick the price was declining before 1972 but started to rise and at a faster rate than in Quebec after the New Brunswick marketing board was implemented.

Impact on volume of production

To the extent that marketing boards allow producer prices to be increased, they should stimulate the development of production. A better farm price should encourage new producers to enter into production, should dissuade others from leaving and should encourage all those already in production to produce more. The same effect no doubt results from increased confidence and reduced uncertainty for all producers following the implementation of a compulsory marketing arrangement guaranteeing equal and fair access to the market.

TABLE 1 *Geometric rate of growth of the price of some fruits and vegetables, Quebec, Ontario, British Columbia and New Brunswick, 1958–78*

	Percentage rate of growth		
A – Vegetables Period 1958–76	Quebec	Ontario	British Columbia
Beets	3.03	3.78	8.52
Carrots	2.01	3.15	4.57
Celery	2.47	5.39	5.79
Onions	3.41	7.76	4.72
Cucumbers	2.86	5.10	6.02
Lettuce	4.32	5.52	4.07
Fresh Corn	2.15	2.23	2.18
B – Apples	Quebec	Ontario	New Brunswick
1958–68	3.88	6.01	
1969–76	11.80	16.87	
1958–71	1.35		–0.08
1972–76	0.05		3.87

This hypothesis was examined by looking at the evolution of the share of the Canadian market occupied by provinces in which there are marketing boards, as compared to Quebec where there was no marketing board for fruits and vegetables over the period 1958–76. The results showed that in five of the seven cases considered a province with a marketing board (Ontario or British Columbia) had increased its share. In hog production on the other hand the reverse was observed. The production increased more rapidly in Quebec where there was no marketing board. From that we can only conclude that there are many factors affecting the change over time of an industry output, of which the existence of marketing boards without supply management is one.

Impact on consumer prices
Since the operation of a marketing board without supply management does not, by itself, imply any increase in the degree of protection of domestic production, and since the level of production is expected to rise it can hardly be expected that the consumer price may be greatly affected by such a board. In fact, after a marketing board is established, the consumer price should have the same relationship to the price of the principal foreign supplier of this product as it had prior to the existence of the board.

I did not analyse data in order to test this hypothesis. Instead I relied on the findings of economists who studied the question of the consumers' interest in marketing boards for the Canadian Consumer Council (Forbes). In the case of hogs, the study indicated that marketing boards seem to produce a slight rise in farm price levels, but one which is not large enough to be perceived at the consumer level.

Likewise in the case of fruits and vegetables the report concluded that marketing boards have little or no effect on consumer interests except in one specific case, grape processing in Ontario and British Columbia. The report also concluded that tariffs rather than marketing boards harmed consumer interests. However no precise indication was given of the effect that tariff protection would have been raised because of the implementation of a marketing board.

2 MARKETING BOARDS WITH SUPPLY MANAGEMENT

The analysis carried out thus far tends to show that marketing boards without supply management powers, by reorganizing the bargaining relationships between producers and processors of farm products, allow producers to capture a larger share of the dollar spent by the consumer (higher farm price without comparable absolute consumer price increases). These gains realized by producers can only be rather limited. The manoeuvring room as regards prices afforded by increased bargaining power is definitely limited.

One means of raising prices to a much greater extent, when the protection of domestic production is adequate (high tariffs or quantitative import restriction) or can be increased, is to regulate production or marketing so as to reduce the total quantity of a product to be placed on the market. This is the power which has been demanded and obtained by producers who have succeeded in establishing marketing boards with supply management. Let us now look at the impacts of these boards that have been observed thus far.

Impacts on producer and consumer price levels
Supply management is practised in Canada in dairy and poultry production. I will not report any empirical research work with respect to dairy product prices because, in this case, production as well as prices are fully administered by the federal government through its price support and surplus removal programme. The objective of raising (and stabilizing) prices is assumed to be obtained almost by definition.

The price impact is examined mostly for eggs and turkeys, for which there are national marketing agencies operating quota systems since 1972 and 1973. Moreover protection of domestic production is obtained through import quotas. They are really "pure" cases in which it is possible for supply management to show its capability to significantly affect prices. A price impact is also expected for broiler production although there was no national marketing board before 1978, but only provincial boards with an informal agreement since 1972 between Ontario and Quebec to share the market and manage supply on that basis.

The authors who have examined the impact of marketing boards on poultry product prices are unanimous in reporting a very significant impact. Forbes has pointed out that the consumer interest is not being served as well as it could be by the poultry industry in Canada. He argues that prices are much higher than they need to be and that they are capitalized into poultry quotas under marketing board control. Menzies has noted that prior to the early 1970s producer prices for broilers were within 5 to 8 cents of US prices. Since 1973 Canadian prices have been 10 to 12 cents per pound over those of US producers. Thus the spread has doubled. A similar situation has developed for turkey producer prices. Finally since 1973 the egg producer price spread between Canada and the US increased from 0 to around 15 cents per dozen.

The data which I gathered suggest that, after the very important price rise of the 1972–73 period in both countries, the Canadian poultry boards succeeded in maintaining the higher prices dictated by the production cost formulae (high grain prices) while the US price got back close to its level prior to the grain crisis.

Impact on price stability
The price stabilization impact of marketing boards has been questioned by Loyns and Martin and Warley. They suggest that this impact is probably less important than advocates of marketing boards tend to suggest.

I believe however that Loyns in his study has gathered data prior to the period in which this stabilization impact really occurred (his empirical analysis) covered data up to 1975 and the national supply management schemes were then too recently implemented). Martin and Warley, in my opinion, were looking for more stabilization impact than marketing boards can provide. As I suggested previously, a stabilization impact should be expected only in the cases of boards with supply management. Even in this case production has to be isolated from foreign source of supply or foreign source of instability. Beyond industrial milk, which is disregarded here, this is the case only for the poultry boards. The results reported by Martin and Warley in these cases effectively supply evidence for significant price stabilization impacts particularly at the farm level. Similar results were obtained by Proulx and St-Louis.

Impact on industry output
Supply management should normally reduce the industry output, maybe not in absolute terms but at least as compared to what it would have been in the absence of the marketing board. Otherwise there would be no need for supply management.

To provide some support for this hypothesis we compared egg and turkey production before and after 1972 and 1973 in Canada and the United States. Egg production in Canada started to decline after 1972. But a similar trend was observed in the US. In the case of turkeys on the contrary, production declined in Canada after 1973 while it increased in the US. Also in support of the hypothesis we observed that from 1965 to 1971 the province of Quebec (no marketing board in that period) was rapidly increasing its share of the Canadian broiler market, while that of Ontario, where a quota was functioning, was declining. A quota system was set up in Quebec in 1971 and after that the respective share of the two provinces stabilized.

Impacts on farm productivity
The most direct impacts that marketing boards have are probably those on prices and production which have been discussed thus far. There are certainly other impacts like on farm productivity which, to my knowledge, have not yet been studied. This is certainly an important research need because the long run competitive position of the agricultural sectors regulated by boards depends on productivity changes that may be induced by the most direct and immediate impacts they have on prices.

On this point we are almost limited to speculation about the direction in which it will work. One may argue that the higher farm prices that marketing boards provide will give farmers an incentive and the financial means to carry out modernization investments which will in turn reduce costs. Conversely, one may suggest that farmers will rely on their market power to avoid seeking ways to reduce cost. In other words the loosening of the "cost price squeeze" will slow down productivity efforts and gains. A corollary of that would be to say that high prices protect inefficient producers who will then remain in production. In opposition someone else may argue that high quota values will lead to concentration of production within the hands of the most efficient producers.

These are empirical questions on which observations will have to be made. The only observation I have made on this point thus far is related to dairy production. Historically the average farm price of milk has been higher in British Columbia than elsewhere in Canada and particularly in Quebec where there is much lower proportion of milk produced for fluid consumption (higher prices). Average milk productivity per cow is much higher in British Columbia than elsewhere in Canada and particularly than in Quebec. This, at least, does not suggest that high prices lead to poor productivity.

SOME PERFORMANCE ELEMENTS

The discussion thus far has indicated that marketing boards without supply management by improving the bargaining position of farmers and their access to markets have had the impact of increasing farm price without important negative impacts on consumers. Marketing boards with supply management powers have had the impact of raising farm as well as consumer price levels and of improving price stability especially at the farm level. Except for the impact on consumer prices these results are, as we have seen, exactly what was intended by governments when they adopted the legislation allowing these boards to be created. The legislators were very probably aware that the desired results (significant improvement of farmer's position) could not be attained without consumer price rises, and they accepted that choice as being appropriate. Thus we can, very probably, say that marketing boards are reaching their primary objective, an objective which happens to be the major purpose of public policies with respect to agriculture over the last fifty years in most developed countries. I believe this is an extremely positive performance element. It is extremely positive for another reason: the objective is reached mostly under producer initiative rather than direct government intervention. Producers highly value this opportunity to take care of themselves by themselves, even though the powers they have are not absolute, the government remaining always in a position to remove the import controls without which the most important power cannot be exercised. When import controls are removed, North American market conditions prevail.

The next questions are: to what extent does the reaching of this objective conflict with other important objectives of Canadian farm and food policy and are there ways to avoid these conflicts? A great deal more analytical work is needed before one can supply answers to these questions. The impacts on farm productivity and costs, marketing efficiency, the margins of processors of farm products[1] and the cost of running these boards have to be measured carefully. From these impacts depends the long run capacity of our farming sector to provide the consumer with an adequate supply of food at "reasonable" prices, an obviously important other objective of farm and food policy.

I will limit my discussion of that point here to what I believe is the most important criticism which is addressed to marketing boards: the fact that part of the supply management benefits are capitalized into quota values. It is alleged that the cost of possession of these quotas will eventually be included in the production cost formulas and since it does not correspond to any productive resource it has no *raison d'être*. It imposes an unnecessary burden on the consumer and the competitive position of the farm sector thus regulated deteriorates.

Even if, at present, the cost of owning the quota does not enter directly into calculation of the cost of production, I do not question that this will eventually occur, when most of these production rights will have changed hands. I first note that the capitalization of the benefits of higher product prices into quota values does not seem to me a more important problem than capitalization into land values under other forms of marketing arrangements. But my basic question is: how heavy is the burden for the consumers? Table 2 reports data and calculations made to provide an indication of the importance of this burden. The first line shows the approximate value of production quotas in Quebec by mid-1978 for all the products under supply management.

The second line transforms this value into a cost of owing the quota per unit of production. This cost is then expressed as a percentage of the prices received by the producer and paid by the consumer. It is clear that the cost of owning the quota is fairly high when expressed as a percentage of the farm price. Since this farm price of agricultural products has become a relatively small component in the retail price of food, at least for certain products, this cost represents a much lower percentage of the consumer price. This lead us to the view that the problem of the value of quotas is not a very serious one for the consumer. To bring out this point, we have calculated that the cost of quota ownership for the products in question, assuming this cost is completely passed on to the consumer and taking into account per caput consumption, means an annual addition per-consumer expenditure of $7.82. Elimination of this cost would affect the proportion of disposable income which the average consumer spends on food by less than 1 per cent.

Therefore, it seems to me that this aspect of the problem is less important than it is sometimes suggested. It could become more important if quota values began to increase in a really dramatic way.

The other aspect of this question of quota values is the impact on the competitive position of the farm sector under supply management. Assuming that supply management has no positive farm productivity impact and the total cost of owning the quota is transferred to the price of the product it is obvious that the competitiveness of the industry is importantly affected. A firm willing to export a product on a highly competitive market will be seriously harmed by price rises of between 1.8 and 3.7 cents. There seems then to be a danger that supply management condemns Canada to produce only for its own market. This may be a problem less important than it looks however since supply management is generally practised only in production oriented towards domestic consumption. I do not see, in any case, what is the incentive to practise supply management of a product produced for export unless under agreement with other exporting countries.

CONCLUDING REMARKS

This paper tends to suggest that marketing boards in Canada have had thus far extremely positive impacts in providing farmers with an efficient means of obtaining, on the market, the "adequate" return to their labour and capital that has been the major objective of farm policies over decades. It would be surprising if this could have been achieved without some less desirable effects. One of these is the problem of quota values which almost necessarily accompanies supply management practices.

I have argued that this problem may be less severe than other people argue. It does not mean that I am not concerned by the fact that quota values seem to be continuously rising and might reach levels at which they will be more damaging. For me this is an indication that supply management agencies may have difficulty in assessing correctly at what level the price of the products should be set in order to allow efficient producers to be "adequately" remunerated for their resources. This is the very difficult

TABLE 2 *Current value of production quotas and importance of quota ownership costs in comparisons to prices at producer and consumer levels, Quebec 1978*

Fresh milk	Industrial milk	Eggs	Broilers	Turkeys
		Quota value		
$10.00/100#	$7.50/100#	$7.00/ hen	$4.00/ sq.ft.	$2.50 sq.ft.
		Per-unit cost of ownership		
2.5c/ quart	75c/cwt.	3.7c/doz.	2.5c/#	1.8c/#
		Ownership cost: as a % of farm price		
7.5%	6.6%	5.6%	7.1%	3.8%
		Ownership cost: as a % of consumer price		
4.4%	—	4.0%	2.7%	1.8%
		Annual cost to the consumer		
$2.05	$4.19	$0.68	$0.73	$0.17

540   *Yvon Proulx*

question which they have to answer when they determined the total quantity that will clear the market at this "desired" price.

I will suggest, in conclusion, that we use quota values and their evolution as an indicator of whether the price at which the product should be sold has been correctly assessed. If the price of the product is too high, as may be the case in some products right now, there would usually be a great many current or potential producers who seek to purchase quotas relative to the number of quota owners willing to sell – thus a tendency for the quota value to rise.

My suggestion is to introduce in the production cost formulae used to determine the level of the desired price a correction factor intended to take into account the evolution of quota values. When quota values are rising the formula would suggest a correction down of the desired product prices. I have no more details to provide on that point but I think it might be useful to look in this direction rather than to turn to administratively determined market sharing quotas or to the disruption of marketing boards.

NOTE

[1] On this point I can only report the conflicting views of Menzies who suggests that processors' margins have increased and that of Funk and Rice who suggest that they have decreased.

REFERENCES

Agriculture Canada Marketing Boards Statistics, 1958 and 1976–77.
Forbes, J.D. "A Report on the Consumer Interest in Marketing Boards", Consumer Research Council, Ottawa Sept. 1974.
Funk, T.F. and Rice, M.T. "Effects of Marketing Boards on the Agri-business Sector", Proceedings Joint Annual Meeting AAEA–CAES, Blackburg, Virginia, CJAE, August 1978.
Hiscocks, G.A. "Market Regulations in Canada", Canadian Farm Economics Branch, *Agriculture Canada*, June 1972, p. 20.
Martin, L.J. and Warley, T.K. "The Role of Marketing Boards in Stabilizing Commodity Markets", Proceedings Joint Annual Meeting AAEA–CAES, Blackburg, Virginia, CJAE, August 1978.
Menzies, E.L. "Impacts of Alternative Marketing Strategies in the Poultry Industry", paper presented at the National Poultry Seminar, Ottawa 3–5 April 1978.
Proulx, Y. and St-Louis, R. "Plans conjoints et gestion de l'offre; un essai d'évaluation de leurs impacts", Département d'économie rurale, Université Laval, October 1978 (published in 1979 in *Economie Rurale*, France).

Contributors: T.K. WARLEY, G.E. SCHUH, V. NAZARENKO and
J. HILLMAN

Panel Discussion on State Trading Agencies*

T.K. WARLEY

There is some ambiguity about the definition of "state trading agencies".
A recent conference on state trading defined state trading as ". . . exporting and importing on government defined transaction terms".[1] For
agricultural economists accustomed to a situation in which national
agricultural programmes determine the parameters and the performance
of markets, this will probably be too broad a definition. On the other
hand, the distinction drawn in the programme of this conference between
state trading agencies and parastatal agencies is certainly too fine. For
instance, the Canadian Wheat Board is a crown corporation, responsible
to the federal Parliament. It is clear that international transactions are
conducted by a variety of public and quasi-public agencies of considerable hetereogeneity. They include operating agencies of government,
quasi-independent crown corporations, producer-controlled marketing
boards with monopolistic–monopsonistic powers, and private companies
with exclusive trading rights. The distinctions are of more than semantic
interest since it can be anticipated that different institutional forms are
matched by different objectives, operating practices, degrees of market
power and effects on markets. I believe that we shall require sharper
definitions – indeed an analytic taxonomy – if we are to learn to understand the influence of "state trading" on market performance.

It is a mistake to associate state trading only with the centrally planned
economies, though these countries certainly do conduct most of their
external transactions through operating agencies of government. It is also
a fact that a majority of developing countries manage their importing and
exporting activities through state operated or controlled trading agencies.
Furthermore, they play a prominent role in some developed market
economies, witness Japan's Food Import Agency, the Australian Wheat
Board or the Liquor Control Boards that are found in most of Canada's
provinces. One would like to know more about why nations engage in

* This replaced the paper by Sergio Chazaro who was unable to be present.

541

542   *T.K. Warley, G.E. Schuh, V. Nazarenko and J. Hillman*

state trading – usually on a selective, commodity-specific basis – for such knowledge would throw light upon the nexus between national domestic sectoral and trade policies, and upon the structural, behavioural and performance attributes of international commodity markets. One can hypothesize about some of the factors which dispose toward state trading. These include: compatibility with ideological principles, an extension abroad of internal economic planning and management systems, the more effective integration of domestic farm and food policies and agricultural trade policies, the desire to create original market power or to countervail the power of others, and so on. These hypotheses need testing in order to establish the necessary and sufficient conditions that induce governments to embrace this form of trade management.

We do not have good information about the extent of state trading. Such information as we do have suggests that it covers a surprisingly large proportion of international transactions. For instance, Baldwin has noted that in 1976 over 30 per cent of US exports were purchased by state enterprises, and over 40 per cent of America's merchandise imports were supplied by foreign state-owned or state-controlled firms.[2] McCalla and Schmitz have calculated that the proportion of world trade in wheat which involved only private traders is small and declining, involving only 5 per cent of wheat trade in 1973–77. That is, 95 per cent of world trade in wheat involved a state trader on at least one side of the transaction. State trader to state trader transactions accounted for fully a third of all world wheat trade in the period.[3] Improving our information in this area is a task that might well be undertaken by UNCTAD.

As to the future, three factors can be cited that might cause state trading to grow in importance. First, it is expected that the centrally planned economies and the developing countries – all of which use state trading – will become more fully integrated into the world trading system. Second, the negotiation of a wider range of international commodity agreements would be likely to lead to the expansion of state trading, for if production, stocks, market shares and prices were increasingly managed it could not be expected that the conduct of trade would be unregulated. Finally, there may be some induced development of state trading arrangements in response to their existence elsewhere. For instance, there are groups in the United States that have urged the formation of a single-selling-desk export agency for US grains in order that the US might better control the volume, direction and terms of its foreign grain sales.

The existence and importance of state trading agencies in general international trade and, more particularly, in trade in agricultural commodities has a number of implications for those agricultural economists who interest themselves in trade matters.

Firstly, in our role as teachers we should ensure that due attention is paid to institutional characteristics of markets in our courses on international commodity marketing.

Second, in our role as analysts we should be concerned about our ability to handle the influence of state trading agencies in empirical models of world commodity markets. Our basic theoretical constructs may be inadequate. For instance, received trade theory deals primarily with producers, consumers and governments and commonly neglects market intermediaries. And the theory of oligopoly, which is obviously pertinent, is characterized by its general inadequacy and its propensity to point to indeterminate market outcomes. Indeed, given that we are dealing with oligopsonistic market structures in which the types of trading agencies differ, in which the objective functions of those agencies are different and are usually unknown, and in which the degree of market power of each agency is uncertain, then one would be rather pessimistic about our ability realistically to model particular commodity markets.

A third area that should attract our interest is to determine the influence of state trading agencies on particular aspects of the functioning of markets for agricultural products. For example, it would seem reasonable to expect some relationship between the presence and behaviour of state trading agencies in a market and the latter's price formation and discovery mechanisms and their stability. Thus, it makes a difference to the functioning of future markets whether they are used by major state trading entities or not, and the unequal access to information of the USSR's monopsonistic grain import agency and the US's private traders was unquestionably a factor in the instabilities in world grain markets that we witnessed in the earlier years of this decade.

Finally, those agricultural economists who are concerned about the future of the multilateral trading system will find much of interest in the relationship of state trading to the GATT. State trading is the antithesis of that precept of the GATT that assumes that trade will be conducted primarily, and to an expanding degree, by private entities acting at arm's length for profit. The drafters of the Agreement recognized the existence of state trading agencies and, under Article XVII, required that they should act in a non-discriminatory manner and that their transactions should be governed by commercial considerations. Not surprisingly, this Article has had little influence on their activities, partly because many countries with state trading enterprises are not signatories to the Agreement, partly because they were presumably established by national authorities precisely because market forms and norms were judged to be inappropriate. By common consent, something will have to be done about the position of state and parastatal trading agencies in the world trading system, not least because of their growing importance and because of their association with hard-to-prove dumping and predatory procurement practices. Possibilities include amplification and strengthening of Article XVII of the Agreement, the articulation of a more general code to govern trade relations between market and command economies, and perhaps even changing national marketing institutions in order to deal more effectively with the state trading agencies of other countries.

REFERENCES

[1]International Conference on State Trading in Industrialized and Developing Countries, Centre for International Business Studies, Ecole des Hautes Études Commerciales, Montreal, 19–20 April 1979.
[2]Baldwin, R.E. "Beyond the Tokyo Round Negotiations", Thames Essay No. 22, Trade Policy Research Centre, London 1979.
[3]McCalla, A.F. and Andrew Schmitz "State Trading in Grains", University of California, Davis April 1979, mimeo.

G. EDWARD SCHUH – *Challenges for Agricultural Economists Working in State Trading Agencies*

The perspective I shall take in preparing these comments is that of an exporting country. State trading agencies will have somewhat different perspectives and functions, depending on whether they are primarily concerned with exporting or importing.

My vantage point will be primarily that of the United States of America. We, of course, have no state trading agency. But, to the extent that increasing agricultural exports is an important policy goal, agricultural economists working in the government conduct their analysis and attempt to influence policy in much the same way as if they were in a state trading agency.

Agricultural economists in such a situation would have to deal with at least six sets of issues:

1   *Sorting out the comparative advantage of the agriculture in their respective countries*. This is probably the most neglected aspect of what we can do as economists. Policy-makers in some countries would like, of course, to repeal the "laws" of comparative advantage. Similarly, many analysts are so struck by the degree of intervention associated with both domestic agricultural policies and trade policies that they believe it futile to even ask the comparative advantage question.

Both these perspectives are misguided. Over time, at least since the end of World War II, the international trading system has gradually evolved towards one of freer and freer markets. Moreover, sound policy probably lies in guiding the allocation of resources towards that best suited to a country's natural comparative advantage. Hence, even though short term economic conditions and trade interventions may preclude the realization of a country's comparative advantage, an analysis of what the longer term perspective has to offer can provide important clues to policy-makers.

The recent trade conflicts between Mexico and the United States offer insights into the disadvantages of not taking a longer term perspective. The United States has been threatened by imports of tomatoes from Mexico, which it alleges benefit either from export subsidies or from mere dumping. It has threatened retaliation, and in general, contributed to tense relations between the two countries. In doing this, it has failed to recognize that in the longer term, Mexico may offer a market for US exports of cereals of the order of 5–10 million tons of grain per year. If it were to look to the future instead of being dominated by short term considerations, it might take a more liberal stance with the Mexican tomato imports.

But Mexico appears to be equally short-sighted. Basing its argument on the past, it seems to feel that its main goal is to increase exports at any cost. But if its petroleum reserves prove to be as promising as recent reports suggest, exporting agricultural products is not likely to be an important factor influencing its rate of growth in the future. It too, could take a more flexible stance.

2 *Careful evaluation of trade policies*. At least four classes of problem emerge under this rubric. The first is to analyse the barriers to trade erected by other countries. Once these barriers are understood, the possibilities of dealing with them are greater, either by direct attack or through negotiation.

Second, there is a need to analyse and understand own-country trade policies and objectives, and to verify that these policies and objectives are not subverted. In the case of the US, the section 22 provisions come immediately to mind. But there are more general trade provisions as well.

Third, there is the need to protect markets from penetration by third countries, especially if these markets are being lost by means of export subsidies and other predatory practices. This last year, the European Community made important inroads into US grain markets in Latin America by means of export subsidies. Agricultural economists can identify such inroads and attempt to understand the influence of such things as export subsidies. This provides a sounder basis for stopping or alleviating such practices.

Finally, there is the possibility of devising creative responses to the trade policies of other countries. For example, Andy Schmitz and his colleagues have argued that the tariff imposed by the European Community on grain imports is consistent with an optimal or scientific tariff. If that is the case, it may be possible to devise an optimal export subsidy to offset it.

3 *Understanding development processes*. Fostering economic development in other countries may be the most important means of expanding agricultural exports. As an example, some of the largest US markets at this time are in those countries that in the past were major recipients of foreign aid, and in particular, of food aid shipments. This is understandable, for in the case of low income countries, an increase in income per caput leads to an increase in food consumption. Understanding development processes, therefore, provides a means of knowing where to focus market development efforts.

Similarly, a great deal of market development can be associated with the introduction of new, improved production practices. The most obvious example is the introduction of improved feeding practices. Back of that, of course, is the introduction of improved breeding stock that demands the use of high quality rations.

4   *Exchange rate policies.* The importance of different exchange rate regimes was discussed in an earlier paper at this conference. In the present context, the main issue is the relative movements in exchange rates among competing exporters, because a country can be more or less competitive depending on what its exchange rate is doing relative to that of competing exporters. Of special importance here is the need to sort out nominal shifts in exchange rates which reflect only differential rates of inflation from shifts in the real exchange rates which reflect more basic forces.

5   *The importance of the internal–external trade-off.* Policy-makers in an exporting country always have to be conscious of potential conflicts between the external gains from more trade and the domestic conflicts which expanded trade may create. An obvious example of a conflict within agriculture is that between livestock producers and grain producers when the main export product is feed grain. Other things being equal, greater exports imply higher domestic grain prices and, hence, higher costs for livestock producers.

More generally, larger exports may mean higher food costs for the domestic consumer. Political pressures under these circumstances can lead to quotas, an embargo, or other restrictions on trade. Hence, it is important to know what the internal–external trade-offs are in order to devise a more rational export policy.

6   *Understanding why economic policies are what they are.* Given the importance of government policies and interventions in most of our economies, one cannot develop much of a market strategy without understanding the policies of other countries. Moreover, it is as important to understand *why* governments do what they do as it is to understand the effects of the policies once they are implemented. This area of analysis and research is badly neglected by most agricultural economists. By such neglect we are ignoring a large part of what is important in the world around us.

V. NAZARENKO – *The part played by agricultural economists in state trading bodies*

When analysing the role of the agricultural economist in State trading organizations one should proceed from the traditional work usually performed by such specialists. As a rule the major part of this task is of an analytical character. Market situations may be analysed from several viewpoints:

(a) *Conjuncture analysis* and study of current market changes.

(b) *Structural analysis* and study of comparatively long term trends, importance of certain commodities in agricultural production and trade, prospects for development, correlation and interchangeability of certain commodities.

(c) *Regional analysis.* Such a method of analysis is bound up with the study of the territorial distribution of agricultural production in the country, trends in changing sources of the major kinds of agricultural products, the role of separate regions in current agricultural production and possibilities for increase of commodity resources.

(d) *Institutional analysis*. The institutional analysis is bound up with study of methods of organization and management of production and trade of agricultural commodities, and governmental regulation of the agrarian branch of economy.

(e) *Technological analysis*. Analysis of such character is necessary to find out major trends in the development of agricultural practices and technology and the corresponding effect of these trends on agricultural output, commodity resources and volume of trade.

Besides analytical work, an agricultural economist's role may be quite important in elaboration of trade recommendations of various kinds, for instance, the study of problems of comparative benefits of production and the preparation on its basis of recommendations aimed at more rational labour distribution in a separate country as well as in economic communities and in the world as a whole. Naturally, this, first of all, calls for detailed investigations into prime cost of agricultural production and comparisons of prime costs in separate regions in each country as well as internationally. As an example of the latter we may cite the continuous work carried out in the COMECON countries aimed at the elaboration of comparable methods for the calculation of the prime cost of agricultural produce, and further comparison of prime cost indices aimed at further effective distribution of labour in the field of agriculture among COMECON countries, based on these methods.

It goes without saying that this work of comparing prime costs in different countries is methodologically extremely complicated. Nevertheless, it is of vital scientific importance so far as studying the prospects for international distribution of labour in agriculture is concerned.

J. HILLMAN – *A new mode of agricultural protectionism*

Though the massive intervention of the state in economic processes between World Wars I and II appeared to be entirely new at the time, the general philosophy was as old as mercantilism itself. Over most of the new systems of trade regulation which arose during the 1930s might be written Thomas Mun's seventeenth century precept "We must ever observe this rule: to sell more to strangers yearly than we buy of theirs in value". New types of intervention in international trade – and in production processes contingent to trading practices – were new only in the sense that they adapted old devices to modern monetary and administrative conditions in what was essentially a reversion to the primitive ideas and trade practices of the seventeenth century. The setting was new, but the idea of and desire for "a favourable balance of trade" was very old.

After the financial and commercial breakdown in the 1930s when the major trading countries found themselves with low agricultural prices and mounting surpluses, they reverted to the most rudimentary forms of mercantilism: credit and exchange controls (their mercantilist predecessors were concerned with precious metals), reduced imports, increased home production, and increased exports. The result was trade distortion, rising budgetary costs, and widespread misallocation of resources in agricultural production throughout the world.

Behind the visible signs of economic stress, manifested in currency depreciation, capital movement, and exchange control, were more fundamental economic disequilibria brought on by the contractions of export markets and the decline in world prices for agricultural products. Cause and effect were interrelated, and the chain of events led inevitably to more protection.

The reduction in industrial imports by debtor countries (developing countries, as they would be called today) and their strenuous export efforts led to increased passive import balances in the trade of creditor countries. Quantitative import restrictions were erected against foreign export promotion. A good example of this was the case of France. But the great bulk of cheap agricultural exports was directed at traditional free trade countries – Britain, the Netherlands, and a few others – all of which in turn took steps to protect their domestic agriculture. In some cases, the flood of exports breached even the high tariff barriers of European industrial countries which had always protected their peasant agricultures.

Many European countries were bound by commercial treaties and conventions which had stabilized their tariff duties. This fact, coupled with the sterling devaluation in September 1931, brought further pressure on their inefficient farm production due to price reductions on exports from Commonwealth countries. For example, a French or Swiss peasant already faced with cheap Australian wheat and wool suddenly found domestic prices for these products halved in terms of francs. The costs of peasant agriculture being relatively fixed, such surplus product dumping and foreign exchange manipulation could not be offset by corresponding currency devaluation in this instance because of the lively memory of post-World War I inflation, especially in the peasant communities of Germany. Finding themselves "boxed in" by economic and political circumstances, these countries understandably turned to new, direct, more effective trade restrictions.

The new agricultural protectionism was radically different in nature and scope from the protective tariff in that it involved a philosophy which assumed a role for government of direct intervention in the production and marketing processes. Particularly affected at first were internationally traded products. A vast array of non-tariff barriers supplemented tariffs in protectionist orthodoxy, and public intervention became an accepted norm for domestic agricultural adjustment.

Most of the effective trade restrictions on agricultural products that countries have adopted since the early 1930s have been but adjuncts to their domestic farm policies, which is to say that nations have not developed a separate and identifiable trade policy for farm products.

Trade restrictions of a wide variety have been developed to make possible the functioning of domestic price and income policies as well as many programmes which do not have specific and identifiable price and income objectives. In the latter category lies almost all of the regulatory and indirect protectionism which has emerged over the years.

Import licensing systems were introduced and soon developed into quantitative import quotas as measures of trade restriction. Tariff quotas had been an integral part of commercial treaties since the mid-1920s, but the outright use of quotas on a large scale for agricultural protection occurred only after France initiated the practice in 1931. The restriction of imports by this technique spread rapidly during the depression years and is widely used today as a protective device, particularly in connection with domestic agricultural programmes.

Quotas on agricultural imports have also been associated with other devices such as licence fees and exchange controls to protect agricultural and raw material producers and distributors from foreign competition. During that decade of chaos in world trade, the 1930s, veterinary, quarantine, and other regulations were strictly enforced. Also, an entirely new and complicated apparatus of state trading, monetary, and indirect protectionism was rapidly developed and put into practice.

Ultimately, the most significant form of protection for agriculture, which began on a large scale during the depression of the 1930s, derives from the direct intervention by the central government in the domestic production and marketing processes. Since that time, techniques of intervention have been applied in most countries, mainly to bolster returns to agricultural producers of individual commodities and to enable them to earn incomes higher than they would without intervention and protection. This intervention has resulted in wide-scale distortions in world prices and trade, large costs to taxpayers and consumers, and uneconomic expansion of farm production in the industrial countries, with corresponding ill effects upon associated countries. Today, supplemented and effectuated by other non-tariff obstacles applied at national borders, they have replaced import taxes as the principal method of agricultural protection.

From a historical standpoint, in the period between World War I and World War II, we saw farmers and agriculturists again in the forefront arguing for protection and against adjustments in resource use in agricultural industries and the related rural sector. Economic conditions differed somewhat between the 1930s and the late nineteenth century, but the protagonists were the same. Particular national positions have changed little, but governmental agricultural and related programmes and policies undertaken in the 1930s and after World War II affected international and commercial activities as the protective tariff had never done. Experiences of these and past eras give credence to the generalization that wars and depressions usually lead to increases in protection, whereas periods of peace and prosperity encourage movements toward free trade. It could be observed rightly that the European Economic Community (EEC) and the Common Agricultural Policy (CAP) would hardly have achieved their current success except for the boom period in economic activity following World War II. Also it is unlikely that the United States could have followed its simultaneous policies of protection and surplus disposal of the past twenty years except in a period of exceptional economic growth, and increasing demand for, or disposal of, food and fibre.

It might seem unwarranted to draw comparisons between these confused early days of the new agricultural protectionism and the situation facing world agriculture and trade in the 1970s. Yet, there are sufficient similarities – as to both their nature and intensity – in the elements to give cause for concern. In the former situation, once the collapse of international monetary equilibrium gathered momentum, there was an interplay of cause and effect, one currency depreciation leading to another, and one country's trade restrictions provoking retaliation from others throughout the world. It was obvious that successive stages of protection could be justified in each country by its own urgent economic considerations.

What was not so obvious was that, however urgent those considerations might have seemed, they were not the fundamental causes, but instead the consequences, of the breakdown in the international economy. The real causes were deeper and lay in the gradual hardening of national economic policies until flexible adjustments became impossible. How far is the world down that same road today, despite current levels of prosperity and despite the institutional and political changes that have been made in order to stabilize monetary and trade conditions and to prevent a recurrence of catastrophic protectionism? There is certainly cause for concern in that governments have been slow to comprehend the need for flexibility in their national agricultural policies and have recently even shown tendencies toward thwarting readjustment in their agricultural sectors. Furthermore, state trading appears to have emerged as an extremely formidable problem in liberalizing world trade in agricultural products.

The large grain purchases by the Soviet Union in 1972, the partial cancellation of US grain sales to the Soviet Union in 1974, and the increasing importance of the People's Republic of China as an agricultural importer have focussed attention on appropriate methods for dealing with exports to and imports from planned economies. Problems involved in exporting agricultural products to them should not be minimized if, as many experts believe, those countries will continue to purchase large quantities of grain from the market economies.

Planned and centrally controlled economies like those of the USSR and China have a considerable degree of monopsony power in agricultural markets. This power presents great problems to major grain exporters, such as the United States with its private traders and even to Australia and Canada with their state marketing agencies. Marketing monopsony in the case of the Soviet Union is exacerbated by the year-to-year variability in its grain production, which accounts for a large fraction of world grain production variability.

How to accommodate to such monopsonies in the likelihood of their continued purchase of farm products, especially when monopsony is reinforced by natural variation in supplies in the purchasing countries, presents a large problem to farmers and the marketing structures of market-oriented economies. One reaction to such uncertainty would be the "natural" response, or unilateral control of supplies – in this case, exports. Such a response would, if perfected, create the essential elements of a state controlled oligopoly–oligospony situation which might be even more unstable than several situations since World War II when the Soviets entered the world grain market. Certainly there would be grave dangers to farmers and to the agricultural marketing structures of market-oriented economies if they turned toward monopoly techniques in response.

Problems created by state trading and related monopoly–monopsony conditions of demand and supply in world trade of agricultural products can be solved partially through better information, especially about total world supplies. Improved information and the rational decisions which might flow therefrom are to be preferred to the confrontation of buyers and sellers acting in ignorance. The alternative of shared information on matters relevant to potential imports and exports is discussed in a recent publication of the United States Department of Agriculture. This general alternative was further explored at the Rome World Food Conference in late 1974.

A large part of the advantage of monopolist and monopsonist in international trading consists of having a monopoly on information and using it skillfully. In the 1972 grain purchase, the USSR used its monopoly on information skillfully; so this one purchase set the tone for destablizing scepticism and reaction in subsequent trading: witness the confusion surrounding the 1974 Soviet grain purchase from the United States and its cancellation. It is not clear that such secrecy was in the long term interests of the Soviet Union because now any seller who may be approached becomes suspicious and wary. Such may be the general case in state-controlled trading situations.

Finally, because of the tendency of modern economies toward control brought about by the concentration of decision-making power in administrative machinery, there is danger of essentially economic decisions turning more toward purely political considerations. Market factors in such cases become dominated by extra-market factors. Non-tariff barriers in their most complex, regulatory forms exist and flourish in the guessing game of administrative bureaucracy.

JOHN M. CONNOR*

Foreign Food Firms: Their Participation in and Competitive Impact on the US Food and Tobacco Manufacturing Sector

The United States has long been recognized as the leading source-country for private foreign direct investment (FDI). In 1976, US residents owned approximately 49 per cent of the world's stock of FDI (CTC 1978). Less appreciated, however, is the fact that the US is also the world's largest host-country for FDI, a position only recently wrested from Canada.[1]

Foreign direct investment has in the course of the twentieth century largely supplanted portfolio investment as a device for the international transfer of private capital. FDI, which typically takes the form of debt or equity ownership of a foreign affiliate, implies a distinctly stronger degree of management control over an investment than does the purchase of bonds from a foreign institution. Unlike portfolio transactions, FDI flows have been directed mainly toward the manufacturing sectors of recipient countries (the oil-exporting countries being an obvious exception). Moreover, these flows have, among the developed market economies, been characterized by industrial interpenetration; that is, within a broadly defined manufacturing industry, FDI generally passes simultaneously in both directions between any two capital-exporting countries. Finally, in contrast to bond markets with their numerous small investors, FDI is carried out solely by a relatively small number of large corporations. To study FDI is tantamount to studying the multi-national corporation (MNC).

Therein lies the source of much of the public's concern over inward foreign investment. Foreign entities, most of them large and highly diversified, make decisions about the disposition of local resources on the basis of a global profit-maximizing strategy. Some of these decisions inevitably clash with the national welfare-maximizing criteria of host-country governments. The initially favourable balance of payments effect of a particular investment is in time reversed as dividend, interest, and royalty payments mount. As the proportion of international trade among affiliated firms rises, fears are expressed that considerations other than comparative advantage may affect the direction of trade. The decisions made

* The views expressed in this paper are not necessarily those of the USDA. The author was heavily assisted by Howard Nash.

552

by MNCs on the location of production can seriously impinge on such national goals as high employment, stable investment, and balanced growth. The efforts of host countries to attract investment can lead to a disadvantageous bidding-away of potential tax benefits. Labour organizations often feel that the power of the strike is diminished by the geographic spread of firms and worry about the imposition of alien labour practices. Finally, several host countries are concerned about the potential loss of economic sovereignty that attends large amounts of foreign ownership or the "denationalization" of certain key industries. Implicit in most of these criticisms is the notion that domestic industry is workably competitive and that domestic profit maximization is closer to the social optimum than a global maximization criterion.

The concerns that were listed above are reinforced by what is known about the peculiar nature of the modern multi-national firm.[2] They are generally large, complex organizations: the flows of information and authority follow multi-layered routes and require numerous co-ordinative management functions. MNCs tend to market a wide array of products, and their products or production technologies generally either incorporate relatively recent vintages of technology or exhibit the results of fairly intensive product differentiation efforts. Evidence for this characterization of MNCs is best provided by the findings of the Harvard Multi-national Project. For a large sample of US companies, they found that US MNCs displayed significantly higher levels of product diversification, progressiveness (R & D-to-sales ratios), and product differentiation (advertising-to-sales ratios) than the rest of the 500 largest industrial firms (Vernon 1971). These same characteristics are also known to be associated with oligopolistic markets; MNCs tend to inhabit highly concentrated industries in their home countries (Wolf 1977) as well as in their foreign markets (White 1974, Connor 1977). Partly as a result, MNCs are more profitable than their more domestic counterparts: they earn higher profits on their foreign than on their domestic assets (Newfarmer and Mueller 1975) and have higher domestic returns as a result of their foreign involvement (Bergsten, Horst, and Moran 1978). Many host-country industries clearly face a strong threat of restructuring due to the entry of powerful foreign firms. Whether competition is intensified or not remains, however, an open question.

Defenders of MNCs typically base their arguments on the increased efficiency of the allocation of resources world-wide, especially physical and financial capital, intangible assets such as patentable technology, and highly trained managers. These international transfers may also result in the more efficient utilization of host-country resources. Such claims are very difficult to establish definitively, and many of them are second-best arguments in that they assume that intra-firm allocation is superior to imperfect markets for these factors of production.

Foreign direct investment into the US food and tobacco manufacturing industries presents a researcher with a particularly interesting case study. First, this sector is only infrequently considered a prime example of one with heavy MNC presence; automobiles, machinery, chemicals, and electronics rightly come first to mind. Yet, as we shall see, FDI is of above-average importance for food and tobacco. Second, these industries do not appear to fit very well the economic models developed to explain FDI: the sector is normally regarded as technologically "mature" and composed primarily of relatively standardized (or homogeneous) products. If this is true, then one of the prime justifications for FDI – its role in the international transfer of technology – undercut. Third, FDI in the food manufacturing sector has not raised nearly as much public concern as foreign investment in agricultural land, despite the fact that both absolutely and proportionately, FDI in the former is much larger and management control appears to be more centralized than the latter. Finally, the question arises as to why FDI would be extensive in a country like the US that already has a substantial population of its own successful food and tobacco multi-nationals. One would expect firms with the ability to do so to resist incursions into their home-base markets.

The principal purpose of this paper is to investigate the extent of the participation in the US food and tobacco manufacturing sector by "foreign food firms" and to determine their motives and competitive impact of their FDI.[3] The general plan of the paper is first to examine what can be learned from aggregate, government-collected data on FDI. For this stage, the new benchmark study of FDI in the US in 1974 will be utilized (DOC 1976). Then, an original data set of the world's largest non-US food and tobacco manufacturing firms (FFFs) will be analysed. Results of a regression analysis of the determinants of FDI by these firms will be presented. Finally, the paper will briefly consider the adequacy of US policy toward FDI, in the light of these findings, to capture the potential benefits for FDI.

PATTERNS OF FOREIGN DIRECT INVESTMENT

In 1979, the total stock of FDI from the developed market economies will have reached about $425 billion, from a mere $105 billion in 1967.[4] During 1971–76, average annual dollar growth was 13 per cent, a rate that was roughly double the GNP growth of the source-countries. In recent years about 47 per cent of all FDI from the major capital-exporting countries has been in manufacturing (excluding petroleum), and has been rising relative to other sectors (CTC 1978).

The share of world FDI originating from the US has fallen since the early 1950s (from over 60 per cent to 49 per cent now), as have the shares of the UK and France. While the world shares of West Germany, Switzerland and Japan have risen, ownership of FDI has not become more dispersed: the seven largest source-countries have accounted for about 88 per cent of all developed-country FDI over the whole 1967–76 period. Also, most FDI flows to only a few developed economies; the US, UK, Canada, and West Germany have received almost 50 per cent of all FDI in recent years. The proportion of FDI going to the developing countries has fallen to only about 25 per cent of the total (CTC 1978).

Outward FDI in manufacturing has tended to occur intensively in only a few industries. The major industry groups in which US firms have invested abroad were petroleum, non-electric machinery, transportation equipment, and chemicals (including drugs and toiletries), in order of their absolute amounts of FDI.[5] Food manufacturing ranks about fifth among the 20 major industry groups (Newfarmer and Mueller 1975). In terms of the proportion of foreign to total assets or sales, food manufacturing would rank relatively lower; one study places food processing ninth in terms of the degree of its multinationality (Vernon 1971 : 14). Tobacco processing ranks quite low by both absolute and relative standards, probably because many countries have state monopolies in this industry and because exporting is fairly inexpensive for tobacco products. In 1976, food and tobacco manufacturing accounted for about 9 per cent of the stock of all US manufacturing FDI (*Survey of Current Business*).

Almost all of the US FDI in food processing lies in Western Europe (43 per cent), Canada (28 per cent), and Latin America (16 per cent) (Table 1). The estimated proportion of host-country sales by US affiliates varies considerably by area; for Europe and Latin America it is low, about 2 and 7 per cent, respectively (Hufbauer and Adler 1968); for Canada it is high, 46 per cent (MITC 1975). A recent study documents that US MNC sales were 26 per cent of total Mexican food processing sales and 3 per cent of Brazilian sales in 1970 (Newfarmer and Mueller 1975); MNC tobacco sales were 84 per cent and 0 per cent of the total for the two countries, respectively.

FDI INTO THE US FOOD AND TOBACCO PROCESSING INDUSTRIES

Data on *inward* FDI into the US food and tobacco processing sector are quite detailed because of a recent "benchmark" census of FDI by the US Department of Commerce (DOC 1976). This benchmark survey, the first since 1959, was prompted by Congressional hearings investigating whether there was adequate data to decide if the US public's "fear of foreign capital invasion" was justified (Foreign Economic Policy 1974).

That survey concluded that FDI into the US at year end 1974 totalled $26.5 billion.[6] Between 1959 and 1972, total FDI rose by 6.5 per cent annually, but during 1973–77 the average annual increase was 16.4 per cent, reaching $34.1 billion in 1977. The total book assets of these foreign affiliates, 60 per cent of which are wholly owned, was $174.3 billion in 1974.

Manufacturing accounts for 40 per cent of all FDI in the US and is the fastest growing sector. The benchmark survey also determined that 17 per cent of all manufacturing FDI was in food processing and 3 per cent in tobacco; the $1.6 billion in food and tobacco processing FDI has

556   *John M. Connor*

TABLE 1   *US foreign direct investment in the food and tobacco manufacturing industries, 1929–76*

		Value of US foreign direct investment[1] in			
Year	Canada	Europe	Latin America	Other areas	All areas
		Million dollars			
1929	25	38	118	8	190
1940	110	56	62	17	245
1950	214	67	182	34	496
1957	320	149	201	53	723
1963	467	326	300	141	1,234
1966	600	597	365	209	1,771
1975	1,369	2,032	720	604	4,725
1977	1,519	2,435	869	714	5,537

Sources: Bruchey (1976, 1976a) and *Survey of Current Business*, various issues.
[1] Foreign direct investment is measured by the value of US residents' net equity in and loans to foreign affiliates. Up to 1950 tobacco processing was included in these data.

increased at an average annual rate of 11 per cent over 1974–77. Food manufacturing ranks third among the 20 major industry groups (after chemicals and petroleum) in terms of total FDI; tobacco ranks eighth.[7] Outward US FDI in food and tobacco manufacturing is roughly two and one-half times inward FDI in those industries.

The 1974 benchmark survey provided a breakdown of inward food manufacturing FDI into six major industry groups for the first time in 1974. Most US affiliates were primarily classified in beverages (50 per cent of FDI and 24 per cent of sales) and "miscellaneous foods" (34 per cent and 27 per cent); grain and bakery products accounted for the least investment (0.4 per cent), while meat, dairy, and preserved fruits and vegetables amounted to only 2 per cent to 9 per cent each. Thus, more than half of all FFF activity in the US involves such industries as alcoholic beverages, candy, margarine, coffee, tea, and snack foods – all highly differentiated products.

FDI in US food manufacturing is highly concentrated in terms of its geographical origin: Canada alone owns 41.0 per cent. Other prominent source countries are: Switzerland (24.7 per cent), the UK (15.8 per cent), the Netherlands (6.8 per cent), France (4.6 per cent), and Belgium (2.1 per cent). Japan accounts for only 1.0 per cent and no other country approaches as much as 0.5 per cent (Table 2). Of course, these FDI proportions are based on book asset components and may not translate into a similar sales or total asset distribution. The net sales of foreign food firms were primarily Swiss (27 per cent), Canadian 24 per cent), British (22 per cent), and other EEC-owned entities (23 per cent).

The estimated total assets of these foreign food and tobacco manufacturing affiliates ($5,119 million) were 6.1 per cent of all US food and tobacco manufacturers according to IRS figures; their net sales were about 4.0 per cent of the US total. Foreign-owned firms in the US handle a portion of US trade that is out of proportion to their sales or asset position. In 1974, US affiliates of foreign firms sold 24.5 per cent of the values of all US merchandise trade; they bought 30.4 per cent of all such imports. These foreign affiliates (both manufacturing and nonmanufacturing) originated 80 per cent of all US exports and 29 per cent of all US imports of food and tobacco manufacturers (DOC 1976: I, p. 36). On average, 36 per cent of all exports and 74 of all imports of these companies are *intra*-firm transactions. Most trade by US affiliates is with the parent firm's home country, especially for Canadian and Japanese subsidiaries.

Foreign direct investment in food and tobacco manufacturing has increased twenty-eight-fold over 1934–77 (Table 3). In recent years, inward FDI has increased at an average annual rate of 11 per cent, almost double the rate of outward FDI in these industries. As a proportion of all inward FDI in manufacturing, food and tobacco investment is about 16 per cent today, but was twice as high in the 1950s.

TABLE 2 *Selected data on foreign food manufacturing activities in the US by country of parent company, 1974*

Country of owner	Foreign direct investment in food mfg.	Total assets of food mfg. affiliates	Net sales of food mfg. affiliates	Merchandise trade of affiliates[2]	
				Exports	Imports
		Per cent			
Canada	40.[1]	41.3	24.2	0.3	12.9
Switzerland	24.7	23.8	27.3	0.3	7.6
U.K.	15.8	15.6	21.6	2.0	26.3
Netherlands	6.8[1]	7.7	9.9	(*)	(*)
France	0.3[1]	1.3	(*)	(*)	(*)
West Germany	0.2	0.1	0.1	0.0	0.0
Other Europe	6.7[1]	4.9	13.3	49.2	6.2
Japan	1.0[1]	3.7	2.4	28.4	26.2
Latin America	3.5[1]	1.6	1.2	20.1	20.8
Other	0.9[1]	0.1	0.0		
		Million dollars			
Total	1,384	3,864	5,534	12,117	3,118

Source: DOC (1976).
[1] Estimated from other ratios, residuals, or nearby years.
(*) Included in "Other Europe".
[2] Trade in SITC 0 + 1, which includes some unprocessed foods and tobacco products.

TABLE 3   *Foreign direct investment in the US food and tobacco manufacturing industries, selected years, 1934–77*

	Value of foreign direct investment		
Year	Food manufacturing	Tobacco manufacturing	Total as a proportion of all manufacturing
	Million dollars		*Per cent*
1934	64	13[1]	14
1937	97	19	16
1941	150	29	24
1959	758[1]	173	38
1974	1,384	244[1]	20
1977	1,834	324[1]	16

Sources: Wilkins (1977); DOC (1976); *Survey of Current Business*.
[1] Estimated from other ratios and residuals.

Occasional surveys of inward FDI provide useful information on the main dimensions of the phenomenon. They are limited, however, by the increasing diversification of the parent companies and their affiliates and by their rules forbidding disclosure of information on individual companies. Little can be learned of the participation of foreign firms in particular markets, nor do official data lend themselves to analyses of industrial organization.

PARTICIPATION OF THE LARGEST NON–US FOOD FIRMS

One approach that can reveal much about the competitive behaviour of foreign direct investors in particular markets is to collect detailed data on the major actors, their histories, and their market environments. Collecting data in this way is fraught with numerous empirical difficulties regarding the multiplicity of languages, differing accounting practices, and incompatible industrial classification schemes. Nevertheless, a summary of the results of one such search is reported in this section, and an analysis is performed on these data in the next section (details will be found in Connor 1980).

Studies of FDI using firms as the unit of analysis are not plentiful, and most of them have focussed on US MNCs (e.g., Horst 1974, Wilkins 1974). Some exceptions include Franko (1976) on Europe and Tsurumi (1976) on Japan. In the present study, we searched for all non-US food and tobacco processing firms with global sales exceeding $350 million in 1974 or 1975; also large diversified firms with food or tobacco as a major, but not necessarily principal, line of business are included if that segment totalled at least $100 million.[8] Foreign subsidiaries of US-based corporations are excluded.

In 1975 there were 117 foreign food firms (FFFs) meeting this criteria. Out of those 117 FFFs, 34 have significant US investments in the US food or tobacco sector. This finding is fairly close to that of a special study by the US Chamber of Commerce (using US Department of Commerce data) which found 26 food and tobacco companies with FDI in the US (Foreign Economic Policy 1974).

The 1974 benchmark survey showed that two-thirds or more of the net sales of FFF affiliates were made in markets characterized by more highly processed foods. The present study confirms that finding: most of the FFFs with US FDI have principal products like candy, sauces, alcoholic beverages, coffee, tea, snacks, and cigarettes. Further support for the notion that FFFs market mainly highly differentiated products in the US comes from 1975 media advertising data: they account for fully 11.1 per cent of all advertising. Since FFF affiliates account for only 4.04 per cent of the net US sales of processed foods and tobacco, that implies that their advertising-to-sales ratios (a common measure of product differentiation) are nearly three times as high as domestic US firms.

These FFFs display all the usual characteristics of MNCs. They are on average quite large ($1,204 million in sales) and fairly profitable entities (9.3 per cent return on equity). They are highly diversified for the most part and have complex corporate structures to handle their dispersed operations. (Some exceptions to this general rule include a few specialized beer and sugar firms, some dairy co-operatives, and state-owned cigarette or alcohol monopolies). They generally inhabit highly concentrated industries in their home countries: the average weighted four-firm sales concentration ratio for 68 of the FFFs for which data were available was 73 per cent. This average is 35 per cent higher than the weighted average concentration of all US industries in 1972 (adjusted for local markets). Finally, the weighted market shares of the FFFs in their home markets averaged 35 per cent. Such high market shares are indicative of well-entrenched oligopolists; strong market positions are known from other empirical work to generate substantial market power (Connor 1977). High shares coupled with highly concentrated home markets also imply that growth-minded companies have a more difficult time expanding their sales in their domestic markets; firms in such situations may be more likely to seek foreign expansion.

SOME DETERMINANTS OF FOREIGN DIRECT INVESTMENT

Our measure used for the propensity of FFFs to invest in the US, is the ratio of US food sales to total company sales (FDIR). The measure used to capture the extent of US market penetration is the extent of media advertising by the FFF relative to total advertising in the five-digit SIC product class (MAS). The market advertising share is a decent proxy for the sales shares of nationally marketed consumer goods, but it reveals little about produce goods or private label products sold.

Regression analysis was used to relate several independent factors to each of these FDI measures. The symbols and data sources are given in Connor (1980), as is a somewhat more elaborate justification for their inclusion.

Macro economic factors
Two variables were introduced to model home-country and US similarities in taste:

1 PCGNP per caput GNP of the home country, and
2 PCAD per caput advertising expenditures of the home country.

Both variables are expected to exert a positive influence of investment and penetration. In addition, to test the ideas of cultural proximity, a separate subset of UK and Canadian firms was run.

Market structure factors
Several variables were designed to capture the influence of both home-country and US market structure dimensions on the FDI performance of the food firms in our sample:

1 HMS home-country weighted market share for food and tobacco products only,
2 HCR home-country four-firm weighted sales concentration ratio for food and tobacco only,
3 HADS home-country weighted firm advertising-to-sales ratio for food and tobacco products only,
4 UCR same as HCR, but only for the US food industries in which the FFF participates,
5 MES minimum efficient plant scale as a percentage of the US market(s), a measure of scale barriers to entry,
6 NETIMP net industry imports, a measure of the ease of foreign entry by export,
7 GEOG the Collins-Preston index of geographical US dispersion of production, a correction for the understatement in UCR due to regional markets,
8 and MP the extent of multiplant ownership in the industries in which the FFF participates.

For reasons given in the section above, HMS, HCR, HADS, and NETIMP are expected to yield positive signs; MES and GEOG should be negative. UCR should be specified as an upward-bending parabola, but if the range of values is too restricted either one slope or the other will dominate a non-linear specification. For the MAS levels, the outcomes for MES and NETIMP are indeterminate.

Firm-level factors

The following variables were included as potential explanatory factors in our regression model:

1 SIZE firm sales size,
2 HDIV product sales diversification using a Herfindahl index,
3 FOOD the extent of firm specialization in food and tobacco manufacturing,
4 OWN a classifactory variable taking a value of 1 if the firm is government-owned, co-operatively owned, or privately held.

We anticipate SIZE, HDIV, and FOOD, to be positive, but OWN to be negative. For the market penetration variables, the outcome for FOOD is *a priori* indeterminate.

REGRESSION RESULTS

The ordinary least-squares regression results are given in Tables 4 and 5. In order to reduce the overwhelming effect that a few large values might have on our results, the dependent variables have been transformed by taking their square root.

Results explaining FDIR

Equations 5.1 and 5.2 show our basic regression results for all 117 FFFs and for the 100 FFFs for which home-country concentration (HCR) data were available. The only significant national factor affecting investment is per caput advertising expenditure. Among the market structure factors examined, only home-country intensity (HADS) is significant; UCR, NETIMP, and MES have the expected signs, but are not significant. Home-country market share (not shown in Table 4) also had a positive impact on FDIR. Finally, four of the variables designed to capture individual firm characteristics are highly significant and correctly signed. Large, highly diversified, publicly owned firms with experience in food product marketing display a marked tendency to invest in the US.

Equations 5.3 and 5.4 attempt to clarify the effect that socio-economic proximity may have on the FDI propensity of firms. Equation 5.3 excludes two sets of firms whose economies appear to be the more dissimilar to the US: several less developed countries and Japan. Equation 5.4 narrows the concept of proximity even further by excluding all but Canadian and British firms; this relatively simple model explains over 50 per cent of the variation in FDIR. For these firms, SIZE no longer has any influence on FDI, but multi-plant operations (MP) do.[9]

Results Explaining MAS

Regression estimates for the 34 investor FFFs using their shares of media advertising expenditures as an index of market position are shown in Table 5.[10] The fit of these models is closer than that of Table 4; Equation

TABLE 4   *Regression results explaining the propensity to invest (FDIR) in the US food and tobacco manufacturing industries by the largest non-US food and tobacco manufacturing firms, 1975*

Equation no.	Constant	Independent variables[1]											General statistics[2]		
		PCAD	HCR	HADS	UCR	NETIMP	MES	SIZE	HDIV	FOOD	OWN	MP	R^2	F	n
5.1	-0.25	0.01^a (5.24)		0.02^b (2.34)	-0.00 (0.13)	0.002 (1.64)	-0.004 (0.65)	0.00002^a (2.41)	0.11^b (1.79)	0.0008^b (1.66)	-0.09^a (2.40)		0.37	7.1^a	117
5.2	0.38	0.01^a (6.19)	0.0008 (1.00)	0.01^b (1.92)	-0.00 (0.35)	0.002 (1.38)	-0.005 (0.77)	0.00002^a (2.79)	0.16^b (2.76)	0.0015^a (2.98)	-0.06^c (1.60)		0.48	8.3^a	100
5.3	-0.40	0.01^a (4.23)		0.02^b (1.85)		0.003 (1.56)		0.00002^b (2.15)	0.23^a (2.87)	0.0016^a (2.40)	-0.08^c (1.64)		0.45	7.7^a	73
5.4	-0.56		0.006^a (2.58)	0.03^b (1.97)	-0.007^b (2.12)				0.44^b (3.29)	0.0019^b (1.87)		0.41^b (2.21)	0.51	5.4^a	38

[1] Regression coefficients shown with t statistics in parentheses below. The superscripts a, b, and c indicate statistical significance at 1, 5 and 10 per cent, respectively.

[2] R^2 = coefficient of determination, F = calculated F statistic, n = number of observations.

Source: Data compiled by the author.

TABLE 5 Regression results explaining market advertising share (MAS) in the US food and tobacco manufacturing industries by the largest non-US food and tobacco manufacturing firms, 1975

Equation no.	Constant	Independent variables[1]										General statistics[2]		
		PCGNP	HADS	UCR	HCR	GEOG	MES	HMS	SIZE	FOOD	MP	R^2	F	n
6.1	-1.89	0.00 (0.21)	0.18[a] (1.42)	0.010 (0.43)	0.023 (1.25)	-0.009 (1.12)	0.65[b] (2.48)		0.0003[a] (2.94)			0.64	5.1[a]	28
6.2	0.31	0.00[c] (1.36)	0.07 (0.42)	-0.040 (1.22)		-0.020[b] (1.94)	0.80[a] (2.87)	0.0004[b] (1.94)	0.0003[a] (2.90)	0.023[c] (1.53)	-2.17 (1.35)	0.79	5.4[a]	23

[1] Regression coefficients shown with t statistics in parentheses below. The superscripts, a, b and c indicate statistical significance at 1, 5 and 10 per cent, respectively.

[2] R^2 = coefficient of determination, F = calculated F statistics, n = number of observations.

Source: Data compiled by the author.

6.2 explains nearly four-fifths of the variance in MAS. Most of the variables behave as expected. Either national income or advertising intensity are positive influences, but not both simultaneously. Concentration is not significant, but market share and technical barriers to entry (GEOG, MES) are. Size and food specialization are again important positive factors. Multiplant ownership may explain the investment decision, but it has no signficant influence on the success of FFF market penetration in the US.

CONCLUSIONS

The models tested above do not provide a comprehensive explanation of the manifold forces impelling MNCs to invest abroad. Yet they do confirm that both firm organization and market structures are key determinants of FDI in the US food and tobacco manufacturing industries. Large diversified firms, publicly owned, marketing highly differentiated products, originating from countries with high advertising per caput are the most prone to invest in the US. Some degree of socio-economic proximity between the home-country and the US appears to strengthen these relationships. In addition, high home-country industry concentration speeds the flow of capital internationally, but there is no evidence that high barriers to industry entry deter FDI.[11]

Most of the same factors influence the relative success of FFFs in establishing and maintaining market shares. Firm product diversification is not important, but high home-market shares, firm size, and high host-country scale barriers all impact positively on market penetration.

There are few economic factors omitted from our analysis; the desire to spread demand risk internationally and the technological progressiveness of the firms are two such factors. Besides the problem of data availability, the level of technology was ignored in the belief that differences among food processing firms in this regard are relatively unimportant. However, the empirical results should be judged in the light of fairly severe data limitations for several variables. We relied for much of the information on annual financial reports of companies; these vary in quality and in accounting standards. Many of the "home-country" market structure variables were developed in spite of gaps in the data.[12]

Further entry by foreign food firms into the US food and tobacco manufacturing sector seems like a safe prediction. Japanese, West German, French, and Scandinavian food firms appear to be under-represented in the present mix of investors. Moreover, the continuing trend in the US toward higher levels of concentration, advertising, and profitability will attract more foreign firms anxious to increase their sale and profits in a market that is generally less regulated than their home countries.

The US has traditionally espoused a neutral attitude toward FDI. In part, this policy stance has evolved because of the presumed analogy between the mutual benefits of free trade and the international, intrafirm movement of production inputs by MNCs. Furthermore, the entry of additional sellers into the market has generally been held to improve industry performance.

Both of these presumptions are open to serious question. FDI appears to be markedly different from pure trade – it is not easily explained by factors relating to national comparative advantage, but more by several firm and industry-specific characteristics. It seems clear that international movements of capital are not neutral to national factor shares or even income shares among investing countries. FDI probably increases the national income of recipient countries and the labour incomes in host countries; it also tilts the balance of incomes in the home country from labour to the owners of capital (Frank and Freeman 1978). The evidence presented here gives limited support to the view that FDI is motivated in part by the desire to obtain or retain market power. The policy decisions of recipient countries should at least consider this factor when evaluating the presumed efficiency or income gains from foreign direct investment.

NOTES

[1] Official data show that the stocks of inward FDI in 1975 were $39 billion in Canada and $27 billion in the United States. A more detailed examination of Canadian data reveals that 35 to 40 per cent of Canada's FDI is owned by non-residents, primarily from the US. Thus, over one-third of Canada's inward FDI is owned by affiliates whose ultimate parents are non-Canadian corporations using their Canadian affiliates as conduits for investments in third countries (CTC 1978: 241). As late as 1967, FDI in Canada exceeded that in the US, even after making this adjustment. During the 1960s, the United Kingdom also had slightly more inward FDI than the US. These comparisons are sensitive to the definition used for FDI, especially the level of foreign ownership chosen as a criterion of foreign control, and to the choice of currency.

[2] In the discussion that follows, attention will be restricted to horizontal rather than vertical investments. Raw materials ventures tend to be markedly different in motive and impact than geographic extensions of markets (Caves 1974).

[3] Lest I be accused of rampant parochialism, let me assure the reader that the term foreign food firms was chosen solely for its euphonious and alliterative qualities and not for any pejorative purpose.

[4] I use the American meaning for billion (one thousand million) throughout this paper. FDI by the less developed countries is negligible, except for what passes through tax-haven countries like Panama.

[5] The industrial nomenclatures of most countries categorize petroleum as an extractive industry or as a separate sector because it is so highly vertically integrated. For domestic censuses, the US classifies petroleum *refining* as a manufacturing activity; for FDI surveys, petroleum is broken out as a separate sector.

[6] FDI is defined as the net value of foreign residents' claims on their US affiliates' equity and debt. An affiliate is counted as foreign-controlled if the foreign parent owns 10 per cent or more of the voting stock and if the affiliate has at least $100,000 in assets or revenues. Previous sample surveys for 1974 had underestimated FDI by $3.6 billion.

[7] Agricultural enterprises account for only 0.2 per cent of total FDI, in contrast to the 6.1 per cent for food and tobacco manufacturing. Grocery wholesaling, food stores, and eating and drinking places account for a further 1.1 per cent of FDI in the US. Thus, investment in the food system, broadly defined, amounts to 7.0 per cent of all FDIs in the US.

[8] "Food" includes beverages and animal feeds, but excluded some fresh foods. Sales were

translated into US dollars at average annual exchange rates; where possible excise taxes, tariffs, and intra-company sales are netted. A major source for our indexes of penetration into US markets was a tape of all US food and tobacco plants in 1975.

[9] Because PCAD is so close in Canada and the UK, it is dropped from the model; similarly, so few UK firms are privately or co-operatively owned that OWN is dropped.

[10] Equations 6.1 and 6.2 use all the 34 firms for which HCR and HMS data are available, respectively.

[11] Other factors tested without success were: (1) the cost disadvantage due to small scale entry, (2) firm export/sales ratio, (3) size of US market, (4) US tariff barriers, (5) firm growth, (6) firm profitability, (7) firm financial leverage, and (8) the extent of joint venture arrangements of the FFF with a US counterpart.

[12] This applies particularly to market share and comparable concentration data. Also for three companies (Nestlé, Unilever, and George Weston Holdings) averages of more than one "home" country were employed.

REFERENCES

Bergsten, D. Fred, Thomas Horst, and Theodore H. Moran (1978), *American Multinationals and American Interests*, Brookings, Washington.

Bruchey, Stuart (ed.) (1976) *Statistics on American Business Abroad 1950–1975*, Arno Press, New York. (1976a) *Estimates of United States Direct Foreign Investment, 1929–1943 and 1947*, Arno Press, New York.

Caves, Richard E. (1974) "Causes of Direct Investment: Foreign Firms' Shares in Canadian and United Kingdom Manufacturing Industries", *Rev. Econ. & Stat*, 56, pp. 279–93.

CTC (Commission on Transnational Corporations of the United Nations) (1978) "Transnational Corporations in World Development: A Re-Examination", UN, New York.

Committee on Foreign Affairs (1974) US House of Representatives, "Foreign Investment in the United States, Hearings before the Subcommittee on Foreign Economic Policy", US Government Printing Office, Washington.

Connor, John M. (1977) *The Market Power of Multinationals: A Quantitative Analysis of US Corporations in Brazil and Mexico*, Praeger, New York. (1980) "Foreign Food Firms", a Working Paper of North Central Regional Project NC 117, Madison, Wisconsin (forthcoming).

Connor, John M. and Loys L. Mather (1978) "Directory of the 200 Largest US Food and Tobacco Processing Firms, 1975", US Department of Agriculture, Washington.

Connor, John M. and Willard F. Mueller (1978) "The Shaping of Market Structures by Multi-Nationals", *Industrial Organization Rev*. 6, No. 2.

DOC (US Department of Commerce) (1976) "Foreign Direct Investment in the United States", Vol. 2. US Government Printing Office, Washington.

Foreign Economic Policy Subcommittee (1974) US House of Representatives "Foreign Investment in the United States", US Government Printing Office, Washington.

Frank, Robert H. and Richard T. Freeman (1978) *Distributional Consequences of Direct Foreign Investment*, Academic Press, New York.

Franko, Lawrence G. (1976) *The European Multinationals*, Greylock, Stanford.

Horst, Thomas (1974) *At Home Abroad: A Study of the Domestic and Foreign Operations of the American Food-Processing Industry*, Ballinger, Cambridge.

Hufbauer, G.D. and F.M. Adler (1968) "Overseas Manufacturing Investment and the Balance of Payments", US Treasury Department, Washington.

MITC (Ministry of Industry, Trade and Commerce of Canada) (1975) *Annual Report under the Corporations and Labour Unions Act*, Ottawa.

Newfarmer, Richard and Willard F. Mueller (1975) "Multinational Corporations in Brazil and Mexico", a report to the US Senate Subcommittee on Multinational Corporations, US Government Printing Office, Washington.

Tsurumi, Yoshi (1976) *The Japanese Are Coming*, Ballinger, Cambridge.

Vernon, Raymond (1971) *Sovereignty at Bay*, Basic Books, New York.

White, Lawrence J. (1974) *Industrial Concentration and Economic Power in Pakistan*,

Princeton University Press, Princeton.

Wilkins, Mira (1974) *The Maturing of Multinational Enterprises*, Harvard University Press, Cambridge. (1977) (ed.) *Foreign Investments in the US*, Arno Press, New York.

Wolf, Bernard, (1977) "Industrial Diversification and Internationalization: Some Empirical Evidence", *J. Ind. Econ*, 26, pp. 177–91.

DISCUSSION OPENING – ALFREDO CADENAS

This paper, as the author emphasized in his presentation, is an abbreviated version of a larger research study in which a more elaborate treatment is given to the chosen subject, that is; the preservation of market competition in the US food and tobacco sector in view of the oligopolistic practices undertaken by multi-nationals.

This opener, claiming from the start no special expertise on the subject other than a general knowledge of the issues and problems presented by multi-national corporations in developing countries, feels that one cannot but praise J.M. Connor's paper for having done a very fine job. His extensive use of previous studies, the pertinent literature citations, the compilation of data from numerous and widely dispersed documents, and the utilization of empirical analysis on which to base policy prescription, all deserve, I believe, high marks. Furthermore, I find the topic covered in the paper very interesting for, at least, three reasons.

First, because it represents the work of a pioneer and a good example of subject matter research in which facts and values pertaining to the theme of multi-national enterprises acting in the food and tobacco manufacturing sector of the US are examined. Also because it gives a clear diagnosis of problems as viewed by the American public and, besides, because some policy recommendations are discussed once an empirical (regression analysis) study is utilized to test several hypotheses which were inspired from industrial organization theory.

Second, because, to my understanding, there are few studies based on industrial organization theory as a subdiscipline of economic analysis. In this respect, I would dare to say that we agricultural economists in market-oriented economies have pretty much neglected the use of industrial organization principles in our own area of enquiry.

The third reason why I think the paper has great value is that studies about the participation and competitive impact of investments made by multi-nationals on the food and tobacco sector are of recognized and increasing importance in countries of different economic development. The paper should be commended, therefore, since it really provides a pattern which might be replicated in the investigation of a vast array of problems and issues relevant to other countries.

It seems to me that the purpose of the study is clearly spelled out in the paper. Its principal objectives are carefully to describe the participation of foreign firms in the US food and tobacco sector and secondly, to determine what are the motives and the competitive impact of the direct investment originated in these foreign firms.

There is, however, a third objective implicit in the presentation which, from my own perspective, deserves a more complete treatment; and it is the evaluation of presently existing US policies in the light of the findings of the regression study and the policy prescriptions which might be alternatives derived from them in order to capture the potential benefits of foreign direct investment.

This opener believes that, while one might say that the first two are fully accomplished in the paper, further elaboration and discussion of the policy recommendation is needed since there are many conflicting views and philosophical and even ideological positions involved.

More specifically I would like to have reactions from the author to the issue of nationalization versus regulation of already established firms as it seems to be the case in many developing countries. In this same context, I would appreciate further elaboration on the likely implications arising from the practice of screening foreign investments on a case-by-case basis with social benefit–cost analysis required for all large proposed investments. (This has been recently advocated in the US). Also I would like to hear about the implications of international codes of conduct being enforced by international or supranational agencies.

Finally, I would like to have further comments from the author on two quite specific points of his paper. The first has to do with the US food and tobacco sector. It seems to me that the results from the model could be predetermined depending on whether data on the fibre subsector and food retailing and wholesaling operations are retained in the model. The second item refers to the rationale, logic or economic theory behind the choosing of some independent variables used in the econometric model from which, afterwards, most conclusions and policy recommendations are derived – for example, advertising expenditures per caput of the multi-national's home country as determinant of the propensity to invest and the size of direct investment of foreign firms participating in the US food and tobacco sector. It seems to me that prior to using it in the regression model, a statement is needed making explicit whether the relationship is proven through logical or empirical experiment, or else, that the independent variable is only a proxy which cannot be used or is without value for policy analysis.

GENERAL DISCUSSION – RAPPORTEUR: W.H. HUNTER

Commenting on the opener's remarks concerning nationalization policy, the author felt that nationalization, which in manufacturing industry was more common in LDCs than in MDCs, was not a realistic policy alternative in the US. Rather, regulation, both directly (to close off potential inflows of FDI in areas such as communications) and through the widening of the use of anti-trust legislation, was followed and was more likely to be followed as a course of action in the US. The principle of "Potential Competitor Loss" could also be used to control FDI and could provide a means of implementing a tougher take-over policy. Social benefit/cost analysis of multi-national corporations' (MNCs) activities would be a useful tool, so long as it encompassed estimates of the benefits and costs of "competition". The "International Code of Conduct" for MNCs, presently being promoted by OECD, would not, it was felt, have great impact on MNC's activities in the field of FDI.

Asked to speak on FDI in Canada, the Chairman (Murray Hawkins) indicated that this was particularly high in Canada in general and in food retailing in Western Canada in particular, with one firm holding a dominant position, to the extent that profit and marginal analysis of the food retailing industry in the area was of little value.

Attention was drawn to the possible relationship between FDI and the demand characteristics for products such as tobacco, oil and fats, and alcohol i.e. those with an unfavourable public image, which are included in the definition of food and tobacco manufacturing.

The author concurred with a suggestion that regression analysis had no cause/effect implications and reiterated his use of the term "determinants" to describe the factors influencing FDI.

Noting the conclusions in the paper that technical barriers to the entry of Foreign Food Firms (FFF) to the US were of a minimal nature, it was suggested that this may have stemmed from the interests of US food and agricultural firms in investing overseas and therefore of a policy on their part of maintaining a reasonable balance between the outflow and inflow of FDI.

In reply, the author felt that his analysis represented a move towards a more objective method of answering the question whether FDI was "good or bad" for a country: a question which hitherto had been considered only in terms of a value-judgement.

Participants in the discussion included Ludvig I. Madsen, Edward Karpoff, Edith H. Whetham and Edward C. Schultz.

ECKHARD RAPELIUS and ADOLF WEBER

The World Agricultural Input Industries as Factors of Rural Change*

INTRODUCTION

To increase food production per caput agricultural input industries play an increasing role. They are key factors of rural change in a dynamic world of population and income growth. They determine the welfare of rural and other people all over the world. Agricultural economists have acquired the skills to assist decision-makers in identifying and analysing the pertinent problems at the farm and at the agricultural sector level. However, the increasing international dimension and the economics of the agricultural input industries have to be properly understood. Otherwise, they become a burden and not a benefit to the farming community.

Agricultural input industries provide agriculture with seed, feed, water, agricultural chemicals and farm machinery. Some inputs are locally bound, like seed and water, and others are ubiquitous goods. They can be produced, transported and applied almost everywhere. In this study we intend to deal only with the latter category: chemicals and machinery. To be detailed enough on a worldwide basis we only treat the nitrogen and tractor industries. In section two the characteristics of these industries are considered. Sections three and four explain the international dimension and development of nitrogen and tractor production. In section five the main conclusions are drawn and proposals are made.

The key working hypothesis in our study is that poor factor endowments and smaller domestic markets are unfavourable for nitrogen and tractor production. Such production tends to increase the price of agricultural inputs. We assert that the basic tendencies of economies of scale in nitrogen and tractor production can be observed throughout the world regardless of the economic system. Whether nitrogen and tractors should be produced domestically or imported has to be judged in any well thought out development policy designed to increase food production.

* The research on which this paper is based was partly supported by the Sonderforschungs-sbereich 86: Weltwirtschaft und Internationale Wirtschafs-beziehungen.

2 CHARACTERISTICS OF THE TRACTOR AND NITROGEN INDUSTRY

Minimum size. Both industries use a sophisticated technology. In the establishment of a new plant, technical and economic reasons require a minimum size. The minimmum size in each industry varies according to site, costs of capital and material inputs, requirements for skilled labour, infrastructure and other factors. For a tractor plant built by a producer of autocars or a big multi-national firm to gain a strategic entry into an expanding market it reduces the minimum size to begin production. FAO [6, p. 203, 235] assumed in 1969, that the respective plants should not produce less than 10,000 tractors annually or 150,000 tons of nitrogen. Other authors claimed in 1972 and 1975[3,9] 20,000 tractors or 300,000 tons of nitrogen should be the minimum size. Further, there is evidence that economies of scale as well as production as in distribution in both industries are the most decisive element in reducing costs: the larger the plant the lower the average cost per unit of output.

Capital requirements. To establish a new plant heavy capital requirements are necessary. A tractor plant with an annual output of 20,000 tractors in 1968[7], (p. 47) needed a capital outlay of 142 million US$ (thereof 53 per cent for production and 47 per cent for wholesale distribution). The investment costs for a nitrogen plant of 300,000 t with the necessary facilities (storage, replacement parts etc.) have been estimated in 1975 to be 100 million US$[10] (p. 6). In the meantime inflation may have increased the reported absolute capital requirements.

Operating costs. In the nitrogen industry capital and maintenance costs account for 50 per cent. A crude analysis of the operating costs per unit of output reveals that raw materials (e.g. natural gas, coke, coal, oil) to be processed are a decisive cost item. Assuming a 100 per cent level of utilization of an ammonia plant and low prices for the natural gas used to derive hydrogen, the percentage for raw materials reaches 28 per cent and with higher prices 39 per cent.[5] Other sizeable parts of costs are energy and water, but labour costs only account for 5 per cent. Depending on the annual output level in the tractor industry the costs for material are about 70 per cent, 15 per cent for capital and 15 per cent for labour.[7] (p. 198) Labour costs increase comparatively in the tractor industry, because the costs of the distribution system and services after the sale have to be included.

Different risks of market entry. Despite similarities in both industries some differences are important to note. They mainly concern the transfer of knowledge and productive capacity, the type of decision-makers involved, and the risk-sharing between them. In the nitrogen industry selling the licence to apply the technical process, the engineering and the final construction of the plant might be done by three different firms. Even if selling the licence, the engineering and the construction of the new plant would be done by one firm the market risks of selling the plant's nitrogen output is completely separated from the original supplier of the

technology. In the tractor industry the owner of the licence and the final
operation of the plant is in the hand of the same firm in market
economies. The risk of building an inappropriate and inefficient plant or
of having misjudged the initial size and growth of demand will be therefore assumed by the tractor firm investing abroad. That means that in the
nitrogen industry there is no institutionalized risk-sharing between the
foreign contractor and the domestic nitrogen producer. The funding is
initiated and done very often by government bodies. This might be
detrimental to farmers, because at later stages an internationally non-
competitive nitrogen plant might be unduly protected beyond the infant
stage by tariffs, quotas, or subsidies to mask an earlier defective decision.
If the tractor firm's capital was exclusively provided by the foreign firm
the need to protect the domestic market against international competition might not be similarly the government's obligation.

   The sequence of establishing nitrogen and tractor industries. The challenge to establish both industries is in each country dictated by the size
and growth of the respective demand. In a general classification, there are
two types of agriculture. In the first type, people, who earn their livelihood from agriculture, are increasing absolutely in numbers. In the
second type, the agricultural labour force decreases absolutely and relatively. The first is the situation in most developing countries, the second in
industrial countries. The first group of countries has fast increasing land
prices. They have to favour land productivity by augmenting fertilizer
application. Industrial countries have to cope with fast rising prices of
agricultural labour. They therefore emphasize labour saving and support
simultaneously land saving technologies. The unlimited divisibility of
fertilizer permits application at the lowest level of labour productivity.
However, to repay the capital outlay for the smallest tractor a minimum
level of labour productivity is required. Developing countries with
domestic markets of sufficient size have in any defendable growth
strategy for agricultural input industries to recognize that the nitrogen
industry has to precede the tractor industry given that land prices increase
faster than the prices of labour.

3   STRUCTURE AND DEVELOPMENT OF THE WORLD'S NITROGEN INDUSTRY

The distribution of the various size classes of nitrogen plants is shown in
Table 1. The smaller plants are mainly situated in developing countries.
Plants with more than 300,000 tons of capacity were in 1975 exclusively
in industrial and oil exporting countries (Map 1). The trend to build larger
plant sizes continues. Until the sixties the production of ammonia was
considered a rather mature technology. Since then the large-scale
ammonia plant has become technically feasible.

   The history of plant sizes in a German chemical company in Graph 1
shows this dramatic increase. A classical Haber-Bosch plant in 1913 had

an annual capacity of 1,320 tons N. Since then, the size of newly established technical units of ammonia plants has grown to 54,000 tons in 1956. But due to recent technical innovations the capacity reached 429,000 tons in 1972. The energy consumption per tons of ammonia dropped from 88 GJ to 33 GJ as well as the investment decreased per unit of output. Nitrogen complexes surpassing the million tons combining several technical units have already been erected or are in the planning stage.

The history of the world's nitrogen production shows – compared to tractor production – a higher growth (Graphs 2(a) and 2(b)). The larger industrial countries lose their market share gradually. Economies of scale and competition among firms will assist them to stabilize nitrogen prices despite rising energy prices. This situation compares very favourably with the high prices farmers have generally to pay in developing countries when nitrogen mostly comes from small and technically old-fashioned plants.[9] (p. 72) Rising energy prices and the lack of possibilities to exploit similar economies of scale do not facilitate the task of keeping fertilizer prices down.

Economies of scale in nitrogen production continue beyond 300,000 tons. At present, 150 plants of this size could satisfy the world's nitrogen demand and could even meet the expected growth in demand until the year 2000. Nowadays, the domestic market is big enough in only 29 countries (out of 152) to host a nitrogen plant of desirable size. Only one country in South America, two in Africa and four in Asia (excluding China, India, and Japan) have a sufficient market size.

To avoid a total dependency on the world nitrogen market governments with small domestic markets tend to favour the erection of nitrogen plants. A contractor of a nitrogen plant will sell any desired size of plant. But he does not share the risks of marketing the production. On the other

TABLE 1   *Distribution of size classes of nitrogen plants*

Worlda 1973

Plant Capacity in 1,000 tons N(p.a.)	Number of plants
> 700	2
501–700	4
401–500	12
301–400	23
< 300	324
	365

a Without China, North Korea and other non-reporting countries.
Source: The British Sulphur Corporation. World Fertilizer Atlas 1973.

MAP 1

Location of the Twenty Largest Nitrogen Plants in the World, 1976

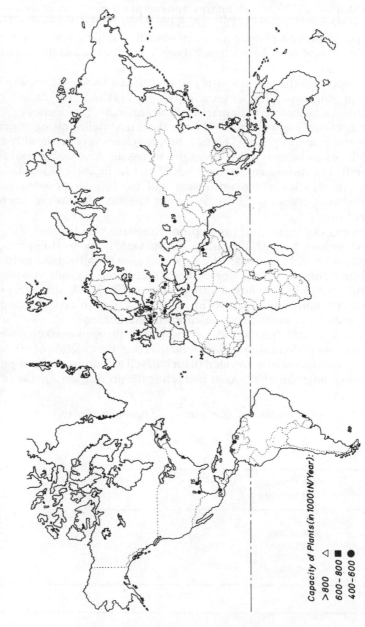

Capacity of Plants (in 1000 t N/Year):

△ >800

■ 600 - 800

● 400 - 600

GRAPH 1

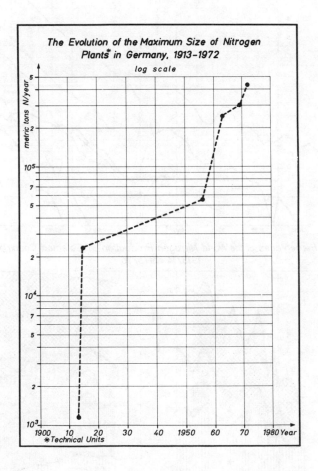

GRAPH 2

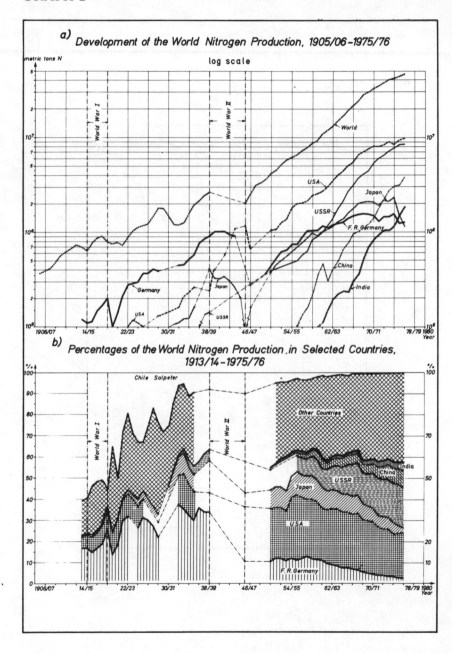

a) *Development of the World Nitrogen Production, 1905/06–1975/76*

b) *Percentages of the World Nitrogen Production in Selected Countries, 1913/14–1975/76*

MAP 2

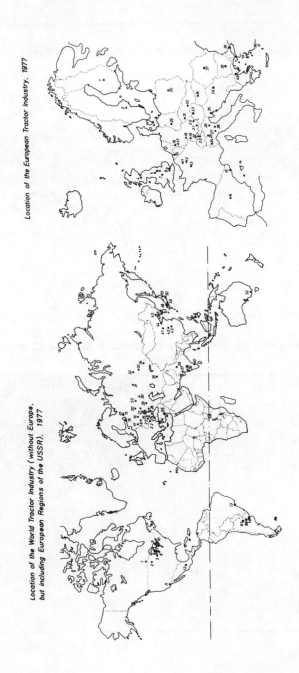

Location of the World Tractor Industry (without Europe, but including European Regions of the USSR). 1977

Location of the European Tractor Industry. 1977

GRAPH 3

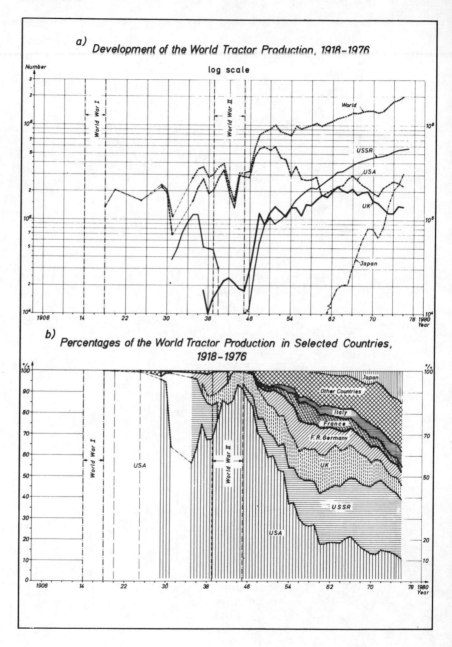

a) Development of the World Tractor Production, 1918-1976

b) Percentages of the World Tractor Production in Selected Countries, 1918-1976

hand the separation of functions may facilitate and encourage bilateral and multilateral financing. Thus it fortifies the tendency that plants which are too small will be erected. Heavy subsidization programmes are very often the consequence, because farmers need economic incentives to increase food production. Careful economic analysis by independent engineers and agricultural economists could help to evaluate the benefits and costs of building a plant. Further the world market can hardly be considered a rescuer for the surplus nitrogen, because the established large scale producers can offer lower prices and manage better the needed marketing logistics in foreign markets.

4 STRUCTURE AND DEVELOPMENT OF THE WORLD'S TRACTOR INDUSTRY

The locations of the main tractor plants are shown in Map 2. The plants are concentrated in the main crop areas of industrialized countries or in large countries like India and China. The world's tractor industry is composed of about 130 plants in 90 locations in 35 different countries.* Eleven locations are reported for North America, 22 for the USSR, six can be found in the UK and West Germany, five are in India, Italy and China. 10 European countries only count for one tractor producing location.

In 1976 the average yearly output of a tractor plant was 15,000 units. The difference in size of the annual output of tractor plants within and between countries is marked. We find the largest plants in industrialized countries. They may reach an annual output of nearly 100,000 tractors (like in the UK or the USSR), but many plants produce less than 5,000 tractors or below the minimum size. If they do not produce a very specific tractor for a small group of customers or sell in a protected national market they can hardly be considered efficient producers, because they lack the possibility of exploiting economies of scale available to large plants.

If we assume for an extremely rough calculation a world of free trade among countries and three versions of plant size, two questions arise: what would be the theoretically needed number of plants to satisfy a yearly demand of 1.83 million tractors, as in 1976, and how many countries would be involved in producing tractors for replacement? Assuming plant sizes of 10,000, 20,000 or 100,000 tractors, the world would need 183, 92 or 18 plants respectively. In 1976, out of 178 countries only 31 countries produced more than 10,000 tractors, 21 countries more than 20,000 tractors and only six countries produced more than 100,000 tractors for the domestic market and for export.

It would be wrong to argue that the difference between actual plant and

---

* Many locations have more than one tractor plant, therefore the number of plants exceeds the number of locations. Countries only assembling tractors or producing less than 1,000 tractors are excluded.

potential plant sizes should be eliminated in the future by implementing only the largest plants. Many other factors have to be considered. Large tractor plants in industrial countries are the result of a long development process, where the demand density and the logistics of production and marketing permit the attainment of such sizes. The observed differences between actual and potential sizes are however an indication of how difficult it is in an international framework to start production with a plant which is too small.

Graphs 3(a) and (b) reveal that total tractor production increased since World War II. Single countries enter tractor production through the stages of growth, saturation, and decline at different points in time. The decline of tractor production occurred in the USA in the early fifties and in the UK in the seventies. The USSR seems to have entered the saturation phase now. The recent stormy growth of Japan's tractor production demonstrates the effects of fast rising prices for labour in agriculture. They induce a fast increasing demand for tractors in a comparatively large domestic market. Countries or firms which do not share such favourable take-off conditions have to pay the price if they begin tractor production too early.

In the planned economies of Eastern Europe the USSR has the dominant position with a share of 80 per cent (Graph 4a). The economies of scale in tractor production are independent of the economic system. Therefore, Bulgaria, the German Democratic Republic and Hungary may give up tractor production one day by mutual agreement. In open market economies many small tractor plants which pioneered several decades ago have had to be closed due to powerful international competitors. The largest firms have plants in several countries. Production and distribution to meet specific demands can be tailored at international scale. Despite their tradition and their superiority in research, marketing, and full-line programmes, the combined total market share of the largest five international tractor firms has certainly not increased (Graph 4b) since Japanese firms entered the market in the sixties. Observations show that market prices for tractors between the industrial and the developing countries differ sharply.[4,6] Governments in countries with higher tractor prices tend to protect tractor production unduly against international competition. To make things worse, in promoting mechanization many governments create credit programmes to facilitate tractor purchases, which further increase the total costs of agricultural mechanization.

5   CONCLUSIONS

In general the production process is economically efficient, if the factors of production – labour, capital, raw materials, energy – are applied in proportion to their marginal costs. Since the availability and cost of these four factors vary between rich and poor countries and the proportions the

GRAPH 4

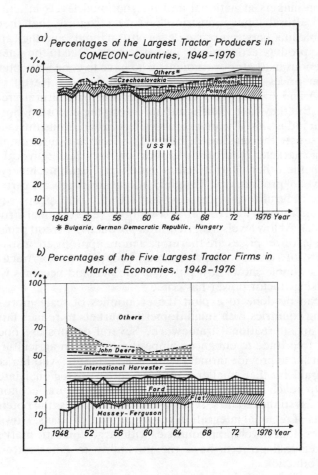

a) Percentages of the Largest Tractor Producers in COMECON-Countries, 1948-1976

* Bulgaria, German Democratic Republic, Hungary

b) Percentages of the Five Largest Tractor Firms in Market Economies, 1948-1976

factors have in production are technically quite fixed, industrial countries can generally produce nitrogen and tractors at lower costs. Due to the larger size of the domestic market industrial countries additionally benefit from large economies of scale in production and distribution. Among the more agriculturally oriented countries and disregarding factor price differences those countries with a small domestic market would have the highest disadvantage in producing nitrogen and tractors.

Decision-makers at national and international levels in and for the main agricultural input industries have to recognize that there is an unavoidable link between pricing agricultural inputs and the capacity of farmers to produce economically and efficiently. Due to the smallness of the indigenous markets governments who have to cope with internationally higher prices for domestically produced nitrogen (fertilizer, pesticides etc.) and tractors very often implement agricultural credit programmes. But they have to differentiate among the importance of agricultural input industries. The divisibility of fertilizer permits the tailoring of credit to satisfy the smallest demand. The yield and rural employment increasing character of fertilizer application has an unequivocal positive effect. On the other hand, tractors and agricultural machinery need a certain level of productivity. The yield increasing effects are certainly less than those of fertilizer, the employment effect to rural peoples might be negative under very unfavourable conditions (e.g. bimodal structure of agriculture). At low levels of agricultural productivity credit programmes to reduce fertilizer prices are therefore a more appropriate instrument to the welfare of rural people than credit programmes for tractors. The Japanese example shows how powerful the demand becomes when the time of using tractor power has come.

What can be done to exploit the economies of scale more fully in developing countries with small domestic markets to reduce farm input prices in an international framework? Several options are open. One would be free trade to enhance competition between agricultural input firms in order to provide farmers with cheaper inputs. Another course of action would be that smaller countries agree on regional integration projects to reach a sufficient market size. Agricultural economic and agri-business studies could serve as useful tools to assess the potential and constraints of regional integration versus national projects. However, we would stress that developing countries with large domestic markets even without regional projects have the possibility to enter fertilizer and tractor production.

The knowledge of designing, managing and operating agricultural input industries at several levels is very scattered. It is not an easily accessible public good. To use the agricultural input industries as factors of rural change more research with an international dimension is required. This might be considered as the final raison d'être for having undertaken this investigation.

[1] Appl, M. "A Brief History of Ammonia Production from the Early Days to the Present", *Nitrogen*, London, March/April 1976 (reprint).
[2] Belter, Andrea A. "Standorte, Struktur und Entwicklung der Weltdüngemittelindustrie", Diplomarbeit (thesis), Kiel 1977.
[3] Carney, M. *Industrialization in a Latin American Common Market*, Washington DC 1972.
[4] Dagnino Pastore, J.M. *La Industria del Tractor en la Argentina*, Tomo I–III, Buenos Aires 1966.
[5] Esaki, M. "Nitrogenous Fertilizer and Raw Material Problems", *Chemical Economy & Engineering Review*, Tokyo, Vol. 7, No. 3, March 1975, pp. 12–30.
[6] FAO "Provisional Indicative World Plan for Agricultural Development", Vol. 1. Rome 1969.
[7] Kudrle, R. *Agricultural Tractors: A World Industry Study*, Cambridge, Mass. 1975.
[8] MacDonald, N.B., W.F. Barnicke, F.W. Judge and K.E. Hansen "Farm Tractor Production Costs: A Study in Economies of Scale", Royal Commission on Farm Machinery, Study No. 2, Ottawa 1969.
[9] Mai, D. "Düngemittelsubventionierung im Entwicklungsprozeß", (Sozialökonomische Schriften zur Agrarentwicklung, Nr. 26.) Saarbrücken 1977.
[10] Mukherjee, S.K. "World Trend in Nitrogen Industry. Design Philosophy of Large Capacity Ammonia Plants. A Practical Approach," *Fertilizer News*, New Delhi, Vol. 21, December 1976, pp. 3–8.
[11] Rapelius, E. "Standorte, Struktur und Entwicklung der Weltschlepperindustrie", Diplomarbeit (thesis), Kiel 1974.
[12] Weber, A. and E. Rapelius "Erscheinungsformen und Konsequenzen der internationalen Konzentration der Agroindustrie", (Schriften der Gesellschaft für Wirtschafts- sund Sozialwissenschaften des Landbaues, Bd. 16), (in print).

DISCUSSION OPENING – ALLAN N. RAE

When I read the title of this paper, I expected to hear discussion of the manner in which the world agricultural input industries had acted as the agents, or determining agents, of rural change. That is, I expected a broad, international coverage of the major input industries and examples of the various ways in which the evolution of these industries had determined, moderated or accelerated rural change. And because the focus is on rural change, I expected discussion to centre on the influence of the input industries on such things as the level and distribution of rural incomes, rural employment, farm structure, resource use and productivity. Since the input industries are often involved in selling new technology, the latter's importance in determining rural change, e.g. unemployment, surplus production, low incomes and so on, could have been covered. I would also have thought that the market structure of at least the major input industries would be important, e.g. its effect on pricing behaviour. Energy prices and their resultant rural effects are an obvious example.

However, I must confess that the paper disappointed me somewhat. It chose to concentrate on only two input industries; those supplying nitrogen and tractors. It then went on to develop a hypothesis that I would have thought obvious – that such industries possess economies of size, so that if established in regions where such economies cannot be achieved, then the costs of these inputs will be higher than if size economies in production were achieved. In my opinion, that tells us little about the impact of the world input industries on rural change. The authors appear critical of past efforts to establish nitrogen and tractor plants in developing countries with only small domestic markets. Because production costs will likely be high, various forms of assistance will be required, and they are critical of "undue" protection of tractor production in developing countries.

I think there is another question that is the really interesting one, namely: "Why do countries, even in well thought out development programmes, decide to construct small scale nitrogen or tractor industries?" If the developing country's objectives include the boosting of rural activity and the conservation of foreign exchange, then the construction of such small-scale industries may not be a bad idea. And of course, they are acting no differently than the industrialized countries (i.e. the large-scale input producers) who protect their agricultural *output* industries. I would have liked the paper to include a cost–benefit analysis of establishing small-scale input plants in developing countries, which aim to boost rural activity and save foreign exchange – it would surely be useful to know just how great or small the welfare losses really are, since economic efficiency is not the only consideration of policy makers.

In their paper, the authors suggest possible welfare gains and losses, e.g. the yield and employment-increasing effects of fertilizers and maybe negative employment effects of mechanization, but some evidence of these gains and losses in a benefit–cost framework would have added greatly to the paper.

Two of the solutions put forward by the authors are the freeing of international trade in such inputs, and market and production integration by the small countries. But given the political realities and uncertainties of today's world, such suggestions are rather simplistic and do not, in my opinion, get us very far.

GENERAL DISCUSSION – RAPPORTEUR: F. BONNIEUX

The following points were raised in the general discussion:

Was too much emphasis being placed on tractors and chemicals as agents of rural change?

Does tractor production necessarily require large investment? (cf. paper by Khan, p. 88.)

What policies are needed to correct the undesirable developments described in the paper?

To what extent might LDCs substitute organic fertilizers (manure) for those inorganic fertilizers which require large inputs of energy?

Multi-national companies might not necessarily set up plants in a country in order to take advantage of an internal demand; but merely to take advantage of cheaper labour there.

There was also a question regarding the comparability of data on tractor units.

In reply, the authors agreed that other agents of rural change were important but felt that the tractor and fertilizer industries needed special attention because of the large amounts of capital involved and perhaps wrongly allocated in LDCs. There was also some evidence that low investment tractor production was not always successful. They felt that while some degree of substitution by manure was possible, much of this was ruled out by the high nutritive requirements of the new high-yielding varieties of plants. Regarding comparability, only four-wheel tractors of 10 hp and over were included in the analysis (which therefore excludes garden tractors). Unfortunately horse-power data are not available on a world basis.

Participants in the discussion included Judith Heyer, A. Mohammad, Caleb W.W. Wangia, Heinrich Niederboster and Joseph Klatzmann.

SECTION VI

Disciplinary

HEINZ–ULRICH THIMM

The Challenges for Western European Teachers of Agricultural Economics in Educating for Agrarian Change in their Own and Developing Countries

INTRODUCTION

Some historical changes which seem to have influenced the teaching of agricultural economics at university level in Western Europe over the past fifty years are traced in this paper. An attempt is also made to point to some accomplishments of our profession as well as to challenge present teachers with issues felt to be of future importance on the European agricultural scene and in developing countries.

Three restrictions have to be kept in mind. (1) It is impossible to find a common denominator for the development of agricultural economics at all European universities. National history and differences of educational systems are frequently not comparable. Conclusions therefore only reflect a general tendency, not a detailed account. (2) Teaching agricultural economics can be treated in a very broad way including textbooks, journal publications, extension service. A narrower approach must be taken in this short paper; undergraduate and post-graduate curricula only are analysed. (3) Measuring teaching accomplishments is almost impossible. Neither particular agricultural policy decisions nor farm management performance can be traced back to teaching activities directly, except in individual case studies. Usually the general hope of all educators is that teaching accomplishes something good, leaving the definition of "good" to the students and to their employers.

ESTABLISHMENT OF THE DISCIPLINE

Agricultural economics at the university level in Europe was established before or shortly after World War I. The biological sciences of crop and animal production had reached their limitations and gave way to economic analysis of the real farm situation where plants and animals had

The author is indebted for very helpful comments and corrections to Dr D.A.G. Green, Department of Agricultural Economics, University College of Wales, Aberystwyth.

589

to be produced for a market with a number of socio-economic determinants influencing the resulting prices, costs and incomes. It is interesting to note that the establishment of the first Chair of Agricultural Economics in Britain had to wait till 1929 while teaching economic subjects in agricultural curricula started much earlier. On the Continent and in Britain farm management won early recognition as the leading field. Agricultural Marketing, the first Chair of Agricultural Marketing in Europe was established also in 1929 at Berlin University, followed in importance, recognizing the general need for market information and policy advice on important state intervention schemes, e.g. marketing boards, deficiency payments, tariff agreements. The major agrarian changes of that period had certainly been the massive introduction of biological technologies into the production process and the instability of farm incomes, following the slow-down of economic activities ending in the Great Depression. Together with general economics, rural sociology (this not in Britain), and agricultural policy the macro fields of agricultural economics were firmly established before or shortly after World War II and were not further subdivided later. The separation of micro and macro disciplines however appeared to be irrevocable, reflecting the growing complexity of agricultural development.

The diversification of the micro field into production economics and farm management started before World War II but, under American influence, only reached its peak in the 1960s and 1970s. The introduction of mechanized technologies into the small family farm structure of European countries necessitated changes in the production pattern, farm sizes and the degree of enterprise specialization. This in turn demanded more theoretical analysis for the optimal combination of production factors as well as more guidance in applied farm problems. On the Continent, extension was introduced as a teaching subject, but it was not connected with the practical extension service, as was the case in the USA. The plant and animal production sciences had by now accepted the fact that agricultural economics would stay as part of the general degree structure. If there was any need to offer more hours of a particular subject field, the introduction of specialized undergraduate streams became unavoidable. In most parts of Europe, there remained at least a common basis for first and second year agricultural students before specialization starts. This contrasts again with developments in the USA where far reaching specialization was introduced quite early, reflecting job opportunities in a growing agribusiness sector, while in Europe the majority of graduates from agricultural faculties was absorbed by the public service for administration and extension. Only in Britain, because of larger farm sizes, a majority of graduates could hope for management positions in practical agriculture. A European agriculture, caught between rising land and labour productivity and decreasing income elasticities of demand, still needed graduates who were generalists in the sense of being able to find solutions to the totality of individual and social farm needs as well as to satisfy consumer demands for a balanced food supply.

TABLE 1 *Establishment of major teaching disciplines in agricultural economics, Europe 1920–80*

Time Period	before 1929	1930–45	1946–60	1961–80
Agrarian changes	Introduction of biological technologies	Introduction of intensive farm systems	Introduction of mechanised technologies	Increase in farm size and specialization
Micro			Production Economics →	Production Economics
			Enterprise Management →	Enterprise Management
		Farm Management ———————		Farm Management
			Home Economics →	Home Economics
		Extension ——		Extension
FARM ECONOMICS				Environment Economics
				Regional Planning
		General Economics ———————		General Economics
			Agricultural Marketing →	Agricultural Marketing
		Agricultural Policy ———————		Agricultural Policy
Macro			International Development →	International Development
		Rural Sociology ———————		Rural Sociology
Agrarian changes	Instability of farm income low consumer demand, rural urban migration	Increasing state intervention, war production schemes, marketing boards	Rising purchasing power; agri-business growth, price and income policies	Increasing European integration, surplus production, development issues

While during the first post World War II period, teaching micro agricultural economics was mainly following events, the discipline was later able to catch up, anticipating more what will happen on the farm level if circumstances change. But it seems that the micro field has reached a certain stage where besides methodological advances particular new factual insights can be obtained only by turning purposefully to problem-solving techniques. The recent introduction of special enterprise courses such as livestock management, or the rediscovery of home economics, and entry into environmental fields as well as systems analysis and decision theory may indicate some new approaches. In contrast, the macro fields of agricultural economics had less difficulty of change anticipation, the problems of rural–urban migration, price policy issues, parity income demands, and structural changes of agriculture figured prominently in their teaching syllabuses which embrace forecasting future problem areas of the European Common Market. Interestingly, a final observation is that during the 1960s the micro fields of agricultural economics certainly lost ground as teaching subjects in favour of macro fields, especially in Britain.

The present structure of agricultural economics teaching disciplines in Europe is equally the result of agrarian developments and changes in educational policies which lead to large increases in educational expenditures to transform the "élite university" into a normal tertiary training institution. The latter allowed the employment of larger numbers of professors and lecturers who then looked for identification as specialists in research and, consequently, in teaching. This facilitated an additional interest in important subjects like international development, regional planning, resource economics and certainly into quantitative methods which made large inroads into all disciplines. At Tables 1 and 2 an attempt is made to summarize the stages of development of agricultural economics as teaching disciplines and to present a European example of a teaching syllabus for undergraduates leading to the degree of Bachelor of Science in Agriculture. In addition, of course, various programmes of post-graduate training are available leading to degrees of Master of Science or Doctor of Philosophy in Agricultural Economics.

ACCOMPLISHMENTS

Over the last fifty years the accomplishments of agricultural economics as a teaching discipline may be summarized as follows: (1) Firm establishment of agricultural economics as an equal part of the general agricultural curriculum in competition with plant and animal sciences. (2) Firm establishment of agricultural economics as specialized streams of undergraduates and post-graduate training, turning out nearly the same number of specialists as in plant and animal sciences. (3) Firm establishment of agricultural economics as a distinct teaching profession with its own methods and technical language; not always understood and appreciated by our colleagues in other disciplines or by the public.

There are generally mixed feelings about the consequences of separating agricultural economics from the other disciplines. No doubt without specialization the contribution of agricultural faculties for solving complex farm problems would be minimal in a dynamic development process. Moreover there is no question that job specialization necessitated specialized training streams for job preparation. But one question should be allowed: will further specialization lead to isolation, where each discipline will concentrate on teaching its own students only, not any longer trying to find a total approach to agriculture? The real test of our accomplishments appears to lie in the attitude of the various disciplines to each other, looking for complementarity rather than differentiation. Is agricultural economics needed by other disciplines, or vice versa? Should a present trend be reversed that specialists are no longer aware that agriculture is a profession which combines biological, technical, economic, and social elements? Is there a danger that the profession turns to irrelevant fields because of too much specialization in agricultural economics? Is G. Johnson's "quest for relevance in agricultural economics"[1] a real issue in

TABLE 2 *A European example: syllabus of selected agricultural courses, Wye College, UK, Prospectus 1978/80*

Economics: Principles relating to the production, pricing and distribution of goods and services. An introduction to national income and international trade concepts. Theories of economic growth, demand and welfare economics. National income and social accounting. Inter-regional and international trade. Time and space dimensions of economic activities.

Management: The management function and the development of the firm; theory of the firm; decision-making criteria, risk and uncertainty. Structure, functioning and performance of organizations and the behaviour of individuals and groups within them. Information for marketing, production and financial planning and control. Analysis of the financial results of farm and horicultural businesses. Planning techniques: budgets, gross margins, programme planning, introduction to linear programming. Economic aspects of the main farm and horticultural enterprises. Resource Use Economics: mechanization, labour, capital. Labour management.

Marketing: Systems of marketing agricultural products and their evolution. Marketing institutions in Britain and the rest of the EEC. Marketing of the principal agricultural and horticultural commodities. Marketing of goods and services to farmers. The study of marketing as an activity. Marketing objectives, market research, measurement and forecasting of demand. Planning and organizational control of marketing. Examination of problems in marketing farm produce and in marketing of goods and services to farmers.

Agricultural Policy: The social significance of demographic structure and trends. Occupational and family structures. Labour mobility. Scope and methods of rural sociology. Social institutions in rural areas. Land tenure. Patterns of rural change in developed and developing countries. The background of European agriculture: geographical, historical, political and social. Agricultural regions, and the characteristics: farm size, land tenure, farming systems, production, income levels. Producers' groups, co-operatives and other forms of market integration. Food consumption patterns and trends. The impact of world trade.

Land Use: The spatial aspects of man's activities on land. Land use statistics and classification. Rural and urban land use structure and change in Britain and other countries. Comparative land use. Land conversion and competition. Living space and land use planning. the locations of agricultural and industrial production. The location of urban and rural land uses. Settlement patterns and central place theory. Principles of land-use planning appraisal. Rural and recreation planning. Regional planning.

Agrarian Development: Nature of traditional agriculture in developing countries. Problems of modernizing traditional agriculture. Role of agriculture in the development of tropical economics. Strategies for rural development. Rich countries' contribution to development.

Statistics: Introduction to the measurement of micro- and macro-variables. The major series of British economic statistics and their sources. Censuses and surveys. Problems of international comparison. Probability. Theoretical and empirical frequency distribution. Theory of sampling. Hypotheses and significance tests. Analysis of variance. Simple and multiple correlation and regression. Analysis of time-series. Introduction to the construction of macro-economic models. Illustrations from economic data.

Operation Analysis: Work study. Network analysis. Programming techniques. Simulation methods. Replacement theory. Systems analysis.

Economics of the Agricultural Industry: Agriculture and economic growth. Productivity and Incomes. Structural adjustment. Resource availability. The market for farm and horticultural products. World trade patterns; food surpluses and aid programmes.

European Agriculture and Policy: The background of European agriculture: geographical, historical, political and social. Agricultural regions and their characteristics: Farm size, land tenure, farming systems, production, income levels. Producers' groups, co-operatives and other forms of market integration. Food consumption patterns and trends. The impact of world trade.

the teaching field, to be taken to heart before new challenges lead to more specialization? The limits are reached where single facts and methods taught leave students in the dark about how to solve the total problem with which they are confronted in agriculture.

What have macro and micro agricultural economics accomplished in their particular fields? In general the contact hours devoted to each field are similar. In the macro subjects students get a fair introduction to the principles of income generation in agriculture, the links between agriculture and the economy as well as the determinants of economic growth. But is the concept taught: what a "healthy" agriculture might be? What is still typical rural? Are agrarian changes leading unavoidably to a non-agrarian society which, consequently, does not need agricultural economics as a separate field any longer?

In the micro subjects, students are introduced to a balanced view of the farm and its enterprises as business units, using gross margin analysis and dynamic programming methods. But in Europe there appears a danger of some agricultural economists becoming irrelevant model builders, creating illusions about attainable precision through statistical methodology. Or they break into the domain of other disciplines, instead of bringing into their own field the insights of the behavioural sciences to explain more realistically than economics alone can do the individual and social decision-making process.

Summing up this section of the deliberation, it appears that our profession has done an outstanding job in pushing our subject into agricultural curricula: the demand for our product (students) has steadily increased and usually agricultural economics graduates in Europe have so far no difficulty in finding jobs. But there is no evidence that teaching of agricultural economics has influenced any major agricultural policy decision in Europe. Nor do agricultural economists appear to have anticipated social and technical changes better than other disciplines. Many individual teachers may be convinced that they have; there is no way to answer this question for the profession in total.

STUDENTS – THE RECIPIENTS OF TEACHING

Who are the students? Students of agriculture have changed all over the world during these fifty years. They come now with largely non-farm backgrounds, their entrance standards are lower compared with the previous élite university; they are looking for a wider range of careers in administration, research, and teaching as well as in agriculture and related business fields. They will frequently have to compete against graduates from economics, business, law, very often they may have to serve conflicting interests (farmers, commerce, administration). They have certainly other personal values about economic growth, politics, environment, and resource use, compared with a generation ago. Does this influence our teaching? Are the students élitists, generalists, specialists? Are they from developing countries? If students change, how are educational goals changed? Too many times the students may feel that they are not trained to be problem solvers in agriculture but merely recipients of our knowledge and they have to find its relevance for themselves. Will more emphasis on teaching skills in problem identification and definition avoid this impression? "The crucial agricultural problems and issues before our society make it desirable for agricultural economics teaching to be oriented to these problems and to appropriate approaches for solving them. Solving these problems also requires disciplinary excellence. For the most part, this means both (1) learning experiences with or in multi-disciplinary, problem solving studies and efforts and (2) hardcore disciplinary training in economic theory and quantitative techniques".[2] Are curricula in Europe following this line without reservation?

TEACHERS – THE INSTRUMENT OF TEACHING

Who are the European teachers of agricultural economics? In the beginning teachers naturally came from the biological fields and turned to economics for personal interest, today nearly all are products of their own discipline, having spent most of their professional life at academic institutions. Links with practical agricultural problems are by research projects only, not through any prolonged management or executive position. They are normally: (1) free to teach and research what appears relevant. (2) used to lecturing instead of guiding (passive learning), (3) looking more for acknowledgement through publications than through teaching performance, (4) taking their teaching ability for granted, doing little for improvement, and (5) not interested to be organized as teachers and to evaluate their teaching performance.

Previously a few great personalities who shaped the start of our discipline dominated the field of teaching. The time period since World War II witnessed a rapid change from the old European university to an institution where larger numbers of younger lecturers were given the responsibility of teaching. Schools of thought are no longer a real issue, curricula look quite similar throughout Europe. The majority of agricultural economics teachers has international experience, reads foreign literature and sustains links with other countries. Freedom of teaching and research, the precious ideal of European universities, allows teachers to transfer their own research results into teaching material. Within certain limits this seems to be an advantage. However, there is no real feedback system telling the teacher that his selection of research topics and teaching subjects was good or bad. Can there be one? Assessment of the value of research for teaching may be achieved by an organized dialogue between the academician, policy decision-makers, and practical farming public. Agricultural economists in Europe could be more aggressive in taking their economic reasoning to their fellow biological and technical scientists. They must insist that economics is as much an integral part of curricula in agriculture as any other subject presented to specialist students. As newcomers in the academic treatment of agricultural subjects, European agricultural economists have fallen into the same trap new disciplines usually do: they develop a language not understood by normal people. Will they remedy the situation as soon as possible? Finally, what is the teacher's greatest problem? Probably, to integrate into one person as teacher, specialized in agricultural economics, the necessary general knowledge to be relevant for the students and, as researcher, the acknowledged specialization to be promoted in an academic career. This does not seem to be a particular European problem only.

COURSE-WORK – THE SUBJECT MATTER OF TEACHING

The previous habit of European professors to read to students (the British "reader" reminds us of this tradition!) what they should be able to read themselves in the library has not died out. Especially in undergraduate work the larger lecture has still its dominant place. In post-graduate work, it is the other way around. It contrast to the United States, coursework for PhD candidates is the exception, not the rule in Europe. Here seminars where students present their work from field data and literature reviews are more important. On both levels, other types of participatory approaches such as the use of case studies and team learning are experimented with. But there is no evidence that agricultural economists are most innovative to improve teaching methods and instruments. Overloaded timetables and dependency on classroom work for undergraduates are more a problem on the Continent than in the UK, where the number of contact hours with staff is, on average, only half that in Germany. Would it be a mistake to allow students to select more for themselves rather than to provide strict timetables? An MSc degree in agricultural economics by thesis and coursework has become accepted practice in Britain, not on the Continent where a two-level degree structure (diploma and PhD) prevails. The diploma, usually with a thesis requirement, takes a minimum of four years after thirteen years of primary and secondary education. Many continental universities, therefore, rate their first degree as equivalent to the American or British MSc or MA degrees.

Teaching and examinations are linked. If "agrarian change" matters in the later life of graduates, are European examination methods up-to-date to examine the capability of anticipating change? The oral and essay type examination dominates with the hope that thinking ability can be tested better this way than using multiple choice questions. Again there is no empirical proof. The fact that both systems work and give results which allow one to differentiate between good and less good students is interesting. In general European teachers still favour more (but not exclusively!) subjective types of examination, compared with the USA where "objectivity" is part of the educational creed.

AGRICULTURAL ECONOMISTS IN DEVELOPING COUNTRIES

How have agricultural economists of the European teaching tradition performed while attached to foreign universities? Some people argue, that this type of partnership has been a great contribution. Others say that it had been the root of all evil because it prevents developing countries from creating (their own) indigenous institutions. The fact is that European teachers have taken heavy responsibility in duplicating their home university structures the world over. Have they produced the kind of graduate that society needs? Not everything has gone wrong but present trends in the rural development of a number of countries cast doubts on the ability of graduates to cope with the complex problems. If universities "are not rooted in local soil, except for the buildings"[3]) there is great danger that Western standards of teaching agricultural economics might not be relevant for development. The trouble is that there are so few people around who can say what is relevant. "We have to get beyond the idea of being missionaries for our own institutions and collaborate with the colleagues of developing countries in the invention of more appropriate institutions".[4]

Agricultural economics curricula in poor countries seldom differ from the European universities of the teachers. Are the agrarian changes really so similar to justify this? If the quest for relevance in Europe is essential how appropriate must be such a quest in developing countries where training resources are so expensive and only available for the "happy few". If demand for knowledge in agricultural economics is derived from demand for more effective institutional performance, then Ruttan rightly demands the replacement of theories of consumer, entrepreneurs, firms and markets, at least partly, by theories of collective action, human capital formation, bureaucratic behaviour. Where many factors seem to be very static, induced social change becomes a major concern. The decision on direction and depth of social change is the responsibility of the country itself but the agricultural economist teaching there must be acquainted with the local problems of poverty and unemployment, equity and growth, bottlenecks and productivity increases, deficiencies of infrastructure and the reality of power struggle; subjects he would never touch in Europe. Who else is there to design agricultural curricula for development if not the agricultural economist?

In addition, agricultural economics teachers must insist on practical training periods for their students in order to keep them in touch with the real rural world; many students would just like to escape from rural life by obtaining the degree for which they are studying. agricultural economists can only avoid the danger of being too theoretical if they turn to a case study approach early on at the undergraduate level. This implies that teaching can only be relevant if the flow of knowledge is not a one-way affair: the teacher has to learn as much as his students. If the ultimate goal of his teaching is the induced change of the "rural village" then he must realize the reasons which may exist for rejecting any particular programme, that the "rejection of an important technical package (the content of most extension messages) is normally a rejection of its social implication."[5] For example, many teachers have stressed the role of the progressive farmers and the impact of trickle-down effects in a society structure completely different from ours. Such teaching therefore remained wishful thinking in the majority of cases.

To plan coursework in developing countries necessitates a search for a different set of agrarian changes compared with Europe. They are less universal but more regional and local. They are less technical in the beginning but more of an institutional character. They are less stable but fluctuating quite heavily with frequent changes of political leadership and with world market developments. Where European countries are able to protect their farmers from income fluctuations, developing countries may not be able to at all. Does this very fact change our teaching? Training needs in agricultural economics must also be derived from the job needs which exist in the economy. It is therefore essential to know enough about the jobs graduates will be looking for in developing countries.

The question whether or not European agricultural economists should actively promote post-graduate studies in developing countries has recently received much interest. Surely, if the basic decision to have a university at all has been taken, then the university has to be a real one, with facilities for local research which can be fruitfully transformed into relevant teaching material. To attract highly qualified people for staff, opportunities for research and training for higher degrees become essential. Such programmes serve three additional purposes: (1) Support a university's international standing needed for its self-respect. (2) Enlarge considerably the country's potential for local applied research. (3) Keep many bright young students in the country who are lost to the development of their country if studying abroad. To be instrumental in the establishment of relevant post-graduate courses, especially in Africa and Latin America, seems to me one of the great challenges to agricultural economists who care to help developing countries to achieve their goals.

CHALLENGES AHEAD FOR TEACHING AGRICULTURAL ECONOMICS

This final section contains a subjective view of future changes which will challenge the teaching profession. Their discussion here has the objective of clarifying how relevance can be achieved? To begin with I think we have to extend G. Johnson's "quest for relevance" to a "quest for proper institutions to determine what relevant is". Agricultural economists have to take part in creating them by shifting their emphasis from maximization–minimization analysis to dialogues with others about the ends of production and the social and environmental costs involved. The major concern of mankind is no longer the problem of productivity of factors as such but to decide whether or not certain things which technically can be produced are needed at all. The same question is valid about teaching: is everything which is researched also to be taught? More and more selection is necessary because of the mass of material available. Values enter the argument and the responsibility of perceiving the total problem in full perspective. We will have to be fair to our students not only by admitting that economics is just one aspect of agriculture but also by encouraging them to look actively to other aspects of the problem. Institutions to determine what is relevant for future teaching cannot come from inside the university alone; a thorough cross-fertilization is needed from all the fields our students will have to work in. The minimum starting point is the immediate introduction of a regular exchange of ideas about syllabi contents among all colleagues of agricultural faculties, an exercise which is currently non-existent.

On the macro-level, important challenges to teachers can be identified as follows: (1) Regional rural decision-making processes will gain importance with a simultaneously diminishing role of agriculture in European integration policies. (2) Increasing awareness that individual and social values about the role of agriculture are in dynamic change with far-reaching impacts on policies and institutions will be needed by students. (3) Future agrarian changes may still have more differentiating impact than in the past and may lead to more disparities between farms and regions. (4) Agribusiness growth will continue, influencing the self-comprehension of agriculture considerably. (5) Agricultural potential in industrialized countries will adjust to a "new economic order" where developing countries demand an equal share of prosperity. (6) Insights into the finality of quite a number of inputs presently used in agricultural production will require new teaching content about environmental economics. (7) The still growing role of government in European agriculture will necessitate a larger share of teaching about bureaucratic behaviour and individual reaction. (8) More dependencies among nations will develop. Do we have an adequate theory of division of labour among rich and poor countries which anticipates world-wide needs for human dignity at the end of this century?

On the micro-level again eight major areas will challenge the future agricultural economics teacher: (1) While farm planning under uncertainty (especially weather risks) remains an issue, the European Community guarantees most prices, so certainty at that level has increased and teaching has to include this fact. (2) Further increases in enterprise specialization need special attention in teaching to look for risk distribution, also into non-agricultural activities. (3) Many small land owners need encouragement not to be full-time farmers any longer and to supplement their income from other employment. Is this a teaching issue? (4) Planning for further growth of the remaining farms should be an essential part of teaching, as long as farm size in most parts of Europe are far below the necessary income generating capacity. (5) Further growth means heavy financial investment for which students demand intensive instruction on liquidity problems, optimal debt volume, farm-household and household-farm transfer problems. (6) Further agribusiness growth means need for information about possibilities of active partnership of farmers in larger commercial business firms, including corporative farming and processing. (7) Farm planning by objectives will necessitate emphasis on "teaching by objectives" to instruct for solving particular individual or regional farm problems with instruments of the decision theory. (8) The teaching of individual decision-making processes on farms may have to be complemented by advice how to motivate and to implement collective action in families, groups and institutions.

SUMMARY

In this paper it has been argued that European teachers of agricultural economics have responded to agrarian changes by establishing relevant disciplines and designing appropriate syllabi. But accomplishments cannot be measured, except in individual case studies; they are assumed as long as graduates find suitable employment. Teaching performance of agricultural economists at university level still takes second place to research acknowledgement through publications. Challenges in the future will come from further political advances of the European integration policy and a worldwide "new economic order" influencing farm prices and investment decisions, and from the further growth of the agribusiness complex, as well as through changing individual and social values about production goals, resources use, and rural life styles.

NOTES

[1] Glenn L. Johnson "The Quest for Relevance in Agricultural Economics", *American Journal of Agricultural Economics*, 53, 5 (December 1971), pp. 728–39.

[2] Glenn L. Johnson, op. cit., p. 733–4.

[3] Wu Ten-Yao "Higher education for whom and for what?" *Conference Proceedings: Higher Education and the masses*, Singapore Sept. 1977, p. 5.

[4] Vernon W. Ruttan "Technical and Institutional Change", *Proceedings of XVth Conference of the International Association of Agricultural Economists: Future of Agriculture*, São Paulo, Brazil 1974, p. 75.

[5] Philip M. Mbithi "Transfer of useful knowledge in agricultural development in Kenya", *Agricultural Administration*, Vol. 1, No. 4 (1974), p. 79.

REFERENCES

British Council *Agricultural Education in Europe*, Commonwealth Agricultural Bureaux, Farnham Royal 1977.

Gordon, M.S. (ed.) *Higher Education and the Labour Market*, McGraw-Hill Book Co., New York 1974.

Johnson, G.L. "The Quest for Relevance in Agricultural Economics", *American Journal of Agricultural Economics*, 53, 5 (1971).

Kuhnen, F. "The Role of Agricultural Colleges in Modern Society", *Zeitsch f. ausld. Landw.*, Heft 2, 1974.

Lindstrom, U.B. "Is our Teaching Good Enough?" Workshop Paper, Association of Faculties of Agriculture in Africa (AFAA), 1975.

Mbithi, P.M. "Transfer of Useful Knowledge in Agricultural Development in Kenya", *Agric. Administration*, Vol. 1, No. 4 (1974).

Niehaus, H. "Betrachtungen über den Einfluß der Berufsbildung und anderer Faktoren auf den Betriebserfolg der Landwirte", *Berichte über Landwirtschaft*, Vol. 49, 1971, pp. 1–18.

Nix, J. "Farm Management: The State of the Art", paper presented at a Meeting of the British Agricultural Economics Society, 6–9 April 1979.

Nsekela, A.J. "The University's Changing Role in a Developing Country: The Tanzanian Case", *Journal of Administration Overseas*, Vol. XVII, No. 2 (1978).

Ruttan, V.W. "Technical and Institutional Change", *Proceedings of XVth Conference of IAAE: Future of Agriculture*, São Paulo, Brazil 1974.

Schmitt, G. "Zur frühen Geschichte der landwirtschaftlichen Marktforschung in Deutschland", *Landwirtschaftliche Marktforschung in Deutschland*, BLV–Verlag, München, ,1967, pp. 17–40.

Thimm, H.U. (ed.) Report on "Post-graduate Training in Agricultural Economics at African Universities", Deutsche Stifung für Internationale Entwicklung, Seminar in Nairobi (Kenya), September 1976.

Thompson, K.W. and Fogel, B.R. *Higher Education and Social Change*, Praeger, New York 1976.

Thurow, L. *Investment in Human Capital*, Wadworth Publ. Co., Belmont 1970.

Tinberger, J. "The Role of the University in the Development Process", paper presented at a NUFFIC–Symposium, The Hague (The Netherlands) 1977.

Wu Ten-Yao "Higher Education – for Whom and for What?" paper presented at a conference on "Higher Education and the Masses", Singapore 1977.

DISCUSSION OPENING – CHRISTINA DAVID

I will focus my comments on the challenge for teaching agricultural economics for agrarian change on less developed countries at the graduate level.

The most insightful and significant part of Dr Thimm's paper, I think, is his observation about the performance of the agricultural economics programme and I quote, "Neither particular agricultural policy decisions nor management performance can be traced back to teaching activities directly except in individual case studies". Again, later he says, "there is no evidence that teaching of agricultural economics has influenced any major agricultural policy decision in Europe. Nor do agricultural economists appear to have anticipated social and technical changes better than other disciplines".

A similar view was expressed by Alex McCalla in reviewing the agricultural and food policy decision making process in LDCs: "Decisions relating to food and agriculture were made at the presidential and cabinet levels with the inputs of ministries of finance, commerce and central banks and much less with the input of ministries of agriculture – agricultural policy researchers doing micro-research are not connected with the policy process and macro-policy researchers lack contact with micro-research".

While I think that those observations reflect the basic shortcoming of agricultural economics programmes in LDCs, I have a somewhat different opinion of what is the source of this problem and therefore what should be the direction for relevance of the programmes.

After reading Dr Thimm's paper and joining the discussion group on curriculum development, I think I am beginning to understand the limitations of the agricultural economic programme in developed countries to the needs of the rural sector in the LDCs. The problems are not only in the complete reliance on the traditional framework of perfect and independent markets, independent farm and household decision-making, lack of exposure to comparative economic systems, in the preoccupation with the study of American related institutions, in the relatively thin and declining expertise in international development issues and so forth. These problems have been articulated in previous conferences. Let me suggest, however, that the programme's emphasis on farm management and the consequent insufficient attention in training economists who will be capable of agricultural production and development analysis for policy-making as well as for educating future agricultural economists are important problems.

Although teachers may think farm management is a tool for understanding farm behaviour which can be used in policy-making, we frequently observe that students feel that through farm management courses, one can make better allocative decisions than the less educated farmers. In the context of the agricultural sector in many LDCs, especially in Asia where farms are very small and farm cultivation is relatively simple, training farm managers in universities is not a priority. They will not be hired by small farmers, they will feel too educated to go back to farming, and they will not necessarily be able to allocate resources more efficiently. At least in Asia, the fact that small farmers are allocatively efficient is well documented. Farmers make the kind of decisions that economists would recommend, using instinct instead of highly complex quadratic programming. Moreover, careful analysis of sources of inefficiency shows that technical inefficiency is more important than allocative inefficiency.

Agricultural economists cannot directly contribute to the development of new technology and it is not obvious that agricultural economists can teach the new farming technology more effectively than extension specialists, agronomists, rural sociologists or trained farmers. Farm management is no doubt useful in extension and agriculture programmes, but a broader economics training is required to analyse the nature of the appropriate technological development.

Thus I differ from Dr Thimm's prescription for increasing the contribution of agricultural economists towards improving rural welfare in LDCs. Dr Thimm suggests that we broaden the programme by more communication, agriculture, and sociology courses. That is, make agricultural economists more of an agriculturalist or extension specialist, or rural sociologist. More appropriate, I think in the LDC context is to broaden towards more economics, international trade, monetary theory, welfare, economics and produce agricultural economists who are stronger *economists*. This judgement is based on my belief that small farmers in LDCs are poor not because they are not allocating resources efficiently but because they have much less initial wealth and opportunities, they have low productivity in the technical sense, they have less developed product, input, and financial markets, and they are victims of inappropriate policies and market interventions.

Let me make two other small points. First, you will note that I did not stress the teaching of quantitative methods. Of course it is very important but I feel that quantitative methods should be used in sharpening our analytical skills as economists. At this time many agricultural economics programmes in the US have not adequately taught students the limitations of quantitative methods. All too often graduate students learn more about programming techniques than about economic analysis.

Second, I have also often wondered why agricultural economists in less developed countries frequently equate research with data collection or surveys. This is not to say that data and field experience are not important. The mentality that surveys are a necessary part of a good agricultural economics programme, however, has detracted from more efficient and improved data collection efforts in LDCs, i.e. institutionalization of farm management surveys and research in reducing sampling and non-sampling errors. Agricultural economists have not adequately recognized the role of a sampling survey statistician nor the sociologist in this task. On the other hand, large data sets collected by agricultural economists are frequently under analysed.

GENERAL DISCUSSION – RAPPORTEUR: RICHARD F. BATES

The following points emerged in the general discussion. It was stated that the Wye College curriculum included in the paper was incomplete in two respects. Firstly, it was confined to undergraduate courses, but there are also post-graduate courses which go further than the courses listed. Secondly, the list omitted the following undergraduate courses: Mathematics for Economists: Concepts and Methods in Social Science; and Introduction to Computers and Computing.

In the paper it was stated that "There is no evidence that teaching of agricultural economics has influenced any major agricultural policy decision in Europe." It may be true that no evidence on this point is available, but this does not mean that none could be obtained. It was suggested that many of the major policy decisions have been prepared mainly by members of secretariats of international agencies and by national civil servants and if these people were asked whether their training in agricultural economics had been of any professional value to them, the answer would generally be positive. As far as British policy is concerned, many consider that the 1947 Agriculture Act has been of fundamental importance in the history of postwar agricultural policy; and it is not difficult to trace in the drafting of that Act the hand of civil servants who had received formal training in agricultural economics as part of their university education.

The division between micro and macro aspects of agricultural economics is not as clearly defined today as it was in the past, especially in the Eastern European countries. It was held that in the teaching of micro economics general problems should be looked at carefully.

With regard to macro economics the problems of the food industries and the agricultural industries must be dealt with.

The question as to whether the problems of LDCs, e.g. the equitable distribution of income, should not be included in the undergraduate courses in the United Kingdom was raised.

In reply, Professor Thimm agreed that agricultural economists have to accept that farmers in LDCs may be more rational than they have been given credit for with regard to the allocation of their resources. He stated, however, that there will have to be a change in the allocation of resources in these countries if the people are to produce for the market in the future. He therefore thought that there was a place for farm management courses in these countries.

He stated that there is a problem of how to measure the accomplishments of teachers. It is probably best to leave the definition of what is good to the employers of agricultural economists.

With regard to the division between macro and micro economics the Eastern European countries have gone further than any other countries in integrating the two fields. The problem has however been taken care of in the courses given in many Western European institutions.

He felt that the problems arising in LDCs have to receive greater emphasis in the teaching of agricultural economics in Western European institutions. The emphasis on these problems has up to now depended on the interests of teachers primarily and students only secondarily. Teachers are now showing a greater awareness of the problems associated with LDCs and hence we need not be too pessimistic about the inclusion of relevant courses in the future. At present there are a number of European students visiting LDCs and acquainting themselves with the problems. This knowledge will be brought back and used to benefit agricultural economics courses in the future.

Participants in the discussion included Denis K. Britton, Mieczslaw Adamowicz and John R. Raeburn.

CHRISTOPHER RITSON

Accomplishments and Opportunities for Agricultural Economists on the Theoretical Front*

I was asked to summarize, briefly, the history of the work of agricultural economists around the world working at the disciplinary level, and to look forward in more detail at the opportunities, problems and challenges. This task may seem more suited to several years' work from an entire research institute than to one agricultural economist given only a few weeks in the middle of a busy university term. Indeed, even without the constraint of time and space, it is arguable that no one agricultural economist could be expected to have a sufficiently comprehensive, yet nevertheless detailed, knowledge of our discipline to be able to do justice to all theoretical accomplishments and opportunities. For this reason, I have chosen to devote much of my paper to an attempt at providing criteria which might enable us to judge what are the theoretical accomplishments of agricultural economists and where the main challenges and opportunities lie, rather than to allow my own views on this subject, obviously coloured by personal experience and interests, to dominate. The paper, therefore, proceeds first in the form of suggested answers to four questions: what part of the work of agricultural economists can be described as agricultural economic theory? What is the role of theory in agricultural economics? How can we judge whether or not a theory is a good one? What constitutes an "advance" in economic theory? This is followed by a suggested framework for categorizing theoretical contributions. Finally, I give a personal impression of accomplishments and opportunities.

Throughout I use the term "agricultural economic theory" to refer to the contributions of agricultural economists working at the disciplinary level. Whether or not there is such a thing as *agricultural* economic theory, rather than merely the application of economic theory to agriculture, is something of a pedantic point which I leave aside.

¹ I would like to thank Professor Ashton of Newcastle University, Professor Marsh of Aberdeen University and Professors McInerney and Tuck of Reading University for their helpful comments on an earlier draft.

WHAT IS AGRICULTURAL ECONOMIC THEORY?

The word "theory" has a well defined and well accepted meaning. Nonetheless, when attempting to categorize a piece of research in agricultural economics, the distinctions can become blurred.

Perhaps the most straightforward definition is to say that a theory attempts to explain processes, or relationships between variables. A more precise definition[1] would be that a theory consists of:

(a) an assertion that a given set of phenomena exhibit some element of pattern, and

(b) a specification of that pattern sufficiently full to enable certain elements to be filled in if enough is known about the rest; this embraces both prediction and questions involving unobserved or unobservable simultaneous events.

To give one example, the theory of the supply of a farm product attempts to explain the process by which the quantity supplied of the product per time period increases (if it does) when the price of an input falls. The explanation might be quite complex, involving typically an assumption about behaviour – an objective function – and interrelationships between many variables. Because the relationships involved are essentially quantitiative ones, agricultural economists have increasingly found it convenient to present theory as formal models described with the aid of mathematical equations, in symbolic or diagrammatic form.

The above paragraph implies that quite a lot of research by agricultural economists can be said to include a theoretical component. Can we identify any significant areas of research which do not involve theory? In fact it is arguable that virtually all of the work of agricultural economists involves theory to a greater or lesser extent. But clearly, some areas are more directly founded in economic theory than others and, for the purposes of this paper, I suggest three areas which can be excluded.

First, there is the work which merely attempts to assemble data of relevance to agricultural economics: "How many farms are located in a particular area?" "What did they produce?" "How have product prices changed over time?" This is the descriptive part of agricultural economics – the work which aims to paint a picture of the economics of agriculture or food in a particular place or time – the picture that the theory attempts to explain. The main function of this kind of work is to assemble relevant factual material, and theory is not about facts but about relationships.

Even here there are, of course, exceptions. For example, there is at present in the UK a lively debate over the "cost" of membership of the European Community. (This cost is mainly attributable to the Common Agricultural Policy.) But the debate is essentially a theoretical one, with estimates of this cost (e.g. Bacon and Godley, 1979) challenged, not on grounds of accuracy, but on the basis of disagreement over what it is that one should be attempting to measure (Ashton et al, 1979).

Second, I think we can exclude much econometric work. On occasions, the econometrician takes a theory off the shelf, as it were, and then simply attempts to identify the specific form that the relationships, incorporated in that theory, take in the particular example to which his data relates. Thus the theory predicts that the quantity supplied will increase if the price of an input falls; the econometrician predicts by how much in the case of, say, corn in the USA. However, much of the work of econometricians does of course contribute to the advance of agricultural economic theory, for a number of econometric exercises may provide information which indicates the relative importance of the different variables within the theory and may indicate the validity of alternative theories. Indeed, one role of econometrics, as a discipline, is to test alternative economic theories.

The third area which I think can be excluded is the development of techniques to aid private decision-makers, or public authorities, to take decisions which fulfil their objectives. The main work of agricultural economists in this area has been in the field of farm management, but increasingly this work has also covered food distribution and marketing – "marketing management" – as well as the application of techniques to deal with things like discounting and risk in the analysis of public projects and policies. Again, of course, this kind of work may well make a contribution to agricultural economic theory (as well as sometimes being founded in mathematical or statistical theory). The farm management expert may be able to throw light on producer objectives and economic relationships within the farm. He may need to develop the theory of the farm firm himself to help him in his management work, and for this reason the subjects of farm management and farm production economics have tended to advance hand in hand, with many distinguished agricultural economists contributing to both subjects.

Finally, I should emphasize that, for the purposes of this paper, I am restricting theory to "economic theory". I have already mentioned "mathematical theory", and there is much other theoretical research which forms part of what we sometimes term "agricultural economics and related disciplines" but which is not rooted in economic theory. Examples of this are the work of rural sociologists and the application of the behavioural sciences in agricultural marketing.

WHAT IS THE ROLE OF THEORY IN AGRICULTURAL ECONOMICS?

The *raison d'être* of the discipline of agricultural economics is that there are important, and distinct, problems to be found in the agricultural and food sectors of an economy. The role of theory is to aid in the solution of these problems.

Whenever it is possible to argue that the actual state of affairs differs from the desired state of affairs, a problem can be said to exist. In the context of agricultural economics, economic problems vary from those associated with individual farm producers and food consumers, to those involving the extent to which events in agriculture are consistent with national objectives, through to problems at a global level (such as "the world food problem"). Since theory attempts to identify relationships between variables in an economic system, theoretical knowledge should provide increased ability to control events within the system; by the judicious manipulation of certain variables, the actual state of affairs can be moved in the direction of the desired state of affairs.[2]

WHEN IS A THEORY A GOOD ONE?

Ideally, there is only one way in which we can judge whether or not a theory is a successful one, and that is to test it. Unfortunately, in the case of economic theory, this is often simply not possible because of the lack of scope for experimental verification. Hypotheses, particularly on large scale or long run issues, or where the predicted outcome is not directly measurable (as with individual and collective utility), have to become established doctrine by argument. Because of this there will always, presumably, be more scope for error, uncertainty and disagreement in the case of economic theory than with the physical sciences.

In judging the merits of a theory in agricultural economics we should ask first whether it is relevant to important issues – important in the sense that they involve what are thought to be significant problems. Second, are the relationships postulated within the theory, as well as its predictions, credible in the light of what has been observed to occur? In other words, it is possible to test the accuracy of some theories, or aspects of theories, by investigating how reliable they are at predicting events which are observed to occur.

To illustrate this, let me cite two theories, one which comes out well on this basis and one which does not. The first is the so-called cobweb theory (or theorem). This is a very simple theory which can be expressed as three equations: quantity demanded of a product in time period n is a function of price in time period n; quantity supplied of the product in time period n is a function of price in time period $n-1$; and quantity supplied in time period n equals quantity demanded in time period n.

The theory is not much liked by many agricultural economists, perhaps because it seems to offer an over-simplified explanation of fluctuating prices. It is even not much liked by many students who find it difficult to accept that producers should continue to fail to forecast prices accurately in spite of the evidence of cycles. Yet the theory works. Agricultural economists continue to observe regular cyclical price movements for many agricultural commodities and the cobweb theory, particularly when refined to include a decision time lag, as well as one due to the biological production process, and to incorporate a supply response which is elastic only over an intermediate price range, provides a good explanation of these cycles.

The second theory is that of the perverse supply curve, which is once again much in vogue in Western Europe, where we are told continually that it is no use cutting prices to reduce surplus production, since farmers will only respond by increasing output. Admittedly this is not a view held by many theoretical agricultural economists, though students of agricultural economics, when confronted with the theory, find it intuitively very reasonable. Curiously, many who take the view that a reduction in product price will lead to an increase in output do not regard this so much as an alternative theory, but more as good sound common sense which just goes to show that theoretical economists are not well informed about what goes on in the "real world".

The theory itself is a perfectly respectable one. It is based on the view that for the small peasant producer, and even the larger family farm, the appropriate behavioural hypothesis will be the objective of maximizing the collective utility of the farm family, which will be derived from a combination of income from farming and leisure. Inasmuch as there is a trade-off between level of farm output and leisure, and particularly where there are few purchased inputs, it follows that a fall in product price could (though not necessarily will) lead to an increase in output. In its simplest form, the theory incorporates a producer objective of a single target income, and in these circumstances it follows that a reduction in product price will lead to an increase in output.

However, to the best of my knowledge there is very little evidence to suggest that supply is related negatively to product price – at the sector level, anyway. On the other hand there is a mass of evidence throughout the world to suggest that if prices go up output goes up, and if prices go down output goes down, or at least is less than it would otherwise have been.

It is perhaps worth emphasizing that the fact that two agricultural economists hold very different views concerning future patterns of prices, production, land use or whatever, does not necessarily imply that they accept different theories. It is true that different theories – in the sense of different views of the functional relationships involved or the nature of the objective function (as in the case of the perverse supply curve) – may well lead to different predictions about the future. But different predictions will also be the outcome if agricultural economists hold different views on likely future changes in exogenously determined variables.

A good example of this is provided by the conflicting views concerning food surplus and food shortage, where many of the agricultural economists involved perhaps believe that they take a different theoretical approach from agricultural economists who have come to different conclusions. However, these views do not necessarily involve a theoretical inconsistency. Both groups of agricultural economists would accept that the longer term evolution of food prices is a consequence of changing conditions of supply and demand; both groups would also probably accept that the main factors affecting the longer term development of demand for food products are real incomes and population growth and, affecting the growth in supply, technological and institutional progress and resource accumulation. If agricultural economists take different views concerning the extent to which quantity supplied or demanded is likely to respond to changes in these variables – for example, different views on the magnitude of the relevant income elasticities – then different predictions on the likely future course of world food prices will result. But equally, if they hold similar views concerning the functional relationships involved, but different views concerning the likely future changes in the values of the variable themselves, they will predict different outcomes. An assumption of rising real incomes, low population growth, and technological progress in agriculture, will lead to one set of conclusions; assumptions of rapid population growth, low productivity improvement and capital accumulation insufficient to offset diminishing returns to land, will lead to another.

WHAT CONSTITUTES AN ADVANCE IN AGRICULTURAL ECONOMIC THEORY?

Existing theory may be erroneous or incomplete. In addition, changes in the power of the means of observation and intervention may make theoretical development relevant which was not previously.

Another reason for the advance of agricultural economic theory is that existing theory may no longer be relevant because the functional relationships have themselves changed over time. For example, in a particular country, agricultural production, once dominated by small peasant producers, may have gradually come under the control of modern commercial farming. A modified theory of supply and resource use may now be required. More dramatically, a major land reform might replace an agricultural sector dominated by large estates and employed labour, by one with a structure involving thousands, or millions, of small independent land owner-producers. Clearly, a new approach in the theory of the behaviour of the agricultural sector will be required, not because the old approach was necessarily incorrect, but because the production relationships themselves have changed.

An aspect of this is emphasized by Gordon (1976) in his presidential address to the American Economic Association:

> I turn now . . . from rigour and relevance to the fact that we live in a world that is continually changing . . . to what extent does the changing institutional environment affect the relevance of the analytical tools that we use and the assumptions that we make about the determinants of individual and group behaviour?

Another possible reason for the advance of agricultural economic theory is that an approach which provides a sound basis for analysis in one part of the world may not be applicable elsewhere. In this context, many agricultural economists have been concerned that theories developed in the economically advanced countries might provide incorrect, or at least incomplete, explanations of economic events in the developing countries.

The response to these various stimuli may be the development of new theory. On the other hand it may take the form of a process of refinement; not developing a new explanation, but improving and refining existing theories. Either kind of contribution could reasonably be called an advance in agricultural economic theory. To use an analogy from land economics, the theoretical front possesses an intensive as well as an extensive margin. One example of advance on the intensive margin is the contribution of powerful mathematical notations. An agricultural and food production and distribution system can involve countless inter-related variables. Arguably, one sign of a good economist is the ability to investigate the complex set of probable reactions to some given economic change, rather than to see merely a set of two-dimensional relationships, all aided by a *ceteris paribus* assumption. Sometimes the interrelationships involved in a theory may be so complex that the theory can only properly be understood if it is set down as a formal model. Thus the formal mathematical model may help the original researcher to clarify his ideas and, more particularly, to communicate them to his fellow agricultural economists. However, a word of caution is appropriate here. There may be occasions when the agile mind can see important relationships beyond the confines of a formal model.

The use of mathematical techniques in agricultural economics may also have extended the theoretical margin. I am thinking of examples such as the impact on the theory of the farm firm of linear and dynamic programming.

CATEGORIZING CONTRIBUTIONS TO AGRICULTURAL ECONOMIC THEORY

There are many possible ways of categorizing agricultural economic theory, none wholly satisfactory. Theory relates to the working of a system and any subdivision of the system will be to some extent arbitrary and for many purposes not essential. Probably the most helpful method of subdivision for the purposes of this paper[3] is to take that part of an economic system which is normally regarded as coming within the agricultural economist's sphere of interest, as illustrated in Figure 1, and then to distinguish within this a set of major subsectors. In this way, Table 1 suggests five main areas in which theoretical agricultural economists work, namely (1) rural resources; (2) farm production; (3) agricultural marketing and distribution; (4) food consumption; (5) international trade in agricultural products. The table gives some examples of theoretical work under the various categories. They are only examples – the table is not intended to be exhaustive, though most contributors to agricultural economic theory which come to mind do seem to fit reasonably well into this framework.

The main drawback of this kind of distinction is, of course, that many

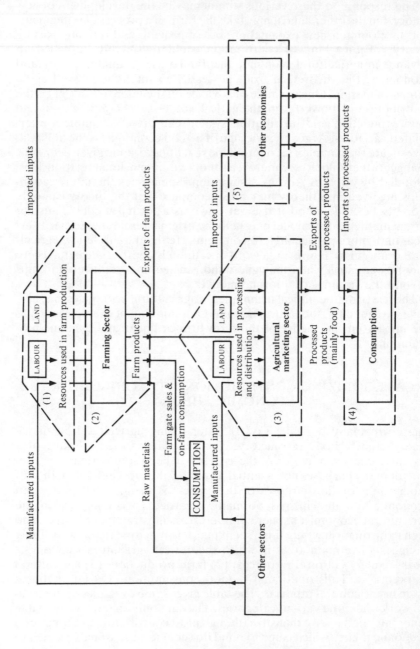

FIG. 1 *Source:* Adapted from Ritson (1977)

TABLE 1.

	Rural Resources (1)	Farm Production (2)	Agricultural Marketing and Food Manufacturing and Distribution (3)	Food Consumption (4)	International Trade in Agricultural Products (5)
Explanatory Theory	Theory of Resource Allocation. Determination of prices in factory markets	Theory of the behaviour of farm firms	Impact of market structure on marketing margins	Demand Theory	Explaining movements in world food prices
Prescriptive Theory	Land Tenure Policies. Optimum allocation of national resources	Measuring producer satisfaction. Impact on producer welfare of farm support policies	Assessing the efficiency of market support and stabilisation policies	Measuring consumer satisfaction	Impact of trade policies on producer and consumer welfare

agricultural economists are ultimately interested in a theory which encompasses the operation of the entire agricultural and food production system, and indeed its interaction with the rest of economic activity, for example, the impact of developments in consumer demand for food products on international trade in farm products, or implications of a changing agricultural trade balance for the performance of the economy as a whole. So in addition to the kind of contributions listed in the table, one would also expect theoretical contributions directed specifically towards the interaction between the components.

One way in which this is done is by lifting a predictive relationships from one area and inserting it in another. Thus the theory of the farm firm is concerned with the way farms will react, in terms of what they produce and the inputs they use, to changing economic circumstances, and this allows us to derive a supply response to changes in product prices and a demand response to input price changes. Both these relationships are founded in the theory of the farm firm, but one relationship is also central to the behaviour of agricultural product markets and the other to the theory of agricultural resource use.

The table makes a second distinction, between what I have called "explanatory" (or predictive) theory and "prescriptive" (or problem-solving) theory. I am not suggesting that there are two *kinds* of economic theory. But I think it is possible in many cases to identify alternative emphases in theoretical work. On the one hand there are contributions directed towards explanations of some aspect of how the agricultural and food system operates and which can, if successful, be used to predict the consequences of some economic change, but which do not, in general, attempt to pass comment on the desirability or otherwise of the predicted developments. On the other hand, there are contributions directed specifically towards problem solving, where the main interest is the relationship between any particular set of circumstances within the agricultural and food system and individual and collective welfare.[4]

Of course not all contributions will fall neatly into one or other of these approaches; often the approaches will have to go together. For example, the economist who wishes to investigate the social consequences of existing land tenure arrangements may have to develop an explanatory theory before he can do so; the economist who wishes to assess the merits of alternative agricultural trade policies may need to develop a model of the interaction between national markets in farm products. A good example of the latter is Josling's article "Government Price Policies and the Structure of International Trade" (1978). The article is directed towards "improving" the performance of international agricultural markets and world food security. But first the article develops a predictive model of the structure of international agricultural trade based on the assumption that Governments have a target level for domestic farm product prices, and that trade is the consequence of the reaction of domestic producers and consumers to that price target, irrespective of developments on world markets.

This distinction will often therefore do no more than indicate the "flavour" of a piece of research rather than provide a categorical classification. Nevertheless I believe it to be a helpful one because it emphasizes that there is a normative element in virtually all agricultural economic theory. Even a simple "pure" explanatory theory of, say, the behaviour of an agricultural product market will probably have been developed because of a perceived problem associated with the behaviour of the market and implicit in the problem will be assumptions about certain individual or collective objectives.

ACCOMPLISHMENTS AND OPPORTUNITIES

A framework for categorizing theoretical contributions, together with criteria for judging their effectiveness, provides in principle the opportunity for a review of the accomplishments of agricultural economists at the theoretical level. However, no one agricultural economist is likely to be sufficiently informed concerning recent theoretical developments throughout the discipline to be able to provide an authoritative review of this kind. I have already made some comments which indicate my "view" on accomplishments. In summary, and very tentatively, I suggest that, of the five areas covered in the columns in Table 1, the theory of the farm firm is the most well developed within the discipline. The food consumer also seems to be a well researched and generally predictable animal, and another success of agricultural economic analysis is surely the accumulation of fairly reliable elasticity estimates, particularly on the demand side. Second, I would suggest that, in general, explanatory theory is more successful than prescriptive theory. But this is not to suggest that agricultural economists taking the prescriptive approach have accomplished little; rather it indicates the greater complexity of the issues raised by welfare theory and (to quote Gordon again) human welfare is a "concept that will not go away no matter how uncomfortable it makes the economic theorist". In this context, I think the development of formal analysis of the welfare effects of agricultural policies must be a strong candidate for the most important advance in agricultural economic theory over the last decade.

Third, at both levels, my impression is that it is in the area of time related problems that many of the current opportunities for useful work lie. This applies particularly to inter-temporal questions of resource allocation. Another example is the problems which occur when attempting to assess the implications of food price instability for consumers.

Looking to the future, I suggest two areas where a "challenge" can be said to face agricultural economists working at the disciplinary level. The first is the need to present agricultural economic theory in such a way that its practical significance is comprehensible and convincing to decision-makers, particularly in the field of public policy. I can illustrate this by the use of an example which, as it happens, it also consistent with my remarks that the greater theoretical problems concern both time related questions and prescriptive theory.

The author of a (justly) respected book on the *Economic Analysis of Agricultural Projects* (Gittinger, 1972), while discussing the choice of an appropriate discount rate, comments, "A third rate sometimes suggested is the social rate of return, a rate, which it is suggested, more adequately reflects the time preference of society as a whole than does the opportunity cost of capital. Although interesting in theory, it is too difficult to identify in practice to be commonly used for agricultural project analysis". As a consequence, "In practice, the rate chosen is simply rule of thumb: twelve per cent seems to be the popular choice and almost all countries seem to think it lies somewhere between eight per cent and fifteen per cent".

The author of this book is, in effect, reporting a failure of theoretical economics. The theoretical analysis surrounding the choice of a social discount rate is of little value if the arguments involved are so complex that the issue is ignored by those who take public investment decisions. Yet the issue is immensely important, affecting decisions over resource depletion and land use – indeed the whole of the future world economic environment. Unless a relatively low discount rate is used, economic analysis can rarely justify a public decision which involves a present cost, but a benefit far into the future. For example, "the seal of official approval for the use of ten per cent as a discount rate in land use economics, set by the recent Treasury cost–benefit of forestry, would seem, temporarily at least, to end the British forester's hope of an economic rationale for upland afforestation. No matter how many social benefits were dragged into the analysis, the study team found it impossible to achieve a positive net present worth for new planting". (Price, 1973)[5]

The second area which seems to me to provide a challenge to theoretical agricultural economists concerns what I will call, heroically, "World Welfare". Agricultural economists have sometimes been nervous about becoming involved in the kind of theoretical questions which I have termed in this paper "prescriptive", believing that such an approach required personal value judgements. But gradually it has been realized that, where it is possible to identify government objectives, in particular reflecting income distribution and collective goods, then it is quite possible to tackle these questions by positive method. This has paved the way for the work of agricultural economists in such areas as agricultural policy, cost–benefit analysis, land use studies and resource economics. Most of this work has been at a national level, assessing alternative policies relative to national objectives.

In the international arena, most work has been of the explanatory kind; prescriptive theory has still been seen in terms of national interest, for example the mutual advantages associated with trade liberalization.

The issues surrounding the "new international economic order" have perhaps made many question the adequacy, on its own, of traditional theoretical approaches to agricultural production, consumption and trade at the world level. There may be an analogy here with the difficulty that some economists have experienced in tackling welfare theory at a national level. In a sense, just as a nation is composed of many individuals attempting to fulfil personal objectives, so the world is composed of nations attempting to fulfil national objectives. Correspondingly, just as predictive theory at the national level is based on the assumption that individuals seek the maximum attainment of personal objectives, so trade theory assumes a world in which sovereign states seek maximum attainment of national objectives. This raises the question of whether there is an analogous step, at the world level, to that taken by agricultural economists who have undertaken policy studies at the national level and found it necessary to develop theory beyond traditional ideas of economic efficiency and to incorporate distributional and environmental objectives. A theoretical approach to resource allocation and product distribution, which restricts itself to the Paretian principle, must be as inadequate at the world level as it is at the national level. But the task of incorporating realistic distributional objectives into a positive analysis of international agricultural economic policies is clearly a formidable one.

One of the more interesting developments in agricultural economics in recent years has been that, whereas previously a significant proportion of the profession seemed to split into economists interested in agricultural problems in economically advanced countries and those concerned with agriculture in low income countries, increasingly both are concerned with world problems. Some work in the field of trade policy does now attempt to work within the confines of what one might call "world" objectives, such as world food security and price stability. Perhaps in the 1980s we may see a new fusion in agricultural economic theory, concerned with problems common to many countries, and more particularly, achieving patterns of production and resource use directed towards the interests of the world viewed as a whole.

NOTES

[1] I am here quoting R.H. Tuck.

[2] This way of presenting the problem-solving role of theory in agricultural economics is attributable to John McInerney.

[3] An alternative is suggested by McInerney (1976): "If economics is to be functional as an applied discipline . . . it needs to identify problem situations and group them into types which share a common thread in economic terms – whether that thread is a common objective to be satisfied, common constraints on choice, or a requirement for a common analytical approach".

[4] This distinction is somewhat analogous to that which identifies the subject matter of Volume 3 of a *Survey of Agricultural Economic Literature* (1977) – "Economics of Welfare, Development and Natural Resources". The five columns in Table 1 also bear some resemblance to the way the subject matter of Volume One of the *Survey* (Traditional Fields of Agricultural Economics) is divided.

[5] In fact, upland afforestation has gone ahead, with or without the approval of economic analysis (and the UK Treasury has also recently "come down" from ten per cent). But how many longer term investment proposals fail because the plan is apparently "uneconomic"? Is the well known difficulty experienced by aid-giving organizations when searching for "suitable" projects partly the consequence of discounting the future too heavily?

REFERENCES

Ashton, J. et al. "Measuring the Costs of the Common Agricultural Policy", London, *Agra Europe*, 23 February 1979.

Bacon, R. and Godley, W. "The *Real* Cost of the Market", London, *The Guardian*, 1 February 1979.

Gittinger, J.P. *Economic Analysis of Agricultural Projects*, Johns Hopkins, Baltimore and London 1972.

Gordon, R.A. "Rigor and Relevance in a Changing Institutional Setting", *American Economic Review*, Vol. 66, No. 1, March 1976.

Josling, T.E. "Government Price Policies and the Structure of International Trade", *Journal of Agricultural Economics*, Vol. XXVIII, No. 3, 1977.

Martin, L.R. (ed.) *A Survey of Agricultural Economics Literature*, (3 volumes), Minneapolis, University of Minnesota Press, 1977.

McInerney, J.P. "The Simple Analytics of Natural Resource Economics", *Journal of Agricultural Economics*, Vol. XXVII, No. 1, January 1976.

Price, C. "To the Future: With Indifference or Concern? The Social Discount Rate and its Implications in Land Use", *Journal of Agricultural Economics*, Vol. XXIV, No. 2, 1973.

Ritson, C. *Agricultural Economics: Principles and Policy*, London, Crosby Lockwood Staples, New York, St. Martins Press, 1977.

DISCUSSION OPENING – RICHARD A. KING

Professor Ritson has offered us a lucid and comprehensive view of the role of economic theory in the field of agricultural economics. He emphasizes the need to present theory to decision-makers in a comprehensive and convincing fashion. He closes with a call for a more complete world view within which agrarian development strategies are considered. His observations bring to mind a number of features of economic theory that are, in some respects, unique to the work of agricultural economists.

With respect to possible refinements of economic theory, it is common
for agricultural economists to work in a world of inelastic market
demand. Most economics texts fail to provide students with an understanding of the relationship between inelastic demand and negative marginal revenue. Economic models that are built around positive marginal
revenue functions cannot possibly convey the real world setting within
which agricultural policy choices are made.

In Figure 1 Professor Ritson provides a convincing picture of the
interdependencies that characterize the food and fibre sectors of an
economy. These interdependencies are often missing from the theoretical
constructs found in many theory books. To make matters worse, one finds
many partial models that purport to describe the real world in sufficient
detail to allow policy prescriptions when in fact far too much has been
"held constant".

The spatial arrangement of resources and economic activity play a
central role in any analysis of rural change. Far too many economics
students complete their formal graduate study without ever hearing the
name of von Thünen, in spite of the fact that his work has been elaborated
upon for over a century and a half.

The level of aggregation found in many theoretical treatments is inappropriate for sound evaluation of policy alternatives. Only when the
impact upon the various participant groups can be identified is it reasonable to suppose that decision makers will find the results of economic
analysis to be convincing.

Current or proposed policies cannot be evaluated in a vacuum.
Agricultural economists are sensitive to the need for weighing alternative
courses of action. Theoretical arguments that serve to discredit a particular choice without specifying one or more options that are clearly superior
are likely to carry little weight. Economic growth literature, in particular,
is full of examples where choices are so obscure as to be worthless for
decision-making purposes.

Near optimum solutions get little attention in many theoretical models.
Agricultural economists have long been aware of the value of looking at
the benefits and costs of close alternatives, whether at farm, marketing
firm or system levels.

Finally, agricultural economists are confronted with the need for
theoretical models that go beyond profit maximization or cost minimization. As has been emphasized at this conference by several speakers,
efficiency, equity and security dimensions of private and public choice
call for more complete theoretical models.

GENERAL DISCUSSION – RAPPORTEUR: RICHARD F. BATES

In the general discussion the view was expressed that the theory of the
farm-household relationship and consumer theory, especially with regard
to the nutrition and income-expenditure relationship, were important

fields of investigation in LDCs and were not covered in the paper.

It was also pointed out that there are many different theories in economics. Economic theory cannot be assumed to be a monolith. The different theories do not necessarily mesh together to make a unit.

In reply, Professor Ritson said that with regard to the statement that there were many independent theories, this was in fact correct and that the statement merely elaborated and complemented that which he had already quoted in his paper.

With regard to "World Welfare" he was of the belief that agricultural economists could make a real contribution towards assisting decision and policy makers in evaluating the impact of measures on different groups within economies.

Participants in the discussion included Chandrahas H. Shah, Clark Edwards, and Indra Jit Singh.

JOSEPH SEBESTYÉN*

Accomplishments, Opportunities and Needs of Agricultural Economists vis-à-vis Quantitative Techniques

Should we speak of techniques only? Is it not a degradation of our activity? For a short answer to all possible questions, economics has begun to resemble physics in shaping out a formalized language and this happens in the branch of agricultural economics too.

Complaints and criticisms because of formalism and alleged overvaluation of techniques can often be heard. I borrow the words of Waugh: a complex world requires appropriate techniques. Since the world has always been complex for people living in it, techniques as appropriate as possible are always needed. If we spend a little time reading from the history of human activity, especially economics and science, we find that the world by necessity created the quantitative means required. And considering the role of agriculture in the well-organized states of antiquity, we may see that measurement of land and products, grain storage and processing, food distribution, earthworks for irrigation and flood control, distribution of water for irrigation, etc., were the creators of demand for gadgets, known by us as elements of functional analysis or linear algebra, 4000 years ago in the Sumerian state. Similar things can be learned from ancient China and Egypt. The *Concise History of Mathematics* by Struik, *Science Awakening* by van der Waerden, *Science and Civilization in China* by Needham and other books can furnish useful knowledge to economists.

1 FROM THE RECORDS OF ACCOMPLISHMENTS

In the following we shall see something like separate still photographs taken out from a moving picture. They are meant to show segments from the process of building up the present inventory of tools at the disposal of agricultural economics.

1 *Beginnings for input–output relationships*
While natural sciences became the main companion of mathematics, the relations to economic activity developed rather in the background. A sign from 1610: A. Serra mentioned input–output relationships. For agriculture, Quesnay gave a figure according to which 1,000 francs of annual advances were assumed to produce an output of 2,500 francs. We may

* Read by Michel Petit

regard it as the parameter of a linear function through the origin. This figure had been used by Saint-Péravy in his *Mémoire*, criticized by Turgot in 1767. Reading thoroughly Turgot's argument, we may recognize a view which later became known as the law of variable proportions, and a cubic parabola lies behind the somewhat complicated verbal description of two segments. Thünen, relying on his own observations at Tellow, stated a diminishing marginal return for manuring potatoes. His description of the procedure for seeking the maximum of a function shows that he knew what he spoke of. (His location theory might rather be mentioned in connection with spatial models.)

2   *The role of farm accounting and cost calculations*
From Thünen's letter to his brother Friedrich (31 December 1820): "Nature answers, in any economy, what I am looking for, and everybody, even the scientifically trained farmer must learn from a long and expensive experience, since one does not take the pains of making records, thus all experience ever gathered goes lost again". [My apologies for the hasty, approximate translation from the German!]

The development of accounting and cost calculation offers good examples in a number of countries. Now I would mention only a few names: that of Laur, Horring, Rheinwald, Preuschen and Heuser, often heard in discussions when the accounting and cost calculation system for a sample of co-operative farms had been set up, more than twenty years ago. Besides their merits for the science and practice of farm management and advisory work, I would like to point to their merits for mathematical modelling. As a result of the activity of experts of agricultural accounting and cost calculations in various countries, mathematical model building found a rich inventory of requisites: sets of coefficients on one hand, systemic thinking, shaping out a model structure, goal setting, formation of possible farming situations on the other. Input–output analysis, mathematical programming, simulation and other techniques would be in a much weaker position without this heritage.

3   *Calculation of effects of weather upon yields*
Dependence on weather of yields in agriculture inspired many people all over the world to search for ways of measuring the influence of meteorological conditions. So was it with a group of outstanding Russian statisticians who, working under Tsarist as well as Soviet rule, made thorough time series analyses of crop yields as influenced by weather. Obukhov, Chetverikov and Yastremsky must be mentioned concerning the huge research work assigned to the Central Statistical Bureau in 1921–23, based upon 1883–1915 time series data for numerous regions. Soviet authorities considered these studies, seeking answers to the following questions, important:

(a) How large are the oscillations between years in the yields of crops in different locations of Russia?
(b) What kind of relationship exists between the changes of yields of

neighbouring years?

(c) Is it possible to arrange the territories into regions showing synchronous oscillations of yields?

(d) How close are the correlations between yields of different crops?

The Vestnik Statistiki reported about answers given by the research group to question (c) for two crops and to question (d) for six crops.

In 1923, at a meeting of evaluation of the project, Slutsky emphasized the great *practical importance* of the work done.

A great personality in the organization of mathematical economic research and planning in the Soviet Union, V.S. Nemchinov, also came from this group of economists–statisticians. Starting from time series covering 25 years, collected by Obukhov, he investigated the effect of precipitation and evaporation by phenological phases. In 1937–39, he fitted weather response functions for three strains of summer wheat. In 1934, he made a cross section study based on data from the 35 pieces of land of the acreage under winter wheat in a sovkhoz, using variables for meteorology, wheat variety, inputs and agrotechnical measures. This type of combined analysis had been continued by others, e.g. Peregudov, in later decades too.

Meteorologists and statisticians have done much work of strong mathematical-economic orientation in many countries and numerous economists were engaged in similar activities. To save space, let the Russians represent them too!

4 *A line of quantification from biology to economics*
To Liebig's law of the minimum and its modification by Mayer into a relative minimum Zöller added in 1867 his findings about a square-root-type response to fertilizer. Wollny's experiments led to a statement about an optimal dosage not independent from other conditions, the response being viewed as a kink of two linear segments. In 1898/99 Duclaux gave a cubic response curve resulting from the opposite effects of two factor components. After this came Mitscherlich's statement in 1909 and its formalization often referred to as the Mitscherlich-Baule function. The experimentation led him to an important correction in economic phraseology (although he also seems not to have united the two segments of the response curve, verbally described by Turgot on two separate pages of his *Réflexions*) saying that the increments of returns and not total returns diminish before reaching the maximum of the response curve.

In the USA, Spillman published in 1924 a book containing his views and that of E. Lang on the "law of diminishing returns". The treatment was of a physiological–biological character, with inferences in the domain of economics. In 1933 his bulletin on fertilizer experiments came out and agricultural scientists became acquainted with the Spillman function.

5 *The "big explosion" and examples of a learning process*
Studies in response to prices by Black (1924) and Bean (1929) and an article by T.W. Schultz on research must be mentioned before I try to give

a picture about a stream of studies using the devices offered by mathematicians, non-agricultural econometricians and OR specialists. Agricultural economists were eager to make use of the new facilities for a more intensive study of the problems they faced.

Let this stream of early applications be exemplified by American studies in several fields:

(a) Production functions: E. Jensen (1942) on dairy production; Tintner-Brownlee (1944) on derivation of production functions from farm records; Atkinson-Klein (1945) on cattle fattening; Heady (1946) on production functions from a random sample of farms; Monroe (1949) on non-linear systems for estimating animal nutrition requiements; Heady-Pesek-Brown (1955) on response surfaces and optima in fertilization.

(b) Linear programming: Waugh (1951) on a minimum-cost dairy feed; C. Hildreth-Reiter (1951) on choice of crop rotations; Fischer-Schruben (1953) on feed mixing with different prices; King (1953) on applications of activity analysis; Heady (1954) on logical aspects of linear programming; Swanson (1956) on fertilizer mixing.

(c) Risk and uncertainty: Heisig (1946) on income stability in high risk farming areas; Schickele (1949) on farm business survival under extreme weather risks; Schickele (1950) on adaptation to income uncertainty; Heady-Kehrberg-Jebe (1954) on instability and choices with crops; Babbar-Tintner-Heady (1955) on programming with variations in input coefficients.

Such a type of development can be observed in a number of countries, others had a different order of application. In the Soviet agricultural economic research, mathematical programming has had the first place for a long time although they could have learned upon a very important experience gathered in the past for doing production function studies on a broad scale (literature in this field began to pour in the 1970s), and the achievements in national and regional input–output analysis had to a great extent been connected with the tough and wise efforts of V.S. Nemchinov, a person so closely linked with agriculture. As to Hungary, production function studies preceded the application of input–output analysis and mathematical programming in agriculture while for industry and national econony an opposite sequence can be recognized, even considering the start of building of national econometric models. In India, crop response studies came out years before reports based upon other techniques appeared.

To add a non-agricultural aspect to the sketch of diffusion given above, let us have a look at developments in non-agricultural sciences, in comparison with that in agricultural economics, as represented by general input–output, interregional input–output and Markov analysis (many other, maybe better, examples could be found, of course), according to references taken from papers written by agricultural economists.

(a) Spread of general input–output to agricultural economics:

Non-agricultural sciences	Agricultural economics
1951 Leontief	1952 Bachman, Fox-Norcross
1953 Leontief, Cenenery- Clark-Cao-Pinna	1953 Peterson
1954 Dorfman	

(b) Spread of regional-interregional input–output to agricultural economics:

Non-agricultural sciences	Agricultural economics
1951 Isard	1953 Fox
1952 Moses	1956 Schnittker
1953 Isard, Leontief	1958 Schnittker-Heady, Carter,
1956 Chenery	Ram
1957 Teibout	1959 Carter-Heady

(c) Spread of Markov analysis to agricultural economics:

Non-agricultural sciences	Agricultural economics
1952 Müller	1961 Judge-Swanson
1953 Goodman	1962 Judge-Swanson, Bostwick,
1955 Prais	Padberg
1956 Hart-Prais, Sittler	1965 Lee-Judge-Takayama
1957 Bellman, Anderson- Goodman	1966 Steffen-Neumann
1958 Goodman, Adelman	1967 G. Müller, E. Hanf,
1959 Madansky	Stanton-Kettunen
1960 Howard	1968 Kislev Amiad
1962 Wolfe-Dantzig	1969 Hallberg
1963 Telser	1970 Lee-Judge-Zellner
1967 De Gheelinck-Eppen	1974 C.H. Hanf-E. Hanf

Not only a "big bang" period showed the eagerness of agricultural economists to make good use of the means and thoughts produced in mathematics, statistics and other sciences, often rewarding the inventors by elaboration of extensions and presentation of new issues: so was it before, so will it also continue in the future.

The lists above reflect difference between fields, as far as speed of reaction is concerned. These differences may depend on the field of invention and first application: communication and learning is much easier in the case of closely related fields (the timetables for general and interregional input–output show the quick turning of the interest to the issues more directly important for agriculture even in case of the same technique). The requirements in date, computing facilities, demand and fashion also influence the learning process, probably in all fields of science.

6 *A selection from the recent activity in non-socialist countries*
The abundance produced by the 1960s and 70s is amazing. In all parts of the world interesting work has been done, in many cases directly in the service of economic planning, and the findings have often been valuable for natural and social scientists, administrators and politicians. Doing injustice to persons, countries and fields of research by not mentioning them here is unavoidable. This situation leads me to direct attention to a book of great value (although it may not be news for the majority): Volume 2 of a survey in agricultural economics (G.G. Judge, R.H. Dayet et al., *Quantitative Methods in Agricultural Economics*, 1940s to 1970s), published by the Minnesota University Press in 1977. Thus only a few representatives of new steps, rather randomly selected, will be mentioned here in a telegram style, from a few fields.

Input–output: besides the shift to regional–interregional problems, national models have often been used for projections serving purposes of agricultural policies. An example may be the study by Schluter-Heady (1975).

Mathematical programming: large systems were developed, mostly having a space and/or time aspect, for linear models I mention the CHAC by Duloy-Norton (1972), two US crop models by Taylor-van Blokland-Swanson-Frohberg (1977) and an analysis of alternative energy policies by Dvoskin-Heady-Burton (1978).

Behavioural equations were included in the Australian model APMAA reported by Kennedy (1973) and Monypenny-Walter (1976).

Risk and uncertainty have been a favourite topic. A long list may be represented by Renborg (1963), McInerney (1967), Boussard-Petit (1967), Boussard (1969, 1971), Hazell (1971) and Schiefer (1977).

Based upon Day's pioneering work, recursive programming has widely spread, used for projecting more realistic normative supply responses and development paths like in Schaller-Dean (1965), in the USDA project and in de Haen-Heidhues (1973).

From the studies using dynamic programming in a Markov process I mention that of Kislev-Amiad (1968).

Game theory: Dillon (1962) sung the requiem of this technique but its return to life is proven by recent papers by, e.g. McInerney (1969), Hazell (1970), Kawaguchi-Maruyama (1972), Ali ben Zaid Salmi (1976).

Monte Carlo technique: a more efficient procedure had been developed by Carlsson-Hovmark-Lindgren (1969) for farm planning. Dent-Bryne used it for investment planning. Bögemann (1977) compared the Monte Carlo procedure with mixed integer programming.

Simulation: besides the well-known MSU models for Nigeria (Manetsch et al., 1971) and South Korea (Rossmiller et al., 1972), one should mention the GOL, of world-wide coverage for grains, oilseeds and livestock (Rokjo et al., 1978, Regier, 1978).

Some other title would be suitable for a series of studies made by an ISU–Thai team for purposes of development policies for Thailand's agriculture. Demand for food, single crop models, recursive programming for regional and national agriculture, a transportation model and an econometric model for the evaluation of Thailand's rice export possibilities can be found, among others, in this complex.

Computerization of the planning process: as examples, the GEMAGRI from France (Boussard, 1972) and the Computerized Farm Planning from the United Kingdom (James, 1971) may be mentioned.

7 From the activity of Socialist countries

Problems emerging in the course of the development of economic planning required analyses different from the traditional ones. These countries had scientists with some experience gained in prewar research, and information came from countries with advanced econometric and OR activity. Now the agricultural economists engaged in OR and econometrics use about the same inventory of tools as in most non-socialist countries.

In 1967, studies from various countries were put together into a book in Moscow. The majority of them dealt with linear programming on the enterprise, farm, regional or national level (one parametric, two of them with non-linear programming, one with CPM, one with input–output, one with transportation, one with information streams, three of them with general problems of modelling).

Linear programming studies being most common and known abroad, I will not go into details. For introducing yield uncertainty into programming, I mention Teresa Marszalkowicz from Poland and Sieglinde Schmuntzsch-Hahn from the German Democratic Republic.

As a continuation of the reponse and yield variability studies of the 1920s–30s, I refer to three books from the Soviet Union: K.G. Tregubov *Mathematical methods of analysis of relationships in agricultural production*, (in Russian), Kolos, Moscow 1972; M.M. Yuzbashev *Methods of studying the dynamics of distributions and relationships*, (in Russian), Statistika, Moscow 1974; O.P. Krastin *Uses of regression analysis in agricultural economic research*, (in Russian), Zinatne, Riga 1976.

It is of interest how agriculture appears in the model systems elaborated for planning the development of vast territories. This is why I direct attention to two books from Kazakhstan: O. Kaldybaev and S. Bayzakov *Mathematical methods in planning and control of regional economy*, (in Russian), Nauka, Alam-Ata 1977; and S. Djandosov, S. Bayzakov and A. Esentugelov *Systems analysis in regional planning* (in Russian), Kazakhstan, Alma-Ata 1976.

The development of the cotton sector in the Soviet Union goes on according to the complex programme HLOPOK (Cotton). Treatment of location of production and processing, irrigation, repair, demand forecasts by systems of models for national, regional, sectoral, intersectoral and agro-industrial-complex levels can be found in a collection of studies edited by N.P. Fedorenko, G.M. Abdullaev et al. *Optimization problems of the development of the national cotton complex* (in Russian), Nauka, Moscow 1975.

There is a co-ordinated effort in the COMECON countries to develop an "automated control system" for agriculture. This would involve information flows, data banks, methods of analysis, model systems, computer hardware and software, training of personnel for purposes of analyses, quick elaboration of consequences of possible policy changes, variants of plans for helping decision-makers from the farm to the government level.

II A FEW WORDS ABOUT NEEDS AND OPPORTUNITIES

Many papers have dealt with this issue viewed from different angles. Let us remember, e.g., the writings by Glenn L. Johnson! Here I would like only to emphasize a few points.

1 *Some needs concerning the use of quantitative techniques*
First of all, agricultural economists must understand each other. We must accept that quantitative techniques involve both quite simple (but very important calculations) and very complicated computations. Different conceptions are often clashing but in a good organization they should reveal their theoretical, political etc. character and not hide behind techniques. Of course, views may differ concerning the treatment of a problem and the choice of the appropriate techniques.

If one starts from the characteristics of the matter to be handled, one can more easily avoid neglect of qualitative judgements and over-emphasising quantifications.

Better understanding between researchers and users of results is needed. The decision-makers, too, should make efforts, but the greater part of the task is on the researchers' side. They must find a language of clarity. However, researchers may also require understanding. If a decision-maker becomes mad when inconvenient outcomes of some planned steps are pointed out by careful analysis it is not the researchers who should be blamed.

To increase understanding between disciplines is a necessity: without this no co-operation in attacking complex problems may be successful.

I have often read complaints about placing too high a value on so-called "sterile disciplinary" results, at the expense of those serving practice. The opposite situation also is a real danger: overpreference for today's utility hampers preparedness to meet tomorrow's problems.

At the Nairobi Conference the issue of non-neutrality of the model builders was touched on. The acceptance of the social and political responsibility of the agricultural economists handling refined mathematical tools is a real need (particularly if we consider working in foreign countries).

2   *Sources of opportunities concerning quantitative techniques*

Mathematicians, statisticians and co-operating natural and social scientists have developed methods and computing facilities, and they do not seem to stop doing so. Thus one can hardly complain about lack of material for learning

The world-wide expansion of learning and practical experience opens up new territories for activity: local analysts and international teams may be expected to work on a much broader scale.

The growing demand for greater completeness enforces more intensive co-operation between people from various fields. Part of our failures have been due to poor knowledge of achievements in other disciplines but sometimes to lack of a necessary knowledge in a particular field representing a backward linkage, eventually a forward linkage. In genetics and in the domain of physiological processes there is a considerable amount of qualitative and quantitative knowledge to be used by agricultural economists. However, they can ask many questions relevant for their models which require further research in biology.

Sociology, psychology, organization research may also offer valuable information for people using quantitative techniques and may similarly receive questions leading to new lines of research. Since we live in the present world, it is preferable to have such a communication with political scientists too. Efforts toward linkage of national models offer one of possible reasons for justification.

DISCUSSION OPENING – FERNANDO C. PERES

This is a very interesting paper, especially for those of us who do not know how research is done in socialist countries.

Though the paper is entitled "Accomplishments, Opportunities and Needs of Agricultural Economists, *vis-à-vis* Quantitative Techniques" it emphasizes the *Accomplishments* and puts less emphasis on the *Needs*. Because I think it deals with the accomplishments part so well, I will stick mainly with the *needs* of agricultural economists in terms of quantitative techniques.

In the historical review, the paper places more emphasis on the use of mathematics for building the models and less emphasis on the testing. Testing the models requires a lot of mathematics to compute and understand all the statistics.

In fact, one can notice, by reading the paper, that economics can claim the status of a science already. Its methods are being used by researchers working under very different values or ideologies. We may make a "parenthesis" here and add to the review the book by Mishiro Morishima on Marxism which requires a lot of mathematics to be understood. He has shown that Marxist theory and neoclassical theory have a lot more in common than is generally thought to be the case. On the other hand, let me disagree with Professor E.O. Heady when he says that agricultural economists are generally well trained in quantitative methods. I think it is very difficult for many of us to understand Professor Morishima's work and consequently to be able to know many of these similarities between neoclassical and Marxist theory.

With respect to this, there is a point on which I would like to have Professor Petit's clarifying comments. As mentioned in the paper, the development of the economic tools followed different patterns in socialist and in western countries. We can understand socialist emphasis on "normative" models. The point is – is there any reason for research from socialist countries not doing (or starting at a later time to do) what we call "positive" economics? I think this is a relevant question in the sense that from the paper I could not know if statistical testing of the models is considered important by Joseph Sebeystén. If so, that indicates some more requirements in terms of mathematical training.

Let us talk a little more about how much mathematical training is required by agricultural economists. I guess nobody would argue with Waugh, as quoted in the paper, "A complex world requires appropriate techniques".

Specifically, in economics, one may think of what economy in writing and in research time could have been realized if John Maynard Keynes had taken his time and used his known mathematical abilities to put into equations what he *meant* in his writings. (It is said that Keynes did not like to use mathematics in economics, which is a shame.)

The British philosopher Bertrand Russell said, "The scope of all sciences is to reduce it to physics". One can argue that the general trend in our profession is just the opposite; that we should devote some of our time to looking to some *normative* kind of research, such as discussing the equity issues embodied in the work we do. If we accept Gunnar Myrdal's view that the most social scientists can do, in the sense of being objective, is to be explicit in their assumptions, then the need for the use of mathematics in economics becomes clear. The big advantage of mathematics is that it assures us that we will not violate our assumptions if we follow its rules. Of course, the assumptions we make may or may not be good approximations of reality and in this sense our journal editors could play a very important role in selecting papers to be published on a basis of their relevance in terms of realism, instead of elegancy or sophistication. Mathematics should not be blamed for people's lack of realism.

Another important point, which I think should be raised, follows from the fact that we are being urged to do problem-solving research, instead of doing, mostly, disciplinary work. Problem-solving research is, by necessity, interdisciplinary work. In doing this kind of work (which has not been a strong characteristic of our profession), we need a common language and I would like to quote Dantzing when he says "Mathematics is the language of science".

Maybe, I can give a testimony here from the Brazilian experience. Since the origin of our higher education system, it was mainly linked to the French system which was not, by tradition, mathematically oriented.

(I am referring to the social sciences.) We have not been able, until recently, to do team work and I suspect that other scientists did not accept us because we did not speak their language. Now the paper agrees with the need for some mathematics. My point is – I don't see any danger of our research being too mathematical. The way I see it is that one can be blamed for not going deeply enough into the phenomena one is studying. But to put the model into equation format and consequently, to be able to do quantitative predictions is superior (in terms of the advancement of science) to simple description. The point is not one of saying that descriptive works should not be done. What I am trying to say is that after the description of the situation one must put it into equations to be able to make useful predictions. Definitely a system of two equations with two unknowns gives us more information than the statement that X influences Y and X is influenced by Y in an interactive way.

Finally, a word about the big non-normative multisectoral models that are being built, as far as I know, by Western countries – the Fed-Mit-Pennsylvanian State Model, the Brookings Institution Model, etc. As mentioned before, a lot of mathematics is required if one wants to take a position on the relevance (in statistical terms) of these models. Even if one does not agree, based on statistical ground, that there is any relevance in building them, I would argue that they may be very useful in explaining all the calculations we make here in our computer system. Explaining those guesses requires a lot of mathematical training.

The paper also lacks any mention of cost–benefit analysis, maybe because a lot of value judgement is involved.

GENERAL DISCUSSION – RAPPORTEUR: I. TAKAHASHI

Dr Sebestyén's paper covered voluminous accomplishments in agricultural economics from the seventeenth century to the present, in both socialist and non-socialist countries, and in other fields of science which had close links with agricultural economics. The discussion on his paper was, however, mainly concentrated on the narrowly limited area of the *needs* of the agricultural economist, on which Dr Sebestyén's paper put less emphasis.

Two comments were made by others on the discussion opener's opinion of the use of mathematics. The first comment pointed out that mathematics was not always the expression of the whole truth in spite of its value and of its usefulness. The econometrician was faced with two constraints: the first came from his theoretical view of the problem. The results would be different between two methods; one fitting demand and supply curves separately based on the assumption that there was a lag between the action of supply and that of demand, and the other fitting together the two curves by means of simultaneous equations. The second constraint came from the method used by the econometrician. In this context examples were given.

The other comment on the discussion opener's opinion concerned the necessity of balancing quantitative and descriptive works. It was said that the proper balance should depend on the type of problem studied and, in some cases, quantifying attempts might result in some regression rather than progress of knowledge.

Finally, it was suggested that Dr Sebestyén's paper should include a full list of references for publication in the Proceedings Volume of the conference.

In reply, Michel Petit questioned whether we really knew if there was a lack of "positive" economics in socialist countries, as the literature is not readily available. If it is true, we should seek the reasons in the study of the philosophical foundation of investigations done in these countries.

On the use of mathematics he felt that Sebestyén would agree with Dr Peres, although he himself felt closer to Dr Dubos who had called attention to the limitations of all econometric works.

Participants in the discussion included Michel Petit (who read the paper on behalf of the author, who was not able to attend, and also responded to the discussion), Jean Dubos and Laurent R. Martens.

DARRELL F. FIENUP and HAROLD M. RILEY*

Training Agricultural Economists to Serve the Needs of a Changing World

Universities in the United States of America have built substantial teaching and research capabilities in international agricultural development since World War II. During the 1960s faculty members had many opportunities for overseas assignments in technical assistance projects and they were strongly encouraged to participate. It was also a period when increasing numbers of foreign students enrolled in US master's and PhD training programmes.

Demand for US graduate training by LDC students has continued at a high level through the 1970s. Studies by Stevenson[2] show a total of 9,600 graduate students entering MS and PhD programmes in some fifty US Departments of Agricultural Economics between 1969 and 1978. Thirty per cent (2,900) came from LDCs. In the period since 1974 about two-thirds came for MS training and one-third for PhDs. Over one-third came from Asia and one-fourth from Latin America. Twenty per cent came from Africa and an equal percentage from the Middle East. Numbers from Asia and Latin America have declined in the last ten years, while the flow of students from Africa and the Middle East has increased. Average yearly enrollment of new LDC students in US universities has increased about 20 per cent in the past four years, compared to the previous five.

The figures cited above reflect the continuing growth in demand for agricultural economists in the developing countries. Agricultural economics is a very new profession in the majority of LDCs and few countries have been able to initiate and/or consolidate their own graduate training programmes. There have been major increases in demand for MS level training from Africa and the Middle East where local training capabilities are very limited. With few exceptions, all LDCs need more PhD trained professionals to staff their teaching and research programmes.

At the same time that LDC demand for US training has continued to

* The authors acknowledge the contributions of the International Committee of the American Agricultural Economics Association to the study reported in this paper.[1]

increase, support for US university-based international work has substantially declined. Young US agricultural economists receive little encouragement to work in the development area and there are fewer opportunities for overseas contact and experience. This has left the US academic community with some sense of frustration as to how to maintain competencies in the economics of agricultural development and still serve the needs of LDC students who constitute over 30 per cent of graduate enrollments.

The training of foreign students has been an area of long-standing concern to the American Agricultural Economics Association (AAEA). In 1974, three regional seminars on international training were held prior to the AAEA annual meeting, where the conclusions and recommendations for improvement were presented. One of the recommendations was to make a follow-up study of former graduate students from LDCs to determine their current employment and training needs, and to obtain an evaluation of their US graduate training.[3]

In 1978, the International Committee of the AAEA obtained funds from the US Agency for International Development (AID) to conduct a major study with LDC alumni of US graduate programmes in agricultural economics on needs and strategies for improving US training in international agricultural development. This paper is based on the findings of the AAEA-sponsored study.

The basic source of information and data comes from 653 LDC agricultural economists, representing 79 countries, who studied in US universities over the past 15 years. These 653 respondents completed an eight-page questionnaire which was initially sent to nearly 2,200 LDC alumni of 52 US Departments of Economics and Agricultural Economics. In addition to the mail survey, in-depth studies were conducted in ten countries.[4] Major employers of agricultural economists, including graduate teaching and research centres, ministries of agriculture and national planning agencies, were personally interviewed to get their views on the usefulness of agricultural economists and their training needs. Leading professionals in each country were also asked to evaluate the strengths and weaknesses of US versus home country training and the country's needs in developing a more viable agricultural economics profession.

Principal objectives of the AAEA study were to (a) determine what has happened to LDC alumni of US universities in terms of residence and employment, (b) obtain an evaluation from LDC alumni of their US course work, thesis research, language training and programme guidance, (c) appraise agricultural economics training and research capabilities in the developing countries, including their current and future needs for training, and (d) assess possible ways the US profession can help strengthen these capacities in the LDCs. The purpose of this paper is to summarize results of the AAEA study and offer some conclusions relative to the objectives listed above.

EMPLOYMENT AND RESIDENCE OF ALUMNI OF
US UNIVERSITIES

LDC agricultural economists trained in US universities are generally working in jobs for which they were trained. Over 40 per cent held university positions; another 40 per cent work in government, including ministries of agriculture, national planning and other state agencies; about 10 per cent work for private businesses and as professional consultants and advisors; and 10 per cent work for international agencies and foundations. Actual positions currently held coincide reasonably well with what the alumni indicated their goals were when studying in US graduate schools. The major divergence is the relatively high proportion working in administration positions in LDC governments and universities (30 per cent) compared to less than 4 per cent who indicated administration as their first employment goal.

Eighty per cent of LDC alumni of US graduate schools are still living and working in their countries of origin. On a regional basis Asia has lost the most US trained professionals (31 per cent) compared to a maximum of 15 per cent in any other region. On an overall basis 92 per cent of those with MS degrees only are still working in their home countries compared to 75 per cent of the PhDs. International development agencies and US universities have been the principal employers of PhDs who have emigrated from their countries of origin.

EVALUATION OF US TRAINING

The essential components of US graduate training in agricultural economics include completion of a set of formal academic courses, plus research experience through writing a thesis or research paper. Most graduate programmes have minimum course requirements in economic theory, quantitative methods, and in the basic subject matter areas of agricultural economics. The thesis research is designed to utilize economic theory and methods in a problem-solving activity. Masters and PhD degrees have similar objectives with the PhD having greater depth and breadth, and major emphasis on the research component.

In the AAEA study, LDC professionals were asked to evaluate their US course work and thesis research experience. What would they change if they were to repeat the process? What were the strengths and weaknesses of their US training and how could it be improved? What effect did this training have on their professional career development? Answers to these questions are important for US universities who continue to enroll large numbers of LDC students, and for the agencies and governments who provide support for their education.

Fourteen areas in which agricultural economists normally take formal courses were listed in the survey questionnaire. Each LDC respondent was asked to indicate the number of courses taken in each area and to rank them as: extremely useful, very useful, moderately useful, slightly useful, a waste of time, or cannot tell. Space was also provided to write in courses not included on the list.

Courses in economic theory and quantitative methods were considered most valuable by the alumni surveyed. The top three areas in order of importance were micro economics, statistics and econometrics, and production economics. From 78 to 85 per cent of respondents ranked these courses as either extremely or very useful. Next in importance were macro economics, economics of agricultural development, mathematics, agricultural marketing, and linear programming, with 66 per cent or more of the respondents ranking these courses in the two top categories of usefulness.

Courses considered least useful were agricultural policy, trade and trade policy, land and resource economics, agribusiness, history of economic thought, and comparative economic systems. Many of these courses tend to be highly oriented to US and developed country institutions and situations. It is hypothesized that these rankings would improve if the courses were more relevant to LDC conditions.

Some consistent differences exist in the ranking of courses between respondents with PhDs and those with the MS only. PhDs consistently rank theory and methods courses higher and institutional courses lower than respondents with MS degrees. Those with higher levels of training evidently put greater value on analytical skills and tools needed for research. The PhDs also give more importance to history of economic thought and comparative economic systems, but even so, these courses still had low rankings.

When asked what courses they wish they had emphasized more when in graduate school, over 30 per cent of the responses were in the area of quantitative methods. Nearly one-fourth of the responses included traditional agricultural economics courses, with emphasis on marketing and agribusiness. There was little interest in giving greater emphasis to micro or macro economic theory, indicating most felt they had gotten enough theory when in graduate school. Again, PhDs were more interested in quantitative methods than were those with MS degrees.

There were essentially two areas of work where respondents would have liked more courses. One area was agricultural sector planning and policy analysis, including project development and evaluation (over 18 per cent of responses). These are topics which are not widely offered in US graduate programmes. Another area often discussed, but where LDC students usually do not get training, is in management and public administration. Ten per cent of the responses were in this area.

Nearly two-thirds of the survey respondents wrote master's theses. Ninety per cent of this group felt it had been more useful, or just as useful, as course work in their training programmes. Experience in the application of theory and quantitative techniques in problem analysis was considered extremely valuable.

Over half of the survey respondents with PhDs recommended doing theses using an LDC problem and data, but to do most of the analysis and writing at the degree-granting US university. The major advantage is to become knowledgeable and contribute to the solution of a home country problem, yet close to the thesis committee and other US university infrastructure to facilitate degree completion. Only 15 per cent recommended doing all the PhD thesis research in the home country. The major problems are lack of thesis guidance and supporting services. Also, many become so involved in job responsibilities at home that no time is left for the thesis. Actual procedures used for thesis completion by the PhDs in the sample were approximately one-third each in the two approaches indicated above. The remaining one-third did their theses in the US on a US problem.

Major strengths, weaknesses and ways to improve US training were explored in the country studies. The strengths coincide with the findings of the mail survey. Most important is the comprehensive training in theory and quantitative methods which provides students with a strong conceptual and analytical orientation. Flexibility in programme and the depth and range of courses were also emphasized. It was felt that the course work structure gave a wider exposure to subject matter and prepared graduates to work in many areas. Good student–professor relations and infrastructure for research and learning were further positive aspects of US training.

Weaknesses of US graduate training in agricultural economics are found mainly in the lack of faculty perception of and application to LDC problems. Many would like to see more attention given to the political, social, and institutional factors in development. There is a need to "bridge the gap" between theory and application, to be aware of the shortcomings of neoclassical theory as well as its strengths in analysis. Another gap may be the lack of attention to Marxist-Socialist ideology. Students trained in the US are usually not well prepared to discuss intelligently the issues of alternative economic systems. Economic theory and quantitative methods taught in the US are considered very useful in countries such as Tanzania, but they stress that only mature students should come to the US in order to put their training in proper perspective.

Both employers and professional agricultural economists suggested that US training could be greatly improved if more professors had real knowledge and experience of LDCs, especially for student advising. It was also felt that courses should be broadened to include application to LDC problems and conditions. Many would like to see more attention given to economic development strategies and also to the more practical aspects of project planning and appraisal, marketing, and management studies. All seem to agree that LDC students need a broad range of training, including more application of theory and methods to their problems. Some changes can and should be made, but often there are time and funding constraints that limit students in taking advantage of what is available.

Employers of agricultural economists in the LDCs are somewhat more critical of US training than professional agricultural economists. However, the same strengths and weaknesses are emphasized. US training is recognized for its rigour and strong analytical tools. It contributes substantially to the overall development of the student by giving a broader perspective of problems with emphasis on the scientific approach in analysis. This is considered especially important for training PhDs. At the same time, there is concern about the lack of focus and application to LDC problems. Some would like to see US training broadened to include more interdisciplinary work. When adequate MS training is available locally, most employers prefer it to US training. There is concern about those going to the US becoming disorientated to their local situations, especially when they are away for more than two years.

It is clear that much can be done to improve the relevance and application of US training to LDC problems and needs. Better student guidance, more international content in existing courses, and some new offerings in areas where LDC alumni indicate special concerns are some of the needed improvements. There was, however, little indication that the basic structure and content of training should be changed. Over 75 per cent of the respondents to the mail survey indicated US training had been extremely useful for their career development.

THE DEVELOPMENT OF AGRICULTURAL ECONOMICS IN THE LDCs

Although US universities have a strong commitment to the training of professionals from the LDCs, there is an underlying long term goal of assisting these countries in the development of their own graduate training capabilities. But this is a process that takes decades and the experience of the past thirty years indicate that it is often an elusive goal to achieve.

The level of professional development and the capacity to train agricultural economists varies widely among geographic regions, and among countries within these regions. Asia seems to have much greater professional agricultural economics capability than the other two regions. MS level training programmes are relatively well developed in several countries, including Japan, India, the Philippines, Thailand, Malaysia, Taiwan and Korea. Some of these countries also have PhD programmes. Within Latin America, Brazil currently has the most viable graduate training programmes in agricultural economics, while programmes previously established in Argentina, Chile, Colombia, and Peru no longer exist, or have been seriously weakened by political shifts within these countries. On the African continent, Nigeria has the strongest agricultural training capabilities, although Egypt, Kenya and Tanzania are also offering graduate degrees. Most African countries have very limited capacity for professional agricultural economics training.

The AAEA surveys in ten countries confirmed a widely held belief that the demand for agricultural economists continues to exceed LDC training capabilities. Employers indicate a growing need for BS and MS level agricultural economists to fill staff positions in government ministries, credit institutions and parastatal marketing agencies. PhD trained economists are increasingly sought for positions in planning units, research institutions, and as faculty members in local universities. In LDCs that have moved up toward the middle income range there emerges a rapidly growing demand in the agribusiness sector for agricultural economists with BS and MS level training.

In countries where MS level training exists, employers generally expressed a preference for locally trained individuals over those trained in the US or other developed countries. They supported this preference with the observation that locally trained professionals are more familiar with local social and economic problems. However, professionally trained agricultural economists identified what they considered to be major weaknesses of existing master's programmes. These included: (1) lack of qualified faculty, (2) narrowness of course offerings, (3) lack of depth in many courses, and (4) inadequate teaching materials and computing equipment. It was felt that the faculty resource constraint is often worsened by the relatively low university salaries, making it necessary for professors to seek other part-time employment, or teach as a supplemental source of income while employed elsewhere on a full-time basis. In either case, graduate students have relatively little contact with their professors and very limited research supervision.

WAYS THE US CAN HELP STRENGTHEN LDC PROFESSIONS

In countries with limited professional capacity, the study indicates a continuing need for both MS and PhD level training in the US. In countries which have made substantial progress in establishing local training capabilities, there is a desire for US training at the PhD level in conjunction with several collaborative arrangements that would strengthen their own local institutions.

Joint degree offerings between a LDC and US university was posed as a means of combining the strengths of US university course offerings in basic subject matter with additional course work and applied research experience within the student's own country. However, due to the complexities of university degree-granting procedures, LDC professionals were sceptical about the administration of a joint degree programme. Several preferred more flexible arrangements that would enable students to obtain their degree from their own local university with an opportunity to spend one to two years in a developed country university taking course work and participating in other professional development activities. Upon completion of this portion of the graduate programme, the candidate would return to his local university to complete the research requirement for the degree.

Shared thesis advising, involving professors from US and LDC universities, is an option that had considerable appeal, both as a means of carrying out a "joint degree" programme and as a means of strengthening the training of students actually completing degrees with developed country universities. Several advantages of this arrangement were noted. For the student it provides an opportunity to complete a degree programme that has greater immediate relevance to the problems of his country. He is separated for a shorter period of time from his home environment. For the LDC university there is a potential advantage in having a qualified US professor collaborating with the student and other faculty members in the development of a research activity which not only produces a thesis, but also contributes to institution-building. For the US universities it provides an opportunity to develop a longer term institutional linkage that enhances the professional capacity of their faculties and, thereby strengthens their own graduate training programmes. Some possible disadvantages of "shared thesis advising" are the additional time for completion of degrees and added costs. There was also a concern that the degree candidate might become heavily pressured to teach and assume other professional responsibilities which would prevent completion of the thesis.

Joint research projects involving professionals from developed or less developed countries were seen as a means of extending shared thesis advising into a broader programme of research. Collaborative research teams could be formed to carry out contract research projects of importance to LDC governments and international development agencies. This would provide opportunities for further development of the research skills of young LDC professionals, while contributing to the need for research inputs into local development programmes. Collaborative research was also seen as a means to maintain viable long term professional networks that could bring together the efforts of experienced LDC and US researchers on important LDC problems. The difficulties of funding and administering these arrangements were recognized.

Several of the LDC professionals who have obtained PhDs abroad expressed a desire for sabbatical-type opportunities to upgrade their professional skills. Many feel relatively isolated from the mainstream of the agricultural economics profession. Some expressed the view that sabbatical programmes need to be carefully planned and rigourously administered. Others pointed out the high opportunity costs in countries with very limited numbers of trained agricultural economists.

In countries with the least professional capacity, there was a keen interest in having developed country professors for both short term and longer term assignments with the local universities. In the more advanced of the LDCs, there was an expressed/interest in faculty exchange arrangements with US universities that would provide mutually beneficial professional development activities.

Employers and professional economists in the LDCs recognized that all training needs of agricultural economists cannot be met through formal degree programmes. Some gaps are bound to exist in any recent graduate's education, due to time restrictions or curriculum limitations at the degree-granting institution. Even more important is the need periodically to update past training and learn new analytical techniques and/or concepts needed for better job performance. There is a tendency for LDC professionals to become isolated from the mainstream of professional development. Interaction with peers in their own countries also is often more limited and difficult.

Approximately 35 per cent of the mail survey respondents had participated in special, non-degree training programmes since receiving their US degrees. Additional areas for short courses most desired by LDC professionals included quantitative methods, agricultural sector planning and policy analysis. Management and administration were also mentioned frequently. US universities have not been active in this type of training, but it offers promising possibilities both for delivery in LDCs and on US campuses.

CONCLUSIONS AND RECOMMENDATIONS

The demand for agricultural economists in the developing countries considerably exceeds their capabilities to train MS and PhD professionals. For the past two decades a large part of this training has been provided by the US and other developed country universities. Our assessment is that these needs for US training and collaboration in LDC institution-building will continue at least through the 1980s. Even those countries with the strongest capabilities in agricultural economics want to expand their relationships with US professionals and universities. LDC enrollment in US master's programmes has continued to be high, but should decline somewhat in the next decade. Demand for PhD training will remain strong as will the need to form better linkages between the more developed and developing professions.

The major recommendations that are suggested by the study are as follows:

US Graduate Programmes

US graduate training in agricultural economics is highly regarded by LDC professionals and their employers. The basic structure of formal course-work and writing a thesis should be maintained.

Economic theory, quantitative methods, production economics and economic development should continue to constitute the subject matter core of graduate programmes.

Courses with a high institutional content, especially those related to US conditions are least useful to LDC students. There is a special need to introduce LDC problems and examples into courses such as marketing, policy, agribusiness and resource economics.

Additional courses should be given in agricultural planning and policy analysis, project design and evaluation, and primary data collection and analysis. These courses should be specifically designed for LDC students and for those from the US who want to work in developing countries.

The thesis option should be used for training LDC students at the master's level whenever possible. PhD students need to develop theses on problems from their own countries. Where possible, arrangements should be made to provide for data collection and initial analysis in the home country, with final writing and thesis defence in the US university.

Every US Department of Agricultural Economics that wants to maintain a significant LDC student group, should have several faculty members with a major commitment and continuing experience in international agricultural development. These professors would teach some of the key courses for LDC students, advise them on their academic programmes, and serve as advisors in thesis research.

Within the limits of time and resources, LDC students should be trained broadly because of the many roles they must fill at home. Courses in public administration and management should be part of the programme.

Strengthening LDC training and research programmes
LDC professionals have a very positive attitude towards more collaboration with US agricultural economists. Joint degree arrangements, shared thesis advising and training more PhDs in the US are most commonly recommended. There is also a continuing need to increase LDC faculty competence through post-doctoral programmes, short courses, and seminar activities. Specific recommendations are as follows:

There is a pressing need to continue training PhDs outside the developing countries. Even a country like India, with its own doctoral programmes, wants to keep some US-trained PhDs flowing into their professional group. Most LDCs have no doctoral training capabilities and the rest have extremely limited capabilities for PhD training. PhDs are greatly needed to staff academic programmes and to guide and conduct research.

Joint degrees and shared thesis advising should become a growing dimension of the collaborative relationships between LDC and US universities. US course work can provide needed background in theory, quantitative analysis and research methodology. LDC course work can give a greater understanding of local development problems and institutions. The combination of course work can then be drawn upon in planning and conducting thesis research. In some instances, thesis advising may be shared by professors from both LDC and US universities.

Joint research projects can extend the collaborative arrangements linking the LDC and US universities, but usually require considerable initiative to arrange and finance. International funding agencies are showing greater interest in collaborative research programmes.

Post-doctoral sabbaticals in the US should be considered for LDC professionals who have at least five years of active experience in their home universities or research institutes since completing their doctoral studies. These awards should be reserved for outstanding young professionals with a serious commitment to continued teaching and research in their own countries. In countries like India, Brazil, Egypt and Nigeria, where the profession is reasonably well developed, there is a great need for more mature leadership to help define national policy issues, set research priorities and give guidance to graduate training.

Short courses, seminars and workshops should be given greater emphasis in a comprehensive strategy for professional development. These can be planned and carried out with LDC institutions collaborating with US university faculty and international development agencies.

Professional associations are an important complement to developing strong professions of agricultural economics in the countries surveyed. They can do much to promote greater communication and interaction among professionals and help alleviate problems of isolation. National meetings, workshops, seminars, and publication of a journal are some principal means used to facilitate peer review and professional development. Formation of LDC associations should be encouraged by the IAAE and other associations like AAEA.

NOTES

[1] This paper is a preliminary report on the AAEA study. A more complete report will be available in late 1979.

[2] Stevenson, Russell "Graduate Students from Less Developed Countries: The Continuing Demand for US Training", *AJAE*, Vol. 61, No. 1, February 1979, pp. 104–6; also, "US Graduate Students from Less Developed Countries", *AJAE*, Vol. 56, No. 4, November 1974, pp. 816–8.

[3] "International Training in Agricultural Economic Development," L.P. Schertz, A.R. Stevenson, and A.M. Weisblat, editors, published for the International Committee of the AAEA, Agricultural Development Council, 1976.

[4] These countries include India, Indonesia, Nepal, Kenya, Nigeria, Tanzania, Egypt, Brazil, Colombia, and Guatemala. The country surveys provide a useful supplement to the mail survey, but should be regarded as a series of case studies, rather than a representative sample of country situations.

DISCUSSION OPENING – G. STEFFEN

First I would like to express our thanks to Dr Fienup and Dr Riley for their contribution about training agricultural economists in a changing world. I am sure that we can take this as a basis for a useful discussion.

An important result is the fact that 80 per cent of the LDCs' agricultural economists are working in universities and governments. These jobs must be very attractive.

A high proportion of the alumni changed their goals, especially to administrative positions. Could we know more about the reasons why administrative work is so attractive in comparison to other activities?

It seems to me a success for my American colleagues that about 80 per cent of the former students ranked economic theory and quantitative methods as most valuable. In my experience these subjects are not easy to teach. I am not sure that European students will evaluate our lessons about theory in the same manner.

Concerning the PhD thesis, more than 50 per cent of the survey respondents thought it was better to write the thesis at a US university. I wish to ask whether this method will give good results compared to the alternative of writing the thesis at the home university. It might be difficult to get the necessary data or to see the real problem which should be solved.

Interesting recommendations have been made to improve the development of agricultural economics in the LDCs. One proposal which seems to me very effective is to involve professors from the US in teaching and research activities. Do you believe that the present capacities of your own universities are big enough to do two jobs – teaching and research work in your own universities *and* abroad? Or will extra funds be needed to pay for additional staff? I see some difficulties in European countries with an increasing number of students, if the state is not ready to pay more money for additional staff who will work in LDCs.

My final comment is that it would be useful to do similar research work to evaluate the activities of other countries which are involved in the same work. For this purpose it is necessary to develop some criteria to judge the work in different countries so that we can compare the results.

GENERAL DISCUSSION – RAPPORTEUR: C. PEMBERTON

In the general discussion the view was expressed that there was need for a similar study every five to ten years. This would show up differences which will occur when US graduates teach their own students. Second and third generation responses are needed. The major role of US training appeared to be to provide individuals for governmental institutions and universities in the LDCs. But was the training of workers to deal with problems of the countryside adequately covered?

One speaker with long experience of bringing students from developing countries to the US for training felt that at the beginning he had confidence that the students would get training relevant to problems of their own farms and marketing systems but as the orientation of US training moved towards theory and mathematical procedures, he now had less confidence that US training could equip LDC students to deal with practical problems. Academics in Asia are very scholarly in their attitudes and tend to insulate themselves from real problems. Such an orientation allows these students to obtain high grades in the US universities, but they do not have to come to grips with practical problems. For these reasons he felt that there may be a bias in the sample of scholastic-oriented persons and was not confident that there had been success in training for solving farming problems.

Valid suggestions were given in the paper on follow-up training for US graduates in the LDCs, but some comments on how these recommendations may be implemented would be welcomed.

In reply to the last point, Dr Riley agreed that publication of the results of the AAEA study was not sufficient in itself. Workshops would be held with US universities and international organizations to discuss the results, and some discussion of the results took place at the last AAEA meeting in Washington. The long term strategy must be to have all training for LDC agricultural economists in the LDCs. A start had been made with MSc programmes in different countries. For a longer period it is likely that PhD training will take place in the US but the results of the study indicate better ways of carrying this out.

In answer to the question expressing concern over the relevance of training of LDC students in the US Dr Fienup felt that there was a declining role for US institutions to train LDC students, especially at the MSc level. MSc level training was best kept pertinent to local conditions by having this training done in the LDCs and the results of the country studies supported this view. Similarly US universities cannot train LDC agricultural economists effectively for work in the countryside of LDCs. This should be done in the LDCs. He agreed that second generation training would be more relevant to local conditions.

Regarding the opener's remarks about US professors holding jobs at home and in the LDCs, this would have to be studied further. Many young professors in the US desert their interest in development studies because of lack of tenured positions and research funding. Manpower will be needed to provide such training in the LDCs.

Participants in the discussion included Rufus O. Adegboye, Vance W. Edmondson, Ardron B. Lewis, Donald S. Ferguson.

MICHEL PETIT

Teaching Marxist Economics to Agricultural Economics Students in non-Marxist Countries

The relevance of Marxism to economics as a discipline remains unfortunately a very controversial subject. Marx himself asserted that his main task was to transform the world and not to interpret it. According to Lenin, "Marx' contribution, materialism and scientific socialism, constitutes the theory and the programme of the workers' movement in all civilized countries".[1] Many economists, more or less consciously influenced by positivism, as a philosophy of science, adamantly reject such a position, asserting that the purpose of scientific investigation is to seek truth, i.e. to understand the world, whereas changing it would belong to the realm of action. Personally, while I can see the advantages of distinguishing between thinking and doing, I am also conscious of the limits of this distinction which implies, *inter alia*, two untenable positions: on the one hand, a complete division of labour between scientists and decision-makers and, on the other hand, the idea that it is possible to draw a line between what economists say as scientists and what they say as citizens. Whatever one may think about these philosophical positions, the essential point is that even to non-Marxists wanting to understand the world, Marx has something important to offer. This is the fundamental point which justifies this paper. Those who are not convinced might consider that Marxist economists are a fact of life and that we have to live with them.

It should be clear that I do not consider myself to be a Marxist[2] and, as a result, I am not a specialist of Marx. However, I have accepted the invitation to present a paper on teaching Marxist economics to agricultural economics students because I am convinced that Marxism is important for all economists. In particular, in countries where Marxism is not the official doctrine of the State (the definition which I give to the expression non-Marxist countries in the title of this paper), teaching Marxist economics is a very effective pedagogical method to make students conscious of the limits of the neoclassical approach which remains, in my view, a very useful tool of analysis. The words neoclassical approach should be taken here as describing a general intellectual attitude, *vis-à-vis* economic problems, belonging to the analytical tradition illustrated by economists since Alfred Marshall and Leon Walras, including Keynes and the post Keynesians and today all the Nobel prize winners. In addition, teaching Marxist economics has the advantage of helping students understand better the theoretical basis of the ideological conflicts so apparent in many societies. Very often students having a very limited training in economics are full of prejudices, of one sort or another, dictated by a sentimental adherence to some vague ideology. It is essential that future economists subject these prejudices to rigourous tests of internal logical consistency and consistency with experience. The purpose is not to preach a doctrine to them but to develop their positive critical mind.

Of course the paper draws on our experience of more than ten years of teaching at ENSSAA[3] where Marxism has always been part of the curriculum. However, given the specific nature of ENSSAA students (agricultural graduates with limited background in economics who are trained to become civil servants of the Ministry of Agriculture, mainly involved in technical agricultural education), our experience is not directly transferable to most university situations. However, I have tried to derive lessons of somewhat general validity. First, we will discuss how a presentation of Marxist economics as a general economic development theory can clearly point out either the main limitations of the neoclassical theories or the partial nature of the analyses usually conducted by economists belonging to the neoclassical tradition. In the second part of the paper, the emphasis will be placed on a few specific problems in agricultural economics. Here again it will be pointed out that Marxist contributions can be viewed as very complementary to neoclassical analyses.

1   PRESENTING MARXIST ECONOMICS AS A GENERAL THEORY OF ECONOMIC DEVELOPMENT

Marx' main contribution to economics is the theory of the capitalist mode of production and, more generally, the analysis of historical economic development in terms of modes of production.

In this perspective, Marxist authors often point out what they call the "apologetic nature of bourgeois economics". The thrust of the criticism was already expressed by Marx when he wrote: "By saying that the present relationships – the bourgeois production relationships – are natural, economists imply that these are the relationships within which wealth is created and productive forces develop themselves according to the laws of nature. Thus . . . these relationships must always regulate society".[4] Is it not true that many agricultural economists trained in the neoclassical tradition, relying on a theoretical framework where models of individual behaviour occupy a privileged position, tend to point out the advantages of market adjustments without giving sufficient attention to the specific conditions under which markets operate and develop? The common expression "market imperfections" is itself revealing; it does suggest that a little intelligence, plus perhaps a little political courage, will suffice to "correct" the imperfections. The Marxist contribution here is to raise relevant questions relative to the causes of the development of these imperfections, causes which should be fully investigated before prescribing any correction.

Taking institutions as given (as we too often do), is also related to a common slant, among agricultural economists towards *production at the expense of distribution*. Marx' theory is useful to warn the students against that slant. Placing class struggle at the centre of human history has the advantage of calling attention to the many conflicts of interest raised by any economic development process. Of course the positive contribution of the neoclassical income distribution theory must be emphasized. Relating the returns to factors of production to their marginal productivity is certainly very useful in empirical analyses. But Marx' differential treatment of labour and capital, with his concepts of labour value and exploitation on which production relationships and then modes of production are constructed, provides a very interesting point of view for the investigation of the relationship between economic growth and income distribution. With such a reference framework in the back of one's mind, considering that the welfare of the poor can only be increased through economic growth and looking only afterwards at income distribution is not tenable. Emphasizing social classes as the essential categories to be taken into account in the analysis of income distribution has the advantage of providing a clue for linking economic and social or political analyses. In that sense the concept is superior to the neoclassical approach which is expressed in terms of returns to factors of production. But the advantage is only limited, as Marx' main classes in the capitalist mode of production, the workers and the capitalists, are precisely defined in terms of the factors of production, i.e. labour and capital, which they supply. The other classes are always sources of difficulties in empirical analysis. In spite of these difficulties, the concepts of social classes and social production relationships can be taken as sources of interesting questions regarding the relationships between growth of production, income distribution and the dynamics of social change.

Beyond thus calling our attention to clearly important aspects of economic phenomena which economists trained in the neoclassical tradition tend to overlook, even though neoclassical economics has something to say about them, the Marxist approach has two other general merits: its treatment of the relationships among social sciences and its reliance on dialectics as contrasted to analytical logic. The expression "Marxist approach" is used here to describe a general intellectual attitude with respect to social phenomena. All economists agree that their discipline deals only with partial aspects of human behaviour. Thanks in particular to the new household economics,[5] we know that *the domain of economic investigation* can be broader than that which traditional text books indicate. Yet even the tentatives of the "Chicago school" cannot give us full satisfaction. *Clearly human phenomena have a unity. Other social sciences have made contributions to their understanding* and we do not know how to relate together their bodies of knowledge. This failure can perhaps best be illustrated with an example. The adoption of innovations is an important question for agricultural economists both from a theoretical and from a practical standpoint. Rural sociologists have done considerable work on this subject.[6] Much econometric work has also been done on it, a pioneer in the field being Zvi Griliches.[7] At one point a controversy opposed economists and sociologists; Griliches argued that the major determinants of the rate of technical change were economic variables, sociological variables being only important in determining who will be the first or the last to adopt a new practice in a given area. Under pressure from sociologists pointing out that if economic reasons were the only basis for adoption improved practices would be adopted as soon as their economic advantages could be demonstrated, Griliches relented, writing that there was no point in opposing one factor to another in order to explain the speed of adoption. The controversy abated then but one must confess that, if it had the advantage of pointing out the relevance of both economics and sociology for studying the adoption of innovations, very little knowledge was gained regarding the relationship between these two social sciences. It is now my conviction that this sterility comes from viewing the domains of the various social sciences as juxtaposed. This view leads to intellectual imperialism, the extension of one's domain being only possible at the expense of another. The controversy between Griliches and the sociologists Rogers and Havens can probably be interpreted in these terms. By contrast, the Marxist approach provides a different clue. Conflicts of interest are central in Marx' view of economic phenomena; they can also be essential in the analysis of society by sociologists. Such an analysis is not without problems but it does open a very interesting perspective.[8] Marx' approach is also relevant in political science. For instance, few can disagree with Beteille when he writes: "The Eighteenth Brumaire is a masterly analysis of the complex interplay of interests among the different classes and strata in mid-nineteenth century France". In the same perspective, the State is viewed as part of the whole social formation. This point of view must be contrasted with the neoclassical tradition which places the State as exogenous to most economic models.[9]

We touch here upon the *differences between analytical and dialectical logics*. The former is at the basis of many scientific disciplines, including the neoclassical tradition; the use of the latter was particularly illustrated by Marx and Freud, the creator of psychoanalysis. The root of the difference lies in the very conception of change.[10] For dialectics, being and becoming are intimately related, e.g. the sources of a change in a society must be found in its internal contradictions. For analytical logic, a change in one variable is always related to a change in another. Hence, any phenomenon can be analysed in terms of a system of variables, influencing each other – the endogenous variables – but also influenced by other variables determined outside the system (the exogenous variables), any system being always a subsystem of a more global system. Yet as Georgescu-Roegen points out: "actuality – we must stress the point – is seamless. Hence, violence is done to it as Analysis slices it into discretely distinct pieces in order to facilitate our understanding".[11] This is, I feel, a clear statement of the philosophical position underlying my conviction that Marxism can help agricultural economists trained in the neoclassical tradition to become more conscious of the limitations of their analytical tools. In my own teaching experience, I have found this statement quite helpful to the students. In a way, this point of view can be validated by considering a few contributions to our understanding of agricultural problems made by economists belonging to the Marxist tradition. These contributions will be the object of the second part of this paper.

2 CONTRIBUTION OF MARXIST AUTHORS TO THE ANALYSIS OF A FEW PROBLEMS IN AGRICULTURAL ECONOMICS

This is, of course, not the place to attempt a complete review of the Marxist literature on agriculture. For the purpose of this paper, it will be sufficient to choose a few cases illustrating the fruitfulness of a Marxist approach and its complementarity with neoclassical analyses. The two questions discussed below: the survival of family farms in French agriculture and the analysis of rural development and rural poverty on a world scale naturally reflect our own preoccupations at ENSSAA; but the relevance of these questions for all agricultural economists is so obvious that it does not seem necessary to present a more elaborate justification for discussing them here.

1 *The survival of family farms in French agriculture*
Marx seems to have been convinced that, in due time, the peasant farm would disappear and that capitalist production relationships would develop within agriculture as well as within other sectors.[12] At the end of the 19th century Kautsky re-examined this question[13] because it had direct political implications then. His investigation followed discussions regarding "the agrarian programme of the German socialist democracy at the Frankfurt and Breslau Conventions".[14] The question arose because "without any doubt – and, we shall henceforth accept this as demonstrated – agriculture does not develop according to the same process as industry; it follows specific laws".[15] The main point is the observation made at the end of the nineteenth century, and to a certain extent still valid today, that small peasant farms coexist with large farms. Kautsky however emphasizes that "according to Marx' method, one must not only ask the question whether or not the small farm has a future in agriculture; one must on the contrary investigate all the transformations experienced by agriculture during the reign of capitalist production. One must seek if

and how capital takes over agriculture, revolutionizes it, shakes down the former forms of production and creates the necessity of new forms".[16] Accordingly, Kautsky proceeds to explain why small peasant farms can coexist with large farms employing wage labourers in spite of the technical superiority which he attributes to the latter. He sees the factors of resistance of small peasant farms in the possibility for peasants to secure a complementary income through employment in large farms and, when employment is not available, in their ability to work more and consume less. But, Kautsky concluded that industry had produced "the technical and scientific conditions of the new, rational agriculture, which revolutionized it through machines and artificial fertilizers, through the microscope and the chemistry laboratory, and thus established the superiority of the large capitalist farm on the small peasant farm".[17] Clearly these ideas on the technical superiority of large farms are essentially shared by agricultural policy-makers in many socialist countries of Eastern Europe.[18] Yet, in Western Europe, the evolution of farm structure since the beginning of the twentieth century does not seem to confirm this superiority even though the influence of industry, as Kautsky foresaw, has been very large. This discrepancy raises a question which contemporary Marxist agricultural economists have discussed at great length, particularly in France. J. Cavailhes[19] gives a clear statement of the problem: "the development of capitalism has been translated into a growing concentration and centralization of the means of production and into an increase in the number of wage earners as compared to other workers; . . . But nothing of the sort occurred in the agricultural sector: wage working is regressing, the concentration of the means of production does take place as a long term trend but it progresses at an outstandingly slow rate as compared to the rate of concentration in industrial branches, the centralization of capital does not occur. Such a situation calls for an explanation and many Marxists have undertaken this task".

In a seminal article Servolin[20] argued that peasant farms belong to a specific mode of production, called "small merchant production", which is confronted to and transformed by the mode of capitalist production but not dissolved into it. What takes place is the reproduction and enlargement of farms belonging to the mode of small merchant production. The small producer is forced "to produce more and more for a more and more unified market, to buy larger and larger quantities of input and more and more expensive equipment, to resort more and more to credit". Precisely because family farms can do that, they are more efficient than large capitalist farms would be. Actually one does not really need to be Marxist to reach this conclusion. Servolin quotes Glenn Johnson whom he characterizes as a very "orthodox American agricultural economist" who wrote: "A cynic might even assert that the family farm is an institution which functions to entice farm families to supply batches of labour and capital at sub-standard rates of return in order to supply the general economy with agricultural products at bargain prices".[21] But the main point is that Servolin places the argument in a Marxist perspective: the development of these farms belonging to the mode of small merchant production "requires, and thus permits at the same time, the development of an industrial, commercial, and financial capital to which the farm is linked more and more closely".

These ideas can play a very useful role in a teaching process, because they clearly suggest the possibility of building a theoretical framework for a global analysis of the dynamic process of agricultural development, pointing out the interplay of various social forces. The fact that many contemporary French Marxist authors have criticized Servolin's argument, claiming that he has misinterpreted Marx, adds to rather than detracts from the interests of having students read his writings. The controversy itself is very instructive about the difficulties of using complex theoretical concepts in empirical analyses.

In theoretical terms, Servolin's argument is based on recent developments[22] regarding the articulation between two modes of production. In agricultural economics several criticisms have been made. Thus Barthelemy and Blanc note that the Marxist tradition has perhaps emphasized too much the existence of a labour process often encountered in industry and perfectly adapted to capitalist production relationships. As a result, the opposition between the small family farm and the large capitalist farm has claimed too much attention leading to the neglect of an "original social form: the large family farm of the well-to-do peasantry".[23] However, "the fundamental question which remains to be solved is to understand the reasons of this strengthening" (of the family character of production units in agriculture). They reject Servolin's analysis in terms of two modes of production arguing that the very concept of mode of production concerns the organization of a whole society at a given time.

J. Cavailhes[24] gives a more radical criticism of Servolin's theoretical concepts. Using Lenin's analysis of the decomposition of the peasantry, he argues that family farms must essentially be viewed as belonging to the "petite bourgeoisie", i.e. a class in transition: most of its elements are called to join the ranks of the proletariat, a few being able to become capitalists. The latter keep up the hopes of those whose fate is not yet clear. This argument has the great merit of taking account of the process of massive elimination of the peasantry in France, as in many other Western countries, as well as of the ambiguous ideological and political positions taken by French peasants for more than a century.

Other authors such as Evrard, Hassan, and Viau[25] and to a lesser extent Mollard,[26] stressing the role of agribusiness industries, argue that, even though farmers sell agricultural products and not their labour force, the relationship with the capitalist of the agro-food sector is tantamount to an exploitative relationship.

Admittedly, this brief review of the French literature on the subject is not complete. But it should be sufficient to make the point that controversies are lively and raise important theoretical and empirical questions which provide a very good training field for agricultural economics students. It should be clear also from this example that the contributions made by Marxist authors are very complementary with those made by economists belonging to the neoclassical tradition. If Marxists grossly neglect micro economic processes, including even the different behaviour of farmers from various economic stata (differences which should be of great importance in their own approach), they call our attention to the interplay of social forces shaping any process of economic development and, as such, the long term dynamics of changes in agriculture, which neoclassical analyses tackle often piece by piece and not as a whole. A somewhat similar point can be made on the example of rural development viewed on a world scale.

2 Rural development and rural poverty: the necessity of world perspective

Although this topic is only occasionally taught at ENSSAA, where our students' preoccupations are mainly centred on the problems of French agriculture, it is important enough to be discussed here in a paper written for an international audience. The starting point may be the inadequacy of the very concept of underdevelopment. W. Rostow's fundamental work[27] on the stages of economic growth provides a systematic framework of analysis for the process of development, assumed to be universal, all countries following the same path but having reached different stages on that path. This approach has been very eloquently criticized by Frank[28] and Amin[29]. It neglects the historical relationships between developed and developing economies which have totally transformed the societies of the Third World. This judgement is analogous to Levi Strauss' criticism of what he calls "social evolutionism",[30] a pseudo-scientific attempt "to suppress the diversity of cultures while pretending to fully recognize it. For if one treats the different states which human societies, whether old or far away, are in as stages or steps of an unique development which, starting from the same point, must have them converge towards the same goal, one sees that diversity is only apparent." Later he asserts that civilization implies the coexistence of cultures presenting a maximum of diversity among themselves.

Coming back to economic development, one can of course argue that all theories are made of simplifying assumptions. Thus it may be perfectly legitimate, in the study of development processes, to ignore the relationship between developed and developing countries. Granting this point, the least which can be expected of the analyst is to remember this simplifying assumption, which bears its own limitations in terms of positive analysis and which has, besides, important ideological and political consequences. In this respect the existence of an alternative theory, based on the concepts of centre and periphery of the mode of capitalist production[31] and that of unequal exchange[32] with the resulting necessary deterioration of the terms of trade, can play a very useful role, at least as a reminder of the limits of the neoclassical approach.[33] The authors of this world theory of development have not said much about agriculture. In a brief overview, S. Amin[34] argues that social formations of the periphery are generally dominated by agrarian capitalism which, it is true, can take several forms. More interestingly perhaps, the writings of some agricultural experts, such as R. Dumont, although not specifically framed in terms of the centre-periphery concepts, seem to be consistent with this general approach.[35] Stressing that the famous book, *Limits to Growth*, sponsored by the Club of Rome, has shown the physical impossibility of generalizing the consumption pattern of Western countries, particularly the USA, to the whole world, Dumont clearly accuses the capitalist economy to be engaged "in a quasi-irreversible movement", which, if it is not checked, will lead mankind to catastrophe. The importance of these issues is obvious, but they may be too broad to provide a very good training ground for students who need to learn how to confront theoretical developments with precise information, i.e. how to test specific hypotheses. In this perspective de Janvry's recent writings present a great interest, since they are attempts to discuss specific agricultural development questions (agrarian reforms in Latin America,[36] rural development programmes[36] technological and institutional innovations,[37] in an explicit theoretical framework using several key Marxist concepts. They do provide interesting insights on the stakes in terms of social conflicts involved in the corresponding very concrete policy issues. A more recent paper[38] elaborates the theoretical framework. The two authors distinguish five levels of analysis (organization of the peasant household, its economic logic, mechanism of surplus extraction, insertion of peasants within particular modes of production, dynamics of transformation of the peasantry) and show that this classification permits them to present a consistent set of data on the peasantry in the northern Sierra Department of Cajamarca (Peru). If this framework can be fruitfully employed in other studies, it will provide a useful link towards the badly needed integration of micro economic phenomena in the Marxist approach.

   In total, this approach can provide students with a better consciousness of the interplay of social forces, based on economic interests, involved in any process of rural development. In particular, there is here a logical explanation of the widespread "urban bias" so often denounced by neoclassical economists analysing agricultural and food policies in developing countries.[39] The case for the analysis of policy issues in terms of an analytical political economy appears very convincing and it can probably be considered as definitively made.

   Given however the very broad issues tackled by the approach, many questions remain open, hence a rigid aherence to the conclusions reached so far would be a dogmatic attitude which should certainly be denounced. We touch here upon a very serious difficulty of the intellectual position taken in this whole paper: most Marxist authors believe in the superiority of their approach, hence they do not accept the complementarity advocated here. That does not make the dialogue with them very easy.

CONCLUSION

The main argument developed here has been that the Marxist and the neoclassical approaches can be very complementary in the training of agricultural economics students. In particular in "non-Marxist countries", Marxist economics can be very useful in pointing out the most basic – often implicit – assumptions of neoclassical theories and the limitations of analyses conducted in the neoclassical tradition. In this respect, the well known general contributions of Marxism (historical perspective, emphasis on conflicts of interest based on the economic position of social groups determined by their place in the production process, bridges with other social sciences, reliance on dialectical rather than analytical logic) are very significant. In addition, recent writings by Marxist authors on two important questions for agricultural economists; the place of family farms in a capitalist mode of production and the analysis of rural development and poverty in a world perspective, illustrate the contributions which a Marxist approach can add to analyses conducted in the neoclassical tradition. Although more specific, the main contributions here again are expressed in terms of historical perspective, globality of the phenomena studied, and conflicts among social groups.

But when presenting this complementarity to students, one is faced with various difficulties. First, and probably most important, is that Marxist colleagues are not convinced of this complementarity. They certainly do not have a monolithic point of view but most would essentially agree with Amin when he writes about the "art of management" produced by the academic economic "science": the very nature of the problems tackled by this art – maximization of some variable (profit or product) under given constraints (in particular "resource scarcity" constraints) at a given time in a given system (here the mode of capitalist production, a point seldom acknowledged) prevents one from seeing in this set of techniques an alternative to the social science.[40] The philosophical pluralism which I advocate is condemned as eclecticism, i.e. as ultimately inconsistent, by Marxists. In a sense, our institutional position at ENSSAA is such that we must tolerate each other, no one having the power to evict others. Our peaceful coexistence, imposed by the necessity to deal with our institutional environment, rests on a minimum, somewhat tacit, consensus regarding some necessary criteria for good research. These are roughly the classical tests of internal logical consistency, consistency with experience, and communicability.[41] However controversies are raised in the very process of applying these tests. Dialectics is prone to evade the tests of consistency because, when faced with an apparent inconsistency, the analyst is always tempted to stress a contradiction which had remained in the background of the argumentation so far but which appears as a legitimate part of the over-all dialectical reasoning. Conversely, analyses conducted in the neoclassical tradition appear always to be tackling very partial problems and thus to fail the test of consistency with a broad enough set of observations.

Another difficulty is due to the intellectual uneasiness with which students are left after they have been exposed to a pluralistic teaching programme. The danger here is that they decide, since the "teachers" cannot agree among themselves, that the choice of an ideological position is a purely personal matter which cannot be subjected to any rigourous test. It is actually very difficult to judge whether or not this danger is real and for what proportion of the student body. My own feeling is that our teaching programme does lead the students to question their *a priori* ideological commitments, and contributes to make them more conscious of the limitations of the theories which they will use in empirical analyses. If that conviction is borne out, we could say that the programme is successful in moving outward the frontier of objective knowledge and in reducing the ideological domain. In my view, this would be a success. I am however perfectly conscious that expressing it this way reflects a philosophical point of view about the relationship between science and ideology which is not shared unanimously, particularly not by Marxists.

NOTES AND REFERENCES

[1] Lenin, V. *Marx, Engels, Marxisme*, Ed. de Moscou, p. 12, as quoted by J. Cavailhes.

[2] The term, as used here, should be taken in its philosophical connotation.

[3] ENSSAA = Ecole Nationale Supérieure des Sciences Agronomiques Appliquées, Dijon.

[4] Marx, K. *Misère de la philosophie* (translated from the French text in *Oeuvres*, Tome I, NRF, Paris 1963.

[5] See, for instance, Becker, G.S. "A Theory of the Allocation of Time", *Economic Journal* 75, pp. 493–517, 1965 and Nerlave, M. "Economic Growth and Population", Perspectives of the "New Home Economics" (revised version of *JPE* article) ADC Reprint, November 1974.

[6] See, for instance, Rogers, E.M. *Diffusion of Innovations*, Free Press, New York 1960.

[7] Griliches, Z. "Hybrid Corn: An Exploration in the Economics of Technical Change", *Econometrica*, 25, pp. 501–22, 1957.

[8] Beteille, A. "Marxism and Modern Sociology", *Six Essays in Comparative Sociology*, Oxford University Press, Delhi 1974.

[9] An exogenous variable can be important in the analysis, but the analysis ignores how it is determined thus the feedback effect of the system on the exogenous variable is neglected. For a rigorous definition see Johnston, J. *Econometric Methods*, McGraw Hill, New York 1963, p. 232.

[10] Petit, M. "Relationships among various aspects of agricultural changes", *European Review of Agricultural Economics*, 3–2/3 (TACAC Special Issue), 1975.

[11] Georgescu-Roegen, N. "Process Analysis and the Neoclassical Theory of Production", *American Journal of Agricultural Economics*, 54, 2 (May 1972), p. 281–2.

[12] Marx, K. *Le Capital*, ch. XV, 10 in *Oeuvres* – Economie, Collection La Pleiade, Paris, p. 996.

[13] Kautsky, K. *La question agraire, Etude sur les tendances de l'agriculture moderne*, Ed. Française, Giard et Brière, Paris 1900, facsimile, Maspero, 1970.

[14] Ibid., first sentence of the Preface.

[15] Ibid., p. 5.

[16] Ibid., p. 6.

[17] Ibid., p. 448.

[18] See, for instance, Brossier, J. and Petit, M. "Un exemple d'agriculture socialiste: l'agriculture bulgare", *Etudes Rurales*, 60, pp. 55–72, Oct.-Dec. 1975.

656 *Michel Petit*

[19] Cavailhes, J. "L'analyse léniniste de la décomposition de la paysannerie et son actualité", *Critiques de l'Economie Politique*, No. 23, Jan.-March 1976, pp. 110–42.

[20] Servolin, C. "L'absorption de l'agriculture dans le mode de production capiliste", *l'Univers politique des paysans*, A. Colin, Paris 1972.

[21] Johnson, G.L. "The Modern Family Farm and its Problems" in Economic Problems of Agriculture in Industrial Societies. Proceedings of a Conference held in Rome in 1965 by the International Economic Association, MacMillan, 1969.

[22] See Althusser, L. and Balibar, E. *Lire Le Capital*, Maspero, Paris 2nd. edition, 1970.

[23] Blanc, M. and Barthelemy, D. *Le Procès de travail capitaliste et le développement d'une agriculture familiale dans la France contemporaine*, INRA, série Economie et Sociologie Rurales, Dijon 1974.

[24] Cavailhes, J. op. cit.

[25] Evrard, P., Hassan, D. and Viau, C. *Petite agriculture et capitalisme*, INRA Série Economie et Sociologie Rurales, Paris 1976.

[26] Mollard, A. *L'exploitation du travail paysan*, Thèse Université Sciences Sociales, Grenoble 1975.

[27] Rostow, W.W. *The Stages of Economic Growth*, Cambridge 1960.

[28] Frank, A.G. "The development of underdevelopment", *Monthly Review*, No. 4, 1966.

[29] Amin, S. *L'accumulation à l'échelle mondiale*, IFAN, Dakar and Anthroposh Paris 1970.

[30] Levi Strauss, C. *Race et histoire*, essay written in 1952 for UNESCO, Paris, Gonthier, 1974.

[31] Amin, S. *op. cit*. De Janvry credits Raul Prebish with the first introduction of the centre-periphery concept.

[32] Emmanuel, A. *L'échange inégal*, Maspero, Paris 1969.

[33] A clear and concise presentation of the essential argument, bypassing the intricate theoretical foundations, can be found in Furtado, C. *Le mythe du développement économique*, Anthropos, Paris 1976.

[34] Amin, S. "Le développement inégal", *Essai sur les formations sociales du capitalisme périphérique*, Ed. De Minuit, Paris 1973, pp. 292–6.

[35] In *l'Utopie ou la mort*, Seuil, Paris 1973, Dumont quotes Emmanuel, Amin, Frank, Jalée, Bairoch, Mende in the same footnote.

[36] De Janvry, A. "The Political Economy of Rural Development in Latin America: An Interpretation", *American Journal of Agricultural Economics*, 57, 3, Aug. 1975, pp. 490–9.

[37] De Janvry, A. "Inducement of Technological and Institutional Innovation: an Interpretative Framework", in *Resource Allocation and Productivity in National and International Agricultural Research*, (ed.) Arnolt, T.A. et al., University of Minnesota Press, Minneapolis 1977, pp. 551–63.

[38] De Janvry, A. and Deere, C.D. "A Theoretical Framework for the Empirical Analysis of Peasants", unpublished, University of California, Berkeley mimeo, 1978.

[39] For a recent and comprehensive presentation of this point of view, see Schultz, T.W. (ed.) *Distortions of Agricultural Incentives*, Indiana University Press, Bloomington 1978.

[40] i.e. Marxism; from Amin, S. *L'accumulation à l'échelle mondiale*, op. cit., p. 20.

[41] For a clear definition of these terms, see Johnson, G.L. and Zerby, L.K. *What Economists Do About Values*, Michigan State University, East Lansing 1973, p. 222–7.

DISCUSSION OPENING – RODOLFO HOFFMAN

The paper by Professor Petit is indeed very interesting and provocative.

Because of the short period of time that I have to make my comments, I will use it to stress the points where I disagree with the author. My criticism begins with the title: what is a non-Marxist country? The definition given in the text is "a country where Marxism is not the official doctrine of the State". That is quite different from the concept of a capitalist (versus socialist) country. Why stress what is declared as official doctrine of the State and not the social relations of production of the country? I would add that Professor Petit teaches in a capitalist democracy.

One does not like to be labelled. One likes to believe that one is, in some sense, original. Professor Petit says that he does not consider himself a Marxist. To make a similar statement about myself – I do not consider myself a neoclassic economist.

Professor Petit states, more than once, that the Marxist approach is complementary to neoclassical analyses. My opinion is that some parts and instruments of the neoclassical analyses are complementary to Marxist economics; but that some aspects of the two approaches are antagonistic and, therefore, incompatible.

Professor Petit tell us that he is accused of eclecticism. Let me dwell upon the meaning of the word eclecticism. The consideration of a vast field of knowledge, including different schools of thought, and selection of ideas, looking for a new synthesis, is good eclecticism. I try to be eclectic in this sense. But putting together ideas of different schools of thought that are sometimes incompatible, without making a new synthesis, that is bad eclecticism.

Let me illustrate with a point where it seems to me that Professor Petit is making bad eclecticism. In the third paragraph of section 1, he says that the neoclassical income distribution theory and the Marxist theory (including the concepts of labour value and exploitation) are both useful. I agree that the marginal approach is useful in determining the most profitable level of fertilizer per acre of some crop or, remembering Von Thünen's contribution, the most profitable quantity of labour to harvest a potato field. But I do not consider these to be questions of political economics. These are praxiological problems. When one comes to the macro economic problems of the functional distribution of income, I think that the Marxist approach and the neoclassical approach using the aggregated production function are absolutely incompatible. After the so-called Cambridge controversy on the theory of capital, one does not need to be a Marxist to disagree with the aggregated production function approach to explain income distribution. In my opinion, the "usefulness" of this approach is as an ideological defence of the capitalist system, intending to show that the functional distribution of income is technically determined.

I agree with Professor Petit when he stresses the unity of the social sciences. I agree also that one has something to learn from both the neoclassical and the Marxist approaches. But frequently, when the two approaches seem to be complementary, they are really considering different problems that should be considered as parts of distinct, even if related, scientific disciplines. I have in mind the distinction between praxiology, the science of rational behaviour, and political economics, as was stressed by Oskar Lange. The frequent reference to Robinson Crusoe in neoclassical textbooks shows that what is being considered is *not* a *social* science.

I agree with Professor Petit in his main.thesis that "even to non-Marxists wanting to understand the world, Marx has something important to offer". But in many important aspects, it is clear that the Marxist and the neoclassical approaches are antagonistic and that, in order to be coherent, one has to adopt one *or* the other.

GENERAL DISCUSSION – RAPPORTEUR: CLARK EDWARDS

In the discussion it was felt that we did not need to seek a synthesis between Marxism and neoclassical economics, as suggested by the opener. Michel Petit was being objective about a subjective topic – he provided a basis for truth seeking and problem solving without dogmatism. The conclusion that those in non-Marxist countries can benefit from an understanding of Marxism which was reached by Petit, was a reasonable one. Some theories, such as the theory of dependence which was introduced into Latin America during the 1950s, may be considered Marxist. However, they have been proposed by economists who had probably not read Marx and who certainly were not Marxist. The different theories complement each other.

Marxism was derived from classical economics and, as noted by Petit, has many parallels with neoclassical economics. From a theoretical viewpoint, Marxism and neoclassical theory are very much the same, but from a political viewpoint they are quite different.

Marxism has also made interesting contributions to Keynesian macro economics. Keynes referred to Marx's theory of money in which Marx controverted the classical proportion, known as Say's Law, that supply creates its own demand. Marx explained how hoarding (saving to Keynes) reduces aggregate demand and leads to an economic crisis. Marx indicated that the focus shifts from hoarding to bank reserves as a country reaches a higher stage of growth. In neoclassical economics the role of money is sterile, in that a change in the money supply will not affect real flows of commodities or relative prices. For both Marx and Keynes, the quantity of money can influence aggregate income, output, employment, and the price level.

In reply, Professor Petit concluded that we need to understand both Marxist and neoclassical theories. They have much in common, they illuminate each other, and they focus on different problems.

Participants in the discussion included James R. Simpson, Alberto Valdes, Victor Nazarenko, and Clark Edwards.

TAMÁS I. FÉNYES*

Potential Applicability of Certain Socialistic Farming Practices for Rural Development in Non-Socialist Less Developed Countries

1 INTRODUCTION

There is no satisfactory theory of rural change for the LDCs.[1] The common element of all theoretical approaches is that they represent partial constructions which analyse a limited aspect of the possible causes for poverty and the possibilities for improvement in the less developed world. Integration of these partial theories into a general theory of development has not yet been accomplished; prospects for such integration are also not promising because of widespread differences among different countries and among regions within a country.

The theoretician of change needs to make detailed examinations over time of an adequate sample of societies (Mcloughlin 1970:10). Byerlee and Eicher (1972) state that: "Until better theory can be developed and more solid micro-level data collected, economists are limited in advising policy makers on problems of employment in rural areas". Collinson (1973) in reference to macro-planners, says that "their experience during the 1960s has created an awareness that development plans are missing a link with the dominant type of production unit in agriculture, the small-holder".

Smallholdings are generally too small to generate incomes above the poverty line. According to World Bank statistics (1975) about 80 million smallholdings in Asia, Africa and Latin America have less than two hectares of land each. Most of these smallholdings are used for traditional low-yielding subsistence production.

In spite of the differences among less developed areas of the world,[2] it is possible to investigate methods intended to reduce poverty and consequently increase production and raise productivity.

The main aim of this paper – within its limited scope – is to recognize the objectives of the different theories or approaches of agrarian change.[3] I propose, however, to concentrate more on methods of agricultural production, especially on the potential applicability of socialistic farming

* The author acknowledges useful comments by Professor J.A. Groenewald of the University of Pretoria.

659

practices[4] in non-socialistic countries.

The inclusion of socialistic farming practices may well fit into the "unimodal" strategy advocated by Johnston as well as into the "unified" approach[5] especially in two respects: Firstly, widespread participation of the rural population in a progressive modernization process and secondly, understanding that development strategy must rely on the interdependence of social progress and raising production.[6]

Inclusion of socialistic farming practices into development efforts of non-socialistic countries may be an important element in comprehensive rural development.

2 CAPITALIST VERSUS SOCIALIST AGRICULTURE

The less developed nations of the world, mostly with dualistic economies, who want to modernize agriculture and obtain rural change including continuous raises in living standards of the rural population have to choose between:

(a) establishing state farms and/or projects;
(b) organizing collective farms with various degrees of co-operative practices;
(c) encouraging capitalistic farming practices by the more enterprising members of the farming community; and
(d) finding a suitable combination of (a), (b) and (c), so as to use the advantages of each system without destroying those aspects of the social structure which do not necessarily hamper the development process.

The well known advantages of the free enterprise system based on private ownership of land and other means of production, such as security of tenure, competition, which leads to innovations etc., may contribute to higher production, more investment, larger exports and price stability.

By creating incentives for maximum individual growth and a favourable climate for private investment, rapid progress has been achieved in some countries, mostly in the developed world. In general this has not happened in LDCs copying the capitalistic model. Although their average agricultural production has increased by 3 per cent per year over the past two or three decades, there was very little alleviation of the general poverty and in some cases the situation worsened.

With regard to socialistic practices it is said that "the worst enemy of socialism is bad economic performance" (Svendsen, 1967). There is certainly a lot of truth in this statement, but with the shift from the growth-oriented policies to the approach of aggregate growth as a social objective it is perhaps necessary to have a fresh look at the possible combination of private, state and collective farming practices for the purpose of integrated rural development.

Possibly because of accepted ideology, many countries favour only the

Left or the Right. Every developing country obviously must find its own solution to its specific problems in the light of its political, social and economic circumstances.

The switch from capitalistic to socialistic farming practices is generally associated with changes in government, redistributive land reform and a decrease in production for at least some time.

My concern here is the possibility of introducing socialistic farming practices without such drastic changes; in other words a "peaceful co-existence"[7] of the state, collective and private agricultural sector within a basically capitalistic LDC. This diversification of systems may have certain advantages:

1   a healthy competition may develop between the more progressive individual farmers who have chosen the capitalistic way;
2   competition may also develop between the state and collective agricultural sectors; and
3   a competititon may be generated between the private and non-private sectors.

Thus a platform can be created where, with the assistance and protection of the government (especially regarding general economic policy, consolidation of holdings, creation of infrastructure, communication facilities, marketing of products etc.) the rural population itself could decide which system is more desired and must ultimately be followed.

Pure capitalistic exercises have often provided a large measure of agricultural growth and individual freedom, but also greater inequality.

Socialistic China entered the field of development as a latecomer "ignoring the accepted beliefs of western development experts and the most sober tenets of orthodox marxism" (Ward 78:XI) and achieved rural change in a relatively short time.

The applicability of socialistic farming practices will depend on the specific needs and problems of particular countries, especially on the willingness of privileged classes to share welfare with the rural poor and on the willingness of governments to assist in meeting the basic needs of the entire population. The highly successful performance of Israeli kibbutzim can obviously not be obtained in countries with a social organization not fitted to the kibbutz structure.

3   A FRAMEWORK FOR RURAL DEVELOPMENT

Aziz (1978:99–104) identified five key elements for long run rural development:

1   more equitable distribution of land and other rural resources in order to provide greater opportunities to the poorest segments of the rural population to meet their minimum needs;
2   organization of farming and other related activities, including land and water development on a collective or co-operative basis so as to

achieve a fuller utilization of available physical and human
resources and a more equitable distribution of future income;

3   diversification of the rural economy within agriculture, including
small and medium scale agro-based industries to expand employment opportunities and income generation, and thus to improve the
pattern of rural life;

4   an active policy of social development through the expansion of
social services and the improvement of social relations;

5   political and administrative capacity for the planning and
implementation of this strategy, to provide linkages with the rest of
the economy and protect legitimate interests of the rural population.

An intimate knowledge of the whole rural system is a prerequisite for the
successful implementation of such a long term development framework.[8]
Therefore it is necessary to undertake micro-level surveys and studies
concerning:

1   agricultural potential, including growth potential;

2   farm income surveys (also to monitor projects already in operation,
to compare estimates with factual results);

3   farm classification surveys (crops, livestock, mixed etc);

4   detailed studies of the family farm as an economic unit, including
acceptability research.

Acceptability surveys and such studies may serve as useful aids to determine immediate minimum needs for the improvement of rural life and
also to determine the prospective areas for introducing socialistic farming
practices.

Mosher's classification (1971) of rural areas into:

1   areas of immediate growth potential;

2   future growth potential areas; and

3   low growth potential areas

can serve as a guide for priorities and suitability of different systems –
private, collective or state – of agricultural production, especially when it
is combined with socio-political aspects of the development process.

Detailed studies of family smallholdings may indicate specific problems, attitudes and preferences of individual farmers – the most important production unit in less developed agriculture.

4   METHODS OF INCORPORATING SOCIALISTIC FARMING
PRACTICES

Introduction of a socialistic agricultural sector is usually accompanied by
mass collectivization and nationalization with the concommitant destruction of social structure without the guarantee of increased production and
a happier life for a long time.

The most prominent exception in this regard is Israel's co-operative settlements.

In view of the socio-economic conditions in rural Africa, Frank (1968) regards the Moshav Ovdim formula as potentially the best pattern of land settlement for inducing and accelerating rural progress because it may lead to:

(a) an increase in the productivity of land and labour; and
(b) an increase in the ratio of earners as a result of the reduction of disguised unemployment, the creation of new fields of occupation, and rational organization measures.

The establishment and incorporation of such a kind of settlement must be considered not only from the view point of the technical and economic potentialities which it offers, but rather in the first instance from its acceptability by the rural society concerned.

Nationalization and collectivization are generally realized only after a change in government. In Africa, with its traditional land tenure systems, that kind of "painful" land reform is not necessary and often not successful.

Traditional communal land tenure systems of Africa may render redistributive arrangements unnecessary, whilst at the same time tipping scales in favour of voluntary socialist forms even in a non-socialist political environment, even though usufructuary land tenure systems are not without their own limitations.

The Ujamaa approach was for instance initially an expression of the characteristic social relationships, existing in the extended family groups of many traditional African societies. It includes the basic principles of:

(a) equality, mutual respect and love;
(b) a common obligation to work; and
(c) collective control of capital goods and land.

It is still too early to judge the ultimate results of the Ujamaa strategy; the fact that it is based on principles of co-operation and socialism in the traditional African society may however offer interesting solutions towards the emerging new structures of collective agricultural production, decision-making, control and finally towards more egalitarian rural development approaches.

One of the greatest obstacles to the introduction of socialistic farming is the fact that, as a rule, an owner of land is not willing to give up his right to land even if he can be convinced that essential economic advantages would ensue (Schiller 1969 p. 28). This problem does not pertain to large parts of Africa partly because of the traditional pattern of group ownership and communal rights. The great disparities in connection with the distribution of land in Latin America, Asia and the Middle East require however, attention with regard to land reform. The question is more likely to be which type of land reform will serve the particular needs of specific countries. While pressure on the land is increasing and the average man–land ratio is worsening, it appears that land reforms intended to redistribute land more equally do not necessarily lead to the desired long term solution (Warriner, 1964). Economical farm units distributed among progressive prospective farmers may soon become uneconomic units.[9]

On the other hand experience of socialist countries clearly shows that certain – mainly labour intensive – branches of agricultural production are difficult to manage under large scale socialist methods. Formation of collective or co-operative farms and state farms for large scale production and the granting of household plots for private labour intensive production – as it is generally practised by socialist countries[10] – seems to be an alternative solution which should be considered.

Formation of co-operative and collective farms must proceed voluntarily and the establishment of state farms or projects through the buying up (by the government) of large estates coming up for sale. The overcoming of political, institutional and technological obstacles requires careful planning and preparation, forming part of the overall strategy of economic development, and conducted in a national economic basis.

Experience in many parts of the underdeveloped world has shown that the furtherance of capitalistic farming practices by a limited number of progressive farmers, government or internationally sponsored agricultural development projects has a very limited impact on the well being of the rural population as a whole.

Nevertheless a number of intermediate or partial solutions may contribute in opening ways for the adoption of a comprehensive strategy or rural development.

A viable model of rural development must necessarily take into account the specific political and social circumstances in the country concerned.

The alternative programmes may include:

1   *Small farmer co-operatives*
The degree of co-operative practices will vary according to the specific needs of the rural community; the ownership of land may either remain private or become communal but the land must be physically pooled for purposes of cultivation. The development of collective farming – the USSR and other European countries from artel, machine and tractor stations to the Kolkhoz – may provide valuable examples for the planners. As a starting point the establishment of service co-operatives seems to be the easiest for most countries.

2   *Private ownership with state management*
(a) The emphasis here is on a high degree of management provided by the state. It is a specially suitable approach for newly reclaimed land. After the initial stage of the application it could be converted into a co-operative enterprise;

(b) Co-operative or communal ownership with private management.
Good examples of this way of combining group ownership with private management can be found in South Africa where private individuals and

companies offer valuable management and consultative services to African small farmers.

There are various methods of approach for such project development (Fényes and Groenewald 1977:5):

on a consultation basis where the government provides the funds and a company handles the management;

on an agency basis where a company also contributes part of the funds and therefore also shares in the profits to recover capital invested, after which the agent may sell his part to local inhabitants;

a public company may be formed in which all shareholders make a contribution to development and all of them share on a pro rata basis in the profit.

Further considerations in this connection may, for example be:

a co-operative unit perhaps on a small group or extended family basis; or

a company in which a certain amount of the shares are held by permanent workers.

3   State projects

Various state or state sponsored projects with or without foreign aid is undertaken in many parts of the world. Mainly capital and managerial intensive projects such as irrigation schemes with the inclusion of the rural people as employees and not farmers can result in high production (De Villiers 1978:8).

The ultimate success of project farming depends mainly on the degree of participation of the local community and on the demonstration effect.

Lele (1975) in summarizing the experiences gained from 18 rural development projects in Africa gives a rather gloomy picture of the possibilities of raising the productivity of the rural poor and integrating the low income groups into processes of planned development. Most of these projects did however have some positive effects, although smaller than desired.

The sources of the relative failures are traced to one-sided economic growth targets in earlier periods at the expense of income distribution, in the limited technical know-how available during the first development decade, in a lack of appreciation of socio-institutional problems and the scarcity of qualified staff resulting in planning inefficiencies.

4   Other alternatives

There are various other alternatives for rural development such as special packages for target groups (World Bank 1975), area development projects, rural works programmes for the landless, representing mainly partial solutions and usually less socialistic by nature and therefore only by implication relevant for the purpose of this paper.

5   THE QUESTION OF FARM MANAGEMENT

According to some writers (Hartzenberg 1977:75, Little 1964) the most important limiting factor amongst the many causes of underdevelopment lies in the human being and its limited managerial ability.

The concept of farm management and its practical implementation needs modification as far as the smallholders of the LDCs are concerned (Fényes 1979:33). Individual farm management advice is too expensive when the opportunity costs of qualified management advisers are taken into account. Without drastic changes to the system and with the assumption that the education-oriented farm management approach is applied, it appears that there are two areas in particular, where the general management approach in a modified form can be usefully applied in the smallholder agriculture, namely:

1   An intensive group management or representative management approach, where acceptability research, family and way of life, education and the non-farm use of resources should receive more attention than is the case in the developed sector; and
2   an improved information system through the media, published works and extension services (Fényes 1979:34).

Here again the incorporation of socialistic farming practices possibly will contribute substantially to the objectives of improved management under conditions of less development.

6   THE ROLE OF AGRICULTURAL ECONOMISTS IN THE PROCESS OF RURAL CHANGE

With the development of new (partial) theories and approaches of agricultural and rural development and especially with the recognition of the multidisciplinary nature of our task, agricultural economists should play a vital role in the development of LD areas.

The actual tasks will depend on specific circumstances but will probably include (Campbell 1975:53):

1   teaching at various levels;
2   undertaking research relating to development in a multidisciplinary base, namely with the co-operation of other disciplines like geography, political science, anthropology, sociology etc.;
3   providing expertize as a member of an aid mission or technical assistance programme;
4   actual service with the government or parastatals.

The main shift in attitude to tackle our "new" challenge probably will include to give the subject a more "human face" by incorporating sociological aspects, continuously investigating the acceptability or our proposals and the recognition of the fact that agricultural growth is only one (although still important) factor and as a sole measure cannot change the general picture of rural poverty.

7 CONCLUSIONS

The search for comprehensive rural development theories and strategies must start with the recognition of the fact that a development strategy that aims at creating a consumer society on the western model is neither feasible nor desirable. As Aziz (78:XV) said "the main focus must be on meeting the basic needs of the entire population rather than on providing western levels of consumption to a privileged minority".

History has already proved that socialistic farming practices have a better potential of inducing rural progress in LDCs than capitalistic practices. The question is how to implement socialistic farming practices into non-socialist less developed countries.

A distinction must be made between countries with antagonistic differences between the owners of the land and the rural poor and African countries with their traditional communal tenures which may foster desirable ideals of mutual help and provide social security. This could offer a foundation for modern co-operative agriculture.

In either case careful macro and micro level studies, including acceptability research are prerequisites for implementation.

Socialist practices must be introduced on a voluntary basis. Where land reform is necessary, the owners must, as far as possible, be compensated both for the reason of humanity and to avoid disruption. Private practices, in reasonable scale, must however be allowed. Another important point in favour of socialistic farming practices is the applicability of high standard management, educational and welfare programmes for the rural population at large.

NOTES

[1] A survey of development theories is presented by Bonnet and Reichelt, (1972, pp. 23–9).

[2] A useful description of the contrasts and similarities of Asia and Africa is to be found in Hunter (1969).

[3] e.g. Clifton Wharton's triple stage system, the "Stage" theories of Perkins-Witt, Johnston-Mellor, Hill-Mosher, the minimum package approach, the comprehensive approach and the sector and other special programmes. Hayami and Ruttan's "induced" development model, and Johnston's distinction between "unimodal" and "biomodal" strategies.

[4] For the purpose of this paper socialistic farming practices are defined as state and co-operative agricultural enterprises where land and other means of production are owned by the state or owned collectively and the production–distribution process is performed on a collective basis.

[5] See Resolution No. 2681 (XXV) passed by the UN General Assembly 1970.12.11.

[6] In social progress one may include amongst other elements motivation for higher commercial production, a sense of general progress and in this respect social progress can be

regarded as a pre-condition for raising production in at least certain parts of the LD world.

[7] There are many examples of this co-existence in different parts of the world for example in Poland, Israel, Yugoslavia, the Punjab in India, and in a lesser extent the household plots allocated to collective farm members and state farm employees in the socialist countries.

[8] Wright (1972) concludes that environmental information needed for development planning is grossly inadequate. Proposed detailed studies oriented towards systems analysis of biophysical processes governing productivity must include investigations into farming practices and socio-economic factors.

[9] The average availability of arable land per caput of agricultural population in developing countries is far less than one hectare.

[10] The existence of household plots seems to be permanent in most socialistic countries. The household plot assisted small farmers during the transitory period, straight after their entry into the collective, making it easier to adjust their working and living habits, allow members another source of income and tying down an over-supply of labour. In addition state farms and co-operatives did not supply agricultural produce in sufficient variety, quality and of enough quantity for domestic consumption and exports but household plots did. This fact created an uneasy situation for Marxist policy makers believing in the elimination of all sorts of private small scale production.. They argued that this situation would disturb the socialist evolution of property and production relations in agriculture. At one stage for instance the household plots were totally abolished in Bulgaria, but this measure was not successful and in the first half of 1976 a broad campaign was conducted in Hungary favouring surviving small scale agricultural production that had been attacked so much earlier (Lázár 1976:72). This changing attitude represents the realization that the existence of small scale production in socialist countries is not only possible but extremely advantageous.

REFERENCES

Aziz, Sartaj (1978) *Rural Development – Learning from China*, The Macmillan Company, London.

Bohnet, M. and Reichelt, H. (1972) "Applied Research and its Impact on Economic Development: the East African Case", IFO–Instituut für Wirtschaftforschung, München, Afrika-Studien 70, Weltforum-Verlag GMBH.

Byerlee D. and Eicher, C.K. (1972) "African Rural Employment Study", Paper No. 1, Rural Employment Migration and Economic Development, Michigan State University.

Campbell, D.R. (1975) "The role of agricultural economists in the development process", *Canadian Journal of Agricultural Economics* 1975, CAES Annual Meeting Proceedings.

Collinson, M.P. (1973) "Transferring technology to developing economies: the example of applying farm management economics in African Agriculture", European Regional Conference Oxford.

De Villiers, A. (1978) "A new approach for the planning and development of smallholder irrigation schemes in the Black States of South Africa", *Agrekon*, Vol. 17, No. 4.

Fényes, T.I. (1979) "Planning of a farm management programme for traditional agriculture", *South African Journal of Agricultural Economics*, Vol. 1, No. 1.

Fényes, T.I. and Groenewald, J.A. (1977) "Socialistic Enterprise Forms in Agriculture VII: Potential application in Agriculture in Africa", *Agrekon*, Vol. 16, No. 3.

Frank, Michael (1978) *Co-operative land settlements in Israel and their relevance to African countries*, Kyklos-Verlag, Basel.

Hunter, Guy (1969) *Modernizing Peasant Societies. A comparative study in Asia and Africa*, Oxford University Press, New York 1969.

Lázár, I. (1976) "Collective farm and private plot", *The New Hungarian Quarterly*, Vol. XVII, No. 63, Kossuth Printing House, Budapest.

Lele, Uma (1975) *The Design of Rural Development. Lessons from Africa*, John Hopkins Press, Baltimore 1975.

Little, T.M.D. (1964) "Aid to Africa", Overseas Development Institute.

McLoughlin, P.F.M. (ed.) (1970) *African Food Production Systems. Cases and theory*, The John Hopkins Press, Baltimore.

Mosher, A.T. (1971) "To Create a Modern Agriculture", Overseas Development Council, New York.

Svendsen, Knud Erik (1967) "Socialist Problems after the Urusha Declaration", paper read to interdisciplinary seminar Dar Es Salaam; University College (mimco).

Ward, B. (1978) in Foreword for Aziz, S. *Rural Development Learning from China*, The Macmillan Press Ltd., London.

Warriner, Doreen (1964) "Land Reform and Economic Development", in Eicher, Carl K. and Witt, Lawrence W. (eds), *Agriculture in Economic Development*, McGraw Hill Book Company, New York.

World Bank (1973) Land reform sector policy paper.

World Bank (1975) Rural Development Sector Policy Paper, 1975.

Wright, R.L. (1972) "Some perspective in environmental research for agricultural land-use planning in developing countries", Geogorum 10/72.

DISCUSSION OPENING – YEN TIEN CHANG

I feel greatly honoured by being invited to open the discussion of Dr Fényes' paper. Dr Fényes' paper is a well presented work, and is surely one of the masterpieces among the papers at the XVII Conference. As the title of the paper signifies, it is an inquiry into the applicability of socialistic farming practices for rural development in non-socialist less developed countries. It is also, in a sense, an inquiry into the causes of poverty in the less developed world. The main aim of this paper, as stated by the author, is to recognize the objectives of different theories or approaches of agrarian change. The background of this paper is obviously the less developed world, especially African countries.

In the short time available I wish to raise some questions and to make a few remarks on the key points of the paper.

In the first place, there are no clear definitions or delineation of the scope of socialistic farming practices. It is, therefore, difficult for us to discuss the social conditions and co-ordinating measures needed for the introduction of socialistic farming practices in the non-socialist, less developed countries.

Secondly, I doubt that socialistic practices could be in "peaceful co-existence" with state, collective and private farming practices within a capitalistic less developed country. And I want to emphasize the point, as the author mentioned, that the switch from capitalistic to socialistic farming practices is associated with changes in government, redistribution of land and a decrease in production for at least some time; and, that the introduction of socialism usually results in mass collectivization and nationalization with the concomitant destruction of social structure, without the guarantee of increased production and a happier life for a long time. Then, why should we make such a switch? It is a dilemma we have to face.

Thirdly, from the social and psychological aspects, one often finds that the great obstacle to the introduction of socialistic farming is the fact that an owner of land is not willing to give up his right to land even if he can be convinced that essential advantages would follow. This is the case the world over, not only in Africa. It is true that every developing country must find its own solution to its specific problems. There is no panacea for all diseases! And not necessarily every developing country has to introduce socialistic farming practices into its own farming system.

Fourthly, one of the acceptable programmes for rural development is the co-operative system for small farmers. The ownership of land may remain private, but land must be physically pooled for cultivation, so as to enlarge the farm to an efficient size.

In Taiwan we developed an alternative for rural development for small farmers, the "joint operation", which is a programme for small farmers to enlarge their farms to an efficient size. The ownership of land of the small farmers who join the "joint operation" programme remains private; but their land must be pooled together, wiping out all the plot boundaries to facilitate farm machine operation. The "joint operation" farms are usually composed of 10 to 20 hectares and include 30 to 50 small farmers.

Finally, in concluding my comments, I would like to say a few words about the important role played by agricultural economists in the process of rural development. In addition to the four responsibilities listed by the author, there is one thing I want to emphasize for agricultural economists, that is, the abolition of the poverty of the less developed world. Poverty is closely connected with hunger, and hunger is a result of inadequate supply of food. As pointed out by Dr Ojala, in his Kellogg Foundation lecture, millions more people will have to die of hunger or hunger-induced disease, and some 500 million agricultural producers live in absolute or relative poverty. In this connection, agricultural economists should make every effort to promote agricultural growth, so as to increase food production to free the rural poor of the underdeveloped world from hunger. This is the challenge the agricultural economists have to meet and the role they have to play.

GENERAL DISCUSSION – RAPPORTEUR: C. PEMBERTON

In the general discussion one speaker felt that he could not come to the same conclusions as the author, who had stated that the development of collective farming in the USSR and other Eastern European countries from the artel, machine and tractor stations to the Kolkhoz could provide valuable examples for planners; but these were not good examples. Nowhere in East Europe was the change to socialist farming voluntary. Such change was only possible under particular political and economic powers of a group of leaders. No developing country had a similar type of situation. Collaboration in agricultural development existed and if the traditions of each country were used to help them to develop these traditions along modern forms, their efforts may be more successful.

It was also felt that the extended family has declined in actual economic significance in much of Africa. Also that where farming systems are comparatively simple, the variations in production and efficiency amongst individual simple families are very wide. Does not this limit the practical possibilities of voluntary communal farming?

In reply first to the opener, Dr Fényes stated that with respect to Dr Chang's comment on the definition of socialist farming practices, this definition was given in Note 4 of the paper.

As to the question of whether socialist farming practices can co-exist peacefully with private farming, Note 7 of the paper provided several examples of co-existence in both socialist and capitalist countries, e.g. Poland and Yugoslavia and Israel and India. Poland and Yugoslavia present interesting situations, since in these socialist countries over 70 per cent of agricultural land is in private ownership. He had little details on the situation in India, but Israel is certainly capitalistic and the kibbutzim is usually considered to be a socialist farming practice, and there is peaceful co-existence there.

Regarding the general discussion, he believed that the experience of socialist countries may provide examples to developing countries because the socialists made mistakes which developing countries can benefit from. For example, he had mentioned Bulgaria which abolished household plots and then allowed them to return. The fact that the introduction of socialist farming in East Europe was non-voluntary was well known. The main concern however is that socialist farming in these countries has eliminated rural poverty, has provided fixed incomes and social security to farmers and, along with their medical schemes, has meant that these countries are away ahead in the developing world.

His experience with the extended family system was mainly in northern South Africa, Lesotho, Botswana and Zimbabwe Rhodesia.

Participants in the discussion included Eberhard J. Schinke and John R. Raeburn.

YAIR MUNDLAK*

Agricultural Growth – Formulation, Evaluation and Policy Consequences

INTRODUCTION

Most of the world's population still lives in countries that are largely rural, and the development of such countries is of general interest. The development of a rural economy is largely related to the development of its agricultural sector. The agricultural sector is not isolated; it is interdependent with the rest of the economy through the factor and product markets, and changes in such markets affect all major sources. This interdependence must be taken into account when important policy questions and measures are considered and evaluated. Specifically, the effects of changes in resource endowment and in supply of final or intermediate products (for instance, due to foreign aid) cannot be limited to one sector, and the feedback cannot be ignored. That, of course, also holds true with respect to price policies, changes in technologies, and any other important measures.

In order to be able to assess the consequences of development policies, it is necessary to understand the process of growth. The distinction between the two concepts is made here in order to emphasize that the concept of development implies some intervention in the process of economic growth. Intervention is generally motivated by the desire to achieve targets, such as higher rates of growth or improvement in the distribution of income or consumption, and it will result in altering the process of growth. A full understanding of these results requires evaluating them within a dynamic framework which allows comparison of the growth paths that will occur under different intervention measures in any given economy.

There are various models that deal with sectoral growth in the context of general equilibrium. However, much of the discussion on economic growth is inspired by stylized facts. The casual observer can easily discover that while the style has remained fairly constant over a long period of time, the facts vary greatly over time and space. Thus, it is suggested that more insight can be gained by concentrating on the facts. This is the

* I am indebted to George M. Kuznets for commenting on an earlier draft.

theme of the approach discussed in this paper. We start by stating the current views on the sources of growth and thereby establish two points. First, that capital accumulation may be more prominent in growth generation than is usually considered and second that improving resource allocation may contribute greatly to growth, as explained in the section devoted to that subject. Intersectoral factor mobility is given analytical prominence as an essential element in the construction of a proper growth model. The various components of this analysis are then drawn together to sketch the framework guiding the research centered at IFPRI. The whole subject of growth is sometimes viewed ambivalently by researchers and policy makers. Some reflections on this point conclude the paper.

SOURCES OF GROWTH AND SOME IMPLICATIONS

An increase in output per caput is achieved by an increase in the ratio of resources to population and by improving the resource utilization. At present, in most countries, aside from population, the resources that are accumulated are aggregated into one variable, capital. There are different forms of capital and in various discussions it is useful to distinguish between some forms and particularly between physical and human capital. However, the common feature of the various forms of capital is that they are financed by sacrificing present consumption and consequently the value of capital formation in any year is simply the value of the sacrificed consumption. The relevance of this basic point will become clear below.

The improvement in the utilization of resources is referred to as technical change. As with capital, there are various forms of technical change. For some purposes they can be aggregated. A common form of aggregation is to consider the marginal affect of technical change on output which leads to the measurement of technical change as a residual.[1]

One of the most important subjects related to our understanding of economic growth is the quantification of the contribution of the two sources, capital accumulation and technical change, to economic growth. Such a quantification may be viewed as an empirical question, but not a very simple one. If the two components are assumed to be independent, it turns out that the direct contribution of capital accumulation to growth is small relative to that of the residual technical change.[2] Taking it at face value, this result is somewhat unsatisfactory for it does not explain why some countries and some periods are blessed with a large residual technical change whereas others are not. It is more tempting to disaggregate the residual technical change to some postulated sources. This is basically the position taken by writers like Jorgenson and Griliches (1967), and Dennison (1974). One postulated source is the improvement in the qualities of inputs. Improvement in the quality of labour is attributed largely to an increase in the amount of human capital embedded in labour. Human capital is generated by schooling, training, health etc.[3]

The works of Schultz (1960, 1961) and Becker (1962), established the prominence of education in the production of human capital. Once variables that contribute to productivity, such as education or research, are identified, they can be introduced explicitly into the production function. This was the approach of Griliches in his work on the Productivity Growth of US Agriculture. [Griliches, 1963, 1964]. The introduction of such variables into the production functions indicate that they are important and as such, they provide an explanation for sources of growth. In as much as this identification of source of growth is important, it should be emphasized that increasing the level of these variables requires resources. This is basically suggested in the name "human capital". Consequently, the degree to which these sources of growth can be exploited by any given country is limited by the amount of savings which the country can generate, domestically and from abroad.

It may be useful to elaborate further on this point. The technology available to the economy at any given point in time consists of a distribution of techniques which, among other things vary in their capital intensities.[4] It is possible that more than one technique can be employed simultaneously. As the overall capital labour ratio in the economy increases there is a shift from the low to the high capital–labour techniques.[5] This intuitive result has very far reaching implications. It is applicable to human capital as well as to physical capital and it is applicable in both ways. Not only that accumulation results in capital intensive activities but also further use of capital (human and physical) intensive activities requires capital accumulation. Thus it is not sufficient to list for a country the portfolio of promising investments. The country should have the means for the implementation of this portfolio. To make the argument more concrete, reference can be made to the green revolution where the planting of the high yielding varieties had to be combined with other inputs as well as knowledge generated in schools, by extension service and by experiment stations. All these have somehow to be financed.

Another source of growth is the interindustry shift of resources (Kuznets, 1946). Such a shift results from a decision by firms and individuals. As it constitutes an important element of our discussion, we devote the next section to a discussion of some aspects of the micro foundations of resource allocation.

ALLOCATION OF RESOURCES

Competitive conditions require that the prices of a homogeneous factor be equal in all alternative uses. In most economies agricultural wages are lower than non-agricultural wages and therefore a competitive condition is violated. The phenomenon is not transitory; it endures for a long period of time, which can be measured in terms of decades and centuries. However, eventually the gap in sectoral wages diminishes and finally it disappears. Two implications can be drawn from this observation: (1) There are forces in the economy that act in the direction of equating factor prices; (2) The process of resource allocation requires real time. The fact that a response to market prices may not be immediate and requires time for completion is not new and it constitutes the corner stone of distributed lag analysis.

In general, economic analysis of resource allocation which allows for lagged response to economic stimuli treats the time pattern of the response as exogenous to the economic system. Such a treatment has no justification; it may be misleading in that it distorts our views with respect to the operation of the economic system. The very same considerations that have led to the introduction of lagged response can also be used to argue that the path of resource allocation is an endogenous variable, that is a variable whose value at any time is determined within the economic system. This position is taken here with respect to the formulation of the agricultural growth model. However, it is also relevant for the study of the various attributes of the product supply and factor demand at lower levels of aggregation, such as firms or industries.[6]

Generally, models of distributed lags assume that a response of the economic units to a change in the exogenous variables is completed within several periods (usually years). The speed of the response is represented by the coefficient of adjustment. The coefficient of adjustment is given exogenously and the economic analysis becomes largely an interesting statistical exercise in estimation. This observation applies to models assuming constant as well as variable coefficients of adjustment. The latter are determined by fitting a flexible polynomial scheme to the data. It is done in order to capture complex response patterns that cannot be captured by a constant coeffient of adjustment models. However, it should be indicated that allowing for a more detailed description of the response path, when this path is endogenous, has its drawbacks. Different economic conditions may generate very different adjustment paths. An attempt to approximate one such path by another may result in considerable error. Yet, with a variety of technical procedures, some of which are very imaginative, this is essentially the practice in many of the empirical studies, dealing with resource allocation.

A different view on the matter was expressed in two articles dealing with the response of a competitive firm [Mundlak 1966, 1967]. This view can be put forward in a way that will serve the subsequent discussion. As Glenn Johnson emphasized [Johnson, 1956, 1958], at any given point in time the economic unit, firm or farm in our case, possesses various assets yielding positive quasi rents whose capitalized values are above the market prices of the assets. The firm therefore finds it profitable to continue using the assets. Quasi rents are derived from the services that those assets render in production. That means that the production plans of the firm are based on the utilization of such assets and the response of the firm to prices and to price variations depend on the level of such assets. The analysis is generalized directly to other commitments or contractual arrangements in which the firm is engaged. In short, the response of the firm is affected by some fixed factors and as such it is a short run response. Applying it to agriculture, and specifically to farm systems based on family labour, labour can be included among the fixed factors. We return to this problem below. Technically, what this means is that strictly speaking the level of the fixed factors should be included in the short run response functions. But since all economic observations are at best generated by short run equilibrium (rather than long run), it follows that the fixed variables should be included in all the response functions. The evaluation of the quasi rents of such contractual arrangements and consequently the changes that take place in their stocks depend on the firm's views or expectations with respect to the economic environment and specifically with respect to prices. As those change, changes take place in the level of the fixed inputs. It is then necessary to express the behavioural equations for the fixed factors in terms of the relevant prices and the level and nature of the existing commitments.

This approach leads to a recursive system describing the behaviour of the firm in terms of factor demand equations, each equation expressed in terms of the relevant prices and the factors of production which can be considered as fixed over the time domain pertinent to the particular decision. Specifically, when applied to investment, investment is not expressed as a function of outputs, as the flexible accelerator formulation suggests. Instead, it is expressed as a function of prices and rates of returns. This is the essence of the analysis. It deals with a competitive firm with decreasing returns to scale, for otherwise there is no profit maximization solution. The analysis is easily generalized to a non-competitive firm with constant returns to scale or to a competitive firm whose output is determined exogenously and whose domain is optimization is cost minimization.[7]

Before concluding this section it should be indicated that there is another topic which is pertinent to the discussion of resource allocation in agriculture and related empirical analysis. Economic analysis is based on the assumption of profit maximization by the firms. As much as profits are desired they need not be the only criterion for the firm's behaviour. Other considerations such as uncertainty, the leisure component of various activities are also taken into account. Thus it is possible to consider a utility function of the firm in which profits are one of the arguments but not the only one. The firm seeks to maximize utility rather than profits. The optimal solution depends on the utility function and it can be expected to be different from the profit maximization solution [Mundlak, 1971]. The solution of course depends on prices and its behaviour in prices is discussed elsewhere [Mundlak and Volcani, 1973]. Two conclusions of this analysis are pertinent for our discussion. First, under such formulation a consistent discrepancy can be found between the value marginal productivities and factor prices. Such discrepancies may vary among various activities. Second, other things being equal, the partial response of quantities to price variations should be of the same sign as that obtained under profit maximization.

INTERSECTORAL FACTOR MOBILITY

As indicated above, at any point in time there may be factor price differences in the economy. At the sectoral level, except for very mature economies, agricultural wages are lower than non-agricultural wages. Also differences may exist in the rates of return on capital. The direction of the differences in the rates of return is not necessarily the same as that of wages although it is usually believed to be so. Such a belief may serve as an explanation for the widely held idea that agriculture should finance growth. This idea has led to government intervention which has taken various forms in different countries.

Two questions immediately arise: first, why are there differences in factor prices and second what are their consequences. As we deal with a dynamic system, the reasons and the consequences are somewhat related. Wage differences are caused by a differential growth in the excess demand for labour in the two sectors. The demand for factors is derived from a demand for the final product which by itself is subject to differential growth. It is well known that the income elasticity of the agricultural product is less than unity, and therefore the income elasticity of the non-agricultural product is larger than unity. Consequently, the income effect of growth calls for a larger expansion of the non-agricultural sector.[8] In addition to the income effect there is also a price effect which tends to increase the relative price of the labour intensive product. That generates a substitution effect in demand which supplements the income effect on differential growth. It then emerges that there is an overall tendency for a faster development of the non-agricultural sector which affects the demand for labour. However, the demand for labour need not change at the same rate as that of the product demand. As capital accumulates there is a tendency for a substitution of capital for labour. That takes place in both sectors, which implies not only that agriculture expands at a lower rate, as compared to the other sector, but that its demand for labour expands at an even lower rate. If the natural rate of growth of the labour force (assuming a constant rate of participation) is the same in both sectors, we find that this process generates excess supply of labour in agriculture.

To the effect of capital accumulation on differential growth we have to add the effect of technical change. This is more complex in view of the various possibilities which exist. To simplify the exposition we assume that technical change is Hicks' neutral, and of equal rate, in both sectors. Under this assumption, only the income effect exists and it augments the effect of capital accumulation considered above.

The excess supply of agricultural labour generated by the process described above tends to press down agricultural wages while the excess demand in the non-agricultural sector tends to raise wages in that sector. This analysis can be further complicated in various ways but there is no need to do so for the purpose on hand. A similar analysis applies to the rates of return on capital, with only one exception: the accumulation of capital results in a decline in the rate of returns relative to wages and consequently in a factor substitution effect leading to an increase in the demand for capital in both sectors. However, the net effect depends also on the sectoral elasticities of substitution.

Unless the elasticity of substitution in agriculture is large relative to that of the non-agricultural sector, the factor substitution effect will not change the final conclusion of a tendency toward a faster growth in demand for capital in the non-agricultural sector. Whether or not this development leads to excess demand depends also on the generation of sectoral savings. The sectoral savings behaviour has not been sufficiently investigated. However, other things being equal, the permanent income hypothesis might suggest higher savings rates in agriculture since agricultural income is subject to wider fluctuations. This is also supported by some evidence. In any case, higher savings rates in agriculture are in line with the generation of excess supply of capital in agriculture.

In a comparatively static model economy excess supply is automatically corrected by a proper change in prices. Such a correction does not require any time since time does not appear in the analysis either explicitly or implicitly. This is a missing link that has to be added to a model which pretends to explain actual data. This is also what has to be done here in order to trace the consequences of factor price differences. The basic premise is that factors move from a sector of low returns to that of high returns. Thus, there is a continuous off farm migration which comes to a halt only when the wage gap properly measured, disappears. The time rate of migration is postulated to depend on the wage differential itself as well as on the relative size of the two sectors and some additional variables. The dependence of the migration on the wage differential and the size of the sectors makes migration, and thereby labour allocation, an endogenous variable within the system. The larger is the gap, the larger is the rate of migration. Such an approach was applied to cross country, to time series data for Japan and for Argentina.[9] The empirical analysis provides quantitative results for the coefficients in question, all in line with the expected direction. The implication of this approach is that the size of the sectoral labour force at any given point in time is equal to the labour force in the previous period plus the natural rate of growth less migration (migration being negative for the receiving sector).

A somewhat similar approach is taken with respect to capital, except that here only the new savings are allowed to move between sectors. For a closed economy without a government we define an inter-sectoral flow of savings which is equal to the difference between the savings generated within the sector and the investment in the sector. The flow of savings is assumed to depend on the ratio of the sectoral rates of returns.[10] Consequently, the change in the sectoral stock of capital is endogenous within the system. The question is how is such a system postulated to operate. This is taken up in the next section.

A FRAMEWORK FOR SECTORAL GROWTH

We have argued at some length that at any given point in time the intersectoral resource allocation in the economy is pretty much determined. This feature has to be incorporated into the model which should explain the behaviour of the system over time. Consequently, the supply conditions at any point in time are rather simple. The resource allocation and the technology determine the sectoral outputs. Outputs are distributed, in a closed economy without government, between consumption and investment. Demand equations for the final products and for the investment goods together with the fixed supplies determine the product price ratio for that period, simultaneously with the distribution of the various products among the various uses. Given the technology and sectoral resource allocation, factor shadow prices are determined and they in turn determine the flow of resources from a sector of low returns to a sector of high returns. The resource flow, together with population growth and capital accumulation, determine the availability of resources to the two sectors in the next period. Adding the effects of changes in technology, the outputs in the next period are determined and the process repeats itself.

The dynamics of the economy is formulated in terms of a period analysis. The length of the period is determined by a practical matter, by the period of national accounting, which is generally a year. The question is to what extent does the length of the period matter and, specifically, if the period were made very short, say a day, would the behaviour of the economy become closer to that of a competitive economy? The length of the period matters in the same way that it matters in distributed lag analysis [Mundlak, 1961b]. The shorter is the period of analysis, the lower is the rate of adjustment which in our case implies lower migration and flow rates. Thus as the period of analysis approaches zero, the limiting case of this economy diverges from the competitive economy. The economy approaches that of a competitive economy when the period of analysis becomes very long, say a century. But such an analysis, while it may be of interest to future historians, is of no present concern. However, it should be indicated that the higher are the rates of adjustment, the faster will the factor price gaps tend to disappear and therefore, it would require less time for the economy to converge to a competitive economy.

As the time path of the endogenous variables depends, among other things, on the rate of intersectoral factor allocation, the path itself is endogenous in the system. In order to compute the path, the system is expressed as difference equations and a solution is obtained for the various rates of growth in terms of the various parameters which are estimated empirically. The solutions are data specific and the growth scenarios depend on the initial values of the exogenous variables and the parameters.

This model was applied to the Japanese data [Mundlak, 1979]. The model is extended to cover foreign trade and the extended model is being fitted to Argentinian data. The model is further extended to include government and this version will be fitted to Mexican data.[11]

Fitting the model to the data implies a selection of values for the various parameters in question and then generating the time path of the various endogenous variables of interest. The computed time path is compared with the actual data. If the discrepancy is large, some values of the parameters are changed and the computation is repeated. Thus, the criterion is that of a good fit for several equations. The criterion could be made more rigid leading to an optimization technique. We have not gone this far yet since the main problem is that we allow for a change of parameters over time and none of the standard optimization techniques accommodates such a situation. The basic idea is that there is no need to assume that the parameters in question are constant throughout the period, as the standard econometric models do. Once we allow for variable parameters we face a very rich set of possibilities. This is an interesting problem by itself, but beyond the scope of the present discussion.

Once the model is fitted to the data, it is possible to raise various questions. The technical questions are clear. For instance, it is possible to examine the sensitivity of the fit to changes in the parameters and thereby gain a "feel" for the quality of the final estimates of the parameters used in the analysis. A different set of questions to be asked is that of "if–then" questions. That is, deriving scenarios under hypothetical conditions. Several such scenarios were derived with respect to the Japanese economy of which we mention one. It is customary to think that agriculture played an important role in the financing of Japanese economic growth. To examine this hypothesis, the growth of the Japanese economy was simulated under the constraint of no flow of savings from agriculture to the non-agricultural sector. The resulting growth path did not differ a great deal from the basic fit. Thus, the use of a complete model for testing the hypothesis does not support it. On the other hand, a similar computation with respect to labour migration indicates that if labour were not allowed to migrate from agriculture, the development of the economy would have been greatly affected. The calculations start with 1905. Such findings have far reaching policy implications. Specifically, one should question the use of government policies of taxing agriculture in order to finance the non-agricultural sector. We have quoted here only one aspect of this policy and there are other unfavourable aspects which augment the above implications. A recent criticism of such policies evaluated against the background of the Indian experiences were expressed by Mellor [Mellor, 1976].

Finally, the model can be used for examining the consequences of various policies. This is done by generating growth paths under the constraints imposed by the policies. One question that we have ignored thus far is the question of distribution. This question can be handled at various levels. At the technical level it can be easily incorporated into the model. It is also possible to trace the effect of various variables on distribution. Such a treatment is far too broad to be pursued here. However, there is a broader aspect to this issue that is related not only to economic analysis but also to economic policy which we overview in the next section.

SOME REFLECTIONS ON GROWTH AND DISTRIBUTION

The process of economic growth increases the sustained stream of output per caput of a country and thereby facilitates an expansion of consumption per caput. As such it should be viewed favourably, independently of the income level or distribution of the country. This is not always the case. Measures leading to growth are sometimes judged by their effects on distribution as some discussions of the consequences of the green revolution demonstrate. Such a discussion is naturally of interest and has some policy consequences. Yet, attempts to judge steps leading to economic growth solely or largely by their effect on distribution may be very costly in terms of both growth and distribution. This statement should be viewed within an historical perspective. High variance and skewed income distributions are at least as old as recorded history. On the other hand economic growth is a relatively recent phenomenon.[12] It immediately follows that inequality of income distribution cannot be attributed to economic growth, nor for that matter can it be said that inequality necessarily leads to growth.

One may puzzle why the discussion on distribution has been linked to that of growth. Two possibilities come immediately to mind. First, growth expands income, and perhaps it is implicitly assumed that it is easier to affect the distribution of new income than that of existing income. Second, the increasing interest of international agencies that have the ability to affect domestic policies and to link their own views of desirable distribution to the economic assistance that they offer. Also, there is some convenience in assuming that poverty should be largely alleviated through the redistribution of new income since it diverts attention from the consideration of redistribution of the present wealth or income flow. Poverty exists in many countries whose average income can be considered to be above subsistence. If a high premium is placed on the elimination of poverty, through redistribution, there is no need to wait for economic growth to take place.

The purpose of bringing this argument in here is not to point at inconsistent thinking but rather to emphasize that in view of the historical record, the problem of distribution is apparently not as simple as it is sometimes viewed. Inequality in distribution and poverty have existed in countries and periods which are otherwise very different in many other dimensions. Whether or not the reasons for such a phenomenon are fully understood, it is clear that economic growth generates rents in the economic system. However, generation of rents is not specific to economic growth. Any change in the physical, economic, political or social environment which affects economic variables generates rents, positive to some and negative to others. No economic system can be sheltered from changes which generate rents and it is therefore not very productive to concentrate our attention on searching for such shelters. What distinguishes economic growth is not the generation of rents but the openings of new opportunities and important among them are the opportunities which are opened up for labour previously employed in low productivity activities.

Arguments are sometimes posed relating the distribution to the welfare of the low income group. In essence the claim states that it is better to be poor in a poor country than to be poor in a rich country. This claim may seem logical but not necessarily in line with the evidence. In recent years about one million Mexican workers cross the border annually to join the US labour market. This is a choice of people to be relatively poor in a rich country. At the same time, no movement of labour is recorded in the opposite direction, that is, there is no movement of poor people who chose to be poor in a poor country. What seems to matter here is the immediate improvement and the prospects for economically better future which dominate any other considerations. These of course are the elements which are generated by economic growth. The revealed preference of the people whose well being we seek is clear and strong.

Sometimes there is a reluctance to deal with economic growth professionally on the ground that there are some pressing short run problems to be solved and it is therefore a luxury to deal with long run problems such as growth. Such an argument could be understood if economic activities were completely separable and independent over periods, so that the level of activity to day were completely independent of the decisions taken in the past. As this is not the case, decisions taken today do affect the future and it is therefore indeed important to be able to assess their effects. It is a luxury not to do it and luxury cannot be afforded when the income is low.

To conclude, it should be emphasized that the purpose of the foregoing comments is not to minimize the importance of distribution. The purpose is to indicate that if distribution is to be improved and poverty is to be alleviated, it is better to be done by means which achieve this objective. Improvement of the conditions of the poor today at the expense of the poor of tomorrow does not seem to be an appropriate solution. But this appears to be the essence of policies which suppress growth.

NOTES

[1] The term marginal is used here to imply that resources are held constant. This meaning of the residual measure is often overlooked by its critics.

[2] For more details see the discussion by Kennedy and Thirwall (1972).

[3] Cf. Schultz (1979).

[4] The capital labour ratios which minimize cost.

[5] Cf. Danin and Mundlak (1979).

[6] For surveys of distributed lags which also provide some perspective of the dominant

methods see Griliches (1967), Nerlove (1971) and Sims (1974).

[7] This point is sometimes misunderstood. For instance Jorgenson [1974, p. 362] writes: "While such a model would be appropriate under decreasing returns, the empirical evidence we have reviewed supports an assumption of constant returns. For this description of technology Mundlak's distributed lags investment model is inappropriate". An earlier statement reads that "Our overall conclusion is that . . . the degree of returns to scale can be taken to equal unity" (Ibid., p. 360). This statement is more in line with the findings reviewed by Jorgenson. It also accommodates decreasing returns. However, this is a marginal point. The main point is that his statement is based on inadequate evidence. In his paper, he reviewed aggregate production functions whereas the model specifies the function of an individual firm, whose managerial capacity is held constant. The production function of the firm can assumed to be of constant returns to scale in all inputs, including management or entreprenurial capacity. It is less than unity with constant management [Mundlak, 1961a]. Thus doubling the level of management, other things being equal, is likely to result in doubling all inputs and output. Consequently, when dealing with aggregate industry data, and these are the data reviewed by Jorgenson, it is not surprising to find constant returns even though the behaviour of a given firm is subject to decreasing returns since his managerial capacity is fixed. The degree of returns of the industry production function depends to a large extent on the elasticity of the supply function of entreprenurial capacity. Other things being equal, the more elastic this function is, the larger is the tendency for observing constant returns to scale. This is also the justification for using constant returns production function for describing the technological conditions at the sectoral level which is implicit in the discussion below.

[8] For the importance of the income and some other effects, see Schultz (1945).

[9] Chapters 2 and 3 (with Strauss) in [Mundlak, 1979] and a yet unpublished work with Cavallo, D. on Argentina.

[10] This is true whether the flow equation is expressed directly in terms of the differential returns as is the case in the work of Mundlak and Strauss, in (Mundlak, 1979, Ch. 4), or if it is derived from the savings and investment equations, as is the case in the yet unpublished work of Cavallo and Mundlak on Argentina.

[11] The work on Mexico is carried out jointly with Aspe, P. and Triguero, I.

[12] See Kuznets, 1973. Actually, it would be more accurate to talk of modern economic growth as Kuznets does.

REFERENCES

Becker, G.T. (1962) "Investment in Human Capital: A Theoretical Analysis" *Journal of Political Economy* (Supplement).

Danin, Y. and Mundlak, Y. (1979) "The Evolutionary Use of New Techniques" (mimeographed) The Centre for Agricultural Economic Research, (forthcoming).

Dennison, E.F. (1974) *Accounting for United States Economic Growth 1929–1969*, The Brookings Institution.

Griliches, Z. (1963) "Estimates of the Aggregate Agricultural Production Function from Cross Sectional Data", *Journal of Farm Economics*; (1964) "Research Expenditures, Education and the Aggregate Agricultural Production Function", *American Economic Review*; (1967) "Distributed Lags: A Survey", *Econometrica*, 35, pp. 16–49.

Intriligator, M.D. and Kendrick, D.A. (1974) *Frontiers of Quantitive Economics* Vol. II, North Holland/American Elsevier.

Johnson, G.L., (1956) "Problems in Studying Resource Productivity and Size of Business Arising from Managerial Processes" in Heady, Johnson and Hardin (ed.) *Resource Productivity, Returns to Scale and Farm Size*, Iowa University Press, Ames; (1958) "Supply Functions – Some Facts and Notions" in Heady, Diesslin, Jensen and Johnson (ed.) *Agricultural Adjustment Problems in a Growing Economy*, Iowa University Press, Ames.

Jorgenson, D.W. (1974) "Investment and Production: A Review" in Intriligator and Kendrick (1974), op. cit.

684   *Yair Mundlak*

Jorgenson, D. and Griliches, Z. (1967) "The Explanation of Productivity Change", *Review of Economic Studies*, 34:3, pp. 249–83.
Kennedy, C. and Thirwall, A.P. (1972) "Technical Progress: A Survey", *Economic Journal*, pp. 11–72.
Kuznets, S. (1946) *National Income: A Summary of Findings*, NBER, New York; (1973), "Modern Economic Growth: Findings and Reflections" *The American Economic Review*, 63:3, pp. 247–58.
Mellor, J.W. (1976) *The New Economics of Growth*, Cornell University Press, Ithaca.
Mundlak, Y. (1961a) "Empirical Production Function Free of Management Bias", *Journal of Farm Economics*, 43:1, pp. 44–56; (1961b) "Aggregation Over Time in Distributed Lag Models", *International Economic Review* 2:2, pp. 154–63; (1966) "On the Micro-Economic Theory of Distributed Lags", *Review of Economics and Statistics*, pp. 51–60; (1967) "Long-run Coefficients and Distributed Lag Analysis: A Reformulation", *Econometrica*, 35:2, pp. 278–93; (1971) "Maximization with Several Objective Functions", *Proceedings of the International Association of Agricultural Economists*, pp. 441–51; (1979) "Intersectoral Factor Mobility and Agricultural Growth", Washington DC, International Food Policy Research Institute, Research Report 6; and Volcani, Z. (1973) "The Correspondence of Efficiency Frontier as a Generalization of the Cost Function", *International Economic Review*, 14:1, pp. 223–33.
Nerlove, M. (1971) "On Lags in Economic Behaviour", *Econometrica* 40, pp. 221–52.
Schultz, T.W. (1945) *Agriculture in an Unstable Economy*, McGraw-Hill, New York; (1960) "Capital Formation by Education", *Journal of Political Economy*; (1961) "Investment in Human Capital", *American Economic Review*; (1979) "Investment in Population Quality throughout Low Income Countries", mimeograph, University of Chicago, Human Capital Paper 79:1.

DISCUSSION OPENING – FERNANDO C. PERES

In opening the discussion, Fernando Peres felt that more was needed to be known about the tests of validity of the models proposed. The functional format of these models suggested a method of trial and error. This may be acceptable but we need to know more about the qualifications concerning the model. A Monte-Carlo convergence technique might be used here.

The trade-off between growth and distribution might have been presented in other terms. The implication of the paper was that those in favour of improving income distribution are against growth if such growth is suspected of causing maldistribution. But alternative kinds of growth are possible and it is necessary to find ways of achieving growth while at the same time improving income distribution.

GENERAL DISCUSSION – RAPPORTEUR: CLARK EDWARDS

In the general discussion the point was made that in applying such a model as Mundlak's to Japan, attention must be given to phases of growth. Three development phases can be distinguished in Japan's growth; Mundlak's model pertains to phase II. During phase I, however, the flow of savings from agriculture to non-agriculture was significant.

It was also pointed out that the Mundlak model relied upon capital accumulation and technology as its two sources of growth. There were several other sources of growth which are relevant to the problem which Mundlak seeks to solve. If the market for farm products is inelastic and agricultural growth is induced by the accumulation of capital and the adoption of new technology, farm income is likely to fall as output rises. This will inhibit growth. In this case, growth will be stimulated instead by expanding the size of the market both at home and abroad. Spatial systems determining growth, such as improved transportation and access to markets, were not considered by Mundlak. Neither did he consider the role of institution building in agricultural growth.

In reply to the opener's comments, Dr Mundlak said that he did not consider the actual testing of his model to be important. He was concerned to find models which seemed to explain history and which had numerical solutions.

Participants in the discussion included Kazushi Ohkawa and Clark Edwards.

RICHARD H. DAY

Understanding the Development of World Agriculture:
Insights from Adaptive Economics

1 INTRODUCTION

The development of world agriculture involves among other things increasing productivity of labour and land, displacement of farm workers, a shift in the production of farm inputs to the industrial sector, a decline in the economic viability of traditional sources of livelihood, migration of rural workers to urban areas and so forth. These developments lead to a host of adjustment problems in both rural and urban areas, such as unemployment, lagging development of infrastructure in the urbanizing parts of the economy, low income including poor nutrition and in extreme cases starvation on a substantial scale. How is this massive transformation to be understood and how are the concomitant problems to be solved?

Economists often analyse such issues by using the well developed apparatus of neoclassical economics based on ideas of individual optimality, supply–demand equilibrium and social (Pareto) efficiency. In this paper an alternative approach, called adaptive or behavioural economics, is considered which looks at precisely those aspects of real world experience from which the pure economic theory abstracts, namely, limitations in human cognition, supply–demand disequilibrium and social or Pareto inefficiencies and disimprovements.

From the vantage point of this alternative approach, agriculture is seen as a dynamic process that endogenously generates irregular fluctuations and switches in techno-social regimes or phases. In extreme cases phase switches stimulate creative morphogenesis: the invention of new technologies and economic organizations that can restore viability and mediate disequilibrium transactions under newly evolving circumstances.

These ideas are used to suggest a new perspective on the emerging world-wide agro-industrial complex. A growing crisis is seen in the current trends in population, energy utilization, and food production; a crisis whose magnitude, duration, and inception cannot be predicted but whose inevitability and significance can now, on the basis of recent experience, be safely assumed. The avoidance of extreme dislocation will require energetic technical and socio-economic innovation.

2 AGRICULTURAL DEVELOPMENT: A GLOBAL VIEW

For millenia after its emergence the connection between agriculture and population was direct. Most people dwelled on farms or in farming villages, producing food primarily for their own consumption. A crucial surplus did make possible the emergence of a few urban centres. As civilization advanced cities of considerable size emerged. Technology gradually improved and agriculture expanded so that the surplus could continue to support the increasing non-agricultural population. Still, it is only in the last few centuries that development has accelerated to such an extent that some parts of the world are now primarily urban and industrial. In our own time, indeed during the last two decades, those parts of the world that are still dominated by agriculture have commenced this great transformation. As a result cities team with hundreds of thousands of rural immigrants where only backward villages stood a few years ago.

All of this means that much of what is produced by the people who remain in agriculture is sent away from the countryside. The connection between food production, processing and consumption is no longer direct.

The improvements in agriculture that underlie the urban transformation have, in part, been indigenous. Improved plant and animal breeds, and more effective rotations provide examples of such indigenous technological change. Many improvements, however, have required investments in capital that can only come from the industrial sector. The use of internal combustion engines to replace humans, bullocks, and horses provide one prime example. This substitution releases land for human food production on the one hand. It drastically reduced farm labour requirements on the other hand. Tractorization therefore stimulates the rural–urban flow and augments the supply of food to feed the expanding urban mass.

Another example of the substitution of industrially produced goods for farm produced inputs is the use of synthesized nutrients. This has made possible the productive use of land that is otherwise infertile and has augmented still more the productivity of already fertile land.

Such developments amount to an *indirect industrialization of agriculture*, that is, the production of inputs by the non-farm economy to be used for the production of food on farms. It contrasts sharply with the direct industrialization of the production of food, which, though already begun and growing in importance, is not yet having the impact its indirect counterpart has had or is having.

This indirect industrialization not only involves increasing farm productivity and rural–urban migration, it also involves an additional critical characteristic, namely the substitution of fossil fuel for solar energy in food production. This is partly because petroleum and its derivatives are used for the commercial production of both fuel and fertilizer. It is also because industrial production of machinery and other non-farm inputs makes heavy demands on non-solar forms of energy. As a consequence, the Green Revolution has created an agro-industrial complex with corollary dependence of the nutritional well-being of the world's population on the supply of petroleum and other exhaustible resources.

The progress of this development, when viewed from an astronomical time scale, is explosive. Along a time axis stretching from the origin of the earth to the solar heat death trends in population, output, productivity and fossil fuel consumption appear as spikes. From an historical perspective, looking back, let us say, to the origins of civilization, the trends appear as more or less geometrically growing curves.

As we focus attention more narrowly on the contemporary scene, however, the epochal transition becomes less apparent. It tends to recede within a variegated pattern of differential response. In some countries where the process has scarcely begun, agriculture is seemingly stuck in ancient patterns. In others where it is underway, some regions proceed at a faster pace than others. Elsewhere the transformation is more or less complete.

In mature and fully modernized economies the dramatic changes seem to be like the classic "cobweb" phenomenon: rising and falling prices, falling and rising supplies, recurrent problems of income and employment. But in the underdeveloped areas widespread famines break out from time to time on such a scale as to exhaust world resources for disaster relief, thus bringing human suffering to catastrophic levels. In the former setting of classic price, income and trade policy, pundits often urge the movement of resources out of the surplus producing, unstable regions. In the latter setting the opposite position is taken in an effort to move resources into agriculture so as to expand the production of food, thereby raising nutritional levels and providing an increase in the well-being of rural dwellers.

3   THE NEOCLASSICAL INTERPRETATION

Our picture of the growing and fluctuating agro-industrial complex is a dynamic one. It is one of uneven, unbalanced growth, of rapid technological change, of the transformation of ways of life, and of periods of fluctuating fortunes for the producers and consumers of food. This is not the place to survey all the methods of economic analysis that can be brought to bear on understanding this complex picture. But to illustrate why a new perspective is needed I want to remind you briefly of the core features of economic analysis.

First of all, economic individuals are defined who have stationary preferences. Second, firms are defined that have stationary technologies. Third, individuals and firms are assumed to maximize preferences and profits respectively given prices. Fourth, economic equilibrium is defined for transactions among individuals and firms: the demand for commodities must not exceed the supply. Thus, although economic exchanges are decentralized they must be perfectly co-ordinated by the price system.

Fifth, social equilibrium is said to prevail when, at equilibrium prices, each individual and each firm maximizes its goal, and no individual or firm can improve its situation without diminishing the situation of at least one other. Two problems are then analysed within this framework: (1) the existence of equilibria and (2) the way such equilibria change when parameters of the system change. The latter type of comparative statics lies at the heart of much, if not most of what passes for policy analysis by economists.

To have a useful correspondence with the real world such an approach to policy evaluation must rest on two critical assumptions. First, the *real* disequilibrium system must work in such a way as to bring equilibrium about. Second, the transition period of disequilibrium must not be so long and so full of problems as to matter in any significant way. If these two assumptions are fulfilled then it is not necessary to understand the nature of disequilibrium nor is it necessary to design policies specifically to cope with its implications.

Now are the basic assumptions of neoclassical economics a good approximation of economic reality? I take it as an implication of scientific reason and of common sense that they are not. If I am right, they therefore provide an inadequate basis on which to understand actual development and from which to derive workable policy. Additional perspectives are needed and that brings me to the next topic, adaptive economics.

4 ADAPTIVE ECONOMICS AND ECONOMIC DEVELOPMENT

It is to belabour the obvious to observe that human decision-makers possess cognitive limitations, that they are imperfectly co-ordinated, and that they vary absolutely and relatively in the rewards and punishments they receive as a result of action. In contrast to orthodox economic theory adaptive economics explicitly incorporates these basic facts of life. Let us discuss them briefly in turn.

Cognitive limitations include imperfections in perception, memory, reasoning and computational power. We may also include in this category difficulties in formulating consistent preferences on the basis of which rational decisions can be based. These facts mean that rationality is "bounded", to use Herbert Simon's apt phrase, and that it involves learning. One exercises the best judgement one can, given what one knows at the time, observes the results, attempts with more or less energy and skill to acquire more knowledge, plans anew, and carries out the implied actions in response to circumstances as they unfold. In conducting these cognition-behaving sequences resort is made to imitation, rules of thumb, habit, inertia and even thoughtless impulse as well as to rational planning.

Economic models that incorporate these aspects of economizing activity include the rule of thumb behavioural economic models of Cyert and

March (1963); the goal adaptive, adjustment behaviour of March and Simon (1958) and Forrester (1964); the recursive programming approach of Day (1962), Day and Singh (1977), and Day and Cigno (1978); the X-efficiency concepts of Leibenstein (1966), (1976); and the satisficing, selection analyses of Winter (1964), (1971), and Nelson and Winter (1978).

Within complex, interactive settings individuals must reach decisions and behave without the benefit of a complete knowledge of what other participants in the process are doing. Therefore they cannot know in advance whether or not effective co-ordination can occur and whether or not supplies and demands for commodities will equate. Evidently, behaviour must be possible and viability must be maintained through the existence of special *disequilibrium mechanisms*. For example, firms may maintain inventories. In addition specialized institutions whose function is to regulate exchange may exist. Such institutions, which include stores and banks, constitute the marketing and financial systems. These systems must be viewed as instruments for mediating economic transactions among individual decision-makers and economic organizations which function out of equilibrium.

A proliferation of such mechanisms cannot always guarantee existence, however. Bankruptcies of farms, industrial firms and banks in the United States run in the thousands every month. Such events signal the demise of individual enterprises, and the transfer of their resources to other enterprises in the system. During periods of economic breakdown that occur in hyperinflations or depressions, human life itself may be in jeopardy, even in wealthy countries.

It should be noted in passing that socialist economies are not immune from the problems of disequilibrium that we are observing. They are in fact archtypical examples of the larger, hierarchically managed economic organization whose constituent members have all the characteristics of adaptive man and which must therefore display lack of perfect co-ordination. Therefore, they too must possess mechanisms much like those in capitalist countries, for mediating disequilibrium transactions within and among individual enterprises.

How do such disequilibrium systems evolve and what is the character of their historical trajectories? Careful computer simulation and theoretical analysis all point to the possibility that model systems of the character we are discussing need not and often will not converge to economic equilibria even when the latter can be shown to exist. Two striking characteristics of system behaviour emerge instead. First, many variables display irregular oscillations of more or less unpredictable complexity. This suggests that policies of control based on observed system performance may be exceedingly unreliable. Second, the system as a whole is characterized by multiple phases and corollary shifts in structure. Each phase represents a given configuration of economic activity, scarcity and surplus, and associated values. Within this configuration some activities grow more or less explosively, as economic advantage is successfully exploited by some organizations within the system. These growing activities replace uneconomic, obsolescent, or otherwise unsuccessful pursuits which are seen to diminish in importance. A counterpoint of economic growth and decay occurs. Eventually, the prevailing structure gives way as certain components are eliminated altogether or certain activities are abandoned in favour of new ones designed to cope more effectively with current opportunities and scarcities. A characteristic feature of this point–counterpoint of development is that economic activity takes place in overlapping waves involving commodities, technologies and corollary ways of life.

A more extreme feature is the occasional breakdown of the system altogether. These disruptive times provide a focus for the synthetic faculty of mind. New organizations and activities are created that temporarily resolve the internal contradictions that have emerged and that set the system off on a new trajectory of evolution.

5 THE DISEQUILIBRIUM DYNAMICS OF AGRICULTURE

To summarize the adaptive economics perspective in a nutshell, economic change involved unpredictable fluctuations, overlapping waves of growth and demise, periodic breakdowns and organizational morphogenesis. This brings us back to a reconsideration of agriculture. For in what other sector of the economy are these characteristics more evident?

The exasperating unpredictability of farm production is so well known and so universally experienced as not to require comment, except to mention that such unpredictability can now be shown to emerge under some conditions from the internal working of the system without assuming the imposition of random shocks. This would mean that many of agriculture's problems might remain, even if the weather were much more uniform and predictable than it is.

Overlapping waves of development are apparent everywhere we look at the farm scene. New practices, new machines, new cropping patterns, new consumption activities replace the old with astonishing speed in the modern world. One or two decades is enough to bring about a transition in an entire way of life.

In the developed world, where this counterpoint has already been repeated several times, it has come to be expected so that its disruptive effects are no longer so directly experienced. In newly developed areas, however, the changes are disrupting ancient patterns and forcing changes so fundamental as to involve the demise of basic cultural ways of life, and to force the mass relocation of whole peoples. Indeed, in some parts of the world we are seeing the final destruction of paleolithic and neolithic life as the last vestiges of pre-agricultural technology are literally ploughed under by the agricultural–industrial frontier.

Somewhat less cataclysmic, but of fundamental significance, is the growing network of linkages between the industrial and agricultural sectors, and, because of the uneven distribution of resources and peoples around the world, the growing web of interdependencies between the world's various regions, nations and cultures.

Indeed everyone now knows of the petroleum crisis that has emerged as new constraints have been reached and new interactions evolved. The potential and actual instabilities are already apparent and a new generation of policy making is just getting underway that may be expected to lead to new national and international institutions for managing resource scarcity and for distributing world food supplies.

The information, decision and production delays that induce instabilities and fluctuations are lengthened and elaborated as the structure of intrafirm, intersectoral, interregional and international linkages grows more intricate. Ironically, the elaboration of new institutions, new marketing and monetary mechanisms to overcome system constraints and to provide for enhanced viability, adds to the complexity of the system. New decision variables and new decision-makers are added along with corollary information, decision and production delays. The dynamic "order" of the system increases and with it the potential complexity of the patterns of historical behaviour. Thus, the "solution" of each emerging policy problem in terms of elaborated institutional structure contains at its inception the seeds of a new order of socio-economic difficulty that will come in its turn to demand a solution in terms of new technical, social or economic organization.

In the rapidly developing African continent we see this interplay unwinding with alarming speed. Savannahs that once teemed with all manner of primeval life are giving way to modern agricultural technology. The result is an urbanization that rivals in speed the expansion of Los Angeles and other such urban explosions that, on an historical time scale, seems to have emerged suddenly as it were "out of nowhere". Its result has additionally meant the transformation of pre-agricultural peoples into urban dwellers, skipping the agricultural revolution itself; a jump from paleolithic to the agro-industrial age. And it is occurring just at the time as exhaustible resources such as petroleum are no longer growing in supply – the irresistible force of economic development seeminly running head-on against the immovable constraints of land and fossil fuels.

6   A POLICY PERSPECTIVE

Agricultural economists have long been interested in what they have rightly regarded as "adjustment problems". Their goals have often been couched in terms of helping farmers adjust, by which they have meant helping them deal effectively with changing economic opportunities, either by more quickly modifying their mix of agricultural activities, or by pursuing opportunities outside of farming altogether. In so doing, they have in part been pushing for policies of change in the face of the most rapid development in the world's history, when migrations from one way of life to another are taking place all over the world at speeds unprecedented in the annals of human history.

Moreover, they have advocated such changes under the assumption (sometimes implicitly made) that the purpose of policy was to speed up the generation of the new equilibrium that would inevitably follow if the irrational barriers to economic change could be brought down.

If, however, the forces for change are disrupting what are merely temporary accommodations to fundamental disequilibrium conditions; if those forces will lead eventually to new instabilities and threats of breakdown; then the role of centralized economic policy may better lie in new directions. First, policies for *moderating* ongoing adjustments should always be considered. Second, policies focused on *preserving* exhausible resources should receive greater attention. Third, policies for *augmenting* renewable resources should be emphasized at all times. Fourth, *emergency supplies* for meeting inevitable but unpredictable economic and natural disasters with appropriate distribution mechanisms should be put in place on a wider scale than is now done. Fifth, resources devoted to the *free play of the intellect* should be enhanced, for it is out of such free play that creative morphogenesis emerges, which as I have argued in this paper is what overcomes the unpredictable but inevitable crisis that threatens stability and survival even though in the process the seeds of the next challenge to human ingenuity are planted.

Now this last policy presents us with a paradox. For I have advocated a conservative and conservationist approach, while at the same time arguing for fostering the intellectual climate in which new ideas for changing socio-economic structure may flourish. That paradox can never be wholly resolved. It will surely continue to involve an increasing struggle between those forces that wish to preserve and those that wish to create. But, if as I think to be the case, the forces of preservation, however important as moderating influences, cannot overcome inherent instabilities and inevitable crises, then society must have within itself at all times – for its time of need can only poorly be foreseen – a dedicated cadre of socio-economic inventors, innovators and engineers. For it is from this cadre that must come the new organizations and mechanisms that will overcome the crises that would lead to cultural and possibly demographic destruction.

That such destruction is a real possibility must be a fear taken seriously by any student of history and prehistory. The artifacts of wonderous past civilizations warn us of this truth. Thus, while a call for greater resources for the intellectual community is self-serving, it is also a call to social service. For if I am correct, then every scientific paper we write, every thoughtful speech we utter, every discussion, debate or argument intelligently pursued plays its role in the dialectical process by which the human mind seeks to understand and to enhance its own evolution.

REFERENCES

Cyert, R. and March, J. (1963) *The Behavioural Theory of the Firm*, Prentice Hall, Englewood Cliffs, NJ.

Day, R. (1963) *Recursive Programming and Production Response*, North-Holland Publishing Co., Amsterdam, The Netherlands.

Day, R. and Cigno, A. (1978) *Modelling Economic Change: The Recursive Programming Approach*, North-Holland Publishing Co., Amsterdam, The Netherlands.

Day, R. and Groves, T. (1975) *Adaptive Economic Models*, Academic Press, New York.

Day, R. and Singh, I. (1977) *Economic Development as an Adaptive Process: A Green Revolution Case Study*, Cambridge University Press, New York.

Leibenstein, H. (1976) "Allocative Efficiency versus X–Efficiency", *The American Economic Review*, 56.

Leibenstein, H. (1976) *Beyond Economic Man*, Harvard University Press, Cambridge, Mass.

March, J. and Simon, H. (1958) *Organizations*, John Wiley and Sons, New York.

Nelson, R. and Winter, S. (1978) "Forces Generating and Limiting Concentration Under Schumpeterian Competition", *The Bell Journal of Economics*, 9: pp. 524–48.

Winter, S. (1964) "Economic 'Natural Selection' and the Theory of the Firm", *Yale Economic Essays*, 4, pp. 225–72.

Winter, S. (1971) "Satisfying, Selection and the Innovating Remnant", *Quarterly Journal of Economics*, 85, pp. 237–61.

DISCUSSION OPENING – W.H. FURTAN AND S. KULSHRESHTHA

Professor Day has provided this afternoon a very lucid yet highly thought-provoking discussion of an alternative avenue for looking at world agriculture. The purpose of his paper is to present a view of the agricultural adjustment problems based upon the notion of "adaptive behavioural" economics.

Day has correctly identified two parameters of adjustment. The first, which is mainly indigenous, has caused a substitution of capital for labour. The second, the agri-industrial complex, is based largely on non-solar sources of energy. Finally, Day suggests reasons why the neoclassical model does not facilitate an understanding of the adjustment process. In its place he suggests "adaptive economics".

Professor Day has provided us with "what" to look for in the area of disequilibrium economics; but in my opinion he has not led us as to "how to get there". A lack of discussion on how the learning process takes place in the context of world agriculture leaves us in a somewhat confused state. The assumptions regarding the rules under which the adaptation occurs are not clearly specified and thus, after reading the paper, one is left bewildered. Many adaptive models require imposition of rules of learning and constraints within which an individual (or the system) can behave.

From the standpoint of policy making using adaptive economic models one further faces issues such as the optimal degree of aggregation (or disaggregation) of world agriculture and the resulting data requirements. Furthermore, the institutional framework that surrounds the individual system greatly affects the likely behaviour of the individuals over time.

Yet another issue that emerges in the study of any economic system is how to deal with changes in the environment in an *ex ante* framework. Each shock (as an unanticipated change is called) leads to some departure in the behaviour.

The discussion should focus on two things: (1) the ability of the adaptive model to analyse the disequilibrium process of farm adjustment; and (2) what assumptions are implied by the adaptive model. Such discussion might provide some further insights into the usefulness of such an approach in the study of world agriculture.

GENERAL DISCUSSION – RAPPORTEUR: KENNETH H. BAUM

The discussion of Professor Day's paper raised many questions concerning the possible conceptual and application possibilities for testing economic hypotheses and performing quantitative policy analyses. A primary concern of those present was the utilization of adaptive economics as a behavioural approach for rural development and agricultural change research and teaching activities. The assertion that neoclassical modelling approaches may be inadequate theoretical tools for investigating economic disequilibria relative to adaptive economics stimulated many participants' comments in three general areas. First, specification of real world behavioural or resource constraints needs to be more adequately detailed. Second, the particular type and aggregation level of economic problems needed for optimal use of the conceptual framework may vary a great extent and also needs to be explained further. Third, explicit knowledge of the operating processes may be necessary to explain the effect of exogenous shocks on the stability and activity level of the economic system. In addition, both quantitative and qualitative changes may affect the disequilibrium processes of dynamic adjustment. Finally, a question was raised regarding the explanatory relationships among economic disequilibrium processes and class conflicts in terms of adaptive economics.

Professor Day responded to these thoughts by first commenting that the broad economic issues mentioned by the participants are at the core of our economic thinking and simple answers are not readily available. Nevertheless, adaptive economics should be viewed as a cohesive family of concepts, while only a particular set might be utilized in an applied study. The primary goal of the agricultural economist should be to ask how the system in question works, while drawing generously on observations of real world behaviour for derivation of the modelling processes. These processes should not be viewed as *ad hoc* behavioural rules, but rather seen as developed from inductive reasoning utilized to investigate economic theory more fully.

Day explained that the process of economic change and class conflict should be analysed as a natural result of disequilibrium processes. Economic models that "break down" reflect world phenemona where the market process does not work well. Also conflict seems to be endemic where an economic system is successful. Day's final comments expressed an awareness of the difficulty of teaching adaptive economics. But this difficulty is partially a problem of lack of theoretical work to refine the theory into a more rigorous economic theory, which he hoped would be remedied in the future.

Participants in the discussion included N. Meyer, D. Feinup, M.L. Lerohl, George T. Jones and Indra Jit Singh.

C.Y. AHN, INDERJIT SINGH, and LYN SQUIRE*

A Model of an Agricultural Household in a Multi-Crop Economy: the Case of Korea

1 INTRODUCTION

A large part of world agriculture comprises semi-commercial family farms operating in a multi-crop environment. These family farms or agricultural households combine two fundamental units of micro-economic analysis – the household and the farm. Although traditional economic theory has dealt with each separately, in developing agriculture dominated by peasant family farms it is their interdependence that is of crucial importance. Models of such households, therefore, should allow for the integration of production and consumption decisions within the context of a single theory of behaviour. That is, labour supply, household consumption (of goods as well as leisure) and the composition of farm output and resource use (including family labour) should all be determined simultaneously.

Existing models have tended to focus on selected aspects of this simultaneous problem and are, therefore, deficient to some, as yet undetermined, extent. Thus, econometric models have been developed recently which allow for the integration of consumption and production decisions but which do not consider the crop composition decision.[1] On the other hand, linear programming models have had as their main purpose an analysis of the allocation of resources to competing crops, but have not allowed for the simultaneous determination of consumption and production decisions.[2] It is the purpose of this paper to describe one method of extending the empirical applicability of the theory of the farm-household to multi-crop economies by integrating the econometric and linear programming models already available in the literature.

The central idea is to replace the single, econometrically-estimated

* The study reported in this paper has been jointly carried out by the World Bank and the Korea Rural Economics Institute, Seoul. We are grateful to its Director, Dr Dong-Hi Kim for making the Korean rural household survey data available for study and analysis. We are grateful to Ms Susan Chou and S. Janakiram for their help with the heavy statistical work involved. The views expressed represent those of the authors and not necessarily those of the World Bank.

697

profit or production function employed in econometric models of the farm-household with a set of linear production activities which can be analysed by means of linear programming techniques. The net result is that the model determines the allocation of inputs to different production activities as in any linear model of production; in addition, however, it determines the level of profits which are in turn a component of total household income and hence a determinant of household consumption behaviour. Changes in farm technology or in input and output prices on the production side can thus be traced in great detail through profits to elucidate their impact on *household* consumption of both goods and leisure. In turn, the household's demand for its own (farm-produced) output and its labour supply to farm production are no longer treated as exogenous variables but are determined from the consumption side of the model in the light of the household's subjective preference.

The paper is organized as follows. In Section 2, the theoretical model is presented. In Section 3, Korean data are used to assess the quantitative significance of the approach by calculating and comparing household response to changes in input and output prices and technology for two different specifications of the models.[3] First, the household is analysed from the consumption side on the assumption that farm profits are exogenous; this corresponds to the standard econometric approach in consumer demand theory. And second, results are presented for a model in which consumption and production responses are integrated in a theoretically consistent fashion, and farm profits are allowed to reflect production responses to prices and technological change. In Section 4 some of the policy implications that stem from this type of analysis are discussed.

2   A THEORETICAL MODEL

The model of household behaviour describes a semi-commercial family farm with a competitive labour market. The farm also engages in subsistence production in that it retains some part of its output for household consumption. A major part of agriculture in LDCs may be characterized by this type of model which lies intermediately on a continuum between a wholly commercialized farm employing only hired labour and marketing all output and a pure subsistence farm using only family labour and producing solely for home consumption with no marketed surplus.

The planning horizon is assumed to be one agricultural cycle. As a result, decisions relating to the total supply of household factors of production are treated as given. Total household labour availability and total area operated may, therefore, be treated as exogenous variables. Similarly, it is assumed that the household has already made some decision concerning its desired level of saving. The model, therefore, focuses on the short-run determination of the allocation of expenditure to different commodities (including own-consumption and leisure), and the allocation of inputs to different production activities.

Further, it is assumed that there is a market for agricultural and other types of labour and all households participate in the labour market either as buyers or sellers of labour. Thus, the use of labour time and the disposal of output are determined with reference to market wages and prices. In output and input markets, the household is assumed to be a price taker. Finally, it is assumed that land, if rented, is rented by means of fixed charges and that there are no sharecropping or other contractual arrangements which might lead to non-standard profit maximizing conditions.

With these points in mind, the model is formulated in matrix notation as follows:

$$\text{Max } U = \underset{(h \times 1)}{U(C)} \tag{1}$$

$$\text{s.t. } \underset{(1 \times n)}{[1]X_i} \leq \underset{(n \times 1)}{\bar{Z}_i} \qquad i = 1, \ldots k \tag{2}$$

and

$$\underset{(1 \times h)}{P'} \underset{(h \times 1)}{C} = \underset{(1 \times m)}{\prod'} \underset{(m \times 1)}{X} + Y \tag{3}$$

where

C is a (hxl) vector of items consumed (own-consumption and purchased) including leisure;

X_i is a (nxl) vector of land use by crop and technologies on the ith type of land (or other quasi-fixed resources);

$\bar{Z}_i$ is the maximum available quantity of the ith type of land (or quasi-fixed resource);

P is a (hxl) vector of prices of consumed goods including leisure;

$\prod$ is an (mxl) vector of net profits per unit of land by crop and by technology and by land type;

$X' = [x_1, x_2, ,,,x_k]'$; and

Y is Becker's concept of 'full income' and equals the market value of total time available to the household plus any (net) non-labour income.[4]

Thus, the household is assumed to maximize its utility function subject to a land constraint by quality or type (e.g., lowland, upland, irrigated and unirrigated) and a combined income and time constraint. The consumption of family leisure is included on the RHS of equation 3 and is valued at the market wage. The total (family and hired) labour input into crop production, again valued at the market wage, is included on the LHS of equation 3 in the determination of II. The household is a net buyer or seller of labour depending on whether total time available less time allocated to leisure is less than or greater than total labour requirement in production.

It is assumed that technology is linear. Thus for the rth crop on the ith type of land we have:

$$\prod_{ir} = p_r a_{ir} - \sum_j q_j b_{irj}$$

where pr is the price of the rth crop (and hence the rth consumption good), a_{ir} is the yield of the rth crop on the ith type of land, q_j is the price of the jth input, and b_{irj} is the jth input requirement per unit of the ith type of land for the rth crop. As noted above, the total (family and hired) labour requirement is included as one of the inputs.

Forming the Lagrangian expression, we have

$$\text{Max } L = U(C) - \lambda(P'C - \prod{}' X - Y) + \sum_i V_i(\bar{Z}_i - [1]X_i) \qquad (5)$$

The first order Kuhn–Tucker conditions are: [5]

$$\underset{(h \times 1)}{U_c} - \underset{(1 \times 1)}{\lambda} \underset{(h \times 1)}{P} = 0 \qquad (6)$$

$$\underset{(1 \times h)}{P'} \underset{(h \times 1)}{C} - \underset{(1 \times m)}{\prod{}'} \underset{(m \times 1)}{X} - \underset{(1 \times 1)}{Y} = 0 \qquad (7)$$

$$\underset{(1 \times 1)}{\lambda} \underset{(m \times 1)}{\prod} - \underset{(m \times 1)}{V} \leq 0 \qquad (8)$$

$$\underset{(m \times m)}{I} \underset{(m \times 1)}{X} \left[\underset{(1 \times 1)}{\lambda} \underset{(m \times 1)}{\prod} - \underset{(m \times 1)}{V} \right] = 0 \qquad (9)$$

$$\underset{(1 \times 1)}{\bar{Z}_i} \underset{(1 \times n)}{[1]} \underset{(n \times 1)}{X_i} \geq 0 \qquad i = 1, \dots k \qquad (10)$$

$$\underset{(n \times 1)}{V_i} \left[\underset{(1 \times 1)}{\bar{Z}_i} - \underset{(1 \times n)}{[1]} \underset{(n \times 1)}{X_i} \right] = 0 \qquad i = 1, \dots k \qquad (11)$$

where $V' = [V'_1 V'_2 \dots V'_k]$ and I is a unit matrix.

Equations 6 and 7 correspond to the standard first-order conditions of consumer demand theory. Equations 8 to 11 represent the production side of the model. If equation 10 is binding for the ith type of land, then Vi ⩾ 0 represents the shadow price of that type of land. If for the rth crop Πir ⩽ Vi the rth crop will not be grown on the ith type of land. For the sth crop, however, assume that Πis = Vi – in this event the ith type of land will be allocated completely to the sth crop. The model thus produces the standard result of complete specialization by land type. The results also indicate that the production side of the model can be solved independently of the value of λ (the marginal utility of income). Since $Vi = \lambda \Pi is$ where s is the most profitable crop, a comparison between Vi and $\lambda \Pi ir$ for any $r \neq s$ is not affected by the value of λ; λ is a scalar which can be cancelled out, the allocation of land to competing crops being determined exclusively by a comparison of profitability at market prices.[6] The model may be treated, therefore, as a block recursive one, in which production decisions are first determined by profit maximization given the level of maximized profits. For any given farm technology and set of input and output prices, the linear programming model of farm production (using data for a *representative* farm) allows the determination of the level of farm profits, which is then introduced into the consumption side of the model to arrive at the household's expenditure pattern.

The consumption side of the model is specified econometrically to conform to the linear expenditure system. To differentiate between the use of time by dependents and working family members the system is developed in per caput terms. For an individual member of the family the utility function is written as:

$$u = \sum \beta_i \ln (c_i - \gamma_i) \qquad i = 1, \ldots h$$

where ci indicates *per caput* consumption of the ith commodity, and γi are functions of a variety of household characteristics. Dependents are assumed to consume all their available time in the form of leisure and to consume the same quantities of other goods as do working family members. The household utility function is assumed to be identical for each member and additive across individuals, so that summing over the n_1 working family members and the n_2 dependents ($n = n_1 + n_2$), the household consumption problem is to maximize

$$U = \sum u = n_1 \beta_1 \ln (c_1 - \gamma_1) + n_2 \beta_1 \ln (t - \gamma_1) + n \sum_i \beta_i \ln (c_i - \gamma_1)$$

$$\text{s.t. } n_1 wc_1 + \sum_i p_i c_i = \prod{}' X + Y$$

where $i = 2..h$, c_1 = consumption of leisure, t = total time available (= consumption of leisure by dependents), and w is the market wage.

Household characteristics are introduced by making the γs linear functions of household composition; that is,

$$\gamma_i = \alpha_{i0} + \alpha_{i1} n_1 + \alpha_{i2} n_2 \qquad i = 1, \ldots h$$

The solution to this problem is described in Barnum and Squire (forthcoming) and their estimation procedure is followed here. In our case the final set of estimating equations yields estimates of β_i for $i = 2, \ldots h$. The value of β_1 is then obtained by the adding up restriction i.e. that marginal expenditures must exhaust the budget. The transformation of the demand curve for leisure into a supply curve of labour allows us to replace γ_1 by γ_s in all the estimating equations where $\gamma_s = t - \gamma_1$.[7] Accordingly, the estimating equations yield estimates of α_{i0}, α_{i1} and α_{i2} for $i = 2, \ldots h$ and α_{s0}, α_{s1} and α_{s2} where $\alpha_{s0} + \alpha_{s1} n_1 + \alpha_{s2} n_2 = \gamma s$.

3 RESULTS FOR KOREAN AGRICULTURAL HOUSEHOLDS (1970)

The linear expenditure system is estimated for six "commodities": labour supply (s), paddy (c_2), barley (c_3), other farm produce (c_4), market purchased food items (m_1), and market purchased non-food items (m_2).[8] The final results are shown in Table 1.

These estimates, in conjunction with the linear programming production model (not reported here for lack of space), are used to calculate two sets of elasticities:

1 Where household and farm behaviour are treated separately, and the responses of *endogenous* variables in the utility maximization problem (consumption of rice (c_2), barley (c_3) and other farm products (c_4), food purchases (m_1), non-food purchases (m_2) and labour supply (s)) to *exogenous* variables (prices, expenditures and wage rates) are estimated assuming that farm profits are exogenous. These elasticities correspond to those obtained by the standard approach to consumer theory.

TABLE 1 *Estimated parameters of the linear expenditure system for an agricultural household in Korea*[1]

Coefficient	Estimate	T-Statistic	Coefficient	Estimate	T-Statistic
β_1[2]	0.23	—	α_{10}	233.9	(6.71)
β_2	0.05	(4.01)	α_{11}	−27.5	(−3.63)
β_5	0.03	(2.68)	α_{21}	−18.4	(−2.90)
β_6	0.81	(68.32)	α_{40}	4,373.3	(4.84)
α_{s0}	580.30	(8.28)	α_{41}	−649.1	(−3.04)
α_{s2}	73.70	(3.07)	α_{42}	−330.3	(−2.02)
			α_{50}	60,969.6	(4.46)
			α_{51}	−14,056.3	(−4.84)
			α_{52}	−4,775.5	(−1.83)

[1] N = 443 households. Only statistically significant coefficients are reported.

[2] Calculated from the restriction $\dfrac{n_1}{n_1 + n_2} \beta_1 + \beta_2 + \ldots \beta_6 = 1$

and a mean value of 0.5082 for $\dfrac{n_1}{n_1 + n_2}$

2   Where household and farm behaviour are treated jointly and the responses of the endogenous variables incorporate the change in farm profits that may result from any changes in the exogenous variables including technology. These elasticities correspond to the integrated approach we have developed in Section 2. A comparison of the *elasticities* corresponding to these approaches and reported in Table 2 allows an assessment of the quantitative significance of the integrated model.

The first set of elasticities corresponds to those obtained from the linear expenditure system. The results prove to be highly plausible. Consumption of food items responds positively but inelastically to changes in total expenditure,[9] whereas non-food consumption responds positively and elastically while labour supply response is negative and inelastic. The corresponding elasticities obtained by Barnum and Squire (forthcoming) for Malaysian farm-households are 0.52 for paddy, 2.74 for market-purchased food and non-food items and −0.81 for labour supply. The overall pattern of elasticities is thus very similar for the two studies. On the assumption that farm profits are determined exogenously, all own-price elasticities are negative and inelastic. A comparison with the Malaysian results again reveals remarkable similarity. Barnum and Squire (forthcoming) produce estimates of −0.04 for paddy, and −0.07 for labour supply. The consumption side of the household model is therefore adequately captured in our LES estimates as reported in Table 2.

The production side of the model is also captured well as can be seen in Table 3 by comparing the *observed* farm cropping pattern, labour use, production costs and farm profits, with those predicted by the linear programming model of the representative farm. We can proceed to use this model to generate changes in farm profits in response to prices and technology with some degree of confidence.

Of course, one of the basic points of the theory is that in an agricultural household farm profits are not exogenous, but are a function of, among other things, farm input and output prices, wage rates and technology as captured by the production model. If we compare the second set of elasticities estimated by allowing farm profits (and hence total incomes) to vary as a consequence of the impact of input and output prices and wage rates on farm production, the full implications of integrating consumption and production decisions are revealed. Apart from the elasticities with respect to the prices of purchased commodities which do not enter into farm production decisions and with respect to total expenditures which remain the same by definition, *thirteen out of the sixteen remaining elasticities change sign*, while the remaining three are significantly different in magnitude. In addition, the integrated model allows the estimation of elasticities with respect to input prices and technological changes in *farm production* which are not defined for models that focus exclusively on consumption behaviour. These results demonstrate the

TABLE 2   A comparison of selected arc elasticities to test the significance of integrating household production and consumption decisions (Korean agricultural households, 1970)[1]

Elasticity of: With respect to:	Own consumption of Rice (C_2)		Food purchases (M_1)		Non-food purchases (M_2)		Labour supply (S)	
	I	II	I	II	I	II	I	II
Total Expenditures (E)	0.5692	0.5692	0.9167	0.9167	2.76	2.76	2.76	−0.451
Price of Rice (P_2)	−0.1778	0.0104	−0.0645	0.269	−0.1941	0.81	0.0317	−0.1322
Price of Barley (P_3)	−0.0031	0.0625	−0.005	0.1007	−0.0151	0.3031	0.0025	−0.0495
Price of Other Crops (P_4)	−0.0009	0.1178	−0.0015	0.1897	−0.0044	0.5712	0.0007	−0.0932
Price of Food Purchases (P_5)	−0.0147	−0.0147	−0.2494	−0.2494	−0.0715	−0.0715	0.0117	0.0117
Price of Non-Food Purchases (P_6)	−0.041	−0.041	−0.066	−0.066	−0.8665	−0.8665	0.0324	0.0324
Wage Rate (W)	0.1583	0.0097	0.255	0.0156	0.7678	0.047	−0.0020	0.105
Seed Costs (Q_1)	NA[3]	−0.0111	NA	−0.0179	NA	−0.054	NA	0.0088
Fertilizer and Pesticide Costs (Q_2)	NA	−0.0484	NA	−0.078	NA	−0.2349	NA	0.0383
Power Tiller Capacity[2]	NA	0.0019	NA	0.0031	NA	0.0094	NA	−0.0015

[1] The first set of elasticities in the columns marked (I) are computed on the assumption that farm profits (π) are constant. The second set of elasticities in the columns marked (II) are computed on the assumption that farm profits (π) are variable. Changes in farm profits (π) are estimated by using the l.p. production model to trace the impact of discrete changes in exogenous variables. The first set of elasticities correspond to the linear expenditure system alone and in the second set to the integrated model.

[2] This elasticity is obtained by increasing the capacity of power tillers available per household to simulate the impact of changes in mechanical technology from bullocks to power tillers. It should be read as the percentage change in endogenous variables for a 1% change in tiller capacity available.

quantitative significance of the model and indicate the importance of integrating consumption and production decisions in models that examine the behaviour of agricultural households. Several interesting and important policy implications follow.

4 SOME POLICY IMPLICATIONS

To begin with, consider the own and cross-price elasticities for rice, the most important food item (and hence nutrition source) in the household's consumption bundle and the most important crop on the farm. Traditional consumer theory suggests that own-consumption of rice will *decrease* if its price is raised (the estimated elasticity is -0.18), but the integrated model predicts that it will *increase* (the estimated elasticity now being 0.01), because increased prices also mean increased profits (and incomes) for agricultural households thus swamping the price and income effects predicted by consumer theory.[10] Similarly positive elasticities are predicted for food purchases and non-food purchases with respect not only to the price of rice but to the prices of all crops grown on the farm. Thus, while raising farm output prices may have a *negative* impact on the nutritional status of non-farming rural households, it has a *positive* impact on agricultural households. By the same token marketed surplus response is *lower* because own-consumption of farm-produced goods increases rather than decreases in response to increased prices. Non-farm households, however, may benefit from increased wages and employment opportunities because increased output prices also decrease the supply of farm labour as profits and income increase instead of *increasing* it as predicted by consumer theory. The integrated model predicts that households are willing to take *part of their increased incomes in increased leisure*, so that any increased demand for labour in agricultural production (say, through land intensification programmes) will have some spill-over effects on the demand for hired labour (hence the incomes of the landless) even where the farm size is very small because not all the increased demand may be met by an increase in the household's own labour supply to farm production.

Finally, there are the set of elasticities that can be estimated *only for the integrated model* – those with respect to input costs and changes in farm technology. Thus our model correctly predicts reduced expenditures on all commodities and increased work effort as input (seed and fertilizer–pesticide) costs are increased, and increased expenditure and reduced labour supply as the availability of tiller capacity is increased and bullock cultivation is replaced by power tillers in farm operations. Increased availability of power tillers also changes the cropping pattern in favour of vegetables that are highly profitable under tiller technologies, in turn affecting the seasonal demand for labour. Thus even labour displacing technological change, such as the increased use of power tillers, may

TABLE 3   *Observed VS predicted values of farm production*

	Observed from Sample Households[a]	Predicted by Linear Programming Model
Cropping Pattern (%)[b]		
Rice	40.7	43.14
Barley Mixtures	28.2	32.8
Misc. Grains	4.2	1.0
Pulses	12.2	12.1
Potatoes	6.1	1.5
Vegetables	8.6	9.5
Resource Use		
Labour Use (in hours)[c]	2,181.1	2,318.0
Draft Animal Use (hours)	103.6	86.1
Borrowing (in 1970 won)[d]	36,742.0	37,325.0

	Observed from Sample Households	Predicted by Linear Programming Model
Gross Values of Production (in 1970 won)	213,244	224,326
Total Production Costs (in 1970 won)		
Variable Inputs[e]	35,395	42,558
Labour	81,684	85,470
Draft Animals	2,642	2,196
Power Tiller[f]	—	3,648
Interest Charges	4,738	8,958
Total	124,459	142,830
Net Farm Profit	88,785	81,496
Farm Profit per Hectare	70,464	64,679

a   All observed values are from a sample of 443 farm-households.

b   The household survey data do not give information of area sown to various crops except for rice. The observed values are from a national survey of cropped land reported in the *Yearbook of Agriculture and Forestry*, 1971, Ministry of Agriculture and Fisheries, Korea, and a total correspondence between this and the household survey figures is not to be expected. The area planted to orchards, mulberry and tobacco is deleted in computing this cropping pattern because of the very small proportion of total area devoted to these crops.

c   Excludes labour spent on orchards, mulberry and tobacco production which is a very small proportion of total labour use and non-agricultural activities for which no data are available.

d   The interest rate on borrowing charged in the model is 2 per annum and is close to the commercial bank rate. The lending rate in agricultural cooperatives is perhaps low, about 18% – accounting for the overestimation of interest charges in the model.

e   Includes expenses on fertilizers, manure, salt, insecticides and irrigation.

f   No data are available on tiller costs in the household survey.

have some positive effects on the demand for hired labour, even though the total demand for labour declines, because agricultural households may reduce their own labour supply as their incomes increase. Such positive associations between farm mechanization and increased demand for *hired labour* are observed in widely differing farming conditions as in the Indian Punjab, Taiwan, Philippines and in Korea.

CONCLUSIONS

The policy implications discussed here are not in the least exhaustive, but rather indicative of the importance to be attached to the development of an integrated approach to the behaviour of agricultural households. In this paper the theory of the agricultural household was extended to a multi-crop economy. The results from this and other studies that use an integrated approach to production and consumption decisions highlight the need to change our perceptions concerning agricultural household response to economic incentives in developing countries and to revise the design of economic projects and policies accordingly.

NOTES

[1] See, for example, Lau, Lin and Yotopoulos (1978) and Barnum and Squire (forthcoming).

[2] See, for example, Odero-Ogwell and Clayton (1973) and Heyer (1971).

[3] The data are drawn from the Korean Farm Household Economy Survey for 1970.

[4] The model thus had h consumption goods (of which one is leisure), k types of land, n crops, and m (=kxn) different possible crop combinations or activities by land type and technology.

[5] Noting that all C's and λ (the marginal utility of income) are positive.

[6] If, on the other hand, equation 10 is not binding for the ith type of land, that type of land is not cultivated. Once again the solution is independent of λ.

[7] This transformation allows us to avoid specifying total time available (t) in the estimating equations. See Abbott and Ashenfelter (1976).

[8] The labour supply curve is estimated instead of the demand curve for leisure because data on hours worked are usually more readily available than data on hours spent in leisure by family members. This follows from the substitution of $\gamma 1$ by γs above.

[9] Total expenditure (E) is the sum of expenditure on commodities and leisure (valued at the market wage). In computing leisure time, we set t = 2,400 manhours per year; i.e., 8 hours per day for 300 days. On this basis, E = 328,103 won.

[10] Traditional consumer theory includes both price and "income" effects of price changes *but assumes the budget line is fixed*. Our model traces, in addition, the shifts in the *budget* line through farm production and its impact on farm profits and hence total income.

REFERENCES

Abbot, M. and Ashenfelter, O. "Labour Supply Commodity Demand and the Allocation of Time", *Review of Economic Studies*, Vol. 63, pp. 389–412, 1976.
Barnum, H.N. and Squire, Lyn "An Econometric Application of the Theory of the Farm Household", *Journal of Development Economics*, (forthcoming).
Heyer, J. "A Linear Programming Analysis of Constraints on Peasant Farms in Kenya", Food Research Institute Studies in Agricultural Economics, Trade and Development, Stanford University Food Research Institute, Vol. 10, pp. 55–67, 1973.
Lau, L.J.W.L. Lin and Yotopoulos, P.A. "The Linear Logarithmic Expenditure System: An Application to Consumption-Leisure Choice", *Econometrica*, Vol. 46, No. 6, July 1978.
Odero-Ogwell, L. and Clayton, E. "A Regional Programming Approach to Agricultural Sector Analysis", School of Rural Economics and Related Studies, Wye College, 1973.

GENERAL DISCUSSION – RAPPORTEUR: KENNETH H. BAUM

The discussion of this paper centred primarily on methodological issues and assumptions made by the authors in their empirical investigation. The large interest expressed by the audience resulted from the authors' linking consumption and production theory and activities in a programming model of a representative Korean farm. The authors were asked to consider additional research with the model to include non-representative farms to find if their results changed. In particular, questioners were interested to know under what conditions estimated elasticities would reverse signs, and under what conditions one would get opposite results with their model. It was also argued that the use of a linear expenditure system in the model acts to preclude its usefulness for policy analysis. A trade-off must be made between the demand assumptions made in the model and the estimated elasticities. For this reason, modifications of the demand and utility structure were recommended to indicate alternative demand assumptions. It was also noted that the model is quite interesting because a direct investigation of net substitution and income effects may be observed with regard to labour availability and goods consumption in rural areas. This may be especially important for various policy and planning analysis either to increase incomes in rural areas or to promote use of capital. Finally, a number of participants observed that the specification of an endogenous rather than an exogenous labour supply in the model was a step forward in the process of understanding household consumption and production behaviour.

Dr Singh responded to the above observations with an awareness that the modelling procedure was at an early stage of development. Yet the model was still capable of generating useful information. It was indicated that the authors were aware of the limitations the linear expenditure system of demand equations placed on their analyses. Hope was expressed of further model development, recognizing that assumptions made in this area would certainly affect empirical estimation of production and consumption elasticities in the model. Second, Korea has a fairly homogeneous farm structure so a representative farm may be used, although this is not true for other countries and disaggregation may have to occur in other models for a meaningful aggregative policy. Finally, Dr Singh noted that farms can only really determine the amount of labour supplied to non-farm markets if these markets exist, and if rural families participate in these markets.

Participants in the discussion included J. Heyer, Murty K. Narasimha, Bob Wells, Richard H. Day, George T. Jones, Robert L. Thompson and Richard A. King.

Synoptic View

I

This year, 1979, there have been many big international conferences, for instance, UNCTAD V (Manila in August); WCARRD (Rome in July); World Conference on Science and Technology (Vienna in August) and others. But these mammoth conferences did not compete with, and certainly did not put in the shade, our IAAE Conference. More than 730 agricultural economists from over 80 countries and areas of the world have gathered here in Banff, Canada, one of the most beautiful parts of the Canadian Rocky Mountains, to join the 17th Conference of the IAAE and to celebrate a special occasion: the fiftieth anniversary of our Association.

Before I try to give a "Synoptic View" of what I think have been the most important contributions to, and results from, this Conference, I would like first to make a few remarks about the informal, non-academic achievements of this Conference which, in my view, have proven to be necessary pre-conditions without which such free exchange of ideas would not have been possible.

1   Our Banff Conference was not the place to pass politically oriented resolutions and recommendations based on minimum consensus. "The IAAE is neither a pressure group nor an action group" (D. Britton). Our founders had in mind that an IAAE Conference should provide an excellent opportunity for exchanging and discussing agricultural economic research methods and findings exclusively on the basis of individual responsibility and obligation. "Our members are all individual members entitled to speak their own mind" (L. Elmhirst, 1929).

---

* To compile an overview of the wide range of contributions is a difficult task. Many issues that I raise stem from numerous and lengthy discussions throughout the entire conference. Of the many colleagues who made valuable suggestions here at Banff, I would like to mention Professors Koester, Schinke, and v. Urff. A special tribute also goes to Mr Heyne and Mr Liem, who helped to prepare this overview, literally up to the last minute. Nevertheless, my Synoptic View is a rather personal report. Due to lack of time, I had to shorten some passages in the oral presentation.

2   A great number of papers have been presented during the past ten days, most of them elaborating on specific topics and often highly sophisticated and specialized. I believe that this is a reflection of the changing environment in which agricultural economists are now working on a day-to-day basis: the increasing differentiation over time of our discipline.

Nevertheless, many experts in our field are sometimes confronted with the danger of losing sight of the overall social and economic context of the specific problems with which we are working, that is, with the encompassing order of our field. In such case, the agricultural economist might become an "expert dilettante" or amateur.

I remember an article written by Max Weber "On Science". In it, Weber remarks that an amateur may well come up with the same path-breaking invention as the professional researcher. It is likely, however, that the former discovered it accidentally, while in the latter case, inventions are probable events within their respective overall context of interdependency of all factors and elements involved. Let us see the Banff Conference in this light, to identify *specific* subject and area matters within their *general* economic and social context.

I believe, that this 17th Conference has clearly demonstrated that our prime concern is not simply to avoid over-specialization, but to enable specialists in their respective domains to share and discuss specific problems with their colleagues so as to broaden their views, to improve research methods, to make them more widely applicable, and to develop a common terminology; in short, to understand each other better than before.

There is wide agreement now that such dialogue is absolutely necessary in view of the complex nature of the problems rural economics and sociology are confronted with today. No special discipline by itself can be expected to tackle such problems without relying on the support of other disciplines.

3   The IAAE has always emphasized the principle of individual membership, a principle which has been honoured by the Association ever since it was founded in 1929, so that members come to our conferences in their personal capacities in order to take part in free discussions for the mutual benefit of scientific work.

Therefore, I would like to extend our gratitude to the host country, to the Local Organizing Committee, and, last but not least, to our individual members, for their great efforts to live up to such high standards before and during this Conference. This was one of the basic requirements for a successful conference, and, at the same time, a challenge for the IAAE to make every endeavour to uphold this principle in the future.

4   On the occasion of the Golden Anniversary of our Association, please let me recall a statement made by our Founder President in 1929: "We really hope that you will take fullest advantage of everything that is here, and for the time being, make Dartington your home". To our Canadian friends who so efficiently and warm-heartedly prepared the

anniversary reunion in this beautiful environment, I can proudly say today, thank you for letting us make Banff our home for the 1979 Conference.

But this is only half the story of our success. The other half is, and here again I borrow from Leonard Elmhirst, thank you for "gathering (us) together as a family-party rather than a group of specialists".

5   My dear friends and colleagues, a great number of young agricultural economists attended this Conference. Thank you very much for coming. In terms of genealogy, they represent the "fourth generation" of agricultural economists starting from our Founder President and his colleagues S.F. Warren, Carl Ladd, M. Sering and their fellow scholars. I believe that, after 50 years of existence of the IAAE, Elmhirst's remark is equally as accurate today as it was then: We are an "institutional fraternity" of agricultural economists, who, in open discussion, endeavour to overcome the problems facing the rural economy. And I hope that we bridged the gap (which may exist) between the younger and the elder generation. We can only continue through time when our capable younger colleagues feel themselves integrated, "at home", in our Association.

All of you who participated in this Conference contributed toward creating an atmosphere in which such aspirations can materialize, guided and supported by the liberal criticism so many of you felt free to exert. I believe that we should always use this capacity to express ourselves in *positive* terms.

II

A difficult task
The scope of our Conference was truly impressive: 730 participants from some 80 countries contributed, in one form or another, to the success of this symposium, 480 of whom were involved in official duties. In trying to give an overview of the discussions of well over 120 papers, it is almost impossible to give every contribution the consideration it deserves.

I therefore ask you to please excuse the imperfection and incompleteness with which I attempt to review some of the main issues that have been discussed here.

The *structure* of the Conference was the following: On the one hand, the *main topic, Rural Change: The Challenge for Agricultural Economists*, and on the other hand, the *different levels* on which agricultural economists are faced with specific problems.

Between these two *sides* of the "Conference Sandwich", quite a lot of *slices* of different characters, sizes, tastes and flavours have been filled in.

My starting point to deliver the Synoptic View is first to analyse the "mixture" between the two sides of the "Conference Sandwich", then to classify the different elements in relation to sub-topics in the framework of the overall Conference theme, and to make an effort to file the results of the plenary and invited paper level topics under these sub-themes. I have to admit that the selection of these sub-topics has been done by my normative eyes! The result of the classification, divided into "Subjects" and "Methods/Methodology" is the following:

Subjects
Rural poverty
Marketing agricultural products
Using quantitative methods
Decision making/planning
Energy, ecology
Teaching/training agricultural economists
International co-operation

Methods/Methodology
Relation between "politics" and research
Interdisciplinary approach

III

Rural poverty: the great challenge for us
In the Elmhirst Memorial Lecture presented by Sir Arthur Lewis: "Along the fringes of the African and Asian deserts, there we have the largest concentration of human poverty – 500 millions of people", as well as in the Presidential Address by Denis Britton: "Landlessness is increasing, about 500 millions of people have less than the critical minimum energy intake, and their number is increasing", we were given evidence of the first challenge for us at this Conference.

In tackling this, one of the greatest problems of our times, we, as IAAE members, are doing it in line with the relevant history of our Association: "It seems to me one of the first duties of the agricultural economists is to see that the farmer is assured a reasonable standard of living with stability" (Elmhirst, 1930, Cornell). And we should not forget that Elmhirst undertook "one of the earliest attempts at community development in the villages in West Bengal, India, in 1921, which soon dispelled any doubts that disease and lack of technical knowledge leading to poverty, lay at the root of the decay of rural life" (J.R. Currie, 1964). And after World War II, Elmhirst "Went to Bengal as agricultural advisor to try to alleviate the famine conditions there".

Sir Arthur Lewis gave us a clear picture of why in the LDCs food production has failed to keep pace with demand. Taking into account the population growth in the near future (2.2 per cent per year), this would create a market demand in the LDCs one-third greater in 1985 than in 1972/74 merely to maintain consumption per caput (FAO, 1979: increasing food gap of cereals from 72 million tons in 1977/78 to 94 million in 1985). But, and this is the crucial problem, there will still remain a substantial calorie gap, roughly estimated by FAO to add about 25 to 30 million tons to the potential import requirements. "If account is taken of the need to offset inequalities in distribution, the additional requirements for meeting the calorie gap would be almost doubled". And the main problem with which agricultural economists are confronted: "This increased deficit would be felt most in MSAC (Most Seriously Affected Countries) and in low income deficit countries" (FAO), particularly in rural regions.

The following points have been covered on this topic by papers presented here in Banff:

1　The analysis of the levels of absolute poverty and the preconditions for their alleviation in general terms (authors already mentioned) or in case studies (Nepal, Philippines, Tunisia, India, Sri Lanka, Tanzania, Brazil, Korea), very often linked with strategies of how to overcome poverty.

2　The concepts of how to integrate the small farmer, the subsistence households, the landless people, into the overall economy – which is necessary, particularly in the framework of so-called "integrated rural development", in order to combine the different measures taken outside and inside agriculture into a "package-approach". (See: credit schemes, fertilizer programmes, marketing facilities, extension service, etc., and employment facilities outside agriculture.) Many impressive results have been achieved in this respect during this Conference.

3　The *national* planning approach to secure that the "development from below" (the movement of the people) will be efficiently supported by the "decision-making from above". A number of papers have been presented to close the gap between these two levels.

4　The need to achieve national and world food security for assuring stable supplies of food at all times at reasonable prices and the role of international schemes in this context.

5　Further investment needs in LDCs to solve the problems faced.

It seems almost impossible to analyse all the papers and to combine the data presented here. Only a few can be taken into consideration. Let me first examine the level of absolute poverty as elaborated by the World Bank, and the projected decline in the near future in relation to certain assumptions about high economic growth rates in the developing countries and very strong redistributive policies in these nations. There is no doubt that absolute poverty is not likely to be eliminated by the year 2000 (Table 1). World Bank Report I, 1978, (Base Scenario): 600 million people would be living in absolute poverty at the end of the century if growth in developing countries continues at the rates envisaged in the Base Scenario: a decline by one-half in the low income countries and by three-quarters in the middle income countries. The poorest 60 per cent receive 18 to 20 per cent of the increases in income. World Bank Report II, 1979: Low Scenario indicates that there would be 710 million people living in absolute poverty by the year 2000, assuming lower growth rates, and 470 million in the case of higher growth rates and very strong

TABLE 1 *Levels of absolute poverty under alternative scenarios, 1975—2000*

| | 1975[a] | | Simulated Result in 2000[b] | | | | | |
| | | | Base Scenario[c] | | High Scenario | | Low Scenario | |
	Percentage of Population	Millions of Absolute Poor	Percentage of Population	Millions of Absolute Poor	Percentage of Population	Millions of Absolute Poor	Percentage of Population	Millions of Absolute Poor
Low income countries	52	630	22 (27)	440 (540)	17	340	26	520
Middle income counties	16	140	10 (4)	160 (60)	8	130	12	190
All developing countries	37	770	17	600	13	470	20	710

Sources: a) World Bank Report 1978
b) World Bank Report 1979
c) Figures in brackets are estimates taken from (a)

redistributive policies in developing countries.

The fact-finding and the projected decline with respect to the levels of absolute poverty not only have an impact on the design of economic policies, but must also be seen as a challenge in the sense of an ethical-moral responsibility for all of us. And, with great satisfaction, we can confirm that the papers presented and the contributions to the discussions demonstrated explicitly or implicitly a great responsibility in this concern. Thank you all for this engagement!

Taking into account (a) the declaration of principles and programme of action (WCARRD, July 1979) and (b) the recommendation of the so-called "crash-programme" for the LLDs in the next three years and for the next decade (UNCTAD V, May 1979), I would like to make the proposal to evaluate the papers and contribution of our 17th Conference and to present the results to international organizations and national governments. That could be an important contribution in bridging the gap between political recommendations and applied research. Also, a new procedure for monitoring agrarian reform and rural development will have to be developed, and the IAAE could make considerable contributions in this field, for example, (1) in discovering the realities of rural poverty, (2) in developing indicators of rural development in order to monitor progress toward respective national targets, (3) in considering ecological balances and environmental preservation.

Such a response to the challenge of rural poverty has to consider the following points:

1 Integrated rural development has to take into account three fundamental elements: poverty, basic needs and grass-roots participation. There are some very important empirical studies along these lines which have been discussed in Banff.

2 Little is known about the interactions of economic and social structures with development policies, interactions which produce particular patterns of economic growth with differential effects on the poor in rural areas. We have to make tremendous efforts through an interdisciplinary approach to close the gap.

3 Participation by people in the institutions and systems which govern their lives is a basic human right and is essential for social and economic development.

In our research, we should focus on the distribution of power as the basis for realizing the full potential of the rural poor through their active involvement. Sometimes the role of NGOs is neglected, but we know that nothing is viable when it is not supported from below. The old question of Arthur Mosher, ADC, has to be reconsidered: How can we get agriculture moving? Let us go this way. The small farmer has always been called the "backbone" of agricultural development. No doubt, then, the solution of the world food problem can only be found when the participation and the integration of the rural poor can be realized.

Marketing agricultural products

The income situation and the standard of living are closely connected with the efficiency of marketing agricultural products. More than in other fields of our profession, agricultural economics is faced with rapid change and a changing framework which will have tremendous impact on the adjustment process of agriculture. Just as in other areas, we first have to review the "relevant" history of this discipline (Abbott), in order to discover the determining factors of different economic levels of development and of decision-making. All countries, without regard to the different economic and political systems they have, are confronted with similar situations in the field of marketing agricultural products. Let me briefly make the following observations in reference to the presented papers:

(a) In market economies, the agro-business and the concentration in processing and retailing are important factors for the adaptation of agriculture. The fact that agriculture is embedded in our interdependent world (foreign trade as well as foreign private investment) has a great impact on the decision-making process at all levels. Vertical integration has, on the one hand, the advantage that it can better link production and marketing. On the other hand, however, the old traditional ideal, that the farmer is "master of his own situation", has almost completely vanished. Some of the papers have questioned the possibility of countervailing the market-power on the processing and retailing stages by organizations of the farmers themselves.

(b)   In Russia and in other CMEA countries, the national agro-industrial-complexes are one of the major research problems attracting the attention of agricultural economists (Nazarenko). There is, in the context of another type of decision-making, a great need for providing the industrialized agricultural production with food and supply industries.

(c)   Modernizing China's agriculture has to take into account that production, as well as processing of agricultural goods and the establishment of input-industries, could be best handled by commune and brigade-run enterprises, supplying them with the necessary equipment and techniques (Wu Zhan). The vertical integration or incorporation of these entities will be covered by signing contracts with the state. Mr Zhan has pointed out, that this adjustment will change the economic structure of the commune and strengthen its collective economy.

(d)   Last but not least, there is the concept of useful strategies for LDCs to improve food marketing systems (H.J. Mittendorf) and the analysis of factors or constraints influencing the effectiveness of rural marketing systems. We have to be very grateful to the authors Fox, Weber, Kamenidis and others for the empirical work they presented here.

Nevertheless, in my opinion, we need more research on how to integrate small farmers and the rural poor into marketing systems. Still, there are many gaps in empirical research work on how to achieve this, how to gain the confidence of the poor. Some decades ago, some of us had in mind that the concept of rapid industrialization would solve the problem of the development of agriculture automatically. In so far as this strategy is concerned, development policy has failed.

Nowadays, however, and I had this impression here at the Conference as well, some of us analysing that strategy argue that the establishment of physical infrastructures, of farmers' marketing co-operatives, and the co-ordination of vertically organized production–processing–marketing schemes, as well as the building up of rural markets, etc., are sufficient preconditions for aiding the small farmers to step into the modern marketing channels.

These conditions are necessary, but not sufficient to integrate the rural poor and the small farmers. As Ted Schultz has ascertained in his famous book, *Transforming Traditional Agriculture* (1958), a poor farmer is rational, a very poor farmer is even more rational. But this rationality is not always linked with the objective to maximize income and to look for the highest marginal returns of capital investment. A poor farmer involuntarily integrated into an old-fashioned land tenure system and who is in the hands of middle men or money lenders, maximizes the security of his daily subsistence, and income maximization may be one element of it. In this context, I call your attention to Medici's paper presented thirty years ago at the 1949 IAAE Conference in Stresa, Italy, entitled, "Diagnosis and Pathology of Peasant Farming", which still today has its value for our discussion.

It may have been these missing points during the Conference, elaborated in the comments to A.T. Birowo's "Marketing is an essential activity to accelerate the transition from subsistence economy to commercialization of the agricultural economy", that brought together some sixty people, after a long working day, to meet until midnight. This and other spontaneous meetings sponsored by individual members of FAO, were excellent examples of how an "international fraternity of economists" works, and that in addition to a very tight schedule!

Using quantitative methods/tools
You have certainly observed during this Conference that a great number of papers, especially the invited and contributed papers, presented research results by using well established quantitative methods (mathematical programming, simulation, etc.). Of the many examples, I will only mention a few here: C. Csaki developed a simulation model to describe the Hungarian food and agriculture sector; J.M. Connor explained, with a regression model, the penetration of foreign firms in the US food and tobacco industry; C.Y. Ahn, I. Singh, and Lyn Squire, integrated simulation and linear programming models to analyse the firm-household interactions, and so on.

For many years, such quantitative methods have allowed analysts to process and apply more data on more variables and to simulate decision-making at national, as well as at firm, levels.

The papers presented in the last ten days show how familiar we agricultural economists are with the set of quantitative methods, techniques, classified on a systematic and chronological basis by J. Sebestyen.

Using these quantitative methods, techniques, to develop models, we are aware of their limitations in analysis and application. Many critical questions and comments on quantitative methods used or on models developed, which were raised by participants in different discussion sessions, proved once again that, and allow me to quote a phrase from E. Heady, "what is important is that the array of theoretical and quantitative tools available be applied in the context of 'here is a relevant real world problem, what is the most efficient tool for its solution?', rather than to ask 'here is a shiny tool, where is a problem to which I can apply it?' ".

Decision-making/planning procedures and agriculture

The Nairobi Conference three years ago was held under this main topic. The reason for choosing this theme was the following one: in the past, economists viewed objectives and targets as basically set and only searched for the instruments necessary to reach efficiently the aims and goals. Some time ago, economists and political scientists began to analyse the political decision-making process as linked with the setting-up of objectives. Our Banff Conference has continued this line of research work which began in Nairobi.

First of all, it seems very important to exchange information so far as different economic and political systems are concerned. Therefore, we appreciate that after an absence of a quarter of a century we had the opportunity to get first hand information from China (presented by Dr Wu Zhan). Furthermore, information given during conferences in the past, has been supplemented for socialist countries of Eastern Europe by V. Nazarenko, Popov, Sebestyen, Fekete, Schieck, and others. For market economies, new items have been brought into the programme, for example the decision-making process in multi-national firms, in parastatal organizations, and in state trading agencies. I believe, that here in Banff we achieved considerable progress in this research field as a whole.

In centrally planned economies, decision-making at the micro level (optimum size and production structure, investment plans, etc.) is largely determined by the production goals set by government administrations. Planning models for such decisions (H. Schieck and V. Nazarenko) are therefore mainly used to find optimum factor combinations in agriculture, given a certain size and structure of production in the agricultural sector. This specific interrelationship between micro and macro targets also determines the scope for rural change in socialist economies. There is a large fund of experience with the application of agricultural planning models from which both Western countries and developing nations can benefit. For this, more information is needed about (a) the relationship between local, regional and central planning and administration, and (b) about the incorporation of different interests of the target groups involved in, and affected by, the planning process.

For the decision-making process concerning the location of agricultural and connected industrial production, transportation costs play an important role in socialist countries (see the model presented by Schieck, GDR).

Understandably, most advances in our discipline have occurred in relation to the micro analysis of large farmers in the developed world where we are in a position to rely on the well established principles of neoclassical theory and statistical and mathematical methods. In this respect, owing to Professor Heady, I have learned a new word, "economic clones".

In recent years, along with drastically increasing degrees of specialization, industrialization and mechanization in agriculture, the analysis and its policy application of micro-level decision-making for large industrial farms in capitalist as well as in socialist countries, has clearly been centred on the dissemination of improved quantitative methods and computerization in production economics and farm management (E.O. Heady). This process was aided by high levels of standardized education and training for both farmers and agricultural economists. While the rapid application of such highly sophisticated models for analysis and decision-making is topical for large-scale developed agriculture, the situation of the small farmers in the same group of countries leaves much more scope for further activities which, by the way, may well be very similar in many aspects to the problems of small farmers in developing countries.

It has frequently been asserted that we as agricultural economists, though highly concerned about small farmers in the Third World, still appear, by the methods and concepts we use, better equipped to deal with big farms in the industrialized world. The very nature of the problems facing small farmers in the developed countries shows that there is a wide scope for improving our approaches to both groups. And it also shows that what we are advocating abroad, and disputing here at this Conference in terms of rural development, has not been solved for the developed countries either. This is the new old link between the activities of agricultural economists working in industrial and developing countries. And I think that this Conference had much to offer in relation to a clarification of the difficulties we encounter in this area.

There is a tendency to concentrate on small farmers, also in developed countries, for purposes of analysis and guidance. While the analytical problems involved here are similar to those of rural development in the Third World, policy guidance immediately confronts us with the macro issues of agricultural policy in the industrial world.

So far as market economies are concerned, a great number of papers with new approaches have been presented. L.P. Schertz pointed out that "the profession over many years has given substantial attention to equity between the farm and other sectors. Only limited attention has been given to equity within the farm sector and to the distribution problems of those who left agriculture." Various aspects of the question of income policy versus price policy give evidence of the many problems still unsolved. In addition to this, other political considerations have superseded purely agricultural considerations, as in the case of regional integration, particularly with the EEC.

Progress in agriculture has also led to larger disparities between large and small farmers. While the adjustment pressure on small farmers increased steadily, the rest of the economy proved not prosperous enough to facilitate structural change to the extent necessary for supporting out-migration without major frictions. We have been observing a further differentiation within the agricultural sector which was not counterbalanced by faster structural change. As the Conference has shown, this continues to be a major obstacle for developed agriculture and the agricultural policy related to this problem.

Denis Britton's Presidential Address has underlined that the objective of "efficiency of the production factors" received a higher priority than equity in income distribution. Furthermore, low-priority objectives have been neglected in order to minimize costs. In some areas (for example the EC) the political decision makers are confronted with a surplus of agricultural products on the one hand and income disparities for agriculture on the other. In addition, there is a heavy financial burden for the taxpayer. All together, an unsatisfactory situation! First attempts to develop alternatives have been undertaken, some proposals (Schmidt, v. Witzke) have been presented and criticized here in Banff.

The specific relationship between central and local planning agencies promoting agricultural development in developing countries has also been discussed extensively at the Conference. Some of them I already mentioned in relation to the problem of rural poverty. Lizardo de las Casas' paper demonstrated the importance of (central) planning and national policies for local rural development programmes; and Werner Kiene, as discussion opener, has shown the dilemma of planners to find the data basis needed and suggested a positive co-ordination approach of the relevant policies. A.S.P. Brandão presented alternative agricultural models commonly advocated in Latin America, the neoclassical model, a Marxist model, the structuralist model. These different concepts can be compared against the results of project evaluation of rural development.

Judith Heyer forcefully argued the case for a serious re-orientation in our efforts as she warned us that too little has been learned from failures in the past which are still being repeated. Though basically agreeing, many delegates felt this view was too pessimistic and pointed out that, indeed, we can report many positive aspects of improvement projects providing a basis for future tasks.

This Conference drew our attention to a careful analysis of the real conflicts on the local level over what is good for some groups within one locality and not good for others. Thus, the resistance of some groups toward rural development programmes really should be seen as an implicit vote in favour of an alternative strategy. We are called upon to investigate further the complex nature of such phenomena within their full terms of reference.

We have to face the fact that in most developing countries, rural societies are more differentiated than the researcher or project manager would like and that we cannot work on the homogeneity assumption on which many of our models are based. In particular, I refer to the appropriateness and effectiveness of the analytical tools we use in trying to understand and improve (and I word this carefully now) the systems within which small farmers operate. "Within their small, individual allocative domain, they are fine tuning entrepreneurs, tuning so subtly that many experts fail to see how efficient they are." These remarks by T.W. Schultz in 1978 are already classic. Let me elaborate on this point. We agricultural economists demanded adjustment, but sometimes we remained immobile ourselves. And we are, in comparison to the rapid agricultural change, hesitant to adopt the tools and methods necessary fully to comprehend the social and economic structures underlying the decisions of small farmers as they were not apparent at first glance. This conference, dear colleagues, I think has speeded up the rate of adjustment of agricultural economists. Maybe it took us too long to realize that there is indeed efficient adjustment at the small farm level, particularly in developing countries, even if it is not in a way many had wanted or expected it to be. Small farmers have fewer alternatives to choose from, less information, and more constraints than big farmers. Within their respective frames of reference, however, they demonstrate highly flexible and innovative adjustment patterns.

On this "bread and butter" level, as M. Collinson puts it, or this "dirty boots" level, as L. Hardin calls it, there is much scope for direct contribution from the profession. Important steps forward are to be expected, among others, from farming system research so extensively discussed here in Banff.

A new dimension of research: energy analysis of agriculture
For the first time, an IAAE Conference intensively discussed the necessity of having an energy analysis of agriculture. Ulf Renborg familiarized us with his survey on issues commonly discussed among biologists and economists. M. Adamowicz for Eastern Europe, R.I. Adams and W. Rask for Brazil, and W.E. Tyner for Brazil, India and the USA, have presented papers with further details. Based on U. Renborg's paper and the discussions which followed, I came to the following conclusions:

(a) There is a great need for more applied research in this field, and IAAE members should attempt to meet this challenge.

(b) But there is also a great danger that ecologists and economists will be in opposition to each other, and that the national resource economist will be caught in the middle. More than in other fields, we need close co-operation here between the different disciplines, and the IAAE could play a catalytic role in this regard.

(c) Problems related to ecology, energy, environment, etc., will challenge the political decision makers to search for a new orientation for economic policy as a whole.

(d) A revised concept of agricultural policy, deduced from this reorientation, will have a tremendous impact on growth, income and equity in agriculture.

This is still an "unfinished problem", and I am sure that the stimulating papers which I mentioned will provide the basis for further research and for discussion in the 1982 conference.

Regional and international integration and co-operation (supra-national level)
There is no doubt that international co-operation, international agencies and supranational integration are great challenges for our profession. Recalling the papers and comments presented last Saturday, I shall only add some short remarks:

1   First of all, we need a typology of international organizations and co-operation based on the quite different goals involved and the specific legal basis which has been accepted by member states. What I mean has been put forward by V. Nazarenko: COMECON is a type of international co-operation while the EC is a type of supra-national integration.
2   This task is always closely linked with the legal basis. For example, the Treaty of Rome (EEC, 1957) contains the basic principles for the economic integration, including agriculture. In relation to the decision-making process, agricultural economists are working with the same treaty in the relatively different framework of the Council of Ministers, of the Commission, etc. On the other hand, agricultural economists working in research institutes, inside and outside the Common Market, are heavily criticizing the irrational common agricultural policy, and are exploring efficient alternatives.

This opens a new dimension for discussion, and we here in Banff have "detected" some of this terrain; not enough, but, in my opinion, a fruitful first attempt.

The wide range of these problems of international impact is shown, for example, in the paper about floating exchange rates (G.E. Schuh). In the late '70s, world agriculture is integrated into the international division of labour more than ever before. Hence, in the years ahead, rural change greatly depends on the mechanisms which link national to international agriculture. The differential impact of alternative international monetary systems on agricultural stability received much attention at the Conference.

A comparison between the situation before and after 1969, did not give conclusive evidence as to how agriculture is affected by different exchange rate regimes. This lack of evidence was attributed to structural changes in the economic environment of the two periods. Today, theoretical evaluations on the international monetary system always have to take account of the high degree of mobility in the international capital markets. The international interdependency of agricultural prices arises either from exchange rate variations in a floating system or via an equalization of national inflation rates in a system of fixed exchange rates. More theoretical and empirical work is needed in order to fully understand the impact of alternative exchange rate regimes on world agriculture (G.E. Schuh).

Teaching/training agricultural economists
With reference to the role of agricultural economists in different sectors (public/private) and different levels (national/international), I come now to the teaching and training of agricultural economists "to serve the needs of the changing world" (D.F. Fienup and H.M. Riley). H.U. Thimm analysed clearly the historical development of teaching agricultural economists in Western European countries. In view of the fact that the accomplishments cannot be measured exactly, they can only be indirectly assumed through looking at the number of graduate students finding suitable employment. Nevertheless, with regard to those students who come from developing countries, questions were raised whether the subjects they studied in Europe or in the United States really derive from, or focus upon, the needs which exist in their home countries. According to Fienup and Riley, there is some concern about the lack of focus and application to LDCs' problems (poverty and unemployment, equity and growth, power struggle, etc.). In this sense, Marxist-Socialist ideology/economics should be given more attention (Fienup and Riley), and it seemed to M. Petit that teaching Marxist economics could make students aware of the limits and shortcomings of neoclassical theory, as well as its strengths in analysis (Michel Blanc: using the class struggle to study rural economy).

Another aspect of teaching and training agricultural economists is the promotion of post-graduate studies, in general, as well as in special subjects like marketing in developing countries. Despite the fact that in Asia, Africa, and Latin America, many improvements at the university level in respect to quantity and quality of the subjects in agricultural economics have been reported, there are still many problems and faculty resource constraints (Fienup and Riley, D.A.G. Green) to overcome.

Now, what about the teacher? While teaching agricultural economists "(he) has to learn as much as his students" (H.U. Thimm), and in the field of research, for instance, many teachers could be brought "in close contact with reality" (H. Mittendorf). In this sense, many of us teachers in agricultural economics should be well prepared to face a set of new challenges in the future, on the macro as well as on the micro level, some of which were quoted in H.U. Thimm in his paper presented yesterday in the plenary session.

IV

It seems almost impossible to view "synoptically" the wide range of contributions to this conference. Therefore, I will change my viewpoint and go from "subjects" to "methods". Only a few remarks:

1 The relationship between politics and research

In market economies, this problem is heavily discussed. Of course, "today agricultural economics are brought into consultation by governments at every turn, and this wealth of new opportunities and of new responsibility offers its reward in giving new status to the profession". But it also has its risks and uncertainties. In 1947, L.K. Elmhirst asked how, under such considerations, could the professional economist best retain his professional integrity. Heinrich Niehaus, a well known agricultural economist from my area, borrowing from the philosopher Ortega y Gasset, once wrote about the "Glamour and Misery of Agricultural Economics". He was referring to the dilemma in our profession to strive for both practical application of theoretical work and political independence from decision-makers at the same time. This dilemma became apparent also at the Conference, most forcibly presented by Michel Petit, who scrutinized the possibility of drawing a line between thinking and doing, between theory and policy, between understanding the world and trying to change it. Well, we will have to live with this dilemma, and I think we can live with it if we observe certain rules of our profession based on the clear confession of whether we are working in the field of positive or normative economics.

2 The challenge for interdisciplinary work

As at earlier conferences, so here in Banff, we have observed a great need for interdisciplinary research. There is a long tradition in the IAAE of discussing the necessities, the possibilities and the limits of such co-operation. Elmhirst, in 1938 at McDonald College, Canada, remarked that "this challenge to attempt a better synthesis with the sociologists, to adopt gentler, broader, more scientific, more sensitive, more psychological attitudes in relating our economic programmes to rural society, is one that we cannot refuse to accept for much longer."

In relation to the disillusionment which some of us may have experienced in the past, I will only make a short comment:

1   The first challenge for us should be to integrate the wide spread of our own sub-disciplines into the framework of agricultural economics. Banff was a success in this respect.

2   So far as interdisciplinary research is concerned, we have to start with very concrete problems and with clear-cut definitions and goals. Otherwise, we will enter into a struggle absorbing our professional capacity for nothing. What I mean has been put forward by R.W. Herdt in relation to the interdisciplinary work of biologists and social scientists. "Potential Productivity of Modern Rice Technology: The potential productivity has to be realized under the real conditions of a farm taking into account the main constraints." I believe that a similar approach could be found for the interdisciplinary approach to ecologists, economists and natural resource scientists. But caution, everyone of them has his own (second) Bible!

3   In some cases, it seems necessary to me first to gather our specialists around a specific problem, to formulate the objectives, the strategies and then to put "some intelligent questions" to other disciplines.

The interdisciplinary approach is and will be a great challenge for us. It is the common problem with which we are all faced, with no difference in relation to the particular political and economic system.

V

Now, I would like to draw your attention to one important aspect of international co-operation. Many of our colleagues from the developing nations explained to us the difficulties they face communicating the research they are undertaking in their own countries to fellow researchers on other continents and sometimes even within one continent. It is sometimes the case, they argue, that international publishers accept such works only if endorsed and sponsored by scholars and institutions from industrial countries. I think that we can help to overcome this deficiency in two-way communication of research in a double sense: (a) developed countries should accept more responsibility in ensuring that research contributions originating from developing countries be made available for international discussion more readily than still is the case today; (b) Third World countries are called upon to undertake more serious efforts in establishing their own means of research exchange and discussion.

A related problem of international research co-operation has also been raised at this Conference. Agricultural economists from the developing world sometimes find it difficult to gain access to, and to use for their own work, background information on important studies (feasibility, evaluation, etc.) that have been undertaken in their countries by donor governments and institutions. On this account, I appeal to agricultural economists working in such donor institutions to consider the possibility of less formal exchanges of information, not based on an institutional level, with their colleagues from developing countries working on similar problems but with less back-up facilities.

This is, in my view, where the IAAE can support a New International Information Order which is currently being advocated within the UN-system.

VI

Let me come to my closing remarks at the end of our Conference, I think I can say now that Banff was a "mile-stone" for strengthening our IAAE. All of us have co-operated, and we succeeded very well. Thanks to Murray Hawkins and his "Heroes and Honies", who so efficiently supported all of us throughout the Conference, so that these positive results could be reached.

There is a tradition, and who would take the liberty not to observe it on the fiftieth anniversary, to conclude the synoptic view with some words of a famous man, usually a poet. If I am right, our President quoted Shakespeare (United Kingdom!) last time in Nairobi (1976). For a better balance, then, this time I was looking for a German poet, who for me must be Goethe! But, fortunately or not, that has already been done by my colleague from Eastern Europe, Professor Fekete. He quoted Goethe: "Who has the case at heart should take a stand for it – otherwise he does not merit to exert any influence anywhere".

Looking at this quotation, I was obliged to turn to another famous man, but now with a change in both discipline, and area. I found a sentence expressed by the outstanding British economist John Maynard Keynes: "A man never realizes how wrong he can be, when sitting alone and thinking by himself".

In closing, all of us here in Banff have "thought together" in tolerance, in "amiable disagreement", in "group thinking". Let me bridge the early times of our Association with today, to tell you that the Nestor of the American economists, Henry C. Taylor, made a statement in 1952, at East Lansing, Michigan, that he had learned this "group thinking" at seminars in Berlin organized by Max Sering, the first Vice-President of our Association.

I hope that all of us will and can "survive" in his profession by observing the principles which I mentioned: tolerance, amiable disagreement, group thinking. This is the last day of the 17th Conference of our Association. It is the "milestone" with the inscription "Fiftieth Anniversary". It is the crossroad from the first into the second half-century of our Association. Let me express my best wishes for a successful future of the Association in the following way:

> the IAAE shall live, flourish and grow
> for many years to come!
> Longue vie à l'Association Internationale des
> Economistes Ruraux!

And last, but not least, in Latin:

> Societas internationalis oeconomis agriculturae
> Vivat, crescat, floreat ad multos annos.

Thank you, good-bye and a safe journey home!

Index

Abbott, John C., 115, 130, 144, 717
Adamowicz, M., 604, 722
Adams, A., 244
Adams, R.I., 722
Adegboye, Rufus O., 644
Africa, tropical,
  communal land tenure, 663
  conflicts of interest and rural poverty,
    219–22, 225
  "delivery system problem", 222–4
  failures in rural development, 215–30
Agrarian reform, 358–68
  depersonalization of agriculture, 364
  emotional aspect, 361
  key issues, 361–2
  Marxian, 359, 364
  reconstruction of systems, 362–3
Agrawal, Ramesh C., 42, 56, 492
Agricultural Decison Analysis, 39
Agricultural Development Council, 126
Agricultural economics,
  categorizing theoretical contributions,
    611–14
  course-work in, 596
  current areas of activity, 9–10
  decision theory, 31–2, 39
  defining theory of, 606–7
  division of activities in, 9
  education for agrarian change,
    589–604
  educational accomplishments, 592,
    594
  educational challenges, 598–600
  efficiency and equity, 5, 8
  establishment as a discipline, 589–92
  European educational syllabus, 593,
    603
  farm accounting, 621
  growth and distribution, 253–6
  input-output relationships, 620–1, 624
  problem of defining theoretical
    advance, 610–11

problem of proving good theory,
  608–10
research in, 622–7
role of theory in, 607–8
students of, 594–5
teachers of 595–6
theoretical accomplishments and
  opportunities, 614–16
theories of, 248–53
weather and yields, 621–2
work at village level in S. Korea,
  147–57
Agricultural economists,
  accomplishments and opportunities in
    COMECON, 407–15
  accomplishments and opportunities in
    international agencies, 391–406
  accomplishments and opportunities in
    parastatal organizations, 520–9
  accomplishments and opportunities on
    theoretical front, 605–19
  challenge of problem of "getting
    poorer while distributing", 376–7
  in relation to agrarian reform, 365–6,
    367–8
  in state trading agencies, 542–3, 544–7
  mathematics needed, 629, 630
  planning accomplishments, 247–53,
    257–8
  present status and future challenge,
    256, 258–9
  quantitative techniques and, 620–31
  roles in international research institu-
    tions, 479–92
  teaching in developing countries,
    597–8
  teaching Marxist economics to,
    647–58
  training for LDCs, 632–44, 724
  work in centrally managed economies,
    285–98
  work on planning for LDCs, 247–50

728